THE CHANGING DISTRIBUTION OF EARNINGS
IN OECD COUNTRIES

The Rodolfo Debenedetti Lectures

**Public lectures by leading academicians on issues
at the forefront of economic research**

The main purpose of the Rodolfo Debenedetti Lectures is to present to a non-technical readership new and evolving research on topical issues, such as:

- the implications of the ageing of populations;
- long-term trends in income distribution;
- the changing size and composition of welfare states in an integrated Europe;
- labour market reforms and transitions in employment, unemployment and inactivity, and the spread of temporary work;
- international and regional migration;
- the future of trade unions and collective bargaining; and
- the political economy of social welfare reform.

The Scientific Committee in charge of selecting the authors of the Rodolfo Debenedetti Lectures is composed of Giuseppe Bertola (University of Turin), Olivier Blanchard (MIT), Tito Boeri (Bocconi University), and Stephen Nickell (Oxford University).

Previous titles published in the book series include:
Fighting Poverty in the US and Europe by Alberto Alesina and Edward L. Glaeser

fondazione RODOLFO DEBENEDETTI
Via Salasco 5, 20136 Milano
Telefono: (39)-02-58 36 33 41/2
Fax: (39)-02-58 36 33 09
E-mail: info@frdb.org
Internet: www.frdb.org

The Changing Distribution of Earnings in OECD Countries

A. B. ATKINSON

OXFORD
UNIVERSITY PRESS

OXFORD

UNIVERSITY PRESS

Great Clarendon Street, Oxford OX2 6DP

Oxford University Press is a department of the University of Oxford.
It furthers the University's objective of excellence in research, scholarship,
and education by publishing worldwide in

Oxford New York

Auckland Cape Town Dar es Salaam Hong Kong Karachi
Kuala Lumpur Madrid Melbourne Mexico City Nairobi
New Delhi Shanghai Taipei Toronto

With offices in

Argentina Austria Brazil Chile Czech Republic France Greece
Guatemala Hungary Italy Japan Poland Portugal Singapore
South Korea Switzerland Thailand Turkey Ukraine Vietnam

Oxford is a registered trade mark of Oxford University Press
in the UK and in certain other countries

Published in the United States
by Oxford University Press Inc., New York

© A. B. Atkinson 2008

The moral rights of the author have been asserted
Database right Oxford University Press (maker)

First published 2008

British Library Cataloguing in Publication Data

Data available

Library of Congress Cataloging in Publication Data

Data available

Typeset by SPI Publisher Services, Pondicherry, India
Printed in Great Britain
on acid-free paper by
Clays Ltd, St Ives, Suffolk

ISBN 978-0-19-953243-8

1 3 5 7 9 10 8 6 4 2

For Estelle, Gerrard, Evelyn, and Leila

Preface

First, I should thank Tito Boeri for having invited me to give the Debenedetti Lecture at Bocconi University in March 2006. Not only was he a warm and generous host, but his invitation stimulated me to launch the two-year research project reported in this book. The project started in September 2005, when I stepped down as Warden of Nuffield College, Oxford, and has been possible by the support of several institutions. I am most grateful to Nuffield College for electing me as a Senior Research Fellow, and thus allowing me to continue research in this wonderful institution. I thank warmly the Netherlands Institute for Advanced Studies (NIAS) for offering me the Jelle Zijlstra Professorship for the period September 2005 to January 2006. NIAS provides invigorating surroundings and an excellent research environment, which allowed me to devote the concentrated block of time necessary to embark on the data collection for Part III of the book. It was during this period that I began to learn just how much earnings data existed but were not being exploited. The Lecture itself was written while I was visiting the Economic Research Department of the Bank of Italy, where I had stimulating discussions that led me to pursue new directions (I am grateful in particular to Ignazio Visco for emphasizing the importance of looking at the 1970s). The writing of the book was completed while I held a Chaire Blaise Pascal at the Ecole Normale Supérieure, funded by the French government and the Region of Ile-de-France. I was there from April 2006 to March 2007, during which period the Ecole d'Economie de Paris (Paris School of Economics) came into existence. I am grateful to Thomas Piketty, the first Director, for inviting me and allowing me to share in this historic experience. I thank all these institutions for their support, while making clear that none are responsible in any way for the views expressed.

The Lecture draws (in Section 6) on material presented as the Second Ruggles Lecture at the 29th General Conference of the International Association for Research in Income and Wealth (IARIW) at Joensuu, Finland, August 2006. I am most appreciative of Tim Smeeding's invitation to give this lecture in memory of Nancy and Richard Ruggles, and of the helpful comments of participants, notably Stephan Klasen, the editor of the *Review of Income and Wealth*, in which the Ruggles Lecture was published (Atkinson, 2007).

A number of people have contributed greatly to the writing of this book, by allowing me to draw on our joint work and by acting as sounding boards for the ideas expressed. I have drawn heavily on joint work with Andrea

Brandolini, with whom I shared an office at the Bank of Italy. In the case of the Czech Republic, Hungary, and Poland, I have used extensively the research conducted some fifteen years ago in conjunction with John Micklewright of the University of Southampton. The new estimates for Ireland grew out of a suggestion by Brian Nolan of University College Dublin, and we have developed a joint paper on this subject.

Warm thanks are due to those who helped me with the assembly of data for individual countries. Without their assistance, the study would have been impossible. By country, and alphabetically, they are: Jeff Borland, Rob Bray, Andrew Leigh, and Peter Saunders (Australia), Alois Guger (Austria), Miles Corak and Brian Murphy (Canada), Peter Sorensen (Denmark), Markus Jäntti and Antti Katainen (Finland), Brian Nolan (Ireland), Andrea Brandolini, Daniele Franco, and Daniela Monacelli (Italy), Wiemer Salverda and Hans Stegeman (Netherlands), Sylvia Dixon and Brian Easton (New Zealand), Rolf Aaberge (Norway), Facundo Alvaredo and Carlos Farinha Rodrigues (Portugal), Magnus Gustavsson, Erik Liljegren, and Sofia Nilsson (Sweden), Ramses Abul Naga (Switzerland), and Gary Burtless and Tim Smeeding (United States). In undertaking the research for this book I owe a particular debt to the study by Harold Lydall (1968) and to an unpublished manuscript by David Grubb of OECD ('Earnings Inequality in OECD Countries'). These were essential in pointing me as to where to look for sources of earnings data in earlier years. I should also like to thank Paul Swaim of OECD for supplying a more recent vintage of the OECD comparative data on earnings dispersion. I should emphasize that they are in no way responsible for the use that I have made of the data nor for the conclusions reached.

Oxford
June 2007

Contents—Summary

Contents

PART III. NEW EMPIRICAL EVIDENCE FOR 20 OECD COUNTRIES

List of Tables

List of Figures

Introduction and Reader's Guide

Why add to the literature on the distribution of earnings? On my count, there have been some 200 articles on this topic in leading economics journals since 1990. The Bibliography on earnings at the end of this book has around 700 items. More than 75 have 'wage inequality' or 'earnings inequality' in their title. Surely we know what has happened to earnings dispersion? According to the background paper for the 2005 Review of the Jobs Strategy by the OECD,

Gross earnings inequality has increased on average in OECD countries for which data are available. This occurred in countries where labour market performance improved considerably (Australia, the Netherlands), as well as in countries where it deteriorated (Germany, Hungary, Korea and Poland). (Brandt, Burniaux, and Duval, 2005, page 20)

According to the widely cited survey by Katz and Autor,

Overall wage inequality and educational wage differentials have expanded greatly in the United States and the United Kingdom since end of the 1970s. . . . More modest increases in overall wage inequality and skill differentials in the 1980s and 1990s are apparent in most other OECD countries. (1999, page 1465)

Furthermore, there is wide concurrence as to the causes of widening dispersion. Readers of economics textbooks are told that

there is general agreement that the main factor behind the increase in the relative wage of skilled versus unskilled workers is a steady increase in the relative demand for skilled workers. (Blanchard, 1997, page 524)

The steady increase in demand is attributed to two main factors, operating either separately or in combination. One is the impact of globalization, with the jobs of unskilled workers being increasingly exposed to international competition. As it was famously asked by Freeman (1995), 'Are Your Wages Set in Beijing?' The second major factor is technological change biased in favour of skilled workers. This latter explanation has highlighted new technologies (ICT) but it dates back more than 30 years to the 'race between technological development and education' described by Tinbergen in his book *Income Distribution* (1975).

Doubts have, however, been raised about this consensus. The forces described above affect all OECD countries, but it has been observed that changes in earnings dispersion are far from uniform across these countries. Gottschalk and Smeeding (1997) drew attention to the large differences across countries in the trends in wage dispersion; Katz and Autor (1999, page 1502) note the divergences across countries in the patterns of change in the 1980s and 1990s. In the case of the United States, it has become clear that we need to look at the top not the bottom of the earnings distribution. In my 1999 WIDER Annual Lecture, I pointed out that 'the most significant widening is not that at the bottom of the United States earnings distribution. [Earnings dispersion is increasing] because of what is happening higher up the scale' (Atkinson, 1999, page 11). Card and DiNardo have cast doubt on the skill-biased technical change (SBTC) explanation, arguing that 'a key problem for the SBTC hypothesis is that wage inequality stabilized in the 1990s despite continuing advances in computer technology' (2002, page 733). Similarly, Lemieux concludes for the US that 'the magnitude and timing of the growth in residual wage inequality provide little evidence of a pervasive increase in the demand for skill due to skill-biased technological change' (2006, page 461).

Moreover, the changes in earnings dispersion in recent decades have to be compared with those at earlier times. The recent literature has concentrated on the period since the 1970s. For example, the study just cited by Lemieux (2006) covers the period 1973–2003; the recent article by Gottschalk and Danziger (2005) is concerned with the period 1975–2002. But I believe that it is important to set this experience in historical context. Writing about the UK, Machin says,

after showing relative stability for many decades (and a small compression in the 1970s) there has been [since the late 1970s] an inexorable upward trend in the gap between the highest and lowest earners in the labour market. (Machin, 1996, page 62)

But was the earlier period so unexciting?

There is therefore a case for taking a fresh look at the evidence for changes in earnings dispersion in OECD countries and for considering alternative explanations. This is the purpose of the present book. It grows out of the 2006 DeBenedetti Lecture. Converting a sixty-minute lecture into a book is never easy. The lecture tells the 'story', whereas the book has to provide the scientific backing. It is all too easy to lose in the process of conversion the freshness and directness of the lecture. If one takes the lecture and develops each section into a separate chapter, then the general reader may lose the overall perspective provided by the oral presentation.

I have therefore kept Part I (The Lecture) close to the original lecture. The material has been revised and extended, but it seeks to give the main argument in relatively non-technical terms. It is designed for the general reader. There are graphs but very little algebra. The Lecture is short (100 pages) and for many readers, including students, it will I hope be sufficient. It is followed by Part II (Details of the Models) and by Part III (New Empirical Evidence for 20 OECD Countries). These are designed for the reader who wishes to delve further. Part II consists of three notes on the theoretical analysis cited in the Lecture. It is very brief, whereas Part III makes up over half of the book. A considerable part of the research for this book has consisted of the assembly of data, and this is the subject of Part III. The core is provided by the twenty country chapters (Chapters A–T), each of which gives tables of data and an account of the country's experience. The chapters relate the data to those in earlier compilations by Lydall (1968) and the OECD (1993 and 1996) and describe the methods employed.

The structure of the book resembles in some (but not all) respects hypertext. The Lecture itself is structured in sections. The reader interested in theoretical explanations should go to Sections 2, 8, and 9; the reader interested in an overall summary of the recent changes in earnings dispersion should go to Section 4; those who want greater detail should go to Section 5; and those who want a long run perspective should go to Section 6. The Lecture draws on material that is set out more fully in the chapters of Parts II and III. The reader who wishes, for example, to see a fuller explanation of the race between technology and education can go to Note 1 in Part II; the reader who wishes to know why the earnings figures shown in the graph in the Lecture differ from those he or she has seen before can go to Part III and the relevant country chapter. The reader interested in the evidence for, say, Australia can look at the multi-country graphs in Part I and Figure 10, and then go to the Australian country chapter (Chapter A). For the same reason, there is both a general bibliography and a bibliography for each country chapter. This involves some repetition, but I hope that the collection together of references to the earnings distribution in a particular country will aid the reader specifically interested in that country.

The book covers only a small part of the large subject of the distribution of earnings. There are many subjects not covered, such as gender and racial discrimination, cohort effects, immigration, and industrial, regional, or occupational differences. Even within the field covered, there are many contributions that I have neglected. I have tried to refer to these where relevant in the extensive bibliography at the end of the book (not all of which are cited in the text—although I hope the reverse is not true!). I should also acknowledge that, in seeking to cover twenty countries, I have not done justice to the literature of each of those countries, particularly the non-English language literature.

Part I

The Lecture

Why Read This Lecture?

> Earnings inequalities are one of the most tangible subjects... with real implications for each and every individual.
>
> European Commission, 2005, page 164

Why should you read this Lecture? First, it deals, as the European Commission says, with a subject of real significance for everyone: what people are paid and how pay differences are changing over time. From the Lecture, the reader can learn about the ways in which economists analyse the determinants of earnings and how new thinking can be brought to bear (from Sections 2, 7, and 8). The reader will be presented (in Sections 5 and 6) with long run data on the distribution of earnings in 20 OECD countries. Secondly, many of the conclusions are new. The Lecture questions the conventional wisdom. For example, it is widely believed that:

- 'If technology wins the race with education, then the wages of the educated will continue to grow faster than those of the uneducated.'
- 'Since all countries are affected by the same forces of globalization and technological change, their earnings distributions will, sooner or later, all be affected in the same way.'
- 'It is the low paid who are most affected by globalization and technical change.'
- 'The 1950s were a Golden Age of growth and equity.'
- 'The recent rise in earnings dispersion is a shock because the wage distribution has been remarkably stable for decades.'
- 'Germany, unlike the US, has a labour market with rigid unchanging wage differentials.'

The Lecture casts doubt on each of these statements.

1

Introduction: What This Lecture Is About

My concern in this Lecture is with the distribution of *individual earnings*, or how much people are paid as workers. This is related to, but different from, the distribution of household incomes. People often talk about 'earnings' and 'income' as though the terms were interchangeable, but they are not. The earnings of workers are only part of household incomes. As everyone knows, households also receive income from self-employment, capital, rents, and transfers from the private sector, as well as paying taxes and receiving state transfers. A significant proportion of households receive no earned income; this applies, for example, to households where everyone is a pensioner or unemployed. Rising inequality of household incomes may therefore be due to many factors apart from rising earnings differences. The significance of this difference is illustrated by a contrast of the United Kingdom (UK) with the United States (US). Earnings dispersion has widened in the US to a greater extent than it has in the UK; yet for household incomes the Gini coefficient (a commonly used indicator of income inequality) has gone up in the UK by nearly twice the increase found in the US. To explain the relative behaviour of income inequality in the two countries, one has to take account of mechanisms additional to those considered in this Lecture, such as changes in tax and social security policy.

So, if you imagine visiting a household and seeking to collect data relevant to this Lecture, then what you have to ask is: Are you employed as a worker? If so, how much do you get paid? Note that 'workers' include all salaried workers, even top managers (to whom I shall be devoting particular attention), but not the self-employed. It covers part time as well as full time workers. In principle, the information should cover workers in the informal sector of the economy, although they may not be well covered in actual earnings surveys. When recording the pay, you should calculate the total of all earnings, including payments for overtime, shift working, commission and tips, and the thirteenth month salary (paid in some countries). Earnings should be gross of all taxes and social security contributions deducted. Where workers are paid in net terms, the contributions should in principle be added back (when I was employed in Paris, this meant adding back no fewer than thirteen items). The earnings may be recorded as weekly, monthly, or annual earnings. They may be divided by hours worked to give hourly earnings. In whatever form they are recorded, they are an important part of household incomes. According to the 2005 American Community Survey, 82 per cent of total household income in the United States came from earnings (US Census Bureau, 2006, page 8).

There are many questions that can be asked about the resulting distribution of earnings. We may ask about the earnings of different occupations. We may be concerned with the gender gap in pay. We may ask whether people in one region earn more than those in another. Here I am concerned with the overall distribution among *all* workers. What is the shape of the whole earnings distribution? In looking at the outcome for people as workers—what reward do they get from the labour market—I am adopting a particular perspective. For an employer, for example, a job may be equally well done by one full time worker or two part time workers, but for the workers there is an important difference. Moreover, I am interested in workers as individuals, not as members of a class or occupational grouping. Much of the literature deals with skilled and unskilled workers, or educated and uneducated workers, and the changing wage premium earned by skilled (educated) workers. This is a useful analytical device, but it is not the end of the story, and not sufficient on its own to determine the overall distribution of earnings among individuals.

I am deliberately referring to earnings *differences*, or to earnings *dispersion*, not to earnings inequality. Differences in earnings may, or may not, be associated with inequality. Again, people tend to use the terms 'dispersion' and 'inequality' interchangeably, but the former does not imply the latter. People may be paid more, for example, because they have more responsible jobs, or ones that require greater effort. They may, as in the standard human capital model, have invested in past training or education. The recent literature appears to have forgotten the long-standing theory of compensating wage differentials.

The Lecture is largely concerned with *changes* over time in the dispersion of earnings. How is the shape of the distribution changing? Recent interest in this question is largely due to the fact that the US experienced a rise in earnings dispersion in the 1980s. This is illustrated in Figure 1, which shows the movement in the US in the decile ratio, that is the earnings of the person 10 per cent from the top as a multiple of the earnings of the person 10 per cent from the bottom. It is calculated for the hourly earnings of all workers, male and female combined. As is well known, this ratio has widened over the past 25 years. It was around 3.5 whereas it is now around 4.5. In 2005, a person at the bottom decile point in the US earned $7.20 an hour; a person at the top

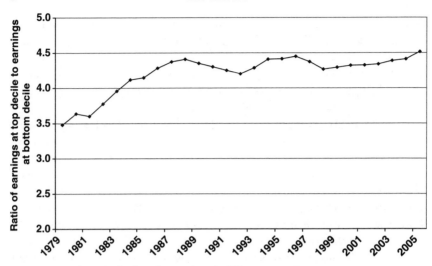

Figure 1 Decile ratio for hourly earnings in US 1979–2005

decile point earned $32.49 an hour. The rise from 3.5 to 4.5 is a rise of over a quarter, and it is not surprising that it has generated a large literature.

In particular, we are concerned with the likely future development of earnings dispersion. Has the rise in the degree of dispersion levelled off? Have we attained a new steady state? Or will the decile ratio continue upwards? In forming a view about future prospects, we need to consider the explanation of the trend so far, and I begin with what has become the textbook story.

2

The Race between Technology and Education: The Textbook Model

The textbook story is usually illustrated by a supply and demand diagram similar to Figure 2, taken from Johnson (1997, page 44). The horizontal axis shows the ratio of skilled to unskilled labour and the vertical axis shows the ratio of the wages of the two groups (assumed otherwise homogeneous). The term 'skilled' is often treated as synonymous with 'educated', and I follow this approach in this exposition of the textbook model. Looking first at the solid lines, we see that the relative demand is a decreasing function of the relative wage. If educated labour becomes relatively more expensive, then firms substitute uneducated labour. At a point in time, the relative supplies are fixed, so that the short run supply curve is vertical. If there is a sudden rise in demand for educated workers, then no increase in supply is immediately forthcoming, so that all that happens is a rise in the relative wage of educated workers.

The response of labour supply is therefore crucial. If 'skills' were fixed, so that the supply curve was vertical in the long run as well as the short run, then the only consequence of an upward shift in demand would be a rise in the relative wages of the skilled. In effect, the lucky skilled people would enjoy an increased 'rent' from their superior ability. However, the number of skilled or educated workers may respond to the rise in relative wages. It becomes increasingly attractive to acquire skills. The supply may shift. Indeed, in the diagram of Johnson (1997) there is assumed to be, in the long run, a horizontal supply curve, as shown by the dotted line in Figure 2.

One situation in which the long run supply curve is horizontal is where people are identical in their capacities and that they choose whether or not to become educated by comparing the present values of earnings. In a simple version of the Mincer–Becker model of human capital formation, people are assumed to maximize the present discounted value of lifetime earnings. If there are no costs of schooling, and people work for the same number of years in total, then the only difference between the earnings profiles is that educated workers enter the labour force later. If T is the length of training, then they start work T years later and retire T years later (of course, in reality they

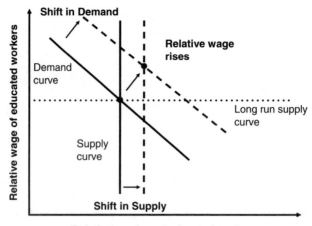

Figure 2 Relative supply and demand: the textbook story

may retire earlier, but this is assumed not to be the case to simplify the comparison). In effect, each year of earning is postponed by T years. This postponement has a cost, since future earnings are worth less. If r is the real interest rate, then wages delayed by T years are worth a fraction e^{-rT}, so that for people to be indifferent between training and not training, the equilibrium wage differential in favour of the educated has to be e^{rT}. There is a wage premium just sufficient to compensate for the costs of training. Putting it differently, if we take natural logarithms, the logarithm of the earnings of the educated are equal to the logarithm of the earnings of the uneducated plus rT. Earnings equations of this type, typically referred to as Mincer equations, are often estimated, with the coefficient r being the return to education.

If people responded immediately to any divergence from the compensating differential, then the economy would move along the long run supply curve (the dotted line in Figure 2). The wage premium would not move from its equilibrium level. In this case, we would *not* observe a rise in the wage differential as a result of the increased demand. We *would* observe a rise in the proportion of educated workers. There would be a structural change in the economy. On the other hand, it does not seem plausible to assume that the supply response is immediate. People take time to recognize and act on the increase in demand. The speed of response depends on the institutions of the labour market and how rapidly they operate. The intermediate case where there is a response, but less than immediate, is shown in Figure 2 by the shifts in the demand and supply curves from the solid lines to the dashed lines. If, as shown, the supply curve shifts less to the right than the demand curve, then the relative wage of educated workers rises. The outcome—increased wage dispersion—is the result of technology winning the race. As Johnson (1997) explains, the extent of the increase in the wage premium depends on the degree of substitution between educated and uneducated labour. If there is a high degree of substitution, then the wage change is smaller.

The textbook story illustrated in Figure 2 seems rather convincing. A major economic phenomenon, touching the lives of many people, can be explained by the supply and demand analysis taught in first year economics. There are however four important elements missing:

- A race is essentially dynamic, but the dynamics are not explicitly modelled.
- The distribution of earnings depends on quantities as well as prices (as where the economy moves along the long run supply curve), so that one cannot look simply at the wage differential.
- The analysis focuses purely on the labour market and ignores the interaction with the capital market.
- The analysis ignores all the developments in labour economics of the past fifty years.

The last of these criticisms is taken up later in the Lecture (in Sections 8 and 9); the others are discussed in turn below.

INTRODUCING DYNAMICS

Central to the supply and demand story is the assumption that the demand curve continues to shift over time. The skill-biased technical progress explanation is based on the view that new technologies continue to be diffused; there was not a single technological shock. The impact of globalization has not been a once-for-all shift, but continues to affect OECD countries as the rest of the world industrializes. What, however, is the effect of a continuing outward shift in the demand curve? Will supply lag further and further behind demand, so that the wage differential rises without limit? Or will the wage differential eventually return to the long run equilibrium level shown by the dotted line in Figure 2?

Putting it differently, if we observe that the wage differential remains constant, can we deduce that the demand curve has ceased to shift? In their critique of the skill-biased technical change (SBTC) hypothesis, Card and DiNardo note that the rise in wage dispersion in the US was concentrated in the early 1980s, and go on to say that 'this suggests a potential problem for the SBTC hypothesis: why did the pace of SBTC slow down after an initial burst during the first few years of the microcomputer revolution?' (2002, page 744). This argument appears to assume that a constant wage differential is inconsistent with a continuously shifting demand curve. However, is it not possible that both supply and demand curves are shifting at the same rate?

In order to understand this question, we need to make explicit the dynamics of the race between technology and education. Moreover, we know from other contexts that the conclusion we reach depends on how the price and quantity adjustments are specified. In a single market, the stability of equilibrium depends on whether quantities or prices adjust. In general equilibrium, the stability of equilibrium depends on the price adjustment process. Surprisingly, the dynamics of wage differentials seem to have been little discussed in the literature of recent years. Yet, there is good historical precedent. In 1959, Arrow and Capron published a paper on dynamic shortage and price rises, with an application to the then shortage of engineers and scientists—an application that seems of contemporary relevance. (See Arrow, 1960, for a multiple market version, and Neugart and Tuinstra, 2003, for a recent explicit treatment of expectation formation.)

The dynamics of the model considered here differ from those of Arrow and Capron (1959), in that my treatment here follows directly from the formulation in Figure 2. At any moment, the supply of educated workers is assumed to be fixed, determined, as Johnson says, by 'past educational investment decisions' (1997, page 44n). When the demand for educated workers begins to shift upwards (at a constant proportionate rate), the immediate outcome is that the skilled wage rises to clear the market. But this is a temporary equilibrium in the sense that, at this higher relative wage, people wish they had acquired skills (on the present value calculation described earlier). The increased wage for educated workers is now more than enough to compensate for the delayed entry to the labour market. Let us now assume, and this is a key assumption, that the relative supply adjusts in proportion to the excess of the wage differential over the long run supply equilibrium level (the dotted line in Figure 2). We can then deduce (for details, see Note 1 in Part II) that the economy approaches a situation in which supply and demand move 'in step' to the right with a wage differential that exceeds the long run supply differential by an amount equal to the ratio of the rate of growth of demand to the speed of supply response. We have a 'semi-equilibrium', semi in the sense that the wage differential has converged to a constant level, but the ratio of educated to uneducated workers rises steadily. This is illustrated in Figure 3, where S_1, S_2, and S_3 denote the supply curves in successive years, and D_1, D_2, and D_3 the demand curves in successive years.

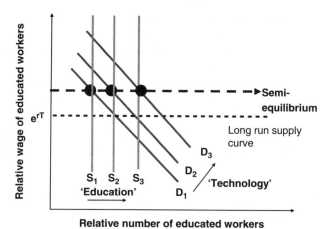

Figure 3 Race between technology and education

The answer to the question posed earlier is therefore that, with one specific set of assumptions, a continuous shift in demand leads, not to a continuous rise in the wage premium, but to a semi-equilibrium where educated workers permanently receive a premium in excess of the long run supply price. This has a number of implications. The results of this dynamic model do appear to undermine the assumption underlying the Card and DiNardo critique: the observation of a constant wage differential is quite consistent with the demand curve continuing to shift. It is just that supply and demand are marching in step. However, such a conclusion would be too hasty, since the overall distribution of earnings depends also on the numbers of skilled and unskilled workers, and these are not constant. The ratio of skilled to unskilled workers is increasing over time in the situation described above. We have to look at quantities as well as prices. I return to this in a moment.

The findings regarding the wage premium itself are important. The observation of a rising premium for educated workers has been taken as evidence that 'the race between education and technology is being lost by schooling' (Jacobs, 2004, page 47). This is consistent with the model described here, but the conclusion needs to be nuanced. The situation shown in Figure 3 is one where one runner can keep up with the leader but never gains sufficiently to catch up. A constant wage premium is not evidence that education has caught up. For that, we have to look at the extent to which there is a wage premium in excess of that required to compensate for the training period. Many such calculations have been made, going back to the pioneering study of earnings in the professions in the United States by Friedman and Kuznets (1945), who calculated the differential required to compensate professional workers (doctors and lawyers, for example) for the longer training required (on average seven years).

The extent of the premium for educated workers can be shown (see Note 1 in Part II) to depend on the rate at which the demand curve is shifting *and* on the speed of response of supply. The more rapid the supply response, the smaller the premium (and with immediate response the premium is zero). This means that even if countries are affected by the same force—a constant shift in demand due to globalization or technical change—their wage distributions may be differently affected if there are differences across countries in speeds of adjustment. The fact that we observe less increase in dispersion in some countries than in others does not undermine the textbook story. A more rapid adjustment of supply to the skills shortage means that a country exhibits a smaller differential. So, if, for example, the Nordic countries have a more responsive education and training system, then they may show a smaller long run rise in the wage premium. If a government succeeds in expanding faster the proportion of the cohort receiving higher education, then the model predicts that there will be a smaller rise in wage dispersion.

FROM SKILLED/UNSKILLED EARNINGS TO THE EARNINGS DISTRIBUTION

As already emphasized, the distribution of earnings among individuals depends both on the wage differential and on the relative proportion of educated workers. Suppose that skill is the only reason for earnings to be different. If we imagine a line up of the total population of earners, then the unskilled come first (remember that we are excluding here the unemployed and the retired). Suppose that the unskilled make up 50 per cent of total earners, so that if we look at, say, the bottom 20 per cent, then they are all unskilled and the top 20 per cent are all skilled. If we know the wage differential, we can then calculate their shares in total earnings. Taking for illustrative purposes a skill premium of 50 per cent (skilled workers earn 50 per cent more than unskilled workers), we can calculate average earnings as $1\frac{1}{4}$ times the unskilled wage, and the share of the bottom fifth as 16 per cent (obtained as 20 per cent divided by $1\frac{1}{4}$) and that of the top fifth as 24 per cent.

What happens to these two groups as the demand and supply curves shift? Their shares of total earnings will clearly be affected if the wage differential changes. But they will change even where the wage differential is constant, as when the demand and supply curves are marching in step. The share received by the bottom 20 per cent depends on their wage relative to the overall average, and the overall average rises as more people become skilled. Suppose that the skilled now make up two-thirds of all workers. The average rises to $1\frac{1}{3}$ times the unskilled wage. The share of the bottom fifth, still all unskilled, becomes 20 per cent divided by $1\frac{1}{3}$, or 15 per cent. The distribution of earnings is therefore affected by the demand shift, even if the supply curve is shifting in line. In this specific sense, the critique of Card and DiNardo (2002) remains valid. If the demand curve is continuing to shift, then we should observe a falling share for the low paid.

It is not perhaps surprising that the share of the unskilled should be falling. But the same argument shows that the share of the top fifth is also falling. Of course, if the wage differential is widening, then they may gain. If, however, we have converged to a semi-equilibrium where the demand and supply curves move in tandem, with a constant wage differential, then those already skilled do not gain any further. But the average continues to rise, and, in the numerical example, the share of the top 20 per cent falls from 24 per cent to $22\frac{1}{2}$ per cent. In fact, we have, in this semi-equilibrium, a situation like that in the famous Kuznets (1955) model of structural change. Instead of a shift in employment from agriculture to industry, we have a shift in the composition of the supply of labour from unskilled to skilled, but the effect on the overall distribution of earnings is the same. There is a quantity change but no change in relative wages (in the semi-equilibrium). The structural change causes the distribution to become more unequal at the bottom and less unequal at the top.

This means that the semi-equilibrium cannot explain a situation where there are increasing shares of top earners. In order to explain this, we need to introduce a further mechanism, generating greater dispersion *within* the skilled group. In order to understand this, we may need to look at the distribution within the upper part of the distribution, distinguishing, for instance, between the upper quartile and the top decile. The theoretical model suggests that we need to redirect our empirical inquiry. It is not sufficient to look, as is commonly done, at the decile ratio, as in Figure 1. We need to distinguish between what is happening at the top and bottom of the distribution.

INTERACTION WITH THE CAPITAL MARKET

Before leaving the supply and demand model, we should note one explanation for rising wage dispersion not so far considered: that there may have been an increase in the long run supply price. One of the merits of the human capital model of earnings is that it builds a link between the markets for labour and capital. This link, however, has not been given sufficient weight in the labour market literature. As we can see from the expression for the long run supply price, the wage differential is an increasing function of the real interest rate (r in the expression e^{rT} for the differential). Here we have a quite different explanation for the rise in earnings dispersion. In the 1980s, real (i.e. after subtracting inflation) interest rates rose to a markedly higher level. Since then they have fallen, but they remain above the level of the 1970s. A higher premium for educated workers may reflect the greater cost of acquiring qualifications. The rise in the interest rate was common to OECD countries, but there are country-specific factors that have affected the cost of financing education. If the opportunity cost of borrowing is a loss of taxed interest income, then the reduction of income tax rates in the US and UK has raised the effective interest rate. We have also to allow for the changes in the degree of government support for education, which mean that the private share of the costs of education has increased.

This alternative line of explanation needs to be taken seriously, since it may have rather different implications. I have deliberately so far referred to earnings *dispersion*, not to earnings *inequality* (except when quoting others). Writers tend to use the terms 'dispersion' and 'inequality' interchangeably, but the former does not imply the latter. Differences in earnings may, or may not, be associated with inequality. If the rise in the college earnings premium is a response to higher borrowing costs, then in terms of the present value of lifetime earnings there *may* be no rise in inequality. I say 'may' because there are likely in fact to be relevant differences across individuals. In the study by Friedman and Kuznets of the professions in the 1930s, they concluded that 'the actual difference between the incomes of professional and non-professional workers seems decidedly larger than the difference that would compensate for the extra capital investment required' (1945, page 84). They went on to say that 'there is nothing surprising about this finding. It is clear that young men [*sic*] are, in fact, not equally free to choose a professional or non-professional career' (1945, page 88). They are restricted, on the one hand, by their level of ability, and, on the other hand, by their access to the capital market. Differences in natural ability play a central role in the theoretical models developed in Sections 8 and 9, such as the superstar theory, and I return to the issue there, but we can see in the present model that the rise in the wage premium may magnify the advantages of the more able and thus increase inequality. In the same way, where young people differ in their capacity to fund education, then the rise in interest rates may have exacerbated this source of genuine inequality. Intergenerational transmission of advantage may in this sense have become more important. What this explanation does is to direct our attention to inequality of access to education and the role of the capital market.

SUMMARY

If we investigate what lies behind the supply and demand story, and the race between technology and education, then we find that, with a specified set of dynamics, the skill wage premium converges to a constant value even where demand is continuing to shift. The extent of the rise depends however on the working of the labour market. Countries that respond more quickly to the need for more educated workers will see a smaller rise in the wage premium. The labour market is in a semi-equilibrium, where demand and supply shift in tandem. But the distribution of individual earnings continues to evolve. The shares of the low paid in total earnings fall; and—more surprisingly—the shares of top earners also fall. To explain rising shares at the top, we have to introduce an explanation for increased dispersion within the educated group. This underlines the need to look separately at the bottom and the top of the distribution when examining the empirical evidence.

3

Taking Data Seriously: Where the Data Come From and How We Should Use Them

In considering the evidence about the dynamics of earnings dispersion, we have to address first the issues of data availability and data quality. In my view, these are issues that economists often take too lightly. People tend to download datasets from the Internet and use them uncritically in econometric analyses. In many articles, all that the reader learns is the significance or otherwise of certain coefficients in an economic model. It is not possible to relate the conclusions back to the underlying data, or to assess the sensitivity of the findings to possible shortcomings of the data. Advances in data handling and in computing have allowed much more sophisticated techniques to be applied but they have at the same time distanced the economist from the data.

I therefore want to spend some time describing the data on earnings distribution and the criteria applied here in using the data. My starting point is the book by Lydall (1968), which was a landmark study of the distribution of earnings. A major contribution was its painstaking assembly of data from different countries and the care devoted to differences in definition. One of the main aims of my research has been to bring up to date the work of Lydall and to assemble a new dataset on the distribution of earnings, although for a smaller number of countries: a subset of the members of the OECD. Like him, I have made extensive use of national sources, drawing on published data from official and from academic studies. I have also drawn heavily on the work of the OECD. In the *Employment Outlook* for 1993 and 1996, and now on its website, the OECD has published data on earnings dispersion that has formed the basis for its own research and for many academic studies. I should also acknowledge the help provided by unpublished research of Grubb (1985) who also took Lydall (1968) as his starting point.

The new dataset is described in detail in Part III, but the main features may be summarized as follows:

- The dataset encompasses 20 OECD countries, covering five Anglo-Saxon countries and Ireland, four Nordic countries, seven countries of Continental Europe, and three countries from Eastern Europe.

- Coverage in time extends back as far as possible so as to allow the recent decades to be placed in historical perspective.

- The dataset is not limited to a single source, or type of source (such as household surveys); it typically contains figures from multiple sources for each country.

- The analysis pays particular attention to the consistency of the series across time, and identifies breaks in the series.

- Quality differences are explicitly treated.

The criteria for selection, the sources used, and the problem of consistency over time are discussed further below.

It should be emphasized that the resulting data are *not* comparable across countries, and no attempt has been made to adjust them to a comparable basis. In this respect, I am following not Lydall (1968), but the OECD, which right from the beginning stressed that its earnings dispersion data are not comparable *across countries*: 'differences between countries in both coverage and definition warn that these data should not be used for international comparisons of the level of dispersion' (OECD, 1993, page 166). This warning has not always been heeded by users of the OECD data, and I return to the issue below.

The countries included, and the time period covered, are shown in Figure 4. The graph shows the earliest year in each case; the series are not necessarily continuous and typically have several gaps. The longest series is that for France, which begins in 1919 and ends in 2004, but there are gaps for the Second World War and in a number of post-war years. The UK series has no gaps, but there is a break in comparability and the series is much shorter, not starting until 1954. The statistics for the US used earlier in Figure 1 are from a source that dates back to the 1940s, but the results are published on different bases at different dates. The end year is shown as 2005 in Figure 4, but in a number of countries the series end in 2004 and in some cases the data series stop earlier: for example, the data for Ireland end in 2000. In some cases, such as Australia and the United Kingdom, the data extend to 2006.

CRITERIA FOR DATA SELECTION AND QUALITY GRADING

In assembling a dataset, we have to establish criteria for data selection. The approach adopted here is influenced by, but departs from, the 'Standard

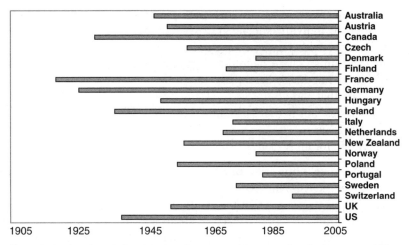

Note: the series do not give data for all years, and there are breaks in comparability

Figure 4 Coverage of data extended back in time

Distribution' approach adopted by Lydall (1968). It departs in the specific criteria adopted (for example, his Standard Distribution relates to male workers, whereas I consider all workers, male and female, wherever possible); and it departs in allowing a variety of definitions (appropriately identified). The latter feature also distinguishes the approach adopted here from har-monization exercises such as those involved in the European Union Structure of Earnings Survey. (I have not used in this study the data from the European Community Household Panel (ECHP), which was input-harmonized. The data are most valuable but cover a relatively short time period.) What is possible in a forward-looking exercise is not possible when seeking to draw together past data drawn from disparate sources. Thus, the data presented below include distributions limited to full year workers and other distribu-tions that also cover part year workers. Some of the data cover workers of all ages; other data are restricted to adult workers. The differences in definition have to be clearly signalled, and taken into account in interpreting the findings, but both types of distribution can aid our understanding.

I differ from earlier studies also in adopting a graded approach to classifica-tion of earnings data. Economists tend to swing between two extreme posi-tions with regard to data quality. They either use any data that can be downloaded, without any consideration of their quality, or they reject any data that depart in any respect from their ideal (for example, considering only household survey micro-data). In my view, we need to adopt an intermediate position, classifying data according to their suitability for the purpose in hand, in the present case the measurement of changes over time in the distribution of individual earnings. As a first step in this direction, I have applied a three-fold classification, parallel to that used in some areas of the national accounts: class A denotes data that are most appropriate, B denotes acceptable, if not ideal, data that may be applied *faute de mieux*, and C denotes data that should not be used. In effect, this divides the useable data into two classes, not perhaps a radical step, but one that serves to signal the data quality issue.

The criteria for an A or B classification, rather than C, are:

1. The data relate to the earnings of *people*, not the earnings of social groups, such as the skilled or unskilled, or cadres, or occupations.
2. The data relate to *individual* earnings, not the total earnings of a household or family.
3. The data relate to actual earnings (typically gross earnings including overtime, bonus payments, commission, holiday or thirteenth month payments), not to wage rates.
4. The data must relate to employees, excluding the self-employed; this is particularly significant at the tails of the distribution.
5. There is national coverage, allowing some exceptions, but not using data relating to particular cities or regions, or confined to urban areas.
6. Coverage of employment is not necessarily complete, but data must cover a major part of the economy.
7. There have to be underlying data on individual earnings, thus ruling out educated guesses by statistical offices based on other data, although not precluding cases where the statistical return aggregates data for individuals (as where employers return the number of employees by ranges of earnings).

The application of these criteria mean, for example, that I classify as C, and hence do not use, data on total income, even where coverage is restricted to those for whom wage or salary income is the primary source (this rules out data for 6 of the 25 countries shown in Tables 5.1 to 5.3 of Lydall (1968)). It means that I do not use data on wage rates.

How are the A and B classifications distinguished? One criterion might be the use of micro-data, rather than reliance on tabulations or grouped data. Where data are grouped into intervals, it is typically necessary to interpolate in order to calculate, say, the top decile. For example, in the UK the percentage earning less than £750 a week may be 88 per cent, and the percentage in the range from £750 to £800 a week may be 4 per cent. If we had access to the micro-data, we could identify the cut-off point that would correspond to 90 per cent, but if we have only interval data we have to interpolate. As has long been recognized, this introduces error. However, I do not feel that we should regard tabulated data as necessarily of significantly lower quality. Where the tabulations were conducted according to the procedures that we would apply if we had the micro-data, and we can interpolate with reasonable accuracy, then there is no reason for not giving an A classification. The error of interpolation depends on the number of ranges, their relation to the key percentiles (bottom 10th, 25th, 50th, 75th, and 90th), and on whether the information includes the interval mean as well as the interval frequency. Where the tabulations only permit an approximate interpolation, then a B classification is applied. The method of interpolation is described in the Introduction to Part III, but I should note here that, in the light of the volume of data involved, and the need for uniformity, I have adopted in most cases a relatively simple approach.

In the same way, I do not require that the data contain information on hours, and I do not limit attention to hourly earnings. Whereas hourly labour costs are the most relevant variable for the employer, my perspective here is that of the employee. For the employee, it is the combined hours–earnings package that is of concern. To be paid €100 for one hour is a very different proposition if only one hour of employment is offered from the situation where this hourly rate applies to a 35-hour week. Moreover, in a number of occupations, 'hours paid for' and 'hours worked' may differ considerably. And a number of empirical studies find that hours are poorly reported: for example, in the case of the French Enquête Emploi, 'as is usually the case for this sort of survey based on individuals' responses to interviews, hours worked are badly reported' (Bonhomme and Robin, 2004, page 19). This is not to suggest that hours are unimportant. In interpreting the evidence, one needs to take account of the difference between distributions of hourly earnings and distributions of weekly, monthly, or annual earnings. The extent of part time employment is important in understanding the distribution of total earnings. But all of hourly, weekly, monthly, and annual earnings are treated here as potentially qualifying for an A classification.

The third possible distinction between A and B classifications relates to the extent of coverage. Earnings data commonly exclude some sectors of employment. The exclusions may relate to agriculture or government service; they may exclude people employed in small enterprises; the data may be truncated at the top or the bottom of the distribution. Given that complete coverage is a counsel of perfection, rarely attained, it does not seem reasonable to relegate distributions from A to B solely on this account. This is especially important when seeking to go back in time. Rather, I suggest that it should be a matter of judgement in each case whether the exclusions are sufficiently important to reduce the classification to B, or indeed C.

VARIETY OF SOURCES

Economists today tend to think of household surveys as the primary micro-data source, but in fact there are many possible sources, including one that I had never previously envisaged. As in the case of distributions of income, information may be available from household surveys, either one-off or repeated panels, from censuses of population, from individual income tax records or other administrative data, or from household surveys linked to administrative records. In the case of earnings, the range of sources is even greater. An individual worker is engaged in a market transaction, and—just as in national accounting—one can make use of information from both sides of the market. One can interrogate the other side of the labour market by surveys of employers. One can use administrative records relating to employers. One can use—a source new to me—information collected in regular censuses of production. We should also note that these may be micro-data at the level of the employer but not for the individual worker: that is, the employer may be asked how many workers are paid in different bands. From this information, we can construct a distribution even though there are no underlying micro-data on individual workers.

A multiplicity of sources is indeed found for different countries in the OECD database. In a number of cases the data are derived from household surveys, such as the US Current Population Survey. In some cases these are panel surveys, such as the German Socio-Economic Panel (GSOEP). In some cases, the household surveys are linked to administrative data, as with the Income Distribution Survey in Finland. In other cases, the data are purely derived from administrative records: in France, the Déclarations Annuelles des Données Sociales (DADS) are the principal source of earnings data. The OECD data in some cases come from employers, as with the New Earnings Survey (NES) in the UK, which is based on a sample of employees but the data are collected from employers. The earlier OECD data showed results for Portugal from the Quadros de Pessoal, which is a census of employers. In this study, I have drawn on all these sources, and on more. A flavour is provided by Table 1, which summarizes the main types of data source and gives examples from those used here.

Table 1. Variety of sources of earnings distribution data in OECD countries

Type of source	Sub-category	Examples
Household survey	Repeated cross-section	*Weekly Earnings of Employees* in Australia; *Microcensus* in Czech Republic; *Household Economic Survey* in New Zealand; *Current Population Survey* in the United States
	Panel	*German Socio-Economic Panel; Living in Ireland Survey;* Bank of Italy *Survey of Household Income and Wealth* (part panel)
Household survey/ linked		*Survey of Labour and Income Dynamics* in Canada; *Income Distribution Survey* in Finland and Sweden
Administrative data	Income tax returns filed by taxpayers	*Income Statistics Register* in Denmark; *Longitudinal Administrative Databank* in Canada
	Earnings returns by employers to tax and social security administrations	*Déclarations Annuelles des Données Sociales;* in France; *Lohnsteuerstatistik* in Austria and Germany; *Istituto Nazionale per la Providenza Sociale* data in Italy
Employer survey	Census of employers	*Quadros de Pessoal* in Portugal
	Sample of employers/ sample of their employees	*Gehalts- und Lohnstrukturerhebung* in Germany; *Enquête Suisse sur la structure des salaries/Schweizerische Lohnstrukturerhebung* in Switzerland
	Sample of employees/ information obtained by contacting employers	*New Earnings Survey* in the United Kingdom
Census of Population		*Census of the Population* in Canada, Finland, Norway, and the United States
Census of Production		*Census of Industrial Production* in Ireland
Combination of sources		*LoonStrukturOnderzoeken* in the Netherlands

Within countries, the multiplicity of sources means that we may have alternative series. In the UK, for example, data on earnings have in the past been available both from the employer survey (the NES) and from household surveys, such as the Family Expenditure Survey, and from the income tax records. In Germany, the OECD database is based on the German Socio-Economic Panel, a household survey, but there are also earnings data from the *Gehalts- und Lohnerhebung*, a survey of employers, and from the wage tax data. These other sources can augment the household survey data in two respects: they can provide an alternative picture of earnings dispersion in the years covered, and they can provide data for years not covered, typically earlier parts of the period.

DATA ACROSS COUNTRIES

One major reason why the OECD warn against using their data for comparisons across countries is that the data for different countries are drawn from different sources. These differences in sources mean that data are not necessarily comparable across different countries. An employer reports the earnings of a worker in his establishment, and cannot give the total where a person has multiple employments. Even for the same employment, the responses by the employer may differ from those given by the employee. Hours of work are an example. The employer is likely to report contractual hours; the employee may report hours actually worked. Administrative records may be more accurate than recall by survey respondents; they may also be less complete on account of non-reported earnings. Data based on tax or social security records will reflect the specific features of each country's tax and social security systems.

The detailed accounts provided in Part III will allow the reader to examine some of the consequences of these differences of source within a single country. The level of dispersion varies considerably in a number of cases, such as the difference between the employer survey and income tax-based estimates in the UK, the difference between the social security data and the household survey results for Italy, or the difference between employer survey and household survey in Germany. The differences can change radically the position of a country in an international comparison. For example, from Figure K.2 we can see that the bottom decile in Italy in the 1990s can be either over 70 per cent of the median (social security data) or under 60 per cent (Bank of Italy Survey of Household Income and Wealth).

A second important source of non-comparability is difference in coverage. This may be related to the differences in sources: for example, a social security system may not cover public administration, and these workers may not be covered by statistics drawn from the social security records. Or there may be differences in the definition of the population covered. Atkinson and Brandolini (2006, Table 14.3) summarize some of the differences among the 15 countries covered by the OECD 1993 dataset. The data for Australia are limited to non-managerial workers. The data for Australia, Belgium, and Portugal are limited to full time workers. Canada, Germany, and Italy further require that the workers have worked a full year. In the case of the United Kingdom, the earnings refer to those of the current pay period (week or month). In some cases the data are top coded, and in two cases there is a bottom code. The data for four countries exclude agriculture.

Readers will nonetheless be interested in cross-country comparisons. I have therefore shown in Figure 5 the results from the European Structure of Earnings Survey (SES), a four-yearly survey designed to be comparable across countries. It covers 15 of the 20 countries studied here. The data relate to 2002 (except that the data for Germany relate to 2001). The pattern shown across countries is not perhaps surprising, with the Nordic countries having the lowest dispersion, with the central mainland European countries towards the middle, and the southern European countries (but not Italy) tending to have greater dispersion. The UK and the former Communist countries (but not the Czech Republic) tended to have the highest decile ratios. It should be noted that, while the SES is a major resource, it has limitations that affect the degree of comparability. Its coverage in 2002 was limited to enterprises with at least ten employees. Its sectoral coverage is partial. Required coverage of sectors was NACE categories C to K (mining, manufacturing, electricity, water and gas, construction, wholesale and retail trade, repairs, hotels and restaurants, transport, storage and communication, financial intermediation, and real estate). Important sectors of the labour force are therefore missing, and the omissions are likely to affect countries differently. For example, the omission of agriculture will differentially affect the United Kingdom and Poland. The omission of the public services will differentially affect Norway and Portugal. Nevertheless, the exploration of

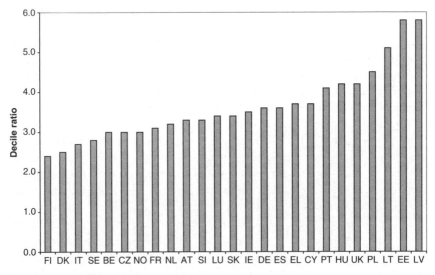

Figure 5 Earnings dispersion in EU25: decile ratio in 2002

the cross-European differences, using sources such as the SES and the ECHP, is a promising avenue (see, for example, Tsakloglou and Cholezas, 2006).

CONSISTENCY OVER TIME

I have emphasized so far the problems of cross-country comparisons, but similar issues of comparability arise over time. The data series presented below are in fact a patchwork for each country of data from different sources, as will be clear to the reader from browsing the charts in Part III. In the case of Australia, the earlier years are covered by income tax data, but the more recent years by employer survey and household survey data. In Canada, the earliest figures are those from the census of population, but this is followed by employer surveys and by household surveys linked to administrative records. In Germany, for example, there is information from the wage tax for earlier years, but in combining the series with more recent evidence from the German Socio-Economic Panel, we have to be careful about the join.

The existence of multiple sources also means that we may have conflicting results regarding the direction of change. This is well illustrated by the following quotation about Canada:

unlike the United States where there is an unambiguous increase in wage inequality [since the early 1980s] existing studies for Canada provide an ambiguous picture on the evolution of wage inequality. On the one hand, studies that look at inequality in hourly wage rates using special supplements to the LFS [Labour Force Survey] generally find little change in overall measures of wage inequality like the variance of log wages. On the other hand, studies that look at inequality in weekly or annual earnings using the Survey of Consumer Finances, the Canadian Census, or administrative tax data tend to find steady growth in earnings inequality. (Boudarbat, Lemieux, and Riddell, 2003, pages 1 and 2)

As this brings out, the alternative may involve a different definition (hourly versus annual earnings) or a different data source (tax data rather than household survey). Or, there may be a combination: one source may not, for example, allow the calculation of hourly, as opposed to annual, earnings. A second example is provided by Italy, where there are three different sources: social security data now used in the OECD LMS database, the Bank of Italy household survey used in earlier OECD compendia, and some limited information from the income tax tabulations. The income tax data, for the 1980s, are broadly in line with the data from the Bank of Italy household survey, in terms of changes over time (it is not surprising that the level is different, since the tax data refer to annual earnings and include part year incomes). But the household survey data depart from the social security data in the 1990s, the former indicating a fall in the bottom decile relative to the median, which may in part be due to the change in survey organization but which may also reflect a fuller coverage of the informal economy.

In certain cases, the differences in the sources may only become apparent when looking at the data. An example is provided by the Netherlands. In 1994 the bottom decile for all workers was 64.3 per cent of the median; a year later, in 1995, the bottom decile had fallen to 61.0 per cent. Such a fall is perfectly possible. However, it prompts the cautious reader to go back to the original source. (The top decile similarly jumps upwards from 165.8 per cent to 171.9 per cent of the median.) When we go back to the source, we discover that 1995 turns out to have been the year in which the current form of the Structure of Earnings Survey was first introduced. Breaks in comparability may occur even when the underlying source is unchanged. An example is provided by France. On examination, it turns out that the estimates supplied by the national statistical office were, for certain years, not based on underlying micro-data (Piketty, 2001, page 665). The data for 1981, 1983, and 1990 are estimates by Institut National de la Statistique et des Etudes Economiques (INSEE), not based on the employer declarations for those years, which were not analysed on account of the workload arising from the censuses of 1982 and 1990 (see Chapter G). While the estimates were no doubt well-founded, they cannot be treated as comparable with other observations. Another example, much discussed in the United States, is the impact of the changes made by the US Census Bureau with effect from the 1993 Current Population Survey. These included the fact that the data collection method changed from paper and pencil to computer-assisted interviewing, and a substantial increase in the top code permitted for earnings. As noted in Chapter T in Part III, the Census Bureau believe that the former change may have stimulated a higher response rate from high-earning individuals. There is in fact a continuing process of upgrading the estimation procedures: for example, the implementation of new control totals as they become available from the Census of Population. The Census Bureau website contains a very helpful chart listing of the significant changes; changes are listed for 22 of the 52 years covered by the period 1949 to 2000.

Problems of comparability over time may arise not on account of changes in the data collection or analysis, but because a constant instrument of measurement is being applied in changing circumstances. An example is provided by Hungary, where a personal income tax was introduced in 1988, and at the same time the gross pay was adjusted so as to compensate. The top decile jumped from 164 per cent of the median to 183 per cent, but this should not be taken as a measure of increased dispersion. The impact of employer-provided health insurance in the United States is a second example. Such health insurance payments form part of total compensation but are not included in money wages, an omission that takes on particular significance in view of their rise as a percentage of total compensation (Burtless, 2007). The implications for measured dispersion are not immediately clear. While the coverage of employer-sponsored plans is likely to favour the better paid, the value may rise less than proportionately with earnings. The impact has been examined empirically by Pierce, who finds that 'inequality growth in broader measures of compensation slightly exceeds wage inequality growth over the 1981–1997 period' (2001, page 1493).

The material assembled here is not, therefore, a neat dataset that can be downloaded and used directly for statistical estimation. The user has to look at the data and exercise judgement as to how the series can be used for the purpose at hand. It may be quite reasonable to chain different series, using overlapping values, and this practice has been followed here. But it requires care and awareness of the implications of selecting one source over another. This applies particularly to the question of measuring the extent of change in dispersion over time.

METRICS AND LANGUAGE

Much of the recent US literature has been motivated by the size of the increase in wage differentials. The following quotation from Juhn, Murphy, and Pierce is typical: 'in this paper we have identified the enormous increase in wage inequality among male workers over the past two decades' (1993, page 441). The same applies to other countries where differentials have widened: 'it is now well established that, over the last fifteen years, the dispersion of male earnings in Canada has widened considerably' (Beaudry and Green, 2000, page 907). Referring to the earlier movement in the opposite direction, in this case in Sweden, Edin and Holmlund say that 'wage inequality declined precipitously during the 1960s and 1970s. There was a sharp reduction in overall wage dispersion' (1995, page 307). On the other hand, there are countries where differentials have not increased so noticeably. According to a paper published by the Office of the Prime Minister of Finland, 'changes over time in individual pay differentials have been quite modest during the last two decades' (Vartiainen, 1998, section 2.2).

Adjectives such as 'enormous' or 'modest' and adverbs such as 'precipitously' do however raise questions as to the metric that is being applied. How large does an increase have to be in order for us to describe it as 'enormous'?

Presumably the increase has to be larger than one described as 'considerable', but how much larger? How small does a change have to be in order that we can apply the description 'modest'? Is the change measured absolutely or as a rate of change over time? Would the same change have been less noteworthy if it had taken place over four, rather than two, decades?

The need for clarity is particularly important when contrasting changes in different countries. The surveys by Gottschalk and Smeeding, and by Katz and Autor, have rightly stressed the differences across countries, as summarized in the following excerpts:

Almost all industrial economies experienced *some* increase in wage inequality among prime-age males during the 1980s (Germany and Italy are the exceptions)....But *large* differences in trends also exist across countries, with earnings inequality increasing most in the United States and the United Kingdom and least in the Nordic countries. (Gottschalk and Smeeding, 1997, page 636, italics added)

The United States and the United Kingdom experienced *sharp* increases in overall wage inequality...The pattern of declining wage inequality apparent throughout the OECD (except the United States) in the 1970s ceased in the 1980s and 1990s in almost all nations (with Germany and Norway as possible exceptions). Canada, Australia, Japan, and Sweden had *modest* increases in wage inequality...Wage differentials and inequality narrowed through the mid-1980s in Italy and France with *some hint* of expanding in France in the late 1980s and with a *large* increase in inequality in Italy in the 1990s...New Zealand also shows *large* increases in inequality. (Katz and Autor, 1999, pages 1502–3, italics added)

But the terms italicized need to be defined. Most importantly, how large does a change have to be in order to be registered? The bottom decile falling from 50 per cent of the median to 49.9 per cent clearly does not qualify, but what about a fall to 48 per cent?

The issue of the choice of metric is rarely discussed. There is indeed a contrast between the sophistication of the econometric methods applied to earnings data and the looseness of the vocabulary of economists in their statistical descriptions. I should stress that this is, as much as anything, self-criticism, since I have employed such undefined adjectives frequently in the past. By way of making amends, I would like to make clear the criteria applied here. Any such criteria are, of course, largely arbitrary, and the only merits I claim for the conventions described below are (a) that they are explicit and (b) that they do not seem unreasonable.

In considering changes over a period of decades, I require for a change to 'register' that there be a 5 per cent change in a percentile (defined relative to the median), or a 10 per cent change in the decile ratio. I take percentage changes since the values vary according to the definition of earnings (for example, annual earnings are more dispersed than current month earnings). For a bottom decile of 50 per cent, it means that a fall is registered if the decile goes below 47.5 per cent. For a top decile of 200, a rise to 210 would qualify as a 'rise'. It should be noted that I am not referring here to sampling errors (which vary with the source); rather I have in mind a judgement based on the economic significance. If real earnings grow on average at an annual rate of at least $\frac{1}{2}$ per cent, then a 5 per cent fall relative to the median over a decade is still consistent with positive real earnings growth. Or, viewed in terms of Figure 5, a rise of 5 per cent in the top decile would move Norway one place to the right; the same change in Portugal would move it two places but still leave it below Poland.

If it takes a variation outside the band (± 5 per cent) to register, then it seems reasonable to define gradations. Again the following conventions are arbitrary, but I have taken a rise or fall of 10 per cent or more as being 'significant', and a change of 20 per cent or more as being 'large'. In the case of the bottom decile, this would mean a fall from 50 per cent to 45 per cent to qualify as 'significant', and a fall to 40 per cent to qualify as 'large'. In the case of the top decile, it would mean a rise from 200 to 220 to qualify as 'significant', and a rise to 240 to qualify as 'large'. Such a grading may appear to set the bar too high. It is indeed the case that the US top decile rose 'only' from 195 to 223 per cent of the median between 1980 and 2000, which would therefore be described as a 'significant' but not 'large' increase. On the other hand, there have been changes of greater magnitude, including at earlier dates in the US. In comparative terms (using the data in Figure 5), a rise of 20 per cent in the top decile would make Norway like Germany; combined with a simultaneous fall of 20 per cent in the bottom decile, such a change would make the Norwegian distribution like that of Poland.

SUMMARY

Assembly of a dataset requires explicit criteria for data selection, criteria that need to be tailored to the purpose at hand. The purpose here is to examine the changes over time in the dispersion of the earnings of individual employees. I have adopted a graded approach to data quality. In some cases, data have been rejected (classification C); in other cases, data are classified as B (acceptable if not ideal), rather than A (most appropriate). Restricting attention to series classified as A or B, there is still a rich range of sources about the distribution of earnings on which I have drawn in order to give as full a picture as possible. At the same time, the sources can yield rather different results, and are not

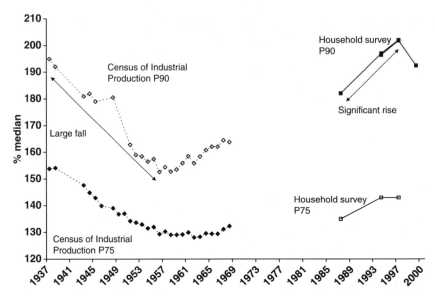

Figure 6 Ireland upper part of distribution 1937–2000

necessarily comparable over time. The data presented below are best seen as a patchwork rather than as a single, unified series. Finally, I have set out conventions for registering the extent of change.

The approach adopted here to data may be summarized in terms of the series for the upper part of the earnings distribution in Ireland shown in Figure 6, which illustrates several of the points made in this section. It makes use of a source (the Census of Industrial Production) that—with the notable exception of Stark (1977)—has been neglected; it contains data of varying quality (the Census of Production data are only graded B on account of their limited coverage); the top decile exhibited a 'large' fall from the 1930s to the 1950s, and a 'significant' rise in the 1980s and 1990s.

4

The Changes in Dispersion since 1980

There are certainly good reasons to expect there have been changes in the degree of earnings dispersion in the past 25 years. Reading the history of labour market developments in the 20 countries, I am struck by the emphasis on the extent of change. This applies not only to the formerly Communist countries, and not only to well known cases such as the UK and the Netherlands, but also to countries such as Canada and Australia:

In the 1990s, Canada's labour market was characterized by a number of major changes in relation to the previous decade. A greater integration of the Canadian and United States economies (with increased north-south trade flows), increased globalization writ more large, rapid technological change, shifting modes and organization of production, demographic shifts (such as immigration activity), and structural changes to employment contributed to significant workplace and labour market changes. (Beach, Finnie, and Gray, 2003, page S42)

In the period since the 1960s there have been many dramatic changes in the Australian labour market. Increases in the labour force participation of females, the growth of part-time employment and a shift in the composition of employment from manufacturing to service sectors. (Borland, 1997, page 28)

What has been the impact on the distribution of earnings? One virtue of concentrating on the changes since 1980 is that the data for the recent decades are fuller and more reliable. We have fewer of the problems examined in the previous section. All but Switzerland provide data going back to the 1980s, even if in some cases the series starts after 1980 (and in some cases cannot be continued beyond the late 1990s). The series used for the 19 countries are listed in Table 2, together with notes. For more information about the sources, the reader is referred to the relevant country chapter in Part III. In general, the change since 1980 is calculated by taking the difference in a three-year average centred on 1981 and the average of the three most recent years, although this is limited by the availability of data (see the final column of Table 2). So that, for the United States, the average for 2003, 2004, and 2005 is compared with the average for 1979, 1980, and 1981. The aim of the averaging is to reduce the influence of year-to-year fluctuations. The data relate to gross

Table 2. Data sources used in analysis of change in earnings dispersion since 1980

Country (abbreviation in graphs)	Source	Notes
Australia (AL)	*Weekly Earnings of Employees* survey	Data 1979–81 averaged to 2001–3 averaged. Use of *Employee Earnings and Hours* employer survey leads to different findings for changes in bottom decile
Austria (AT)	Earnings statistics of the Austrian Association of Social Insurance Funds and *Lohnsteuerstatistik*	Linked social security and wage tax series, assuming no change from 1996 to 1997 (hence grade B)
Canada (CA)	*Survey of Consumer Finances*	1981 single year to 1994 single year
Czech Republic (CZ)	Census of enterprises	1979 and 1981 averaged to 1999 single year, linked to earlier series for Czechoslovakia
Denmark (DK)	Tax registers	1980–1 averaged to 2001–3 averaged, linked series
Finland (FI)	*Income Distribution Survey*	1980 single year to 2000–2 averaged
France (FR)	*Déclarations Annuelles des Données Sociales (DADS)*	1979–80 averaged to 2002–4 averaged, ignoring break between 1992 and 1994 Data relate to earnings net of social security contributions
Germany (DE)	*German Socio-Economic Panel*	1984 single year to 2000–2 averaged
Hungary (HU)	Enterprise earnings survey	1980 single year to 2001–3 (1998–2000 for bottom decile) averaged. Allow for introduction of personal income tax in 1988 by assuming change from 1986 to 1989 same as from 1984 to 1986 (hence graded B)
Ireland (IE)	*Living in Ireland Survey*	1987 single year to 2000 single year
Italy (IT)	*Survey of Household Income and Wealth* (Bank of Italy)	Data 1979–81 averaged to 2002 and 2004 averaged
Netherlands (NL)	Employer survey	Data for 1979 single year and 2003–5 averaged; hourly earnings for full time equivalent workers. Allows for break in 1995 by assuming no change between 1994 and 1995 (hence grade B)
New Zealand (NZ)	*Household Economic Survey*	1984 single year to 1997 single year

Norway (NO)	Tax register data	1986 single year and 2000–2 averaged; deciles interpolated from share data (hence graded B)
Poland (PL)	Enterprise survey	1980–1 averaged to 2002 and 2004 averaged; net series linked to gross series
Portugal (PT)	*Quadros de Pessoal*	1982 to 2000 and 2002 averaged
Sweden (SE)	*Income Distribution Survey*	1980–1 averaged to 2002–4 averaged
United Kingdom (UK)	*Annual Survey of Hours and Earnings,* previously *New Earnings Survey*	1979–81 averaged to 2004–6 averaged
United States (US)	*Current Population Survey,* Outgoing Rotation Group	1979–81 averaged to 2003–5 averaged

earnings (with the exception of France, where social security contributions have been deducted) of all workers (male and female) of all ages.

Before describing the findings, I should emphasize that this analysis looks at the distribution of earnings from a particular perspective. I am concerned with earnings as received by workers, not the cost of labour to employers. I am looking at the whole of the labour force, not at particular groups or cohorts. Many of the tables in Part III show the distribution separately for men and women, but here I am not considering the differences by gender. This perspective means that one cannot observe changes within the distribution, such as in the extent of part time working. For this, a different, more detailed analysis is necessary. I focus on the *relative* distribution, in that I look at the top and bottom deciles, each expressed as a proportion of the median. So a fall in the bottom decile means that the earnings of the person at that decile have risen less fast than those of the median worker. Such a fall would be quite consistent with the earnings of both having increased in terms of purchasing power.

In Figure 7 are shown the changes in the top and bottom deciles (expressed as proportions of the median) from 1980 to the early years of this century: that is, a period of some 25 years. Where, in this graph, a country is identified by a # sign, this corresponds to a series graded B, rather than A, or where the linking of different series is considered to be less than fully satisfactory.

What does the graph show? We can see, first, that there *has* been considerable change between the beginning and end of the 25 year period. Sixteen of the 19 countries have a change in either top or bottom decile that is sufficient to 'register' according to the criterion adopted here (indicated by the heavy horizontal lines in Figure 7). More than half of the countries exhibit changes

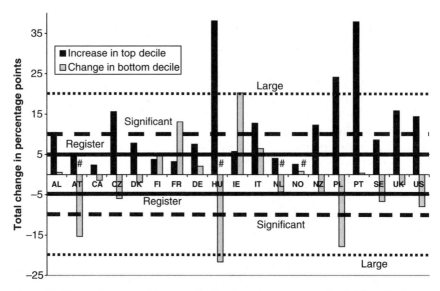

Figure 7 Change in top and bottom deciles (relative to the median) 1980–2004

that meet the criterion of 'significance' according to the standard applied here. Theories of distributional change have therefore some purchase. We are not watching grass grow.

We can see, secondly, the importance of looking separately at the top and bottom deciles. It may be the case that the decile ratio is rising because both top and bottom are moving away from the median. From Figure 7 we can see that this was true in the United States, where the bottom decile fell by more than 5 per cent and the top decile rose by nearly 15 per cent. Both of these changes are sufficient to register. At the same time, even in the United States the changes were not symmetric: the fall in the bottom decile contributed much less than the rise in the top decile. Indeed, the rise in the top decile in the United States qualified as significant.

Which countries had both top and bottom moving outside the range marked by the heavy horizontal lines? One group is clear: the three countries of Eastern Europe. Here the fall in the bottom decile was large enough to register in all three countries, and was significant in Poland and Hungary (where the data are qualified in the light of the need to make an adjustment for the introduction of the personal income tax, hence the #). In all three, the rise in the top decile was large. Clearly, for these countries the period includes the transition to a market economy, and a different set of explanations apply. For this reason, I leave them on one side until the next section. Of the remaining 16 countries, only 4 (Austria, New Zealand, Sweden, and the United States) have top and bottom deciles that move outside the heavy horizontal lines (i.e. fall or rise by 5 per cent or more). For 12 of the 16 countries, the bottom decile does not fall by enough, during this 25 year period, to register. Indeed, in 4 countries the bottom decile *rose* relative to the median by enough to register. The asymmetry noted for the United States applies more generally. For 11 of the 16 countries, the top decile rose by enough to register; indeed for 6 of the 16, the rise met the criterion of being significant. This brings us to the second conclusion: the bulk of the change over this period has been at the top rather than the bottom. The omission of the four countries whose estimates are graded B would not affect this conclusion.

At the same time, the experience of the 16 countries is quite diverse, as has been stressed in earlier reviews of the evidence such as that by Gottschalk and Smeeding (1997) and Katz and Autor (1999). The rise in dispersion in the United States stood out: the broad consensus emerging out of this literature is that while almost all countries experienced some increase in earnings inequality, 'the United States was unusual in the magnitude of the rise in overall inequality' (Gottschalk and Joyce, 1998, page 490). In a comparison of the US, UK, France, and Japan, Katz, Loveman, and Blanchflower concluded that 'all four countries share a pattern of rising wage inequality among both men and women in the 1980s, but the magnitudes of the increases differ substantially. Great Britain and the United States both displayed dramatic increases in wage inequality during the 1980s, while the increase in Japan was much more moderate. France experienced declining inequality until 1984 and a moderate increase from 1984 to 1987' (1993, page 3).

A number of interesting country differences do indeed emerge in Figure 7. For example, the United Kingdom is often seen as transatlantic, but we can see that, in contrast to the experience of the United States, the bottom decile did not fall by enough to register. The difference between (West) Germany and France is noteworthy. Germany is widely regarded as a country with a rigid wage structure. To quote one comparative study, 'the dramatic changes that have been seen in the UK and the US labour markets, which increased the gap between skilled and unskilled workers and inequality within skill groups, have not occurred in West Germany' (Giles, Gosling, Laisney, and Geib, 1998, page 83). Indeed, there was not long ago an article in the *IMF Staff Papers* entitled 'The Unbearable Stability of the German Wage Structure' (Prasad, 2004). But Figure 7 shows Germany as one of the countries registering a rise in the top decile. Diversity may of course be more apparent than real, resulting from the differences in sources and from imposing a common analytical framework that fits some countries less well. It should be noted for example that, if for Australia we had used data from the Employee

Earnings and Hours survey, rather than the Weekly Earnings of Employees survey, then there would have been a reduction in the bottom decile of over 10 per cent. The choice of a different starting date would have affected the conclusions drawn for the Netherlands: starting in 1985, rather than 1979, would have led to the recording of a 5 per cent rise in the top decile and an 8 per cent fall in the bottom decile (in this case the asymmetry is in the opposite direction). This underlines the need to look at the full run of years, not just take isolated points, and this is the approach taken in the next section.

FANNING OUT

I have emphasized the necessity of looking separately at the top and bottom deciles, but we need also to look in more detail at different percentiles. If we examine the upper part of the earnings distribution, then we can see that in a number—but not all—countries there has been a 'fanning out'. This is illustrated year by year by the UK data in Figure 8. In constructing this figure, I have started with all nine deciles of the earnings distribution, from the bottom decile (called P10), up via P20 (the earnings of a person a fifth of the way up the distribution), through the median (P50), to the top decile (P90). In each case the earnings are expressed relative to the median, so that P50 = 1. I have then calculated the *changes* in these percentiles by expressing them relative to their values in 1977, so that a value of 1.1 in Figure 8 means that the percentile has risen by 10 per cent. All start at 1.0, and the median remains there (shown by the dashed line). There is no reason for the percentiles to remain in order, and the reader can see that P20 lies above P30 in some years, which means that P30 had fallen more, relative to its 1977 value, than P20. But in general they do remain in order. The heavy horizontal lines show the 5 per cent range, and it is striking that the bottom 60 per cent remain within these bounds: over the period as a whole, they do not register any change according to the standard applied here. It is true that the bottom decile fell below in the mid 1980s, and remained below until the end of the 1990s. If I had taken a period ending before 2000, then a fall would have been registered. This fall was missed by my earlier analysis considering only the endpoints. But such a conclusion for the period up to 2000 would equally have missed the fact that the bottom decile has been recovering since 1995. Moreover, all the other deciles in the bottom half of the distribution have been broadly stable for the past 30 years. Of particular

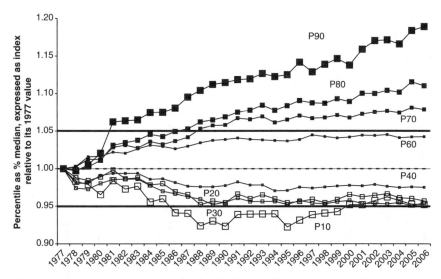

Figure 8 Changes in earnings deciles in the United Kingdom 1977–2006

interest is what is happening above the median. The sixth decile (P60) increased by less than 5 per cent, but all higher deciles increased by more than 5 per cent. The deciles have been increasing progressively more, the higher up the distribution one looks. P70 rose by 8 per cent, P80 by 11 per cent, and P90 by 19 per cent.

This 'fanning out' of the upper part of the distribution has not happened in all countries. It has not taken place in countries such as Denmark, Finland, and France, where we have not observed a registrable rise in dispersion at the top. It does not appear to have taken place in the Czech Republic. But in quite a number of countries we observe a pattern where the upper quartile has grown less than the top decile, and where the top decile has grown less than the top vintile (P95). Figure 9 shows that the pattern holds in ten countries, with a range of countries represented: Anglo-Saxon, Continental European, Nordic, and Eastern European. The periods covered differ (see the note to the Figure), depending on the availability of consistent series, and in some cases series have been linked. (The figures for the United Kingdom relate to a slightly shorter period than those in Figure 8.) The series are all graded A, and it is interesting to note the general agreement of the two series for Germany, covering overlapping, but different, periods. In the case of Switzerland, too, not covered so far in this section, the employer survey data show a fanning out from 1996 to 2004, with P90 rising nearly twice as much as P80 (see Figure R.1 in Part III).

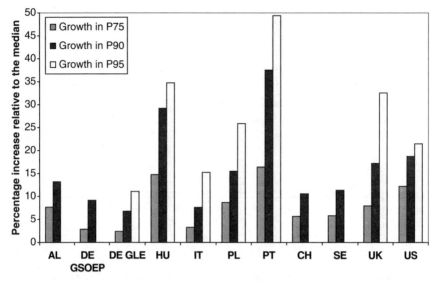

Note: AL 1975–2006; DE GSOEP 1984–1998; DE GLE 1962–1995; HU 1994–2003; IT 1977–2004; PL 1992–2004; PT 1982–2002; CH 1996–2004; SE 1983–2004; UK 1977–2001; US 1973–2005

Figure 9 Fanning out in the upper part of the distribution

CONCLUSIONS

From this first look at the evidence, I draw the following conclusions:

- In most of the 19 countries the distribution of earnings has changed between 1980 and today: for 16 out of 19, either the bottom decile has fallen by 5 per cent or more, or the top decile has risen by 5 per cent or more, and in 7 cases both have happened.

- It is not enough to look just at the decile ratio, which masks the asymmetry in the changes in the distribution; much of the action over the past 25+ years has been in the upper part of the distribution.

- There is diversity in the experience of individual countries, which justifies closer examination, including looking at the full run of years.

- In quite a number of countries, but not all, there has been a 'fanning out' of the upper half of the distribution.

5

Recent History in Full: Was there a Lull before the Storm?

In this section I give a fuller account of the evolution of the distribution of earnings in recent decades, set out graphically in Figures 10–15. Consideration of just the endpoints may mean that we miss significant events within the period, as we have seen with the examples of the Netherlands and the United Kingdom. We have to see the movie as a whole, not just wake up for the denouement. The graphs all start in 1965 (1960 for Figure 14 and 1951 for Figure 15); although in most cases the first data points shown are later. The graphs draw on the data assembled in the country chapters of Part III, to which the reader is referred for the sources. In each case, a selection has had to be made regarding the sources. In this section, I have tended to take those series providing the longest run of years on a consistent basis, but, as we have already seen in the case of Australia, different data sources may yield different conclusions. Each graph typically covers 2 countries, and 13 of the 20 are represented. The data sources are shown in Table 3. The countries not covered, on account of data limitations, are Austria, Denmark, Ireland, the Netherlands, New Zealand, Norway, and Switzerland. The reader can find material for these countries in the country chapters.

The data assembled here are not comparable across countries, so that one cannot draw any conclusions about the relative degrees of dispersion from comparing the different lines in Figures 10–14 (the exception, Figure 15, concerns Eastern Europe, discussed separately below). Any such cross-country comparisons require further research. The data should therefore be considered as a panel of countries with an unknown country difference. To a first approximation, this country difference can be treated as a constant fixed effect, although differences in coverage and in sources may cause the country differences to vary over time. For example, if the earnings data for one country omit farming, the effect may have been larger in the 1960s than today. This qualification needs to be borne in mind. I have also noted that the series cannot be regarded as fully comparable within a country over time. I have however attempted to overcome the main discontinuities by selection of

Table 3. Data sources used in Figures 10–15

Country (abbreviation in graphs)	Source
Australia (AL)	*Employee Earnings and Hours* (Table A.5)
Canada (CA)	*Survey of Consumer Finances* (Table C.3) and *Survey of Labour and Income Dynamics* (Table C.6)
Czech Republic (CZ)	Census of enterprises (Tables D.2, D.3, D.5, and D.6 linked)
Finland (FI)	*Income Distribution Survey* and census of population (Tables F.2 and F.3)
France (FR)	*Déclarations Annuelles des Données Sociales (DADS)* (Tables G.3 and G.7 linked)
Germany (DE)	*German Socio-Economic Panel* (Table H.3), and earlier *Lohnsteuer* (Table H.5)
Hungary (HU)	Enterprise earnings survey (Tables I.1 and I.2 linked, and Table I.4), with break shown for introduction of income tax in 1988
Italy (IT)	*Survey of Household Income and Wealth* (Table K.4)
Poland (PL)	Enterprise survey (Tables O.1 and O.3), linking gross and net series
Portugal (PT)	*Quadros de Pessoal* (Table P.3)
Sweden (SE)	*Income Distribution Survey* (Table Q.5), and earlier *Pensionable Income Register* (Table Q.6)
United Kingdom (UK)	*Annual Survey of Hours and Earnings* (Table S.5) linked to earlier *New Earnings Survey* (Table S.4)
United States (US)	*Current Population Survey*, Outgoing Rotation Group (Table T.4)

series, by linking where appropriate, and by showing breaks where necessary (for example, when the Survey of Consumer Finances was replaced by a new source in Canada).

   With the dataset constructed here, it would be possible to carry out a panel of countries analysis, looking at all countries simultaneously, with country fixed effects as described earlier. A number of interesting studies have used the OECD datasets in this way, such as Wallerstein (1999) and Rueda and Pontusson (2000), who seek to explain variation in the decile ratio as a function of economic and political variables. (For a review of these studies, and those using data on incomes, see Atkinson and Brandolini, 2006.) Here, my analysis is at an earlier stage, in that I want simply to 'look at' the data for each country, to identify the main changes over time and the similarities and dissimilarities across countries in the pattern of evolution. Moreover, I do not limit attention to a single summary statistic; I am interested in differences in experience at different points in the earnings hierarchy. To this end, I show in Figures 10–15 the evolution of the bottom decile, marked by the hollow symbols, the upper quartile (or upper quintile), marked by the smaller solid symbols, and the top decile, marked by the larger solid symbols, each expressed as a percentage of the median. The top decile and upper quartile (quintile) are measured in each case on the left-hand (LH) axis; the bottom decile is measured on the right-hand (RH) axis.

Examination of the recent history in full is of substantive interest. In particular, it is often suggested that the recent rise in dispersion came after a period of stability. Are we in this sense experiencing a 'New Economy'? In the United States, Jones and Weinberg noted that 'the earnings distribution for men remained stable, with a few exceptions, between 1967 and 1980' (2000, page 3). In Australia, the assessment by Keating concluded that the 'increasing inequality of earnings over the last 25 years ... contrasts with what is believed to be a long period of stability or compression of the earnings distribution during most of the twentieth century prior to the mid-1970s' (2003, page 376). In this section, I examine whether there was indeed a 'lull before the storm'.

In Figure 10, I begin with Australia (shown by circles), and the United Kingdom (shown by squares). These are two Anglo-Saxon countries with lengthy periods of conservative governments, but also differing traditions of government involvement in the labour market. As already noted, the different Australian sources tell different stories with regard to the magnitude and indeed direction of changes in earnings dispersion. In Figure 10, I have taken the *Employee Earnings and Hours* series, used in *Australian Social Trends*, but it should be noted that the long run series relates to non-managerial workers, and that the time path differs from that of the *Weekly Earnings of Employees* survey shown in Figure 7. Since the mid-1970s, when the series begins, the bottom decile has fallen by a significant amount, and apart from a possible pause at the end of the 1980s, there has been a fairly steady decline. In contrast, in the United Kingdom, the bottom decile fell from 1977 to 1986, but then levelled off. For the past 20 years there has been effectively no change in the ratio of the bottom decile to the median. For the top decile and upper quartile in Australia, Figure 10 shows a continuing rise over the period, with a pause from the mid-1980s to the mid-1990s. In the United Kingdom, there is a steady rise in both top decile and upper quartile, although the degree of 'fanning out' appears to have increased over time.

In the Australian case, we can say little from these data about what happened before 1980 (the income tax data for the 1950s are discussed in the next section), but from the UK series in Figure 10 we can see that there was definitely not a lull before the storm. Between 1970 and 1977, the bottom decile had risen by 18 per cent, reflecting, among other elements, the impact of redistributive incomes policies and of Equal Pay legislation. The top decile

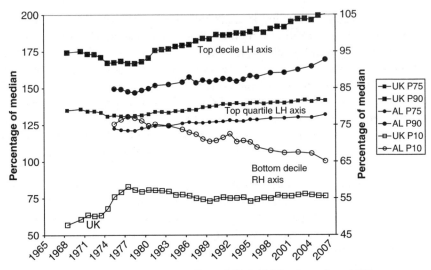

Figure 10 Evolution over time Australia and United Kingdom since 1965

had fallen over that period by 5 per cent. The asymmetry of the subsequent widening is highlighted by the fact that the bottom decile in the United Kingdom remains 13 per cent above its 1970 proportion of the median, whereas the top decile has not only recouped the ground lost in the 1970s but improved its position by 14 per cent compared with 1970. The shift in the distribution would have been missed if we had looked simply at the decile ratio, which turns out to have the same value in 2006 as in 1970. (This will not of course continue to be true if the top decile goes on rising.)

The misleading nature of the decile ratio is further illustrated by the United States. As we saw in the figure from which I started (Figure 1), the ratio has remained broadly constant since the late 1980s: it had the same value in 2004 as in 1988. From Figure 11 we can see however that this constancy is the result of both top and bottom deciles rising. Between 1988 and 2004, both top and bottom deciles (in Figure 11 the United States is shown by circles) rose by $5\frac{1}{2}$ per cent. The history of widening earnings dispersion in the United States since 1973 (the start date for the series used in this graph—data for the 1960s are presented in the next section) is essentially one of a fall in the bottom decile in the 1980s, followed by a recovery, while the top decile trended upwards, with some variation about that trend. As noted earlier, one important characteristic of the United States labour market is the role of employer-sponsored plans for health care, which are an (incomplete) substitute for the social provision found in many other countries. Payments have increased over time, and the distribution of total compensation may have moved in a different way from the distribution of money wages and salaries. The impact has been examined empirically by Pierce, who finds that 'inequality growth in broader measures of compensation slightly exceeds wage inequality growth over the 1981–1997 period' (2001, page 1493). We should however note that, while the fall in the bottom decile is larger for total compensation, it is not large enough to register according to the criteria adopted here (the fall for 1981 to 1997 in the bottom decile of total compensation is 3 per cent, rather than 1 per cent for wages).

The action in the United States earnings distribution is at the top. The degree of 'fanning out' appears to have increased over time: between 1995 and 2005 the upper quintile in the United States simply kept pace with the median, while the top decile continued to rise relative to the median. Moreover, the fanning applies within the top 10 per cent, as is well illustrated by the calculations given to me by Gary Burtless of the Brookings Institution based on the social security (SSA) data: between 1990 and 2005, the top decile rose 14 per cent faster than the median, P95 rose 20 per cent faster, and the top percentile rose 30 per cent faster.

The second country in Figure 11 is Canada (shown by squares). Given its close proximity to the United States, and the close economic links, one may

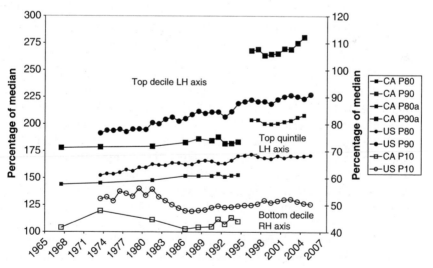

Figure 11 Evolution over time Canada and United States since 1965

expect there to be similarities in the changes in the earnings distributions. The observations shown in Figure 11 for Canada are more of a patchwork than a single continuous annual series, but they provide some visual support for the similarity view. The bottom decile in Canada fell by 14 per cent between 1973 and 1986. The top decile rose by nearly 5 per cent between 1996 and 2004. At the same time, we should note that in Canada, as in Australia, different sources and measures lead to different conclusions. As pointed out by Boudarbat, Lemieux, and Riddell, studies of hourly wage rates using special supplements to the labour force survey find little change in overall measures of wage dispersion, whereas studies of weekly or annual earnings using the Survey of Consumer Finances, or administrative tax data, tend to find increasing earnings dispersion. It is the Survey of Consumer Finances data, and the successor Survey of Labour and Income Dynamics, that are shown in Figure 11.

CONTINENTAL EUROPE

With Figure 12, we cross the Atlantic to Europe, but the diagram demonstrates that we cannot regard Continental Europe as a homogeneous entity. From Figure 7 earlier we saw the differences between the overall changes in the earnings distribution in France and Germany, and Figure 12 shows in more detail the differences in the time paths over the 40-year period. The data for France (shown by squares) come throughout the period from the same source (administrative records) but there are breaks in comparability; the data for Germany (shown by circles) are from two sources: the wage tax data cover the earlier part, and the German Socio-Economic Panel (GSOEP) (used in Figure 7) covers the years since 1984. In the early part of the period, from 1965 to 1980, the top decile in France fell by 7 per cent, whereas the top decile in Germany did not register any change. At the bottom, the changes in France are highly significant: P10 rose by 17 per cent between 1965 and 1980, 1969 stands out. According to Piketty, 'the rupture is clearly identifiable, because it arises from the "events" of May 1968 and the resulting social measures' (2001, page 165, my translation). He goes on to say that this break was 'the result of breaks in the wages policy of the state, and notably in policy towards the minimum wage' (2001, page 165, my translation). The bottom decile fell back after 1969 but after 1972 continued an upward climb that was reinforced by the Mitterrand election in 1981. (No series is shown for the bottom decile for Germany for this period, as the wage tax and employer survey data point in opposite directions—see Chapter H.)

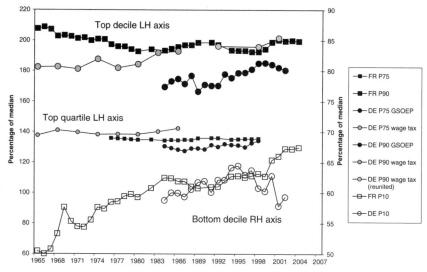

Figure 12 Evolution over time France and (West) Germany since 1965

In France, it was more a case of a storm before a lull, since from the mid-1980s to the end of the 1990s there was registrable change in neither the bottom nor the top decile. It was in Germany that change was more evident, particularly after 1990. The top decile in the GSOEP data rose in that decade by 8 per cent relative to the median. This is supported by the evidence from the employer surveys (not shown in Figure 12), according to which the top decile rose by 7 per cent between 1978 and 1995, and P95 rose by 11 per cent. Between 1995 and 2002 there was a fall of 8 per cent in the bottom decile. Despite earlier claims about the rigidity of wages in the German labour market, the German wage structure does appear to have changed over time. A striking feature of Figure 12 is the divergent movement of the bottom decile in the two countries in recent years. One factor distinguishing the lower part of the distribution in Germany from that in France is the absence of a nationally legislated minimum wage like the SMIC (Salaire Minimum Inter-professionnel de Croissance) in France. The establishment of minimum wage levels has rested on collective agreements, and low paid workers have been affected by changes in industrial structure that impinge on the collective bargaining process. Privatization is here important, since it reduced the protection afforded to the low paid, as has the growth of 'atypical' employ-ment (Buch and Rühmann, 1998) or the evolution of a new 'standard employment relationship' (Bosch, 2004).

The position on Italy and Portugal is shown in Figure 13. At the start of this section, I emphasized the need to see the post-1980 period in historical context. In the case of Italy, the experience of the 1970s appears to have been particularly significant. According to Erickson and Ichino, 'during the 1970s, Italy experienced an impressive compression of wage differentials' (1995, page 265). This is borne out by the evidence in Figure 13 from the Bank of Italy household survey for the upper quartile and top decile (data for Italy are shown by squares). The top decile fell from 177 per cent of the median in 1973 to 143 per cent in 1981, a fall of a fifth. A major element in this compression was the Scala Mobile (SM), a negotiated wage indexation 'escalator', notably following the agreement between workers and employers in 1975. According to Manacorda, 'the SM had a considerable equalizing effect and that it was largely responsible for the fall in inequality between the late 1970s and the mid-1980s' (2004, page 609). The compression at the top in Italy came to a stop in the early 1980s. The bottom decile is shown in Figure 13 as first rising and then falling from the mid-1980s to the mid-1990s, although the social security data (not shown) record a more stable picture. The reasons for the difference (see Chapter K) may lie in the coverage of the two sources: the household survey data having better coverage of the informal sector. Both sources are, however, agreed that the top groups were gaining relative to the median: between 1989 and 2004, the top quintile rose by 8 per cent relative to the median, the top decile by 15 per cent, and P95 by 23 per cent. The 'fanning

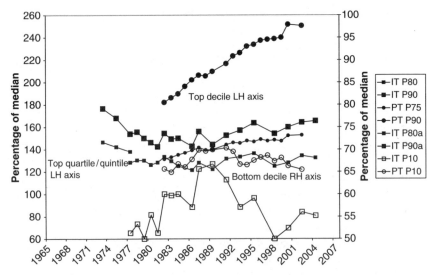

Figure 13 Evolution over time Italy and Portugal since 1965

out' is even clearer in the case of Portugal (shown by circles in Figure 13). The upper quartile in Portugal has risen by 16 per cent since 1982, and the top decile by nearly 40 per cent.

The post-1968 period has been studied carefully in other European countries. The data, for example, assembled for Sweden by Gustavsson (2004) show the quintile ratio for men as falling from 1.86 in 1968 to 1.7 in 1976. As he notes, the period coincided with the heyday of the 'solidarity wage policy' followed by the major trade union confederation, Landsorganisationen (LO). The series for Sweden (shown by circles) in Figure 14 indicates that the bottom decile registered a rise and the top decile a fall between 1975 and 1980. The changes in Finland (shown by squares), which begin in 1971, are larger. (There are two series for Finland, one based on the Census of Population and one on the Income Distribution Survey (used earlier in Figure 7).) The top decile fell by 18 per cent between 1971 and 1981, which is a significant fall by the criteria adopted here, and represented some 3 percentage points per year. The rise in the bottom decile from 1971 to 1985 was as much as 29 per cent, qualifying it as large. As described by Eriksson and Jäntti, in Finland, 'earnings inequality dropped dramatically between 1971 and 1975, and continued to decrease until 1985' (1997, page 1763). For the period after 1980, Figure 7 shows Sweden but not Finland registering a rise in the top decile and a fall in the bottom decile. In Figure 14, this is reflected in the bottom decile

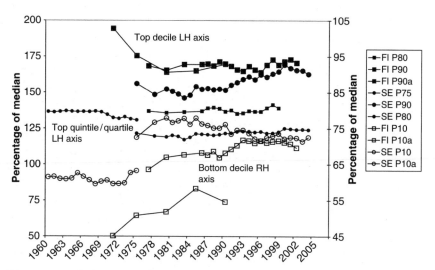

Figure 14 Evolution over time Finland and Sweden since 1960

for Sweden falling below that for Finland (as emphasized, the levels are not in fact comparable) and on the top decile in Sweden 'catching up' that for Finland, although we should note that the top decile turns down in Sweden after 2000. Overall, the distribution appears to have been widening in Sweden from the mid-1980s to 2000, whereas for Finland, the period can fairly be described as one of stability in earnings dispersion.

THE EXPERIENCE OF EASTERN EUROPE

In Figure 15 are shown the distributions of earnings for three Eastern European countries: the Czech Republic, Hungary, and Poland. They are shown on one graph in part to allow the contrasts to be highlighted, and in part because, in this case, the data are reasonably comparable across countries. Earnings data in the three countries in the period up to 1990 were studied in Atkinson and Micklewright (1992) (see also Flemming and Micklewright, 2000). There were differences: for example, the Hungarian data included certain private ventures, but the overall conclusion was that the earnings data used in that study (and here) 'enjoy, by the standards of international comparisons, a high degree of comparability' (1992, page 80).

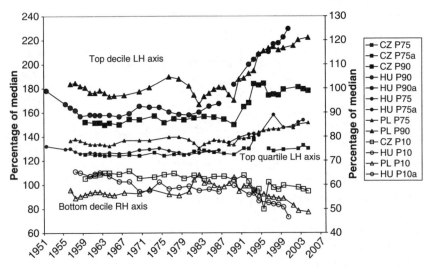

Figure 15 Evolution over time in Czech Republic, Hungary, and Poland since 1951

As in the earlier study by Lydall (1968), we found that earnings dispersion was lowest in Czechoslovakia, followed closely by Hungary, with Poland having a more intermediate position. The Czech performance has been widely recognized: 'as far as income distribution is concerned, Czechoslovakia was...an exception among both Western and Eastern European countries: the range of income inequality here was extremely small and virtually stable over a long period of time. This was true especially for inequality of earnings' (Večernik, 1991, page 237). According to Connor, 'a certain amount of egalitarian sentiment was diffused broadly among the Czech working class—more so perhaps than elsewhere in Eastern Europe. Socialist and labor movements had operated freely in interwar years' (1979, page 221). As it was put by Teichova, 'the desire for greater equality had deep historical roots in the social consciousness of broad segments of society' (1988, page 101). She argues that the narrowing of the skilled/unskilled differential had its origins in the 1930s.

The evidence assembled here in Figure 15 does not go back to the 1930s, but covers the period before and after the ending of Communism in 1989. The squares mark the observations for Czechoslovakia (from 1993 the data relate only to the Czech Republic, before that they cover both the Czech Republic and Slovakia). As is noted by Večernik (1995), the periodic wage surveys only began when the main features of the communist economy were in place. He dates the 'wage revolution' to the beginning of the 1950s, and indeed cites evidence that 'the systematic enforcement of earnings equality in the post-war period...had already begun by December 1945 (when the first regulation started)' (Večernik, 1991, page 238). He later commented that 'the three decades following 1959 were a period of remarkable and perhaps unique stability in the overall earnings distribution' (1995, page 356), and this is borne out by the flatness of the series in Figure 15. Over the period, there were swings in wages policies (see Chapter D), but the top and bottom deciles varied within a range of not much more than 5 per cent.

In the case of Hungary, shown by the circles in Figure 15, we can see some tendency to reduced dispersion in the early 1950s, although not too much weight should be placed on the 1951 observation. There was then broad stability until the mid-1960s, when, as observed by Flakierski (1979), the economic reform process was associated with a rise in dispersion. The bottom decile lost ground between 1968 and 1970 and the top decile increased. These changes were largely reversed in the 1970s. Taking the long run of 30 years from 1956, there was no overall registrable change.

The distribution of earnings in Poland is shown by the triangles in Figure 15. In the early part of the period, up to 1970, the convergence was not enough to register. The 1970s saw a definite increase in the top percentiles: the top decile rose from 166 per cent of the median in 1970 to 177 per cent in 1977, and the top vintile rose from 198 per cent to 210 per cent. This was followed by the labour unrest at the start of the 1980s and the Gdansk Accord of August 1980, which led to relatively equalizing wage adjustments: the bottom decile rises by 7 percentage points, reaching the Czechoslovak level. Flakierski (1986) argues that 'the spectacular drop in relative dispersion of earnings between 1980 and 1982 claimed by the official statistics is probably exaggerated, because the official statistical data in this period of turmoil are particularly unreliable' (1986, page 72). But he goes on to say that 'there is no doubt that even the partial implementation of Solidarity's wage and incomes policies has reduced inequalities' (1986, page 72). The gains, whether real or a statistical illusion, were then lost and, substantially, regained during the rest of the 1980s.

What happened after 1989? According to Večernik, in the Czech Republic,

the transition to a market economy has opened great opportunities for private entrepreneurship, employment in foreign firms, and awards of higher managerial positions. High earnings were accorded to employees in finance and the top echelons of bureaucracy. The possibility was opened for rewarding work differently according to skills and performance. Newly established and foreign firms have had greater liberty in wage settings, and sought to attract highly skilled people by offering considerably higher wages.... After state wage regulation was removed, formerly state-owned companies also began to have greater discretion in rewarding their employees. All of this contributed to a general de-equalizing trend in wages. (Večernik, 2001, page 3)

In considering earnings dispersion before and after 1990, we have of course to take account of the impact on the statistical sources. I have been surprised by the willingness of many commentators to treat the series as continuous before and after the Communist regime. The basis for the enterprise surveys in particular has been greatly changed, with the need to cover the private sector, although there are reasons to expect greater continuity in the case of household surveys. These issues are discussed further in Chapters D, I, and O. Moreover, we have to allow for the impact on the Hungarian figures of the introduction of the personal income tax; a break is shown in Figure 15. Finally, we should bear in mind that higher cash salaries may have replaced benefits in kind, not recorded in the statistics, provided to those at the top of the ladder in the old regime.

The immediate direction of movement after 1989 indicated by the statistics is shown in Figure 15. As we have already seen in Figure 7, the top decile rose and the bottom decile fell. But there are differences between the three countries. The fall in the bottom decile registered in the Czech Republic, was significant in Poland, and was large in Hungary. In the case of the Czech Republic, the series appears to have levelled off since the mid-1990s. At the top, the rise in the top decile has been significant in the Czech Republic but large in the other two countries. The magnitude of these changes should be stressed. In Czechoslovakia, the decile ratio had been as low as 2.3, and was around 2.45 in the mid-1980s, when the figure for Great Britain was around 3.25 (Atkinson and Micklewright, 1992, Table 4.1). By 2000, the decile ratio in the Czech Republic was over 3.0. According to Večernik, 'the Czech wage inequality and structure have been in energetic motion directed towards the Western pattern' (2001, page 13).

In the case of Hungary, Pudney concluded from his analysis of the employer survey and household budget survey data, that 'there is statistically significant evidence of an increase in earnings inequality, which takes Hungary to a degree of inequality comparable with (or even higher than) countries like Britain' (1994, page 273). As noted by Rutkowski (2001, page 11), earnings dispersion in Hungary, in contrast to the Czech case, has tended to increase at a steady rate over the 1990s. Poland appears to be an intermediate case. Some authors have argued that 'the growth in inequality was strongly concentrated during the early stage of the transition' (Rutkowski, 2001, page 11). He attributes this in part to the fact that Poland is a country 'where strong trade unions are successful in protecting the relative earnings position of low paid workers' (2001, page 13). However, the more recent evidence indicates that the widening has recommenced. Between the mid-1990s and 2004, the bottom decile has fallen, and the upper quartile and the top decile have increased. Figure 15 illustrates the 'fanning out' of the distribution, with the top decile out-stripping the upper quartile (and—not shown—P95 shooting ahead of the top decile).

SUMMARY

Examination of the full run of years has revealed considerable diversity of experience, not least in the timing of change. Countries where similarity of experience might have been expected, such as France and Germany, have exhibited different directions of movement. Nevertheless, there are certain themes:

- The late 1960s and 1970s were a period of earnings compression in a number of countries (Finland, France, Italy, Sweden, and the United Kingdom); there was not a lull before the storm, and the falls in the bottom decile after 1980 can be seen as a part reversal of the 1970s compression.

- In many countries, there has been a steady upward movement since 1980 in the top decile (Australia, Canada, Germany, Italy, Portugal, Sweden, the United Kingdom, and the United States).

- The finding of a fanning out at the top is evident for Australia, Germany, Italy, Portugal, Sweden, the United Kingdom, and the United States.

- The three Eastern European countries all showed a move towards increased earnings dispersion with the transition to a market economy, but there are differences, with dispersion being less, and more stable, in the Czech Republic than in Hungary and Poland.

6

A Longer-Run View of the Earnings
Distribution: The Great Compression and
the Golden Age

Looking backward is important not only to understand our past but also as a basis for speculating how the future will evolve. A generation of labour economists in the United Kingdom were much influenced by the view of Sir Henry Phelps Brown that the earnings distribution exhibited remarkable long run stability. Commenting on the British data for 1886 and 1978, Phelps Brown notes how

the average wage in money...has been multiplied by a factor of 64. Differentials between occupations and grades and regions have changed—mostly they have contracted. The distribution of manpower between different jobs and different places has altered radically. Trade unionism has greatly extended its power.... Yet, after 91 years of these changes...the dispersion of individual earnings remains very closely the same. (1977, page 4)

Stability has been regarded as a long-standing feature of the British earnings distribution: 'thus in a period [1886 to 1966] when the level of earnings of adult male manual workers increased by a factor of nearly 16, it appears that their dispersion (measured in percentage terms) changed very little' (Thatcher, 1968, page 163).

Other researchers, particularly in the United States, have emphasized the degree of *change* in earnings dispersion. 'Great Compression' is the term used by Goldin and Margo to describe the narrowing in the United States wage structure in the 1940s: 'when the United States emerged from war and depression, it had not only a considerably lower rate of unemployment, it also had a wage structure more egalitarian than at any time since. Further, the new wage structure remained somewhat intact for several decades' (1992, page 2). They go on to say that 'the movement toward equality in the 1940s was reversed in the post-1970 period' (1992, page 3). As it was put by Katz and Autor, we have returned to the degree of differentiation observed in 1939: 'the entire compression of the wage structure in the 1940s is undone by 1990'

(1999, page 1500). Such a view of changing earnings dispersion has been characterized as a 'Great U-turn' (Bluestone and Harrison, 1988). There are, however, different forms of 'U'. The quotation from Goldin and Margo (1992) suggests that the compression and the reversal were separated by two or more decades of relative stability: that the U had a flat floor during the 1950s and 1960s. They cite the finding of Thurow that 'after the wage differentials of the Great Depression and World War II had become embodied in the labour market for a number of years, they became the new standard...and were regarded as "just" even after the egalitarian pressures of World War II had disappeared' (Thurow, 1975, page 111). Equally, the earlier study by Lydall, after recording 'the substantial fall in dispersion of employee earnings in the United States from 1939 to 1949' (1968, page 177), went on to note that 'when we turn to the period 1949 to 1959 we find a quite different picture. The general picture is one of stability, with a slight tendency to widening dispersion' (Lydall, 1968, page 178). On the other hand, Katz and Autor record that, after the 1940s, 'wage inequality for men then rises in each subsequent decade with an acceleration of the pace of widening inequality in the 1980s' (1999, page 1500). This suggests more of a 'V turn' than a 'U turn'.

The distinction between these two shapes is important since it affects how we view the 'Golden Age' of the third quarter of the twentieth century. As described by Maddison, 'the years 1950–73 were a golden age of unparalleled prosperity' (2005, page 12). In France, the period 1946–1975 was described by Fourastié (1979) as *Les Trentes Glorieuses,* 30 years of growth and redistribution. Writing about the United States, Morris and Western in their survey article for the *Annual Review of Sociology* state that 'the postwar years of prosperity were marked by... relative stability in earnings inequality. The benefits of economic growth were large and widely distributed.... These trends made a dramatic reversal in the early 1970s' (Morris and Western, 1999, page 625). But did all share equally in the growth of that period, as suggested by the flat-bottomed U? Or was the Golden Age characterized by widening earnings dispersion as suggested by the V-shape? If the rising earnings dispersion started in 1950, rather than 1980, then we may have to consider other explanations than those currently in favour, which emphasize the advent of Information and Communication Technologies and the impact of globalization.

From this point, I shall concentrate on five large OECD countries: Canada, France, Germany, the United States, and the UK. Other countries could be added: for example, I have already shown estimates of earnings dispersion for Ireland from the 1930s (in Figure 6). But the five countries illustrate the potential and allow us to contrast experience on two sides of the Atlantic. We

Table 4. Data sources used in Figures 16–20

Country (abbreviation in graphs)	Source
Canada (CA)	As Table 3, and *Census of Population* (Table C.4), *Earnings and Hours of Work in Manufacturing* (Table C.5) and income tax data (Table C.10)
France (FR)	As Table 3, and wage tax data (Table G.4)
Germany (DE)	As Table 3, and social security data (Table H.6) and *Gehalts- und Lohnstrukturerhebung* (Table H.4)
United Kingdom (UK)	As Table 3, and income tax data (Table S.7)
United States (US)	As Table 3, and *Census of Population* (Table T.8 and T.9), *Current Population Reports* tabulations (Table T.10), *Current Population Survey* microdata (Tables T.7 and T.11)

can compare the years of the German 'economic miracle' with the Eisenhower years in the United States.

To go back before 1965, we have to draw on a variety of sources. (The sources are listed in Table 4.) This is well illustrated by the case of Germany. Lydall (1968) gives eight tables of earnings distribution data for West Germany. They cover the years 1950, 1957, and 1961 from the Lohnsteuer (wage tax) statistics, and 1962 from the Gehalts- und Lohnstrukturerhebung (salary and wage survey). The latter survey has been conducted in West Germany for the years 1949, 1951, 1957, 1962, 1966, 1972, 1978, and 1990. These sources may not all be A graded (for example the 1949 survey had only partial geographical coverage), but we can go back in time. Indeed, we can go back before the Second World War (when Germany had different borders). The wage tax statistics have long been used to examine the distribution of earnings in Germany, an early official publication relating to 1926 (*Statistischen Reichsamt*, 1929). A second source of earnings data in the interwar period is provided by the social insurance records, which furnish information for 1929 to 1937. These data were used by Sweezy (1939).

In the same way, for France we can use information from the employer wage tax. The *impôt cédulaire* was introduced in 1914, and from 1919 the fiscal administration began publishing the distribution of earnings by ranges. As pointed out by Piketty (2001, page 31, n2), these returns appeared to have been entirely neglected. The coverage is limited to those above the tax threshold, but the data provide information about the top decile.

In the case of the United Kingdom, the major source of earnings data in recent decades has been the *New Earnings Survey*, an employer survey introduced experimentally in 1968 and established on an annual basis in 1970.

Before 1968, we can, however, obtain evidence from income tax sources: the distributions of *principal source Schedule E income* of individuals that began to be published in the Inland Revenue (IR) *Annual Reports* from 1954/55. The data are not the same: they refer to annual earnings, whereas the employer survey data relate to the current pay period of workers whose pay is not affected by absence. Where the person changes job, it is the sum of earnings from successive principal employments in the tax year, but there is no restriction to full time or full year workers. These differences in definition have to be taken into account in interpreting the series.

For Canada, I have made use of what Lydall described as 'the rich material collected in the Canadian censuses' (1968, page 181). While noting their richness, we have also to recognize that the census moved with the times: for example, the 1931 Census of Canada refers to wage-earners aged 10 and over; the 1941 Census refers to wage-earners aged 14 and over; and the 1971 Census to wage-earners aged 15 and over. In addition to the population censuses, I have also made use of the fact that, from the 1940s, as part of the census of manufactures, statistics were collected for this sector on the distribution of weekly earnings. Initially they covered only wage-earners, but from 1944 salaried employees were also included. The survey was carried out at approximately three-year intervals, and the data used here cover 1944, 1950, 1953, 1956, 1959, 1964, and 1967. The series constructed from the surveys is classified as B, but is of interest for covering a period for which there appears to be no other information relating to the years between the censuses of population.

For the United States, in their study of the Great Compression of the 1940s, Goldin and Margo (1992) make use of an impressive variety of sources, including the census of population, but they do not refer to the annual tables on the distribution of earnings based on the Current Population Survey (CPS) published by the Census Bureau covering years since the 1940s. If one is prepared to use grouped data, then, as pointed out by Burtless (1990), these tabulations provide an unbroken series of earnings data since the Second World War. He used them to calculate the Gini coefficient, which depends on the full distribution; here I have calculated deciles, which place less demanding requirements in terms of interpolation.

As emphasized earlier, the data are a patchwork and not always fully comparable across time. The estimates relate to different definitions of the population: for example, the United States published CPS tabulations refer to all wage-earners, whereas the more recent data refer to full year full time workers. We should not therefore expect the deciles to be at the same level. These breaks in comparability are signalled in the graphs. Similarly, there are differences in the quality of the data. Following the classification suggested in

Section 3, I have not used any series that I would classify as C. I have, however, used series classified as B in addition to those classified as A. In the case of Germany, for example, I have classified the wage tax series prior to 1939 as B, on the grounds that the median has to be obtained from another source. In the graphs the percentiles above the median are again shown with solid symbols, and those below the median by hollow symbols. The deciles are in a medium point size; the quartiles and quintiles are in a smaller point size. The graphs also show in some cases P95, indicated by a solid symbol in larger point size. The different symbols distinguish different sources.

UNITED STATES

The Great Compression stands out in the estimates of Goldin and Margo, based on the Census of Population, shown in Figure 16 by the heavy lines: from 1939 to 1949 the top decile fell and the bottom decile rose by similar amounts (around 14 per cent). In terms of the classification given earlier, these were 'significant' although not 'large' changes. There was compression at both ends—in contrast to the period 1980 to 2004, when the widening was found much more at the top. (In Figure 7, for the United States, the upper bar is about twice the length of the lower bar.) When did the compression take place? Miller (1958) used the 1939 and 1949 Census data, together with the

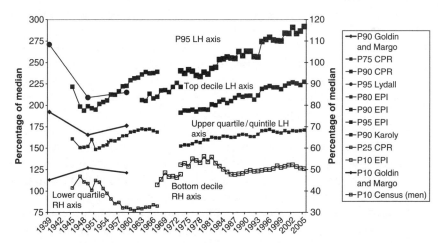

Figure 16 Long run development of earnings dispersion in United States 1939–2005

1945 CPS data, to address this question. He concluded that 'the substantial changes in the relative distribution of wage income took place during the war years.... In contrast, the years immediately following World War II (1947–1949) did not see any change in the relative distribution' (1958, page 356). A different conclusion was reached by Meyers, using data on wages in manufacturing up to 1948, who concluded that 'the trend toward lesser dispersion has not been substantially slowed down since the War' (1950, page 352). Comparing the percentiles for 1945 and 1948 in Figure 16 provides some support for this view. Meyers in seeking to explain the 'marked narrowing of proportionate differentials' in the immediate post-war years cites approvingly the view that the wartime regulation had had lasting effects.

This was, however, to change. Both of the lines in Figure 16 from the Goldin and Margo study turn in the opposite direction after 1949. Comparing 1959 with 1949, we see that the top decile rose by 6 per cent and the bottom decile fell by slightly less than 5 per cent. In fact, from the annual data provided by the CPS tabulations, we can see the time path more clearly. The top decile began to rise immediately in 1952 and the rise continued unchecked until 1964. The rise from 195 per cent of the median in 1951 to 239 per cent in 1964 certainly qualifies as large. The rise in the upper quartile was 16 per cent. The path initiated by the Great Compression in the United States was not a flat-bottomed U but a V, with increased dispersion during the Golden Age of the 1950s and early 1960s. The picture provided by the CPS tabulations is sharper than that from the Census data, but in part, the difference between the results presented here and those from the Census is more apparent than real, since it lies in the timing. In effect, the 1949 Census observation comes two years before the sharp turnaround after 1951, so that the Census figures understate the magnitude of the increase in dispersion during the Golden Age. Of course, the annual CPS estimates are subject to reservations, notably on account of the interpolation necessary when using tabulated data, but there is a systematic year-on-year trend. The V-conclusion does not depend on a couple of isolated years.

At the same time, the conclusion of a rise in dispersion in the United States during the 1950s may appear to contradict that reached by Miller in his analysis of the CPS and of the 1960 Census data, where he finds that 'the entire postwar period was marked by stability in the distribution of wages' (1968, page 76). In fact, his estimates show the share of aggregate wage and salary income received by the bottom fifth as falling from 3.0 per cent in 1951 to 1.8 per cent in 1960, and the share of the top fifth as rising from 41.6 to 46.8 per cent (1968, page 77), which scarcely seems consistent with the conclusion of 'stability'. Indeed, other writers found that there was an upward trend in dispersion. Henle, using the annual CPS data, concluded that there was 'a slow but persistent trend toward inequality' (1972, page 17). Brittain, on the basis of unpublished data from the Social Security Administration (SSA), concluded that the Gini coefficient had 'a very convincing upward trend' (1972, page 106). His estimates show the Gini coefficient rising from 46.9 per cent in 1951 to 49.2 per cent in 1966. The SSA data may have been affected by changes in coverage, but the later estimates of Henle and Ryscavage (1980) using CPS data, showed the Gini coefficient for full year full time male workers rising by 2.7 percentage points in the eight years from 1958 to 1966, a rise of a tenth, which again does not suggest stability. Equally, the estimates of Burtless (1990) show the Gini coefficient (see Table T.10) for male earners as rising from 30.7 per cent in 1951 to 37.6 per cent in 1964, a rise of over a fifth, and the ratio of average earnings in the top tail to the average earnings of the middle quintile group as rising from 174.1 per cent to 199.8 per cent, an increase of 15 per cent. He concludes that 'earnings inequality rose for both men and women over the 1950s' (1990, page 89).

Moreover, we should note that the use of shares (or the Gini coefficient) can give a different impression. The share of the top fifth includes the earnings of all workers above P80 (and the Gini coefficient depends on the top shares). The findings in Figure 16 relate to percentiles. It is quite possible that the distribution has 'tilted' in a fashion that raises the top decile but leaves the share of the top 10 per cent unchanged. In this context, it is interesting to look at the estimates of Piketty and Saez (2003) using income tax data. (These data relate to tax units and are not therefore included in the graphs—but see Table T.13.) They show the top decile as rising (relative to the mean) from 192 per cent to 244 per cent, confirming the findings of Figure 16. In terms of shares, their results show the share of the top 5 per cent as stable (in fact falling by 0.2 percentage points) between 1951 and 1964 but the share of the next 5 per cent as rising from 9.1 to 9.7 per cent. In the same way, the estimates of Brittain, using social security data for individual earnings, show a 1 percentage point fall in the share of the top 5 per cent between 1951 and 1964 (1972, page 107). This indicates a 'tilt' in the upper part of the distribution, where the top decile gained but where those still higher up lost ground.

The findings for the distribution of earnings in the Golden Age need to be reconciled with the observed changes in the distribution of the total income of households. For more recent years, Gottschalk and Danziger found that the distribution of hourly wages of men and the distribution of adjusted family incomes for the period 1975 to 2002 'follow remarkably similar patterns' (2005, page 232). But this need not happen. There are several intervening mechanisms (see, for example, the discussion of the United States case by Karoly and Burtless, 1995) that may have caused the two distributions to move differently. Household income depends on the joint distribution of the earnings of individual household members. There is capital income. There are transfers. There have been significant changes in family size and composition. In his 1972 study, Henle addressed the divergent movement of the distributions of individual earnings and of total income by families. He concluded that these different trends could largely be accounted for by changes in other sources of income, notably increased transfer payments, and by the increasing proportion of families with two or more earners.

What happened to the United States earnings distribution after 1964? Although I have not here, or later, applied rigorous statistical tests, the period between 1965 and 1979 seems to represent a shift of regime. The top decile did not decline, but it stopped rising. The bottom decile (for men) in Figure 16 shows a significant (more than 10 per cent) rise between 1967 and 1973. Then, we had the widening after 1980 discussed in the previous section. Linking the series for men (Census of Population, Current Population Survey tabulations, and Current Population Survey results given by the Census Bureau and Economic Policy Institute (EPI), we find that the top decile fell from 210 per cent of the median in 1939 to 160 per cent in 1951 and then rose, with a pause from 1965 to 1979, to 233 per cent in 2005.

CANADA

Was there also a Great Compression north of the 49th parallel? The comparison of the United States and Canada is of interest if we are seeking to identify the contribution of specifically United States institutional factors, such as the National War Labor Board, and of the United States labour movement. The long run changes in earnings dispersion for Canada are shown in Figure 17. The complexity of the graph is even greater than for the United States in that it combines evidence from five different sources: the Census of Population, the earnings inquiries in manufacturing (both shown with dashed lines to indicate a B grading), the Survey of Consumer Finances, income tax data, and the new dataset combining interview and tax data.

For the period 1941 to 1951, the picture from the Census of Population data is clear. In Canada, as in the United States, there was a large fall in the top decile; indeed the fall was larger in Canada—by a quarter—and is rightly described as 'dramatic' by Lydall (1968, page 182). The upper quartile fell by a similar proportion. Moreover, the fall in the top decile, but not the upper quartile, began in the 1930s. In the same way, the rise in the lower quartile began in the 1930s, whereas between 1941 and 1951 there was no registrable change. So the Great Compression did indeed take place in Canada, with a timing that suggests that it was not confined to the war years.

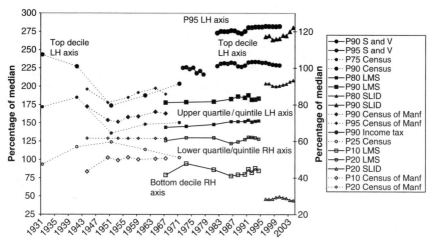

Figure 17 Long run development of earnings dispersion in Canada 1931–2004

Was the compression reversed after 1951? The Census of Population data show a distinct reversal: the top decile rose between 1951 and 1961 and, again, between 1961 and 1971. The total rise was 17 per cent. The bottom decile fell by 14 per cent between 1951 and 1971. For this period, we also have the Census of Manufactures data. The changes from 1944 to 1950 confirm the finding of compression (with the caveat that the data for the two years are not fully comparable). From 1953 to 1964, the top decile and P95 rise steadily, the increase being of the order of 10 per cent. On the other hand, over the same period, the bottom decile did not change. This evidence suggests therefore that the widening during the Golden Age took place at the top of the distribution.

Changes over the period 1965 to 1979 are not easy to discern, since I have not been able to locate a consistent annual series. The differences in the partial series shown are not large enough to be regarded as 'changes' according to the criteria adopted here, apart from the rise in the bottom decile in the second part of the 1960s indicated by the Survey of Consumer Finances data.

UNITED KINGDOM

In the United Kingdom, Routh (1965) constructed an estimate of the individual distribution of earnings for 1911/12 that he compared with the Schedule E income tax data for 1958/59, showing for men a large rise in the bottom

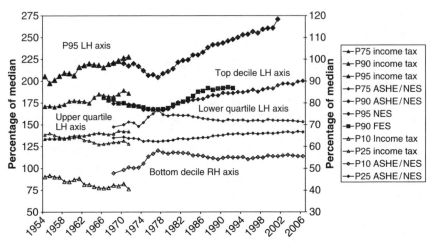

Figure 18 Long run development of earnings dispersion in United Kingdom 1954–2006

decile and a significant fall in the top decile. He also made use of the earnings inquiries carried out by the Ministry of Labour on three occasions (1906, 1938, and 1960). The latter information relates only to manual workers and excludes a number of sectors, including agriculture, mining, railways, and gas, electricity, and water. For this reason, I do not regard it as meeting a B grading, but it is interesting nonetheless to note the conclusion of Routh: 'the egalitarian process observed for men ... must have been the net product of a move to greater equality followed by a less pronounced move away from it' (1965, page 57). In other words, a compression followed by some degree of unwinding up to 1960.

To draw firmer conclusions about the time pattern, more frequent data are needed. Annual data in the UK are available from 1954/5 from the Schedule E tax returns. For the Golden Age of the 1950s and early 1960s, they show (Figure 18) a significant fall in the bottom decile and a rise in the top decile. The extent of the 'unwinding' may have been masked by the fact that some salaries at the top of the scale were failing to keep up with inflation. We have to distinguish between the top decile and the very top of the distribution. As we have seen in the case of the United States, there may have been a 'tilt' at the very top. As is shown in Atkinson and Voitchovsky (2003), over the Golden Age the very top earnings shares were falling. If we examine the change between 1954 and 1965, we find that the top decile rose by 8 per cent relative to the median, but that the top percentile did not register a change, and the top 0.1 percentile (P999) fell by over 10 per cent.

These changes need of course to be interpreted carefully, since the data relate to annual earnings of all workers. The tax-based statistics may have included a larger number of low, part year incomes, although Lydall (1968, page 185) doubts that this can explain all of the change. They may reflect the expansion of part time work and increased labour force participation by women. It may be noted that the estimates of Hill (1959, Table 1) from the Oxford national survey of incomes and savings show upper and lower deciles for men working full time and full year that (at 68.3 per cent and 159.4 per cent, respectively) are close to those from the Family Expenditure Survey (FES) for 1963 (Thatcher, 1968). But there is evidence that widening of the earnings distribution did leave its impression on the literature of the time. In particular, it was in the mid-1960s that concern began to be expressed again about the extent of 'working poor', notably following the publication of *The Poor and the Poorest* (Abel-Smith and Townsend, 1965). The concerns of the 1960s with the persistence of poverty in the United Kingdom had indeed an impact on the policy of successive governments, including the introduction of Equal Pay legislation. Reference must also be made to incomes policies. The focus of United Kingdom incomes policies in the 1970s, under both Conservative and Labour governments, was on the macro-economic problems of the day, but they had a redistributive ingredient. The limit on pay increases introduced by the Conservatives in 1973 was part flat rate and part proportionate; the 1975 Labour pay limit was £6 a week for all. The extent to which incomes policy narrowed differentials is open to debate (see Brown, 1976 and 1979, Dean, 1978, and Chater, 1981), but between 1968 and 1977, as may be seen from Figure 18, there was a large rise in the bottom decile and a fall in the top decile. Taken together with the post-1980 significant rise in the top decile and the fall in the bottom decile, these generate a V form, but the data for the 1950s suggest that it is in fact best seen as part of a W.

FRANCE

What about Continental Europe? Piketty, whose research I have followed in using the wage tax and employer declaration data, stresses the stability of the top and bottom decile over the long run: 'the P10 threshold regains from the end of the 1970s its "habitual" level (around 50 per cent of mean earnings), just like the threshold P90 (around 160 per cent of mean earnings)' (2001, page 212, my translation). The percentiles in Figure 19 are expressed relative to the median, rather than the mean, but show the same findings regarding the beginning and end values. The top and bottom deciles in 1998 are

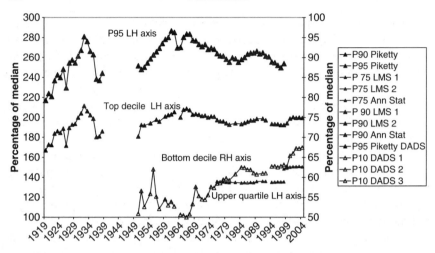

Figure 19 Long run development of earnings dispersion in France 1919–2004

virtually identical to their values in 1950. But, in between, earnings dispersion in France first widened and then narrowed. The top decile rose by nearly 10 per cent from 1951 to 1965, and the bottom decile fell significantly. For at least this part of the Golden Age, there was distinct widening of the distribution of individual earnings. Piketty (2001, pages 207–10) has explained clearly how earlier accounts of the *Les Trentes Glorieuses*, as years of equalization, had been misled by focusing on occupational differentials, and particularly on the salaries of top-ranking civil servants.

As may be seen from Figure 19, the bottom decile rose significantly from 1966 to 1979. The top decile fell by nearly 10 per cent. There was an almost complete reversal of the increased dispersion of the 1950s. As was summarized in the report of Centre d'Etude des Revenus et des Coûts (CERC), 'earnings dispersion widened between 1954 and 1963, the decile ratio increasing by 20 per cent; it remained stable between 1963 and 1967, then closed abruptly in 1968' (CERC, 1976, page 14). The evolution of earnings dispersion in France up to the late 1980s was summarized by CERC in terms of three phases: 'from 1950 to 1966 one sees, despite certain irregularities, a tendency for dispersion to increase. [The period 1966–1985] saw, on the contrary, a significant and regular reduction in inequality, at a stronger rate than the previous rise. Finally, since 1985, one sees a return to widening' (1990, page 1, my translation).

For France, we can go back to 1919 for the top decile (the wage tax data do not cover the lower part of the distribution). This shows a significant fall in the top decile in the 1930s, so that the Great Compression was not limited to

North America. We should however note the turning point in 1936, and the fact that the fall in the top decile from 1932 was preceded by a large rise from 1926. Inevitably it seems, in seeking a pattern, we are led further back in time.

GERMANY

For Germany, we can go back to 1929, and the data, shown in Figure 20, also suggest that the top decile was rising in the late 1920s, to be followed by a reverse in the 1930s. It should be stressed however that the insurance estimates have been assembled from a combination of sources, and are only B graded (although the wage tax data corroborate the changes in the top decile). The continuing decline in the top decile after 1933 appears to run counter to the conclusion reached by Sweezy, who used the same data for earnings, that 'the general picture of the distribution of individual income shows that inequality has increased during the Hitler regime' (1939, page 182). She was referring here to total income as well as earnings, and part of the rise in inequality may have been associated with a general fall in the wage share. Moreover, we should note that our data in Figure 20 also show that the lower quartile was falling. The distribution was becoming more spread out at the

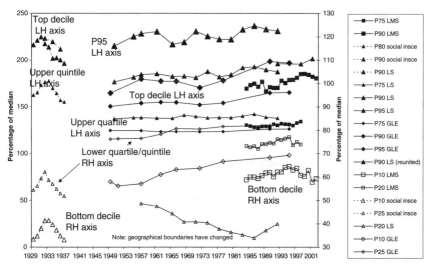

Figure 20 Long run development of earnings dispersion in West Germany 1929–2002

bottom, which is consistent with the direction of change found by Petzina, who describes an unprecedented fall in the share in total income of the bottom 50 percent (1977, page 147). This period clearly warrants closer examination, in particular if we wish to establish what would have happened in the counterfactual situation where Hitler had not come to power. The wage and labour market policies of the Nazi regime are described in Trivanovitch (1937) and Bry (1960, pages 235–7).

Turning to the post-war period for Germany, we should note the obvious differences in territorial coverage (also that West Berlin and Saarland are missing from the earlier years). We can also note the contrast in Figure 20 between the results for the lower quartile from the wage tax and employer surveys. The wage tax data suggest a significant fall between the mid-1950s and the mid-1980s, whereas the employer survey data indicate a rise of 7 per cent between 1951 and 1978 (and a 19 per cent rise in the bottom decile). This may reflect the changing coverage of the wage tax data. If we take the employer survey data, then it appears that the direction of change in Germany during the Golden Age was different from that in other European countries. The bottom decile in Germany rose by over 10 per cent between 1957 and 1966 according to the GLE employer survey, and the lower quartile rose by over 5 per cent. This conclusion is reinforced by the fact that the top percentiles are stable over this period (and the two sources are in general agreement). There does not appear to have been widening of earnings dispersion during the Golden Age. There is no apparent break in the 1960s. From 1950 to the end of the 1970s, the change in the top decile was less than the threshold of 5 per cent, and the bottom decile continued to rise. In the years following 1980, the top decile rose, and splitting the period in two reveals that the bottom decile first rose and then fell.

SUMMARY

The long run earnings data assembled here for five countries certainly cannot be characterized as depicting a picture of 'remarkable stability'. The United Kingdom commentators cited at the beginning of this section were drawing on single isolated years, and it is clear how this can be misleading. One needs to look in much greater detail at the year-by-year changes. With the new data presented here, we can see that the Anglo-Saxon countries have all seen large rises and falls in the deciles; France and Germany have both seen significant rises and falls. As the case of Germany has just illustrated, generalizations about the time path of change do not necessarily hold universally, but there appear to be three distinct phases in the pre-1980 period, which exhibit common features in several—but not all—of the five countries studied:

- compression of the earnings distribution in the 1930s and 1940s (although we lack evidence for the United Kingdom and the series for the United States starts in 1939)
- rise in the top decile of the earnings distribution during the Golden Age from 1950 to the mid-1960s (with the exception of Germany), accompanied in some cases by falls in the bottom decile or lower quartile, and a 'tilt' at the very top
- narrowing of the distribution in the late 1960s and 1970s (stability of top decile in United States and Germany).

These conclusions have been drawn from evidence for just five countries—only a quarter of those studied here (although in terms of population they account for more). There is some evidence for four other countries. In the case of Portugal (Chapter P), there is no evidence either for a compression from the 1930s, or of a rise after 1950, but the evidence is limited to the share of the top 1 per cent. For Australia, Lydall, using income tax data, had found that the 'dispersion [of earnings] of both males and females was growing steadily from 1952–3 to 1962–3' (1968, page 190). In the case of Ireland, we have seen (Figure 6) that there was a fall in the top decile from the 1930s that was reversed in the latter part of the 1950s; although, there is no corresponding fall in the bottom decile (see Chapter J). For New Zealand, there is evidence (Chapter M) that the top decile rose relative to the median between 1958 and 1973, although the changes in the lower half of the distribution were not sufficient to register. These findings for English-speaking countries support the view of Golden Age widening in the upper part of the distribution.

7

What We Are Seeking to Explain

The reader may reasonably feel that the empirical evidence in the previous three sections presents a picture of confusion. Earnings dispersion has tended first in one direction, then in another, reversing again, before settling on the current upwards path. There is diversity across countries in the timing of changes, and apparently similarly placed countries exhibit different changes. In one sense, this is to be expected. When Kuznets advanced his hypothesis of an inverse U-shaped time path (that inequality first grew and then fell as a country developed), he did so on the basis of a handful of data points for four countries. In the dataset described here we cover twenty countries with annual data covering periods of up to 75 years. It is not surprising if such rich data defy simple summary.

At the same time, some general features stand out. If a single-letter summary of the time path of dispersion is required, then over the period since the 1930s a W seems more appropriate than a U or a V. The Great Compression was followed, in all countries apart from Germany, by a rise in dispersion in the Golden Age of the 1950s and early 1960s (with in some cases a tilt at the very top). There was then a change in direction, when dispersion fell, or was stable, in the late 1960s and 1970s. Then, from the latter part of the 1970s, we have the—fairly general—widening of the distribution. In contrast to the earlier period of widening, the changes have been asymmetric, with much of the action in the upper part of the distribution. In quite a number of countries, but not all, there has been a fanning out of the upper percentiles. The different countries studied here share some, but not necessarily all, of these features. There is diversity of experience, and the timing of the changes has not been the same in all countries.

I doubt whether a single all-encompassing explanation can account for the general pattern described above, still less for the departures of individual countries from the pattern. In what follows, I privilege two main explanations—shifting pay norms, and pyramidal/superstar theories. I focus on these, not because I believe that they provide an overarching theory, but because I believe that they warrant more attention. In my 1999 WIDER Lecture (Atkinson, 1999), I argued that the fanning out of the upper part of the earnings distribution in some, but not all, countries could be explained by a shift to a less redistributive pay norm. However, this argument has hardly been recognized in the literature. The superstar model has received more attention, but this attention has concentrated exclusively on the recent rise in top earnings. We need also to see how far it explains the earlier periods when there was compression of the top of the earnings distribution. As noted in the previous section, in some countries the very top percentiles continued to fall in the 1950s (the top decile gaining while those within the top percentile lost).

These are the lines of explanation that I take up in Sections 8 and 9. But they do not preclude other models of the earnings distribution. The shifting of supply and demand curves remains a useful way of approaching the issue (providing that the dynamics are treated explicitly), and these curves are undoubtedly affected to some degree by the forces of technological change and globalization. At the same time, they only provide a starting point, and we need to look at what lies behind. In seeking to understand the working of the labour market, there are indeed more mechanisms than I can treat in this Lecture. These include discrimination, collective bargaining, and the impact of government policy. In my account of the evolution of the earnings distribution, I have focused on the overall distribution, not on the composition by gender or by race. In so doing, I am aware that I have missed an important part of the story. By ignoring, for example, the changing gender composition of the labour force, and the role of gender-based discrimination, I may have obscured the underlying changes. This is why the country chapters all include substantial amounts of information about the distributions among men and women separately. (I should also point out in mitigation that my main text does look at the distribution among all workers, rather than concentrating on men as in the Standard Distribution of Lydall (1968).) At the same time, I believe that one has to be careful in interpreting the impact of compositional changes. Considering the distribution within sub-groups is a valuable way of understanding the determinants of earnings, but I do not accept that one can write off compositional changes as 'spurious'. It is, after all, compositional changes that lie at the heart of the Kuznets explanation of the evolution of income inequality. A good example is provided by the reduced proportion of young workers (for example, in Australia workers aged under 20 were 14 per cent of the total 40 years ago, whereas today they are around 3 per cent). Separate consideration of these workers and of adult workers helps us interpret the changes over time in the earnings distribution, but it would be misleading to concentrate solely on what has happened within these groups. The wages of young adults today reflect their later entry into the labour force.

Entry and exit may affect the composition of the employed population through variation in the levels of unemployment and of migration. Taking the long view, one certainly needs to take account of the revival of employment after the Great Depression, and, conversely, of the rise of European unemployment in the latter decades of the twentieth century. On a year-to-year basis, it would be interesting to carry out a time-series analysis of the changes in earnings dispersion in relation to labour market tightness. Equally, a long view requires consideration of the impact of global labour mobility; and, in the immediate past, the differential experience of the United States and Europe has to be seen in the context of different levels and types of immigration. Concentration of the unemployed or of immigrants at the bottom of the earnings distribution could mean that differences in the levels of unemployment or immigration caused significant changes in the degree of earnings dispersion. In the United Kingdom, in 1970, for example, removal of the bottom 10 per cent of employees would have caused a large (more than 20 per cent) rise in the ratio of the bottom decile to the median. On the other hand, the upper part of the distribution would have been little affected. As has been noted by Piketty and Saez (2007, pages 219–21), entry to and exit from the labour force do not necessarily affect indicators of dispersion such as the top decile as a percentage of the median. Both the top decile and the median are increased in the case described above. The proportionate effect of removing the bottom tenth on any given percentile depends on $(1-F(y))/yf(y)$, where F is the cumulative distribution and f is its derivative with respect to earnings (y). If that ratio were the same at the median and the top decile, then their ratio would be unaffected. (In fact, in the United Kingdom example, the top decile relative to the median falls by some 3 per cent, not enough to register.) Moreover, the example given is an extreme one. In reality, the impact is more diffuse. In the case of immigration, the empirical literature on the relation with wage structures 'has produced a confusing array of results' (Borjas, 1999, page 1734).

I am equally conscious that government policy has profoundly affected the distribution of earnings. The influence of government ranges from a total society-wide impact, as with the Nazi regime in Germany, to specific labour market policies in democratic countries. Reference has already been made to the wartime regulation of earnings in the United States, to the consequences of May 1968 for labour market policy in France, and to the centralized wage bargaining in Sweden. Earnings are also affected by other strands of government policy, a recent example being provided by the privatization of state enterprises, with consequences for the workers who had previously been protected by pay agreements. These influences are considered in a number of the country chapters in Part III. Another important omission, of which I, as author of a textbook on public finance, am particularly aware concerns the impact of taxation. Progressive taxation of earnings may well have an impact on gross wages. The recent rise in dispersion may reflect reductions in income tax rates, particularly at the top, where this has caused increased effort or hours, or has led to earnings being paid in a form that appears in the statistics rather than in other forms (such as fringe benefits). It may have shifted the balance between earned income and capital income. These fiscal consider-ations are undoubtedly part of the explanation, although I am not convinced that they are the whole story.

Finally, the Bibliography at the end of the book contains a number of references to these important subjects, and those concerned with gender differentials, collective bargaining, minimum wages, and product market regulation/privatization are listed at the outset.

8

A Behavioural Model of Change in
Differentials: The 'Fanning Out' at the
Top of the Earnings Distribution

Reliance on a simple supply and demand analysis ignores the developments in
labour economics of the past half century, notably the contribution of search
theory, which treats explicitly the process by which workers search for jobs
and firms advertise vacancies. These are important features of the real-world
labour market, as every reader will know. Students leaving university do not
automatically acquire jobs that are commensurate with their talents and skills.
They have to seek out possible employers. Equally employers do not simply
hire those standing outside the factory or dock gates. There is a process of
costly matching. This has always been the case. Villiers (1949) in his account
of the last days of trading under sail, describes vividly the problems faced by
seamen in finding a ship that was in commission, and of the masters of those
ships in finding suitable crew.

Central to this approach is the notion of a surplus being generated by a
job match. Given that the probability of making such a match is less than
100 per cent—workers may search in vain, and firms may advertise and get no
suitable applicants—there has to be a positive surplus to offset the positive
costs of searching and of creating a job vacancy. There is an element of
indeterminacy, since supply and demand only place bounds on the market
wage, allowing scope for bargaining about the division of the surplus,

Having come together, the firm and worker have a joint surplus ... there is a wage that
makes the worker indifferent between taking this job and waiting for his next job
opportunity. There is a wage that makes the firm indifferent between hiring this
worker and waiting for the next available worker. The bargaining problem is to agree
on a wage between these two limits. (Diamond, 1982, page 219)

In the job search literature, the surplus is typically assumed to be shared out as a
result of a process of bilateral bargaining, the division reflecting relative bargaining power. The bargaining over the surplus may be at the level of the individual
worker or may be collective. I concentrate here on individual pay determination.

Where there is a degree of indeterminacy of the market equilibrium, pay norms may play a role. Concepts of equity have long been discussed in the psychological literature on the determination of pay (see, for example, Weick, 1966 and Lawler and O'Gara, 1967). Amongst labour economists, they have often been seen as an alternative to economic explanations. Phelps Brown opens his *The Inequality of Pay* (1977) by contrasting the economist's approach with that of the sociologist. The former sees people as engaged in rational, impersonal transactions; the latter sees people as interacting as members of a social entity. Wood in his *A Theory of Pay* (1978) contrasts 'normative and anomic pressures', the latter being non-normative explanations. But the role of social norms is increasingly been recognized by economists (see, to give just two examples, Schlicht, 1998 and Rotemberg, 2002). The approaches are complementary rather than competitive. For example, the introduction of a notion of fairness or equity may provide a route to removing the indeterminacy where 'individual incentives are not by themselves generally sufficient to determine a unique equilibrium' (MacLeod and Malcomson, 1998, page 400). Observance of social norms may be consistent with individual rationality and indeed instrumental in achieving efficient outcomes. Social codes may enter directly into economic behaviour.

The penetration into mainstream economics has accelerated with the rise of interest in behavioural economics, although important contributions were made more than a quarter of a century ago. Of particular relevance here is the pioneering article by Akerlof (1980), who describes a model of the labour market where individual utility depends not only on income but also on reputation, which is based on conformity with the social code. The loss of reputation if one departs from the social code depends on the proportion believing in the code, which is undermined if people cease to observe it. He shows that there may be a long run equilibrium with the persistence of a 'fair', rather than market-clearing, wage.

This reputational approach is applied to the relation between wages and productivity in Atkinson (1999). Suppose that there is a social code, or pay norm, that limits the extent to which, within a group of equally qualified workers, individual earnings increase with actual productivity. (See Note 2 in Part II for details of a version of this kind of model.) Where this code is followed, people are paid a fraction (less than unity) of their productivity plus a uniform amount. Bewley (1999, pages 84–5) refers to studies of such 'wage flattening'. In his own interview study in the United States, he found 'ample evidence that pay differentials often do not fully reflect differences in productivity' (1999, pages 84–5). Such a policy involves a degree of redistribution and lower productivity workers can be expected to subscribe to the pay norm.

But other workers will also accept it, even where they could be paid more if they broke the norm, since—if they believe in the norm—by deviating they would suffer a loss of reputation. The extent of the loss rises with the proportion of jobs that are paid according to the pay norm, so that the proportion of workers adhering to the norm is endogenous. It is this endogeneity that leads to the 'tipping' phenomenon identified by Schelling (1978). Interior equilibria for the proportion believing in the social code may be unstable, and, depending on the initial conditions, a society converges to a high level of conformity with the social code, or to a low level of conformity.

Employers may also be concerned with their reputations. When they create a job, it is determined in advance whether or not it is paid according to the pay norm. The profitability of the job depends not only on the pay but also on the acceptance of the job by the worker with which it is matched. Matching is assumed to follow a random process, but is only successful where either both employer and worker observe the code or neither does. Employers determine their pay policy (i.e. whether or not to observe the social code) on the basis of comparing expected profitability, which depends on the proportion of workers who accept different pay offers. (In a more complex model than that described in Note 2, it will also depend on the characteristics of workers accepting different offers.) The expected profitability of breaking the social code has to exceed the consequential loss of reputation, which is assumed to vary across employers, so that some employers may observe the code while others depart from it. There will therefore be a proportion of jobs which accord with the pay norm. This proportion will depend on how much the employer is willing to 'invest' in reputation.

Where there are multiple possible outcomes, and the 'tipping' phenomenon described above, an exogenous shock may shift the key relationship and switch the society from an equilibrium with a high level of conformity to the pay norm, and hence relatively low wage differentials, to an equilibrium where a much larger proportion of these workers are paid on the basis of their productivity. With this kind of dynamic process, we could well observe movement in one direction for a period, which would then be suddenly reversed. An example of such a 'shock' could be a change in the political climate, perhaps influenced by events in other countries, causing a reduction in the degree of worker support for a redistributive pay norm. Or, there may be a shift on the side of employers. In the past, governments have sought to influence pay levels and relativities through public sector employment, and this leverage has been attenuated in recent decades as a result of privatization. There may well have been a shift in the aggregate behaviour of employers on account of the transfer of state enterprises to private shareholders. As a result, we may observe a move towards a more spread-out distribution.

This line of explanation rests on there being an exogenous shock. One reason why there may have been a shift is that employers may attach more weight to short run profits and less weight to reputation, which is a long run investment. This may be a consequence of the rise in real interest rates identified earlier. Or, it is plausible to suppose that the rate of time discount of firms has increased on account of increased emphasis on shareholder value. Here we have further grounds to link what is happening in the labour market with changes in the capital market. If the model depends on an exogenous shock to explain a change in direction, it still contains an endogenous explanation as to why the same shock may produce different outcomes in different countries. The support for pay norms depends, for instance, on the extent of differences in underlying productivity. Where people are relatively homogeneous, then there is more likely to be adherence to an egalitarian pay norm. Countries may therefore experience different changes in the distribution of earnings.

9

Superstars and Pyramids: Two Complementary Explanations for Changes in Top Earnings

The recent rises in top earnings have been attributed to the 'superstar' phenomenon. This model is rightly associated with Rosen (1981), although he stressed his debt to Alfred Marshall writing at the beginning of the twentieth century. According to the 'superstar' theory, people differ in their talents, which are assumed fixed. The top performer in a field is able to extract a rent that is related to the extent of the market served; those unable to afford to see this superstar go to the next best performer; and so on. Rosen takes the example of opera singers. In the days when there was no broadcasting, and no recording possibilities, you could only hear the top singers in person, so that they played in the largest venues in large cities. The top singers would attract those with the greatest willingness to pay. Those who were less willing to pay would hear lesser stars, or have to make do with the local talent. This means that the earnings of the second-best performer depend on the 'reach' of the top performer, and so on down the range of talent.

Now this reach has been extended by technology. Many years ago, Marshall identified 'the development of new facilities for communication, by which men, who have once attained a commanding position, are enabled to apply their constructive or speculative genius to undertakings vaster, and extending over a wider area, than ever before' (1920, page 685). This raised the earnings of the superstars, who were able to extract more of the rents, while lowering those of the lesser performers, whose audience would desert them in favour of the radio or recordings of top performers. The earnings gradient is tilted in favour of the superstars. In the case of the arts, Marshall noted that 'there was never a time at which moderately good oil paintings sold more cheaply than now and at which first rate paintings sold so dearly' (1920, page 685). Moreover, it is not just technology. It is also trade. Opera singers are now global brands. Lecturing in Milan, I naturally stressed the opera example, but also thought that I should refer to football. As a result of technology that allows games to be followed all round the world, and the globalization of competitions, there is no doubt that the top teams, and hence top players, have secured greatly increased rents, whereas those in lower divisions are struggling (I say this with feeling as a supporter of Nottingham Forest).

There is however a potential problem. The superstar theory points in one direction, at least as far as technology is concerned. The degree of globalization has of course varied over time, but technical progress operates in general to increase the earnings gradient. Yet we have seen that, in a number of countries, top earnings fell in the late 1960s and 1970s, and indeed during the Golden Age of the 1950s some countries saw a tilt against the very top earnings. Moreover, the superstar theory cannot apply to all top earners; there are occupations where remuneration is not individualized in this way.

For these reasons, I suggest combining the superstar theory with the theory of earnings in hierarchical organizations, advanced by Simon (1957) and Lydall (1959). They examined a pyramidal employment structure, with each person in charge of the same number of direct subordinates (the span of control) and where pay rises by a constant increment as one advances up the ladder, so that each person earns a constant multiple of the salary of the person in the rank below them. This can be shown to generate an approximately Pareto tail to the earnings distribution. (The Pareto distribution is such that, wherever you are, the people above you earn on average a constant multiple of your earnings, the multiple being $a/[a-1]$, where a is known as the Pareto exponent. So that $a = 3$ means that people above you earn on average 50 per cent more than you do; $a = 6$ means that people above you earn on average 20 per cent more.) The Pareto exponent in the hierarchical model is equal to the natural logarithm of the span of control divided by the natural logarithm of the salary multiple (1 plus the increment). Examples of a number of pyramidal organizations, and their pay structures, are given by Beckmann (1977), who shows that in the British army at the time the average increment was 22 per cent.

There is in turn a problem with this explanation, as observed by Phelps Brown (1977, page 309), which is that plausible values for the span and increment imply values of the Pareto exponent higher than observed in the actual distribution. If we take the increment as 25 per cent, then a span of control of 6 implies an exponent of 8, and a span of 4 implies an exponent over 6. Even when earnings were least dispersed in the United Kingdom, the estimated Pareto coefficient was around 4.5 (Atkinson and Voitchovsky, 2003). Earnings at the top, as predicted by the hierarchical model, are not sufficiently concentrated. People above you in fact earn more than predicted by the exponent. Lydall also noted (1968, page 133) that there was an inconsistency between the predictions of the hierarchical model and the evidence then available about the relation between firm size and the pay of chief executives (the elasticity in the hierarchical model being equal to the inverse of the Pareto coefficient). Today, we might question how far the hierarchical formula applies all the way up the scale. In 1990, Jensen and Murphy could write that 'on average corporate America pays its most important leaders like bureaucrats' (1990, page 138), but a few years later, when Hall and Liebman (1998) asked 'are CEOs really paid like bureaucrats?', their answer for the United States was negative. As they showed, there was evidence for the United States that executive remuneration, including stock options, had become increasingly responsive to firm performance.

In my view, neither superstar nor hierarchical theory is sufficient on its own. It is for this reason that I propose combining the two explanations. The cumulative frequency at a particular value of earnings consists of those earning superstar rents of this amount plus the members of hierarchical organizations (companies, government agencies, etc.) of the appropriate size. The resulting distribution shows a rising fraction of superstars as we move to higher earnings levels. (See Note 3 in Part II for further details.) From this combination of the two approaches, we can identify three forces leading to greater dispersion at the top:

- increased concentration of superstar rents, resulting from technology and trade
- increasingly steep pay hierarchies in pyramidal organizations
- switch from hierarchical pay to rent-sharing (people paid like salesmen rather than on fixed salary scales).

How far these different forces applied over the period since 1980 needs to be explored in detail. There are *ex ante* grounds for supposing that all three were in operation. Globalization has had an apparent effect on the earnings of sports stars, performers, and creative professionals. Pay hierarchies appear to have become steeper in companies, in civil service organizations, and in universities. Within these organizations, pay is increasingly related to individual performance and individually negotiated. People are rewarded for the business brought in, targets achieved, or publications in top journals, rather than paid according to rank. As we have seen, CEOs are no longer paid like bureaucrats. The balance of employment has shifted with the scaling back of the public sector and with privatizations. These forces operated to different degrees in different countries. Indeed, the impacts may be negatively correlated across countries. As Marshall noted, the emergence of superstars depresses the earnings of those lower down the scale, and the latter may be located in another country. As the top performers extend their reach to supply consumers all round the globe, local stars may find their earnings reduced.

The three elements outlined above may have operated differently in earlier periods. The reach of opera singers may have been continuously extended by the advent of radio, or gramophone records, or CDs, and so on. But the steepness of pay hierarchies may have fallen in the past and the significance of hierarchical pay may have increased in earlier epochs. Not only did organizations move to regularize their pay scales, replacing individualized payments by pay policies, but the organizations themselves became more predominant at the top of the distribution.

10

Conclusions

The first aim of this Lecture has been to examine the way in which economists think about the distribution of earnings. I believe that economists need to take seriously the models they employ, following them through to their logical conclusions. They need to integrate the theoretical discussion with the empirical enquiry, relating the concepts to the observed data. They need to probe the strengths and weaknesses of the variety of sources of information available about the distribution of earnings. The Lecture has tried to follow these dictates.

In Section 2, I argued that the idea of a race between technology and education is appealing, but it is more complex than is suggested by simple textbook supply and demand analysis. A constantly rising demand for educated workers leads—not to a constantly rising wage premium—but to a stable wage differential, the size of which depends on the speed of a country's response to shortages of qualified workers. This means that countries may face the same external shocks (rising demand), but have different outcomes in terms of wage dispersion. Countries that adjust more rapidly will see, on a continuing basis, smaller wage differences. At the same time, the fact that supply and demand are shifting in tandem means that the distribution of individual earning continues to evolve. The shares of the low paid in total earnings fall; and—more surprisingly—the shares of top earners also fall. To explain rising shares at the top, we have therefore to introduce an explanation for increased dispersion within the educated group.

Consideration of shares of total earnings at the end of Section 2 provided a bridge to the empirical evidence, since it is in the form of such relative measures that data are typically presented (although earnings data are typically shown as percentiles relative to the median, rather than shares of total earnings). In Section 3, I described the new dataset assembled here, designed to illuminate the changes over time in the distribution of earnings in 20 OECD countries. As stressed, the data are not comparable *across* countries; that is an exercise that remains to be undertaken. The focus is on comparing the *changes over time* in the different countries. The dataset is a rich source, covering a variety of countries, and drawing on a wide range of types of information. There is a wealth of data about the distribution of earnings that has not been fully exploited, or which has been neglected. We can learn a great deal from the evolution of earnings over a period that extends, in the case of 12 countries, back to the 1950s, and, in 5 cases, back to the 1930s or earlier. The data need however to be used with care. They are often a 'patchwork' rather than a single unified series. They are of variable quality, and I have for this reason introduced a grading system.

The second purpose of the Lecture has been to throw light on the substantive question—how has the distribution of earnings been changing? Has the rise in dispersion in the United States been followed elsewhere? In Section 4, I examined the changes since 1980 in 19 countries (the series for Switzerland not being sufficiently long). In 16 of the 19 countries, either the bottom decile has fallen by 5 per cent or more, or the top decile has risen by 5 per cent or more. In seven cases, both have happened. The findings demonstrate that it is not sufficient to look just at the decile ratio, which masks the asymmetry of the changes. Most of the action has been in the upper part of the distribution. In only seven countries does the bottom decile fall by 5 per cent or more, and three of these are from Eastern Europe and have been engaged in the transition to a market economy. In contrast, in 14 countries (again including the 3 from Eastern Europe), the top decile rose by more than 5 per cent. Indeed, for 6 of the 19, the top decile rose by more than 10 per cent over the period from 1980 to 2004 (or most recent year). Within the upper part of the distribution, in quite a number of countries, there has been a 'fanning out' of the upper part of the distribution. The increase relative to the median is larger the higher one goes up the distribution.

Much analysis of distributional change looks at the beginning and end points of the period studied. The advantage of the data collected here is that we can follow the changes over the years. In Section 5, I considered the time pattern in more detail, going back to 1965 in order to examine the period before the recent increase. How far was the rise in dispersion a reaction to the 1970s? The evidence assembled here shows the late 1960s and 1970s as a period of change. The events of May 1968 left their mark not just in France, and unions achieved earnings compression, as in the solidarity wage policy in Sweden and the Scala Mobile in Italy. The widening post-1980 should be seen in historical context. This experience suggests that for some, but not all, countries the rise in dispersion after 1980 formed the second part of a V.

In Section 6, I took the story back further to a previous period of compression and reaction. In the United States, the first part is well known as the 'Great Compression', but the same fall in dispersion between the 1930s and beginning of the 1950s was observed in Canada and Ireland. Less well known in the United States is the reversal after 1951. The Golden Age of the 1950s and early

1960s was a period when the top decile rose on Australia, Canada, France, Ireland, and the United Kingdom, as well as in the United States. In some of these countries, the bottom decile fell. This earlier V joined to that since 1965 means that, if we want a single letter description, then we are observing a W.

Section 7 provided a bridge back to theoretical explanations, and made clear that those theories privileged here are not the only ones that I consider import-ant. Factors such as discrimination, collective bargaining, and government intervention are all part of the story, but a lecture does not provide space for a proper examination. Instead, I chose to concentrate on two lines of explanation.

In Section 8, I considered a behavioural model of changes in differentials, directed particularly at explaining the fanning out of the upper part of the earnings distribution. It was suggested that we may observe changes in the extent to which earnings are governed by pay norms, these changes corre-sponding to a switch from a redistributive norm to one where people are paid on their individual productivity, or vice versa. An external shock causes an abrupt reversal of direction and convergence to a new equilibrium. This could be caused by a change in the political climate, shifting the degree of conform-ity with the social norm, which is then magnified as more people change their behaviour. It could be caused by a change in the capital market, as where firms become more short term in their outlook, and less willing to invest in establishing a reputation.

In Section 9, I turned to the explanation of top earnings that has received much recent attention: the superstar theory. Here, trade and technology have a clear role in expanding the reach of the most talented, and make the earnings gradient steeper. Local stars may lose out to global superstars. These considerations do not however apply to all top salaries. I have suggested that the superstar explanation be complemented by a model of salaries in hierarchical organizations. Such a theory, where earnings depend on position in a pyramidal organization, cannot be enough on its own either. Indeed, part of the story is, I suggested, that we have seen moves over time between the two types of earnings determination. In the past, we saw the spread of hierarchical organizations, but in recent years we have seen, to differing degrees in different countries, a reversal of the process, so that more people are now paid on an individual basis.

ENVOI

The observed pattern of change over time leads us to speculate about the future. How should the W shape be interpreted? Are we observing variation about a stationary distribution that tends to reassert its hold? Or is there a natural tendency for market economies to generate rising dispersion, only redressed (or held in check) on occasion? The different mechanisms that I have described here provide some basis for speculating about the likely future evolution. But it is important to remember that the distribution of earnings is not outside our control. It is true that governments are constrained by the global economy and by the pace of technological change, but policy has a role. Even in the simple supply and demand model, the extent of the wage differential depends on the speed of response to a shortage of qualified workers. The evolution of pay norms is partly endogenous, and state enterprises can influence the resulting market equilibrium. Conversely, the privatization of state enterprises can affect pay at both the top and the bottom of the distribution. Progressive taxation is still possible. All of these are matters over which citizens have some say; they are not purely spectators of an inevitable process.

Part II

Details of the Models

Note 1

The Dynamics of Supply and Demand

Two types of worker, skilled and unskilled, are available in quantities L_s and L_u, and they receive wages w_s and w_u. The relative wage, w_s/w_u, is denoted by ω. The relative demand for the two types of worker is denoted by $D(\omega)$. If the relative wage of skilled labour rises, then profit-maximizing firms reduce their relative demand to an extent that depends on how easy it is to substitute one kind of labour for another. The ease of substitution is measured by the elasticity of substitution, denoted by σ:

$$D(\omega) = A\omega^{-\sigma} \qquad (I.1)$$

In this expression, A is a parameter that determines the location of the demand curve, and this provides a vehicle for introducing shifts in the relative demand due to technical change or changes in international competitiveness. Let us suppose that A is shifting over time at a constant exponential rate g (i.e. $A = A_o e^{gt}$). Then

$$dlnD/dt = g - \sigma dln\omega/dt \qquad (I.2)$$

where ln denotes the natural logarithm. At any point in time, the relative supply of the two types of worker is fixed at S, and the relative wage ω is assumed to adjust to clear the market, so that

$$D[\omega] = S \qquad (I.3)$$

If supply remains permanently fixed, then from (I.2) the relative wage has to grow at a rate to keep relative demand unchanged, so that it grows at rate g/σ.

Suppose that the supply adjusts according to the difference between the relative wage and the cost of acquiring skills, denoted by e^{rT}, where r is the cost of borrowing and T is the length of time for which entry into the labour force has to be postponed. Suppose too that there is a constant speed of adjustment, β, then

$$dlnS/dt = \beta[\omega - e^{rT}] \qquad (I.4)$$

Equating the growth in supply with that in demand, we can see that

$$\sigma \; dln\omega / dt = g - \beta \; [\omega - e^{rT}] \tag{I.5}$$

If we start with $\omega = e^{rT}$, then the wage will rise, initially at rate g/σ, but as ω rises above e^{rT}, the rate of increase is reduced. The relative wage converges to

$$\omega^* = g/\beta + e^{rT} \tag{I.6}$$

At this semi-equilibrium, both supply and demand are growing at rate g, a situation which can continue since they are *relative* supplies and demands. The parameter σ does not enter the long run wage differential because in the long run we are not moving up or down the demand curve (see Figure 3).

Note 2

A Behavioural Model of Changing Pay Norms

The aim of this note is to describe a simple version of the pay norm model, where the assumptions are chosen to bring out the essence of the argument, rather than to allow for the full richness of strategic behaviour. It is essentially a behavioural model.

People differ in their innate productivity, a, and either work in a job paid according to productivity, in which case they are paid a, or they work in a job following the pay code, where they are paid $\alpha + \beta a$, where α is positive and β is less than 1. A fixed proportion of unemployed workers, λ, independent of their productivity, seek jobs paying according to the pay norm; the remainder seek jobs paying according to productivity.

At any point in time, there are M (market) jobs paying according to productivity and N (norm) jobs paying according to the pay code. The ratio of N to M is defined to be θ, which can vary between 0 and infinity. At any date, a fixed fraction, δ, of these jobs end, and firms are assumed to create enough job vacancies, J, that total employment remains unchanged. The mix of jobs, θ, can however change.

Firms vary their pay according to productivity in one of the two ways described above, but hire workers in the absence of information about their productivity (by assumption, no information is conveyed by the kind of job that they are seeking). It is assumed that the parameters α and β are set such that the expected profit net of wages is the same in the two types of job. (Of course, *ex post* the firm may wish to end the employment of low productivity workers, but this is assumed not to be possible.) The proportion of jobs offered according to the pay code is denoted by μ.

In equilibrium, at any point in time, t, one unemployed worker applies for each vacancy. The probability of an encounter of a firm and a worker producing a match for a pay code job is $\lambda\mu$ and the probability of a match for a market job is $(1-\lambda)(1-\mu)$. This means that employment evolves according to

$$d\ M/dt = (1-\lambda)(1-\mu)J - \delta M; \quad d\ N/dt = \lambda\mu J - \delta N \qquad (\text{II.1})$$

From which it follows that

$$d \ln\theta/dt = \lambda\mu \ J/N - (1-\lambda)(1-\mu)J/M \qquad (II.2)$$

So that (taking out *J/N*) θ rises or falls according as

$$\lambda\mu \ \textit{is greater or less than} \ (1-\lambda)(1-\mu)\theta \qquad (II.3)$$

In Figure II.1, θ rises to the left of the of curve. (In this figure, θ is shown on the horizontal axis; λ on the vertical axis; and μ is assumed constant.)

If both the proportions λ and μ were simply constants, then the economy would converge to a unique value of θ, a weighted combination of the fixed proportions of the two types among workers and firms. But both depend on θ. Let us consider first the endogeneity of λ. It is assumed that a fraction λ_{min} of workers always follow the norm and a fraction $(1-\lambda_{max})$ never does so, but the remainder are influenced by the extent to which the pay code is followed. In the case shown on Figure II.1, the fraction rises linearly once a threshold value of θ is reached, and continues to rise until the maximum value λ_{max} is attained. As may be seen from the diagram, there may now be three intersections: two locally stable equilibria separated by an unstable equilibrium. An economy may approach either of the locally stable equilibria, so that initial conditions matter. Equally, an exogenous shock may cause the economy to shift from one equilibrium to another. Suppose that people become more

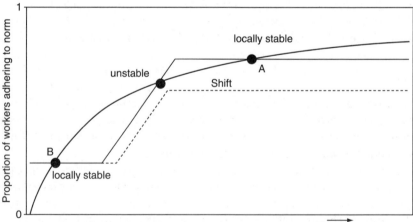

Figure II.1 'Tipping' equilibria

sceptical about the value of social norms, and there is a rise in both the threshold and in the proportion who never follow the norm. This means that an economy initially at A may shift rapidly to B, where a much smaller proportion of jobs are paid according to the redistributive pay norm. We can also see how the experience of different countries may differ, depending on the distribution of values held by their citizens, and the degree of heterogeneity. Where there is a wide range of values of θ over which people are changing their views, the upward-sloping section of the straight line in Figure II.1 is less steep, and hence, for any given threshold, it is less likely that there will be multiple equilibria (i.e. if the slope is sufficiently gentle, it will reach the curve to the right of the point A).

What about employers, whose job offer behaviour has so far been assumed fixed? Firms decide whether to offer either market or pay code jobs according to the probability of filling the jobs (since the creation of job vacancies is costly) and according to the loss of reputation associated with departing from the pay code. The expected profitability of breaking the social code has to exceed the consequential loss of reputation, which is assumed to vary across employers, so that some employers may observe the code while others depart from it. Suppose in fact that, as with workers, there are some employers who always offer market jobs, some who always follow the pay code, and some who decide on the basis of the expected present value (at interest rate r, where for convenience of exposition I switch to using discrete time periods) of profits allowing for the costs associated with the loss of reputation. Since the probability that any given worker encountered will accept the market job is $(1-\lambda)$, the expected present value of offering a market job is as follows, where π denotes the flow of net profit per period (assumed equal for both types of contract) and the present value takes account of the probability δ that the job will terminate:

$$V_M = (1-\lambda)\pi/(r+\delta) + \lambda V_M/(1+r) \qquad (\text{II.4})$$

It is assumed that the firm persists next period with the same strategy in the event of no match being made. Denoting by R the equivalent in terms of profits of the reputational gain from following the norm, we can see that the corresponding expression where following the pay code is

$$V_N = \lambda(\pi + R)/(r+\delta) + (1-\lambda)V_N/(1+r) \qquad (\text{II.5})$$

The firm will choose to follow the pay code if the reputational advantage

R/π *is greater than* $[(1-\lambda)/\lambda] \cdot [1-(1-\lambda)/(1+r)]/[1-\lambda(1+r)]-1$ (II.6)

If the firm were equally likely to encounter the two types of worker, then the right-hand side would be zero. Where λ is smaller than a half, and r positive, the right-hand side is positive and firms only offer pay code jobs where the reputational gain is considered to be sufficient. Moreover, in this situation, the required reputational gain rises with the rate of interest. If firms discount the future more heavily, then they are less likely to be willing to let considerations of reputation outweigh the fact that λ is smaller than a half.

Note 3

Superstars and Pyramids

The model of top earnings described (in words) in Section 9 is a blend of superstar and hierarchical explanations. In the case of the superstar theory, there is no direct link to a functional form for the resulting distribution. At the same time, the 'winner take all' nature of the model (Frank and Cook, 1995) suggests that it can be regarded as an extreme value process. The distribution of earnings in this case is given by the maximum values generated by the results of many separate 'competitions'. If we limit attention to those values exceeding some specified threshold, then for a sufficiently high threshold the distribution function takes on the generalized Pareto form (Embrechts, Klüppelberg, and Mikosch, 1997, page 164 or Coles, 2001, page 75), which has a Pareto upper tail. Here, I assume that the Pareto distribution provides a sufficiently close approximation, so that the cumulative distribution for superstar earnings, $G(y)$, where y denote earnings, is given by

$$1 - G(y) = A y^{-a} \tag{III.1}$$

A is a constant and a is the Pareto coefficient. As noted in the text, this distribution has the property that the mean income above y is given by $a/(a-1)$ times y. A fall, in the Pareto exponent means that this ratio rises and in this sense the distribution favours more the higher paid. Such a shift is shown in Figure III.1, where I have taken logarithms and inverted the relation:

$$lny = (1/a) \, ln[A/(1 - G(y))] \tag{III.2}$$

The basis for the superstar explanation of rising earnings dispersion is that there has been a fall in a, so that the gradient has become steeper.

The hierarchical theory has been set out by Lydall (1959) and Simon (1957). As they show, with a fixed span of control, c, and a fixed increment of salary, i, as one moves up the ladder, the distribution can be approximated by a Pareto distribution with an exponent equal to $ln\{c\}/ln\{1+i\}$, denoted here by β. (See Lydall, 1968, page 275.) The cumulative distribution for hierarchical earnings, $H(y)$, is given by

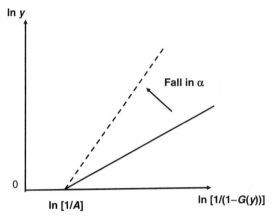

Figure III.1 Superstar shift in earnings gradient

$$1 - H(y) = By^{-\beta} \tag{III.3}$$

Again, the smaller β, the steeper is the salary gradient.

The proposal made here is that the overall distribution should be seen as a combination of the two: a simple mixture. Where θ is the weight on the superstar distribution and $(1-\theta)$ is the weight on the hierarchical distribution, the overall cumulative distribution is given by the following (where $0 < \theta < 1$):

$$1 - F(y) = \theta\, Ay^{-\alpha} + (1-\theta)\, By^{-\beta} \tag{III.4}$$

It is assumed that the gradient is steeper for the superstar element: that is, $\alpha < \beta$. The constants depend on the units in which earnings are measured, but I assume that at $y = 1$, the hierarchical model contributes more, in the sense that $A < B$. Taking logarithms and rearranging,

$$\ln\,[1/(1 - F(y))] = \alpha\, \ln y - \ln A - \ln[\theta + (1-\theta)B/A\ y^{\alpha - \beta}] \tag{III.5}$$

This is depicted in Figure III.2, which is similar to Figure III.1, but shows (i) the line relating to the case where there is pure hierarchy ($\theta = 0$), (ii) the line where there is purely superstars ($\theta = 1$), and (iii) the intermediate case, combining the two ($0 < \theta < 1$), shown by the dashed curve. The last of these requires some explanation. The dashed curve begins at $\ln[1/(\theta A + (1-\theta)B)]$ when $y = 1$, labelled Q in Figure III.2. It intersects the lines at their intersection, P, where variation in θ has no effect. Since by assumption, $\alpha < \beta$,

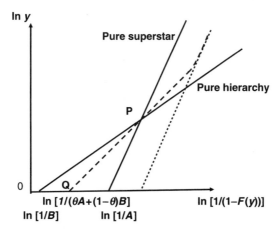

Figure III.2 Combined superstar and hierarchical models

the term in y in (III.5) tends to zero, so that the right-hand side tends to $\alpha\,lny - lnA - ln\theta$. Since θ is less than 1, this asymptote, indicated by the dotted line, is to the right of the pure superstar line.

From Figure III.2, we can see how the percentiles are affected by changes in the parameters. Any given percentile corresponds to a point on the horizontal axis, and the corresponding earnings can be read from the value of lny measured vertically. The effect of a change in α or β can be seen directly in terms of a rotation of the lines about the intercepts on the horizontal axis. A change in θ causes a tilt around the point P. If payment according to the hierarchical model becomes more important (θ falls), the point Q moves to the left and the asymptote moves to the right. There is a clockwise rotation: there is an increase in percentiles below the value corresponding to P and a decrease in higher percentiles.

Part III

New Empirical Evidence for 20 OECD Countries

Introduction to Part III

The main empirical contribution of this book is to assemble data on the distribution of earnings among individuals for 20 OECD countries covering as much as possible of the past 100 years. In this enterprise, I have benefited a great deal from the work of the OECD. In *Employment Outlook* for 1993 and 1996, and later on its Labour Market Statistics (LMS) website, the OECD has published data on earnings dispersion that has formed the basis for its own research and for many academic studies. I have gone beyond the existing OECD sources in two main respects. The first is that I have sought to go further back in time, seeking to set the experience of recent decades in historical perspective; the second is that I have made use of the multiplicity of sources on earnings available in many countries. In both respects, I have been heavily influenced by the path-breaking book by Lydall (1968), a book that is cited here so frequently that it is not referenced separately in the country chapters (nor are the OECD studies). The data presented by Lydall still provide a most valuable resource for researchers wanting to go back before 1965. His Appendix 7 covers an astonishing 36 countries. Of the 20 OECD countries considered here, only Ireland and Switzerland are missing from his Country Tables. In each of the other 18 country chapters, I begin by describing the data available in Lydall (1968). In extending the period to the present day, I have, like Lydall, made extensive use of national sources, drawing on published data from official and academic studies. The information collected here is, with a few exceptions, already available in published form. For many of the countries, earnings data are published in their *Statistical Yearbook*s or in regular statistical publications on earnings.

For each of the 20 countries, there is a separate chapter. Each chapter describes the evidence available on earnings dispersion in the country in question, lists the data in a series of tables with percentiles and, in some cases, decile shares and Gini coefficients, and summarizes the findings in two graphs, covering the upper (Figure x.1) and lower (Figure x.2) parts of the distribution. The value added of the country chapters lies in (1) bringing together information that is at present dispersed (for example in successive issues of *Statistical Yearbook*s), (2) presenting the evidence in a standardized form, in particular by interpolating from tabulations to give percentiles, (3) evaluating the quality of the different sources and applying the A/B/C grading discussed in Part I, and (4) seeking to explain the relation between different series. There then follows for each country a summary of the main features of the evolution of the earnings distribution over the period covered, with references to the literature (for each country there is a separate bibliography). At the beginning of each country chapter, there is a brief description of changes in the geographical boundaries over the twentieth century and in the currency system.

In the course of preparing this part, I have benefited greatly from the help of others with deeper knowledge of the situation in each country. Despite this, I am sure that I have made mistakes in describing or interpreting the data. I should be grateful if readers who identify such errors could let me know at Nuffield College, Oxford.

The tables are modelled on those of Lydall (1968) and are accompanied by notes describing in summary form the coverage, age, sex, industry, occupation, definition of earnings, intensity (full time, part time, full year, etc.), period, limits on the range of earnings, and source. In all cases, the first tables for a country are drawn from the OECD sources cited above: the 1993 and 1996 *Employment Outlooks*, and the LMS website (version downloaded on 17 December 2005). The remaining tables are drawn from official and academic sources. In the tables, I have tried to provide as full information as possible, with, for example, different summary statistics or different coverage. Wherever possible, I have included distributions for males and females separately. This means that some tables contain a very large number of columns. The *Thomas Cook Railway Timetable for Europe* used to have a heading to the Paris–Cherbourg timetable saying that 'this is the most complicated timetable in Europe'. In the present book, the record is held by Table A.5, with 54 columns. It is hoped that, nonetheless, these tables will provide a valuable source for future researchers.

In the graphs, different symbols are used to distinguish different types of source and different percentiles. The types of source are grouped as follows:

- household surveys, shown by squares (■), where earners in a sampled household are interviewed and their earnings recorded; in some cases, earnings records are obtained from tax registers, in which case the data are classified as based on administrative records
- data based on income tax registers or returns, shown by circles (●), where this includes tax registers and social security records
- data derived from social security records or employer returns, shown by triangles (▲)

- Censuses of Population, shown by St Andrew's crosses (**X**)
- employer surveys, shown by diamonds (◆), where information is obtained from employers about the earnings of individual workers, including cases where the information is reported by groups of workers (as in the Irish Census of Industrial Production).

The deciles (P10 at the bottom, P90 at the top) are shown by solid symbols of regular size; the quartiles (P25 for the lower, P75 for the upper), or quintiles (P20, P80) are shown by hollow symbols of the same size; the top vintile (P95) is shown by larger, solid symbols. So that, in Figure x.1, ■ corresponds to the top decile, □ to the top quartile, and ■ to P95. The scales of the Figures x.1 and x.2 vary from country to country, so as to allow the data to be displayed as clearly as possible.

As explained in the Lecture (Section 3), I have applied a grading system to the earnings data. Data graded as C are unacceptable; data graded A are regarded as fit for purpose. In between are data graded B, which have serious limitations but which are sufficiently reliable to be used in the absence of data graded A. The series graded B are listed below:

Australia	Income tax data 1949–62
Canada	Census of manufacturing data 1944–67
	Census of population data 1931–71
	Income tax data (tabulated by total income) 1972–81
Germany	Pre-war wage tax data 1932–36
	Pre-war social insurance data 1929–37
Ireland	Census of industrial production data 1937–68
Netherlands	Data restricted to males in manufacturing 1970–7
Norway	Population census (tabulations) 1980–2001

Where used, these data series are shown by dashed lines in the graphs. As may be seen, they mostly concern earlier years, for which superior data are not available.

SUMMARY

To summarize, the new data

- cover 20 OECD countries each described in the country chapters A–T
- cover as much as possible of the twentieth century (12 of the 20 series start before 1960)

- consider multiple sources for each country
- recognize different levels of quality
- pay particular attention to consistency of the series across time.

I hope that the data will therefore represent a valuable resource for future research. At the same time, the data must be used with care. Many of the qualifications relate to the specific circumstances of the different countries, and are discussed in detail below. There are however three general issues that I discuss in the final part of this Introduction: interpolation, sampling error, and top coding.

INTERPOLATION

In many cases it has been necessary to interpolate tabulated data. In their simplest form, the tabulations show the percentage of people on different ranges of earnings. For example:

Starting point of range	Per cent	Cumulative per cent
1–	15	0
50–	20	15
100–	20	35
125–	20	55
150–	13	75
200–	8	88
300–	4	96

In this example, the upper quartile is 150, but we have to interpolate the top decile, which lies between 200 and 300. It should be noted that in this example, we are assumed to have no information on the mean earnings by range.

The interpolation of *shares* of total earnings in the case where there is also information on the mean earnings by range has been the subject of a large literature. This has shown how upper and lower bounds can be placed, for example, on the share of earnings of, say, the top 10 per cent. The bounds are calculated by making extreme assumptions about the allocation of people within the range (for example, that they are all at the mean, or that they are all at one of the endpoints). These bounds can be tightened when combined with the assumption that the density is non-increasing, which certainly seems a reasonable assumption for the upper part of the earnings distribution. Alternatively, a number of authors make the assumption that the distribution has the Pareto form (see, for example, Piketty, 2003). If the cumulative distribution is written as F(y) where y denotes earnings, the Pareto distribution has the form $1-F(y) = A\, y^{-\alpha}$, where A and α are constants, the latter (alpha) being referred to as the Pareto parameter. In other words, as y rises from 200 to 300, the proportion of people above y falls by a factor $(3/2)^{-\alpha}$. This provides a simple way of estimating the Pareto parameter. In the example above, the proportion above 200 is 12 per cent, and the proportion above 300 is 4 per cent, so it falls by a factor of 3. Taking logarithms shows that α is equal to the logarithm of 3 divided by the logarithm of 1.5, giving a value close to 2.7. It should be noted that this calculation uses only information on the frequencies; if we also had information on the means for the different ranges, then this would provide an alternative, possibly different, estimate of the Pareto parameter.

In the present case, the problem is more difficult than that described above for two reasons. The first is that we are seeking to calculate the percentiles *expressed as a percentage of the median*, not the share expressed relative to a known overall mean. Whereas the overall mean is typically known, the median has to be estimated from the distribution. This complicates the calculation of the upper and lower bounds, in that we have to allow for different extreme assumptions for the median and for the relevant percentile. It also does not seem reasonable to assume that the Pareto distribution holds for the middle and lower parts of the distribution. The second difficulty is that for percentiles, even at the top, we cannot make the same argument about a non-decreasing density that allowed the bounds to be refined in the case of shares (see Atkinson, 2005). The unrefined bounds, on the other hand, are quite wide. In the example shown, the median could lie between 100 and 125, and the top decile between 200 and 300, so that the top decile expressed as a percentage of the median could lie between 160 and 300 per cent.

This example warns us against seeking to interpolate over broad ranges and in general I have not attempted to do this. In the few cases where it proved necessary, the series are graded B on this account. Given therefore that most of the tabulated data contains detailed ranges, and given that no refined bounds are available, I have adopted a relatively simple method: that of linear interpolation of the cumulative frequencies. In other words, the density is assumed to be uniform throughout the range. So that in the example, the top decile is estimated as $200 + (300-200)(2/8) = 225$. The median is estimated as 118.75, so that the top decile is 189 per cent of the median. I appreciate that the linear interpolation is likely to overstate the top decile. In some cases, I have therefore used the *Pareto* assumption. Applying the value of the parameter calculated earlier, we can calculate the value of y required to generate (1–F) equal to 10 per cent as $(12/10)^{1/\alpha}$. This gives a value of around 214.

I have not however done so in general, as it seemed better to use a method that could be applied to all percentiles, rather than make an arbitrary decision as to where the Pareto assumption was appropriate. Also, while the linear assumption may tend to overstate the top decile, there is no reason to suppose that it systematically biases the measurement of the changes over time on which this book focuses. Finally, I should emphasize that the example given above was deliberately simplified in terms of the number of ranges to allow illustration of the method. Much more typical are the Austrian social insurance data for 1968, where there are 45 ranges, each of a width less than 5 per cent of the median.

In certain cases (for example, the UK income tax data) where there is information on the mean earnings for each interval, I have applied the *mean-split histogram* (see Cowell and Mehta, 1982, and Atkinson, 2005).

SAMPLING ERROR

Interpolation has been discussed separately from the issue of sampling error. For a number of the data sources this seems reasonable. In some cases, the data are based on complete enumerations; there is no sampling. In other cases, the samples are sufficiently large that sampling error can effectively be neglected. The Canadian Longitudinal Administrative Databank has a sample of around 1 million. The sample size for the Italian National Social Security Institute (INPS) data in Italy is around 100,000. In the analysis of the United States social security data by Utendorf (1998), the smallest annual sample consists of 982,510 observations.

Where sampling error is likely to be important is in the case of household surveys with modest sample sizes. An example is provided by the Household Economic Survey (HES) on New Zealand, which collects earnings data for some 3,000–4,000 current wage or salary earners. The effect of sampling errors is discussed by Dixon, who concluded that 'sampling errors are relatively large, and survey estimates tend to be volatile from year to year' (Dixon, 1998, page 74). She concludes that the 95 per cent confidence interval for estimates of the top and bottom decile 'are generally around 4–6 percent on either side' (1998, page 75). She goes on to comment that 'given these sampling errors, most of the year-to-year movements in the various measures of . . . earnings inequality are not statistically significant. However, the longer-term changes occurring over periods of five years or more generally *are* large enough to exceed the relevant confidence intervals, and therefore can be treated as meaningful changes' (1998, page 75). While design effects may increase the sampling errors in certain cases, the HES sample *size* is probably one of the smallest encountered in the different sources used here, so that these considerations provide further support for the 5 per cent criterion adopted here for a change to 'register'.

TOP CODING

In a number of cases, estimates of the percentiles are based on micro-data that are subject to top coding. Top coding is commonly applied when releasing data for public use, so as to protect the confidentiality of respondents. The same consideration may lead to top coding being applied to internal data, to which may be added other factors such as the avoidance of coding errors or (in the past) restrictions on computer storage. The existence of top coding is one reason why researchers on earnings have tended to use the top decile or the decile ratio, arguing that top coding is unlikely to affect as much as 10 per cent of observations, whereas it does affect alternative measures such as the share of the top 10 per cent or the Gini coefficient. In other cases, researchers have assigned an arbitrary value to the top-coded observations: for example, Lemieux (2006) multiplies top-coded wages by a factor 1.4.

The implications of top coding are similar to those of seeking to interpolate into an open upper interval, and the issue can be approached by estimating upper and lower bounds, as has recently been discussed by Burkhauser, Feng, and Jenkins (2007). They examine the impact of different procedures on estimates obtained using the United States data from the March Current Population Survey. While the results for size-adjusted household incomes are subject to an increasing top-coding problem, the estimates for individual wages and salaries of full time full year workers are not in practice much affected. The range between the upper and lower bound for the decile ratio, based on the public-use files, in 2004 (a not atypical year) was around 1 per cent. This is well within the margin required for a change to register (10 per cent for the decile ratio).

A

Australia

In the period since the 1960s there have been many dramatic changes in the Australian labour market. Increases in the labour force participation of females, the growth of part-time employment and a shift in the composition of employment from manufacturing to service sectors... Another notable development has been an increase in inequality in the distribution of earnings for workers in Australia.

Borland, 1997, page 28

A.1 Introduction

Australia has had the same geographical boundaries since the Commonwealth of Australia was formed on 1 January 1901. On 14 February 1966, it introduced the Australian dollar in place of the pound, 2 dollars being equal to 1 pound.

Previous Coverage

There are seven tables for Australia in Lydall (1968). One table relates only to New South Wales; the remaining six tables cover Australia for 1949/50, 1952/3, 1955/6, 1958/8, and 1962/3, and are based on income tax data, which are discussed further below.

The OECD tabulations have included the following data for Australia:

1993 (Table A.1): data for men and women separately 1975, 1979–81, 1985–91, relating to non-managerial employees, based on the May employer survey of *Employee Earnings and Hours* (*EEH*).

1996 (Table A.2): data for all workers, and for men and women separately, 1979–95, based on the August household survey *Weekly Earnings of Employees*, an annual supplement to the labour force survey.

LMS (Table A.3): all workers, and men and women separately, 1975–2000, based on the August household survey *Weekly Earnings of Employees*.

Official Publications

Articles on the distribution of earnings in Australia have been published by the Australian Bureau of Statistics (ABS) in *Australian Social Trends*. The May employer survey results have been published as *Employee Earnings and Hours* (ABS Catalogue

No. 6306.0). The results of the August household survey are published under the title *Survey of Employee Earnings, Benefits and Trade Union Membership*, previously *Weekly Earnings of Employees* (ABS Catalogue No. 6310.0).

A.2 Data Sources

According to King, Rimmer, and Rimmer, writing in 1992, 'information on the distribution of employment income in Australia is notoriously patchy and genuinely long-run statistical series are not available' (1992, page 394). It is true that there is no single series covering the whole post-war period, but Australia is nevertheless better placed than a number of other OECD countries. The income tax data have been used by Lydall (1965) to generate estimates for the 1950s; employer surveys of earnings were introduced in the early 1960s; regular household surveys of earnings began in the early 1970s. There is in fact a variety of sources. The main problem is piecing them together: 'patchwork' is a good description.

The richness of sources is accompanied by differences of view about their relative merits. Norris, who uses employer surveys, notes that estimates of earnings dispersion are available from alternative sources such as household (the *Weekly Earnings of Employees*) but comments that 'these are thought to be less reliable' (1977, page 488). King, Rimmer, and Rimmer say that 'the best available data come from the employer survey of the distribution of employees' earnings and hours' (1992, page 394). In official publications on the distribution of earnings, the ABS has tended to rely on data from the *EEH* employer survey. See for example the article by Saunders (2000) in *Australian Social Trends, 2000*. On the other hand, according to Borland and Wilkins, 'the only source of data which appears suitable for a general study of earnings inequality is the [household] Income Distribution Survey' (1996, page 13). Their preference may stem from the availability of micro-data, but it may be noted that the OECD has switched from using the employer survey to using estimates of earnings dispersion based on the household survey of weekly earnings.

In my view, all of the available sources contribute to our understanding of the picture. The fact that, on occasion, they indicate different directions of movement may reflect differences in scope and coverage, as well as underlying differences in the forces shaping the overall distribution. The latter include the changing mix of full time and part time employment, the falling share of youth employment, changes in public policy such as those with respect to taxation and salary sacrifice schemes, and the difference between private and public employment, an aspect emphasized by Nevile and Saunders (1998) and Borland, Hirschberg, and Lye (1998).

Employer Survey of Employee Earnings and Hours (EEH)

The main employer survey containing information on the distribution of earnings—as opposed to average earnings—is that conducted in May (hence cited as the May survey).[1] Selected employers are requested to supply details for only a sample of their employees (randomly selected according to instructions issued by the ABS). The *EEH* was initiated in May 1974,[2] and has moved between being annual and biennial. It was carried out every year from 1974 to 1981. It was then reconstituted in 1983, when a new survey format was introduced: see Gregory (1993, page 70, n16).[3] The ABS noted that the new sampling framework is 'likely to have an effect on the comparability of [the 1983] survey with the 1981 and earlier surveys' (1981, page 1). The survey was then carried out in the following years: 1985–96, 1998, 2000, 2002, 2004, and 2006. The results were used in OECD (1993).

The *EEH* covers all employing organizations both public and private, with the exception of those primarily engaged in agriculture, forestry, and fishing, of private households employing staff, and foreign embassies and consulates. In the *EEH* 2002, data were collected for some 53,000 employees from a sample of approximately 8,000 employers. Adjustments are made for the lag between businesses commencing operation and their inclusion on the business register from which the sample is drawn. In order to understand the coverage of this employer-based sample, it is clearly important to compare the grossed-up numbers with those from other sources, such as household-based surveys. For the years 2002, 2004, and 2006 there are data both including and excluding the amounts covered by 'salary sacrifice' schemes.

The results from the *EEH* have been published in a variety of forms, and Table A.5 contains three main series. The first covers all employees: that is, all ages, full time and part time, and all occupations. The second series is restricted to all full time adult employees. (Prior to 1983, adult workers were defined as those aged 21 and over; from 1983 they also included those aged under 21 who are paid at the adult rate.) It should be noted that the proportion of youth workers (those aged 15–19 as a percentage of all full time employed persons) has fallen from 14 per cent in 1966 to 3 per cent in 2006. The third series is restricted to *non-managerial* full time adult employees. In the 1996

---

[1] There had been a number of earlier surveys including:

- *Survey of wage rates and earnings*, September 1960, covering the actual weekly earnings of adult male, full time employees in the private sector in the last pay-period in September 1960 (see *Labour Report*, No 50)
- *Survey of weekly earnings*, October 1961, covering the actual weekly earnings of adult male, full time employees in the private sector in the last pay-period in October 1961 (Reference S.B. 22)
- *Survey of weekly earnings*, October 1965, covering the actual weekly earnings of male, full time employees in both private and government sectors in the last pay-period in October 1965, but covering only certain industrial groups (*Labour Report*, No 52)

Information about these surveys is provided in *Labour Statistics 1975* (the first year of this publication), page 60, and the Data Appendix to Norris (1977). The analysis of the results by Norris (1977) is summarized in Table A.6.

[2] In May 1971, there was a *Survey of Weekly Earnings (Size Distribution)*, which differed in its sample design.

[3] According to Belchamber, 'there are bugs in the 1983 data' (1996, page 289, n4), although he refers to employment, rather than earnings.

survey, the employees covered were 70.9 per cent full time and 59 per cent were full time and non-managerial. It should be noted that the proportion of workers classified as 'non-managerial' in the survey varies from year to year: for example, for men, the proportion was 81.9 per cent in 1995, 77.5 per cent in 2000, and 81.5 per cent in 2002.[4] There is a fourth, hybrid series, for the years 1978 to 1981, which covers all full time adult employees except those in the government sector.

Household Survey: Survey of Employee Earnings, Benefits and Trade Union Membership

Since 1975 a sample household survey, based on the population survey, has collected information about weekly earnings in August (it is referred to as the August survey).This survey is the *Survey of Employee Earnings, Benefits and Trade Union Membership*, referred to here as 'Survey of Employee Earnings'; it was previously called *Weekly Earnings of Employees*. This survey is used in the OECD (1996) and LMS compilations. The estimates relate to all persons aged 15 and over (in August 1990 restricted to those aged 15–69) who are employees in their main job, with certain exceptions such as members of the permanent defence forces, and non-Australians on tour. The sample results are re-weighted using population benchmarks. The 1975 results relate to all jobs and hours worked, whereas subsequent survey publications show results both for all jobs and for the main job. Imputation for missing data was only introduced in 2004; prior to that the earnings of around 9.5 per cent of full time employees (in 2003) 'could not be determined'. It should be noted that the survey, in contrast to that discussed below, uses a single person in the household to respond on behalf of all members; this method is likely to produce less reliable answers.

Survey of Income and Housing Costs (SIHC)

A second source of earnings data from households is the *Survey of Income and Housing Costs (SIHC)*, introduced on a (more or less) annual basis with effect from 1994/5. The SIHC was run in conjunction with the Monthly Population Survey (MPS), with a sample of around 650 dwellings being selected each month from the responding units in the MPS. This means that the 1994/5 SIHC contained earnings data collected on a continuous basis over the period July 1994 to June 1995. Over the year, the sampling means that around 15,500 persons over the age of 15 are included in the sample, and of these about 85 per cent respond. A complex weighting procedure is applied to ensure that the resulting estimates conform to population statistics benchmarks. As of 2003/4, the SIHC has reverted to being a biennial household survey (and made a number of other changes). The survey covers persons resident in private dwellings throughout Australia, apart from people living in remote and sparsely populated areas of the Northern Territory.

    The SIHC replaced the previous special survey, known as the *Income Distribution Survey* (IDS), which was conducted every four to five years: 1968/9, 1973/4, 1978/9,

---

[4] I am grateful to Rob Bray for drawing my attention to this point and for supplying these figures.

1981/2, 1985/6, and 1989/90. The IDS differed in that the survey was conducted over a limited period (for example 2 months), compared with the 12-month period of the SIHC. Other differences included changes in the survey weighting and estimation procedures, to the population in scope, and to interviewing methods. The impact of the replacement of IDS by SIHC is discussed by Saunders, who notes that 'there are legitimate concerns about how far this change has affected comparisons that span this change' (2005, page 11). He cites the findings of Siminski, Saunders, and Bradbury (2003) that the ratio of reported total earnings to the national accounts totals increased by around 5 percentage points between 1990 and 1994/5, which was 'potentially enough to explain the observed increase in inequality over this period' (2005, page 11, n10). For this reason, in Table A.7, a break is shown in the series between 1990 and 1994/5.

Borland and Kennedy (1998) base their work on the IDS/SIHC unit record files for 1982, 1986, 1990, and 1994/5, using the current usual weekly earnings in main job (in 1982, sample is restricted to employees with only one job). Their results are largely presented in the form of changes, and are not summarized in the tables here. Saunders (2005) uses the unit record files for 1986, 1990, 1994/5, 1995/6, 1997/8, 1999/2000, and 2000/1. His results are summarized in Table A.7.

Survey of Trade Union Members

Information on trade union membership was collected in a survey that started in 1976, and was conducted every two years from 1986 to 1996 (from 1997 onwards, trade union membership is covered by the *Survey of Employee Earnings, Benefits and Trade Union Membership*). Data on weekly earnings in main job are available from 1986 to 1994 and were used by Borland (1996) to examine the effect of union membership. The earnings data are in grouped form, and Borland applied a linear interpolation to the cumulative frequencies. The survey was conducted as a supplement to the Labour Force Survey. The results were published in *Survey of Trade Union Members* (6325.0).

Income Tax Data

The income tax data do not calibrate incomes according to total wages and salaries. As explained in Lydall (1965), the construction of time series estimates from this source involves concentrating on those in the category 'Occupation 1', which consists of individuals with less than £100 of non-wage and salary income (less than £50 in 1949). He did however have access to special information tabulating income of other wage and salary earners for the two years 1953/4 and 1959/60, which allowed him to estimate the distribution including those missing from Occupation 1. This shows major differences at the very top, but the top decile was quite close: for men, it was 146 per cent of the median in 1953/4, compared with 144 per cent for Occupation 1, and 153 per cent and 150 per cent, respectively for women (Lydall, 1965, Table II). For 1959/60, the figures for men were 161 per cent and 156 per cent, and for women they were identical. His estimates based on Occupation 1 (from Lydall (1965) and Lydall

(1968)) are given in Table A.4. In view of the fact that they exclude employees with significant non-wage income, I have classified the series as B.

Comparison of Different Sources

A number of studies have considered the differences between the sources. Gregory (1993) compares the estimates of employment growth obtained from the May employer survey and the August household survey for the period 1976 to 1990. He shows that male employment growth is considerably less in the May survey, and suggests that 'this difference raises questions about the coverage of the ABS business register used for the May survey' (1993, page 66, n11).

Borland and Kennedy (1998) make a comparison of the August survey with the SIHC. They compare the percentage change between 1982 and 1994/5 in real main job earnings by decile for full time employees. For male employees, the reported pattern of change by decile does not appear particularly close, but there is a good correspondence in the case of female employees.

Saunders compares the SIHC with the May survey for 1994 and 2000. He finds that 'although the two series are very similar at the higher percentiles, there are marked differences lower down the distribution, which suggests that there may be some under-statement of wage incomes among low-wage employees in the SIHC' (2005, page 14). However he notes that, if this were the case, one would expect it to show up in aggregate comparisons, whereas Siminski, Saunders, Waseem, and Bradbury (2003) show that the ratio of income survey totals for employed persons to labour force survey totals are between 98.3 per cent and 101.1 per cent for the years 1982 to 1997/8.

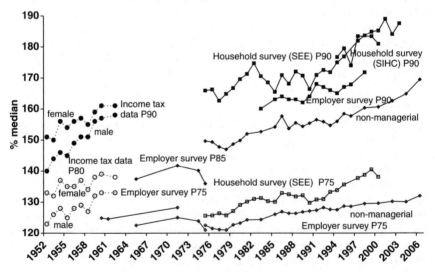

Figure A.1 AUSTRALIA upper part of the distribution 1952–2006

Sources: Table A.3, columns D and F; Table A.4, columns I, J, O and P; Table A.5, columns X, AN, and AP; Table A.6, columns C, G, and H; Table A.7, column B.

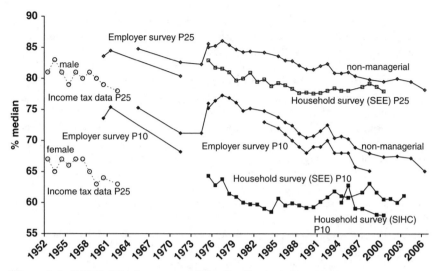

Figure A.2 AUSTRALIA lower part of the distribution 1952–2006

Sources: Table A.3, columns A and C; Table A.4, columns H and N; Table A.5, columns S, AK, and AM; Table A.6, columns A, B, E, and F; Table A.7, column A.

While there is some degree of agreement, these findings mean that we should not be surprised if there are differences in the recorded changes in earnings dispersion over time.

Summary

As already indicated, there is not one single source of evidence about the evolution of the distribution of earnings in Australia. From the mid-1970s, there are both employer and household surveys, and the latter are of two different types. Each of these sources has comparative strengths and weaknesses. Their merits have varied over time, as have the implications of their shortcomings in the context of a changing labour market and of changing public policies. It is not therefore surprising that they may show differing patterns of change over time, as is illustrated in Figures A.1 and A.2 for a selection of series.

A.3 What Happened?

Increased earnings dispersion in Australia is not a new story. In his study using income tax data, Lydall found that the 'dispersion [of earnings] of both males and females was growing steadily from 1952–3 to 1962–3' (1968, page 190). He went on to say that 'we do not know whether this was mainly a reaction to a period of compression of differentials during the early post-war years or was indicative of some more fundamental changes' (1968, pages 190–1). From Figures A.1 and A.2, it may be seen that the lower quartile for women fell by 6 per cent between 1952 and 1962, although the fall for men was less than 5 per cent. The top decile for women rose, over the same period, by 7 per cent, and that for men by 13 per cent. On this basis, Australia experienced definite widening of the earnings distribution during the Golden Age, although it should be noted that these series are graded B.

A link to the 1970s is provided by the estimates of Norris (from Table A.6). In his analysis of these figures, he draws a distinction between short run fluctuations and long run developments. The considerable year to year movement in his estimates (shown in Figures A.1 and A.2) is attributed by him to the actions of the Arbitration Commission. These aside, Norris concludes 'there was little change in the dispersion of earnings over the whole period 1960 to 1975' (1977, page 486). It is true that there were no registrable changes in the upper percentiles over this period, and that, if the bottom decile fell by more than 5 per cent, the fall was largely (although not entirely) reversed. The picture may therefore be described either as one of overall stability or of a U-shaped path for the bottom decile, relative to the median, over the 15-year period from 1960 to 1975.

From 1975, we can use both the employer survey (EEH) and the household surveys: Survey of Employee Earnings (SEE) and Survey of Income and Housing Costs (SIHC). I start with the lower part of the distribution, of particular interest in view of the Accord, an agreement on incomes policy reached in 1983. As shown in Figure A.2, in the second half of the 1970s and early 1980s both types of source show that the lower percentiles were falling, relative to the median. The fall is shown as larger by the SEE household survey data: the bottom decile fell by 10 per cent between 1975 and 1984. For the next few years, the sources disagree about the direction of movement, which is important in assessing the impact of the Accord. As noted by King, Rimmer, and Rimmer, 'it is part of the folklore of the Australian labour market that the country's centralized system of wage determination imposes a damaging rigidity... which prevents wages from adjusting rapidly in response to shifts in labour supply and demand' (1992, page 391). King, Rimmer, and Rimmer go on to suggest that, as far as wage rigidity is concerned, 'the folklore is quite wrong', citing as evidence that 'the Accord has not wholly reversed this trend [to increased dispersion] and, on some measures, the growth of inequality has actually accelerated since 1983' (1992, page 410). This is, however, based on the employer survey data, whereas Borland and Kennedy conclude, using the SIHC household survey data, that 'between 1982 and 1990 there was little change in the measures of overall earnings inequality' (1998, page 14). This is shown in the SEE data in Figure A.2, where it should however be noted that the lower quartile fell between 1982 and 1990 (although not enough to register).

More recently, since 1990, the SEE household survey data in Figure A.2 suggest that there was little overall change in the bottom decile from 1980 to 2003, whereas again the employer survey evidence suggests a fall in both the bottom decile and lower quartile: the bottom decile fell by 8 per cent between 1990 and 2006. In recent years, the figures have been affected by the expansion of salary sacrifice among lower earners: if the 'salary sacrificed' is included, the fall in the bottom decile between 2002 and 2006 is reduced from 2.4 to 1.4 percentage points.[5] Over the whole period

---

[5] I am most grateful to Rob Bray for drawing this to my attention and supplying the figures.

from 1975 to 2006, the EEH data show the bottom decile as falling by 13.5 per cent, qualifying as 'significant', and the lower quartile by 8 per cent.

In the upper part of the distribution (Figure A.1), the two sources are in broad agreement. The top decile in the household survey rose by 13 per cent between 1975 and 2003, whereas in the employer survey the rise up to 2004 was 10 per cent. The upper quartile rose by, respectively, 10 per cent and 6 per cent. There is some evidence of a pause from 1983 to the early 1990s, but the upward tendency was resumed. As described by Saunders, 'the difference between the earnings of full time adult employees at the top end of the earnings scale and those at the bottom has continued to rise through the 1990s' (Saunders, 2000).

In the literature, there has been considerable discussion of the possible explanations. Australia's position in the world economy means that there is much interest in the effect of globalization. Murtough, Pearson, and Wreford (1998) examine the impact of trade liberalization on the Australian earnings distribution. Using a computable general equilibrium model, they conclude that 'none of the analytical approaches... provides strong support for the claim that reduced trade barriers have increased Australia's earnings inequality or unemployment' (1998, page xiii). Borland (1996) examines the consequences of the decline in the density of union membership between 1986 and 1994, He finds that there is some contribution to the rise in dispersion among men workers, but that 'the main cause of changes in earnings dispersion for both male and female employees has been an increase in the dispersion of earnings of non-union employees' (1996, page 237). Keating (2003) has indeed argued that the main force at work has been changing employment structure, rather than changing pay relativities.

Summary

The Australian data have demonstrated how different sources can tell different stories with regard to the magnitude and indeed direction of changes in earnings dispersion. Nonetheless, some conclusions may be risked. The overall picture in Figures A.1 and A.2 is one of a widening earnings distribution throughout the period. Widening took place during the Golden Age of the 1950s; there was a possible reversal in the early 1970s; this was followed by renewed widening (with possibly a pause in the 1980s); widening resumed in the 1990s, and appears to have continued into this century.

Table A.1. Australia: OECD (1993)

	Column			
	A	B	C	D
	Male		Female	
	P10	P90	P10	P90
1976	75	150	77	137
1979	74	148	80	140
1980	74	149	78	143
1981	74	154	78	144
1985	72	154	78	148
1986	71	158	77	148
1987	71	153	76	147
1988	70	156	75	148
1989	69	154	74	148
1990	70	156	75	147
1991	70	159	75	149
1992	71	157	75	152
1993	69	156	75	152
1994	69	158	74	151
1995	68	161	74	151

Coverage	All
Industry	Exc. armed forces, agriculture and certain other categories, such as domestic service
Age	All
Sex	See headings
Occupation	Non-managerial employees
Definition	Gross
Intensity	FT receiving pay in May reference period
Period	Weekly
Limits	None
Source	OECD (1993, Table 5.2)
Original source	Employer survey *Distribution and Composition of Employee Earnings and Hours* ABS catalogue 6306.0
Notes	(1) Change in sampling frame from 1983 onwards (see OECD, 1996, page 100); (2) Data 1992 to 1995 updated from OECD 1996 page 100

Table A.2. Australia: OECD (1996)

	A	B	C	D	E	F
	All		Male		Female	
	P10	P90	P10	P90	P10	P90
1979	61	167	62	169	63	150
1980	60	170	63	170	60	153
1981	60	168	61	174	61	151
1982	60	173	61	173	59	155
1983	59	171	61	168	58	160
1984	58	169	61	167	59	159
1985	61	166	62	162	60	158
1986	60	171	61	170	60	163
1987	60	168	61	170	61	161
1988	60	172	60	172	60	159
1989	59	170	60	168	61	159
1990	59	166	60	162	61	159
1991	60	171	61	174	62	162
1992	61	172	61	179	63	162
1993	62	172	61	176	63	159
1994	61	175	60	177	63	159
1995	61	177	60	175	63	160

Coverage	All
Industry	All
Age	All
Sex	See headings
Occupation	All
Definition	Gross
Intensity	FT in main job
Period	Weekly
Limits	None
Source	OECD (1996, Table 3.1)
Original source	Household survey *Weekly Earnings of Employees*, ABS Catalogue 6310.0, interpolated by OECD

Table A.3. Australia: OECD (LMS)

			All						Male						Female			
	A	B	C	D	E	F	G	H	I	J	K	L	M	N	O	P	Q	R
	P10	P20	P25	P75	P80	P90	P10	P20	P25	P75	P80	P90	P10	P20	P25	P75	P80	P90
1975	64.3	79.1	82.9	125.6	134.9	165.9	68.3	79.9	83.5	126.6	136.0	166.2	63.3	78.0	83.5	119.3	124.8	144.0
1976	62.8	77.0	81.8	125.7	135.1	166.2	65.4	78.0	81.8	125.8	135.2	165.4	61.9	78.6	82.5	120.6	126.2	147.6
1977	63.8	76.7	81.6	126.4	134.4	162.6	66.1	78.2	82.2	126.4	136.2	164.9	61.3	76.8	81.7	118.3	124.6	145.8
1978	61.5	76.0	81.0	125.7	134.6	164.8	63.5	77.1	81.3	126.0	134.4	163.5	61.7	76.0	81.2	120.8	127.3	147.4
1979	60.9	75.0	79.7	127.1	134.9	166.7	61.5	76.1	80.5	126.3	138.0	168.3	62.8	76.2	81.1	122.0	127.4	150.6
1980	60.0	75.2	80.0	129.0	140.0	169.5	62.5	76.3	81.7	131.3	140.2	170.5	60.4	74.2	80.2	122.5	130.2	153.8
1981	59.7	75.0	80.9	130.1	139.0	171.2	60.7	76.6	81.0	130.2	140.1	173.4	60.7	74.8	80.1	121.8	128.6	152.4
1982	59.7	75.4	79.5	131.0	141.0	174.6	60.4	74.1	78.2	129.4	139.2	173.0	58.6	74.6	80.6	121.6	129.7	154.7
1983	59.0	75.3	79.9	131.3	140.3	170.5	61.0	75.3	79.5	130.5	139.3	167.9	58.2	73.1	79.1	124.5	132.9	159.8
1984	58.5	73.6	78.8	130.2	140.2	168.5	61.1	74.7	79.2	130.7	142.2	167.5	58.9	74.4	79.3	123.7	131.5	158.9
1985	60.7	74.8	79.3	130.0	140.5	165.5	61.9	75.4	80.1	131.4	140.3	162.2	59.9	75.6	81.5	123.3	131.7	157.8
1986	59.6	73.6	78.9	132.9	142.4	170.8	61.0	74.3	78.5	132.2	141.4	169.6	59.7	75.2	80.3	127.1	136.5	162.6
1987	59.9	74.1	78.4	132.5	140.9	168.1	61.2	74.3	79.0	131.6	140.0	170.1	61.2	75.2	79.7	127.9	137.0	161.2
1988	59.6	73.0	77.7	131.8	140.7	172.0	59.6	73.3	78.0	132.0	142.0	172.4	60.3	75.1	80.6	129.1	138.3	159.4
1989	59.2	73.6	77.8	132.1	142.0	170.6	59.8	72.9	77.6	132.7	142.7	168.6	61.2	75.9	80.6	130.2	137.3	159.1
1990	59.3	72.6	77.6	129.7	139.4	166.4	59.6	73.1	77.8	130.9	141.0	161.6	60.7	75.6	80.5	127.7	135.8	159.0
1991	60.1	73.1	77.7	130.8	141.5	170.9	60.9	73.4	78.3	133.2	143.8	174.0	62.1	75.6	79.8	127.2	135.8	161.9

Year																		
1992	60.9	73.7	78.0	130.9	141.9	172.5	61.2	73.8	78.3	134.0	144.3	178.9	63.2	75.8	80.5	126.8	136.1	162.3
1993	61.8	74.0	78.4	133.2	143.1	171.8	61.2	73.6	78.1	135.1	144.7	176.6	63.3	76.0	80.0	127.1	135.7	159.7
1994	61.1	73.4	78.0	133.8	143.7	174.9	60.2	72.6	77.4	135.4	145.3	176.6	62.7	75.3	79.5	127.2	136.1	159.0
1995	60.8	73.4	78.1	135.6	145.1	176.8	59.6	71.7	76.6	136.0	146.3	175.1	63.2	75.2	79.7	128.7	137.6	159.8
1997	61.7	74.2	78.7	137.7	147.3	181.8	60.4	71.5	75.8	135.3	145.6	178.7	62.7	76.0	80.2	130.5	139.8	164.0
1998	63.1	74.6	79.2	138.7	148.0	183.6	61.5	72.8	76.9	138.1	150.5	187.2	63.9	76.1	80.4	130.0	141.4	163.2
1999	61.7	73.3	78.7	140.5	150.9	184.8	59.0	71.9	76.6	140.1	151.7	187.9	62.0	74.5	79.5	132.3	142.7	166.3
2000	60.5	73.3	78.0	138.0	149.1	185.2	58.5	71.1	75.9	138.5	150.3	185.2	64.1	75.8	81.3	133.2	143.2	169.9
2001	60.6					188.9	59.3					195.5	61.6					169.0
2002	60.0					184.0	57.5					187.5	64.0					164.1
2003	61.1					187.5	62.0					191.1	64.3					166.7

Coverage	All
Industry	All
Age	All
Sex	See headings
Occupation	All
Definition	Gross
Intensity	FT in main job (all jobs prior to 1988)
Period	Weekly
Limits	None
Source	OECD LMS, 2001 to 2003 supplied by OECD
Original source	Household survey, *Survey of Employee Earnings*
Note	OECD interpolations of published data

Table A.4. Australia: Income tax data (Lydall)

	A	B	C	D	E	F	G	H	I	J	K	L	M	N	O	P	Q	R
Column	All						Male						Female					
	P15	P25	P80	P90	P95	P99	P15	P25	P80	P90	P95	P99	P15	P25	P80	P90	P95	P99
1949	51	66	135	155	179	238	61	81	123	140	157	221	51	67	133	151	167	216
1952	49	66	130	149	169	231		83	126	144	162	217		65	132	150	166	211
1953								81	128	146	165	225		67	137	156	173	228
1954																		
1955							61	79	125	145	170	238	49	66	135	154	175	235
1956								81	128	149	170	237		67	135	156	176	235
1957								80	129	151	175	243		67	137	157	178	237
1958	47	64	136	162	188	262	62	81	127	151	176	244	49	65	134	155	176	238
1959								80	132	156	178	250		63	138	159	180	243
1960								79	133	157	181	255		64	139	161	183	254
1962	44	63	143	173	202	289	59	78	133	158	185		46	63	138	161	185	259

Coverage	Occupation 1: i.e. all workers with less than £100 of non-wage or salary income (£50 in 1949)
Industry	All
Age	All
Sex	See headings
Occupation	All
Definition	Taxable employment income, including occupational pensions
Intensity	All
Period	Annual, for tax year commencing 1 July, so 1949 refers to 1949–50 etc.
Limits	Excludes those below exemption limit (£105)
Source	Lydall (1965, Table VI) and (1968, Tables AL-1, AL-2 and AL-3)
Original source	Income tax *Reports of the Commissioner of Taxation*

Table A.5. Australia: Employee Earnings and Hours (EEH)

	A	B	C	D	E	F	G	H	I	J	K	L	M	N	O	P	Q	R	
Column	All — All employees FT and PT						Male						Female						Source
	P10	P20	P25	P75	P80	P90	P10	P20	P25	P75	P80	P90	P10	P20	P25	P75	P80	P90	EEH denotes Employee Earnings and Hours; AST denotes Australian Social Trends
1975	50.8	73.4	79.3	128.8	137.1	165.5	62.1	77.2	81.5	126.7	135.1	161.0	46.4	66.2	74.6	119.6	125.2	145.6	Labour Statistics 1975, p 71
1976	49.8	73.3	80.0	128.3	137.8	166.1	61.6	76.8	80.9	126.9	135.4	162.0	44.0	64.2	72.4	118.8	125.1	144.4	Labour Statistics 1976, pp 75–6
1977	50.0	73.9	80.2	128.2	137.0	164.4	62.2	77.5	81.6	126.8	135.4	161.6	43.2	63.8	72.4	118.8	125.2	145.9	EEH 6306.0, Tables 1 and 7
1978	50.2	73.8	80.0	129.0	137.0	163.1	63.1	77.1	81.0	126.5	134.4	159.8	43.7	64.1	72.7	119.6	126.2	147.0	EEH 6306.0, Tables 1, 6 and 12
1979	49.0	73.1	79.4	129.7	138.5	165.6	61.3	76.0	80.1	128.0	136.2	161.0	41.8	63.0	72.4	120.5	127.5	148.1	EEH 6306.0, Tables 1, 6 and 12
1980	49.1	72.5	78.5	130.1	139.0	166.2	62.4	75.9	80.1	127.8	136.2	161.0	42.5	62.9	71.8	121.9	129.4	151.7	EEH 6306.0, Tables 6, 10 and 13
1981	48.5	71.8	78.4	130.8	139.9	168.5	60.7	75.4	79.7	129.3	138.0	164.0	41.4	62.6	71.6	122.4	129.7	152.7	EEH 6306.0, Tables 6, 10 and 13
1983																			AST 1994
1985																			AST 2000
1986																			AST 1994
1987																			AST 2000
1988	26.8	51.7	63.0	143.3	155.4	189.7													AST 1994
1989																			AST 2000
1990																			AST 1994
1991																			AST 2000
1992																			AST 1994
1993	32.1	59.1	70.5	139.2	149.5	179.7	44.2	69.3	74.0	134.0	144.2	176.3	27.6	50.7	61.5	135.6	145.1	177.2	EEH 1993, Tables 1, 4 and 8
1994	30.4	57.2	68.5	138.8	149.7	180.2	42.3	68.8	73.6	134.7	143.7	175.2	26.7	48.4	60.4	135.9	146.0	178.3	EEH 1994, Tables 1, 6 and 10
1995	28.5	53.9	66.5	140.8	150.7	184.6	37.9	66.9	73.2	135.6	146.5	182.4	24.9	46.5	56.6	136.1	146.1	178.8	EEH 1995, Tables 1, 8 and 17
1996	27.6	53.1	64.8	142.1	153.6	186.2	36.6	64.2	71.8	136.6	146.7	179.0	24.2	46.5	57.0	138.3	149.5	182.6	EEH 1996, Tables 1, 8 and 15
1998	26.8	51.7	63.0	143.3	155.4	189.7	33.7	61.0	70.1	138.8	150.0	186.1	23.7	45.7	56.5	139.6	151.2	186.1	EEH 1998, Tables 1, 7 and 14
2000	27.6	51.2	63.1	144.4	156.9	193.1	35.0	63.0	70.4	140.0	151.1	189.6	24.2	46.9	56.6	140.8	153.3	189.1	EEH 2000, Tables 6 and 14
2002	27.9	52.0	62.5	141.7	155.1	190.9	37.2	63.7	70.9	138.7	150.7	187.6	24.4	46.9	56.9	141.4	153.2	189.5	EEH 2002, Tables 6 and 13
2004	28.0	51.9	62.2	142.8	156.2	195.7	34.8	62.4	70.6	141.2	153.6	194.5	24.6	47.6	58.1	142.4	154.5	191.4	EEH 2004, Table 5 and Datacube
2006																			EEH 2006, supplied by R Bray

(*Continued*)

Table A.5. (*Continued*)

			All					Male						Female			
			FT adult (prior to 1983 excludes managerial employees in government sector)														
	S	T	U	V	W	X	Y	Z	AA	AB	AC	AD	AE	AF	AG	AH	AI	AJ
	P10	P20	P25	P75	P80	P90	P10	P20	P25	P75	P80	P90	P10	P20	P25	P75	P80	P90
1975																		
1976																		
1977																		
1978	75.2	81.2	84.0	123.1	129.8	150.9	74.3	81.1	84.3	122.7	129.7	150.3	80.6	87.1	89.5	118.5	124.3	140.5
1979	74.7	80.7	83.6	124.7	131.6	153.0	73.2	80.1	83.5	124.0	130.6	151.2	80.7	86.7	89.0	118.2	123.7	141.0
1980	73.2	80.0	83.1	124.7	132.0	153.3	72.8	80.0	83.3	124.2	131.1	151.5	79.3	85.5	88.1	119.8	125.9	143.6
1981	73.4	80.0	83.1	125.5	132.8	155.9	72.2	79.5	82.8	124.8	132.1	154.3	78.9	85.5	88.0	119.8	126.1	144.0
1983	73.0					160.0	72.0					160.0	78.0					150.0
1985	72.0					163.0	70.0					162.0	78.0					150.0
1986	71.0					164.0	69.0					164.0	77.0					151.0
1987	70.0					163.0	69.0					162.0	75.0					150.0
1988	69.0					163.0	68.0					163.0	74.0					152.0
1989	68.0					162.0	66.0					163.0	73.0					151.0
1990	69.0					164.0	67.0					164.0	74.0					149.0
1991	69.0					168.0	67.0					166.0	74.0					154.0
1992	70.0					167.0	67.0					168.0	73.0					155.0
1993	68.0	75.4	78.8	130.1	139.0	166.0	65.0	73.8	78.1	129.9	139.2	169.0	73.0	79.6	83.0	129.5	136.1	155.0
1994	68.0	75.7	79.1	130.1	138.6	165.0	65.0	73.7	77.7	129.9	138.6	167.0	73.0	79.9	83.4	126.9	135.3	154.0
1995	68.0	75.8	79.6	131.2	139.7	167.0	65.0	73.4	76.7	130.6	139.2	169.0	72.0	79.8	83.0	127.1	135.8	154.0
1996	65.7	74.7	78.0	130.0	138.9	167.8	63.9	72.4	76.8	130.5	139.9	170.3	70.8	78.4	81.8	127.3	134.8	152.7
1998	65.1	74.1	78.1	131.7	140.5	171.7	62.5	72.2	76.8	132.5	141.9	175.6	69.7	78.1	81.4	129.1	137.3	155.0
2000																		
2002																		
2004																		
2006																		

(*Continued*)

Table A.5. (*Concluded*)

| | | All FT adult Non-managerial | | | | | Column Male | | | | | | Female | | | | | |
	AK	AL	AM	AN	AO	AP	AQ	AR	AS	AT	AU	AV	AW	AX	AY	AZ	BA	BB
	P10	P20	P25	P75	P80	P90	P10	P20	P25	P75	P80	P90	P10	P20	P25	P75	P80	P90
1975	75.2	82.1	85.1	122.5	128.7	149.6	76.0	82.6	85.5	121.0	128.3	147.6	80.1	86.5	88.8	115.3	120.3	137.4
1976	76.5	82.6	85.3	121.5	128.7	149.3	75.9	82.5	85.4	121.5	127.7	148.7	80.5	87.5	89.7	116.3	122.1	137.1
1977	77.3	83.5	86.1	121.1	127.6	147.7	76.7	83.0	85.8	120.6	127.2	146.9	81.3	87.3	89.9	116.3	121.9	138.2
1978	76.9	82.8	85.4	121.0	127.6	146.9	76.0	82.3	85.3	120.7	126.9	145.6	81.0	87.4	89.7	117.7	123.7	139.4
1979	76.1	82.0	84.7	122.7	129.3	148.6	74.9	81.4	84.5	122.2	128.6	147.5	81.1	87.0	89.2	117.7	122.9	139.8
1980	74.8	81.4	84.3	123.2	129.9	149.8	74.4	81.2	84.3	122.5	129.2	148.1	79.7	85.8	88.3	119.1	125.3	142.5
1981	75.2	81.5	84.4	124.3	131.0	151.9	74.1	80.9	84.0	123.7	130.8	152.4	79.4	85.9	88.3	119.1	125.2	143.3
1983	74.8		84.2	124.4		152.6												
1985	73.8		83.6	126.0		154.1												
1986	72.9		82.9	126.9		157.6												
1987	72.4		82.8	126.3		153.6												
1988	71.1		82.1	126.3		155.5												
1989	70.5		81.5	126.8		154.3												
1990	70.7		81.4	127.1		155.4												
1991	71.5		82.0	127.4		156.5												
1992	72.5		82.4	128.2		155.9												
1993	70.4	77.6	80.9	127.6	135.2	154.6	68.9	76.4	79.9	127.0	134.3	156.7	74.4	80.7	84.0	127.2	134.7	152.1
1994	70.7	78.0	80.8	127.5	135.1	155.9	68.8	76.3	79.7	127.7	134.6	157.5	74.3	81.0	84.5	125.0	132.9	150.4
1995	70.3	77.7	81.0	128.7	136.1	158.4	67.5	75.6	79.0	127.8	135.1	160.8	73.6	80.9	83.9	124.8	133.0	150.4
1996	68.9	77.0	80.4	128.6	134.7	157.7	66.8	75.0	78.6	127.0	135.0	160.4	72.7	80.0	83.2	125.3	132.8	148.0
1998	68.0	76.1	79.8	129.5	136.3	160.3	65.6	74.5	78.5	128.7	137.0	163.1	71.9	79.3	82.5	127.3	135.3	150.0
2000	67.4	75.3	79.5	129.6	135.8	160.5	65.0	73.3	77.5	128.2	136.8	162.9	71.5	78.8	82.1	126.3	135.0	151.8
2002	67.5	76.3	80.0	130.2	137.6	162.5	65.9	74.5	78.7	129.3	138.3	164.3	70.6	78.8	81.8	125.3	132.9	152.0
2004	67.2	75.3	79.5	130.0	138.7	164.8	65.8	74.3	78.4	131.9	141.1	170.2	69.6	77.1	80.5	125.6	134.0	154.9
2006	65.1		78.2	131.9		169.4												

Coverage   All
Age   All
Occupation   See headings
Intensity   See headings
Limits   None
Original source   May survey, *Employee Earnings and Hours*
Notes   (1) Prior to 1983 adult defined as 21+, from 1982 includes also those paid at adult rate; (2) Interpolation, where necessary, is linear on the cumulative distribution

Industry   All
Sex   See headings
Definition   Gross
Period   Weekly
Source   sources following column R

Table A.6. Australia: Analyses of EEH and earlier surveys

								Column					
A	B	C	D	E	F	G	H	I	J	K	L	M	N
All occupations				Non-managerial employees									
								Share of bottom quintile	Share of middle quintile	Share of top quintile	Share of bottom quintile	Share of middle quintile	Share of top quintile
P10	P25	P75	P85	P10	P25	P75	P85						
1960 73.6	83.6	124.9	142.7										
1961 75.4	84.5	124.6	143.2										
1965				75.3	84.8	122.5	137.4						
1971 68.2	80.4	128.2		71.2	82.6	125.0	141.7						
1974				71.2	82.3	123.9	140.1						
1975				76.0	85.6	121.0	135.9						
1976								14.00	19.52	22.78	14.84	19.98	21.63
1981								13.69	19.29	23.15	14.96	19.74	22.21
1986								13.18	19.19	23.81	14.55	19.62	19.68
1989								12.94	19.45	23.45	14.01	19.68	22.76
1995				65.6	79.0	127.8							

Coverage	All
Industry	All
Age	Adults (21 and over), workers paid as adults included up to 1971
Sex	M except for columns L–N
Occupation	See headings
Definition	Gross wages and salaries
Intensity	FT
Period	Weekly
Limits	None
Source	Norris (1977, Table 4), except 1995 added from Borland (1999, Table 2) and columns I–N from King, Rimmer, and Rimmer (1992, Table 3)
Original source	Employer surveys, *Survey of Weekly Earnings (Size Distribution)*, and *EEH*
Note	Borland also gives 1995 figure for top decile

Table A.7. Australia: Survey of Income and Housing Costs (SIHC)

						Column						
	A	B	C	D	E	F	G	H	I	J	K	L
		All				Male				Female		
	P10	P90	P95	Gini	P10	P90	P95	Gini	P10	P90	P95	Gini
1986	60.7	168.0	197.8	23.4	61.5	171.0	200.1	23.2	62.9	154.9	176.5	20.3
1990	62.1	171.2	203.8	23.8	63.8	172.9	211.4	24.3	64.7	155.5	175.7	20.3
1994	60.0	176.6	218.3	27.5	60.3	179.5	224.2	28.5	60.2	158.3	184.1	23.5
1995	62.8	179.4	215.1	26.6	58.4	183.4	224.9	28.1	66.6	163.6	187.9	21.9
1996	59.0	173.9	219.2	26.8	57.8	184.8	233.3	27.8	64.6	163.0	187.4	22.8
1997	59.0	183.3	227.8	27.6	56.2	185.4	230.8	28.9	61.9	165.3	183.5	22.7
1999	58.1	183.3	234.4	28.1	56.5	196.6	240.8	29.3	60.1	163.4	184.0	23.8
2000	58.0	180.9	219.9	28.0	55.5	190.9	236.7	29.5	65.0	162.6	192.2	23.3

Coverage	All
Industry	All
Age	15 to 64
Sex	See headings
Occupation	All
Definition	Gross wages and salaries
Intensity	FT
Period	Annual
Limits	None
Source	Saunders (2005, Table 5)
Original source	SIHC, previously Income Distribution Survey (IDS)
Note	Change from IDS to SIHC may have affected comparability between 1990 and 1994 (see text)

Bibliography

Australian Bureau of Statistics, 1981, *Earnings and Hours of Employees, Distribution and Composition, May 1981 (Preliminary)*, Catalogue 6305.0.

—— 1995, *Australian Social Trends 1995*, Canberra.

—— 1997, *Income Distribution in Australia 1995–6*, ABS Catalogue 6523.0, Canberra.

—— 1999, *Income Distribution in Australia 1997–8*, ABS Catalogue 6523.0, Canberra.

—— 2001, *Income Distribution Australia 1999–2000*, ABS Catalogue 6523.0, Canberra.

—— 2002, 'Upgrading household income distribution statistics', in *Australian Economic Indicators*, April, ABS Catalogue 1350.0, Canberra.

—— 2002a, *Measuring Australia's Progress*, ABS Catalogue 1370.0, Canberra.

—— 2003, *Household Income and Income Distribution Australia 2000–01*, ABS Catalogue 6523.0, Canberra.

—— 2003a, 'Revised household income distribution statistics', in *Australian Economic Indicators*, ABS Catalogue 1350.0, Canberra.

Belchamber, G, 1996, 'Disappearing middle or vanishing bottom? A comment on Gregory', *Economic Record*, vol 72: 287–93.

Borland, J, 1996, 'Union effects on earnings dispersion in Australia, 1986–1994', *British Journal of Industrial Relations*, vol 34: 237–48.

—— 1997, 'Earnings and inequality in Australia', RSSS Annual Report, Australian National University, Canberra.

—— 1999, 'Earnings inequality in Australia: Changes, causes and consequences', *Economic Record*, vol 75: 177–202.

—— Hirschberg, J and Lye, J, 1998, 'Earnings of public sector and private sector employees in Australia: Is there a difference?', *Economic Record*, vol 74: 36–53.

—— and Kennedy, S, 1998, 'Earnings inequality in Australia in the 1980s and 1990s', Centre for Economic Policy Research, Australian National University.

—— and Wilkins, R, 1996, 'Earning inequality in Australia', *Economic Record*, vol 72: 7–23.

Gregory, R G, 1993, 'Aspects of Australian and US living standards: The disappointing decades 1970–1990', *Economic Record*, vol 69: 61–76.

Keating, M, 2003, 'The labour market and inequality', *Australian Economic Review*, vol 36: 374–96.

King, J E, Rimmer, R J, and Rimmer, S M, 1992, 'The law of the shrinking middle: Inequality of earnings in Australia', *Scottish Journal of Political Economy*, vol 39: 391–412.

Lydall, H F, 1965, 'The dispersion of employment incomes in Australia', *Economic Record*, vol 41: 549–69.

McGuire, P, 1994, 'Changes in earnings dispersion in Australia 1975–1992', *Labour Economics and Productivity*, vol 6: 27–53.

Murtough, G, Pearson, K, and Wreford, P, 1998, *Trade Liberalisation and Earnings Distribution in Australia*, Industry Commission Staff Research Paper, AGPS, Canberra.

Nevile, J W and Saunders, P, 1998, 'Globalization and the return to education in Australia', *Economic Record*, vol 74: 279–85.

Norris, K, 1977, 'The dispersion of earnings in Australia', *Economic Record*, vol 53: 475–89.

—— and Mclean, B, 1999, 'Changes in earnings inequality, 1975 to 1998', *Australian Bulletin of Labour*, vol 25: 23–31.

Richardson, S, 1999, *Reshaping the Labour Market: Regulation, Efficiency and Equality in Australia*, Cambridge University Press, Melbourne.

Saunders, P, 1996, 'Unpacking inequality: Wage incomes, disposable incomes and living standards', in *The Industry Commission Conference on Equity, Efficiency and Welfare, Conference Proceedings*, The Industry Commission, Melbourne.

—— 2000, 'Trends in earnings distribution', in *Australian Social Trends, 2000*, Australian Bureau of Statistics, Canberra.

—— 2005, 'Reviewing recent trends in wage income inequality in Australia', in R Lanbury and J Isaacs, editors, *Rewriting the Rules: Labour Market Deregulation in Australia*, Federation Press, Sydney.

Siminski, P, Saunders, P, and Bradbury, B, 2003, 'Reviewing the inter-temporal consistency of ABS household income data through comparisons with external aggregates', *Australian Economic Review*, vol 36: 333–49.

—— —— Waseem, S, and Bradbury, B, 2003, 'Assessing the quality and inter-temporal comparability of ABS household income distribution statistics', SPRC Discussion Paper No 123, University of New South Wales.

B

Austria

Inequality has been growing significantly over the past three decades. In recent history, there have been only two phases when the unequal distribution of before-tax wages and salaries either did not get worse or even improved slightly: in the early 1970s...and, even more, in 1991–92....In between, wage inequality grew consistently, fuelled chiefly by a high dynamism at the edges: top incomes rose briskly while...the bottom income groups lost out.

Guger and Marterbauer, 2005, page 627

B.1 Introduction

The First Republic of Austria was established in 1918, after the end of the Austro-Hungarian monarchy. The country was annexed by Germany in 1938, and occupied by Allied Forces after the Second World War. The Second Republic was founded in 1945, and the treaty of independence signed in 1955. Austria joined the European Union in 1995. The country adopted the euro in 2002.

Previous Coverage

Lydall (1968) contains data for 1957 based on the wage tax statistics, also used here, and data for 1926, 1947, 1953, and 1960 for earnings in unionized firms in Vienna (not used here on the grounds that its coverage was insufficient to warrant a B grade).

Austria is included in two of the OECD compilations (a single year, 1996, is given in the downloaded LMS):

1993 (Table B.1): total, and men and women separately, 1980 and 1987–91, includes P80 in addition to P10 and P90, from the earnings statistics (Lohnstufenstatistik) of the Hauptverband der Österreichischen Sozialversicherungsträger (Austrian Association of Social Insurance Funds).

1996 (Table B.2): total, and men and women separately, 1980 and 1987–1994, includes P80 in addition to P10 and P90, from the same source as Table B.1; Annex contains data from the Mikrozensus on net earnings 1981–93 (see Table B.3).

Official Publications

The Statistical Yearbook of Austria was known as the *Statistisches Handbuch* and is now the *Statistisches Jahrbuch*, referred to here as *SJ*. Over the years, it has contained data from the Lohnstufenstatistik, published from 1966, and from the wage tax statistics (Lohnsteuerstatistik). Data from the Lohnsteuerstatistik have in addition been published in the periodical *Statistische Nachrichten*, and in separate publications entitled *Lohnsteuerstatistik.*

B.2 Data Sources

Referring to the 'Standard distribution of adult full time workers in all sectors' of Lydall (1968), Chaloupek notes the problems of securing data that conform to any such standard: 'unfortunately [in Austria] the data are either not available in this form or not useable. Data must therefore be based on a distribution of earnings that does not match the standard distribution' (1981, page 83, my translation). He goes on to note that neither of the two principal sources in Austria covers the entire employed population. These two sources are based on administrative records: the earnings statistics of the Austrian Association of Social Insurance Funds (whose data have been used in the OECD compilations), and the wage tax statistics. The social insurance earnings data were assembled twice-yearly from 1953, whereas the wage tax statistics have been made available for selected years (1953, 1957, and then every three years from 1964 to 1982, 1987, and annually from 1994). These two administrative sources have been supplemented by the *Mikrozensus*, which is a household survey, and in 1996 an employer survey of the *Structure of Earnings* was introduced. These data sources are described in turn.

Lohnstufenstatistik (Earnings Statistics of the Austrian Association of Social Insurance Funds)

The social insurance data are provided by the Hauptverband des Österreichischen Sozialversicherungsträger (HV). They are derived from the administrative records of the social security system, and relate to gross earnings as defined for the purposes of social security contributions. There is a potential problem of multiple entries where people are registered more than once. The conclusion of the HV was however that multiple records were in practice unimportant (Chaloupek, 1981, page 90). Until 1987 (see below), the figures included apprentices, who varied as a proportion from 7.8 per cent of *arbeiter* in 1953 to 13.8 per cent in 1979. As noted by Chaloupek (1981, page 92), this may affect the bottom two deciles and their comparability over time, although he does not believe that the main conclusions should be changed.

There have been two major changes in the comparability of the published data. With effect from 1987, the data include supplementary payments such as annual bonuses: earnings are one-twelfth of total annual earnings, in place of earnings in particular month. At the same time, apprentices were excluded. As may be seen from the figures for 1987, given on both the old and new basis, this made a major difference. The median rose from 13,467 schilling to 15,991 schilling, and the lower quartile rose from 69.9 per cent to 73.1 per cent of the median (*SJ* 1990, page 149). With effect from 1989, the data covered *pragmatisierten Beamten der Gebietskörperschaften*, who were previously excluded (see *SJ* 1990, page 145). According to Chaloupek (1981, page 90), this meant that the statistics previously covered only a third of public officials, but this change had a smaller impact on the shape of the distribution—see Table B.4.

The principal limitation of the social insurance data is that they are truncated at the upper earnings ceiling (all higher amounts being returned in this single class). The ceiling was 7,575 schilling in 1970, 14,850 in 1979. In each year, about 10 per cent of observations are affected: in the 1970s, the maximum was 13.3 per cent for all workers (for men, the percentage is higher). Christl (1980) makes estimates of the decile shares, and of summary measures such as the Gini coefficient, by assuming a lognormal distribution. He also assumes a constant frequency within earnings classes of the tabulated data, noting that the classes are sufficiently detailed to mean that no serious interpolation error is introduced.

The Lohnstufenstatistik were used by Chaloupek (1981), but the results are given in the form of growth rates per decile, not allowing the levels of the percentiles to be deduced. The shares of different decile groups and the Gini coefficients are calculated by Christl (1980)—see Table B.5. The Lohnstufenstatistik from 1970 are used by Guger and Marterbauer (2005)—see Table B.6—who also calculate income shares.

The Lohnstufenstatistik were published from 1966 (data relating to 1965) in the *SJ*. These data have been used to construct Table B.4. This uses the published deciles where available (covering years from 1988 to 1996), and applies a linear interpolation elsewhere, for all years where the truncation was below 10 per cent. Where the truncation affected more than 10 per cent (1972 to 1977, 1980, 1983–4, and 1987), a Pareto extrapolation was made, using the upper two points on the cumulative frequency curve. A table providing quartiles on a consistent basis for 1980 and the 1990s was published in the *SJ* for 1998, 1999–2000, and 2001, and this is the basis for the figures for 1996 to 1999.

Lohnsteuerstatistik (Wage Tax Statistics)

The wage tax is a special form of income tax. The earnings of employees (and pension income) are not taxed via a tax declaration but by withholding at source via the Lohnsteuer. The employer (or employers in the case of multiple jobs) is required to make an annual return (the Lohnzettel), and these returns are the basis for the Lohnsteuerstatistik. Income returned in this way is classified as 'full year' where it applies to 11 months or more. In a small proportion of cases (1.45 per cent in 2003), the returns lack the necessary information on working period. Where there are multiple returns for one person, they are combined to form a single person record. In 2003, 16.9 per cent of persons had multiple returns, and 7.1 million returns were reduced to 5.8 million persons. In the earlier analyses, all returns were processed in producing the statistics; from 1967 a sample was taken; from 1987 again all returns were processed. The Lohnsteuer statistics cover a sizeable number of pensioners, but the analysis of earnings data is based on employees. In 2005, there were a total of 5.9 million wage tax payers, of whom 2.2 million were pensioners. The statistics distinguish between those in employment for the entire year, and those employed for only part of the year. Results are given both for full year and for all workers.

The wage tax statistics have been assembled for 1953, 1957, at three-yearly intervals from 1964 to 1982, and have been annual since 1994. The results of the analysis of the wage tax statistics for 1953 and 1957 were published in *Steuerstatistiken*. For 1964, tables were published in *Statistische Nachrichten*. Since 1970, reports on the *Lohnsteuerstatistik* have been published. The tabulations are often very detailed. The 1964 tables contain no fewer than 72 ranges; in the top category of full year workers there were 34 men and 2 women. Data on the distribution of earnings from the wage tax statistics are now published in the *SJ*, including a series standardized for the number of days worked (see Table B.8).

The wage tax statistics have the advantage, compared with the social security data, that there is no truncation at the top. Moreover, the tabulations are published in considerable detail, particularly for earlier years. On the other hand, as was explained in the report on the 1953 statistics, 'there are significant difficulties with respect to the return of the wage tax cards' (Österreichischen Statistischen Zentralamt, 1957, page 25, my translation). The coverage of returns was significantly incomplete: in 1953, 550,000 Lohnsteuerkarten, about a quarter, were not delivered by employers. This shortfall particularly concerned lower paid workers: in 1953, 30 per cent of the missing returns related to workers in agriculture and forestry (Chaloupek, 1981, page 86).

Chaloupek (1981, page 87) presents an analysis of the coverage of the wage tax statistics. He shows that the total recorded in the wage tax statistics is between 75 per cent and 79 per cent of the national accounts total for 1953 and 1964 to 1973 (for 1957 the figure falls to 66 per cent). He converts the amounts recorded in the wage tax statistics into full time equivalents (FTE), using the recorded average earnings of full year workers, and then compares the FTE figure with the recorded employment statistics, which yields in all years except 1957 a figure close to 74 per cent. However, the breakdown into 'arbeiter' and 'angestellte und beamte' shows that the composition in 1953 was noticeably different from that in 1964. Taken together, these considerations lead him to be cautious about using the data prior to 1964. It should also be noted that the figures given in the published report on the 1957 data include pensioners (see Österreichischen Statistischen Zentralamt, 1957, page 28). For this reason, and on account of the significantly larger shortfall of total earnings noted above, the estimates for 1957 need to be treated with caution.

The Lohnsteuerstatistik were used by Chaloupek (1981), who gives the deciles for 1973 (page 94), but only in the form of growth rates per decile for other years, not including 1973, so that the levels of the percentiles cannot be deduced. The shares of different decile groups and the Gini coefficients are calculated by Guger and Marterbauer (2005)—see Table B.8.

Mikrozensus

The Mikrozensus is a representative 1 per cent national household survey, Each quarter around 4,500 'new' households are interviewed, who remain in the survey for 5 quarters, so that the total sample at any date is 22,500. In odd-numbered years the Mikrozensus collects information on net earnings. (Until 1993, net earnings included child allowances.) However, while households are required to answer the demographic questions, answers to the income questions are not obligatory, and there is a high rate of item non-response on the earnings question. According to Fersterer and Winter-Ebmer (1999, Table 3), the non-response rate for men rose from 22 per cent in 1981 to 54 per cent in 1997. Moreover, in 1981 the rate of non-response was considerably higher among those with a university education (38 per cent for men, compared with 22 per cent overall), although the gap had disappeared by 1997. This is likely to mean that higher earnings were under-represented in 1981, but not in 1997, affecting the measured changes over time.

Verdienststrukturerhebung VESTE (Structure of Earnings Survey)

The Structure of Earnings Survey was first carried out for the year 1996. From 2002, it is to be carried out every four years. It is a survey of enterprises with at least ten employees in manufacturing and services, with the exceptions of public administration and defence, compulsory social security, education, health and social work, and other community, social, and personal service activities. It collects detailed information about earnings, employment, and the characteristics of the enterprise. This survey is part of the European Structure of Earnings Survey, referred to in Part I.

Comparison of Sources

According to Chaloupek (1978 and 1981), the social security data provide a more stable source for time series analysis, particularly for the period before 1964. Guger

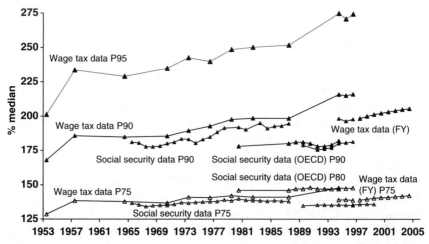

Figure B.1 AUSTRIA upper part of the distribution 1953–2004

Sources: Table B.2, columns B and C; Table B.4, columns C and E; Table B.7, columns D, F, G, U, and W; Table B.8, columns V and X.

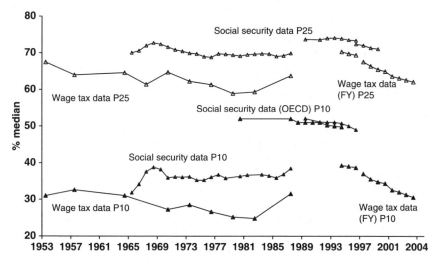

Figure B.2 AUSTRIA lower part of the distribution 1953–2004

Sources: Table B.2, column A; Table B.4, columns A and B; Table B.7, columns A and C; Table B.8, columns S and U.

and Marterbauer (2005) compare the social security and earnings tax statistics. They emphasize the fuller coverage of high and low incomes in the earnings tax statistics, noting that the share of the bottom 20 per cent is less than 3 per cent in the latter statistics post-1994 (Table B.8), compared with 7 per cent in the social security statistics.

Summary

In studying the evolution of the earnings distribution in Austria, we have two important sources: the social security data and the wage tax statistics. The evidence from these two sources is summarized in Figures B.1 and B.2. The wage tax figures relate to all workers; the series restricted to full year workers shows a similar time path, although the overall increase in the upper percentiles is smaller.

B.3 What Happened?

From the evidence about manual workers in unionized firms in Vienna, Lydall concluded that from 1926 to 1960 'on the whole, there has been remarkably little change over a third of a century' (Lydall, 1968, pages 187–8). But this evidence is very partial. There could have been changes in the position of manual workers vis-à-vis non-manual workers, in the impact of unionization, and the circumstances of Vienna may not have been typical. While it may be reasonable, in the absence of better sources, to accept data with incomplete coverage, the evidence cited by Lydall seems to me too limited to draw the conclusion that the Austrian earnings distribution was stable. Indeed, others have pointed to significant change. Guger (1989, page 190) describes a levelling of earnings as having taken place in the immediate post-war years, citing Steindl (1958). He notes the special circumstances after the war, which gave rise to new earnings structures, and to the role of the principle of solidarity in union wage policy. The wage–price agreement of 1947 to 1951 contributed to the levelling of wage differentials. Steindl compared the results of analyses of the wage tax statistics for 1933 with those for 1953, and found that wage dispersion had decreased.

In his account of the developments from 1953 to 1979, Christl starts by stressing how Austria had seen in this period 'remarkable changes in demographic, socio-economic and political structure' (1980, page 203). Nonetheless, there were important continuities. In particular, the determination of pay has been heavily influenced by the social partners and labour market institutions (see, for example, Karlhofer and Ladurner (1993)). As just noted, price and wage policies were employed in the immediate post-war period, and a formal social partnership, involving unions, employers, and government, was established in 1957 in the form of the Parity Commission for Prices and Wages (Paritätische Kommission für Preis- und Lohnfragen). The social security earnings data 1953 are analysed by Christl (1980), whose results in terms of shares and the Gini coefficient are shown in Table B.5. Christl (1980) identifies three sub-periods up to 1979. In the first, from 1953 to 1964, there was a 'strong increase in inequality' (1980, page 199). The calculated Gini coefficient for earnings rose from 26 per cent in 1953 to 31 per cent in 1964, with the major part of the increase taking place between 1953 and 1957, when wage bargaining was more decentralized, and before the establishment of the Parity Commission. This suggests that the labour market institutions put in place in the latter part of the 1950s brought to an end the rise in dispersion in the first part of the Golden Age. From Figure B.2, we can see that the wage tax statistics show a widening at the top: there was a rise of 10 per cent in the top decile and of 7 per cent in the upper quartile. But we saw earlier that the wage tax data before 1964 should be treated with some caution.

After 1964 there was, according to Christl, a period of reduction in earnings dispersion, and finally a period of broad stability for the share of the bottom 10 per cent but a rise in the top earnings shares. For Guger and Marterbauer (2005), the social security data show the period 1970 to 1976 as one of stability, but there then followed a rise in dispersion until 1981 (see Table B.6). The Gini coefficient rose by 2 percentage points between 1976 and 1981, as did the share of the top 20 per cent. As may be seen from Figure B.1, for the changes in the upper part of the distribution the social security data and the wage tax statistics show a similar pattern over this period. The top decile in the wage tax statistics rose by 7 per cent between 1964 and 1978. There was no apparent narrowing post-1968. If there was a decline in the early 1970s, it was not large enough to register. The picture at the bottom is less clear. As may be seen from Figure B.2, the two series move in different directions in the 1960s. The lower quartile shows a fall of 9 per cent between 1970 and 1979 according to the wage tax statistics but a fall of less than 5 per cent according to the social security data.

Table B.1. Austria: OECD (1993)

	A	B	C	D	Column E	F	G	H	I
		All			Male			Female	
	P10	P80	P90	P10	P80	P90	P10	P80	P90
1980	52	146	178	62	139	162	52	141	174
1987	52	146	180	61	141	165	51	144	177
1988	51	147	181	61	143	167	51	145	178
1989	51	147	181	60	143	165	52	145	179
1990	51	148	180	60	143		51	145	179
1991	51	147	178	60	142		50	146	180

Coverage	All
Industry	All
Age	All
Sex	See headings
Occupation	All except for most civil servants and for apprentices
Definition	Gross earnings, inc. special payments such as holiday and Christmas pay
Intensity	All
Period	Monthly standardized taking account of recorded days of insurance contributions
Limits	Earnings above maximum contribution recorded at that level
Source	OECD (1993, Table 5.2)
Original source	Earnings Statistics of the Austrian Association of Social Insurance Funds
Notes	(1) Figures have been constructed on a consistent basis, allowing later years to be compared with 1980 (e.g. omitting the majority of Beamte)

Moreover, we should note that Gusenleitner, Winter-Ebmer, and Zweimüller, using their own sample of the social security earnings data, find that 'the period from 1972 until 1977 was characterized by a trend towards more equality' (1998, page 8). This conclusion is based on the Gini coefficient, which they show as falling by some $2\frac{1}{2}$ percentage points (Figure 1). They go on to point out that the aggregate Gini coefficient conceals changes at different points in the distribution. In the 1970s, gains were made particularly at the bottom, which they link to the social democratic government elected in 1970. It is possible that this improvement is not captured by the percentiles shown in Figures B.1 and B.2.

For Gusenleitner, Winter-Ebmer, and Zweimüller, the period from 1977 is charac-terized by a 'steady rise in inequality' (1998, page 8). From Figures B.1 and B.2, it appears that this tendency was more apparent in the 1990s than in the 1980s. During the 1980s, as observed by Guger and Marterbauer (2005, page 617), there was only a 'light' tendency for dispersion to increase. The lower percentiles actually turned upward. On the other hand, from the late 1980s, there was a clear widening of the distribution. The wage tax statistics show an 8 per cent fall in the bottom decile between 1997 and 2004; there was a rise in the top decile over the same period, although it fell just short of 5 per cent.

Table B.2. Austria: OECD (1996)

	A	B	C	D	Column E	F	G	H	I
		All			Male			Female	
	P10	P80	P90	P10	P80	P90	P10	P80	P90
1980	52	146	178	62	139	162	52	141	174
1987	52	146	180	61	141	165	51	144	177
1988	51	147	181	61	143	167	51	145	178
1989	51	147	181	60	143	165	52	145	179
1990	51	148	180	60	143		51	145	179
1991	51	147	178	60	142		50	146	180
1992	50	147	178	60	143		50	146	181
1993	50	147	179	60	143		50	146	181
1994	50	147	182	60	144		49	147	182

Coverage	All
Industry	All
Age	All
Sex	See headings
Occupation	All except for most civil servants and for apprentices
Definition	Gross earnings, inc. special payments such as holiday and Christmas pay
Intensity	All
Period	Monthly standardized taking account of recorded days of insurance contributions
Limits	Earnings above maximum contribution recorded at that level
Source	OECD (1996, Table 3.1)
Original source	Earnings Statistics of the Austrian Association of Social Insurance Funds
Notes	(1) Supplied by Austrian Central Statistical Office; (2) Appendix gives figures from SJ inc. civil servants—see Table B.4; (3) Appendix gives figures from Mikrozensus for net earnings—see Table B.3

Summary

Over the period as a whole, there has been a widening in the earnings distribution in Austria. If we compare the wage tax results for 2004 with those for 1964 (linking the series), we find that the top decile has risen by 21 per cent, enough to qualify as large. The upper quartile rose by 10 per cent, so that there has been a degree of 'fanning out'.

Table B.3. Austria: Mikrozensus (OECD)

			Column			
A	B	C	D	E	F
All		Male		Female	
P10	P90	P10	P90	P10	P90
1981	64	161	69	159	66	158
1983	66	157	71	154	67	155
1985	63	160	68	161	61	159
1987	67	150	70	161	66	156
1989	62	162	65	166	62	160
1991	64	156	67	166	65	165
1993	63	160	66	175	63	171

Coverage	All
Industry	All
Age	All
Sex	All
Occupation	All
Definition	Net earnings
Intensity	All
Period	Monthly, standardized to a 40 hour week
Limits	None
Source	OECD, 1996, Appendix
Original source	Mikrozensus

Table B.4. Austria: Social security data

								Column									Source
	A	B	C	D	E	F	G	H	I	J	K	L	M	N	O	
			All					Male					Female			SJ denotes *Statistisches Jahrbuch*
	P10	P25	P75	P80	P90	P10	P25	P75	P80	P90	P10	P25	P75	P80	P90	
1965	31.8	70.0	136.7	147.5	181.0	41.0	76.0	130.2	139.5		31.2	69.3	129.1	138.0	166.5	SJ 1966, page 275
1966	34.1	70.6	135.6	146.0	180.5	44.5	76.5	130.1	139.7	172.3	32.5	69.8	128.9	138.2	167.7	SJ 1967, page 265
1967	37.6	72.0	134.2	144.4	177.7	51.6	77.7	128.9	138.2	170.3	35.5	71.2	128.2	136.7	165.8	SJ 1968, page 286
1968	38.8	72.7	134.8	144.9	177.7	52.4	77.2	128.9	137.9	168.8	36.8	72.1	127.5	136.8	164.9	SJ 1969, page 300
1969	38.2	72.4	135.1	145.2	178.2	51.5	77.0	129.8	139.1	170.3	34.8	71.1	128.3	137.5	165.4	SJ 1970, page 291
1970	35.9	71.6	135.0	145.6	180.0	47.8	76.6	130.3	139.6		35.2	70.5	128.3	137.3	165.7	SJ 1971, page 313
1971	36.2	70.8	135.8	146.3	181.0	46.2	76.4	130.6	140.2		37.0	71.0	128.7	137.6	167.3	SJ 1972, page 311
1972	36.1	70.5	137.1	148.3	183.4	45.8	75.8	131.8	141.7		37.3	70.5	130.3	139.6	171.3	SJ 1973, page 322
1973	36.2	69.9	136.8	147.9	183.1	43.7	75.5	131.2	141.5		38.5	70.7	131.2	141.3	172.7	SJ 1974, page 342
1974	35.3	69.7	137.3	147.8	180.3	41.6	75.4	130.6	139.9		38.0	68.9	130.7	140.8	172.5	SJ 1975, page 354
1975	35.3	69.0	137.6	148.2	183.0	39.3	75.0	130.9	140.5		38.1	68.8	131.0	140.9	173.0	SJ 1976, page 360
1976	36.1	68.8	137.8	149.2	184.8	40.0	75.1	131.8	142.0		38.6	68.9	131.7	141.9	174.5	SJ 1977, page 363
1977	36.8	69.7	138.0	149.5	188.4	41.4	75.0	133.3	144.0		39.2	70.4	132.1	142.7	175.6	SJ 1978, page 356
1978	35.8	69.6	139.1	151.1	191.3	38.8	75.0	134.2	145.5		38.1	69.6	131.5	142.0	176.4	SJ 1979, page 362
1979		69.4	138.5				74.3	133.9				69.8	131.6			
1980	36.3	69.2	139.8	152.2	191.9	39.3	73.6	133.5	144.5		39.1	69.4	131.3	141.5	176.6	SJ 1983, page 180
1981	36.7	69.5	138.9	150.9	190.2	40.0	74.3	133.1	144.4		38.6	69.4	131.0	141.9	175.5	SJ 1983, page 180
1982		69.6	138.6				75.0	134.3				69.5	132.5			
1983	36.8	69.8	138.5	151.1	194.9	39.3	75.3	134.9	149.1		39.6	69.7	133.6	144.6	180.0	SJ 1983, page 180
1984	36.5	69.7	138.1	150.4	191.0	40.2	74.9	134.2	146.4		39.0	69.9	132.9	145.0	178.1	SJ 1984, page 181

Year																Source
1985	35.9	69.0	138.6	150.4	192.7	39.3	74.3	134.5	147.2		38.4	69.6	133.5	145.0	177.5	SJ 1985, page 181
1986	36.9	69.2	138.1	151.2	192.8	39.4	74.6	133.9	147.0		38.2	69.5	133.5	144.1	177.3	SJ 1986, page 164
1987	38.5	69.9	138.0	149.9	194.6	45.2	74.9	134.0	146.4		40.6	69.6	133.6	144.5	178.3	SJ 1987, page 182
1987*		73.1	134.9				78.1	131.4				74.1	133.5			SJ 1989, Table 9.02
1988	51.1	72.8	135.4	146.6	181.4	60.6	78.0	132.1	142.8	167.0	51.2	74.0	133.9	144.6	178.1	
1989		72.9	135.8				78.0	132.9				74.0	134.2			
1989*	52.1	73.7	134.8	146.0	178.7	62.8	79.0	132.6	142.8		51.0	73.5	135.3	146.7	180.5	SJ 1990, Table 9.02
1990																
1991	51.1	73.6	135.4	146.4	175.5	61.6	78.5	132.4	142.2		50.0	73.0	135.9	147.9	183.0	SJ 1992, Tabsle 9.02
1992	51.0	74.0	135.5	146.6	176.1	61.9	78.6	132.6	142.6		49.8	72.7	136.0	147.8	183.7	SJ 1993, Table 9.02
1993	51.0	74.1	135.3	146.4	176.9	62.0	78.8	132.4	142.7		49.2	72.4	136.3	148.4	184.6	SJ 1994, Table 9.02
1994	50.7	73.9	135.5	146.9	180.1	62.1	78.8	133.0	143.7		49.2	72.3	137.1	149.2	186.0	SJ 1995, Table 9.02
1995	50.0	73.5	135.3	146.7	180.6	61.9	78.9	132.9	143.8		48.8	72.0	137.6	149.7	186.7	SJ 1996, Table 9.02
1996	49.0	73.4	135.2	146.8	181.2	61.8	78.8	133.1	144.2		47.9	71.6	138.1	150.1	187.1	SJ 1997, Table 9.02
1996*		72.3	135.5				78.1	133.2				71.9	136.5			SJ 1998 Table 9.06
1997		72.0	135.8				78.1	133.4				71.6	136.9			SJ 1999–2000, Table 9.08
1998		71.3	136.0				78.0	133.5				70.9	137.5			SJ 2001, Table 9.08
1999		71.1	135.9				77.9	133.5				70.9	138.1			SJ 2001, Table 9.08

Coverage   All; before 1989 excludes prag. Beamte

Industry   All

Age   All, inc. apprentices up to 1987

Sex   All and M and F

Occupation   All

Definition   Gross, exc. overtime, holiday pay, special payments up to 1987

Intensity   All

Period   Monthly (July or August unless underlined, when January); annual from 1988

Limits   None

Source   See final column and SJ 1990 Table 9.05, SJ 1988 Table 9.03, SJ 1985 Table 9.02, SJ 1981 Table 9.02

Original source   Lohnstufenstatistik of Hauptverbandes (HV) des Öesterreichischen Sozialversicherungstraeger.

Notes   (1) Entries in italics are interpolated from tabulations; see text for description of Pareto extrapolation of P90 for certain years; (2) 1989 to 1994 given in OECD 1996 Appendix.

Table B.5. Austria: Social security data (Christl)

| | A | B | C | D | E |
			Column		
	Gini	Share of bottom 10%	Share of bottom 20%	Share of top 20%	Share of top 10%
1953	26.0	2.2	7.2	33.3	19.3
1957	30.1	1.8	6.2	36.5	21.5
1964	30.9	1.8	6.3	37.4	22.5
1967	29.0	2.1	7.0	36.4	21.8
1970	29.3	2.0	6.8	36.6	21.8
1975	30.2	2.2	6.7	37.0	22.1
1979	31.5	2.2	6.6	38.5	23.4

Coverage	All; excludes prag. Beamte
Industry	All
Age	All
Sex	All
Occupation	All
Definition	Gross, exc. overtime, holiday pay, special payments
Intensity	All
Period	Monthly
Limits	None
Source	Christl, 1980, Tables 1 and 3
Original source	Lohnstufenstatistik of the Hauptverbandes des Öesterreichischen Sozialversicherungstraeger, WIFO calculations

Table B.6. Austria: Social security data (Guger and Marterbauer)

	A	B	C	Column D	E	F
	Gini	Share of bottom 20%	Share of next 20%	Share of middle 20%	Share of next 20%	Share of top 20%
1970	29.3	6.8	14.3	18.7	23.6	36.6
1976	29.2	6.8	14.1	18.7	24.2	36.3
1981	31.4	6.6	13.6	17.9	23.3	38.6
1987	31.6	6.9	13.5	17.8	23.0	38.8
1987 new	29.6	7.4	13.9	18.1	23.1	37.6
1990	30.2	7.3	13.7	17.9	23.0	38.2
1995	30.6	7.3	13.6	17.7	22.6	38.7
2000	31.7	7.1	13.3	17.6	22.4	39.6
2000 new	31.1	7.4	13.4	17.5	22.3	39.3
2001	31.0	7.4	13.5	17.6	22.4	39.1
2002	31.3	7.3	13.4	17.5	22.3	39.5
2003	31.2	7.2	13.4	17.6	22.5	39.3

Coverage	All; excludes Beamte up to 1989
Industry	All
Age	All, inc. apprentices up to 1987
Sex	All
Occupation	All
Definition	Gross, exc. overtime, holiday pay, special payments up to 1987
Intensity	All
Period	Monthly (July); annual from 1987
Limits	None
Source	Guger and Marterbauer 2005, Table 1
Original source	Lohnstufenstatistik of the Hauptverbandes des Öesterreichischen Sozialversicherungstraeger, WIFO calculations

Table B.7. Austria: Wage tax statistics

Column groups: **A–H** = All (FY and PY): A=P10, B=P20, C=P25, D=P75, E=P80, F=P90, G=P95, H=P99 · **I, J, K, M** = Male: I=P10, J=P25, K=P75, M=P90 · **N–Q** = Female: N=P10, O=P25, P=P75, Q=P90

	A	B	C	D	E	F	G	H	I	J	K	M	N	O	P	Q	Source
	P10	P20	P25	P75	P80	P90	P95	P99	P10	P25	P75	P90	P10	P25	P75	P90	
1953	31.0	56.9	67.5	128.6	138.9	168.0	201.2	320.5	39.0	74.1	127.1	162.5	24.7	57.2	128.2	160.4	Steuerstatistiken 1953, pages 80–3
1957	32.6	55.8	64.0	138.5	148.4	185.7	233.5	379.0	41.1	72.1	130.0	180.2	31.9	62.6	141.9	197.8	Steuerstatistiken 1957, pages 36–43
1964	31.0	54.6	64.6	137.9	148.8	184.9	229.0	383.8	38.3	74.2	130.6	174.3	31.3	61.1	137.5	189.1	SN 1968, issue 11, pages 800–3
1967		53.1	61.4	136.2	147.8	182.0	225.6	389.9	40.8	74.3	129.7	172.6			141.8	191.6	LSS 1970, page xiii
1970	27.2	54.7	64.7	136.8	147.2	185.5	234.8	390.4	32.6	73.3	129.9	177.2	27.4	62.2	136.7	185.9	LSS 1970, pages 98 and 99
1970	29.5	54.5	64.2	138.0	148.7	187.1	236.4	390.1	34.7	73.3	130.6	178.4	30.6	63.0	138.6	191.0	
1973	26.7	51.5	62.2	141.0	151.3	189.5	242.5	390.9									LSS 1973, page 108
1973	28.5	52.3	62.3	142.0	152.9	191.9	245.5	393.0									
1976	26.6	50.1	61.3	140.7	156.1	192.8	239.8	396.8									LSS 1976, pages 102 and 103
1979	25.2	47.5	58.9	142.1	154.2	197.6	248.5	407.2	26.3	69.7	135.4	188.4	25.8	58.3	135.4	188.4	LSS 1979, pages 128, 129, 132, and 133
1982	24.8	48.1	59.4	141.1	154.2	198.5	250.1	413.5	26.9	69.7	135.6	190.8	25.3	58.7	141.7	195.7	LSS 1982, page 26
1987	31.6	54.1	63.8	141.1	152.5	198.4	251.7	418.6	35.0	72.1	137.5	195.9	31.8	62.5	141.4	192.8	LSS 1987, pages 46 and 48
1994	15.9	37.5	49.7	147.8	161.9	215.7	274.7	498.8	18.7	61.1	142.2	207.9	15.6	45.6	155.1	220.9	LSS 1994, pages 40, 42, 46, and 48
1995		38.0	50.3	147.3	162.1	214.9	270.7	493.2	19.3	62.6	142.1	208.5		45.9	154.5	221.5	LSS 1995, pages 40, 42, 46, and 48
1996		37.2	49.3	147.7	162.8	215.9	274.3	486.0	18.5	61.3	141.9	209.6		44.9	155.2	222.0	LSS 1996, pages 56, 58, 62, and 64

SN denotes *Statistische Nachrichten*; LSS denotes *Lohnsteuerstatistik*

(*Continued*)

Table B.7. (*Continued*)

					All FY only					Male				Female		
Column	R	S	T	U	V	W	X	Y	Z	AA	AB	AC	AD	AE	AF	AG
	P10	P20	P25	P75	P80	P90	P95	P99	P10	P25	P75	P90	P10	P25	P75	P90
1953	50.4	73.4	79.3	126.5	134.7	161.7	194.2		64.5	82.9	124.9	160.6	40.6	75.7	121.5	153.0
1957	39.4	60.5	69.0	134.0	144.4	183.2	229.2	368.5	52.5	77.0	128.6	178.0	39.0	68.2	139.2	191.3
1964	41.7	63.6	70.8	134.0	144.6	178.6	222.2	371.1	56.3	77.9	128.5	172.5	45.3	70.7	134.1	182.7
1994	39.3	61.9	70.3	139.1	152.0	198.2	252.0	450.5	53.0	76.5	137.9	199.0	35.9	66.7	141.4	193.4
1995	39.1	61.7	69.7	139.3	152.3	196.4	250.7	444.1	54.4	76.7	138.3	198.0	35.3	66.2	141.9	195.4
1996	38.7	61.5	69.4	138.9	152.2	197.8	250.6	428.3	54.5	76.4	137.7	198.4	35.2	65.7	141.5	195.3

Coverage	All
Industry	All
Age	All, inc. apprentices
Sex	See headings
Occupation	All
Definition	Gross
Intensity	See headings
Period	Annual
Limits	None
Source	See sources following column Q
Original source	Lohnsteuerstatistik
Note	The figures in italics include pensioners; Sources remain the same throughout the table.

Table B.8. Austria: Wage tax data in Statistical Yearbook

						Column													
	A	B	C	D	E	F	G	H	I	J	K	L	M	N	O	P	Q	R	Source
	All FY and PY						Male						Female						
	P10	P20	P25	P75	P80	P90	P10	P20	P25	P75	P80	P90	P10	P20	P25	P75	P80	P90	SJ denotes *Statistisches Jahrbuch*
1996	14.7	41.4	53.9	145.4	160.0	210.2	21.8	55.6	67.6	140.7	155.3	205.9	12.0	34.6	47.5	152.7	168.2	216.7	SJ 1998, page 162
1997	14.4	40.6	53.1	145.0	159.6	209.9	21.2	55.6	68.1	140.5	155.2	206.0	12.2	34.0	47.1	153.8	169.6	218.5	SJ 1999–2000, page 195
1998	13.8	39.3	51.8	146.1	160.9	212.5	19.9	54.3	67.1	141.1	156.1	207.8	12.1	33.3	46.5	155.9	172.2	222.3	SJ 2001, page 198
1999	13.2	38.2	50.7	147.2	162.3	214.1	18.6	53.3	66.4	141.5	156.5	208.3	12.0	32.8	46.1	158.1	174.8	226.7	SJ 2002, page 199
2000	13.0	37.7	50.2	147.5	162.8	215.4	18.3	52.8	66.2	141.8	157.1	209.6	12.2	32.5	46.0	158.6	175.7	228.2	SJ 2003, page 198
2001	12.8	36.9	49.3	147.6	162.8	214.9	16.6	50.6	64.8	141.7	157.0	208.9	12.3	32.8	46.3	158.9	175.6	227.6	SJ 2004, page 204
2002			48.5	148.5					62.6	142.2					46.3	158.9			
2003			47.4	149.5					61.0	142.6					45.1	160.5			
2004	11.6	34.5	47.1	150.1	165.8	218.8	14.2	45.0	60.2	143.0	158.3	209.4	11.9	31.3	45.0	161.1	178.4	232.2	SJ 2007, page 228

(Continued)

Table B.8. (*Continued*)

			All						Male						Female			
			Standardized by days worked															
	S	T	U	V	W	X	Y	Z	AA	AB	AC	AD	AE	AF	AG	AH	AI	AJ
	P10	P20	P25	P75	P80	P90	P10	P20	P25	P75	P80	P90	P10	P20	P25	P75	P80	P90
1996																		
1997	37.0	59.2	67.6	139.0	152.1	198.3	52.7	70.9	76.5	136.4	150.0	197.3	31.4	54.7	63.9	144.4	158.0	201.3
1998	35.5	57.9	66.4	139.7	153.0	199.9	51.2	70.3	76.1	137.0	150.8	198.8	30.6	53.9	63.1	145.7	159.6	203.7
1999	34.8	56.8	65.5	140.4	154.0	201.2	50.4	70.2	76.0	137.5	151.5	199.9	30.1	53.6	62.7	146.9	161.2	206.8
2000	34.3	56.3	64.9	140.7	154.5	202.1	49.7	69.9	75.9	137.7	151.9	200.6	30.0	53.4	62.4	147.4	161.9	208.1
2001	32.6	54.6	63.6	140.9	154.9	203.1	46.8	69.1	75.5	138.1	152.5	202.0	28.5	52.3	61.4	147.9	162.4	208.7
2002																		
2003																		
2004	30.6	52.8	62.1	142.2	156.6	205.4	43.1	67.3	74.3	139.0	153.4	202.8	26.9	50.9	60.2	149.6	164.6	212.9

Coverage All
Industry All
Age Excludes apprentices
Sex See headings
Occupation All
Definition Gross
Intensity See headings
Period Annual
Limits None
Source See sources following column R
Original Source Lohnsteuerstatistik

Table B.9. Austria: Wage tax statistics (Guger and Marterbauer)

	A	B	C	D	E	Column F	G	H	I
	Wage taxpayers		Workers						
	All	FY men	All	FY men	All	All	All	All	All
					Share of	Share of	Share of	Share of	Share of
	Gini	Gini	Gini	Gini	bottom 20%	next 20%	middle 20%	next 20%	top 20%
1970	33.8	27.1							
1976	34.6	27.4	34.9		4.8	12.7	18.3	24	40.2
1982	35.7	28.7	36.4		4.5	12.4	18	23.9	41.2
1987	38.9		35.0		5.4	12.7	17.7	23.1	41.0
1991	39.3		30.7		7.4	13.7	17.5	22.6	38.8
1992			31.3		6.9	13.7	17.6	22.7	39.1
1994			41.3	30.4	2.8	10.8	17.7	24.1	44.6
1995	43.1	34.5	41.0	30.2	2.9	10.9	17.7	24.1	44.4
1999	44.5	36.0	42.9	31.3	2.6	10.3	17.5	24.0	45.5
2000	44.8	36.7	43.3	32.0	2.5	10.2	17.4	24.2	45.7
2001	44.2	35.4	42.9	31.0	2.5	10.0	17.4	24.3	45.8
2002	44.3	35.5	43.2	31.2	2.4	9.9	17.4	24.4	45.9
2003	44.5	35.6	43.6	31.1	2.3	9.7	17.4	24.5	46.1

Coverage	See headings
Industry	All
Age	All
Sex	See headings
Occupation	All
Definition	Gross
Intensity	See headings
Period	Annual
Limits	None
Source	Guger and Marterbauer 2005, Table 2
Original source	Lohnsteuerstatistik

Bibliography

Chaloupek, G, 1978, 'Die Verteilung der persönichen Einkommensverteilung in Österreich, II Die Arbeitsverdienste', *Wirtschaft und Gesellschaft*, no 2.

—— 1981, 'Die Verteilung der Einkommen aus unabständiger Arbeit in Österreich 1953 bis 1979', in H Suppanz and M Wagner, *Einkommensverteilung in Österreich, Ein einführender Überblick*, Verlag für Geschichte und Politik, Vienna.

—— 1984, 'Lohnentwicklung und Einkommensverteilung bei schwachem Wirtschaftswachstum', *Wirtschaft und Gesellschaft*, vol 10: 483–98.

Christl, J, 1980, 'Entwicklungstendenzen in der österreichischen Lohn- und Gehalts-pyramide zwischen 1953 und 1979', *Empirica*, vol 11: 47–57.

Fersterer, J and Winter-Ebmer, R, 1999, 'Are Austrian returns to education falling over time?', IZA Discussion Paper No 72.

Guger, A, 1989, 'Einkommensverteilung und Verteilungspolitik in Österreich', in H Abele, E Nowotny, S Schleicher, and G Winckler, editors, *Handbuch der Öster-reichischen Wirtschaftspolitik*, Manz, Vienna.

—— and Marterbauer, M, 2005, 'Langfristige Tendenzen der Einkommensverteilung in Österreich', WIFO Monatsberichte 9/2005.

Gusenleitner, R, Winter-Ebmer, R, and Zweimüller, J, 1998, 'The distribution of earnings in Austria 1972–1991', *Allgemeines Statistisches Archiv*, vol 82: 275–90.

Hofer, H and Pichelmann, K 1997, 'A note on earning inequality in Austria', HIS, Vienna.

Karlhofer, F and Ladurner, U, 1993, 'The Austrian labour market: Description and analysis of structures and institutions', in J Hartog and J Theeuwes, editors, *Labour Market Contracts and Institutions: A Cross-National Comparison*, North-Holland, Amsterdam.

Österreichischen Statistischen Zentralamt, 1957, *Steuerstatistiken 1953*, Vienna.

—— 1961, *Steuerstatistiken 1957*, Beiträge zur Österreichischen Statistik, vol 68, Vienna.

Steindl, J, 1958, 'Die Stichtung der persönlichen Einkommen in Österreich', *Monats-berichte des Österreichischen Instituts für Wirtschaftsforschung*, 31 (Beilage 32).

C

Canada

It is now well established that, over the last fifteen years, the dispersion of male earnings in Canada has widened considerably.

Beaudry and Green, 2000, page 907

C.1 Introduction

The British North America Act brought Canada into being as a confederation from 1 July 1867. In 1931, the Statute of Westminster affirmed the independence of Canada. In 1949, Newfoundland joined Canada as the tenth province of Canada.

Previous Coverage

Canadian data are included in all of the OECD compilations:

1993 (Table C.1): 1973, 1981, 1986, 1990, supplied by Statistics Canada, taken from the Survey of Consumer Finances (SCF), with adjustments made by Statistics Canada to improve coverage and comparability between the years shown.

1996 (Table C.2): 1981, 1986, 1988, 1990–4, supplied by Statistics Canada, taken from the SCF, with adjustments made by Statistics Canada to improve coverage and comparability between the years shown.

LMS (Table C.3): data for the same years as OECD (1996), based on the SCF, with adjustments made by Statistics Canada to improve coverage and comparability between the years shown, with more detail in terms of percentiles, and with the addition of 1967 and 1973, the latter being the same as in OECD (1993).

Official Publications

A variety of statistics on the distribution of earnings have been published at different times—see below.

C.2 Data Sources

The Statistics Canada website contains a most useful 'global view of surveys', classified according to theme. In the case of 'Labour Market and Income Data', it tabulates a number of surveys, indicating whether they contain data on earnings. Those relevant to the whole population include the Survey of Consumer Finances, the Labour

Market Activity Survey, both now replaced by the Survey of Labour and Income Dynamics, and the Longitudinal Administrative Databank. These are discussed in turn, as is the Canadian Census of Population and other earlier sources, such as the survey of earnings and hours in manufacturing. Blackburn and Bloom (1993, Table 7A.1) give a valuable tabular survey of studies of earnings dispersion (and income inequality) in Canada.

Survey of Consumer Finances (SCF)

The SCF was an annual supplement to the Labour Force Survey,[6] carried out in April of each year, collecting information about income in the preceding year. Starting in the early 1950s,[7] Statistics Canada carried out periodic surveys, usually every two years, of the incomes of families and individuals. The regular SCF was instituted in April 1972, providing data for 1971, and was then carried out every two years, until it became annual in the 1980s. The final year was 1999, containing data relating to incomes in 1998. The sample size was 35,000 households, and all persons aged 15 and over were interviewed. The sample is re-weighted in line with the Statistics Canada sampling frame. Coverage was complete apart from residents of the Yukon and Northwest Territories, persons living on Indian reserves or in institutions, and full time members of the armed forces. The exclusions amounted to less than 3 per cent of the population aged 15 and over. Information was collected on annual income in the preceding calendar year, broken down by source, and on employment, including weeks worked (although not information that allows the hourly wage rate to be calculated). According to Statistics Canada, 'most data are conceptually consistent since 1971'. As noted above, the data are the basis for the OECD figures reproduced here in Tables C.1–C.3.

Statistics Canada has made available micro-data from the SCF in public-use files, and these have been the basis for extensive research. The form of these files has varied. The 1971 to 1979 public-use files relate to households, providing information on the earnings of the household head and spouse, but not covering other workers in the household; from 1981 they relate to individuals, including, for example, working children who live with their parents (see Blackburn and Bloom, 1993, page 253). The first year for which the public-use file covers all workers is therefore 1981. Prior to 1977, the public-use files did not include information where there was item non-response for income, whereas from 1977 observations with imputed income values are included (see Dooley, 1986, page 146). Dooley attributes to this change in procedure more than half of the growth in his sample from 13,098 in 1971 to 19,778 in 1981. He noted that the imputed observations

---

[6] The LFS is a monthly household survey, with a sample of some 53,000 households. Households are first interviewed in person and then interviewed by telephone for the next five months. It covers all persons aged 15 and over in the non-institutional population, excluding persons living in the Northwest Territories or Nunavut, or on Indian Reserves. The Yukon is surveyed but not included in the national totals.

[7] See Goldberg and Poduluk (1957) for a discussion of the 1952 Income Survey of non-farm households; the results are published in Dominion Bureau of Statistics (1954).

could not be identified, but there is no reason to suppose that they were distributed in the same way as those reporting earnings.

The SCF data have been used in a large number of studies of earnings dispersion. Blackburn and Bloom (1993) consider the distribution of annual earnings in 1979 and 1987 among men aged 25–64 who worked full time and full year and who were household heads or married to household heads (the reasons for this restriction have been described above). Dooley (1987) considers the distribution of annual and weekly earnings over the period 1971 to 1982, and finds no clear trend in dispersion. Burbidge, Magee and Robb (1997) employ 15 years of SCF data from 1971 to 1991 to examine weekly earnings for full time full year workers who reported positive earnings. They draw attention to the sensitivity of the variance of log(earnings) to outlying observations, noting that bottom truncation causes a particularly large reduction in the variance: falling for men in 1971, for example, from 0.28 to 0.19. Richardson (1997) considers weekly earnings from 1981 to 1992 (see Table C.7). Wolfson and Murphy (1998) make use of special tabulations of the SCF, not subject to top coding, for 1974, 1985, and 1995. They consider the distribution of total employment income, including self-employment income. Picot (1998) uses SCF data for selected years between 1975 and 1995 (see Table C.8).

Labour Market Activity Survey (LMAS)

The LMAS was a supplement to the Labour Force Survey, collecting retrospective information for a 12-month period in an initial interview, and obtaining information for a second 12-month period from a second interview a year later. It covered the Canadian non-institutional population, excluding persons living in the Yukon, the Northwest Territories, or on Indian Reserves. The data are weighted as in the LFS but with allowance for additional non-response to the LMAS, and with a readjustment to account for independent province–age–sex population projections.

The LMAS data have been used by, among others, Morissette (1995), Doiron and Barrett (1996), DiNardo and Lemieux (1997), and Card, Kramarz, and Lemieux (1999), in conjunction with the 1981 Survey of Work History, which was also a supplement to the Labour Force Survey.

Survey of Labour and Income Dynamics (SLID)

The SLID has replaced the SCF and the LMAS, and provides data on labour market activity, earnings, and other sources of income. A new panel is introduced every three years, starting in 1993, and remains in the survey for six years. At any date there are two panels, each with 15,000 to 30,000 households. Information is collected at a January interview on labour market activity in the previous calendar year; information is collected at a May interview on income in the previous calendar year (if respondents agree to their tax file being consulted, then this interview is waived). Coverage of the civilian population is complete apart from residents of the Yukon and Northwest Territories, persons living on Indian reserves or in institutions. Table C.6 contains the deciles from the SLID data 1996–2004, as supplied by Statistics Canada. They cover all workers.

Although the SLID has replaced the SCF as a source of information on earnings, the two sources are not fully comparable. In particular, earnings are reported by the respondents in the SCF but administrative data are used for most respondents in the SLID (Boudarbat, Lemieux, and Riddell, 2003, page 7). There has, to a substantial degree, been a move from household survey data to administrative data. The survey element has, moreover, become a panel, with the associated problem of attrition.

Longitudinal Administrative Databank (Income Tax Data)

The Longitudinal Administrative Databank (LAD) consists of a 20 per cent (originally 10 per cent—see Beach and Finnie, 2004) longitudinal sample of people identified on the personal tax file (T1). It contains information on individual and family-level annual earnings (but no information on hours or wage rates). The income tax returns provide information on wages and salaries, commission from employment, taxable allowances and benefits, bonuses, directors' fees, and the value of stock options exercised. The LAD data are first available for the year 1982. Once selected, individuals remain in the sample whenever they appear in the annual T1 Family File tax file; in addition there is a sample of new filers. Coverage in 1996 was 96 per cent of the official population estimates. Detailed information is available about income by source, relating to the tax year. The LAD data from 1982 to 1992 are used by Finnie (1997 and 1997a)—see Table C.9. The LAD data from 1982 to 1997 are used by Beach, Finnie, and Gray (2003). Earnings dispersion for their 'broad estimation sample' is summarized in Table C.8. As they note, the purpose of their sample selection conditions is to 'approximate Statistics Canada's concept of "All paid workers" while excluding those with only limited attachment to the labour market' (2003, page S45). The sample sizes were around 500,000 for men and women.

In addition to the sample drawn from the T1 file, there is the T-4 Supplementary Tax File. It is constructed by merging information from the forms issued by employers (the T-4 supplementary tax forms) with T1 personal tax records. The T-4 forms have to be issued where tax or social security contributions are deducted or where annual earnings exceed a (modest) threshold. The T-4 File is used by Morissette and Bérubé (1996), and by Baker and Solon (2003), who argue that the file, being based on employers' reports, has advantages over the T1 file, where filing may have varied over time.

The income tax data over a longer run of years have been used by Saez and Veall (2005) in their study of top earnings, where they relate the tax data to external control totals. They report that total employment income is stable at around 95 per cent of the national accounts figures for wages and salaries, excluding supplementary labour income. The total number of returns with positive wages and salaries fluctuates around 100 per cent of the national accounts figure for the total of full time plus part time employees. The estimates cover all employees, part time and full time, and part year as well as full year. The estimates of Saez and Veall (2005) fall into two parts. For the most recent years, they use the Longitudinal Administrative Databank to classify individual returns by total wage and salary income. These results are shown in Table C.10, and cover the period 1982–2000. It should be noted that these percentiles are expressed relative to the mean, since the median is not given. Saez and Veall also present estimates for the earlier period 1972–81, but these are based on the tabulation of individuals by total taxable income, not by total earnings. I have used these figures, and also made alternative estimates as shown in Table C.10, columns G–K. These differ from those of Saez and Veall in that I have not used the published brackets (which relate to total income). Rather I have used the cumulative frequencies and cumulative amounts to interpolate the Lorenz curve, and hence obtain the implied earnings intervals. The fact that the underlying data are ranked by income and not by earnings means that they are given a B grade.

Canadian Census

In the Canadian Census, 20 per cent of the population are asked an additional set of questions (the 'long form'), covering earnings and labour market activity. Statistics Canada makes available a Census Public Use Sample Tape, containing information (in 1986) for about 2 per cent of the population (around 500,000 persons). Questions are asked about earnings in the previous calendar year. Earnings are top-coded: $100,000 for 1980, $140,000 for 1985, $200,000 for both 1990 and 1995.

According to Boudarbat, Lemieux, and Riddell, 'the Census is superior to the SCF/SLID for measuring the evolution of the wage structure in Canada' (2003, page 7). It is certainly the only source that provides a long time series. At the same time, the results are not fully comparable across time. For example, the published results of the 1971 Census of Canada refers to wage-earners aged 15 and over; the 1941 Census refers to wage-earners aged 14 and over; and the 1931 Census to wage-earners aged 10 and over. There is also a difference between using the micro-data and interpolating from published tables with broad ranges, as has been done here in Table C.4. In this case, there is a considerable margin of error, and the series is classified as B.

Earnings and Hours of Work in Manufacturing[8]

Prior to 1950, as part of the census of manufactures, statistics were collected for this sector on the distribution of weekly earnings. Initially they covered only wage-earners, but from 1944 salaried employees were also included. The data in Table C.5 date from 1944, in that I judged that figures covering only wage-earners were too limited. The next survey, which had been transferred to the Employment Section of the Labour Division, was in 1950 (referring to the last pay period in October of that year). The 1944 and 1950 data are 'not strictly comparable, largely because the earlier surveys included establishments employing less than 15 persons and were conducted for a different period of the year. Also the 1944 survey reflected wartime conditions' (Dominion Bureau of Statistics, 1961, page 93).

The survey was carried at approximately three-year intervals, and the data in Table C.5 cover 1944, 1950, 1953, 1956, 1959, 1964, and 1967. As described by the Dominion Bureau of Statistics (1966, Commentary), the survey covered some

---

[8] I owe this reference to McDougall (1947). He makes use of information about the earnings by different occupations (with uniform rates) in the railways, drawn from *Statistics of Steam Railways of Canada*.

11,000 establishments, comprising around 90 per cent of the employees in manufacturing. Information was collected on the number of employees by 16 classes of weekly earnings. The exclusion of establishments employing fewer than 15 workers reduces the degree of representativeness of the data, as does evidently the restriction to manufacturing. For these reasons, the series is classified as B. The series is however of interest for covering a period for which there appears to be no other information relating to the years between the censuses of population.

Comparison of Sources

The findings based on the LAD (tax file T1) data are compared with those based on the SCF data by Finnie: 'despite differences in the sample selection criteria employed across the various studies, the LAD results reported here are qualitatively quite similar. The magnitudes of the increases in inequality tend to be somewhat greater than those reported by others, but the precise period over which the inequality trends are assessed has a significant impact on the results—and on the comparisons' (1997, page 98). He advocates the use of three-year averages. Baker and Solon conclude that, as far as overall dispersion is concerned, 'it is reassuring that the SCF data and our data based on tax reports tell the same story' (2003, pages 294–5). In contrast, Morissette and Bérubé conclude from their comparison of the two sources that 'while the numbers from the two data sources are very similar for the bottom and middle quintile, the tax file suggests that real earnings in the upper part of the distribution have increased more in the eighties than SCF data would suggest' (1996, page 4).

An interesting study, which deals with both differences in sources and differences in methods, is MacPhail (2000). She compares the SCF for 1981 and 1989 with the 1981 Survey of Work History (SWH) and 1989 Labour Market Activity Survey (LMAS). She finds that the latter report an increase in the Gini coefficient of 1.83 percentage points, compared with 2.67 in the SCF. She attributes this to the 'greater capture of high earnings observations' in the SCF. Her analysis demonstrates the sensitivity of summary indicators such as the Gini coefficient to top coding and to the exclusion of outliers.

Summary

There are earnings data for Canada covering more than 70 years. They are drawn from a variety of sources, not all of which can be shown in Figures C.1 and C.2. The graphs are 'anchored' by the OECD version of the SCF series, which has the twin merits of having been prepared by Statistics Canada with adjustments to improve comparability and of covering a long span of years (1967 to 1994). For the more recent period, I have shown the series based on the replacement source: the Survey of Labour and Income Dynamics (SLID), and the income tax series. (The income tax based series in Figure C.1 for the years 1982–2000 have been multiplied by 1.15 to allow for the fact that the relevant percentiles in Table C.9 are expressed relative to the mean.) The earlier series, graded B, are drawn from the manufacturing earnings inquiry, and the census of population.

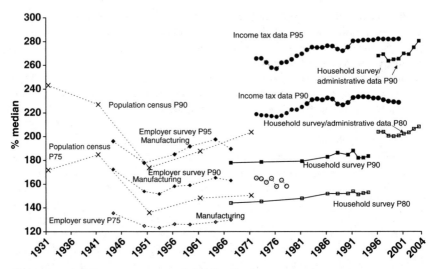

Figure C.1 CANADA upper part of the distribution 1931–2004

Sources: Table C.3, columns C and D; Table C.4, columns U and V; Table C.5, columns D, F, and G; Table C.6, columns B and C; Table C.10, columns A, B, and I.

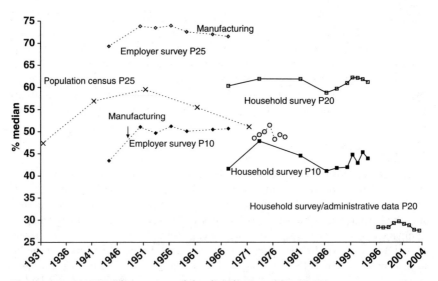

Figure C.2 CANADA lower part of the distribution 1931–2004

Sources: Table C.3, columns A and B; Table C.4, column T; Table C.5, columns A and C; Table C.6, column A; Table C.10, column H.

C.3 What Happened?

Views about what has happened to earnings dispersion in Canada are divided:

Unlike the United States where there is an unambiguous increase in wage inequality [since the early 1980s] existing studies for Canada provide an ambiguous picture on the evolution of wage inequality. On the one hand, studies that look at inequality in hourly wage rates using special supplements to the LFS generally find little change in overall measures of wage inequality like the variance of log wages. On the other hand, studies that look at inequality in weekly or annual earnings using the Survey of Consumer Finances, the Canadian Census, or administrative tax data tend to find steady growth in earnings inequality. (Boudarbat, Lemieux, and Riddell, 2003, pages 1 and 2)

This refers to the period after 1980, but I begin with the early part of the period, covered by the Census of Population data. One has to bear in mind that the census data are not fully comparable with those for recent years, and the percentiles have had to be interpolated from broad ranges. But the overall picture for the first part of the period is clear: the earnings distribution narrowed. In Canada, as in the US, there was a fall in the top decile; indeed the fall was larger in Canada: by nearly 30 per cent between 1931 and 1951, which is clearly a large fall. The upper quintile rose between 1931 and 1941, but then fell by a third. The lower quartile rose by 25.5 per cent between 1931 and 1951. Lydall seems quite justified in describing these events as 'dramatic' (1968, page 182).

Moreover, the narrowing was reversed after 1951. There is only decennial data from the population census, but the rises in the top decile and in the upper quartile from 1951 to 1971 were both in excess of 10 per cent. Over the same period, the lower quintile fell by 14 per cent. The census data indicate a clear return to a more dispersed distribution. Further evidence is provided by the employer surveys, although these have to be doubly qualified: they relate only to manufacturing, and 1944 is not fully comparable with the later data. The results in Figure C.2 suggest stability, rather than a fall, in the lower part of the distribution (although we should note that the bottom decile for men fell by 5 per cent between 1953 and 1964). In the upper part of the distribution, the results from the employer surveys move more closely in line with the census of population figures, particularly the top decile and P95, at least up to 1964. The top decile rose by 9 per cent between 1953 and 1964. At the top, at least, the Golden Age appears to have been a period of rising earnings dispersion.

The latter part of the 1960s and early 1970s saw, according to the SCF data, a significant improvement in the bottom decile, which increased by 15 per cent between 1967 and 1973. This conclusion is fragile, since it relies simply on two observations, but we may note that the lower quintile in the (B graded) income tax series (shown by hollow circles in Figure C.2) is moving in a parallel direction in the early to middle 1970s. At the top (Figure C.1) there are no registrable changes. There is therefore limited evidence for a post-1968 narrowing in Canada.

The rise in the bottom decile was followed by a fall: from 1973 to 1986 there was a decline of 14 per cent in the bottom decile, the fall being steeper for men and women taken separately (see Table C.3). There was a smaller fall of 5 per cent in the lower quintile. In view of the cyclical element (see below), however, it is important to look at the changes year by year. The estimates of Richardson (1997) suggest (see Table C.7) that the fall took place at the beginning of the 1980s. After the early 1980s, the bottom percentiles and shares tended, if anything, to recover some of the ground lost. There is no sign during this period of a continuing downward trend. The position at the top is shown in Figure C.1. In the case of the household survey data (SCF), for neither the top quintile nor the top decile is there a registrable change. This may reflect differences in the experience of sub-groups of the population. Burbidge, Magee, and Robb find over 1971 to 1991 'statistically significant and large increases in inequality for males with low levels of education and experience coexist with more modest changes in inequality for those with average education and experience and actual declines in inequality for older, more experienced workers with a university degree' (1997, page 181). Picot notes that relative stability in the overall dispersion of earnings 'is the result of a number of *offsetting* trends. . . . Inequality increased significantly among male workers . . . however it fell among female workers' (1998, page 25). We should also note the increases at the top shown by the income tax data: the top decile and P95 both increased by 7 per cent in the ten years between 1976 and 1986.

Turning to the 1990s, we see that the labour market changed significantly. According to Beach, Finnie, and Gray,

in the 1990s, Canada's labour market was characterized by a number of major changes in relation to the previous decade. A greater integration of the Canadian and United States economies (with increased north-south trade flows), increased globalization writ more large, rapid technological change, shifting modes and organization of production, demographic shifts (such as immigration activity), and structural changes to employment contributed to significant workplace and labour market changes. (Beach, Finnie, and Gray, 2003, page S42)

Their study, based on the Longitudinal Administrative Database (derived from tax returns) shows a rise in the top decile of 9 per cent between 1989 and 1997—see Table C.9. In Figure C.1, the most recent SLID data show a rise of 6 per cent in the top decile from 2000 to 2004. At the bottom, there is no registrable sign of a decline.

Conclusions reached concerning changes over time in dispersion may be influenced by the definitions adopted. SCF collected data on annual earnings, from which it is possible to calculate weekly earnings, by dividing by weeks worked, but 'it is difficult to obtain reliable data on the hourly wage rate from the SCF' (Picot, 1998, page 20). The same disadvantage applies to the LAD data. This is important since a number of authors have found 'that in Canada hourly wage inequality grew much more slowly than weekly earnings inequality' (DiNardo and Lemieux, 1997, page 636). These authors use the 1981 Survey of Work History and the 1988 Labour Market Activity Survey. For weekly earnings, the bottom decile fell from 44 per cent of the median to 39 per cent, and the top decile rose from 176 per cent to 185 per cent. In contrast, for hourly earnings, the fall in the bottom decile was smaller (from 49 to 46) and the rise in the top decile was not registrable (from 177 to 179). Morissette (1995) using the same sources argues that the modest rise in dispersion of hourly earnings in the early

1980s was 'because increases in between-group inequality—due to the widening gap between young and older workers—were offset by decreases in hourly wage dispersion within age groups' (1995, page 11). Doiron and Barrett (1996) make a similar argument with regard to the earnings of men and women: for both groups there was a decline in the dispersion of hourly earnings.

In the Canadian literature, there has been considerable discussion of the relationship between unemployment and the inequality of market income: Sharpe and Zyblock (1997), for example, suggest that a third of the rise in the Gini coefficient for market income between 1975 and 1994 can be attributed to higher unemployment. Osberg noted that 'the influence of the recession of the early 1980s, the expansion of the 1984 to 1989 period and the contraction of 1989–1994 show up in the fluctuations [of the Gini index] but over the 1975 to 1994 period as a whole there is little change' (1997, page 158). These findings refer to families and to the employed and unemployed. Examination of the impact of unemployment on the dispersion of individual earnings among the employed led Richardson (1997) to conclude that wage dispersion is anticyclical, rising in recession and falling during recovery.

Earnings instability has also been studied: see for example, Kennedy (1989), Beach and Finnie (1998), Beach, Finnie, and Gray (2003), and Baker and Solon (2003). The longitudinal administrative datasets have proved particularly valuable tools in this respect. From their analysis of the T-4 Supplementary Tax File data from 1976 to 1992, Baker and Solon conclude that 'the rise in inequality has stemmed from upward trends in both [persistent and transitory] components. Thus Canada's growth in annual earnings inequality signifies an increase in long-run inequality, as well as an increase in earnings instability' (2003, page 317).

Summary

I have highlighted the difficulties in reaching conclusions about the changes in earnings dispersion in Canada in recent decades. The pictures drawn here (Figures C.1 and C.2) underscore the problems associated with the absence of a single, authoritative series covering the past 25 years. The graphs also underline the fact that the changes in recent decades—a fall in the bottom decile in the early 1980s, and a rise in the top decile in the later 1980s (and possibly after 2000)—are smaller in magnitude than the 'dramatic' reduction in dispersion from 1931 to 1951, and are not dissimilar to the widening that characterized the Golden Age of the 1950s and early 1960s.

Table C.1. Canada: OECD (1993)

			Column			
	A	B	C	D	E	F
	All		Male		Female	
	P10	P90	P10	P90	P10	P90
1973	48	179	52	167	55	170
1981	45	179	48	167	47	176
1986	41	183	42	168	41	176
1988			45	171		
1990	42	185	44	175	44	175

Coverage	All
Industry	All
Age	All
Sex	See headings
Occupation	All
Definition	Gross
Intensity	FT FY
Period	Annual
Limits	None
Source	OECD (1993, Table 5.2)
Original source	Survey of Consumer Finances
Note	Supplied by Statistics Canada, with adjustments to improve coverage and comparability

Table C.2. Canada: OECD (1996)

	A	B	C	D	E	F
	\<center\>Column\</center\>					
	\<center\>All\</center\>		\<center\>Male\</center\>		\<center\>Female\</center\>	
	P10	P90	P10	P90	P10	P90
1981	45	179	48	167	47	176
1986	41	183	42	168	41	176
1988	42	186	45	171	45	186
1990	42	185	44	175	44	175
1991	45	188	44	175	46	178
1992	43	182	44	174	45	179
1993	45	182	46	173	48	184
1994	44	184	46	173	44	178

Coverage	All
Industry	All
Age	All
Sex	See headings
Occupation	All
Definition	Gross
Intensity	FT FY
Period	Annual
Limits	None
Source	OECD (1996, Table 3.1)
Original source	Survey of Consumer Finances
Notes	(1) Supplied by Statistics Canada, with adjustments to improve coverage and comparability; (2) All = Same as OECD (1993) up to 1990

Table C.3. Canada: OECD (LMS)

						Column					
A	B	C	D	E	F	G	H	I	J	K	L
		All				Male				Female	
P10	P20	P80	P90	P10	P20	P80	P90	P10	P20	P80	P90
1967	41.6	60.3	144.0	177.9	44.6	65.3	139.3	170.3	41.3	64.8	140.1	167.0
1973	47.8	61.9	145.3	178.6	51.8	67.8	139.4	166.9	55.4	71.1	141.8	170.2
1981	44.6	61.9	147.9	179.3	48.2	67.0	139.9	167.4	47.2	65.9	144.4	176.3
1986	41.1	58.8	151.9	182.9	41.6	61.0	139.1	168.2	41.5	59.7	147.4	176.0
1988	41.8	59.7	151.9	186.3	44.9	62.5	144.2	170.5	44.7	61.0	149.9	185.7
1990	41.9	60.9	152.0	184.7	43.9	62.9	145.8	174.9	43.9	62.8	146.2	174.5
1991	44.8	62.2	153.9	188.1	44.5	62.8	144.5	174.8	46.4	61.8	144.0	177.9
1992	42.9	62.1	151.1	182.0	44.3	63.0	144.0	174.0	45.3	61.3	147.1	179.1
1993	45.3	61.8	152.4	182.2	45.6	61.0	145.2	172.8	47.6	65.2	148.9	184.1
1994	43.9	61.2	153.0	183.5	45.9	63.2	144.7	172.8	44.4	59.8	147.3	177.8

Coverage	All
Industry	All
Age	All
Sex	See headings
Occupation	All
Definition	Gross
Intensity	FT FY
Period	Annual
Limits	None
Source	Downloaded from OECD website December 2005
Original source	Survey of Consumer Finances
Note	Supplied by Statistics Canada, with adjustments to improve coverage and comparability

Table C.4. Canada: Census of Population

	A	B	C	D	E	F	G	H	I	J
	All*			All*			Male*			
	P20	P80	P25	P80	P90	P95	P25	P80	P90	P95
1931	21.4	188.2	51	196	259	332	49	186	243	317
1941				183	242	305			215	271
1951	35.0	154.7	59	146	175	209	65	137	164	194
1961			56	154	189	230	64	145	176	214
1971										
	Goldberg and Poduluk (1956, Table II, median interpolated from Table I); 1951 data from 1952 Income Survey		Lydall (1968, Table CA-3), not using 'less reliable estimates'				Lydall (1968, Table CA-1), not using 'less reliable estimates'			

(*Continued*)

Table C.4. (*Continued*)

	K	L	M	N	O	P	Q	R	S	T	U	V
	Female*				All**				All			
	P25	P80	P90	P95	P25	P80	P90	P95	P10	P25	P75	P90
1931	57	187	238	284					21.8	47.4	171.9	243.2
1941			234	283					26.9	56.9	184.8	227.0
1951	48	153	179	203	80	132	156	189	26.3	59.5	136.0	173.8
1961	50	159	188	221	77	137	166	203	22.6	55.5	148.2	187.7
1971	Lydall (1968, Table CA-2), not using 'less reliable estimates'				Lydall (1968, Table CA-10)				18.1	51.1	150.4	203.7

Interpolated from 1931 Census of Canada, vol V, p 78, 1951 Census of Canada, vol V, Table 14 (for 1941), 1961 Census of Canada, vol III, Table 9 (for 1951 and 1961), 1971 Census of Canada, vol III, Part 1, Table 39

Coverage	All
Industry	All
Age	All
Sex	See headings
Occupation	All
Definition	Gross taxable wages and salaries
Intensity	See headings
Period	Annual
Limits	None
Sources	Indicated below columns
Notes	*All classified as wage earners at time of Census, with positive earnings in year
	**Full year workers

Table C.5. Canada: Earnings and Hours of Work in Manufacturing

	All (A–G)							Male (H–M)						Female (N–S)						
	A	B	C	D	E	F	G	H	I	J	K	L	M	N	O	P	Q	R	S	Sources*
	P10	P20	P25	P75	P80	P90	P95	P10	P20	P25	P75	P80	P90	P10	P20	P25	P75	P80	P90	
1944	43.4	61.6	69.3	135.5	146.7	172.4	196.0	52.5	67.4	73.5	129.0	136.1	158.9	52.31	64.23	70.19	134.39	141.30	163.84	GR 1958, page 94
1950	51.0	67.1	73.8	124.8	132.3	153.8	177.8	62.7	76.4	81.0	121.1	127.8	147.6	54.63	70.29	75.78	124.19	129.86	146.18	E and H, 1950, pages 30–35
1953	49.7	66.8	73.5	123.2	130.2	151.6		63.7	77.6	82.3	119.9	125.4	148.5	55.38	69.26	74.99	125.73	132.15	148.96	E and H, 1953, pages 32–37
1956	51.2	67.2	74.0	126.3	133.6	158.2	185.0	62.4	76.1	81.7	122.3	129.7	151.5	52.94	69.05	75.03	126.53	133.53	151.94	E and H, 1956, pages 32–37
1959	50.1	65.9	72.6	126.0	133.9	159.1	191.6	62.0	75.9	80.9	122.7	130.4	154.6	51.92	68.09	73.73	127.77	135.00	152.44	E and H, 1959, pages 40–45
1964	50.5	65.5	72.0	128.1	136.4	165.4	197.5	60.2	74.7	79.7	123.8	133.1	160.0	57.48	71.81	77.17	126.41	133.44	152.50	E and H, 1964, pages 39–44
1967	50.7	65.2	71.5	129.9	137.7	163.1	189.5	59.9	73.7	79.2	125.1	132.9	154.5	57.95	72.01	77.79	125.12	132.73	151.83	E and H, 1967, pages 40–43

Coverage	All
Industry	Manufacturing
Age	All
Sex	See heading
Occupation	All
Definition	Gross taxable wages and salaries
Intensity	All
Period	Weekly
Limits	Establishments employing 15 or more persons (from 1950)
Source	See final column
Original source	Annual Survey of Earnings and Hours
Notes	1944 data not fully comparable—see text

*GR denotes *General Review of the Manufacturing Industries of Canada*; E and H denotes *Earnings and Hours of Work in Manufacturing*

Table C.6. Canada: Survey of Labour and Income Dynamics (SLID)

| | | | | | Column | | | | |
	A	B	C	D	E	F	G	H	I
		All			Male			Female	
	P20	P80	P90	P20	P80	P90	P20	P80	P90
1996	28.4	203.9	268.0	28.1	190.6	239.0	32.3	203.1	271.5
1997	28.3	203.8	269.2	30.0	209.8	272.3	28.1	189.8	245.1
1998	28.4	200.5	263.6	27.6	191.5	243.1	31.2	202.7	267.7
1999	29.3	200.1	264.8	30.4	212.2	276.5	29.7	192.3	248.3
2000	29.7	200.7	265.3	29.2	188.3	250.0	30.0	209.7	278.6
2001	29.1	202.2	269.8	29.8	205.5	268.0	27.4	193.9	248.7
2002	28.8	203.3	269.2	28.4	187.4	237.6	28.6	208.9	277.4
2003	27.8	206.3	275.0	31.5	201.4	265.4	27.0	195.9	252.6
2004	27.6	208.2	280.5	28.3	186.4	235.4	29.1	208.5	282.9

Coverage	All
Industry	All
Age	All
Sex	See headings
Occupation	All
Definition	Gross taxable wages and salaries
Intensity	All
Period	All
Limits	None
Source	Supplied by Statistics Canada
Original source	Survey of Labour and Income Dynamics

Table C.7. Canada: Survey of Consumer Finances (Richardson)

	A	B	C	D	E	F	G	H	I
					Column				
	Male		Female				All		
						Share of bottom 10%	Share of bottom 20%	Share of top 20%	Share of top 10%
	P10	P90	P10	P90	Gini				
1981	34.3	175.0	29.3	202.5	37.3	1.89	7.60	39.76	23.86
1982	30.6	181.0	28.1	207.0	38.1	1.77	7.18	40.36	24.28
1984	28.6	184.0	29.3	208.0	36.7	1.85	7.32	40.73	24.54
1985	29.5	188.0	28.8	214.0	39.4	1.78	7.09	42.16	26.01
1986	30.9	188.5	28.5	211.0	40.7	1.77	7.06	42.28	26.48
1987	30.1	186.5	27.5	210.0	40.5	1.78	7.17	41.31	25.19
1988	30.0	184.5	29.1	209.0	40.2	1.83	7.25	41.57	25.59
1989	31.0	186.5	28.5	204.0	38.5	1.83	7.32	40.96	24.89
1990	29.7	193.5	28.4	207.0	41.2	1.75	7.04	41.89	25.93
1991	30.9	194.0	27.5	209.0	39.9	1.73	7.01	41.59	25.44
1992	26.1	192.0	26.0	215.0	39.9	1.59	6.50	41.87	25.61

Coverage	Civilian workers, excluding those who received any self employment income
Industry	All
Age	All 16 and over
Sex	See headings
Occupation	All
Definition	Gross wages and salaries
Intensity	All who worked at least one hour during the survey year
Period	Annual wage and salary income divided by weeks worked
Limits	Excludes those with computed hourly wage less than half minimum wage (or similar conditions); in 1981 and 1982 a number of people (59 in 1982) with exceptionally high incomes were excluded
Source	Richardson (1997, Table 1 and Figures 2 and 3)
Original source	SCF
Note	Entries in italics read from graph

Table C.8. Canada: Survey of Consumer Finances (Picot)

	Column		
	A	B	C
	All	Male	Female
	Gini	Gini	Gini
1975	39.6	33.9	39.6
1981	40.3	34.7	41.3
1984	42.2	38.6	42.1
1986	41.8	38.0	41.7
1988	41.8	37.8	41.7
1989	40.8	37.4	40.3
1990	41.7	38.4	41.2
1991	42.0	39.4	41.3
1993	42.8	40.5	42.4
1994	42.3	40.0	41.6
1995	41.9	39.5	41.9

Coverage	All
Industry	All
Age	17–64
Sex	See headings
Occupation	All
Definition	Gross wages and salaries
Intensity	With positive employment income but excluding persons with self-employment earnings
Period	Annual wage and salary income divided by weeks worked
Limits	None
Source	Picot (1998, Table A-1)
Original source	SCF

Table C.9. Canada: LAD data

					Column				
	A	B	C	D	E	F	G	H	I
	All	Male	Female		Male			Female	
						Var			Var
	Gini	Gini	Gini	P10	P90	of log	P10	P90	of log
1982	38.4	34.4	37.4	26.9	181.1	0.6537	23.8	207.3	0.7194
1983	39.1	35.5	37.8	22.9	184.2	0.7355	22.5	212.8	0.7629
1984	39.3	35.5	38.0	23.3	184.3	0.7303	23.1	216.7	0.7646
1985	39.3	35.4	38.1	23.9	183.9	0.7174	23.0	216.6	0.7670
1986	39.4	35.5	38.3	24.3	185.0	0.7045	22.8	215.9	0.7686
1987	39.3	35.5	38.3	25.5	184.8	0.6812	23.3	215.0	0.7609
1988	39.5	36.0	38.0	27.2	185.1	0.6568	24.0	211.5	0.7428
1989	40.1	37.2	37.8	29.6	182.6	0.6211	24.9	204.2	0.7104
1990	39.8	37.2	37.9	27.3	187.6	0.6635	24.6	209.5	0.7229
1991	40.3	38.0	38.5	23.2	194.6	0.7672	22.5	216.2	0.7809
1992	40.6	38.6	39.1	21.9	195.9	0.8021	22.4	218.1	0.8034
1993				21.9	197.9	0.8096	21.9	219.0	0.8093
1994				23.1	198.5	0.7937	22.4	217.8	0.8042
1995				23.4	199.1	0.7881	22.5	218.3	0.7989
1996				23.3	201.5	0.7995	23.0	219.2	0.8039
1997				26.6	198.9	0.7313	24.8	214.9	0.7477
	Finnie (1997, Table 2)			Beach, Finnie, and Gray (2003 Tables 1, 2 and 3), broad estimating sample					

Coverage	All
Industry	All
Age	Aged 20 to 64, not full time students
Sex	See headings
Occupation	Excludes those whose net self employment income exceeded wage and salary income, or $1,000 (1992$) for columns A–C
Definition	Gross taxable wages and salaries
Intensity	All
Period	Annual
Limits	Excludes those who received less than $1,000 (in 1997$) wage and salary income (1992$ for columns A–C)
Source	Indicated below columns
Original source	LAD

Table C.10. Canada: Income tax data

	Column										
	A	B	C	D	E	F	G	H	I	J	K
	Defined relative to the mean			Share of top 10%	Share of top 5%	Share of top 1%	Defined relative to median				
	P90	P95	P99				P10	P25	P75	P90	P95
1972	190.3	231.0	371.2	27.2	16.8	5.6	23.4	48.5	165.1	225.3	270.7
1973	189.5	231.1	374.8	27.3	16.9	5.8	23.4	49.3	164.5	226.1	273.2
1974	189.3	228.1	369.5	26.9	16.6	5.7	23.2	50.0	161.5	223.5	268.3
1975	188.9	224.2	370.8	27.0	16.6	5.8	24.3	51.4	164.8	225.6	273.1
1976	188.4	223.6	355.8	26.2	16.0	5.2	23.2	48.3	158.0	217.9	253.7
1977	189.3	227.9	346.1	26.1	15.8	5.0	24.0	49.3	163.3	221.1	264.0
1978	191.1	228.4	328.5	25.8	15.4	4.7	23.4	48.8	158.3	216.3	256.2
1979	193.6	230.3	328.8	26.3	15.7	5.1					
1980	193.6	233.0	351.0	26.7	16.1	5.3					
1981	195.6	234.5	343.6	26.4	15.8	4.9					
1982	198.0	237.4	353.2	27.4	16.6	5.6					
1983	200.9	239.4	351.7	27.5	16.6	5.5					
1984	201.4	239.1	353.3	27.7	16.7	5.7					
1985	200.8	239.1	353.5	27.8	16.9	5.8					
1986	202.1	240.3	358.2	28.0	17.0	5.9					
1987	201.4	240.1	361.5	28.3	17.4	6.2					
1988	197.7	237.9	369.0	29.0	18.3	7.1					
1989	197.1	236.7	372.4	29.4	18.7	7.6					
1990	198.7	239.3	371.6	29.1	18.2	6.9					
1991	202.4	243.9	374.7	29.2	18.2	6.8					
1992	202.9	243.9	371.7	29.2	18.2	6.8					
1993	203.0	244.5	372.8	29.6	18.5	7.1					
1994	202.8	244.5	377.9	29.8	18.7	7.2					
1995	202.0	244.6	388.7	30.2	19.1	7.6					
1996	202.0	245.4	398.9	30.7	19.7	8.1					
1997	200.8	245.2	414.0	31.7	20.6	8.9					
1998	199.7	245.2	424.9	32.2	21.2	9.3					
1999	199.2	245.1	430.9	32.4	21.4	9.5					
2000	198.9	245.3	437.5	33.5	22.6	10.5					

Coverage	All
Industry	All
Age	All
Sex	All
Occupation	All
Definition	Gross taxable wages and salaries
Intensity	All
Period	Annual
Limits	None
Source	Columns A–F from Saez and Veall (2004, Tables D1, D2, and D3); columns G–K interpolated from Taxation Statistics using interval means (not brackets)
Original source	Taxation Statistics and LAD
Note	Estimates for 1972–81 based on tabulations by total taxable income

Bibliography

Abowd, J M and Lemieux, T, 1993, 'The effects of product market competition on collective bargaining agreements: The case of foreign competition in Canada', *Quarterly Journal of Economics*, vol 108: 983–1014.

Baker, M and Solon, G, 2003, 'Earnings dynamics and inequality among Canadian men, 1976–1992: Evidence from longitudinal income tax records', *Journal of Labor Economics*, vol 21: 289–321.

Bar-Or, Y, Burbidge, J, Maggie, L, and Robb, A L, 1995, 'The wage premium to a university education in Canada, 1971–1991', *Journal of Labor Economics*, vol 13: 762–94.

Beach, C M and Finnie, R, 1998, 'Earnings mobility 1982–1994: Women gaining ground and lower paid males slipping', *Canadian Business Economics*, vol 6: 3–25.

—— and —— 2004, 'A longitudinal analysis of earnings change in Canada', *Canadian Journal of Economics*, vol 37: 219–40.

—— —— and Gray, D, 2003, 'Earnings variability and earnings instability of women and men in Canada: How do the 1990s compare to the 1980s?', *Canadian Public Policy*, vol 29: S41–S63.

—— and Slotsve, G A, 1996, *Are We Becoming Two Societies? Income Polarisation and the Myth of the Declining Middle Class in Canada*, C D Howe Institute, Toronto.

—— —— and Vaillancourt, F, 1996, 'Inequality and polarization of earnings in Canada, 1981–1992', Queen's University, Kingston.

Beaudry, P and Green, D, 2000, 'Cohort patterns in Canadian earnings: Assessing the role of skill premia in inequality trends', *Canadian Journal of Economics*, vol 33: 907–36.

Blackburn, M L and Bloom, D E, 1993, 'The distribution of family incomes: measuring and explaining changes in the 1980s for Canada and the United States', in D Card and R B Freeman, editors, *Small Differences That Matter*, University of Chicago Press, Chicago.

Boudarbat, B, Lemieux, T, and Riddell, W C, 2003, 'Recent trends in wage inequality and the wage structure in Canada', discussion paper, University of British Columbia.

Burbidge, J, Magee, L, and Robb, A L, 1997, 'Canadian wage inequality over the last two decades', *Empirical Economics*, vol 22: 181–203.

Card, D, Kramarz, F, and Lemieux, T, 1999, 'Changes in the structure of wages and employment: A comparison of the United States, Canada and France', *Canadian Journal of Economics*, vol 32: 705–46.

Chaykowski, R P and Slotsve, G A, 2002, 'Earnings inequality and unions in Canada', *British Journal of Industrial Relations*, vol 40: 493–519.

DiNardo, J and Lemieux, T, 1997, 'Diverging male wage inequality in the United States and Canada, 1981–1988: Do institutions explain the difference?', *Industrial and Labor Relations Review*, vol 50: 629–51.

Doiron, D and Barrett, G F, 1996, 'Inequality in male and female earnings: The role of hours and wages', *Review of Economics and Statistics*, vol 78: 410–20.

Dominion Bureau of Statistics (Statistics Canada), 1940, *Weekly Earnings of Male and Female Wage-Earners Employed in the Manufacturing Industries of Canada, 1934–36*, Ottawa.

—— 1954, *Distribution of Non-Farm Incomes in Canada, by Size*, Ottawa.

—— 1961, *General Review of the Manufacturing Industries of Canada, 1958*, Ottawa.

—— 1966, *Earnings and Hours of Work in Manufacturing 1964*, Ottawa.

Donald, S G, Green, D A, and Paarsch, H J, 2000, 'Differences in wage distributions between Canada and the United States: An application of a flexible estimator of distribution functions in the presence of covariates', *Review of Economic Studies*, vol 67: 609–33.

Dooley, M D, 1986, 'The overeducated Canadian? Changes in the relationship among earnings, education, and age for Canadian men: 1971–1981', *Canadian Journal of Economics*, vol 19: 142–59.

—— 1987, 'Within-cohort earnings inequality among Canadian men: 1971–1982', *Relations Industrielles*, vol 42: 594–609.

Finnie, R, 1997, 'Stasis and change: Trends in earnings levels and inequality: 1982–1992', *Canadian Business Economics*, vol 5: 84–107.

—— 1997a, 'The distribution of earnings in a dynamic context, 1982–92', Applied Research Branch Working Paper W-97-3E.b, Human Resources Development Canada, Ottawa.

—— 1997b, 'Unequal inequality? The distribution of individual earnings by province, 1982–94', Applied Research Branch Working Paper, Human Resources Development Canada, Ottawa.

Freeman, R B and Needles, K, 1993, 'Skill differentials in Canada in an era of rising labor market inequality', in D Card and R Freeman, editors, *Small Differences that Matter*, University of Chicago Press, Chicago.

Gera, S and Grenier, G, 1994, 'Inter-industry wage differentials and efficiency wages: Some Canadian evidence', *Canadian Journal of Economics*, vol 27: 81–100.

—— Gu, W and Lin, Z, 2001, 'Technology and the demand for skills in Canada: An industry-level analysis', *Canadian Journal of Economics*, vol 34: 132–48.

Goldberg, S A and Podoluk, J, 1957, 'Income size distribution statistics in Canada: A survey and some analysis', *Income and Wealth*, series VI: 155–201.

Kennedy, B, 1989, 'Mobility and instability in Canadian earnings', *Canadian Journal of Economics*, vol 22: 383–94.

Lemieux, T, 1993, 'Unions and wage inequality in Canada and the United States', in D Card and R Freeman, editors, *Small Differences that Matter*, University of Chicago Press, Chicago.

McDougall, J L, 1947, 'The distribution of income among wage workers in railway employment, 1939–47', *Canadian Journal of Economics and Political Science*, vol 13: 248–55.

MacPhail, F, 1998, 'Increased earnings inequality and macroeconomic performance: The case of Canada in the 1980s', *International Review of Applied Economics*, vol. 12: 333–59.

MacPhail, F, 2000, 'Are estimates of earnings inequality sensitive to measurement choices? A case study of Canada in the 1980s', *Applied Economics*, vol. 32: 845–60.

Morissette, R, 1995, 'Has inequality in weekly earnings increased in Canada?', Statistics Canada Analytical Studies Branch Research Paper No 80.

—— and Bérubé, C, 1996, 'Longitudinal aspects of earnings inequality in Canada', Statistics Canada Analytical Studies Branch Research Paper No 94.

—— Myles, J, and Picot, G, 1993, 'What is happening to earnings inequality in Canada?', Statistics Canada Analytical Studies Branch Research Paper No 60.

—— —— and —— 1994, 'Earnings inequality and the distribution of working time in Canada', *Canadian Business Economics*, vol 2: 3–16.

—— —— and —— 1996, 'Earnings polarization in Canada: 1969–1991 Reform', in K Banting and C Beach, editors, *Labour Market Polarization and Social Policy*, School of Policy Studies, Queen's University, Kingston, Ontario.

Murphy, K J, Riddell, W C, and Romer, P M, 1998?, 'Wages, skill and technology in the United States and Canada', in E Helpman, editor, *General Purpose Technologies*, MIT Press, Cambridge.

Osberg, L, 1997, 'Economic growth, income distribution and economic welfare in Canada, 1975–1994', *North American Journal of Economics and Finance*, vol 8: 153–66.

Picot, G, 1996, 'Working time, wages and earnings inequality among men and women in Canada, 1981–93', Statistics Canada.

—— 1997, 'What is happening to earnings inequality in Canada in the 1990s?', *Canadian Business Economics*, vol 6: 65–83.

—— 1998, 'What is happening to earnings inequality and youth wages in the 1990s?', Statistics Canada Analytical Studies Branch Research Paper No 116.

—— Myles, J, and Wannell, T, 1990, 'Good jobs/bad jobs and the declining middle: 1967–1986', Statistics Canada Analytical Studies Branch Research Paper No 28.

Richardson, D H, 1997, 'Changes in the distribution of wages in Canada, 1981–1992', *Canadian Journal of Economics*, vol 30: 622–43.

Riddell, W C, 1995, 'Unionization in Canada and the United States: A tale of two countries', in D Card and R Freeman, editors, *Small Differences that Matter*, University of Chicago Press, Chicago.

Saez, E and Veall, M, 2005, 'The evolution of high incomes in Northern America: Lessons from Canadian evidence', *American Economic Review*, vol 95: 831–49.

Sharpe, A and Zyblock, M, 1997, 'Macroeconomic performance and income distribution in Canada', *North American Journal of Economics and Finance*, vol 8: 167–99.

Smeeding, T, 1999, 'Income inequality: Is Canada different or just behind the times?', plenary lecture presented to the Canadian Economic Association, Toronto.

Wolfson, M C and Murphy, B B, 1998, 'New views on inequality trends in Canada and the United States', Statistics Canada Analytical Studies Branch Research Paper No 124.

Zyblock, M, 1996, 'Individual earnings inequality and polarization: An exploration into sub-population trends in Canada, 1981 to 1993', Applied Research Branch Working Paper W-96-8E, Human Resources Development Canada, Ottawa.

D

Czech Republic

> As far as income distribution is concerned, Czechoslovakia was...an exception among both Western and Eastern European countries: the range of income inequality here was extremely small and virtually stable over a long period of time. This was true especially for inequality of earnings.
>
> Večernik, 1991, page 237

D.1 Introduction

Czechoslovakia was formed as an independent republic in 1918. In 1938, part of the country was annexed by Germany. The republic was reconstituted, with the loss of Ruthenia, after the Second World War. In the democratic elections of 1946, the Communists were the largest party in the governing coalition; they took over control in February 1948. The USSR invaded in August 1968 to displace the Dubçek government. The Communist regime was replaced in December 1989. On 1 January 1993, Czechoslovakia split into two: the Czech Republic (considered here) and the Slovak Republic (considered here only as part of Czechoslovakia). The Czech Republic joined the European Union on 1 May 2004.

Previous Coverage

Lydall (1968) contains one table for Czechoslovakia, based on data from the Official Yearbook for 1965; it gives data for 1962 and 1964. In his rank order of countries (Table 5.5), Czechoslovakia has the least dispersion.

The Czech Republic is included in the OECD (1996) and OECD (LMS) compilations:

1996 (Table D.1): for full time workers, gross earnings (including self-employed income)

1988 and 1992, from Microcensus of 1989 and 1993, published in Večernik (1995).

LMS (Table D.2): for full time workers, gross monthly earnings 1996, 1997, and 1999 (with further data supplied by OECD for 1998 and 2002–3), from enterprise survey of earnings.

Official Publications

Prior to the 1980s, a basic table on dispersion of earnings was published in the Statistical Yearbook (these were the data used by Lydall). Atkinson and Micklewright (1992) assembled these data and brought them together with the data contained in a 1990 publication of the Statistical Office providing a consistent time-series of data on the Czechoslovak labour market (FSU, 1990), of which only 100 copies were printed. These data are set out in Table D.5.

D.2 Data Sources

The main sources of data on earnings for Czechoslovakia/Czech Republic are censuses/surveys of employers and household surveys.

Employer Censuses and Surveys

Periodic investigations of earnings have been conducted by or for the Czech Statistical Office. Atkinson and Micklewright (1992, Section S.1) describe the 100 per cent census of enterprises in the state sector and the non-agricultural cooperative sector, requiring information on the number of employees in discrete bands of gross earnings. From 1959 to 1979, the information referred to earnings in May; from 1981 to earnings in November. Up to 1992, it was a complete census (Rutkowski, 1996, page 5). The coverage of private firms was extended in the 1990s: until 1992 only companies with 100 and more employees were included, the cut-off then being lowered to 25 workers, and 20 workers from 1997 (Večernik, 2001, page 4). Banking and insurance were included without limit. The mechanics have changed over the 1990s:

between 1993–1995, information on wage distribution was estimated combining various sources, in 1996 and 1997 wage surveys were again collected as a sample survey for units with 1–999 employees and full coverage of larger organizations... Since 1998, database of *Information System on Average Wage* administered by private company Trexima for the Ministry of Labour and Social Affairs has been used instead of wage surveys. (Večernik, 2001, page 4)

From 2004, information for the business sector is taken from the Average Earnings Survey and combined with information on the non-business sector from the information system of the Ministry of Finance. This forms the basis for the Structure of Earnings Survey.

Data from these sources are reported in Table D.3, the first part of Table D.4, and Tables D.5 and D.6.

Microcensus

The Microcensus is a household survey, supplemented by information from employers, from which results are available since 1958 (see Atkinson and Micklewright, 1992, page

248). They were conducted every three to five years, and sampled between 0.5 and 2 per cent of all households. Information was collected on income in the preceding calendar year, with earnings being notified by employers. The 1996 Microcensus was conducted in March 1997, collecting information about yearly incomes in 1996, and sampled 1 per cent, or 28,148 households (Večernik and Stepankova, 2003, page 185).

Data from this source are reported in Tables D.1 and D.4.

Economic Expectations and Attitudes Survey (EEA)

The EEA is a household survey, conducted by the Institute of Sociology of the Academy of Sciences, with a sample (in November 1994) of 864. The survey started in 1990, and was carried out annually from 1993 to 1998.

Data from this source are reported in Table D.4.

Comparison of Sources

The comparison of sources is particularly important in this case, since we have to consider both the differences in sources at a point in time and the impact on the different sources of the 1989 political changes. The basis for the enterprise surveys in particular has been greatly changed, with the need to cover the private sector. I have noted above some of the changes in the sample basis over the 1990s. There are good reasons to expect greater continuity in the case of household surveys. In this respect, it is valuable that Verčernik (2001) has compared the results from the wage surveys with those from the Microcensus and from the Economic Expectations and Attitudes Survey. As may be seen from Table D.5, the decile shares show some divergences. He points out that the Microcensus shows a fall in the share of the bottom 10 per cent from 1992 to 1996, not reflected in wage surveys. Nonetheless, the immediate direction of movement after 1989 is the same, and the top shares move similarly.

Summary

The results from employer censuses/surveys are summarized in Figures D.1 and D.2 (from 1993, the data relate only to the Czech Republic). Caution must be exercised in comparing figures before and after 1989, and this is marked by a heavy vertical line. With this qualification, the data allow us to examine changes in overall earnings dispersion over a 45-year period.

D.3 What Happened?

There has been considerable discussion of 'Czech egalitarianism', a phrase used by Connor (1979), who suggests three main explanations.[9] One explanation is purely economic: that the Czechoslovak economy was relatively advanced, and 'skill and literacy were simply not scarce enough to command high prices' (Connor, 1979, page 221).

---

[9] I owe this reference to Večernik (1991).

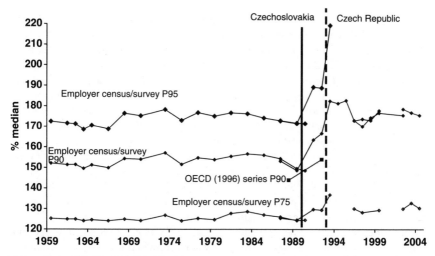

Figure D.1 CZECHOSLOVAKIA/CZECH REPUBLIC upper part of the distribution 1959–2004

Sources: Table D.1, column B; Table D.2, columns D and F; Table D.3, columns C and D; Table D.5, columns D, E, and F; Table D.6, columns D, E, and F.

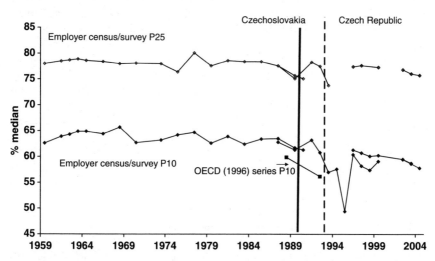

Figure D.2 CZECHOSLOVAKIA/CZECH REPUBLIC lower part of the distribution 1959–2004

Sources: Table D.1, column A; Table D.2, columns A and C; Table D.3, columns A and B; Table D.5, columns B and C; Table D.6, columns B and C.

This may explain the difference from other Eastern European countries, but does not explain the difference from Western European countries with comparable levels of skill and literacy. The other explanations offered by Connor are specifically Czecho-slovak. One is the negative function of an egalitarian incomes policy in preventing political dissatisfaction, with Czechoslovakia occupying an outlying position because it was 'the only socialist country that had been a functioning democracy in the interwar years' (Connor, 1979, page 222). One has however to ask how equality could serve such a function, and here we come back to the first explanation: 'a certain amount of egalitarian sentiment was diffused broadly among the Czech working class—more so perhaps than elsewhere in Eastern Europe. Socialist and labor move-ments had operated freely in interwar years' (1979, page 221). As it was put by Teichova, 'the desire for greater equality had deep historical roots in the social consciousness of broad segments of society' (1988, page 101). She argues that the narrowing of the skilled/unskilled differential had its origins in the 1930s.

The evidence assembled here does not go back to the 1930s. As is noted by Večernik (1995), the periodic wage surveys only began when the main features of the communist economy were in place. He dates the 'wage revolution' to the beginning of the 1950s, and indeed cites evidence that 'the systematic enforcement of earnings equality in the post-war period...had already begun by December 1945 (when the first regulation started)' (Večernik, 1991, page 238). The period covered in Figures D.1 and D.2 starts in 1959, and Večernik comments that 'the three decades following 1959 were a period of remarkable and perhaps unique stability in the overall earnings distribution' (1995, page 356). In a broad sense, this is true, but—as he goes on to say—there were still important changes taking place. Moreover, some of these affected the overall distribution. The bottom decile increased by 5 per cent from 1959 to 1968, leading the decile ratio to fall from 2.43 in 1959 to 2.35 in 1968.

Concerns about the performance of the Czech economy did indeed lead critics of the regime (such as Šik, 1966) to argue that the narrowing of differentials was responsible for the slow growth of productivity. This was couched in terms of the necessary return to investment in education (see Phelps Brown, 1977, page 48). According to Adam, 'Czechoslovak ruling groups have always been somewhat aware of the detrimental effects of wage leveling' (1972, page 170), and the 1968 action programme of the Communist Party envisaged a widening of wage differentials. As may be seen from Figure D.1, the top decile rose by some 5 per cent from 1966 to 1973.

The two changes identified were the largest observed. Over the period 1959–89 as a whole, the limit of variation for the top and bottom decile does not exceed 5 per cent. Applying this criterion, we arrive at the same conclusion as Večernik regarding the stability of the earnings. The stability of the deciles is indeed remarkable when compared with the changes taking place at the same time in market economies. There was no apparent widening of dispersion in the early 1960s, nor a post-1968 compression.

What, however, happened after 1989? According to Večernik,

the transition to a market economy has opened great opportunities for private entrepreneurship, employment in foreign firms, and awards of higher managerial positions. High earnings were accorded to employees in finance and the top echelons of bureaucracy. The possibility was opened for rewarding work differently according to skills and performance. Newly established and foreign firms have had greater liberty in wage settings, and sought to attract highly skilled people by offering considerably higher wages.... After state wage regulation was removed, formerly state-owned companies also began to have greater discretion in rewarding their employees. All of this contributed to a general de-equalizing trend in wages. (Večernik, 2001, page 3)

In considering earnings dispersion before and after 1990, we have to take account of the impact on the statistical sources. As noted earlier, the basis for the enterprise surveys used in Figures D.1 and D.2 has been greatly changed, with the need to cover the private sector. In this respect, it is reassuring that the results from the Microcensus and from the Economic Expectations and Attitudes Survey are reasonably consistent with those shown in Figures D.1 and D.2. The immediate direction of movement after 1989 is the same. Overall, there is a widening. As Verčernik observes, the ratio of the average earnings of the top decile relative to those of the bottom decile is approaching 6:1, whereas it was closer to 3:1 before 1989. The top decile rose by 12 per cent between 1989 and 1992. On the other hand, the relative decline at the bottom was 'modest' (Rutkowski, 2001, page 12). In the immediate period of transition to a market economy, most of the widening in Czechoslovakia/Czech Republic was at the top. It is of course possible that this reflects the replacement by higher cash salaries of benefits in kind, not recorded in the statistics, provided to those at the top of the ladder in the old regime.[10] This is a further reason for caution in drawing conclusions about the impact of the transition on earnings dispersion.

The period of transition discussed so far was one of falling average real wages (see for example Rutkowski, 1996, Table 1), so that a fall in the relative position of the bottom decile implied an even larger fall in their purchasing power. Since then, in the Czech Republic and elsewhere, average real wages have risen. We now have sufficient observations to form a view, not just about the transition, but also about the evolution of earnings dispersion in the market economy phase. Has there been a continuing trend towards widening, or was there a once-for-all realignment? Inspection of Figures D.1 and D.2 suggests that the action after 1993 was more at the bottom: the bottom decile fell by 7 per cent between 1993 and 2004. The top decile and upper quartile appear to have levelled off. According to Večernik, 'the Czech wage inequality and structure have been in energetic motion directed towards the Western pattern' (2001, page 13), but there is no evidence in Figure D.1 of a continuing fanning out at the top.

---

[10] For discussion of non-cash benefits under Communism, see Atkinson and Micklewright (1992), Chapter 6.

Summary

The distribution of earnings in Czechoslovakia was broadly stable for the 30-year period from 1959 to 1989. The move to a market economy led to a widening of differentials in the upper part of the distribution. Since 1993 there has been a fall in the bottom decile, but to date the upper part does not appear to be following the pattern of widening observed in many other countries.

Table D.1. Czech Republic: OECD (1996)

	Column	
	A	B
	P10	P90
1988	59.9	144.0
1992	56.2	154.0

Coverage	All
Industry	All
Age	All
Sex	All
Occupation	All
Definition	Gross (inc. self-employment income)
Intensity	FT
Limits	None
Source	OECD (1996, Table 3.1)
Original source	Microcensus

Table D.2. Czech Republic: OECD (LMS)

	A	B	C	D	E	F	G	H	I	J	K	L	M	N	O	P	Q	R
			All						Males						Females			
Column																		
	P10	P20	P25	P75	P80	P90	P10	P20	P25	P75	P80	P90	P10	P20	P25	P75	P80	P90
1996	61.3	72.6	77.4	130.1	139.6	173.0	65.1	75.5	79.8	128.7	139.0	171.3	63.1	73.2	77.6	131.1	140.4	170.6
1997	60.7	72.7	77.6	128.2	137.8	170.0	65.3	75.7	80.0	127.6	137.6	173.2	62.2	72.5	77.3	128.1	135.6	161.6
1998	60.1					174.4												
1999	60.3	72.2	77.3	129.3	139.8	176.7	64.2	74.9	79.3	129.9	140.2	177.9	61.7	72.2	77.0	128.0	135.9	162.7
2002	59.5					175.5	63.7					180.9	60.4					164.1
2003	58.7						63.0					181.8	59.5					163.9

Coverage	Workers in enterprises with 25 or more employees
Industry	All
Age	All
Sex	See headings
Occupation	All
Definition	Gross
Intensity	FT and full year
Period	Month
Limits	None
Source	Downloaded from OECD website December 2005 and supplied by OECD
Original source	Census of enterprises

Table D.3. Czech Republic: Structure of Earnings Survey (SEE)

								Column					
	A	B	C	D	E	F	G	H	I	J	K	L
		All				Male				Female		
	P10	P25	P75	P90	P10	P25	P75	P90	P10	P25	P75	P90
2002	59.46	76.84	130.04	178.54	63.45	78.98	133.09	183.11	60.35	75.23	128.96	169.45
2003	58.64	76.06	132.80	176.82	62.82	78.13	132.37	189.49	59.46	74.45	130.00	166.11
2004	57.79	75.75	130.31	175.51	61.75	77.73	130.83	180.00	57.89	74.12	129.74	164.79

Coverage   All
Industry   All
Age   All
Sex   All and M and F
Occupation   All
Definition   Gross
Intensity   FT
Period   Month
Limits   None
Source   Structure of Earnings Survey: Czech Statistical Office website
Note   Interpolated linearly

Table D.4. Czech Republic: Employer and household surveys (Večernik)

Employer survey

	A	B	C	D	E	F	G	H	I	J	K	L
	Share of decile group 1	Share of decile group 2	Share of decile group 3	Share of decile group 4	Share of decile group 5	Share of decile group 6	Share of decile group 7	Share of decile group 8	Share of decile group 9	Share of decile group 10	Gini	Robin Hood Index
1989	4.7	6.5	7.3	8.2	9.1	10.1	11.0	12.2	13.7	17.2		14.1
1993	4.4	5.6	6.6	7.4	8.4	9.4	10.7	12.2	14.6	20.7		18.2
1997	4.6	5.9	6.9	7.7	8.5	9.3	10.2	11.0	13.1	22.8		17.1
1999	4.4	5.8	6.7	7.5	8.3	9.1	10.1	11.4	13.8	22.9		18.2

Microcensus

	M	N	O	P	Q	R	S	T	U	V	W	X
1988	5.3	6.6	7.4	8.3	9.2	10.0	10.9	12.0	13.3	17.0	19.0	13.2
1992	5.0	6.1	6.9	7.7	8.5	9.4	10.4	11.7	13.8	20.5	23.0	16.4
1996	3.9	5.5	6.6	7.5	8.4	9.4	10.4	11.8	14.1	22.4	24.0	18.7

Economic Expectations and Attitudes survey

	Y	Z	AA	AB	AC	AD	AE	AF	AG	AH	AI	AJ
1992	4.5	5.6	6.4	7.2	8.1	9.0	10.5	12.1	14.1	22.6	27.0	19.3
1993	4.5	5.7	6.5	7.1	7.9	8.8	10.1	11.7	13.9	23.8	27.0	19.5
1994	4.5	5.1	6.4	7.2	8.1	8.9	10.3	11.8	14.2	23.5	28.0	19.8

Coverage	All
Industry	All
Age	All
Sex	All
Occupation	All
Definition	Gross (inc. monthly equivalent of bonuses and allowances); net for EEA Survey
Intensity	FT
Period	Monthly
Limits	None
Sources	Večernik 2001 Table 1 and Večernik 1995 Table 1
Original sources	See headings
Note	*Economic Expectations and Attitudes Survey* data for 1992 relate to January 1993

Table D.5. Czech Republic: Census of enterprises

	A	B	C	D	E	F	G	H	I	J	K	L	M	N	O	P	Q	R	S	T	U	V
Column				All							Male							Female				
	P05	P10	P25	P75	P90	P95	P99	Gini	P05	P10	P25	P75	P90	P95	Gini	P05	P10	P25	P75	P90	P95	Gini
1959	54.4	62.6	78.0	125.2	152.1	172.5	224.0	19.6	58.6	68.1	83.2	119.5	142.7	161.2	16.8	62.3	70.5	83.8	117.5	136.8	151.4	14.9
1961	56.5	63.9	78.5	124.9	151.4	171.6	220.4	19.1	61.3	70.2	84.2	119.0	141.9	159.5	16.1	65.3	72.1	84.8	115.9	134.7	147.8	13.9
1962	57.0	64.3	78.7	124.9	151.5	171.3	219.4	19.0	61.9	70.6	84.4	118.8	141.7	158.8	15.9	65.8	72.5	85.1	115.8	134.3	147.3	13.7
1963	58.2	64.9	78.9	124.1	149.6	168.6	214.9	18.5	62.9	71.4	84.9	118.0	140.0	156.4	15.4	67.7	73.6	85.5	115.4	133.5	146.6	13.3
1964	57.8	64.9	78.6	124.6	151.3	170.6	217.3	18.8	62.8	71.6	84.7	118.2	141.0	157.2	15.3	67.9	73.3	85.3	115.0	134.6	147.4	13.5
1966	57.7	64.4	78.4	124.1	149.9	168.8	216.0	18.7	63.2	72.0	85.2	117.8	139.9	156.5	15.3	64.7	72.6	85.6	116.2	135.1	149.4	14.0
1968	54.6	65.7	78.0	124.9	154.4	176.5	231.3	19.4	61.5	73.5	83.4	119.9	145.0	164.9	16.1	64.1	71.9	87.2	119.9	143.6	156.7	15.0
1970	57.9	62.7	78.1	124.2	154.1	175.3	233.1	19.8	60.0	70.4	84.8	118.9	145.6	163.9	16.6	63.1	72.1	83.6	119.0	140.8	160.6	15.7
1973	56.7	63.2	78.0	126.8	157.2	178.3	235.5	19.7	63.5	68.2	83.3	121.5	146.4	165.6	16.6	65.9	71.4	85.1	121.2	145.6	167.9	16.4
1975	54.3	64.2	76.4	124.1	151.6	173.0	231.4	19.5	61.4	70.6	83.3	120.3	145.1	165.0	16.7	64.5	71.3	84.3	120.1	145.3	165.6	16.3
1977	55.2	64.7	80.1	125.3	154.8	176.8	234.9	19.5	60.4	69.8	83.3	119.6	145.5	165.3	16.8	63.6	70.8	83.4	117.9	146.3	164.4	16.4
1979	56.6	62.6	77.6	124.7	153.9	175.1	231.0	19.6	60.1	69.5	82.7	120.3	144.3	163.4	16.7	62.7	72.5	83.6	120.1	146.1	163.0	16.4
1981	56.7	63.9	78.6	127.7	155.5	176.7		19.7														
1983	56.3	62.4	78.4	128.6	156.1	176.3		19.8														
1985	55.2	63.4	78.4	127.0	156.1	174.2		19.8														
1987	54.9	63.5	77.6	126.0	154.4	172.9		19.8	59.6	68.9	82.0	120.6	139.9	160.5	16.2	58.7	72.7	85.9	122.6	148.7	169.6	17.2
1989	53.5	61.7	75.7	124.3	149.6	171.7		19.8	61.2	68.2	85.9	121.4	143.6	165.7	16.2	59.3	73.0	83.4	122.9	150.3	171.5	16.6
1989 CR	53.0	61.3	75.1	124.5	148.6	171.5		19.8	60.6	67.5	86.3	120.7	143.8	166.7	16.2	60.0	72.2	83.0	122.8	150.2	170.9	16.8

Coverage   Exc. those working in private sector, in agricultural cooperatives, members of armed forces, and employees of Communist Party

Industry   All

Age   All

Sex   All and M and F

Occupation   All

Definition   Gross inc. overtime and allowances but not annual bonuses

Intensity   FT

Period   Month of May until 1979; November from 1981

Limits   None

Source   Atkinson and Micklewright (AM), Tables CSE 1,2,3, and 5

Original source   Census of enterprises

Notes   (1) see A+M section S.6 on interpolation method; P99 obtained by Pareto interpolation of individual ranges; (2) same information, for fewer years, given by Večerník (1991), Table 3, slight differences in interpolation; (3) covers Czechoslovakia, except 1989 CR

Table D.6. Czech Republic: Census of enterprises (Rutkowski)

	A	B	C	D	E	Column F	G	H	I
	P05	P10	P25	P75	P90	P95	Gini	Share of bottom 20%	Share of top 20%
1987	54.5	62.8	77.6	125.4	153.2	172.8	19.8	%	30.5
1988								11.6	30.3
1989	53.0	61.3	75.1	124.5	148.7	171.5	19.8	11.6	30.1
1990								11.5	31.5
1991	55.2	63.2	78.3	129.7	163.5	189.2	21.0	11.3	32.8
1992	54.4	60.8	77.5	129.4	166.7	188.8	21.2	11.2	32.3
1993	51.4	57.0	73.8	136.8	182.4	219.2	25.7	9.9	35.7
1994		57.6			181.3		25.9		
1995		49.4			182.7		28.2		
1996		60.4			172.9		25.5		
1997		58.2			173.7		26.0		
1998		57.4			173.0		25.8		
1999		59.1			177.8		25.7		

Coverage	All
Industry	All
Age	All
Sex	All
Occupation	All
Definition	Gross (inc. monthly equivalent of bonuses and allowances)
Intensity	FT
Period	Monthly
Limits	None
Sources	Rutkowski 1996, Tables 3 and 4, Annex, and 2001 Table 1
Original source	Census of enterprises
Note	These figures relate to the Czech Republic

Bibliography

Adam, J, 1972, 'Wage differentials in Czechoslovakia', *Industrial Relations*, vol 11: 157–71.

Atkinson, A B and Micklewright, J, 1992, *Economic Transformation in Eastern Europe and the Distribution of Income*, Cambridge University Press, Cambridge.

Connor, W D, 1979, *Socialism, Politics and Equality: Hierarchy and Change in Eastern Europe and the USSR*, Columbia University Press, New York.

Federální Statisticky Úřad, 1990, *Časové řady základnich ukazateů statisticky práce*, FSU, Prague.

Flemming, J S and Micklewright. J, 1999, 'Income distribution, economic systems and transition', in A B Atkinson and F Bourguignon, editors, *Handbook of Income Distribution*, Elsevier, Amsterdam.

Myant, M, 1989, *The Czechoslovak Economy 1948–1988*, Cambridge University Press, Cambridge.

Phelps Brown, E H, 1977, *The Inequality of Pay*, Oxford University Press, Oxford.

Rutkowski, J, 1996, *Changes in the Wage Structure during Economic Transition in Central and Eastern Europe*, World Bank Technical Paper 340.

—— 2001, 'Earnings inequality in transition economies of Central Europe: Trends and patterns during the 1990s', World Bank SP Discussion Paper 0117.

Šik, O, 1966, 'Contribution to the analysis of our economic development' (in Czech), *Politická ekonomie*, no 1.

Teichova, A, 1988, *The Czechoslovak Economy 1918–1980*, Routledge, London.

Večernik, J, 1991, 'Earnings distribution in Czechoslovakia: Intertemporal changes and international comparison', *European Sociological Review*, vol 7: 237–52.

—— 1995, 'Changing earnings distribution in the Czech Republic: Survey evidence from 1988–1994', *Economics of Transition*, vol 3: 355–71.

—— 2001, 'Earnings disparities in the Czech Republic: Evidence of the past decade and cross-national comparison', William Davidson Institute Working Paper No 373, May 2001.

—— and Stepankova, P, 2003, 'Households, work and flexibility', Chapter 5 in *HWF Survey Report by Countries*, HWF Research Report No 2, Institute for Advanced Studies, Vienna.

E

Denmark

The impression is that the dispersion of the incomes of full time employees is relatively narrow compared to other countries and has become more equal in Denmark from 1986 to 1991, while there has been a trend towards greater inequality in a number of other countries (including the UK and the USA).

Madsen, 1999, page 17

E.1 Introduction

In 1920 North Schleswig was reunited with Denmark following a plebiscite. The Faroe Islands acquired home rule in 1948 and Greenland in 1979. In 1973 Denmark joined the European Communities.

Previous Coverage

Denmark is included in the following OECD compilations:

1993 (Table E.1): all workers 1980, 1981, 1985, to 1990, based on the tax registers, information supplied by Niels Westergård-Nielsen.

1996 (Table E.2): all workers 1980 to 1990, based on the tax registers, information supplied by Niels Westergård-Nielsen.

LMS (Table E.3): all workers 1980 to 1990, based on the tax registers, information supplied by Niels Westergård-Nielsen, essentially the same as OECD (1996), with additional percentiles.

Official Publications

Information about the distribution of earnings is published in the Official Yearbook (*Statistisk Årbog*), giving medians and quartiles for sectors (private and government).

E.2 Data Sources

The main sources of information in Denmark about the distribution of earnings are the income tax returns and surveys of employers, combined with information about government employment.

Tax Registers

The tax-related income statistics (*Skatteorienteret indkomststatistik*) are based on the Income Statistics Register, which has been constructed since 1970. Information before 1983 was based on the Tax Return Survey, derived from a sample of income tax returns. The data cover people who are aged 15 or over at the end of the year and who are liable to pay tax in the year concerned, mainly comprising people with a permanent address in Denmark. Income is gross taxable income before labour market contributions are deducted. Statistics Denmark note that 'the income data are generally of high quality inasmuch as they come from administrative registers' (website, 1 January 2006), but they go on to say that 'use of administrative registers for statistical purposes may cause problems concerning the statistics' since 'information and data of direct importance to the administrative authority are more reliable than information and data without that kind of importance' (website, 1 January 2006). This qualification may apply to the hours information. The results in Tables E.1 to E.3 are obtained by dividing annual earned income by annual hours worked; the results in Table E.5 relate to annual earned income. These results differ, as may be seen by comparing the tables for the years where they overlap.

Earnings Surveys

In collaboration with the employers' confederations, Statistics Denmark collects data about earnings from employers with more than ten full time employees. Enterprises in agriculture and fisheries are excluded. Employees covered are those on 'normal terms'. Apprentices and young people under the age of 18 are included. Information is collected on total earnings including pension contributions and income in the form of fringe benefits liable to tax. Information is collected on total hours worked, which are understood to mean the number of hours actually performed by an employee. (The above information is derived from the 'Declaration of Content' in the Statbank of Statistics Denmark.) The statistics in Table E.4 relate both to the private sector and to central government, where a similar conceptual framework is applied. The statistics are published in *Løn*, appearing in the series *Statistiske Efterretninger* (Statistical News).

Summary

Figures E.1 and E.2 combine the data available from the sources described above. The series based on employer surveys relate to the private sector.

E.3 What Happened?

The evidence for the distribution of earnings in Denmark relates only to the past 30 years. It is nonetheless of considerable interest, since the Danish labour market is often regarded as a model of labour market reform. It is the home of 'flexicurity'.

In his study of 'Denmark: Flexibility, security and labour market success', Madsen attributes the 'narrow dispersion and relative stability' of relative earnings in Denmark to (a) wage negotiations being largely concerned with relativities and

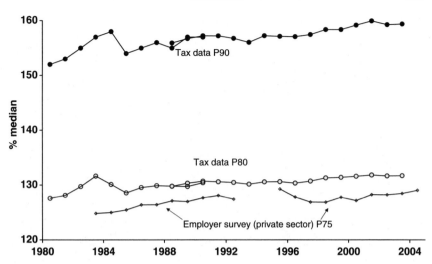

Figure E.1 DENMARK upper part of the distribution 1980–2004

Sources: Table E.2, column B; Table E.3, column C; Table E.4, column B; Table E.5, columns C and D.

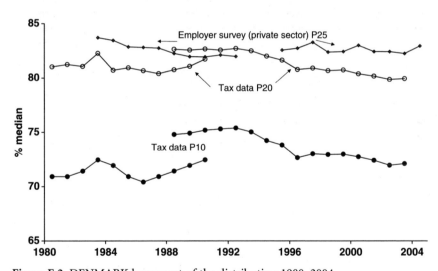

Figure E.2 DENMARK lower part of the distribution 1980–2004

Sources: Table E.2, column A; Table E.3, column B; Table E.4, column A; Table E.5, columns A and B.

(b) unemployment benefits setting a floor to wages. To what extent has this picture been disturbed by the labour market reform programme? From Figure E.2, we can see that the bottom decile and quintile tended downwards since 1992, but that the magnitude of the fall did not exceed 4 per cent in either case. This was preceded by a period when there was no overall trend in the lowest deciles. Indeed, the data from Table E.5 (not shown in Figure E.2) indicate a rise in the bottom decile relative to the median of 5.5 per cent between 1980 and 1988.

At the top, Figure E.1 shows a steady rise in the top decile and in the top quintile. This rise may lie behind the rise in the overall variance of logarithms of earnings reported for a sample of individuals in Denmark aged 30–56 by Diaz-Serrano, Hartog, and Nielsen (2003, Table 4). But the magnitude of the rise in Figure E.1 is small. Between 1980 and 2003, the top quintile rose by 3.2 per cent and the top decile by 4.9 per cent. It is therefore only the top decile that comes close to a registrable change according to the criteria adopted here. Indeed if we look at the top percentile (Table E.5), then we see a rise of 9.1 per cent from 1980 to 2003.

Summary

In Denmark, the direction of movement, at least in recent years, has been towards widening earnings dispersion, but the magnitude has been too small to register according to the criteria adopted in this study. It is only at the top, particularly the top percentile, that the widening is large enough to register.

Table E.1. Denmark: OECD (1993)

	Column	
	A	B
	P10	P90
1980	71	152
1981	71	153
1985	71	154
1986	70	155
1987	71	156
1988	71	155
1989	72	157
1990	73	157

Coverage	All
Industry	All
Age	All
Sex	All
Occupation	All
Definition	Gross annual wage income divided by annual hours worked
Intensity	All
Period	Hourly
Limits	Excludes persons with wage rates lower than 80% of minimum wage
Source	OECD (1993, Table 5.2)
Original source	Tax registers
Note	Supplied by N Westergård-Nielsen

Table E.2. Denmark: OECD (1996)

	Column	
	A	B
	P10	P90
1980	71	152
1981	71	153
1982	71	155
1983	72	157
1984	72	158
1985	71	154
1986	70	155
1987	71	156
1988	71	155
1989	72	157
1990	72	157

Coverage	All
Industry	All
Age	All
Sex	All
Occupation	All
Definition	Gross annual wage income divided by annual hours worked
Intensity	All
Period	Hourly
Limits	Excludes persons with wage rates lower than 80% of minimum wage
Original source	OECD (1996, Table 3.1)
Source	Tax registers
Note	Supplied by N Westergård-Nielsen

Table E.3. Denmark: OECD (LMS)

| | Column | | | |
	A	B	C	D
	P10	P20	P80	P90
1980	70.7	81.0	127.6	151.7
1981	70.3	81.3	128.1	153.1
1982	71.6	81.1	129.7	155.4
1983	72.2	82.3	131.6	157.0
1984	71.1	80.7	130.1	157.8
1985	71.4	81.0	128.6	153.6
1986	70.5	80.7	129.5	155.7
1987	71.1	80.4	129.9	155.7
1988	71.2	80.8	129.8	155.8
1989	72.1	81.1	129.7	155.9
1990	73.0	81.7	130.4	157.4

Coverage	All
Industry	All
Age	All
Sex	All
Occupation	All
Definition	Gross annual wage income divided by annual hours worked
Intensity	All
Period	Hourly
Limits	Excludes persons with wage rates lower than 80% of minimum wage
Source	Downloaded from OECD website December 2005
Original source	Tax registers
Notes	(1) Supplied by N Westergård-Nielsen; (2) Essentially the same as OECD (1996)

Table E.4. Denmark: Employer surveys

						Column						
	A	B	C	D	E	F	G	H	I	J	K	L
	Private Sector						Central government					
	All		Male		Female		All		Male		Female	
	P25	P75	P25	P75	P25	P75	P25	P75	P25	P75	P25	P75
1983	83.7	124.8	82.7	123.3	89.3	113.6						
1984	83.5	125.0	82.4	123.8	88.9	114.3						
1985	82.9	125.5	82.2	124.6	87.8	114.7						
1986	82.8	126.4	81.7	124.4	87.1	115.2						
1987	82.8	126.4	82.1	125.9	87.3	115.7						
1988	82.3	127.1	81.5	126.0	87.6	116.5						
1989	82.0	127.0	81.6	126.4	87.3	116.8						
1990	81.9	127.7	81.3	126.0	87.0	117.0						
1991	82.1	128.1	80.7	126.6	86.1	116.6						
1992	82.0	127.4	80.6	126.1	86.2	117.0						
1995	82.6	129.3	83.1	133.2	81.4	125.7						
1996	82.7	127.8	82.7	131.5	82.6	122.9	87.4	121.0	85.7	122.6	89.5	116.4
1997	83.3	126.9	83.3	129.8	82.5	122.5	87.3	119.6	86.3	121.0	89.1	115.9
1998	82.4	126.9	82.9	129.6	81.6	124.1	86.8	120.1	85.5	121.6	88.5	116.3
1999	82.4	127.8	82.7	131.8	82.3	123.4	86.2	122.2	85.0	122.2	87.6	119.3
2000	83.0	127.2	83.1	130.5	82.6	122.9	85.5	122.8	83.8	122.8	88.0	120.3
2001	82.4	128.2	82.8	131.5	81.8	124.2	85.2	123.4	83.4	123.2	87.8	121.6
2002	82.4	128.2	83.0	130.5	81.6	125.6	85.2	122.3	84.4	122.4	87.4	122.5
2003	82.3	128.5	82.8	130.9	81.4	125.4	85.0	122.9	84.0	122.5	87.0	122.7
2004	82.9	129.0	83.7	132.0	81.9	125.8	84.1	122.2	82.7	121.6	86.6	122.7

Coverage	All measured-day workers and fixed salary earners
Industry	See headings
Age	Exc. young people and trainees
Sex	See headings
Occupation	All
Definition	Gross, excluding over time and bonuses
Intensity	All
Period	Hourly
Limits	None
Source	Statistics Denmark, downloaded January 2006
Original source	Employer surveys
Note	(1) Break in 1995; (2) Information from 1995 published in Statistical Yearbook

Table E.5. Denmark: Tax register data

								Column						
A	B	C	D	E	F	G	H	I	J	K	L	M	N	O
		All					Male					Female		
P10	P20	P80	P90	P99	P10	P20	P80	P90	P99	P10	P20	P80	P90	P99
1980 70.9	81.3	130.8	156.7	268.4	74.6	81.6	131.2	156.4	273.4	68.8	80.8	119.7	134.5	198.6
1988 74.8	82.6	129.8	155.9	268.1	75.3	82.0	132.0	157.8	276.6	76.1	84.4	119.7	134.4	198.2
1989 74.9	82.6	130.3	156.7	270.9	74.9	81.6	132.6	159.7	280.6	76.9	84.7	120.1	135.0	203.2
1990 75.2	82.7	130.7	157.2	272.0	74.8	81.5	133.0	159.7	279.7	77.7	85.0	120.9	136.0	204.3
1991 75.3	82.6	130.6	157.2	267.9	74.8	81.7	133.1	160.3	277.6	77.9	85.1	121.3	136.4	203.6
1992 75.4	82.7	130.5	156.8	266.8	75.1	81.6	132.8	159.6	275.5	77.9	85.3	121.1	136.3	205.1
1993 75.0	82.5	130.2	156.1	264.4	74.9	81.4	132.6	159.2	272.7	77.2	84.8	122.1	136.8	204.8
1994 74.2	82.0	130.6	157.2	270.9	74.5	81.5	133.3	160.3	282.3	75.8	83.9	122.2	137.2	211.0
1995 73.8	81.6	130.6	157.1	275.0	74.2	81.4	133.1	159.8	288.4	75.9	83.8	122.7	138.1	211.1
1996 72.7	80.8	130.4	157.1	276.2	73.9	81.0	133.2	160.4	288.0	75.1	83.3	123.8	139.3	216.3
1997 73.0	80.9	130.7	157.5	278.5	73.9	81.1	133.3	161.0	291.0	75.8	83.4	123.5	139.5	215.2
1998 73.0	80.7	131.3	158.4	280.7	73.4	80.6	134.1	162.4	296.2	75.8	83.1	123.9	140.3	218.3
1999 73.0	80.7	131.4	158.4	282.7	73.8	81.1	134.0	162.2	298.9	75.9	83.2	123.8	141.0	220.0
2000 72.7	80.4	131.6	159.2	287.4	73.3	80.6	134.2	164.1	302.0	75.6	82.9	124.2	141.3	225.4
2001 72.4	80.2	131.8	159.9	291.4	72.9	80.3	134.5	164.4	308.5	75.4	82.7	124.8	142.7	229.7
2002 72.0	79.9	131.7	159.3	294.1	72.7	80.2	134.5	164.4	311.7	74.9	82.2	124.7	142.4	229.3
2003 72.1	80.0	131.7	159.4	292.8	72.7	80.3	134.5	164.3	311.5	74.9	82.1	124.8	143.1	230.5

Coverage	All
Industry	All
Age	All
Sex	See headings
Occupation	All
Definition	Gross annual wage income
Intensity	All
Period	Annual
Limits	None
Source	Tax registers
Note	Supplied by P Sørensen

Bibliography

Asplund, R, Bingley, P, and Westergård-Nielsen, N, 1998, 'Wage mobility in Denmark and Finland', in R Asplund, P J Sloane, and I Theodossiou, editors, *Low Pat and Earnings Mobility in Europe*, Edward Elgar, Cheltenham.

Bjerke, K, 1970, 'An analysis of the distribution of wages in Copenhagen in the second quarter of 1951', *Review of Income and Wealth*, series 16: 333–51.

Björklund, A, 2000, 'Going different ways: Labour market policy in Denmark and Sweden', in G Esping-Andersen and M Regini, editors, *Why Deregulate Labour Markets?*, Oxford University Press, Oxford.

Diaz-Serrano, L, Hartog, J, and Nielsen, H S, 2003, 'Compensating wage differentials for schooling risk in Denmark', IZA Discussion Paper 963.

Drescher, J, 1999, 'Income inequality decomposition by income source and by population subgroups: A theoretical overview and the empirical case of Denmark', LIS Working Paper 209.

Lausten, M, 1995, 'Inter-industry wage differentials in Denmark?', Centre for Labour Market and Social Research, Aarhus University.

Madsen, P K, 1999, 'Denmark: Flexibility, security and labour market success', ILO Employment and Training Paper 53, ILO, Geneva.

F

Finland

Finland does not stand out either as an economy of particularly high nor of particularly low dispersion. Furthermore, changes over time in individual pay differentials have been quite modest during the last two decades.

Vartiainen, 1998, published by the Prime Minister's Office

F.1 Introduction

The Parliament of Finland celebrated its centenary in 2006 and 2007. The republic ceded a substantial amount of territory to the Soviet Union in the Treaty of 1940 and subsequent treaties after the Second World War. Finland joined the European Union in 1995 and adopted the euro in 2002.

Previous Coverage

Lydall (1968) included one table for Finland giving estimates only for 1960, based on income tax data, and relating to total income, not earnings.

Finland was not included in the OECD (1993) compilation. It is covered in:

1996 (Table F.1), which covers all workers, and men and women separately, for 1980, 1983, and 1986 to 1994, based on the *Income Distribution Survey*.

LMS (Table F.2) dataset covers all workers, and men and women separately, for 1977, 1980, 1983, and 1986 to 1999, based on the *Income Distribution Survey*.

Official Publications

No information on the distribution of earnings is published in the Statistical Yearbook.

F.2 Data Sources

As in other Nordic countries, the basic sources of earnings data are administrative records, derived from the operation of the income tax, linked in the case of Finland to the Income Distribution Survey and to the Census of Population, and surveys of employers. Since 1995, there is the Structure of Earnings Survey, formed by combining data collected by employer organizations from their members with those from wage and salary inquiries by Statistics Finland.

Income Distribution Survey (IDS)

According to Uusitalo, 'the best source of data on the Finnish wage structure is the Income Distribution Survey' (2002, page 70). The survey dates from 1977 and has been carried out annually, apart from 1981 and 1985. It combines an interview survey of households with data on earnings (and other income) taken from administrative records. The survey has a rotating panel design, whereby each household is interviewed in two consecutive years. There is a degree of non-response (around 20 per cent) and the results are re-weighted to allow for non-response. The sample size in 1977 was some 47,000 households and 100,000 individuals.

The IDS is used by the OECD (1996) and OECD (LMS). The data for 1977 to 1995 have been used by Uusitalo (2002).

Census of Population

Starting in 1970,[11] Statistics Finland has compiled a data file based on the quinquennial population censuses linked to the tax register data on income, including separate information on earnings. From 1970, the use of register data increased continuously, and from 1990 the general population census was fully replaced by register-based information.

The census data file contains information on all those living in Finland in the census year, with their individual characteristics (such as education and occupation), their earnings, and the number of months worked full time and part time. Earnings equal taxable wage income including fringe benefits and fees. Since the earnings data are taken from the records of the tax authorities, they 'are considered to be of high quality' (Eriksson and Jäntti, 1997, page 1765). The data are, however, top-coded, Statistics Finland imputing the average earnings to all observations above the top-code cut-off (approximately the top percentile). Moreover, the data for 1970 in fact relate to incomes in 1971, whereas other variables relate to 1970, so that some people with relevant earnings in 1971 are omitted. There is also no information for this year on months worked, so that this year is 'somewhat problematic' (Eriksson and Jäntti, 1997, page 1766). The sample sizes ranged from around 180,000 in 1970 to around 200,000 in 1990.

The census data for 1971, 1975, 1980, 1985, and 1990 are analysed by Eriksson and Jäntti (1997), who include all persons who were wage earners and aged between 25 and 64 years. They exclude all those earning less than 100 Finnish marks (in 1990 prices).

Structure of Earnings Surveys

The Structure of Earnings Survey, carried out since 1995, is formed by combining data collected by employer organizations from their members with those from wage and salary inquiries by Statistics Finland. The survey collects information on hourly,

---

[11] 'It has not been possible to combine data on income with the data of earlier population censuses' (Statistics Finland, 1975, page 28).

monthly, and annual earnings of wage and salary earners, classified by sector, industry, occupation, education, gender, type of employment relationship, form of remuneration, and region. (Information from the website of Statistics Finland, 'Description of Statistics'.) The information on individual earnings from the Confederation of Finnish Industry and Employers (TT) is used in the study by Meyersson-Milgrom, Petersen, and Asplund (2002).

The findings from the Structure of Earnings Survey from 1995 to 2004 are summarized in Table F.4.

Comparison of Sources

As far as the Income Distribution Survey and the Census are concerned, the source in both cases is the same: the tax registers. The differences lie in the choice of sample. From Figure F.2, it appears that the bottom decile is lower in the sample drawn from the population census file. There is, however, little difference at the top: the top decile in 1990 was 169.7 per cent of the median in the census data of Eriksson and Jäntti (1997), compared with 170.0 per cent in the IDS data of the OECD.

Comparisons have also been made of the tax register data with those collected in household surveys. In the first wave of the European Community Household Panel in Finland in 1996, data on earnings were collected by interview, and these reported earnings have been compared with register data by Nordberg, Pentitilä, and Sandström (2001). They found that the greatest difference was in the number of cases of zero earnings. A much larger proportion had earnings but reported no earnings in the interview than vice versa. A third of the reported zeroes in the interview responses were 'false' according to the register data. This affected the lower decile but had relatively little impact on the median or upper percentiles. As a result, the top decile was 174.2 per cent of the median in the interview data, compared with 170.9 per cent in the register data. In contrast the bottom decile was 18.8 per cent in the interview data, compared with 25.6 per cent in the register data. Where earnings are reported, they concluded that 'the answers are quite reliable suffering only a modest level of net underreporting for low and medium income levels' (2001, page 6).

Summary

The available information about the distribution of earnings in Finland is shown in Figures F.1 and F.2, which combine Census of Population, Income Distribution Survey data, and results from the Structure of Earnings Survey from 1995.

F.3 What Happened?

The period of the 1970s and early 1980s was one of narrowing earnings differentials in Finland: 'earnings inequality dropped dramatically between 1971 and 1975, and continued to decrease until 1985' (Eriksson and Jäntti, 1997, page 1763). The top decile fell by 18 per cent between 1971 and 1981, which is a significant fall by the criteria adopted here, and represented some 3 percentage points per year. The rise in the bottom decile from 1971 to 1985 was as much as 29 per cent, qualifying it as large.

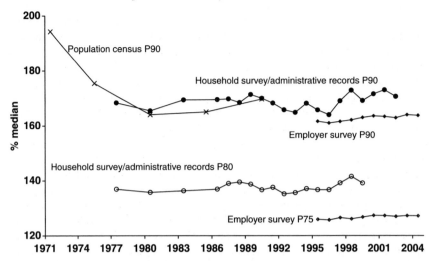

Figure F.1 FINLAND upper part of the distribution 1971–2004

Sources: Table F.2, columns C and D; Table F.3, column B; Table F.4, columns C and D.

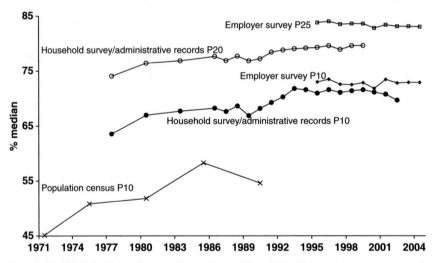

Figure F.2 FINLAND lower part of the distribution 1971–2004

Sources: Table F.2, columns A and B; Table F.3, column A; Table F.4, columns A and B.

Although we have noted that the estimates for 1970 may be less reliable, the rise in the bottom decile from 1975 to 1985 is still 15 per cent. Moreover, the narrowing at the bottom is picked up in the Income Distribution Survey (IDS) data starting in 1977: the increase between then and 1993 being 13 per cent.

The continuing rise in the bottom decile observed in the IDS series in Figure F.2 may appear to conflict with the conclusion of Eriksson and Jäntti from the Census of Population data that 'from 1985 to 1990 there was a substantial increase in the inequality of earnings, comparable in magnitude to that found in the U.K. and the U.S.' (1997, page 1763). The two sources do suggest a slightly different picture. It is possible that there was a reversal in the late 1980s. According to Meyersson-Milgrom, Petersen, and Asplund, 'the pay range seems to have widened somewhat during the late 1980s and narrowed again during the recession of the early 1990s' (2002, page 7). But the magnitude was not sufficient to register according to the criteria adopted here. As is noted by Santamäki-Vuori and Parviainen, 'as to developments since the early 1980s, the changes in individual wage dispersion have been moderate' (1996, page 43). They go on to draw attention to the impact of lower employment (employment in Finland fell by around a fifth between 1989 and the early 1990s). They note that 46 per cent of the women who became unemployed in 1992 had been in the lowest quintile of the earnings distribution in 1991 and that only 4 per cent had been in the highest quintile.

The overall impression of the past two decades is one of stability. The top decile in 1986 was 169.5 per cent of the median; in 2002 it was 170.6 per cent. The bottom decile was 68.2 per cent in 1986 and 69.7 per cent in 2002. If the period is taken as a whole, the decile ratio did not move enough to register.

Summary

There was a large, indeed significant, fall in earnings dispersion in Finland from the 1970s to the mid-1980s, after which the distribution remained stable in the sense that the observed changes were not large enough to register.

Table F.1. Finland: OECD (1996)

			Column			
	A	B	C	D	E	F
	All		Male		Female	
	P10	P90	P10	P90	P10	P90
1980	67	165	68	167	71	147
1983	68	169	68	170	72	149
1986	68	170	67	173	71	151
1987	68	170	66	169	71	155
1988	68	168	66	169	73	157
1989	67	171	66	173	72	157
1990	68	170	67	172	73	154
1991	69	168	68	171	73	152
1992	70	166	69	170	74	150
1993	72	165	69	165	77	150
1994	71	170	68	173	77	152

Coverage	All
Industry	All
Age	All
Sex	See headings
Occupation	All
Definition	Gross
Intensity	FT+FY
Period	Annual
Limits	None
Source	OECD (1996, Table 3.1)
Original source	*Income Distribution Survey*
Note	Deciles supplied by Statistics Finland

Table F.2. Finland: OECD (LMS)

						Column					
A	B	C	D	E	F	G	H	I	J	K	L
		All				Male				Female	
P10	P20	P80	P90	P10	P20	P80	P90	P10	P20	P80	P90
1977 63.5	74.1	136.9	168.4	66.8	77.8	136.4	169.0	68.3	78.2	128.3	150.4
1980 67.0	76.4	135.8	165.5	68.4	78.0	134.4	166.5	71.4	81.0	126.3	146.8
1983 67.7	76.9	136.3	169.4	67.6	78.2	136.8	169.7	72.2	81.8	126.5	149.1
1986 68.2	77.7	136.9	169.5	66.5	77.3	137.6	172.6	71.3	81.1	127.9	150.6
1987 67.6	76.9	139.0	169.8	66.3	76.4	139.2	169.4	71.2	81.5	130.1	155.5
1988 68.6	77.7	139.5	168.4	66.2	76.4	137.6	169.0	73.3	82.3	129.7	156.9
1989 66.9	76.9	138.7	171.4	66.2	76.7	138.0	173.1	72.3	81.2	129.6	157.3
1990 68.2	77.2	136.7	170.0	67.1	76.6	138.1	172.3	72.7	81.4	129.4	153.8
1991 69.3	78.4	137.6	168.3	68.1	77.7	138.5	170.8	73.1	81.6	129.7	151.9
1992 70.3	78.8	135.2	165.8	69.2	77.7	135.3	170.0	73.3	81.4	128.4	150.5
1993 71.8	79.0	135.6	164.8	69.3	77.4	135.5	165.1	76.7	83.8	128.5	150.2
1994 71.6	79.2	137.1	168.2	68.4	76.7	137.4	172.4	77.1	83.9	127.9	149.9
1995 70.9	79.3	136.7	165.7	68.8	76.9	135.6	166.2	75.6	83.4	129.0	152.9
1996 71.6	79.6	136.7	164.0	69.0	77.2	134.9	161.6	76.0	83.6	130.6	153.3
1997 71.1	78.9	139.2	169.0	67.4	75.8	137.8	168.7	76.1	83.1	130.0	155.6
1998 71.4	79.6	141.5	172.9	67.8	76.7	141.0	172.2	74.9	83.3	127.7	152.4
1999 71.6	79.6	139.1	169.1	68.0	78.0	137.3	167.8	77.7	84.7	131.2	157.4
2000 71.1			171.5								
2001 70.7			173.0								
2002 69.7			170.6								

Coverage	All
Industry	All
Age	All
Sex	See headings
Occupation	All
Definition	Gross
Intensity	FT FY
Period	Annual
Limits	None
Source	Downloaded from OECD website December 2005; 2000–2 supplied by OECD
Original source	*Income Distribution Survey*
Note	Deciles supplied by Statistics Finland

Table F.3. Finland: Population census

	A	B	C	D	E	F
			Column			
	All		Male		Female	
	P10	P90	P10	P90	P10	P90
1971	45.1	194.3	45.8	190.4	47.4	176.8
1975	50.8	175.4	55.5	168.2	50.0	156.2
1980	51.8	164.0	56.2	161.9	51.6	147.6
1985	58.3	165.0	63.5	164.2	55.5	148.9
1990	54.6	169.7	61.4	168.0	51.5	154.0

Coverage	All
Industry	All
Age	25–64
Sex	See headings
Occupation	All
Definition	Gross wage and salaries from all sources inc. own work income
Intensity	All
Period	Annual
Limits	None
Source	Eriksson and Jäntti, 1997, Table 2
Original source	Quinquennial population census

Table F.4. Finland: Structure of Earnings Survey

						Column					
A	B	C	D	E	F	G	H	I	J	K	L
		All				Male				Female	
P10	P25	P75	P90	P10	P25	P75	P90	P10	P25	P75	P90
1995	73.0	83.8	125.9	161.6	71.5	82.8	126.3	162.1	76.5	87.0	119.8	149.4
1996	73.5	84.0	125.7	161.0	72.0	83.0	126.6	162.7	76.7	87.0	120.0	149.5
1997	72.5	83.5	126.5	161.5	70.6	82.3	126.5	161.7	76.2	86.8	120.2	150.5
1998	72.5	83.6	126.1	162.1	70.4	81.9	126.3	162.6	76.1	86.8	120.3	150.6
1999	72.8	83.6	126.7	163.0	71.0	82.3	126.6	162.8	76.4	86.8	120.5	151.9
2000	71.8	82.8	127.3	163.6	69.7	81.6	126.8	163.1	75.8	86.4	121.4	153.2
2001	73.4	83.4	127.2	163.3	70.6	81.8	127.0	163.2	77.8	87.1	120.9	153.1
2002	72.8	83.1	127.0	162.9	70.3	81.7	126.4	162.4	77.3	86.8	121.0	153.2
2003	72.9	83.1	127.2	164.0	70.0	81.7	127.2	164.2	77.3	86.8	121.1	153.8
2004	72.9	83.0	127.2	163.7	70.1	81.8	127.0	164.5	77.3	86.7	121.2	153.8

Coverage	All
Industry	All
Age	All
Sex	See Headings
Occupation	All
Definition	Gross wages and salaries
Intensity	All
Period	Monthly
Limits	None
Source	Statistics Finland
Original source	Employer surveys and earnings inquiries

Bibliography

Böckerman, P, Laaksonen, S, and Vainiomäki, J (2006), 'Micro-level evidence on wage rigidities in Finland', Labour Institute for Economic Research Discussion Paper 219, Helsinki.

Eriksson, T and Jäntti, M, 1997, 'The distribution of earnings in Finland 1971–1990', *European Economic Review*, vol 41: 1736–79.

Meyersson-Milgrom, E M, Petersen, T, and Asplund, R, 2002, 'Pay, risk, and productivity. The case of Finland, 1980–1996', *Finnish Economic Papers*, vol 15: 3–23.

Nordberg, L, Penttilä, I, and Sandström, S, 2001, 'Earnings data from surveys and registers. Experiences from the Finnish Community Household Panel Survey in 1996', Intermediate Workshop of CHINTEX, Helsinki, November 2001.

Santamäki-Vuori, T and Parviainen, S, 1996, *The Labour Market in Finland*, ECOTEC Research and Consulting, Helsinki.

Statistics Finland, 1975, *Population Census 1970*, Volume XIII, Central Statistical Office of Finland, Helsinki.

Uusitalo, R, 1998, 'Trends in between- and within-group earnings inequality in Finland', Research Institute of the Finnish Economy, Discussion Paper 611.

—— 2002, 'Changes in the Finnish wage structure: Will demand and supply do?', *Scandinavian Journal of Economics*, vol 104: 69–85.

Vainiomäki, J and Laaksonen, S, 1995, 'Inter-industry wage differentials in Finland: Evidence from longitudinal census data for 1975–85', *Labour Economics*, vol 2: 161–73.

Vartiainen, J, 1998, *The Labour Market in Finland: Institutions and Outcomes*, Prime Minister's Office, Publications Series 1998/2, Helsinki.

G

France

Over the long period, the evolution of the dispersion of earnings in France may perhaps be separated schematically into two periods: a first going from the beginning of the 1960s to around the mid-1980s, when one saw a narrowing of earnings dispersion; a second, which started in the middle of the 1980s, when one observes an inverse movement, but to a relatively weak extent.

Bontout et al, 2001, page 301, my translation

G.1 Introduction

The chapter refers to Metropolitan France. In 1935, a plebiscite led to the Saarland, which had been part of France since 1918, joining Germany. Otherwise, the country has had the same geographical boundaries throughout the period. France adopted the euro in 2002.

Previous Coverage

Lydall (1968) contains 15 tables for France, based on the employer returns *Déclarations Annuelles des Données Sociales (DADS)*. In addition, he includes a table with earnings data for the tobacco industry and railways for 1891–5, from March (1898).

France is covered by all the OECD compilations:

1993 (Table G.1): all workers, and men and women separately for various years 1973 to 1988, from the DADS.

1996 (Table G.2): all workers 1979–95, and men and women separately for 1979 to 1994, from the DADS.

LMS (Table G.3): all workers for all years 1950 to 1998 (except 1953 and 1958—and 1981, 1983, and 1990—see below), and men and women separately for 1950, 1955, 1960, 1965, 1970, and 1975–98, from the DADS.

Official Publications

Information on the distribution of earnings, based on the DADS, is published in recent editions of the Statistical Yearbook (*Annuaire Statistique*). The French statistical office (INSEE) has published a number of long time series of earnings distribution data, based on the DADS, entitled *Séries Longues sur les Salaires* in the series INSEE Résultats (see Bibliography).

G.2 Data Sources

France is unusual in having a unified source of earnings data covering nearly the entire post-war period, based on administrative records supplied by employers (the DADS), which builds on an earlier wage tax source going back to 1919. This and other sources are described below. It should be noted at the outset that the French earnings data relate to earnings net of employee social security contributions (but before deduction of income tax).[12]

Déclarations Annuelles des Données Sociales (DADS)

The principal source of earnings data in France are the declarations (formerly known as 24–60, then DAS, and now as DADS) made by employers annually to the fiscal and social administrations covering the earnings paid to individual employees. The information supplied covers function exercised, level of professional qualification, dates at which earnings started and stopped, intensity of work (full time, part time, etc.), (since 1994) hours paid, the amount of earnings before and after deduction of social security contributions, valuation for tax purposes of benefits in kind, and expenses reimbursed. A first tabulation was published in 1947; the series then became annual in 1950, with certain gaps as described below. Since 1993, the figures have been based on a complete analysis of these returns; prior to 1993 a sample of approximately 1 in 25 was retained for purposes of statistical analysis.

The existence of a unified database on earnings based on the DADS data owes its origins to the work of Baudelot and Lebeaupin, 'Les salaires de 1950 à 1975' (1979), and the data have proved a valuable resource. Their advantages are well described by Friez and Julhès (1998, page 17). Submission of the declaration is compulsory, and the fiscal authorities ensure a response near to 100 per cent. There are few incentives to misstate earnings. The employee would resist any overstatement, since he would be liable for tax on income not received, and the employer would not understate, since this would increase taxable profits. At the same time, the field of coverage is not complete. The DADS does not cover agricultural workers, agents de l'Etat et des collectivités territoriales, and persons employed in domestic work. In the 1990s this meant excluding some 20 per cent of the annual average number of employees. The DADS analysis further excludes all persons working less than 80 per cent of the normal working hours. This reduces the total by a further 20 per cent, so that the results cover around two-thirds of all employees: 12.1 million out of 19.5 million in 1995 (Friez and Julhès, 1998, page 21).

---

[12] For a recent discussion of the difference between gross and net, see Bontout et al (2001). For 1990, their analysis by centiles shows that the proportion paid by the worker was relatively constant at around 20 per cent of gross salary, tailing off slightly above P80.

There are questions surrounding the degree of comparability over time. According to Casaccia and Seroussi, 'the constitution of a homogeneous series is only possible from the beginning of the 1960s' (2000, page 5, my translation). In their Graphique 2, they show 1951–2, separately, 1954 on its own, and then 1956–7, followed by a continuous series from 1959. Moreover, the notes indicate that 'before 1967 the reconstitution of the deciles is fragile' and 'from 1993 a break in the method of processing of the DADS data means that the degree of continuity in the series is open to question' (2000, page 8). Friez and Julhès (1998, pages 17 and 18) distinguish several periods:

- 1950–61, early days of data collection, dominated by restrictions imposed on the field of coverage by virtue of the burden on employers: the Paris region was excluded in 1953 (which means that a third of employees, many of them among the better-paid, were excluded in that year; this year is left out of the LMS data), and from 1955 to 1962 only permanent employees were taken into account for the private sector. No tabulation was published for 1958, which is missing from the LMS database.

- 1962–7, introduction of computer processing allowed the coverage to be extended to all full time employees (and not just permanent employees), and to cover public industrial enterprises and agri-industry.

- 1967–89, a new method of sampling was introduced in 1964, taking employees born in October of even years (approximately 1 in 25), which allowed the processing to combine different declarations for the same employee from the same employer; producing estimates per job; figures were calculated on both bases for 1967 and 1968 to assess the effect (found to be a 'light distortion' (my translation)).

- 1990–2 saw the preparation for a new processing system, and the changes over time need to be treated with caution Friez and Julhès (1998, page 18).

- In 1993 a new processing system was introduced that no longer relied on a sample but covered all jobs, which totalled more than 30 million; coverage was extended to posts, other than fonctionnaires, in La Poste and France Télécom; the results for 1993 have an experimental character which means that they are not comparable with those for 1992 nor 1994. One of the aims of the new processing system was to eliminate cases of low pay that arose on account of part year working or the like, which may have led to a rise in the bottom decile (see Piketty, 2001, page 666, n1).

Finally, we should note that the data for 1981, 1983, and 1990 that appear in the LMS database are estimates by INSEE, not based on the employer declarations for those years, which were not analysed on account of the workload arising from the censuses of 1982 and 1990 (Piketty, 2001, page 665). Moreover, the figures for 1963 were affected by a programming error, which was corrected at the level of the published tables, but which affects a certain number of the unpublished tables used to construct the historical series (Friez and Julhès, 1998, page 19).

In view of these considerations, the DADS-based series shown in Figures G.1 and G.2 exclude the observations for 1963, 1981, 1983, 1990, and 1993. Breaks are shown from 1964, and from 1994, so that the series consists of three segments.

Use of the data for the years 1955 to 1962 has to take account of the restriction of coverage to permanent employees. CERC (1976, page 51) notes that use of this series to study the evolution of wage dispersion between 1955 and 1963 led to significantly different results from those obtained using the series for all full time workers and comparing 1954 with 1963. The consequences have been examined in detail by Piketty (2001), using the tabulations for 1963 given on both bases. I have used in Table G.5 his corrected figures for 1955 to 1957 and 1959 to 1962 (but not 1954). I have also adopted his correction to the median and top decile for 1950, to allow for the exclusion of salaries below a certain level. Finally, I have used his estimate of the top decile in 1947 and assumed a median of 97,500 francs (49.1 per cent had earnings in excess of 100,000).

Employer Wage Tax

Preceding the DADS series was information from the employer wage tax. The impôt cédulaire was introduced in 1914, and from 1919 the fiscal administration began publishing the distribution of earnings by ranges. As pointed out by Piketty (2001, page 31, n2), these returns appeared to have been entirely neglected. The coverage is limited to those above the tax threshold: for example 7.4 per cent of total employees in 1924, rising to 37.1 per cent in 1938 (Piketty, 2001, Tableau D-3). But Piketty suggests that, for the estimation of the upper part of the earnings distribution, the inter-war tabulations have certain advantages compared with the post-war DADS tabulations, including the fact that data are available for all years.

Piketty uses the wage tax data to make estimates of the top part of the distribution from 1919 to 1938. The results, reproduced here in Table G.4, considerably extend the historical scope.

Enquête Emploi (EE)

The French Labour Force Survey *Enquête Emploi* (EE) is a rotating panel of households, containing at any point some 75,000 households and 150,000 individuals aged 15 or more. Households are interviewed three times in March of successive years, a third of the sample being replaced each year. Households are asked to report their net salary in that month. Results for the distribution of earnings from the EE from 1990 to 1998 are given by Piketty (2001, page 676). He notes that there is an understatement of the very top salaries in the EE and for this reason uses the top decile, rather than the shares of total earnings. These are reproduced in Table G.7, together with data for earlier years from the published reports.

Formation et Qualifications Professionelles

Surveys of education and professional qualifications have been undertaken by INSEE for 1970, 1977, 1985, and 1993. They contain information on earnings, education, occupation, and industry. Respondents are asked to report their exact payroll earnings in the year prior to the survey and the number of months of work corresponding to those earnings, with a breakdown into months of full time and part time work. The

1993 survey was based on a sample of 18,000 people aged between 20 and 65; the previous three surveys had samples of approximately 45,000. The surveys have been brought together by Goux and Maurin (2000). See also Wasmer (2001).

Comparison of Data Sources

The DADS and the Enquête Emploi (EE) are compared in Synthèses Number 26 (1999, page 73), it being stressed that the differences, including in the underlying concepts, are numerous. They include:

- The EE refers to individuals, whereas the DADS relates to jobs, so that a person holding two part time jobs appears twice in the DADS but once (for their principal activity in March) in the EE.

- The statement of work intensity (full time, part time) is made by the respondent in the EE, but based on administrative rules in the processing of the DADS.

- Salaries relate to the month in the EE, but are annual in the DADS.

- In the DADS the earnings paid, and the hours worked, correspond to the same period; in the EE, the earnings are those for the last month regularly paid (typically February), whereas the hours worked are those stated as 'normal'. This has consequences for the calculation of hourly earnings.[13] Particular difficulties arise with part time workers.

It is not therefore surprising that the two sources can give different results. Bontout et al note that 'recent research has cast light on the difficulties linked to using the declared earnings in the EE: understatement, due to a lack of knowledge about premia, uncertainty about the concepts (in particular, about the net salary), strong rounding effects as well as a sometimes imprecise statement of the hours of work' (2001, page 302, my translation). This creates a presumption in favour of using the administrative data for our purposes here, but we have to remember that some of the difference may be due to differences in definition, or indeed to shortcomings of the DADS series. The EE results used in Figures G.1 and G.2 are limited to full time workers.

Summary

The series for the distribution of earnings in France shown in Figures G.1 and G.2 cover an impressive period: 85 years. They are a rich source. At the same time, they are pieced together from sources that have evolved and where different methods have been applied at different dates.

---

[13] For example, for full time workers in 1997 the estimated percentage earning less than 1.33 times the minimum wage (SMIC) is close on a monthly basis (28.1 per cent in EE, compared with 27.2 per cent in DADS), but much less close on an hourly basis: 31.1 per cent in the EE, compared with 26.0 per cent in DADS (Synthèses, 1999, page 74).

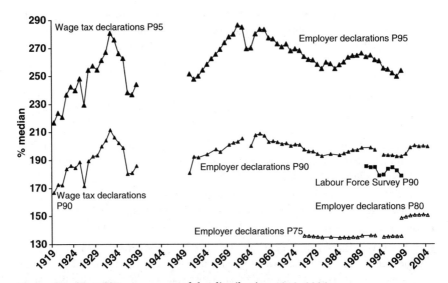

Figure G.1 FRANCE upper part of the distribution 1919–2004

Sources: Table G.3, columns C and D; Table G.4, columns A and B; Table G.5, column A; Table G.6, columns C and D; Table G.7, column I.

Figure G.2 FRANCE lower part of the distribution 1919–2004

Sources: Table G.3, columns A and B; Table G.6, columns A and B; Table G.7, columns F and G.

G.3 What Happened?

One of the virtues of the data for France is that they allow us to consider what happened during the inter-war period, albeit only in the upper part of the distribution. The changes at the top were quite dramatic. The top decile is shown as rising, relative to the median, by over a quarter between 1919 and 1932. Nor was this simply an after-war correction. The rise continued steadily over the 1920s. Piketty (2003) attributes the rise in the early 1930s to the deflationary macroeconomic policy pursued, with higher-paid workers benefiting from nominal wage rigidity. This came sharply to an end in 1936 with the arrival of the Front Populaire.[14] In 1938 the top decile was 12 per cent below its 1932 value, and close to its value in the early 1920s.

Turning now to the post-war period, we can examine both the upper and the lower parts of the distribution. The evolution of earnings dispersion in France up to the late 1980s was summarized by CERC in terms of three phases: 'from 1950 to 1966 one sees, despite certain irregularities, a tendency for dispersion to increase. [The period 1966–85] saw, on the contrary, a significant and regular reduction in inequality, at a stronger rate than the previous rise. Finally, since 1985, one sees a return to widening' (1990, page 1, my translation). The quotation from Bontout et al (2001) at the beginning of the chapter says much the same.

This pattern is clearly illustrated in Figures G.1 and G.2, although it needs to be nuanced. For the overall series, there is little downward trend for the bottom decile in the 1950s (we have to take account of the discontinuities). The widening is much clearer at the top, with both the top decile and the top vintile (P95) increasing. The top decile rose by 6.7 per cent between 1951 and 1962, although interestingly the *share* of the top 10 per cent in 1962 was little higher than in 1951. Since the share reflects what was happening above the top vintile, this points to a 'tilt' at the very top of the distribution.

The post-1968 narrowing is very evident. In two years, 1967 to 1969, the bottom decile jumped 13 per cent, reflecting a changed policy towards the minimum wage. The bottom decile then fell back somewhat, but in 1972 began a steady upward trend that took it to a value 15 per cent higher by 1985. Over the same period, the top decile fell, but by less than 5 per cent. The effect was more marked for the top vintile, which fell overall by 8 per cent between 1967 and 1985. But the main story is what happened at the bottom.

The return to widening of the earnings distribution post-1985 was not large enough to register: neither the top nor the bottom decile showed a change in excess of 5 per cent. In contrast, the bottom decile has risen by some 7 per cent since 1999.

---

[14] Consumer prices fell by about a third in France between 1930 and 1935; by 1937 they had returned to their previous level (Pikety, 2001, Tableau F-1, BMS series).

Summary

The history of the earnings distribution in France since the mid-1980s is one of broad stability and of a recent rise in the bottom decile—standing in contrast to a number of other countries. The previous 65 years were characterized less by stability and more by episodes of change. These episodes have tended to touch differently the upper and lower parts of the distribution. In the inter-war period, we have only evidence for the upper part, but there appears to have been a rise in the top percentiles followed by a fall with the arrival of the Front Populaire. In the Golden Age of the 1950s and early 1960s, earnings dispersion increased on account of the larger increases at the top of the distribution. The gap was narrowed dramatically after the events of May 1968, with the bottom decile jumping upwards, and then from 1972 beginning a period of steady increase until the mid-1980s.

Table G.1. France: OECD (1993)

			Column			
	A	B	C	D	E	F
	All		Male		Female	
	P10	P90	P10	P90	P10	P90
1973	60	197	62	200	65	172
1975	61	198	61	209	62	177
1979	63	193	62	205	65	169
1980	62	191	63	205	64	170
1985	64	193	64	211	66	170
1986	64	194	64	213	64	170
1987	64	195	63	213	63	172
1988	65	193				

Coverage	Excludes those working less than 80% of normal working hours
Industry	Excludes agriculture and general government workers
Age	All
Sex	See headings
Occupation	All
Definition	Net of employee social security contributions (but before deducting income tax)
Intensity	FT, adjusted for annual hours worked to represent full year equivalent earnings
Period	See above
Limits	None
Source	OECD (1993, Table 5.2)
Original source	Déclarations Annuelles des Données Sociales (DADS)
Note	Not including the provisional figures projected using partial indicators

Table G.2. France: OECD (1996)

			Column			
	A	B	C	D	E	F
	All		Male		Female	
	P10	P90	P10	P90	P10	P90
1979	60	194	60	204	63	170
1980	59	193	60	203	62	169
1981	60	193	61	205	61	169
1982	61	194	61	206	61	169
1983	62	194	62	206	63	168
1984	63	193	62	206	64	167
1985	63	195	62	208	64	168
1986	62	196	62	210	62	168
1987	62	197	62	211	62	169
1988	61	197	62	212	61	168
1989	61	199	61	214	61	171
1990	61	199	62	213	60	172
1991	61	199	62	213	60	173
1992	61	197	62	212	59	174
1993	61	199	62	213	59	173
1994	61	199	62	213	58	172

Coverage   Excludes those working less than 80% of normal working hours
Industry   Excludes agriculture and general government workers
Age   All
Sex   See headings
Occupation   All
Definition   Net of employee social security contributions (but before deducting income tax)
Intensity   FT, adjusted for annual hours worked to represent full year equivalent earnings
Period   See above
Limits   None
Source   OECD (1996, Table 3.1)
Original source   Déclarations Annuelles des Données Sociales (DADS)

Table G.3. France: OECD (LMS)

							Column					
	A	B	C	D	E	F	G	H	I	J	K	L
			All				Male				Female	
	P10	P25	P75	P90	P10	P25	P75	P90	P10	P25	P75	P90
1950	50.9			180.8	65.9			185.4				161.9
1951	56.6			192.5								
1952	52.6			191.9								
1954	55.9			194.1								
1955	62.0				58.8				66.9			
1956	55.2			197.7								
1957	52.1			195.8								
1959	54.5			200.9								
1960	53.0			202.3	54.3			205.6	60.8			183.5
1961	53.8			203.1								
1962	52.7			205.4								
1963	50.3			200.0								
1964	50.6			200.0								
1965	50.5			207.7	52.9			208.4	55.2			187.4
1966	50.0			208.8								
1967	50.8			207.3								
1968	53.3			202.8								
1969	57.6			203.4								
1970	55.3			202.7	56.4			209.1	60.8			184.2
1971	54.5			201.4								
1972	54.4			201.9								
1973	55.6			200.0								
1974	57.6			201.0								
1975	57.4			200.7	57.9			207.7	59.8			178.1
1976	58.5	75.9	135.8	197.3	59.4	77.1	137.4	206.1	61.8	79.0	132.8	174.2
1977	58.6	76.1	135.6	196.1	59.4	77.1	137.3	205.5	61.6	78.8	132.0	172.5
1978	59.4	76.6	135.4	196.0	60.1	77.5	137.7	205.9	62.8	79.0	131.2	171.0
1979	59.8	76.7	135.0	194.2	60.2	77.3	137.3	204.4	62.7	78.6	131.1	169.9
1980	59.3	76.5	134.7	192.7	60.1	77.6	137.1	203.1	61.9	78.0	131.8	169.4
1981	60.0	76.7	134.8	193.4	60.5	77.5	137.5	204.6	61.5	78.3	131.3	169.3
1982	60.8	76.8	134.9	194.2	60.9	77.4	137.9	206.1	61.0	78.6	130.8	169.2
1983	61.8	77.2	134.6	193.6	61.6	77.4	137.8	206.1	62.6	79.0	130.5	168.1
1984	62.5	77.4	134.4	193.3	62.2	77.4	137.7	206.1	63.6	79.3	130.2	167.4
1985	62.4	77.3	134.7	194.5	62.2	77.3	138.2	207.9	63.7	79.2	129.8	167.5
1986	61.9	77.2	134.5	195.7	62.2	77.4	138.7	210.4	62.3	78.6	129.9	167.9
1987	61.9	77.4	134.8	196.9	62.3	77.6	139.1	211.2	61.8	78.8	129.5	168.6
1988	61.1	77.1	134.6	196.9	61.7	77.5	139.3	212.4	60.5	78.1	129.1	168.2
1989	60.8	76.7	135.9	198.5	61.3	77.1	139.9	213.5	60.7	77.8	130.5	171.4
1990	60.9	76.8	135.9	198.6	61.7	77.1	139.9	213.3	60.4	77.7	131.2	172.5
1991	61.0	76.8	136.0	198.7	62.0	77.2	140.0	213.1	60.0	77.7	131.8	173.4

(*Continued*)

Table G.3. (*Continued*)

	A	B	C	D	E	F	G	H	I	J	K	L
							Column					
			All				Male				Female	
	P10	P25	P75	P90	P10	P25	P75	P90	P10	P25	P75	P90
1992	61.0	76.7	135.9	197.1	62.1	77.2	140.0	211.7	59.3	77.3	132.1	174.1
1993	60.8	76.6	135.3	195.4	61.7	77.0	139.2	210.9	59.9	76.9	131.1	172.3
1994	62.7	76.9	135.0	193.4	62.8	76.9	138.9	208.2	64.0	77.2	130.6	171.8
1995	62.8	76.9	135.2	193.3	62.7	76.9	138.9	207.9	64.0	77.0	130.5	171.3
1996	62.5	76.6	135.5	193.2	62.5	76.7	139.1	207.5	63.7	76.8	130.9	172.1
1997	62.8	76.8	135.4	192.4	62.7	76.9	139.0	206.4	64.0	77.0	131.0	172.1
1998	63.2	77.1	135.5	192.4	63.0	77.0	139.2	206.3	64.6	77.4	131.1	171.9

Coverage	Excludes those working less than 80% of normal working hours
Industry	Excludes agricultural and general government workers
Age	All
Sex	See headings
Occupation	All
Definition	Net of employee social security contributions (but before deducting income tax)
Intensity	FT, adjusted for annual hours worked to represent full year equivalent earnings
Period	Annual
Limits	None
Source	Downloaded from OECD website December 2005
Original source	Déclarations Annuelles des Données Sociales (DADS)
Notes	(1) Data for 1981, 1983 and 1990 estimates by INSEE, not based on employer declarations; (2) Deciles supplied by INSEE, *Serie longues sur les salaires*

Table G.4. France: Inter-war period (Piketty)

	A	B	C	D	E
			Column		
	Percentiles		Shares		
	P90	P95	Top 10%	Top 5%	Top 1%
1919	166.9	216.9	21.46	13.95	5.62
1920	172.7	223.9	22.09	14.32	5.74
1921	172.3	220.9	21.49	13.78	5.23
1922	183.8	236.8	23.47	15.23	5.91
1923	186.1	242.6	24.50	16.12	6.48
1924	184.6	239.9	24.01	15.71	6.13
1925	188.7	248.3	25.34	16.80	6.85
1926	171.6	229.6	24.09	16.27	6.80
1927	189.5	254.4	26.55	17.89	7.39
1928	192.8	257.4	26.58	17.79	7.32
1929	193.5	254.5	26.46	17.64	7.11
1930	199.9	261.4	26.79	17.71	7.11
1931	204.1	267.2	27.17	17.89	7.02
1932	211.6	280.8	28.13	18.48	7.11
1933	206.3	276.1	27.37	17.98	6.82
1934	202.3	266.3	26.84	17.67	6.71
1935	198.8	262.8	26.62	17.59	6.71
1936	180.3	238.3	24.15	15.96	6.11
1937	180.9	236.9	23.68	15.51	5.93
1938	185.9	244.2	24.50	16.09	6.04

Coverage	All
Industry	All
Age	All
Sex	All
Occupation	All
Definition	Net of employee social security contributions (but before deducting income tax)
Intensity	All
Period	Annual
Limits	None
Source	Piketty (2001, page 64)
Original source	Impôt cédulaire
Note	Percentiles calculated assuming that median is 80% of mean

Table G.5. France: DADS data

			Column		
	A	B	C	D	E
	Percentiles			Shares	
	P95	P99	Top 10%	Top 5%	Top 1%
1947	251.3	476.7	26.94	17.81	6.57
1950	251.6	497.4	24.43	16.29	7.08
1951	247.9	502.0	26.98	17.97	6.99
1952	250.1	500.3	26.82	17.86	6.90
1953	254.4	512.5	26.69	18.14	7.03
1954	258.5	524.2	24.88	17.25	6.71
1955	262.5	536.3	25.49	18.07	7.07
1956	265.7	545.9	25.74	18.58	7.29
1957	269.2	545.3	25.40	18.87	7.19
1958	274.0	572.0	26.02	19.31	7.65
1959	278.1	595.1	27.47	20.37	8.32
1960	280.0	592.5	26.78	20.27	8.21
1961	286.5	608.8	26.40	19.70	8.29
1962	285.0	596.1	27.41	20.11	7.94
1963	269.6	541.6	27.38	17.96	7.71
1964	270.1	549.0	27.24	18.75	7.62
1965	280.2	564.2	28.03	19.15	7.71
1966	283.5	578.4	28.18	19.46	7.94
1967	283.3	585.8	28.39	19.88	8.22
1968	277.3	573.0	28.39	19.40	8.02
1969	276.6	578.2	27.94	19.71	7.95
1970	273.0	537.3	27.47	18.63	6.70
1971	270.9	530.6	27.41	18.53	6.52
1972	272.9	534.3	27.81	19.33	6.64
1973	268.1	516.0	27.28	18.27	6.44
1974	269.5	525.5	27.23	18.37	6.87
1975	268.2	515.4	26.43	18.16	6.33
1976	263.9	506.7	26.93	17.72	6.44
1977	261.7	495.2	26.33	17.13	6.00
1978	261.4	487.8	26.10	16.90	5.79
1979	258.2	476.9	25.96	16.78	5.74
1980	255.2	469.9	25.77	16.63	5.68
1981	259.7	475.6	26.17	16.92	5.82
1982	258.6	471.6	26.00	16.82	5.83
1983	255.1	466.4	25.68	16.64	5.80
1984	257.9	472.4	25.99	16.87	5.91
1985	259.9	469.2	25.92	16.72	5.72
1986	263.3	477.5	26.36	17.15	6.07
1987	264.4	483.4	26.38	17.10	5.91
1988	264.6	478.1	26.25	16.94	5.74
1989	266.3	486.7	26.42	17.09	5.84
1990	263.6	478.3	26.15	16.88	5.77
1991	264.8	477.0	26.25	16.91	5.78

(*Continued*)

Table G.5. (*Continued*)

| | | | Column | | |
	A	B	C	D	E
	Percentiles			Shares	
	P95	P99	Top 10%	Top 5%	Top 1%
1992	261.4	464.0	25.93	16.65	5.66
1993	260.7	470.2	26.24	17.00	6.04
1994	255.4	454.1	25.80	16.62	5.86
1995	254.6	455.9	25.67	16.50	5.75
1996	252.1	444.9	25.38	16.27	5.62
1997	249.6	440.6	25.45	16.31	5.63
1998	253.7	447.8	25.73	16.49	5.69

Coverage	All
Industry	All
Age	All
Sex	All
Occupation	All
Definition	Net of employee social security contributions (but before deducting income tax)
Intensity	All
Period	Annual
Limits	None
Source	Piketty (2001, pages 671, 673, and 675)
Original source	Déclarations Annuelles des Données Sociales (DADS)

Table G.6. France: DADS (Annuaire Statistique)

| | | | | | | | Column | | | | | |
	A	B	C	D	E	F	G	H	I	J	K	L
	All				Male				Female			
	P10	P20	P80	P90	P10	P20	P80	P90	P10	P20	P80	P90
1998	63.2	72.8	148.5	192.4	63.0	72.8	153.5	206.3	64.6	73.5	140.7	171.9
1999	62.7	72.6	149.3	194.2	62.7	72.7	154.7	208.3	64.0	73.1	141.5	173.2
2000	65.4	74.1	150.2	198.8	65.0	73.9	154.4	208.6	67.3	75.5	142.9	178.1
2001	66.0	74.5	150.6	200.2	65.5	74.2	154.7	210.3	68.2	76.2	143.8	180.6
2002	67.2	75.2	150.6	199.5	66.8	75.0	154.8	208.8	69.5	77.1	143.7	180.2
2003	67.2	75.2	150.9	199.9	66.7	75.0	154.9	209.1	69.5	77.1	144.0	180.8
2004	67.4	75.6	150.5	199.5	67.2	75.3	154.5	208.5	70.1	77.7	143.6	180.5

Coverage	Excludes those working less than 80% of normal working hours
Industry	Excludes agricultural and general government workers
Age	All, excluding apprentices and 'stagiares'
Sex	See headings
Occupation	All
Definition	Net of employee social security contributions (but before deducting income tax)
Intensity	FT, adjusted for annual hours worked to represent full year equivalent earnings
Period	Annual
Limits	None
Source	Annuaire Statistique (2003, Table C.03-4, 2004, Table C.03-4 and 2005, Table D.01-4+B2) and INSEE website, March 2006
Original source	Déclarations Annuelles des Données Sociales (DADS)

Table G.7. France: Labour Force Survey

							Column							
A	B	C	D	E	F	G	H	I	J	K	L	M	N	O
		All					FT				FT and private sector			
P10	P25	P75	P90	P99	P10	P25	P75	P90	P99	P10	P25	P75	P90	P99
1984	81.0	133.6												
1985	80.6	135.8												
1986	79.9	132.7												
1987	80.2	132.9												
1988	79.6	132.9												
1989	79.6	132.6												
1990	50.0	76.4	133.3	184.6	396.1	64.4	78.9	131.7	185.4	395.1	64.3	78.5	135.2	197.5	426.4
1991	51.1	76.0	134.4	189.1	395.7	64.9	78.9	133.1	184.6	388.5	64.3	78.6	134.6	197.6	425.0
1992	49.7	76.7	134.9	184.6	399.4	65.0	79.4	133.1	184.8	386.7	64.9	78.8	134.3	194.0	413.3
1993	46.6	74.3	135.2	183.1	388.0	63.5	77.5	131.8	178.8	381.0	64.6	78.6	134.3	192.9	404.2
1994	43.8	73.7	133.9	184.8	385.0	62.5	77.2	131.3	179.4	375.0	64.5	78.5	135.5	195.4	399.5
1995	44.0	73.7	133.5	186.7	376.8	63.9	78.6	135.1	183.5	374.2	65.0	78.0	136.5	195.0	394.3
1996	44.4	73.8	135.3	185.7	395.6	64.0	78.7	133.3	184.6	381.5	64.1	77.2	135.7	192.3	416.7
1997	43.3	73.8	136.5	186.0	393.4	63.9	78.3	132.5	182.4	370.7	64.7	77.5	135.4	189.6	406.3
1998	43.0	73.6	135.1	185.9	381.5	64.4	76.6	131.1	178.6	357.2	66.1	78.8	135.1	189.2	392.9

Coverage	See headings
Industry	All
Age	All
Sex	See headings
Occupation	All
Definition	Includes premia and 13th month payments; net of employee social security contributions
Intensity	See headings
Period	Monthly
Limits	None
Source	1984–8 from *les collections de l'INSEE, series D, Tables PA04bis*, 1989 from *INSEE Resultats, Emploi-Revenus, Table PA04bis*, 1990 onwards from Piketty (2001, page 676)
Original source	Enquête Emploi (Labour Force Survey) from the files distributed by LASMAS

Bibliography

Atkinson, A B, Glaude, M, and Olier, L, 2001, *Inégalités économiques*, La documentation française, Paris.

Baudelot, C and Lebeaupin, A, 1979, 'Les salaires de 1950 à 1975', *Economie et Statistique*, No 113: 15–22.

Bayet, A and Julhès, M, 1996, *Séries Longues sur les Salaires*. INSEE Résultats No 457, Emploi-Revenus, No 105.

Bazen, S, 1991, 'The impact of the minimum wage on earnings and employment in France', *OECD Economic Studies*, vol 16: 199–221.

Bontout, O, Chambaz, C, Lhommeau, B, and Ralle, P, 2001, 'Les effets des prélèvements sociaux sur la dispersion des salaires au cours de la décennie quatre-vingt-dix', in A B Atkinson, M Glaude, and L Olier, *Inégalités économiques*, La documentation française, Paris.

Card, D, Kramarz, F, and Lemieux, T, 1999, 'Changes in the structure of wages and employment: A comparison of the United States, Canada and France', *Canadian Journal of Economics*, vol 32: 705–46.

Casaccia, M and Seroussi, G, 2000, *Séries Longues sur les Salaires*. INSEE Résultats No 735, Emploi-Revenus, No 172.

Centre d'Etudes des Revenus et des Coûts (CERC), 1976, *Dispersion et disparité de salaires en France au cours des vingt dernières années*, Document No 25/26, Paris.

—— 1990, *Formation, mobilité et disparités de salaires depuis quarante ans,* Notes et Graphiques No 10, Paris.

Concialdi, P and Ponthieux, S, 1997, 'Les bas salaires en France, 1983–1997', *Document d'Etudes*, No 15, DARES.

Dugé de Bernonville, L, 1912–13, 'Distribution des salaires et de revenus en divers pays', *Bulletin de la Statistique Générale de la France*, vol 2: 400–36.

Friez, A and Julhès, M, 1998, *Séries Longues sur les Salaires*. INSEE Résultats No 605, Emploi-Revenus, No 136.

Goux, D and Maurin, E, 1999, 'Persistence of inter-industry wage differentials: A reexamination on matched worker–firm panel data', *Journal of Labor Economics*, vol 17: 493–533.

—— 2000, 'The decline in demand for unskilled labour: An empirical method and its application to France', *Review of Economics and Statistics*, vol 82: 596–607.

Haller, M, 1987, 'Positional and sectoral differences in income: Germany, France and the USA', *International Journal of Sociology*, vol 17: 172–90.

Jean, S and Bontout, O, 2000, 'What drove relative wages in France? Structural decomposition analysis in a general equilibrium framework, 1970–1992', Centre for Research on Globalization and Labour Markets Research Paper 2000/8, University of Nottingham.

Katz, L F, Loveman, G, and Blanchflower, D, 1995, 'An international comparison of changes in the structure of wages: France, the United Kingdom and the United States', in R Freeman and L Katz, editors, *Differences and Changes in Wage Structures*, University of Chicago Press, Chicago.

Kramarz, F, Lollivier, S, and Pelé, L-P, 1996, 'Wage inequalities and firm-specific compensation policies in France', *Annales d'Economie et de Statistique*, vol 41/2: 369–86.

March, L, 1898, 'Quelques exemples de distribution des salaires', *Journal de la Société de Statistique de Paris*, vol 39: 193–206.

Margolis, D, 1996, 'Cohort effects and returns to seniority in France', *Annales d'Economie et de Statistique*, vol 41/2: 443–64.

Piketty, T, 2001, *Les hauts revenus en France au 20ème siècle*, Grasset, Paris.

—— 2003, 'Income inequality in France, 1901–1998', *Journal of Political Economy*, vol 111: 1004–42.

Strauss-Kahn, V, 2004, 'The role of globalization in the within-industry shift away from unskilled workers in France' in R E Baldwin and L A Winters, editors, *Challenges to Globalization: Analyzing the Economics*, University of Chicago Press, Chicago.

Synthèses Number 26, 1999, *L'Évolution des Salaires jusqu'en 1997*, INSEE, Paris.

Wasmer, E, 2001, 'Between-group competition in the labour market and the rising returns to skill: US and France 1964–2000', IZA Discussion Paper 292.

H

Germany

The dramatic changes that have been seen in the UK and the US labour markets, which increased the gap between skilled and unskilled workers and inequality within skill groups, have not occurred in West Germany.

Giles, Gosling, Laisney, and Geib, 1998, page 83

H.1 Introduction

The geographical boundaries of Germany have changed considerably over the period, and the coverage of the statistics has changed even more. The first data given below relate to the 1920s, during the Weimar Republic, which was established in 1919. Hitler came to power, and the Third Reich was created, in 1933. In 1935, a plebiscite led to the Saarland, which had been part of France since 1918, joining Germany. After the Second World War, the country, with a different eastern border, was administered in four zones of occupation (American, British, French, and Russian). The three western zones were combined in the Bundesrepublik Deutschland (Federal Republic of West Germany) from 1949. The Saarland rejoined the Bundesrepublik in 1957. The Russian zone became the East German Democratic Republic. In 1990 West and East Germany were reunified.

The currency was the Reichsmark (RM) from 1924 until June 1948, when the Deutschmark (DM) was introduced in West Germany. Germany adopted the euro in 2002.

Previous Coverage

Lydall (1968) gives eight tables of earnings distribution data for West Germany. They cover the years 1950, 1957, and 1961 from the Lohnsteuer (wage tax) statistics, and 1962 from the Gehalts- und Lohnstrukturerhebung (salary and wage survey); historical data are also included, with very limited coverage, for 1896 and 1907.

The OECD tabulations have included the following data for West Germany:

1993 (Table H.1): data for males from 'social security data' (no source given) for 1979, 1980, and 1981; data from the German Socio-Economic Panel for all workers, and men and women separately, from 1983 to 1990, supplied by Viktor Steiner.

1996 (Table H.2): data from German Socio-Economic Panel for all workers, and men and women separately, from 1983 to 1993, supplied by Viktor Steiner.

LMS (Table H.3): data from 1984 to 1998, covering all workers and men and women separately, from the German Socio-Economic Panel.

Official Publications

The *Statistisches Jahrbuch für die Bundesrepublik Deutschland* (Statistical Yearbook), previously the *Statistisches Jahrbuch für das Deutsche Reich*, referred to below as *SJ*, contains earnings distribution data from the wage tax data or from the salary and wage surveys in many issues, although not every year. *Wirtschaft und Statistik*, a monthly publication, referred to below as *WS*, contains articles giving more detail on both sources. The wage tax statistics have been published in separate volumes, originally with the title *Der Steuerabzug vom Arbeitslohn*, in *WS*, then in *Finanzen und Steuern*, Reihe 6, and (from 1974 to 1992) in the series *Finanzen und Steuern*, Fachserie 14, Reihe 7.3.

H.2 Data Sources

Most recent studies of earnings in Germany make use of the German Socio-Economic Panel (GSOEP), which dates from 1984 and was a pioneering panel survey of incomes in Europe, much influenced by the US Panel Study of Income Dynamics at Michigan. There is no doubt that the GSOEP has acted as a considerable stimulus to research on the distribution of earnings, but it is an overstatement to say that 'due to lack of individual and firm level data, wage structures in Germany were "terra incognita" until the mid 1980s' (Frick and Winkelman, 1999, page 2). As evident from Lydall (1968), other sources of data existed earlier and official statistics have been published on the extent of earnings dispersion in Germany for much of the twentieth century. The principal sources are the wage tax (LS) data, which date back to 1926, and the salary and wage survey (GLE), dating back to 1949. These, together with the GSOEP are described below.

Lohnsteuerstatistik

The wage tax (LS) statistics have long been used to examine the distribution of earnings in Germany, an early example in the Anglo-Saxon literature being the article by Sweezy (1939). The first publication that I have located relates to 1926 (Statistischen Reichsamt, 1929). The Foreword explained that the wage tax is not a separate tax, being part of the general income tax, but that the deduction at source of tax due on wage and salary income required a separate statistical procedure, first possible for the year 1926. (There had been prior publications, with results covering large cities, in *SJ* 1928 and in *WS* 1929, No 1.) The LS data were based on the returns made by employers for each individual employee, covering the gross earnings and tax deduction, and the period of employment. The returns included some pensioners. The employer returns were processed at the tax office corresponding to the employee's place of residence. The analysis related to those for whom an employer tax return existed, which included both taxable and non-taxable persons, and the untaxed workers for whom no tax was due and no return was made. The results were published in the form of 12 earnings ranges.

A particular issue concerns deductions from earnings—see Dell (2007). In the LS data, deductions are made from gross earnings for work costs (Werbungskosten) and for other costs (Sonderleistungen) (although these deductions were not made in the figures published for 1926 in *SJ* 1928). There was a minimum default deduction of 240RM allowed in both cases for tax purposes. Dell (2007) adds back the 'other costs' to the LS data, a procedure which seems reasonable since he is concerned with top incomes. However, as explained by the Statistischen Reichsamt (1931, page 4), caution has to be used when considering the lower ranges, since the deductions were only made where the recorded gross wages exceeded 1,200RM. This meant that the ranges below 1,500RM contain both people for whom net earnings are recorded and people for whom gross earnings are recorded. As a result, it does not seem possible to make use of the data for the lowest ranges (below 1,500RM), which means that the data only cover the upper quartile of the earnings distribution. For this reason, I show in Table H.5 only the ratio of the top decile to the upper quartile.

The text commentary to the 1926 analysis noted that it was a year of 'really unfavourable economic conditions', and it is therefore of considerable interest that the exercise was repeated every two years, with the exception of 1930 (when the 'pressure of events' meant that it could not be carried out). The statistics for 1932, 1934, and 1936 differ in two important respects: (i) no deductions are made for work costs or other allowances, and (ii) it is possible to subtract pensioners. There is therefore a break in comparability between the estimates for the 1920s and for the 1930s. The 1936 estimates also differ in including Saarland. (In 1936 Saarland accounted for 1.2 per cent of wage taxpayers, from *SJ* 1941–2, page 577.) Again the wage tax data for these years cover less than 50 per cent of the labour force, and the top deciles in Table H.5 have been expressed relative to the medians obtained from the social security data in Table H.6 (see below). For this reason, the series is classified as B.

In the postwar period, the wage tax statistics continued on the basis of the 'Lohnsteuerkarten' (wage tax cards) returned by employers or workers to the tax office. Results have been published in 1950, 1955, 1957, 1961, 1965, and then every three years. As is noted in the report on the 1950 exercise (*WS*, Dezember 1953, page 560), the returns do not cover certain people with high incomes subject to the income tax, and there was a problem with the non-return of the tax cards, particularly by lower paid workers. These deficiencies have to be corrected by estimation, which in 1950 added 19 per cent to total gross earnings (*WS* Dezember 1953, page 561). The rate of return of wage tax cards improved in successive exercises from 73 per cent in 1950 to 88 per cent in 1961 (*Finanzen und Steuern*, Reihe 6, 1968, page 10) and the adjustment process stopped. Earnings are total earnings including all bonuses and taxable income in kind. The statistical process combines the results from different employments to give total earnings for an individual worker.

The wage tax statistics are the basis for the estimates shown in Table H.5, which have been interpolated linearly from the published tables. From 1968, the tax statistics began to be published on a tax unit basis, combining the earnings of husbands and wives. In that year, there were reported to be 18.7 million tax units (Steuerpflichtige) and 22.0 million taxed individuals (Steuerfälle). (See *Finanzen und Steuern*, Reihe 6, 1968, page 16.) I have throughout used the data for individuals, based on the tables for 'Individualnachweis'.

Social Insurance Data

A second source of earnings data in the interwar period is provided by the social insurance records, which furnish information for 1929 to 1937. These data were used by Sweezy (1939), who argued that 'wage tax statistics which omit tax exempt incomes could not be used because they are very incomplete' (1939, page 181n). This limitation of the wage tax data has already been recognized above. On the other hand, the social insurance data come in two parts which are not readily spliced together and which do not cover all earners. The majority of the records relate to 'Arbeiter' covered by 'Invalidenversicherung', which was compulsory up to monthly earnings of 600RM, although a substantial number of those with earnings above this amount contributed voluntarily. The second part comes from the insurance records of 'Angestellte', covering clerical workers and managers earning less than 7200DM a year. Excluded are officials and higher-paid managers. The total number covered in 1936 was 17.6 million compared with some 23 million covered by the LS data. Wages cover all items of gross earnings, including bonuses and payments in kind. The results are presented separately for the two groups in ranges that do not coincide, and different methods of combining the ranges can lead to differences in the results. For this reason, the resulting estimates are graded as B.

Social security data for the post-war period have been used in a number of studies, such as Abraham and Houseman (1995), whose data are reproduced in Table H.7. A sample of social security data (the Beschäftigtenstichprobe), starting in 1975, is made available by the Institut für Arbeitsmarkt- und Berufsforschung (IAB) of the Bundesanstalt für Arbeit (Federal Employment Service). See Bender et al (1996). Social security contributions are mandatory for employees who earn more than a minimum threshold, with the exception of civil servants, and the data from which the sample is drawn cover about 80 per cent of the employed population. Gross earnings are recorded up to the maximum earnings threshold. The proportion of cases for which earnings are truncated varied in the 1980s between 8 and 11 per cent (Steiner and Wagner, 1998, page 33). The definition of earnings follows the social security law. As is noted by Frick and Winkelmann (1999), such administrative data have the advantage that they have typically been checked by more than one party, since both employers and employees have an interest in accurate recording. They therefore describe these data as 'highly reliable'. On the other hand, their coverage is affected by changes in legislation. A good example is provided by the change of income definition in 1983, extending the coverage of fringe benefits—see Möller (1998, page 171). This particularly affected higher earners: Steiner and Wagner showed that the 80th percentile rose by 6 percentage points between 1983 and 1984 (1998, page 34).

Gehalts- und Lohnstrukturerhebung

The Gehalts- und Lohnstrukturerhebung (GLE) of employers has been conducted in West Germany for the years 1951 (not covering West Berlin or Saarland), 1957 (not covering Saarland), 1962, 1966, 1972, 1978, and 1990. There was an earlier Gehaltserhebung in May 1949 covering certain Bundesländer. The survey was carried out in October (May in 1949 and November in 1951). In 1995 the survey covered the whole of Germany. In between there had been a similar survey covering the reporting period May 1992 in the new Länder and East Berlin.

The survey is addressed to enterprises with ten or more employees. There was (in 1995) a two-stage sampling procedure. First a sample was drawn of 14 per cent of companies and then, from within these companies, a sample of 8 per cent of workers. It covers all workers, full time and part time, excluding those who are not liable for social security contributions (such as home workers). Gross earnings include tips, payments for a 13th month, and holiday pay. The results are published separately for 'Arbeiter' and 'Angestellte', and these have been added. Prior to 1966 the published results were not grossed-up. In the results presented here no allowance has been made for the differing sampling fractions, so that they should be qualified in this respect. Experimentation with an adjustment for 1951 showed that the effect on the bottom decile was small: it was reduced from 56.2 per cent of the median to 55.8 per cent. The top decile was slightly more affected, rising from 155.1 per cent to 157.5 per cent.

The published tables from the GLE are used to obtain percentiles by linear interpolation in Table H.4.

German Socio-Economic Panel (GSOEP)

The GSOEP was launched in Germany in 1984 as a longitudinal household survey containing a wide variety of economic and social information. The first wave was conducted in 1984 in West Germany and included some 12,000 respondents in around 6,000 households. Each year the survey seeks to re-interview the original panel members, together with children reaching the age of 16, and new persons who have joined survey households. In 1990, the panel was extended to East Germany. To allow for panel attrition and for the initial over-sampling of foreigners, the GSOEP provides weighting factors designed to give a representative cross-section for each year. Sample attrition has also been accommodated by including new interviewees. The survey collects detailed information on earnings (including additional payments such as those for holidays and Christmas) and hours worked, and, in addition, has the advantage of providing a great deal of contextual information.

The GSOEP earnings data have been used in the OECD data compilations (Tables H.1 to H.3) and in studies such as Steiner and Wagner (1998). Steiner and Hölzle (2000) use GSOEP data for the 1990s to contrast the earnings distributions in West and East Germany.

Comparison of Different Sources

The relative merits of the social security (IAB) data and the GSOEP are discussed by Steiner and Wagner (1998), Frick and Winkelmann (1999), and others. In order to make a comparison of the findings, it is necessary to match the same definitions (for example excluding civil servants from the GSOEP sample). Steiner and Wagner show that, with the data adjusted in this way, median earnings evolved in a similar way in the two sources between 1983 and 1990, even if they are rather higher in the IAB sample. The findings regarding dispersion are discussed in the next section. On a priori grounds, there are strengths and weaknesses of both data sources, and, as is argued by Frick and Winkelmann, the administrative social security data and the household panel survey (GSOEP) are best regarded as 'complementary'.[15]

Summary

There is a wealth of earnings data for Germany, extending over three-quarters of a century, based on administrative records, employer surveys, and the German Socio-Economic Panel. These are summarized in Figures H.1 and H.2.

H.2 What Happened?

It is widely believed that the distribution of earnings in Germany has been extremely stable in recent decades. Indeed, the title of the recent article by Prasad (2004) is 'The Unbearable Stability of the German Wage Structure'. As is noted by Frick and Winkelmann, the fact that a number of studies found near-constant dispersion in West Germany since the mid-1980s led to this becoming 'virtually a "stylised" fact' (1999, page 6). In part this perceived stability is in contrast to the changes in the US, but it also is based on evidence for a short period: from 1983 when the GSOEP was initiated and the mid-1990s when most of the literature appeared. For example, the top decile from GSOEP rose between 1984 and 1994 by 3.5 per cent, not enough to register according to the criteria applied here.

In my view, we need to place the evidence in a broader time perspective. For Germany, as we have seen, we can go back to 1926. The evidence for this period in Figures H.1 and H.2 must be treated with caution, for the reasons explained above. The estimates based on social insurance data have been assembled from a combination of sources, and are only B graded (although the wage tax data corroborate the changes in the top decile). The continuing decline in the top decile after 1933 appears to run counter to the conclusion reached by Sweezy, who used the same data for earnings, that 'the general picture of the distribution of individual income shows that inequality has increased during the Hitler regime' (1939, page 182). She was referring to total income as well as earnings, and part of the rise in inequality may have been associated with a general fall in the wage share. Moreover, we should note that our

---

[15] Frick and Winkelmann also discuss the *Einkommens- und Verbrauchsstichprobe* (EVS), or Income and Expenditure Survey, and the *Mikrozensus*. As they note, the latter codes earnings in broad categories.

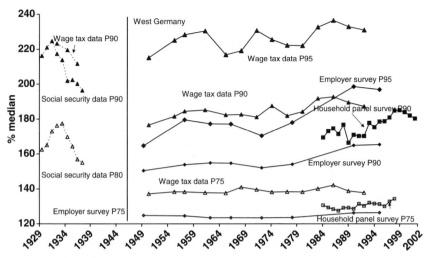

Figure H.1 GERMANY upper part of the distribution 1929–2002

Sources: Table H.3, columns D and F; Table H.4, columns D, F, and G; Table H.5, columns D, F, and G; Table H.6, columns D and E.

data in Figure H.2 also show that the lower quartile was falling. The distribution was becoming more spread out at the bottom, which is consistent with the direction of change found by Petzina, who describes an unprecedented fall in the share in total income of the bottom 50 per cent (1977, page 147). This period clearly warrants closer examination, in particular if we wish to establish what would have happened in the counterfactual situation where Hitler had not come to power.[16]

Turning to the post-war period for Germany, we should note the obvious differences in territorial coverage (also that West Berlin and Saarland are missing from the earliest years). We can also note the contrast in Figure H.2 between the results for the lower quartile from the wage tax and employer surveys. Not only is the quartile much smaller, but also the wage tax data suggest a significant fall between the mid-1950s and the mid-1980s, whereas the employer survey data indicate a rise of 7 per cent between 1951 and 1978 (and a 19 per cent rise in the bottom decile). This may reflect the changing coverage of the wage tax data. If we take the employer survey data, then it appears that the direction of change in Germany during the Golden Age was different from that in other European countries. The bottom decile in Germany rose by over 10 per cent between 1957 and 1966 according to the GLE employer survey, and the lower quartile rose by over 5 per cent. This conclusion is reinforced if we look at Figure H.1, where the top percentiles are stable over this period (and the two sources are in general agreement). There does not appear to have been widening of earnings dispersion during the Golden Age.

[16] The wage and labour market policies of the Nazi regime are described in Trivanovitch (1937) and Bry (1960, pages 235–7).

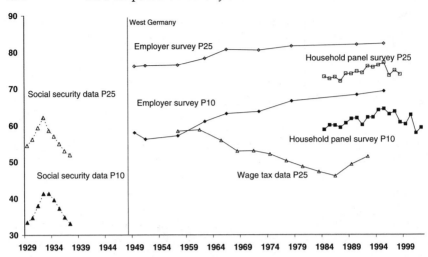

Figure H.2 GERMANY lower part of the distribution 1929–2002

Sources: Table H.3, columns A and B; Table H.4, columns A and C; Table H.5, column B; Table H.6, columns A and C.

By the same token, there does not seem to have been a reaction in terms of earnings dispersion after 1968. The bottom decile, according to the employer survey data, continued to rise: by 5 per cent between 1966 and 1978. The lower quartile did not register any change. The fall in the top decile from 1966 to 1972 was less than 2 per cent (and that in P95 less than 5 per cent). Indeed, for the whole period from 1950 to the end of the 1970s, the change in the top decile was less than the threshold of 5 per cent.

What happened in the 1980s? Steiner and Wagner (1998) make use of the IAB social security data and the GSOEP data for the period 1984 to 1990. They show that the bottom quintile, expressed relative to the median, took essentially the same value in both years in the GSOEP and fell by some 2 per cent in the IAB sample. The top quintile, again as a percentage of the median, was again essentially the same in the GSOEP data, and rose by less than 2 per cent in the IAB sample. They reached the conclusion that there had been little change in this decade. On the other hand, Dustmann, Ludsteck, and Schönberg (2007) find a rise in P85 in the IAB data during the 1980s. If we look further up the distribution, we can see from Figures H.1 and H.2 that the employer surveys provide some support for the view that dispersion has increased. The top decile rose by 7 per cent between 1978 and 1995. In part, this reflects the inclusion of the 1990s, but the rise at the very top started in the 1980s. The P95 in the GLE rose by 11.6 per cent between 1977 and 1990, and the P95 in the wage tax data rose by 6.5 per cent between 1980 and 1986. In the 1990s, the GSOEP data too shows a widening: between 1992 and 2002, the top decile rose by 6 per cent and the bottom decile fell by 8 per cent. There has been therefore a definite rise in the decile ratio in the 1990s (see Gernandt and Pfeiffer, 2006). Moreover, we may note that the employer survey data provide evidence of a fanning out at the top in Germany. Over the whole period 1978 to 1995, when the top decile rose by 7 per cent, the value of P95 rose by 16.5 per cent.

Finally, the findings for East Germany show that the earnings distribution in 1990 was considerably more compressed than in West Germany, but that it widened significantly over the 1990s. The results of Steiner and Hölzle (2000, page 11) for hourly earnings show that the top decile for men in 1990 was 144 per cent of the median, compared with 166 per cent in West Germany. The corresponding figures for the bottom decile were not very different: 71 per cent in East and 69 per cent in West. From 1990 to 1997, the top decile in East Germany rose from 144 per cent to 160 per cent.

Summary

A contrast is often drawn between the German earnings distribution and that in the US, but in recent decades we have seen a similar, if less marked, pattern of change, with a widening of earnings dispersion and a fanning out at the top. It is in the earlier part of the post-war period that the German episode appears to have been different from that in other OECD countries. Finally, the existence for Germany of data for the late 1920s and 1930s allows an insight into a period, and a political experience (the rise of the Nazi dictatorship), whose distributional consequences have been little studied.

Table H.1. Germany: OECD (1993)

				Column			
A	B	C	D	E	F	G	H
German Socio-Economic Panel						Social security data	
All		Male		Female		Male	
P10	P90	P10	P90	P10	P90	P10	P90
1979						67	147
1980						67	147
1981						68	147
1982							
1983	61	163	68	163	59	156	
1985	63	165	70	166	63	158	
1986	63	164	70	166	64	162	
1987	65	164	71	163	65	158	
1988	65	162	71	165	67	158	
1989	67	164	72	165	66	159	
1990	65	164	71	165	66	158	

Coverage	West Germany
Industry	All
Age	All
Sex	See headings
Occupation	All
Definition	Gross
Intensity	FT+FY
Period	Monthly inc. 13th month and other bonuses
Limits	None
Source	OECD (1993, Table 5.2)
Original source	See headings

Table H.2. Germany: OECD (1996)

			Column			
	A	B	C	D	E	F
	All		Male		Female	
	P10	P90	P10	P90	P10	P90
1983	60.6	163.0	68.5	163.0	58.8	156.0
1984	59.5	166.0	67.6	165.0	59.9	160.0
1985	62.9	165.0	70.4	166.0	62.9	158.0
1986	63.3	164.0	69.9	166.0	63.7	162.0
1987	64.5	164.0	70.9	163.0	65.4	158.0
1988	64.5	162.0	70.4	165.0	67.1	158.0
1989	66.7	164.0	71.9	165.0	65.8	159.0
1990	65.4	164.0	71.4	165.0	65.8	158.0
1991	67.1	161.0	74.1	157.0	69.9	162.0
1992	67.6	165.0	73.0	165.0	67.6	157.0
1993	69.4	161.0	73.0	164.0	70.4	159.0

Coverage	West Germany
Industry	All
Age	All
Sex	See headings
Occupation	All
Definition	Gross
Intensity	FT and FY
Period	Monthly inc. 13th month and other bonuses
Limits	None
Source	OECD (1996, Table 3.1)
Original source	German Socio-Economic Panel

Table H.3. Germany: OECD (LMS)

| | | All | | | | | | Male | | | | | | | Female | | | |
| | A | B | C | D | E | F | G | H | I | J | K | L | M | N | O | P | Q | R |
	P10	P20	P25	P75	P80	P90	P10	P20	P25	P75	P80	P90	P10	P20	P25	P75	P80	P90
1984	58.8	73.2	78.4	130.6	138.3	169.4	67.3	77.5	81.4	128.5	137.7	170.1	57.1	71.9	77.8	128.8	138.8	163.7
1985	60.0	72.7	77.8	129.3	140.0	173.2	66.4	76.9	81.0	131.0	139.6	170.7	59.7	72.6	78.5	129.8	139.0	168.5
1986	60.0	73.1	78.0	128.4	140.0	174.7	68.1	77.2	81.0	130.5	142.7	172.6	62.6	73.7	77.9	132.2	138.8	164.7
1987	59.3	72.0	76.7	127.5	136.6	171.5	66.3	76.0	80.6	129.3	140.4	171.8	59.7	73.4	78.5	130.1	139.0	165.2
1988	60.5	74.1	81.2	129.2	141.0	176.8	68.4	77.5	81.2	131.6	143.2	177.1	60.6	73.1	78.4	131.9	137.2	159.8
1989	61.7	74.0	78.8	129.2	139.6	166.4	68.8	78.0	81.4	129.1	140.2	169.3	61.8	74.0	79.0	129.7	136.9	163.3
1990	61.9	74.7	77.1	128.6	138.8	170.9	69.8	78.5	81.6	130.8	140.7	170.3	59.2	72.2	79.2	128.7	137.5	155.2
1991	60.1	74.3	79.3	131.4	141.4	170.2	67.6	77.9	81.9	131.2	138.4	165.9	59.9	71.9	77.1	126.9	133.3	162.8
1992	62.1	76.1	81.2	130.2	139.1	170.2	69.3	79.5	82.9	127.5	138.4	163.2	59.9	74.0	78.1	123.7	133.1	161.7
1993	62.1	75.8	80.7	132.1	142.2	177.8	68.6	78.3	81.2	132.0	143.6	169.7	57.3	73.2	79.0	124.8	134.0	163.2
1994	64.1	76.4	80.9	131.5	140.4	175.4	70.2	79.3	82.8	131.4	143.3	177.8	63.2	76.4	81.3	126.7	135.9	166.4
1995	64.4	77.1	81.3	131.3	141.0	178.6	69.6	77.9	81.4	131.7	142.3	173.7	61.7	75.1	80.9	126.1	133.8	159.5
1996	63.0	73.6	78.5	130.0	140.2	178.8	65.5	76.5	80.3	131.3	144.6	180.8	63.5	76.1	79.1	128.2	136.8	157.8
1997	63.7	75.0	79.4	132.7	140.5	181.0	66.5	76.4	80.0	132.1	142.2	174.7	62.9	75.7	80.1	128.8	134.8	158.8
1998	60.8	73.9	79.4	134.3	142.0	185.0	63.5	74.9	79.5	132.2	146.7	181.5	58.6	75.1	80.2	130.8	137.2	162.8
1999	60.2					185.1	64.1					185.4	59.6					166.9
2000	62.8					184.1	64.8					179.5	64.7					160.2
2001	57.8					182.1	64.0					180.5	54.7					169.2
2002	59.3					180.4	61.0					183.6	58.2					163.1

Coverage   West Germany
Industry   All
Age   All except apprentices
Sex   See headings
Occupation   All
Definition   Gross earnings, inc. 1/12 of supplementary Payments (13th and 14th months), holiday and Christmas allowances
Intensity   FT
Period   Monthly
Limits   None
Source   Downloaded from OECD website December 2005
Original source   German Socio-Economic Panel
Note   Data for 1999–2002 supplied by OECD

Table H.4. Germany: Employer earnings survey (GLE)

Groups: columns A–H = **All**; columns I–P = **Male**; columns Q–X = **Female**. Within each group the percentiles are P10, P20, P25, P75, P80, P90, P95, P99.

Year	A	B	C	D	E	F	G	H	I	J	K	L	M	N	O	P	Q	R	S	T	U	V	W	X	Source*
	P10	P20	P25	P75	P80	P90	P95	P99	P10	P20	P25	P75	P80	P90	P95	P99	P10	P20	P25	P75	P80	P90	P95	P99	
1949	58.0	70.7	76.1	124.8	131.3	150.5	164.7	192.4	70.2	79.9	83.6	119.6	125.2	140.8	150.8	171.9	69.9	80.2	85.0	120.2	125.3	144.6	164.2	208.2	SJ 1954, pages 492 and 498
1951	56.2	70.2	76.3	124.8	132.9	155.1	178.7	244.9	66.3	77.7	82.1	122.8	128.9	150.5	172.1	243.4	57.1	74.4	78.6	126.0	133.3	155.5	177.2	231.3	SJ 1954, pages 492 and 498
1957	57.1	70.5	76.5	124.6	131.8	153.9	179.6	264.8	70.5	80.2	83.8	120.9	127.3	148.0	172.0	265.0	65.7	76.9	81.3	123.3	130.0	151.2	172.3	230.2	SJ 1961, page 512
1962	61.0	73.0	78.3	123.5	129.4	154.9	177.3	248.9	73.3	81.9	85.3	119.9	126.4	151.2	172.8	245.7	70.1	80.2	84.2	119.5	125.0	142.9	161.6	215.6	SJ 1965, pages 517 and 520
1966	63.2	75.6	80.7	123.5	131.2	154.7	177.2	253.1	73.3	81.2	84.7	121.9	128.9	151.6	170.1	251.4		79.2	82.6	121.3	127.1	145.9	164.6	215.6	SJ 1969, page 464 and 467
1972	63.7	75.6	80.5	123.4	130.6	152.1	170.4		73.3	81.4	84.7	121.4	128.0	149.5	164.5		71.0	80.5	84.3	121.2	127.6	146.2	165.0	191.2	SJ 1975, page 474 and 475
1978	66.6	77.6	81.6	123.6	130.7	154.1	178.1	250.4	73.3	81.4	84.5	122.1	129.0	151.8	175.3	247.7	70.5	80.2	83.7	121.1	127.3	146.0	165.1	207.3	SJ 1981, pages 477 and 478
1990	68.3	78.1	82.0	126.3	135.1	164.9	198.7	292.9	73.1	80.6	83.8	126.3	135.2	165.7	198.5		70.7	79.8	83.3	125.5	133.2	156.4	178.6	239.7	SJ 1994, page 624
1995	69.3	78.5	82.3	126.4	135.9	165.4	196.9	279.4	72.7	80.5	83.8	127.2	135.9	165.8	197.0	278.6	69.9	79.1	83.2	125.5	132.9	155.9	176.9	235.2	SJ 1998, pages 598 and 600

Coverage	West Germany
Industry	All
Age	All
Sex	See headings
Occupation	All
Definition	Gross wages and salaries
Intensity	FT
Period	Monthly
Limits	None
Sources	See final column
Original source	Employer survey
Notes	Certain Länder missing for 1949
	* SJ refers to *Statistisches Jahrbuch*

Table H.5. Germany: Wage tax data (Lohnsteuer)

	A	B	C	D	E	F	G	H	I	
					Column					
					All				ratio	
	P10	P20	P25	P75	P80	P90	P95	P99	P90/P75	Source*
1926									1.653	Band 359 page 9
1928									1.596	Band 378, pages 22–3
1932					223.3	305.4	501.1		1.761	Band 492 pages 7, 16 and 21
1934					219.6	288.7	466.2		1.558	Band 492 pages 7, 16 and 21
1936					211.7	266.9	413.4		1.431	Band 530 pages 9, 16 and 25
1950				137.2	146.6	176.6	215.2	337.6	1.288	W+S 1953, Heft 12, page 561
1955FY	37.0	57.7	66.0	131.4	139.8	172.5	215.3	348.9		SJ 1959 page 383
1955		57.8		138.4	148.9	181.6	225.2	375.0	1.312	SJ 1958 pages 382 and 383
1957FY		57.6	65.8	133.0	142.3	172.8	219.4	352.4		SJ 1961 pages 444 and 445
1957		48.6	58.4	138.3	150.7	184.5	228.4	367.4	1.334	SJ 1961 pages 444 and 445
1961FY	38.5	60.3	68.0	131.3	141.3	175.9	221.0	344.2	1.340	SJ 1964 page 452
1961	22.6	47.5	58.8	137.9	147.9	185.2	230.5	358.5	1.343	SJ 1964 page 452
1965FY	33.4	57.7	67.0	130.6	142.1	171.0	206.1	331.7	1.310	SJ 1968 page 408
1965		44.3	55.8	137.7	145.6	182.4	216.9	342.7	1.325	SJ 1968 page 406
1968		40.8	52.9	141.0	151.6	182.7	219.2	349.7	1.295	Lohnsteuer Reihe 7.3, 1968, page 30
1971		40.8	53.0	139.7	147.9	181.2	230.7	338.1	1.297	Lohnsteuer Reihe 7.3, 1971, page 22
1974	17.2	40.4	52.0	138.2	154.7	187.6	225.6	347.4	1.358	Lohnsteuer Reihe 7.3, 1974, page 22
1977	14.9	37.8	50.2	138.4	150.3	181.9	222.3	337.0	1.314	Lohnsteuer Reihe 7.3, 1977, page 25
1980	13.7	36.4	48.7	138.3	149.2	184.3	222.1	335.6		Lohnsteuer Reihe 7.3, 1980, page 36
1983		35.3	47.2	140.2	154.5	191.8	232.7	361.3		Lohnsteuer Reihe 7.3, 1983, page 27
1986	12.8	33.9	46.1	142.2	154.1	192.8	236.6	407.5		Lohnsteuer Reihe 7.3, 1986, page 168
1989	14.3	37.1	49.3	138.9	150.6	189.6	233.0	400.6		Lohnsteuer Reihe 7.3, 1989, page 114
1992	15.8	39.9	51.4	137.9	149.3	187.3	231.1	391.7		Lohnsteuer Reihe 7.3, 1992, page 151
1992	27.6	53.7	63.8	130.9	139.4	165.4	194.7	284.2		Lohnsteuer Reihe 7.3, 1992, page 83
1992	17.8	42.4	53.5	143.0	155.1	196.2	241.9	398.1		as above
1998	19.2	43.8	54.5	141.2	153.8	195.8	244.2	407.0		Lohn- und Einkommensteuer Reihe 7.1, 1998, page 16.
2001	17.7	42.7	53.5	143.9	157.5	201.5	253.9	427.7		Lohn- und Einkommensteuer Reihe 7.1, 2001, page 16.

Coverage	From 1950 to 1992 (first row) = West Germany; 1992 (second row) = East Germany; 1992 (third row) and later = reunited Germany
Industry	All
Age	All
Sex	All
Occupation	All
Definition	Gross wages and salaries
Intensity	See row headings: FY denotes full year workers
Period	Annual
Limits	None
Sources	See final column
Original source	Wage tax statistics
Notes	(1) The estimates for 1932–6 use the medians from the insurance data in Table H.6; (2) 1950 estimates include the 'unbesteuerte'; *Band refers to *Statistik des Deutschen Reichs*; W+S refers to *Wirtschaft und Statistik*; SJ refers to *Statistisches Jahrbuch*

Table H.6. Germany: Pre-war social security data

	A	B	C	D	E	F	
			Column				
	P10	P20	P25	P80	P90	Median RM per year	Source*
1929	33.5	47.6	54.5	162.5	216.2	1,516	VS 1937, Heft III, pages 102 and 107
1930	34.7	49.2	56.1	165.1	221.0	1,472	as above
1931	38.0	52.5	59.3	173.0	224.7	1,318	as above
1932	41.3	55.1	62.1	176.3	217.4	1,128	as above
1933	41.4	52.6	58.6	177.5	213.8	1,092	as above
1934	39.6	50.4	57.0	169.8	201.9	1,157	as above
1935	37.3	47.9	54.9	164.4	202.4	1,234	as above
1936	34.8	45.3	53.0	157.0	200.2	1,328	as above
1937	33.1	43.4	51.9	155.1	196.4	1,411	W+S 1938 2 August page 652

Coverage	All workers
Industry	Exc. government
Age	All
Sex	All
Occupation	All
Definition	Gross
Intensity	All
Period	Year
Limits	None
Source	See final column
Original source	Social security data
Note	*VS refers to *Vierteljahrshefte zur Statistik des Deutschen Reichs*; W+S refers to *Wirtschaft und Statistik*

Table H.7. Germany: Social security data

| | Column | |
| | A | B |
	P10	P90
1976	67.1	
1977	65.8	
1978	66.2	148
1979	66.7	146
1980	67.1	146
1981	66.7	146
1982	68.5	150
1983	68.0	152

Coverage	West Germany
Industry	Exc. government
Age	All
Sex	Male
Occupation	All
Definition	Gross
Intensity	FT for any part of year
Period	Annualized
Limits	Truncated at upper ceiling
Source	Abraham and Houseman (1995, page 377)
Original source	Social security data

Bibliography

Abraham, K G and Houseman, S N, 1995, 'Earnings inequality in Germany' in R B Freeman and L F Katz, editors, *Differences and Changes in Wage Structures*, University of Chicago Press, Chicago.

Anderton, R and Brenton, P, 1998a, 'Trade with the NICs and wage inequality: Evidence from the UK and Germany' in P Brenton and J Pelkmans, editors, *Global Trade and European Workers*, Macmillan, London.

Bauer, T, 1999, 'Educational mismatch and wages in Germany', IZA Discussion Paper No 87.

Beaudry, P and Green, D, 2003, 'Wages and employment in the United States and Germany: What explains the differences?' *American Economic Review*, vol 93: 573–602.

Bender, S, Hilzdegen, J, Rohwer, G, and Rudoph, H, 1996, *Die IAB-Beschäftigten-Stichprobe 1975–1990*, Beiträge zur Arbeitsmarkt- und Berufsforschung 197, Nürnberg.

Biewen, M, 1999, 'Inequality trends in the German income distribution', *Vierteljahreshefte zur Wirtschaftsforschung*, vol 2: 275–83.

Biewen, M, 2000, 'Income inequality in Germany during the 1980s and 1990s', *Review of Income and Wealth*, series 46: 1–19.

Bry, G, 1960, *Wages in Germany, 1871–1945*, Princeton University Press, Princeton.

Dell, F, 2007. 'Top incomes in Germany throughout the twentieth century: 1891–1998', in A B Atkinson and T Piketty, editors, *Top Incomes over the Twentieth Century*, Oxford University Press, Oxford.

Dustmann, C, Ludsteck, J, and Schönberg, U, 2007, 'Revisiting the German wage structure', Discussion Paper.

—— and van Soest, A, 1997, 'Wage structures in the private and public sectors in West Germany', *Fiscal Studies*, vol 18: 225–47.

Fitzenberger, B, Hujer, R, MaCurdy, T, and Schnabel, R, 1995, 'The dynamic structure of wages in Germany, 1976–1984: A cohort analysis', University of Konstanz Discussion Paper 22.

—— —— —— and —— 2001, 'Testing for uniform wage trends in West-Germany: A cohort analysis using quantile regressions for censored data', *Empirical Economics*, vol 26: 41–86.

Frick, B and Winkelmann, K, 1999, 'Pay inequalities in Germany: A review of the literature', University of Greifswald.

Gang, I N and Yun, M-S, 2002, 'Decomposing male inequality change in East Germany during transition', IZA DP 579.

Gernandt, J and Pfeiffer, F, 2006, 'Rising wage inequality in Germany', ZEW Discussion Paper 06-019, Centre for European Economic Research, Mannheim.

Giles, C, Gosling, A, Laisney, F, and Geib, T, 1998, *The Distribution of Income and Wages in the UK and West Germany 1982–1992*, IFS Research Report, London.

Grund, C, 1998, 'Zur Verteilung der Arbeitseinkommen in Westdeutschland', *Vierteljahreshefte zur Wirtschaftsforschung*, vol 1: 30–39.

—— 2002, 'The wage policy of firms—comparative evidence for the U.S. and Germany from personnel data', IZA Discussion Paper 685.

Haller, M, 1987, 'Positional and sectoral differences in income: Germany, France and the USA', *International Journal of Sociology*, vol 17: 172–90.

Kohn, K, 2006, 'Rising wage dispersion, after all! The German wage structure at the turn of the century', IZA Discussion Paper 2098.

Lücke, M, 1999, 'Trade with low-income countries and the relative wages and employment opportunities of the unskilled: An exploratory analysis for West Germany and the UK', in P Brenton and J Pelkmans, editors, *Global Trade and European Workers*, Macmillan, London.

Möller, J, 1998, 'Die Entwicklung der Lohnungleichheit in Deutschland', *Forum der Bundesstatistik*, Band 32: 169–93.

Petzina, D, 1977, *Die deutsche Wirtschaft in der Zwischenkriegszeit*, Franz Steiner Verlag, Wiesbaden.

Prasad, E S, 2004, 'The unbearable stability of the German wage structure: Evidence and interpretation', *IMF Staff Papers*, vol 51: 354–85.

Statistischen Reichsamt, 1929, *Der Steuerabzug vom Arbeitslohn im Jahre 1926*, Statistik des Deutschen Reichs, Band 359, Reimar Hobbing, Berlin.

—— 1931, *Der Steuerabzug vom Arbeitslohn im Jahre 1928*, Statistik des Deutschen Reichs, Band 378, Reimar Hobbing, Berlin.

—— 1937, *Der Steuerabzug vom Arbeitslohn im Jahre 1932 und 1934*, Statistik des Deutschen Reichs, Band 492, Verlag für Sozialpolitik, Wirtschaft und Statistik, Paul Schmidt, Berlin.

—— 1939, *Der Steuerabzug vom Arbeitslohn im Jahre 1936*, Statistik des Deutschen Reichs, Band 530, Verlag für Sozialpolitik, Wirtschaft und Statistik, Paul Schmidt, Berlin.

Steiner, V and Hölzle, T, 2000, 'The development of wages in Germany in the 1990s: Description and explanations', in R Hauser and I Becker, editors, *The Personal Distribution of Income in an International Perspective*, Springer, Berlin.

—— and Wagner, K, 1998, 'Has earnings inequality in Germany changed in the 1980s?', *Zeitschrift für Wirtschafts- und Sozialwissenschaften*, vol 118: 29–59.

Sweezy, M Y, 1939, 'Distribution of wealth and income under the Nazis', *Review of Economics and Statistics*, vol 21: 178–84.

Trivanovitch, V, 1937, *Economic Development of Germany under National Socialism*, National Industrial Conference Board, New York.

Zanchi, L 1992, 'The inter-industry wage structure: Empirical evidence for Germany and a comparison with the U.S. and Sweden', EUI Working Paper ECO 92/76.

I

Hungary

The transition brought about a sharp increase in the dispersion of earnings for all groups.

Ábrahám and Kézdi, 2000, page 16

I.1 Introduction

The Austro-Hungarian Empire ended in 1918, and new borders were set by the Treaty of Trianon in 1920. Following Soviet occupation in 1945, a Communist government was established. There was a Revolution in 1956, suppressed by force. Hungary later moved towards a market economy, and the Communist regime came to an end with the creation of the Third Hungarian Republic in October 1989. Hungary joined the European Union on 1 May 2004.

Previous Coverage

Lydall (1968) includes four tables on Hungary covering 1962, based on the Hungarian Income Survey.

Hungary was not included in the OECD (1993) or (1996) compilations, but is covered by the OECD (LMS) dataset, which contains data for the years 1986, 1989, 1992–4, 1996–2000. In other words, it covers years both before and after the transition from Communism.

Official Publications

The official publication on earnings by the Hungarian Statistical Office is *Fogalkozta-tottság És Kereseti Arányok* (Earnings and Employment), referred to below as FKA. Statistics on the distribution of earnings have been published in the Statistical Yearbook.

I.2 Data Sources

Survey of Earnings

Under the Communist government, information on earnings was collected regularly, starting in 1951, from employers in a September survey (the 1955 and 1956 surveys were in June). Although the form and coverage of the inquiry has varied, it provides a long-running source of earnings data, requiring employers to report the number of men and women receiving monthly earnings within each of a number of ranges. The survey was annual from 1955 to 1962 (with the exception of 1959), then became two-yearly until 1990 (although the data for 1991 do not provide a size distribution). The data are published regularly in FKA, and have been published in less detailed ranges in the annual Statistical Yearbook.

The coverage has varied. Initially, prior to 1970 it was limited to the 'state sector', defined as state-owned enterprises and state-owned farms. From 1970 the data cover the more extensive 'socialized sector', thus adding agricultural and non-agricultural cooperatives. From 1982, private ventures with a legal identity were included where they employed 50 workers or more. In 1991, the survey covered enterprises employing fewer than 50 workers, on a sample basis, the sampling fraction only reaching 100 per cent for enterprises employing more than 300 employees. The number of workers covered is very large: some 150,000 in the mid-1990s. Earnings are defined as gross pay plus the monthly equivalent of annual or other bonus payments, and one-ninth of all additional earnings received between January and September. Excluded from the survey are part time workers (although certain part time workers were included up to 1978). Workers of all ages are covered, but not apprentices. Excluded are also people absent from work for more than three days in September, and those who joined or left during the month. Excluded are the armed forces.

The earnings survey data were analysed in Atkinson and Micklewright (1992), and their results are summarized in Table I.2. The table marks several breaks in continuity, such as the extension in 1970 of coverage from the state sector to the socialized sector. As was stated there, 'the Hungarian earnings distribution consists of four separate segments, each linked by overlapping years' (1992, page 91). Comparison of the results on different bases for the same year shows that these breaks can have a noticeable impact. In Figures I.1 and I.2, the breaks are shown for the bottom decile and top decile but not for the other percentiles. Data from the earnings survey for years after 1988 are shown in Table I.3, based on the work of Rutkowski (1996), and in Table I.4, interpolated from the published tables.

Household Budget Survey (HBS)

The HBS is 'the only regular Hungarian household survey that has been continuously carried out through the Communist and Transformation years' (Redmond and Kattuman, 2001, page 468). It has been carried out every two years (prior to 1983 it was conducted annually with a smaller sample). Prior to 1989, households containing a self-employed member were excluded from the sample. The sampling frame is based on the census of population, but with a non-proportional design, for which weighting factors are applied to the estimates. There is a significant panel element (one third of the sample rotating out every time). The rate of non-response has been about 25 per cent, described by Pudney as 'good in comparison to Western surveys' (1994, page 253). Where a household is contacted and refuses, or cannot be contacted, then another household is drawn to replace it, which allows a target sample size to be attained but does not deal with the problem of differential non-response.

In the HBS, detailed information is collected from household members on their characteristics and income (as well as expenditure, based on a diary). The HBS records earnings on two bases: pay received during the two-month diary-keeping period, and annual earnings. Pudney (1994) shows that the resulting distributions depend sensitively on the choice of earnings measure. In 1991, with annual earnings, the decile ratio is 5.21 but that with two-month earnings is 4.06 (Pudney, 1994, page 259).

Comparison of Sources

A careful comparison of the Earnings Survey (ES) and HBS has been made by Pudney (1994), whose final conclusion is that 'the Household Budget Survey data agrees surprisingly closely with the Earnings Survey, in terms of the characteristics of its sample earnings distribution' (1994, page 273).

Summary

The main source on earnings data in Hungary is the census/survey of employers and the results are summarized in Figures I.1 and I.2. The source dates back to 1951 but it has changed significantly over the period, so that we have a patchwork rather than a single continuous series. In considering the earnings data, it has also to be borne in mind that a personal income tax was introduced in January 1988 and that this was accompanied by a grossing-up of wages. In Figures I.1 and I.2, a vertical line has been drawn at this point, in that the distributions before and after cannot be directly compared.

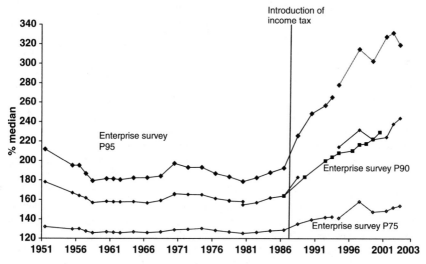

Figure I.1 HUNGARY upper part of the distribution 1951–2003

Sources: Table I.1, column B; Table I.2, columns D, E, and F; Table I.3, columns C and E; Table I.4, columns D, F, and G.

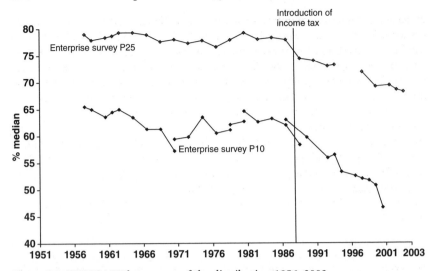

Figure I.2 HUNGARY lower part of the distribution 1956–2003

Sources: Table I.1, column A; Table I.2, columns B and C; Table I.3, column B; Table I.4, column C.

I.3 What Happened?

The 1950s saw a narrowing of earnings dispersion. Although not too much weight should be placed on the 1951 observation, the top decile fell by 6 per cent between 1955 and 1958. There was then no registrable change until the mid-1960s, when, as observed by Flakierski (1979), the economic reform process was associated with a rise in dispersion. The bottom decile lost ground, particularly between 1968 and 1970 (the overall fall in the 1960s was 10 per cent) and the top decile increased by 5 per cent between 1962 and 1970. These changes were reversed in the 1970s, to the extent that the top decile fell by 5 per cent, but the bottom decile did not rise, and fell in the 1980s. Taking the long run of 30 years from 1956, the net impact was that the decile ratio rose from 2.47 to 2.94 (linking together the different series).

If, after an initial period, the Communist regime did not reduce earnings dispersion, the transition to a market economy certainly increased dispersion. Recognizing the effect of the introduction of income tax in 1986, we have to discount the changes at the end of the 1980s, but to the right of the line in Figures I.1 and I.2 the lower percentiles fell and the upper percentiles rose. The bottom decile was 59.7 per cent of the median in 1989, had fallen to 53.3 per cent in 1994, and still further to 50.7 per cent in 1999. This was a significant fall. The top decile was 183 per cent of the median in 1989, rose to 208 per cent in 1994, and further to 222 per cent in 1999. This was a large rise. From his analysis of the ES and HBS data, Pudney concluded that 'there is statistically significant evidence of an increase in earnings inequality, which takes Hungary to a degree of inequality comparable with (or even higher than) countries like Britain' (1994, page 273). As noted by Rutkowski (2001, page 11), earnings dispersion in Hungary, in contrast to a number of other Central European countries, has tended to increase at a steady rate over the 1990s. There have been a number of studies of the factors underlying the evolution of relative wages. These show in general a rise in the return to education. According to Tóth (2004), there has been both an increase in the premium to education and a change in the age profile of earnings, with the better educated having higher earnings at younger ages, and then a flatter profile.

The most recent years in Figures I.1 and I.2 exhibit volatility about a continued widening. This volatility reflects in part government intervention: 'between 2000 and 2003 there were two exogenous wage shocks: the more than doubling of the minimum wage in 2000–2001 and the drastic rise of public sector wages in 2002' (Tóth, 2004, page 85). The Hungarian Central Statistical Office confirms that 'during the 2000–2003 period, earnings were greatly influenced by government measures. These included minimum salary increases of 57 per cent in 2001 and 25 per cent in 2002' (KSH, 2004, page 15).

Summary

The evidence for the Communist period has to be interpreted in the light of the changing coverage of the statistics, but the degree of dispersion went through several cycles, with a widening of differentials registered during the economic reform period. The changes were, however, moderate compared with those after 1989 when there was a significant fall in the bottom decile relative to the median, and a large rise in the top decile, which formed part of a fanning out of the upper part of the distribution.

Table I.1. Hungary: OECD (LMS)

	A	B	C	D	E	F
				Column		
	All		Male		Female	
	P10	P90	P10	P90	P10	P90
1986	63.0	164.0				
1989	59.7	183.3	61.0	180.6	64.5	176.9
1992	55.9	199.9	55.6	199.8	58.4	193.3
1993	56.4	203.9				
1994	53.3	208.1	53.2	213.0	55.1	200.3
1996	52.5	210.4	52.8	213.7	54.8	200.5
1997	52.0	216.8				
1998	51.7	217.6	50.1	225.4	54.7	202.6
1999	50.7	222.4	48.2	232.0	53.6	203.7
2000	46.6	229.4	41.9	212.9	50.7	209.0

Coverage	Excludes workers in private enterprises with fewer than 10 (before 1994, 20) employees
Industry	All
Age	All
Sex	See headings
Occupation	All
Definition	Gross, including 1/12 of non-regular payments from previous year
Intensity	FT
Period	Monthly in May
Limits	None
Source	Downloaded from OECD website December 2005 and supplied by OECD
Original source	Enterprise survey
Note	Change in sampling method from 1992

Table I.2. Hungary: Census of enterprises

	Column																					
	A	B	C	D	E	F	G	H	I	J	K	L	M	N	O	P	Q	R	S	T	U	V
	Socialized sector, inc. PT All											Male						Female				
	P05	P10	P25	P75	P90	P95	P99	Gini	P05	P10	P25	P75	P90	P95	Gini	P05	P10	P25	P75	P90	P95	Gini
1951				132.2	178.1	211.9	284.4	22.7														
1955				129.7	167.0	195.1	261.2	22.2														
1956				130.1	164.1	195.1	257.5	22.2														
1957		65.5	79.0	127.5	161.7	186.7		20.5														
1958		65.0	77.9	125.8	156.9	179.3		20.0														
1960	56.4	63.6	78.4	126.8	158.2	181.5		20.4														
1961	57.5	64.5	78.7	126.3	157.8	181.3		20.1														
1962	56.8	65.0	79.3	125.8	157.7	180.5		20.1														
1964	56.1	63.5	79.3	126.8	157.9	182.3		20.5														
1966	57.0	61.3	78.9	125.9	156.6	182.5		21.0														
1968	55.3	61.3	77.6	126.8	159.2	184.2		21.0														
1970	49.1	57.2	78.3	128.9	165.3	191.5		22.8														
1970 socialized sector	50.5	59.4	78.0	129.0	166.1	197.2	269.5	22.9	57.6	67.7	82.0	125.0	158.8	185.8	20.1	56.6	62.4	79.1	121.9	148.2	172.4	20.0
1972	49.3	59.8	77.3	129.5	165.3	193.1	266.0	22.6	58.5	66.0	81.4	125.4	157.7	183.9	20.0	56.0	62.4	84.0	125.3	156.9	178.2	20.0
1974	52.0	63.5	77.8	130.4	165.1	193.2	262.0	22.1	56.8	65.1	79.7	124.4	155.8	181.1	19.9	55.1	66.1	81.9	122.8	154.0	175.5	19.0
1976	52.8	60.5	76.6	128.3	161.2	186.8	251.5	21.9	57.6	65.7	81.2	123.3	152.6	176.8	19.1	57.7	67.4	80.9	124.9	154.8	176.8	19.0

(*Continued*)

Table I.2. (*Continued*)

		Socialized sector, inc. PT All							Column			Male						Female					
	A	B	C	D	E	F	G	H	I	J	K	L	M	N	O	P	Q	R	S	T	U	V
	P05	P10	P25	P75	P90	P95	P99	Gini	P05	P10	P25	P75	P90	P95	Gini	P05	P10	P25	P75	P90	P95	Gini
1978	53.9	61.1	77.3	126.9	159.2	184.7	253.6	21.4	58.8	67.2	82.1	122.9	152.4	178.4	18.8	59.8	67.0	79.6	125.0	153.3	174.3	19.4
1978 FT only	55.4	62.1	77.9	126.7	158.6	183.4	251.7	20.8	59.2	67.5	82.0	122.9	152.6	178.0	18.7	62.1	68.3	81.1	124.4	153.2	175.3	18.4
1980	55.3	62.7	77.9	126.7	158.1	184.2	250.2	20.7	59.5	67.4	82.0	123.0	152.2	175.8	18.6	61.3	67.7	81.5	124.5	153.3	175.2	18.4
1980 inc. wage supp.	57.2	64.6	79.2	125.3	154.7	178.7		19.7														
1982	55.5	62.6	78.0	126.3	157.0	182.5		20.5	59.4	67.2	82.0	123.5	153.3	177.1	18.6	61.2	68.8	81.6	123.9	151.9	173.9	18.1
1984	54.9	63.2	78.3	127.9	161.8	187.8		21.3	56.8	65.4	80.7	125.5	157.6	183.9	20.2	59.0	66.7	80.4	125.6	156.3	179.0	19.2
1986	54.2	62.0	77.9	128.7	163.9	192.5		22.1	55.4	64.4	80.1	125.9	159.3	187.3	21.0	59.0	66.2	80.0	126.6	158.1	182.7	20.0
1988	50.0	58.3	74.4	135.1	183.0	225.9		26.8	51.1	59.8	76.8	133.1	181.1	225.6	26.4	54.5	62.3	76.7	133.5	177.8	212.0	24.3

Coverage	See headings
Industry	All
Age	All
Sex	All and M and F
Occupation	All
Definition	See headings
Intensity	See headings
Period	Month
Limits	None
Source	Atkinson and Micklewright (AM), Tables HE1–HE4
Original source	Census of enterprises; information provided in bands
Note	See A+M section S.6 on interpolation method; P99 obtained by Pareto interpolation of individual ranges

Table I.3. Hungary: Earnings survey (Rutkowski)

	Column					
	A	B	C	D	E	F
	P10	P25	P75	P90	P95	Gini
1988	58.3	74.4	135.1	183.0	225.9	26.8
1990	57.7	74.0	139.4	196.4	248.6	29.1
1992	56.6	73.0	141.9	201.2	256.9	30.4
1993	55.9	73.2	142.4	205.2	265.3	31.5
1994	54.7			207.4		32.3
1997	51.4			214.0		34.9

Coverage	All
Industry	All
Age	All
Sex	All
Occupation	All
Definition	Gross (inc. monthly equivalent of bonuses and allowances)
Intensity	FT
Period	Monthly
Limits	None
Source	Rutkowski 1996, Tables 3 and 4, and 2001 Table 1
Original source	From September earnings survey

Table I.4. Hungary: FKA

	Column							
	A	B	C	D	E	F	G	
	P10	P20	P25	P75	P80	P90	P95	Source
1994	53.8	66.2	71.9	141.2	157.7	214.4	278.1	FKA 1995, page 63
1997	49.9	65.0	71.9	158.1	175.3	231.9	314.8	FKA 1999, page 80
1999	50.2	63.2	69.2	147.5	163.6	222.0	302.6	FKA 2001 page 121
2001			69.4	148.6	164.5	224.4	327.6	FKA 2005, page 241
2002		64.3	68.5	151.9	168.7	237.9	331.5	FKA 2005, page 241
2003	50.5	62.0	68.2	153.7	170.5	243.9	319.2	FKA 2005, page 241

Coverage	Excludes workers in private enterprises with fewer than 10 (in 1994, 50) employees
Industry	All
Age	All
Sex	See headings
Occupation	All
Definition	Gross (inc. monthly equivalent of bonuses and allowances)
Intensity	FT
Period	Monthly
Limits	None
Sources	See final column
Original source	September earnings survey

Bibliography

Ábrahám, Á and Kézdi, G, 2000, 'Long-run trends in earnings and employment in Hungary, 1872–1996', Budapest Working Papers on the Labour Market, 2000/2.

Andorka, R, Ferge, Z, and Tóth, I, 1996, 'Is Hungary really the least unequal? A discussion of data on income inequality and poverty in Central European Countries', Research Note on Data Presented in the World Development Report 1996, TÁRKI, Budapest.

Atkinson, A B and Micklewright, J, 1992, *Economic Transformation in Eastern Europe and the Distribution of Income*, Cambridge University Press, Cambridge.

Flakierski, H, 1979, 'Economic reform and income distribution in Hungary', *Cambridge Journal of Economics*, vol 3: 15–32.

Havasi, E and Rédei, M, 1997, 'Representativity of the household budget survey sample and validity of HBS income data, 1995', Hungarian Central Statistical Office, Budapest.

Kattuman, P and Redmond, G, 2001, 'Income inequality in early transition: The case of Hungary 1987–1996', *Journal of Comparative Economics*, vol 29: 40–65.

Kertesi, G and Köllö, J, 2000, 'Wage inequality in East-Central Europe', Budapest Working Papers on the Labour Market, 2000/7.

—— and —— 2001, 'Economic transformation and the revaluation of human capital: Hungary, 1986–1999', Budapest Working Papers on the Labour Market, 2001/4.

Kézdi, G, 2002, 'Two phases of labour market transition in Hungary: Inter-sectoral reallocation and skill-biased technological change', University of Michigan.

KSH (Hungarian Central Statistical Office), 2004, *Hungary 2003*, Budapest.

Pittaway, M, 'The reproduction of hierarchy: Skill, working-class culture, and the state in early socialist Hungary', *The Journal of Modern History*, vol 74: 737–69.

Pudney, S, 1994, 'Earnings inequality in Hungary: A comparative analysis of household and enterprise survey data', *Economics of Planning*, vol 27: 251–76.

Redmond, G and Kattuman, P, 2001, 'Employment polarization and inequality in the UK and Hungary', *Cambridge Journal of Economics*, vol 25: 467–80.

Rosser, J B, Rosser, M V, and Ahmed, E, 'Income inequality and the informal economy in transition economies', *Journal of Comparative Economics*, vol 28: 156–71.

Rutkowski, J, 1996, *Changes in the Wage Structure during Economic Transition in Central and Eastern Europe*, World Bank Technical Paper 340.

—— 2001, 'Earnings inequality in transition economies of Central Europe: Trends and patterns during the 1990s', World Bank SP Discussion Paper 0117.

Tóth, I G, 2004, 'Income composition and inequalities in Hungary, 1987–2003', in T Kolosi, G Vukovich, and I G Tóth, editors, *Social Report 2004*, TÁRKI, Budapest.

J

Ireland

The dispersion of earnings in the Republic of Ireland has decreased since 1938, but not since 1960.

Stark, 1977, page 113

J.1 Introduction

In 1921 the treaty was signed creating the independent Irish Free State with effect from December 1922. It had previously been part of the United Kingdom of Great Britain and Ireland (now the United Kingdom of Great Britain and Northern Ireland).The Constitution was amended in 1937, and the Republic of Ireland was established in 1949. Ireland joined the European Communities in 1974. The country adopted the euro in 2002.

Previous Coverage

Ireland was not covered by Lydall (1968): Ireland does not even appear in the index.

Ireland is covered by the OECD (LMS) database, even though it was not covered in the earlier OECD (1993) and OECD (1996) compilations. The OECD (LMS) data, given in Table J.1, cover 1994 and 1997 for all workers and for men and women separately. The source is the *Living in Ireland Survey* carried out by the Economic and Social Research Institute (ESRI) in Dublin.

Official Publications

No official earnings distribution statistics are currently published.

J.2 Data Sources

The main source of earnings data for the past two decades has been the household surveys carried out by ESRI. Until the recent establishment of the Structure of Earnings Survey, there has been no employer-based survey providing data on the Irish earnings distribution. On the other hand, the Census of Industrial Production provides partial information on the distribution of earnings for the earlier period 1937–68.

ESRI Surveys

The first ESRI survey was conducted in 1987 under the title *Survey of Income Distribution, Poverty and Usage of State Services*. The aim was to provide a national sample of the population resident in private households, and the sampling frame was the Register of Electors. The response rate was 64 per cent providing information for a total of 3,294 households. The results have been re-weighted to allow for non-response, and the representativeness validated by comparison with external sources such as the Census of Population and the Labour Force Survey (see Callan et al, 1989). The 1987 survey provides information on gross earnings for about 2,700 employees in sample households. Results are given in Table J.2.

The 1994 *Living in Ireland Survey*, carried out by ESRI, was the first wave of the Irish element of the European Community Household Panel (ECHP). The sampling frame was again the Register of Electors. The response rate was 62.5 per cent providing information for a total of 4,048 households. The results have been re-weighted to allow for non-response, using information from the Labour Force Survey (see Callan et al, 1996). The 1994 survey provides full information on gross earnings for about 3,000 employees in sample households. The same source provides the data for 1997 in Tables J.1 and J.2.

The panel survey suffered a significant degree of attrition, and by 2000 the number of continuing households had fallen from 4,048 to 1,952 (Nolan et al, 2002, Table 2.2). The ESRI supplemented the sample in 2000 by 1,515 households, and the total of 3,467 form the *Living in Ireland Survey*, which is the source of the data in Table J.1. The ECHP consists only of the continuing sample.

Structure of Earnings Survey

The Structure of Earnings Survey collects information on the earnings distribution as part of the harmonized EU-wide survey. It has been carried out in 1996 and 2002. A sample of 10,000 enterprises in private and public sectors is drawn from the Business Register. The sampling frame includes only establishments with at least ten workers, and does not cover agriculture, forestry, fishing, construction, transport, storage and communication, real estate, public administration, defence, education, health and social work, personal services, or domestic service.

No results have been published by the Central Statistical Office, but they are supplied to Eurostat. The data were used in a study of inter-industry differentials by Nolan (2004).

Household Budget Surveys

Household Budget Surveys have been conducted for 1973 (for which micro-data are no longer available) and 1980. As far as I am aware, no use has been made of these surveys to estimate earnings distributions.

Census of Production[17]

In 1937, the Census of Industrial Production (CIP) in Ireland began to collect information about the earnings and hours worked by wage-earners, asking employers

---

[17] I am most grateful to Brian Nolan for drawing my attention to this source. The analysis of the data is developed further in Atkinson and Nolan (2007).

for information about the number of wage-earners by ranges of earnings in a specified week. The published tables show the distribution of earnings separately for men and women, and for workers aged under 18, and 18 years and over. They covered 'all industries', both 'transportable goods' and 'building and services', where the latter included building and construction, laundry, dyeing, and cleaning, gas, water, and electricity works, canals, docks, and harbours, railways, and local authority and government departments.[18] When launching the collection of the Census of Production data, the Department of Industry and Commerce stated that 'one of the objects in asking for these particulars was to obtain statistics which could be related to corresponding information compiled by a number of other countries and thus provide the International Labour Office, Geneva, with data suitable for international comparisons' (1939, page x). The CIP data were used for this purpose by Stark (1977), who compared the distribution of earnings in Ireland with that in Great Britain and in Northern Ireland.

The first report was cautiously optimistic about the quality of the data collected: 'generally, it can be stated that the returns of earnings and hours worked were satisfactorily completed. No data, however, were available which could satisfactorily be used for the purpose of scrutiny of the returns and, as in the case of most newly established series of statistics, complete reliability cannot be placed on their accuracy until corresponding figures for at least a second year are available.' (Department of Industry and Commerce, 1939, page x). The Censuses of Industrial Production went on in fact to provide data not just for 1938 but for the period up to 1968, although the data for 1939 to 1942 were confined to industries producing transportable goods, excluding services, and are not considered here.

The main limitations of the Census of Industrial Production data are those of coverage. Very important for Ireland is the exclusion of agriculture, which in 1937 employed nearly half the labour force, and in 1968 accounted for some 30 per cent of employment. According to Stark (1977, page 102), the CIP data covered approximately 90 per cent of industrial production, but this coverage was still incomplete: it excluded salaried workers, such as clerks, typists, bookkeepers, or managers. Moreover, 'even though the Census is complete in the sense that it covers all the various types of industrial production, many small concerns are omitted owing to the impracticability of obtaining reliable returns from them' (Central Statistics Office, 1951, page 9). All of this means that in 1960, for example, the data relate to some 190,000 workers (male and female, all ages) out of some 1 million employed.

Despite their limited coverage, the data are well worth including in that they cover a period for which little evidence is available. They were the basis for the conclusion of Stark cited at the beginning of this chapter. The CIP data are assembled in Table J.3. In view of the limited coverage, they are classified as grade B.

---

[18] For 1966–8 the distribution is shown separately for building and construction workers; we have assumed that they were all male and added them to the distribution for other sectors.

Summary

The results are summarized in Figures J.1 and J.2. For Ireland, we have a long series for a period not well covered in other countries (from 1937 to 1968), but then a gap until the late 1980s.

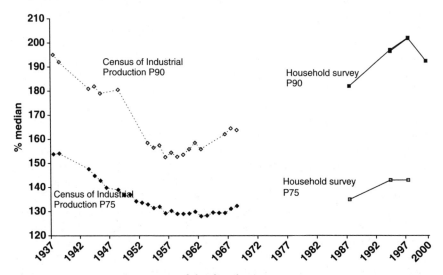

Figure J.1 IRELAND upper part of the distribution 1937–2000

Sources: Table J.1, column F; Table J.2, columns K and L; Table J.3, columns C and D.

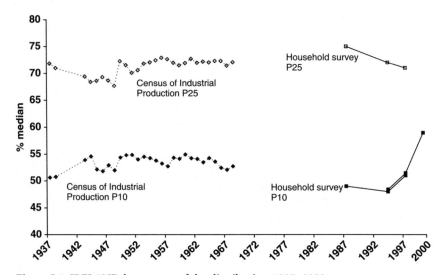

Figure J.2 IRELAND lower part of the distribution 1937–2000

Sources: Table J.1, column A; Table J.2, columns I and J; Table D.3, columns A and B.

J.3 What Happened?

The Irish data provide a long run perspective. Stark (1977) used the Census of Industrial Production data to compare 1938 with 1960 and 1968, showing that for adult male workers there had been a significant fall in the top decile, and a large rise in the bottom decile, over the period as a whole. Here we provide further detail by considering the whole run of years. Starting with the 1930s and 1940s, we can see that the top decile fell by nearly a fifth, the upper quartile fell by over a tenth, and the bottom decile rose by approaching a tenth. Even if the rise at the bottom did not extend to the lower quartile (which fell), the late 1930s and 1940s saw a significant compression of the earnings distribution in Ireland.

What happened in the 1950s and 1960s? Judged by the bottom decile and the lower quartile (Figure J.2), there was a period of stability. Between 1951 and 1968, the bottom decile lay in the range 52.7–54.9 per cent of the median, and the lower quartile lay in the range 70.1–72.9 per cent of the median. In contrast, the upper percentiles demonstrate more of a U-shape, the decline continuing until the mid-1950s but there then being an upward movement. This is most visible for the top decile, which rose from 153 in 1958 to 164 in 1968. To this limited extent, the earlier compression had been unwound.

We now jump to 1987. Summarizing the evidence from the ESRI surveys, Barrett, Fitzgerald, and Nolan note that in the case of hourly earnings of all employees from 1987 to 1994, 'the overall picture is thus of widening dispersion throughout the distribution except at the very bottom' (2002, page 667). From 1994 to 1997, as economic growth accelerated, 'the top decile did continue to move away from the median [but] the bottom decile and bottom quartile now kept pace with the median' (2002, page 667). For the weekly earnings of full time workers, the bottom decile rose as a percentage of the median. This leads them to conclude that 'over the decade as a whole, then, the ratio of the top to the bottom decile increased markedly, but this was concentrated in the period from 1987 to 1994' (2002, page 668). The widening over the period 1987 to 1997 emerges clearly for the upper part of the distribution in Figure J.1. There is a distinct fanning out: the upper quartile rose relative to the median in the ten years by 6 per cent and the top decile by 11 per cent. The reversal for the bottom decile between 1994 and 1997 is evident in Figure J.2, and becomes even more marked between 1997 and 2000.

Summary

The Irish experience illustrates three of the general themes of the Lecture. The period 1937 to 1951 exhibits a significant compression, which is of interest since Ireland was not directly engaged in the Second World War. The latter part of the 1950s and 1960s showed a rise in the top decile. There is then a gap in coverage, but in the period 1987 to 1997 there was a fanning out of the upper part of the earnings distribution.

Table J.1. Ireland: OECD (LMS)

| | | All | | | | | | Male | | | | | | Female | | | |
	A	B	C	D	E	F	G	H	I	J	K	L	M	N	O	P	Q	R
	P10	P20	P25	P75	P80	P90	P10	P20	P25	P75	P80	P90	P10	P20	P25	P75	P80	P90
1994	48.4	65.5			155.2	196.4	50.2	68.0			154.5	196.4	52.2	67.8			159.5	194.1
1997	51.4	65.7	71.4	142.5	156.1	201.8	49.0	66.7	72.3	143.3	158.3	200.0	59.6	68.1	75.3	144.7	154.9	194.5
2000	58.9					192.4	55.1					189.2	60.6					178.5

Coverage   All
Industry   All
Age   All
Sex   See headings
Occupation   All
Definition   Gross
Intensity   FT
Period   Weekly
Limits   None
Source   *Living in Ireland Survey* (ESRI), data for 2000 supplied by Brian Nolan

Table J.2. Ireland: ESRI

	A	B	C	D	E	F	G	H	Column I	J	K	L	M	N	O	P
	FT and PT, hourly earnings Male and female; all ages				FT and PT, weekly earnings Male and female; all ages				FT, weekly earnings Male and female; all ages				FT, hourly Male aged 21 and over			
	P10	P25	P75	P90	P10	P25	P75	P90	P10	P25	P75	P90	P10	P25	P75	P90
1987	47	73	137	196	41	70	139	187	49	75	135	182	63	78	133	179
1994	47	68	150	224	34	65	149	205	48	72	143	197	55	74	142	204
1997	48	69	153	233					51	71	143	202	57	75	144	207

Coverage	All
Industry	All
Age	See headings
Sex	See headings
Occupation	All
Definition	Gross
Intensity	See headings
Period	See headings
Limits	None
Source	Barrett, Callan, and Nolan (1999, Table 1) and Barrett, Fitzgerald, and Nolan (2000, Tables 1, 2, and 4)
Original source	ESRI household surveys

Table J.3. Ireland: Census of Industrial Production

		All			Column Male				Female			
	A	B	C	D	E	F	G	H	I	J	K	L
	P10	P25	P75	P90	P10	P25	P75	P90	P10	P25	P75	P90
1937	50.6	71.9	153.8	195.0	48.3	68.5	143.1	172.0	51.5	74.7	123.3	139.5
1938	50.8	71.0	154.1	192.0	48.3	67.1	139.3	163.6	54.6	76.0	122.3	140.4
1943	53.9	69.5	147.6	180.9	52.1	65.5	133.3	158.8	58.0	77.7	122.6	143.8
1944	54.6	68.4	144.9	181.9	50.5	66.5	133.4	163.1	57.5	79.3	123.2	143.1
1945	52.1	68.6	142.9	179.0	49.4	68.7	131.8		55.7	78.3	121.0	141.3
1946	51.8	69.3	139.9		52.8	68.6	128.3		56.0	78.2	120.4	139.8
1947	52.9	68.7			50.7	65.9			58.7	79.3	120.6	137.8
1948	52.0	67.7	139.0	180.5	50.4	66.6	127.7		57.4	78.6	124.7	142.0
1949	54.4	72.3	136.8		55.6	66.3	127.8		58.5	78.9	121.8	136.4
1950	54.8	71.5	137.0		56.6	70.8	128.1		60.2	80.7	119.6	134.4
1951	54.9	70.1	134.2	162.2	55.9	71.9	125.1	145.7	62.7	80.7	119.6	138.0
1952	54.0	70.6	133.6	158.8	56.9	73.7	125.3	145.2	61.8	81.5	120.0	138.9
1953	54.5	71.8	132.9	158.4	58.8	74.0	124.4	145.0	62.3	83.3	121.6	138.5
1954	54.2	72.0	131.5	156.5	60.2	75.0	123.9	143.9	62.1	82.7	121.1	137.1
1955	53.8	72.4	132.0	157.4	59.1	76.0	124.1	145.3	61.5	81.0	120.1	138.4
1956	53.2	72.9	129.3	152.6	61.6	77.8	122.7	142.1	61.3	80.4	115.2	135.0
1957	52.7	72.6	130.3	154.4	61.6	77.4	123.1	143.8	59.8	80.1	117.4	137.6

1958	54.3	72.0	129.0	152.7	62.0	77.5	121.9	142.8	65.4	84.2	119.2	136.5
1959	54.1	71.5	129.0	153.6	60.2	77.7	121.9	143.9	65.6	84.5	120.0	139.0
1960	54.9	71.9	129.2	155.9	61.0	78.4	122.4	146.9	64.6	82.6	117.7	136.7
1961	54.2	72.7	129.9	158.5	63.2	77.9	122.5	147.9	65.1	82.2	118.9	137.6
1962	54.1	72.0	128.1	155.9	61.6	78.3	121.0	146.9	64.8	84.2	119.5	139.7
1963	53.4	72.2	128.3	158.9	62.1	79.1	123.0	150.2	65.0	83.7	120.8	143.8
1964	54.2	72.0	129.6	161.3	61.8	78.9	123.7	151.8	64.4	82.7	118.7	141.1
1965	53.6	72.3	129.4	162.6	62.8	79.1	123.5	152.7	63.8	82.7	120.4	140.9
1966	52.4	72.3	129.4	162.1	62.5	79.4	124.5	152.4	61.4	82.0	122.8	142.3
1967	52.1	71.5	131.1	164.5	61.1	78.2	125.0	153.7	61.8	81.8	121.9	141.9
1968	52.7	72.1	132.3	163.8	62.6	78.0	126.0	152.5	64.0	80.3	120.4	141.2

Coverage	Wage-earners, excluding salary-earners
Industry	Census of Industrial Production industries, excludes agriculture, commerce and finance, public administration, defence, and personal services
Age	18 and over
Sex	See headings
Occupation	All
Definition	Gross
Intensity	All
Period	Weekly
Limits	None
Source	Census of Industrial Production
Note	Top decile Pareto interpolated, and extrapolated where top interval less than 15 per cent.

Bibliography

Atkinson, A B and Nolan, B, 2007, 'The Changing Distribution of Earnings in Ireland 1937 to 1968', discussion paper.

Barrett, A, Callan, T, and Nolan, B, 1997, 'The earnings distribution and returns to education in Ireland, 1987–94', CEPR Discussion Paper 1679.

—— —— and —— 1999, 'Rising wage inequality, returns to education and labour market institutions; Evidence from Ireland', *British Journal of Industrial Relations*, vol 37: 77–100.

Barrett, A, Fitzgerald, J, and Nolan, B, 2000, 'Earnings inequality, returns to education and immigration into Ireland', IZA Discussion Paper 167.

—— —— and —— 2002, 'Earnings inequality, returns to education and immigration into Ireland', *Labour Economics*, vol 9: 665–80.

Callan, T and Harmon, C, 1999, 'The Economic Returns to Schooling in Ireland', *Labour Economics*, vol 6: 543–50.

—— Nolan, B, Whelan, B J, Hannan, D F, with Creighton, S, 1989, *Poverty, Income and Welfare in Ireland*, Economic and Social Research Institute, Dublin.

—— —— —— Whelan, C T, and Williams, J, 1996, *Poverty in the 1990s: Evidence from the 1994 Living in Ireland Survey*, Oaktree Press, Dublin.

Central Statistics Office, 1949, *Some Statistics of Wages and Hours of Work in 1949*, P. No 9261, Stationery Office, Dublin.

—— 1951, *Some Statistics of Wages, Earnings and Hours of Work in 1951 and Previous Years*, Pr 840, Stationery Office, Dublin.

—— 1953, *Some Statistics of Wages, Earnings and Hours of Work in 1953 and Previous Years*, Pr 2030, Stationery Office, Dublin.

—— 1956, *Statistics of Wages, Earnings and Hours of Work in 1956 and Previous Years*, Pr 3989, Stationery Office, Dublin.

—— 1959, *Statistics of Wages, Earnings and Hours of Work 1959 and Previous Years*, Pr 5235, Stationery Office, Dublin.

—— 1962, *Statistics of Wages, Earnings and Hours of Work 1962 and Previous Years*, Pr 6774, Stationery Office, Dublin.

—— 1965, *Statistics of Wages, Earnings and Hours of Work 1964 and Previous Years*, Pr 8499, Stationery Office, Dublin.

—— 1971, *Statistics of Wages, Earnings and Hours of Work 1970 and Previous Years*, Pr1 2160, Stationery Office, Dublin.

Department of Industry and Commerce, 1939, *Census of Industrial Production, 1937*, Stationery Office, Dublin.

—— 1947, *Census of Industrial Production, 1938–1944*, Stationery Office, Dublin.

—— 1948, *Some Statistics of Wages and Hours of Work in 1946*, P. No 7775, Stationery Office, Dublin.

Nolan, B, 2004, 'Inter-industry wage differentials in Ireland', ESRI, Dublin.

—— Gannon, B, Layte R, Watson, D, Whelan, C T, and Williams, J, 2002, *Monitoring Poverty Trends in Ireland: Results from the 2000 Living in Ireland Survey*, Policy Research Series 45, ESRI, Dublin.

O'Donnell, N, 1998, 'Why did earnings inequality increase in Ireland: 1987–1994?' EUI Working Paper ECO 98/17.

Stark, T, 1977, *The Distribution of Income in Eight Countries*, Background Paper No 4, Royal Commission on the Distribution of Income and Wealth, HMSO, London.

K

Italy

Wage inequality in Italy decreased strongly until the first half of the 1980s and started to increase sharply in the early 1990s, remaining substantially stable in the second part of the decade.

Checchi and Pagani, 2005, page 43, citing the conclusions of
Brandolini, Cipollone, and Sestito, 2002

K.1 Introduction

Italy was a kingdom from the time of its unification in 1861 until 1946, when the present republic was established. The land borders have changed as a result of the addition of Trentino-Alto Adige, Trieste, and Gorizia in 1918 and the loss of territory around Trieste to the former Yugoslavia after the Second World War (a definitive border settlement was reached in 1975). Italy adopted the euro as its currency in 2002.

Previous Coverage

The book by Lydall (1968) contains one table for Italy, relating to 1953–4, based on the *Indagine statistica sui bilanci di famiglie non agricole negli anni 1953–54*. It refers to the monthly expenditure per family, not to earnings, nor to individuals, and does not therefore meet the minimum requirements set for inclusion in this book.

Italy is included in the following OECD compilations:

1993 (Table K.1): men and women separately 1979–81, 1986–7, from Bank of Italy *Survey of Household Income and Wealth (SHIW)*.

1996 (Table K.2): total, and men and women separately, 1979–84, 1986–7, 1989, 1991, and 1993, from *SHIW*.

LMS (Table K.3): total, and men and women separately, 1986 to 1996, based on social security data from the records of the Italian National Social Security Institute (Istituto Nazionale di Previdenza Sociale, *INPS*), supplied by Claudia Villosio.

Official Publications

No earnings data are published in the official yearbook. There is no official publication of earnings data by the statistical office (ISTAT).

K.2 Data Sources

Two major sources of earnings data have provided the basis for a series of studies of earnings dispersion in Italy. The first is the Bank of Italy *SHIW* household survey (for a historical account, see Brandolini, 1999). The second source is provided by the social security records of the Istituto Nazionale di Previdenza Sociale (INPS). In addition, the income tax published tabulations provide an alternative source for the years 1982 to 1989.

Bank of Italy Survey of Household Income and Wealth (SHIW)

The Survey of Household Income and Wealth (*Indagine sui bilanci delle famiglie italiane)* is carried out regularly by a private survey organization on behalf of the Bank of Italy. The survey has the advantage of containing, in addition to the earnings data, a wide range of demographic and labour market variables. From 1965 to 1985 it was conducted annually, then in 1986 and 1987, 1989, 1991, 1993, 1995, 1998, 2000, 2002, and 2004. A historical archive has been assembled (D'Alessio and Faiella, 2000), containing *SHIW* data from 1977 to 2004, which can be downloaded from the Bank of Italy website. These data are shown in Table K.4. I understand from the Bank of Italy that micro-data for earlier years are not available, and that few of the surviving tabulations classify individuals according to their earnings, so that only limited information is available prior to 1977. For the three years 1973, 1975, and 1977, interpolations have been made from the tables of frequencies and mean earnings published in Caligiuri (1978). These are given in Table K.5 (see also Pirrotta and Zen, 1983), but are not fully comparable with those for later years, as may be seen from the differences for the overlap year (1977).

The *SHIW* has evolved significantly over the period since 1977, even if 'the definition of earnings has remained stable, apart from minimal rewording' (Brandolini, Cipollone, and Sestito, 2002, page 257). The survey, and the changing methods over time, are described in detail in Brandolini (1999). The basic survey unit is the household. The sampling design has changed frequently over the period. The target sample size was initially set at 3,000; it was increased to 4,000 in 1981 and 8,000 in 1986. Since 1989 the survey has contained a panel element. The gross response rate has fluctuated considerably. In 1967, it was 66.7 per cent; in 1974 it was 51 per cent; in 1980 it was nearly 70 per cent; and in 1991 it fell to 32.5 per cent (Brandolini, 1999, Table 5). The results have been re-weighted to bring five socio-demographic marginal distributions into line with the population statistics and the labour force survey. Nonetheless, it should be borne in mind that the relatively high level of non-response, and its variation over time, may have affected the representativeness of the survey to varying degrees over time.

The relation between the number of employees covered by the *SHIW* and evidence from the *Labour Force Survey* (the *LFS*) is discussed by Brandolini, Cipollone, and Sestito (2002, Appendix). As they note, the use of adjusted weights brings the *SHIW* figures close to those in the *LFS*. They conclude that the *SHIW* may capture some part of non-regular employment, but that difficulties are encountered in covering secondary jobs. Brandolini (1999) makes comparisons with the national accounts. Employment income is better covered in the *SHIW* than other income categories, and part of the shortfall is attributable to differences in definition (such as the exclusion of the institutional population). For the whole period it is possible to distinguish between main and secondary jobs, and the number of months worked in the job in the year. But the distinction between full time and part time employment can only be made from 1986.

National Social Security Institute Data (INPS)

The National Social Security Institute has made available data from the records supplied by employers when paying social security contributions, and these have allowed the estimates of the distribution of earnings shown in Table K.7. The data contain information about both individual employees (gross annual wage, including overtime and supplements, date of birth, gender, occupation, and weeks worked), and about the employer (industry and size). For discussion of the *INPS* data, see Abbate and Baldassarini (1995), Lucifora (1996), Casavola, Cipollone, and Sestito (1999), and Borgarello and Devicienti (2006).

The data cover some 12½ million workers (according to the INPS *Rapporto Annuale 2004*, page 101). Among those excluded (see Abbate and Baldassarini, 1995, page 118) are farm employees who contribute to a separate social security system, and workers in central and local government. The underlying dataset is the universe of records, and even where samples are drawn, the number of observations is typically large. Contini, Filippi and Villosio (1997), for example, take all workers born on the 10th of March, June, September, and December, a sample of 1 in 91. Each yearly sample includes some 100,000 workers. Comparable data on the public sector for 1981–95, drawn from the Treasury archive, are used by Cappellari (2001).

Income Tax Data

The income tax records have not in general provided tabulations of earnings for employees. For the years 1982 to 1989, however, such a tabulation was provided in the publication *Analisi dei Redditi delle Persone Fisiche Suddivisi per Categorie Omogenee di Contribuenti*, published by the Ministero delle Finanze. For example, Ministero delle Finanze (1992) gives data for the tax year 1989. The table LD4A gives a tabulation for lavoratori dipendenti (dependent workers) by range of annual earned income, together with the mean value for the range. The results in Table K.6 have been interpolated from these data. (There are also data for 1991, but this is limited to declarations Mod 740, excluding those Mod 101 (those with only wage income), and they only cover 9.9 million workers, compared with 14.6 million in 1989. These 1991 data have not been used in Table K.6.)

Comparison of SHIW and INPS Data

The differing findings (see below) regarding earnings dispersion of the Bank of Italy survey (*SHIW*) data and the *INPS* administrative data are discussed by Bardone, Gittleman, and Keese (1998). They note that the *SHIW* data cover all sectors, and that

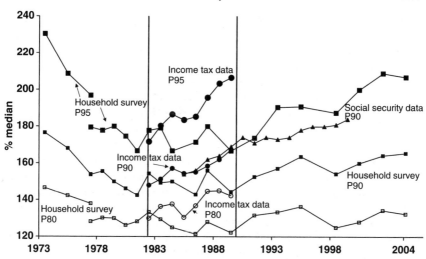

Figure K.1 ITALY upper part of the distribution 1973–2004

Sources: Table K.4, columns C, D, and E; Table K.5, columns G and H; Table K.6, columns E, F, and G; Table K.7, column G.

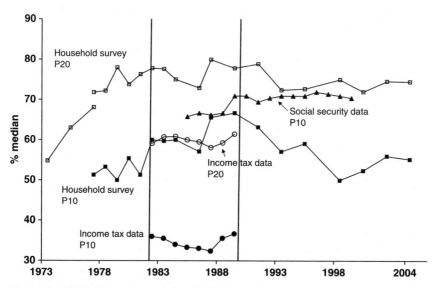

Figure K.2 ITALY lower part of the distribution 1973–2004

Sources: Table K.4, columns A and B; Table K.5, column F; Table K.6, columns A and B; Table K.7, column F.

the *SHIW* data are 'more likely than the *INPS* data to cover workers in the informal sector' (1998, page 27). On the other hand, 'measurement error associated with self-reporting of earnings in the *SHIW* data is probably higher than with pay records provided by firms to the *INPS* (unless firms mis-report earnings to minimize payroll taxes)' (1998, page 27). The *SHIW* sample size is relatively small, and data are not available for all years. These considerations lead them to prefer the *INPS* data, but they recognize that 'each of these two sources has its advantages and disadvantages in terms of coverage, types of earnings data collected and data quality' (1998, page 26).

Summary

The principal findings from the Bank of Italy household survey (*SHIW*), the *INPS* data, and the income tax data, are summarized in Figures K.1 and K.2. The different sources point on occasion in different directions. Notably the *INPS* social security data show the bottom decile as broadly constant in the 1990s, whereas the Bank of Italy household survey data show the bottom decile as falling. But there is sufficient commonality to allow certain conclusions to be drawn.

K.3 What Happened?

In the Lecture, I begin with the period since 1980, but I have emphasized the need to see the recent decades in historical context. In the case of Italy, the experience of the 1970s appears to have been particularly significant.[19] According to Erickson and Ichino, 'during the 1970s, Italy experienced an impressive compression of wage differentials' (1995, page 265). This is borne out by the evidence from the Bank of Italy household survey. We have to bear in mind that the data for these earlier years are probably less reliable, and not fully comparable with later figures, but Figures K.1 and K.2 show a large and sustained decrease in the upper percentiles and a rise in the lower percentiles. The top decile fell from 177 per cent of the median in 1973 to 143 per cent in 1981, a fall of a fifth. A major element in this compression was the Scala Mobile (SM), a negotiated wage indexation 'escalator', notably following the agreement between workers and employers in 1975. According to Visco, writing in 1979, 'one can clearly distinguish a marked tendency for the range of earnings to become narrower, despite the few years which have passed since the conclusion of the 1975 agreement' (1979, page 171). More recently, Manacorda (2004) has estimated the effect of the SM, using the differential effect for men and women and at different percentiles to identify its impact. He concludes that 'the SM had a considerable equalizing effect and that it was largely responsible for the fall in inequality between the late 1970s and the mid-1980s' (2004, page 609).

The compression came to a stop in the early 1980s, as indicated by the first vertical lines in Figures K.1 and K.2. According to Erickson and Ichino, 'most evidence suggests that this compression came to a stop around 1982–83, coincident with a

---

[19] I am most grateful to Ignazio Visco for having drawn this to my attention, and for having given me a number of valuable papers written at the time, including Visco (1979).

major institutional change [in the SM], a major economic change (the slowdown in inflation), a major technological change (industrial restructuring and the computer revolution), and a major political change (the loss of support for unions and their egalitarian pay policies)' (1995, page 265). There was then a fall in the lower percentiles, consistent with the impact of the Scala Mobile being lessened as inflation fell, and as the mechanism was eroded by government decisions. The income tax data suggest some rise in upper percentiles, but this is not mirrored in the household survey data. Moreover, the lower percentiles appear to rise in the latter part of the 1980s. Despite the major changes noted, the social security (*INPS*) data show a decile ratio of 2.34 in 1985 and 2.46 in 1990, a rise of only 5 per cent, and the household survey data show a fall in the decile ratio between 1983 and 1989. In broad terms, there was no great change in the 1980s.

The 1990s evidence from the household surveys, to the right of the second line in Figures K.1 and K.2, shows a clearer picture, as summarized by Checchi and Pagani (2005): wage dispersion increased in the early 1990s, but was stable in the second part of the decade.[20] At the bottom, however, the social security data show a different picture. As discussed earlier, the reasons for the difference may lie in the coverage of the two sources. The household survey may well have better coverage of the informal sector than the social security data. Part of the fall in the bottom decile between 1991 and 1993 may however be attributable to the fact that there was a change in the survey organization. The two sources are however agreed that the top groups were gaining relative to the median—see Figure K.1. In the upper part of the distribution there is a distinct fanning out. Between 1989 and 2004, P80 rose by 8 per cent relative to the median, P90 by 15 per cent, and P95 by 23 per cent. Bardone, Gittleman, and Keese summarize the 1990s as follows: 'both the *SHIW* and *INPS* data suggest that earnings inequality has risen in Italy over the past decade, although they differ somewhat with respect to the timing, magnitude and composition of this increase' (1998, page 28).

Summary

Paraphrasing Manacorda (2004, page 602), we can say that earnings dispersion in Italy decreased in the late 1970s, stayed broadly unchanged in the 1980s, and increased in the 1990s, with a fanning out of the upper percentiles.

---

[20] The Italian labour market experience in recent years is described in Brandolini et al (2005) and Prasad and Utili (1998).

Table K.1. Italy: OECD (1993)

	Column			
	A	B	C	D
	Male		Female	
	P10	P90	P10	P90
1979	67	137	54	129
1980	69	146	60	133
1982	70	150	59	140
1986	73	151	58	131
1987	75	156	64	129

Coverage	All
Industry	Non-farm
Age	18–65
Sex	See headings
Occupation	All
Definition	Net of taxes
Intensity	FT FY
Period	Annual
Limits	None
Source	OECD (1993, Table 5.2)
Original source	Household Survey of the Bank of Italy

Table K.2. Italy: OECD (1996)

	Column											
	A	B	C	D	E	F	G	H	I	J	K	L
	All		Male		Female		FT workers		Male		Female	
	P10	P90	P10	P90	P10	P90	P10	P90	P10	P90	P10	P90
1979	51	150	64	146	44	133						
1980	55	146	61	143	50	133						
1981	53	141	67	146	46	146						
1982	62	150	65	150	50	138						
1983	59	147	65	146	53	142						
1984	60	150	65	150	58	135						
1986	57	143	69	153	54	133	64	143	69	152	65	133
1987	66	160	69	156	61	139	69	160	70	156	68	136
1989	67	144	72	156	64	138	67	144	72	156	75	138
1991	63	153	70	155	61	145	67	151	70	156	67	139
1993	57	160	63	165	53	149	62	157	65	165	60	140

Coverage	All
Industry	All
Age	All
Sex	See headings
Occupation	All
Definition	Net
Intensity	See headings
Period	Monthly
Limits	None
Source	OECD (1996, Table 3.1)
Original source	Household Survey of the Bank of Italy

Table K.3. Italy: OECD (LMS)

	A	B	C	D	E	F	G	H	I	J	K	L
	All				Male				Female			
	P10	P20	P80	P90	P10	P20	P80	P90	P10	P20	P80	P90
1986	68.3	80.0	128.3	151.7	71.9	81.3	126.6	150.0	63.5	80.8	123.1	144.2
1987	68.8	79.7	129.7	157.8	70.6	80.9	695.0	157.4	64.3	80.4	123.2	144.6
1988	68.7	79.1	132.8	161.2	69.4	79.2	130.6	159.7	67.2	82.8	125.9	150.0
1989	72.2	79.2	133.3	163.9	71.4	79.2	132.5	162.3	75.8	85.5	127.4	154.8
1990	71.4	79.2	136.4	167.5	70.7	79.3	135.4	168.3	75.8	84.8	128.8	157.6
1991	70.6	78.8	135.3	164.7	69.2	78.0	133.0	163.7	74.3	82.4	128.4	155.4
1992	70.8	79.8	136.0	168.5	69.5	78.9	133.7	167.4	75.6	83.5	129.5	157.7
1993	70.9	79.6	134.4	166.7	71.4	79.6	134.7	167.3	75.6	82.9	129.3	156.1
1994	71.1	79.4	134.0	166.0	70.6	79.4	134.3	167.6	75.3	82.4	129.4	157.6
1995	71.7	79.8	138.4	172.7	70.5	79.0	137.1	172.4	75.9	83.9	131.0	164.4
1996	72.5	80.4	139.2	173.5	71.3	79.6	138.9	174.1	76.7	83.3	132.2	164.4

Coverage	All
Industry	Excludes agricultural and general government workers
Age	All
Sex	See headings
Occupation	All
Definition	Gross
Intensity	FT
Period	Monthly
Limits	None
Source	Downloaded from OECD website December 2005
Original source	Social security data collected by INPS

Table K.4. Italy: Bank of Italy Survey

	A	B	C	D	E	F	G	H	I	J	K	L	M	N	O	P	Q
									Column								
	All						Shares					Men					
	P10	P20	P80	P90	P95	P99	Share of bottom 10%	Share of bottom 20%	Share of top 20%	Share of top 10%	Gini	P10	P20	P80	P90	P95	P99
1977	51.3	71.8	128.2	153.8	179.5	256.4	3.13	9.24	33.39	19.72	23.8	65.0	75.0	137.5	157.5	187.5	275.0
1978	53.3	72.2	130.2	155.6	177.8	288.9	3.03	9.05	33.92	20.62	24.3	62.5	75.0	125.0	156.3	187.5	312.5
1979	50.0	78.0	130.0	150.0	180.0	300.0	3.13	9.29	32.74	19.71	23.1	63.6	76.4	127.3	145.5	181.8	272.7
1980	55.4	73.8	126.2	146.2	174.6	259.1	3.52	9.99	31.60	18.51	21.3	60.0	77.1	125.7	142.9	171.4	257.1
1981	51.3	76.3	128.2	142.5	166.7	233.3	3.22	9.50	32.13	19.03	22.3	62.5	81.3	127.5	150.0	175.0	250.0
1982	60.0	77.8	133.3	154.4	177.8	266.7	3.77	10.47	31.53	18.35	20.7	64.0	78.0	128.0	150.0	170.0	250.0
1983	59.7	77.6	129.4	149.3	179.1	258.7	3.89	10.41	31.67	18.47	21.0	65.5	77.3	127.3	145.5	181.8	245.5
1984	60.0	75.0	125.0	150.0	166.7	275.0	4.03	10.67	31.84	18.96	20.9	66.4	79.0	126.4	152.7	177.3	300.2
1986	57.1	72.9	121.4	142.9	171.4	250.0	4.19	10.90	31.39	18.34	20.1	69.0	82.8	124.1	151.7	179.3	248.3
1987	65.6	80.0	128.0	156.0	180.0	266.7	4.57	11.37	32.11	19.03	20.4	68.8	78.8	130.0	156.3	187.5	264.1
1989	66.7	77.8	122.2	144.4	166.7	277.8	5.27	12.09	31.68	18.95	19.3	72.2	80.0	133.3	155.6	188.9	333.3
1991	63.2	78.9	131.6	152.6	173.7	263.2	4.92	11.74	31.29	18.28	19.4	70.0	80.0	130.0	150.0	180.0	267.5
1993	57.1	72.4	133.3	157.1	190.5	309.5	3.67	9.78	34.10	20.83	24.1	63.4	74.9	132.2	167.4	198.2	308.4
1995	59.1	72.7	136.4	163.6	190.9	310.9	4.00	10.23	33.97	20.60	23.4	62.5	75.0	133.3	166.7	200.0	333.3
1998	50.0	75.0	125.0	154.2	187.5	291.7	3.23	9.18	33.78	20.48	24.1	60.0	76.0	132.0	160.0	200.0	320.0
2000	52.4	72.0	128.0	160.0	200.0	307.7	3.42	9.50	34.05	20.79	24.0	63.8	76.9	134.6	169.2	200.0	346.2
2002	56.0	74.6	134.3	164.2	209.0	313.4	3.54	9.44	34.05	21.78	25.1	64.3	78.6	140.0	178.6	214.3	342.9
2004	55.2	74.5	132.4	165.5	206.9	306.2	3.76	9.83	35.18	21.34	24.2	66.7	80.0	135.7	173.3	213.3	326.7

(Continued)

Table K.4. (Continued)

	R	S	T	U	V	W	X	Y	Z	AA	AB	AC	AD	AE	AF	AG	AH	AI
		Women					FT						Non-farm males aged 30–50 FY					
	P10	P20	P80	P90	P95	P99	P10	P20	P80	P90	P95	Gini	P10	P20	P80	P90	P95	Gini
1977	40.0	66.7	133.3	156.7	176.0	216.7							71	80	133	156	178	19.1
1978	39.5	63.2	126.3	142.1	157.9	210.5							77	83	135	155	193	19.2
1979	44.4	62.2	124.4	133.3	154.2	200.0							75	83	125	150	183	17.6
1980	46.7	66.7	119.2	133.3	150.0	204.0							77	80	124	155	173	16.7
1981	46.2	64.6	130.8	146.2	161.5	223.1							76	82	122	144	162	16.7
1982	50.0	75.0	125.0	137.5	150.0	206.3							74	79	130	144	167	17.1
1983	48.9	66.7	125.3	141.1	155.6	216.7							75	83	125	150	181	16.3
1984	52.9	73.5	127.5	137.3	152.9	190.7							73	80	123	145	174	17.3
1985	54.2	75.0	125.0	133.3	150.0	200.0	64	77	129	143	171	18.9	77	83	128	154	192	16.5
1986	61.5	76.9	125.4	138.5	161.5	215.4	69	80	130	157	180	19.5	74	83	130	154	186	18.3
1988	63.7	78.1	125.0	137.5	156.3	218.8	67	78	122	144	167	18.7	74	82	128	154	185	18.6
1990	60.5	74.9	126.8	144.1	161.4	201.7	67	77	128	149	174	18.6	73	82	130	155	182	17.8
1992	53.1	69.0	132.6	148.5	164.5	221.8	63	74	130	158	187	22.7	72	80	128	160	184	20.0
1994	50.0	70.0	125.0	150.0	171.4	225.0	68	77	136	163	190	22.0	71	78	133	159	195	20.0

1997	45.5	68.2	122.7	140.9	163.6	234.1	60	76	124	156	180	21.6	73	82	133	156	185	19.6
1999	54.5	68.2	135.5	150.0	172.7	272.7												
2001	49.6	66.2	132.4	158.9	194.5	302.0												
2004	53.8	69.2	130.8	153.8	192.3	276.9												

Coverage	All
Industry	See headings
Age	See headings
Sex	See headings
Occupation	All
Definition	Gross
Intensity	See headings
Period	Monthly, obtained by dividing annual earnings by the number of months worked
Limits	Primary job
Source	Brandolini, Cipollone, and Sestito (2002, pages 236 and 238), updated by Andrea Brandolini
Original source	Household Survey of the Bank of Italy

Table K.5. Italy: Bank of Italy Survey (Earlier estimates)

				Column					
A	B	C	D	E	F	G	H	I
		Shares				Percentiles			
Share of bottom 10%	Share of bottom 20%	Share of top 20%	Share of top 10%	P10	P20	P80	P90	P95
1973	1.8	5.7	39.9	25.4		54.8	146.6	176.5	230.4
1975						63.0	142.3	168.0	208.7
1977	2.2	7.3	34.6	20.5	35.9	68.1	138.0	154.0	196.9
1981	1.8	6.7	33.7	20.0					

Coverage	All
Industry	All
Age	All
Sex	All
Occupation	All
Definition	Net
Intensity	All
Period	Weekly
Limits	None
Source	Caligiuri (1978, pages 368–9) and Pirrotta and Zen (1983, page 19)
Original source	Household Survey of the Bank of Italy

Table K.6. Italy: Income tax data

	A	B	C	D	Column E	F	G	H
	P10	P20	P25	P75	P80	P90	P95	P99
1982	36.0	59.1	66.9	125.0	130.0	148.0	171.7	278.7
1983	35.5	60.7	72.1	126.8	136.4	151.3	180.4	291.5
1984	34.0	60.8	73.8	130.9	137.7	157.1	186.6	311.1
1985	33.3	60.0	69.2	125.3	130.4	154.4	183.6	320.6
1986	33.1	59.5	67.9	123.0	136.8	155.1	185.4	335.0
1987	32.4	58.1	67.1	133.5	144.8	158.5	195.7	347.8
1988	35.6	59.3	69.4	136.6	145.0	162.0	203.4	360.0
1989	36.7	61.5	72.7	135.2	142.2	167.4	206.6	362.4

Coverage	All
Industry	All
Age	All
Sex	Men
Occupation	All
Definition	Gross including overtime and supplements
Intensity	All
Period	Annual
Limits	None
Source	Calculated from tax statistics—see text
Note	P90, P95, and P99 calculated by Pareto interpolation

Table K.7. Italy: Social security data (INPS)

	A	B	C	D	E	F	G	H	I	J	K	L	M
						Column							
	Private sector			Public sector		Private sector							
	Male	FT		Male	FT	All				Male		Female	
	P10	P90	Std dev of logs	P10	P90	P10	P90	Gini	Std dev of logs	P10	P90	P10	P90
1979	70	157	0.42										
1980	71	160	0.38										
1981	72	154	0.37										
1982	73	149	0.36	84	127								
1983	72	155	0.38	85	127								
1984	71	154	0.38	85	128								
1985	71	158	0.40	85	128	65.8	154	19.9	0.36	68.6	149.5	62.4	140.8
1986	71	160	0.40	85	130	66.7	156	20.2	0.36	69.2	152.4	64.7	144.4
1987	70	167	0.41	84	131	66.2	162	21.2	0.38	69.2	157.2	66.0	149.1
1988	69	168	0.42	84	138	66.7	164	21.5	0.38	68.3	160.0	67.9	152.0
1989	69	168	0.41	83	136	70.9	169	21.8	0.38	70.3	164.3	75.9	154.9
1990	69	175	0.43	80	138	70.9	174	23.2	0.40	69.6	167.0	75.6	158.2
1991	68	177	0.43	80	142	69.4	171	22.6	0.39	68.8	167.1	74.6	156.8
1992	68	182	0.44	79	142	70.4	174	22.8	0.39	69.1	169.6	76.1	158.7
1993	68	180	0.45	79	143	70.9	173	22.6	0.39	70.2	168.4	75.9	158.3
1994	66	186	0.48	79	143	70.9	174	22.8	0.39	70.1	169.3	76.0	159.4
1995	65	190	0.48			70.9	178	22.9	0.39	69.9	173.3	76.2	161.6

	Capellari (2000, Table 1)	Capellari (2000a, Table 1)	Borgarello and Devicienti (2006, Table 1)				Borgarello and Devicienti (2001, Table 5)	Borgarello and Devicienti (2001, Table 5)
1996			71.9	180	23.2	0.39	70.6	76.8
1997			71.4	180	23.6	0.40	174.5	163.1
1998			70.9	181	23.9	0.41		
1999			70.4	184	25.7	0.43		
Sources	Capellari (2000, Table 1)	Capellari (2000a, Table 1)	Borgarello and Devicienti (2006, Table 1)				Borgarello and Devicienti (2001, Table 5)	Borgarello and Devicienti (2001, Table 5)

Coverage	See headings
Industry	See headings; excludes agriculture and (apart from columns D and E) central government administration
Age	Columns A to E, born between 1936 and 1959; other columns aged 15–64
Sex	See headings
Occupation	All
Definition	Gross including overtime and supplements
Intensity	See headings
Period	Annual earnings divided by days paid in year
Limits	None
Source	See bottom of table
Original source	INPS social security data

Bibliography

Abbate, C and Baldassarini, A, 1995, 'Contenuto informativo degli archivi INPS e confronto alter fonti sur mercato del lavoro', *Economia e Lavoro*, vol 28: 115–33.

Bardone, L, Gittleman, M, and Keese, M, 1998, 'Causes and consequences of earnings inequality in OECD Countries', *Lavoro e Relazioni Industriali*, vol 2: 13–59.

Bonjour, D and Pacelli, L, 1998, 'Wage formation and the gender wage gap: Do institutions matter? Italy and Switzerland compared', UCL Discussion Paper 98-12, University College London.

Borgarello, A and Devicienti, F, 2001, 'Trends in the Italian earnings distribution, 1985–1996', LABORatorio R Revelli, University of Turin.

—— and —— 2006, 'L'Aumento della disuguaglianza dei salari in Italia: Premi salariali per le "nuove" skill?', *Politica Economica*, vol 22: 69–108.

Brandolini, A, 1999, 'The distribution of personal income in post-war Italy: Source description, data quality, and the time pattern of income inequality', *Giornale degli Economisti ed Annali di Economia*, vol 85: 183–201.

—— Casadio, P, Cipollone, P, Magnani, M, Rosolia, A, and Torrini, R, 2005, 'Employment growth in Italy in the 1990s: Institutional arrangements and market forces', paper presented at the International Conference 'Social Pacts, Employment and Growth: A Reappraisal of Ezio Tarantelli's Thought', Rome, 31 March–2 April 2005.

—— Cipollone, P, and Sestito, P, 2002, 'Earnings dispersion, low pay and household poverty in Italy, 1977–98', in D Cohen, T Piketty, and G Saint-Paul, editors, *The Economics of Rising Inequalities*, Oxford University Press, Oxford.

Caligiuri, G, 1978, 'Evoluzione dei redditi da lavoro dipendente e da pensione nel quinquennio 1973–77', *Bollettino Banc d'Italia*, vol 33: 367–81.

Cappellari, L, 2000, 'The covariance structure of Italian male wages', *Manchester School*, vol 68: 659–84.

—— 2000a, 'The dynamics and inequality of Italian male earnings: Permanent changes or transitory fluctuations?', ISER Working Paper 2000–41.

—— 2001, 'Earnings dynamics and uncertainty in Italy: How do they differ between the private and public sectors?', ISER, University of Essex.

Casavola, P, Cipollone, P, and Sestito, P, 1999, 'Determinants of pay in the Italian labor market: Jobs and workers' in J C Haltiwanger et al, editors, *The Creation and Analysis of Employer–Employee Matched Data*, North-Holland, Amsterdam.

Checchi, D and Pagani, L, 2005, 'The effects of unions on wage inequality: The Italian case in the 1990s', *Politica economica*, vol 21: 43–70.

Contini, B, Filippi, M, and Villosio, C, 1998, 'Earnings mobility in the Italian economy', in R Asplund, P J Sloane, and I Theodossiou, editors, *Low Pay and Earnings Mobility in Europe*, Edward Elgar, Cheltenham.

D'Alessio, G and Faiella, I, 2000, editors, *Archivo storico dell'Indagine sui bilanci delle famiglie italiene, 1977–98*, Banca d'Italia, Rome.

Del Boca, D and Pasqua, S, 2002, 'Employment patterns of husbands and wives and family income distribution in Italy (1977–1998)', IZA Discussion Paper 489.

Dell'Aringa, C and Lucifora, C, 1994, 'Wage dispersion and unionism: Do unions protect low pay?', *International Journal of Manpower*, vol 15: 150–69.

—— Ghinetti, P, and Lucifora, C, 2000, 'Pay inequality and economic performance in Italy: A review of the applied literature', paper prepared for the second PIEP Project meeting at the LSE.

Erickson, C L and Ichino, A C, 1995, 'Wage differentials in Italy: Market forces, institutions and inflation', in R B Freeman and L F Katz, editors, *Differences and Changes in Wage Structures*, University of Chicago Press, Chicago.

Flinn, C J, 2002, 'Labour market structure and welfare: A comparison of Italy and the U.S.', *Review of Economic Studies*, vol 69: 611–45.

Lilla, M, 2005, 'Disuguaglianze salariali in Italia: nouve evidenze dai microdati SHIW', *Politica economica*, vol 21: 71–101.

Lucifora, C, 1996, 'L'analysi del mercato del lavoro con micro-dati: l'utilizzo degli archivi amminstrativi INPS', *Economia e Lavoro*, vol 29: 3–20.

—— 1999, 'Wage inequalities and low pay: The role of labour market institutions', Nota di Lavoro Fondazione Eni Enrico Mattei No 13, FEEM, Milan.

Manacorda, M, 2004, 'Can the Scala Mobile explain the fall and rise of earnings inequality in Italy? A Semiparametric Analysis, 1977–1993', *Journal of Labor Economics*, vol 22: 585–613.

Ministero delle Finanze, 1992, *Analisi dei Redditi delle Persone Fisiche Suddivisi per Categorie Omogenee di Contribuenti*, Rome.

Pirrotta, R and Zen, G, 1983, 'Il reddito da lavoro dipendente nelle indagini campionarie della Banca d'Italia dal 1972 al 1981: evoluzione e determinanti', *Temi di Discussione*, No 26, Bank of Italy.

Prasad, E and Utili, F, 1998, 'The Italian labor market: Stylized facts, institutions and directions for reform', IMF Working Paper 98/42.

Visco, I, 1979, 'The indexation of earnings in Italy: Sectoral analysis and estimates for 1978–79', *Rivista di Politica Economica*, vol 13: 151–83.

L

Netherlands

Wage inequality in the Netherlands has increased over the last twenty years. Although the increase has not been so severe as that in Anglo Saxon countries, it was more than in most other continental European countries.

Stegeman and Waaijers, 2001, page 50

L.1 Introduction

The Netherlands had the same geographical boundaries throughout the period. The country adopted the euro in 2002.

Previous Coverage

The Netherlands is covered by five tables in Lydall (1968). These are based on the income tax statistics (*Inkomensverdeling en vermogensverdeling*) for the years 1949, 1952–4, 1957–9. The figures are based on distributions classified by income, not earnings, and the income tax source is not used here.

The Netherlands is included in all three OECD compilations:

1993 (Table L.1): 1973 to 1990 various years, aged 23–64, weekly earnings for industries 1–8 for 1973, 1975, and 1979, weekly for industries 1–9 for 1979 and 1985, weekly for industries 0–9 for 1985, annual for industries 0–9 for 1985 and 1990. Supplied by Wiemer Salverda, on the basis of data from the half yearly Survey of Earnings for 1972 to 1979 and the yearly Survey of Earnings for 1985 and 1990.

1996 (Table L.2):1981–1994, interpolated by OECD Secretariat from classes of earnings derived from the yearly Survey of Earnings as reported in the publication *Sociaal-Economische Maandstatistiek* (referred to below as *SEM*, previously (before 1984) *Sociale Maandstatistiek*).

LMS (Table L.3): 1977–1999 (only quartiles for 1998), full time full year equivalent workers including overtime and occasional payments, interpolated from classes of earnings derived from the yearly Survey of Earnings as reported in *SEM* and supplied by Central Bureau of Statistics.

Official Publications

For many years, the *Statistical Yearbook of the Netherlands* (SY) contained data on the dispersion of earnings, and these are summarized in Table L.4. In 2005, the Yearbook adopted a new layout and did not include a table on the distribution of earnings.

L.2 Data Sources

As is described below, the sources of information on earnings dispersion in the Netherlands have varied over time, as have the coverage and definitions. The OECD (LMS) series runs from 1977 to 1999, but there is an important break in 1995 with the introduction of the new earnings survey. A distinctive feature of the Netherlands labour market is the high proportion of part-timers, which had reached 46 per cent by 2004 (Salverda, van Klaveren, and van der Mer, 2007, Table 2.1). This is discussed in Section L.3.

Historical Data from Employer Gross Earnings Surveys

The Centraal Bureau voor de Statistiek (CBS) has carried out surveys of employers to obtain information on earnings since 1947. Results on the distribution of earnings are available in the SY for years starting from 1970, although they were initially limited in their industrial coverage, and the published results have been limited by age and gender. The first distribution shown in Table L.4, that for 1970, is limited to manufacturing, and covers only males, aged 25 and over. In view of its limited coverage, it is classified as B. Coverage was extended, and starting from 1977 'all economic activities are covered, excluding agriculture and fishing' (SY, 1980, page 347). The survey was six-monthly, although the results published in the SY relate to October, except for the data for 1984 which relate to April. From October 1984 the survey was annual, and the data began to cover agriculture and fishing. The data in Table L.4 cover all sectors from 1985 onwards. From 1986 the data include overtime and occasional payments.

The series evolved therefore substantially over the period 1970 to 1986. The timeline of changes in definition may be summarized as follows:

1971 data extended to men aged 23 and over in place of 25 and over

1975 data extended to cover private services and construction (previously shown separately)

1977 data extended to cover all sectors except for agriculture and fishing

1978 data cover both men and women

1985 data extended to cover agriculture and fishing, extended to full time workers of all ages, and to include standby workers

1986 overtime and other occasional payments included

A further break in the series occurred in 1995 with the introduction of a new design for the Structure of Earnings Survey, described below. This provided better coverage of low-paid jobs.

Structure of Earnings Surveys (LoonStruktuurOnderzoeken)

The current source of earnings data, dating from 1995, is the Structure of Earnings Survey (SES), or LSO (in Dutch). This has been created by matching three data sources: the business survey on employment and wages (Enquête naar Werkgelegenheid en Lonen, or EWL), the registration system of the social security funds (Verzekerden Administratie), and the Labour Force Survey (used for information on education and occupation). See Nordholt (1997). The employer survey covers all enterprises with employees. It has a complicated design, with information for larger employers taken mainly from registers, whereas for smaller enterprises a sample is taken. The data are to a great extent obtained directly by electronic data capture from payroll administrations. In 1997 the sample size was around 149,000. The EWL data from 1995 to 2003 are available on STATLINE from the CBS website, with two sets of figures for 1999 (voorlopig and nader voorlopig herzien) and for 2000 (voorlopig herzien and nader voorlopig herzien). The differences are due to differences in the methods of re-weighting to bring them into line with the employment statistics (see *Sociaal Economische Maandstatistiek* December 2001 and April 2003). From the percentiles shown in Table L.5 it seems safest to treat the figures as two series (1995–9) and (2000–3). The STATLINE results cover all workers (full time and part time), and are therefore not directly comparable with those in Table L.4 from the Statistical Yearbook.

Socio Economic Panel (SEP)

The SEP is a household survey, in which all household members aged 16 and over are asked each year about their income, employment, ownership of durables, housing, and other circumstances. The sample size is around 5,000. The survey has information on yearly wages.

Survey of Income and Program Users

The Survey of Income and Program Users is the survey lodged with the Luxembourg Income Study. The data for 1983 and 1987 have been used by Gottschalk and Joyce (1998).

Summary

The available data on the distribution of earnings in the Netherlands cannot be seen as a continuous series, and in Figures L.1 and L.2 the breaks are shown clearly. The lack of continuity led Hartog, Oosterbeek, and Teulings to state that 'there is no good time-series information on earnings inequality among individuals in the Netherlands, due to the absence or incomparability of information about particular years' (1993, page 184). This seems too strong a conclusion. The information assembled here has value, even if it cannot be treated as a single series.

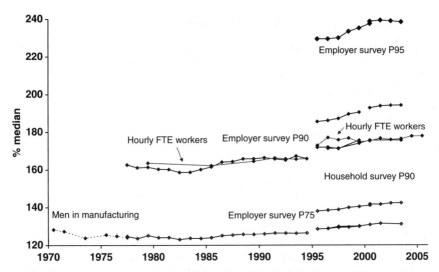

Figure L.1 NETHERLANDS upper part of the distribution 1970–2005

Sources: Table L.3, columns D and F; Table L.4, columns C, D, and L; Table L.5, columns C, D, and E; Table L.6, column B.

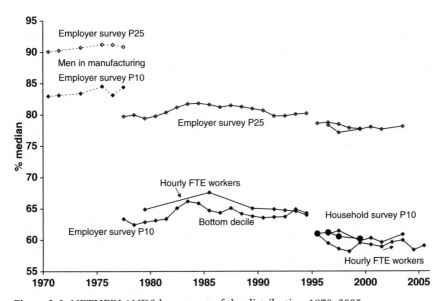

Figure L.2 NETHERLANDS lower part of the distribution 1970–2005

Sources: Table L.3, columns A and C; Table L.4, columns A, B, I, and J; Table L.6, column A.

L.3 What Happened?

A brief history of the Dutch labour market from 1945 to the early 1990s is provided by Hartog, Oosterbeek, and Teulings (1993). They suggest that four broad periods can be distinguished: the early reconstruction period (late 1940s), the golden growth period of the 1950s and 1960s, the problems of the 1970s following the first oil crisis, and the period of recovery in the 1980s. In the Golden Age, strong growth had a major impact on the labour market, and wage differentials were affected by government policy including the minimum wage underpinned by welfare benefits. The minimum wage was raised substantially in 1974 and there was a deliberate government policy to narrow differentials (Hartog and Vriend, 1989). The rise in unemployment in the early 1980s led to the general agreement between the government, unions, and employers (Wassenaar Akkoord of 1982) on the moderation of wage claims. According to Hartog, Oosterbeek, and Teulings, this agreement has had large effects on the outcome of the process of wage formation and these effects lasted for several years (1993, page 185). But from the mid-1980s there was a rise in wage dispersion. According to Stegeman and Waaijers, there was a fall in wages at the bottom of the distribution in the 1980s and a rise at the upper quartile in the 1990s, although they note that 'this rise in inequality is rather moderate compared to the US' (Stegeman and Waaijers, 2001, page 50).

In seeking to trace these changes in earnings dispersion, we face the problem that the data start only at the end of the golden growth period, and they are a patchwork rather than a single series. These breaks mean that we have to be cautious in drawing conclusions. It is should noted for example that the sizeable fall in the OECD LMS data (Table L.3) for the bottom decile from 64.3 in 1994 to 61.0 in 1995 coincides with the introduction of the new earnings survey. (The top decile similarly jumps upwards from 165.8 to 171.9.)

The data for the first part of the 1980s have to be treated with caution in view of their limited coverage. They show a rise in the bottom decile and lower quartile, but not a magnitude to register according to the criteria applied here. The same applied in the upper part of the distribution for the period 1977 to 1983, but the bottom decile rose by 6 per cent between 1978 and 1983. In this sense, the distribution was narrowing in the period of active government intervention described above, although it should be noted that the Statistical Yearbook based figures in Table L.4 show a much less marked rise than the figures given by the OECD (LMS) and shown in Figure L.2. It would be hard to resist the conclusion that the overall distribution was fairly stable from 1970 to 1983, with, if anything, an improvement in the position of those in the lower part of the distribution.

This narrowing was reversed after 1983, in that the bottom decile fell, but again the change is not sufficient to register. The top decile rose, relative to the median, by 5 per cent between 1983 and 1995. In the decade since 1995, there is little sign of a downward trend in the position of the bottom decile or lower quartile. The upper quartile, the top decile, and the top vintile all show a continuing upward movement, but the increase was in all cases less than 5 per cent.

The Netherlands has been described as 'the world champion of part-time work' (Salverda, 1998, page 28). Concentrating on full time workers, as in the series discussed so far, may therefore give a misleading impression of what is happening in the labour market as a whole. The studies by Salverda (1998) and Salverda, van Klaveren, and van der Mer (2007) have taken hourly wages of all workers, expressed as full time equivalents. These series are indicated by arrows in Figure L.2 (at the top they move very similarly to the earlier series and they are not shown in Figure L.1). As Salverda (1998) shows, between 1979 and 1985 there was an improvement in the position of the bottom decile, but this was less than 5 per cent. The improvement was reversed between 1985 and 1994, when the bottom decile fell by 6 per cent. In the latter part of the 1990s, there is more evidence of a decline in the bottom decile when we include part time workers on this basis, but the overall change from 1995 to 2002 is not sufficient to register. These changes at the bottom of the earnings distribution are mirrored in the estimates of the incidence of low pay in Salverda, van Klaveren, and van der Mer (2007, Figure 2.8) that show a rise from 1985 to 1998 and then remain broadly stable.

Summary

The overall distribution of earnings in the Netherlands was fairly stable from 1970 to 1983, with, if anything, an improvement in the position of those in the lower part of the distribution. This was followed by a period from the mid-1980s to the mid-1990s when the top decile increased; the bottom decile may have fallen and the incidence of low pay increased. Since the mid-1990s, any changes in dispersion are not large enough to register according to the criteria applied here.

Table L.1. Netherlands: OECD (1993)

	A	B	C	D	E	F	G	H
	Column							
	All							
	Weekly; exc. overtime, industries 1–8		Weekly; exc. overtime, industries 1–9		Weekly; exc. overtime, industries 0–9		Annual; inc. overtime, industries 0–9	
	P10	P90	P10	P90	P10	P90	P10	P90
1973	76	153						
1975	77	153						
1979	76	154						
1985			74	164	75	160	73	162
1990			75	160			71	164

(*Continued*)

Table L.1. (*Continued*)

				Column							
		Male						Female			
I	J	K	L	M	N	O	P	Q	R	S	T
Weekly; exc. overtime, industries 1–8		Weekly; exc. overtime, industries 1–9		Annual; inc. overtime, industries 1–8		Weekly; exc. overtime, industries 1–8		Weekly; exc. overtime, industries 1–9		Annual; inc. overtime, industries 1–8	
P10	P90	P10	P90	P10	P90	P10	P90	P10	P90	P10	P90
1973 77	154					76	146				
1975 78	153					82	143				
1979 76	154					85	143				
1985		75	166	75	163			76	150	77	143
1990		76	162	72	165			79	143	74	148

Coverage   All
Industry   See headings
Age   23–64
Sex   See headings
Occupation   All
Definition   Gross; see headings
Intensity   FT and Full week
Period   See headings
Limits   None
Source   OECD (1993, Table 5.2); Half yearly survey of earnings 1972 to 1979; Yearly survey of earnings for 1985 and 1989
Note   Calculations made by W Salverda

Table L.2. Netherlands: OECD (1996)

	Column	
	A	B
	P10	P90
1985	64.7	161.5
1986	64.3	164.1
1987	65.1	164.4
1988	64.2	165.8
1989	63.8	165.8
1990	63.5	166.4
1991	63.6	165.7
1992	63.7	165.1
1993	64.9	167.3
1994	64.3	165.8

Coverage	All
Industry	All
Age	All
Sex	All
Occupation	All
Definition	Gross, inc. overtime, holiday pay
Intensity	FT and FY equivalent
Period	Annual
Limits	None
Source	OECD (1996, Table 3.1)
Original source	*Survey of Earnings* data
Note	Interpolated by OECD from distribution by earnings class

Table L.3. Netherlands: OECD (LMS)

	A	B	C	D	E	F	G	H	I	J	K	L	M	N	O	P	Q	R
Column																		
			All						Male						Female			
	P10	P20	P25	P75	P80	P90	P10	P20	P25	P75	P80	P90	P10	P20	P25	P75	P80	P90
1977	63.3	75.2	79.7	124.8	132.8	162.7												
1978	62.4	75.2	80.0	123.6	132.4	161.2												
1979	62.9	74.9	79.4	125.1	132.0	161.4												
1980	63.1	75.1	79.8	124.0	132.2	160.4												
1981	63.4	75.7	80.4	124.1	131.4	160.2												
1982	65.1	76.7	81.2	123.0	131.2	158.7												
1983	66.2	77.5	81.7	123.7	131.9	158.8												
1984	65.8	77.4	81.8	123.6	132.4	160.2												
1985	64.7	77.0	81.6	124.0	132.8	161.5	69.7	79.5	83.4	124.5	133.3	162.0	60.5	77.4	81.8	121.6	127.9	148.9
1986	64.3	76.9	81.2	125.1	134.0	164.1												
1987	65.1	77.4	81.5	125.4	134.4	164.4												
1988	64.2	76.6	81.3	125.8	135.1	165.8												
1989	63.8	76.4	81.0	125.7	134.9	165.8												
1990	63.5	76.3	80.7	125.9	135.2	166.4	66.4	77.7	81.9	125.8	135.3	165.1	59.9	74.8	79.6	124.1	131.7	152.9
1991	63.6	75.1	79.8	126.4	135.1	165.7												
1992	63.7	75.1	79.8	126.3	134.9	165.1												

(Continued)

Table L.3. (*Continued*)

	Column																	
	A	B	C	D	E	F	G	H	I	J	K	L	M	N	O	P	Q	R
			All						Male						Female			
	P10	P20	P25	P75	P80	P90	P10	P20	P25	P75	P80	P90	P10	P20	P25	P75	P80	P90
1993	64.9	75.5	80.1	126.2	135.5	167.3	66.4	77.4	81.6	126.9	135.6	166.0	64.7	76.5	80.8	124.5	131.4	155.2
1994	64.3	75.3	80.2	126.4	135.0	165.8	63.7	75.3	80.1	128.4	138.5	171.7	61.4	74.2	79.3	125.6	133.5	158.6
1995	61.0	73.5	78.6	128.5	138.5	171.9	62.8	74.9	80.1	128.6	138.0	171.9	61.1	73.9	78.9	124.7	133.3	157.3
1996	61.2	73.6	78.8	128.8	138.8	172.0	62.3	75.0	79.8	129.4	138.9	173.0	60.7	73.6	78.4	125.8	133.4	158.5
1997	60.5	73.1	78.5	129.4	138.6	171.2			79.7	129.8					77.7	126.1		
1998			77.9	129.5														
1999	60.1	72.6	77.7	129.9	139.7	175.6	61.8	74.3	79.6	130.1	139.8	175.0	61.3	73.1	77.7	126.7	134.4	160.7

Coverage	All
Industry	All
Age	All
Sex	See headings
Occupation	All
Definition	Gross inc. overtime, holiday and occasional payments
Intensity	FT and full year equivalent
Period	Annual
Limits	None
Source	Downloaded from OECD website December 2005
Original source	Enterprise survey *Survey of Earnings*
Notes	(1) Interpolated by OECD from distribution by earnings class; (2) Unusual in use of full year equivalent

Table L.4. Netherlands: Data from Statistical Yearbook

	Column												
	A	B	C	D	E	F	G	H	I	J	K	L	
	All industries (exc. agric. and fish. before 1985) male and female				Manufacturing, construction and private services male				Manufacturing male				Source*
	P10	P25	P75	P90	P10	P25	P75	P90	P10	P25	P75	P90	
1970									83.0	90.1	113.2	128.3	SY 1971, page 314
1971									83.1	90.3	112.7	127.3	SY 1974, page 306
1973									83.4	90.7	111.2	123.8	SY 1975, page 308
1975					82.0	89.9	112.5	127.8	84.5	91.2	111.0	125.5	SY 1976, page 323
1976					81.2	89.6	112.3	126.7	83.1	91.2	111.5	124.8	SY 1977, page 325
1977					82.6	89.8	112.6	126.8	84.4	90.9	111.4	124.1	SY 1978, page 337
1978	74.2	84.5	124.6	165.2									SY 1980, page 352
1980	74.2	84.6	123.6	163.9									SY 1982, page 357
1981	74.6	84.8	124.2	163.6									SY 1982, page 357
1982	74.7	84.9	123.1	162.1									SY 1983, page 350
1983	75.4	85.4	123.5	161.1									SY 1984, page 348
1984	75.1	85.4	123.7	162.7									SY 1985, page 348
1985	67.8	82.6	122.7	160.3									SY 1986, page 346
1986	64.1	81.2	124.9	163.6									SY 1988, page 350
1987	64.9	81.6	125.3	164.0									SY 1990, page 95
1988	63.8	81.1	125.7	164.6									SY 1991, page 98
1989	63.7	81.0	125.6	165.1									SY 1992, page 123
1990	63.4	80.7	126.0	166.3									SY 1993, page 128
1991	63.3	79.9	126.3	166.2									SY 1994, page 127

(Continued)

Table L.4. (*Continued*)

	Column												
	A	B	C	D	E	F	G	H	I	J	K	L	Source*
	All industries (exc. agric. and fish. before 1985) male and female				Manufacturing, construction and private services male				Manufacturing male				
	P10	P25	P75	P90	P10	P25	P75	P90	P10	P25	P75	P90	
1993	64.9	80.4	126.5	167.5									SY 1995, page 127
1994	63.7	79.9	126.1	165.0									SY 1997, page 126
1996	60.9	78.3	128.8	171.3									SY 1998, page 124
1997	61.4	77.1	129.8	171.4									SY 2000, page 211
1999	59.8	77.7	130.0	174.0									SY 2001, page 221
2000	60.3	78.0	130.8	175.6									SY 2003, page 212
2001	59.6	77.6	131.5	175.6									SY 2004, page 208
2003	60.8	78.1	131.1	175.6									Sociaal-economische trends, 3e kwartaal 2005, page 48

Coverage   All; exc. stand-by workers 1985 and before
Industry   See heading
Age   All; 23 and over 1984 and before, 25 and over in 1970
Sex   See heading
Occupation   All
Definition   Gross, inc. overtime, holiday allowances, special payments, and employee savings scheme contributions from 1986; exc. before
Intensity   FT
Period   Annual; weekly for 1985 and before
Limits   None
Source   See final column
Note   Interpolated linearly
  *SY denotes Statistical Yearbook

Table L.5. Netherlands: STATLINE (CBS)

	A	B	Column C	D	E
	P10	P25	P75	P90	P95
1995	19.0	56.4	138.0	185.6	229.5
1996	17.5	55.3	138.5	186.2	229.5
1997	16.4	54.8	138.8	187.2	230.0
1998	16.7	55.2	139.9	189.6	233.4
1999	17.0	55.1	140.4	190.5	235.2
1999 revised	17.5	55.6	140.4	190.6	235.4
2000	17.6	55.1	141.1	192.3	237.5
2000 revised	17.9	55.1	141.7	192.8	238.7
2001	18.6	55.3	141.6	193.9	239.3
2002	17.9	54.8	142.2	194.2	239.0
2003	18.1	55.0	142.4	194.2	238.5

Coverage	all
Industry	All
Age	All
Sex	All
Occupation	All
Definition	Gross, inc. overtime, holiday allowances, special payments, and employee savings scheme contributions
Intensity	All
Period	Annual
Limits	None
Source	CBS website 13 November 2005

Table L.6. Netherlands: Employer survey (Salverda)

	Column			
	A	B	C	D
	Expressed as FT equivalents		Expressed as headcount	
	P10	P90	P10	P90
1979	64.9	163.6	65.2	165.6
1985	67.6	162.2	68.3	162.8
1989	65.0	164.5	63.7	165.4
1991	64.9	166.2	61.9	167.7
1992	64.7	165.8	62.9	167.2
1993	64.6	165.6	62.8	166.1
1994	63.9	165.9	61.7	166.6
1995	60.8	172.8	58.0	174.9
1996	59.4	177.0	57.0	177.4
1997	58.6	175.9	56.3	175.9
1998	58.1	176.7	55.5	177.3
1999	59.5	174.8	55.6	174.3
2000	59.2	175.3	55.6	177.1
2001	58.9	176.6	55.7	178.4
2002	59.6	175.9	56.6	178.3
2003	59.9	176.4	56.9	179.0
2004	58.4	177.8	54.2	180.9
2005	59.0	177.9	56.1	180.5

Coverage	Exc agriculture
Industry	All
Age	All
Sex	Male
Occupation	All
Definition	Gross wages and salaries
Intensity	All FT and PT, expressed as FT equivalents or headcount (see headings)
Period	Hourly
Limits	None
Source	Salverda, 1998, Table 3.9 and supplied by author, based on tabulations published by CBS, first in SEM, then in 1993 and 1994 Arbeid en Lonen publications, then in STATLINE, 2004 and 2005 kindly provided by CBS
Original source	Employer survey (Loonstructuuronderzoek)
Notes	(1) estimates up to 1989 calculated from micro-data, after that date interpolated from tabulated data; (2) linear interpolation with average hours for six bands of weekly hours of work); (3) there is a break in 1995 with the change in the form of the survey

Bibliography

de Beer, P, 2006, 'Why did earnings inequality increase in the Netherlands in the past two decades?', Amsterdam Institute for Advanced Labour Studies/De Burcht.

Gottschalk, P and Joyce, M, 1998, 'Cross-national differences in the rise in earnings inequality: Market and institutional factors', *Review of Economics and Statistics*, vol 80: 489–502.

Hartog, J, Oosterbeek, H, and Teulings, C, 1993, 'Age, wages and education in the Netherlands', in P Johnson and K F Zimmerman, editors, *Labour markets in an ageing Europe*, Cambridge University Press, Cambridge.

—— and Vriend, N, 1989, 'Post-war international labour mobility: The Netherlands', in I Gordon and A P Thirlwall, editors, *European Factor Mobility*, Macmillan, London.

Nordholt, E S, 1997, 'Imputation in the new Dutch Structure of Earnings Survey (SES)', paper presented at the Conference of European Statisticians, Prague, 14–17 October 1997.

Salverda, W, 1998, 'Incidence and evolution of low-wage employment in the Netherlands and the United States, 1979–1989' in S Bazen, M Gregory, and W Salverda, editors, *Low-Wage Employment in Europe*, Edward Elgar, Cheltenham.

—— van Klaveren, M, and van der Mer, M, editors, 2007, *The Dutch Model of Low-Wage Work*, RSF Project 'Future of Work in Europe', National Monograph.

Stegeman, H and Waaijers, R, 2000, 'Beloningsverhoudingen in Nederland 1979–1998: Ontwikkeling en verklaringen voor de veranderingen in de beloningsstructuur', Centraal Planbureau Document 2000/11.

—— and —— 2001, 'Wage inequality in the Netherlands', *CPB Report*, 2001/1: 50–54.

Weel, B Ter, 1999, 'Changes in job, skill and wage structures: Evidence from the Netherlands 1986–1998', Merit, Maastricht.

M

New Zealand

Like other OECD countries, New Zealand experienced quite marked growth in earnings inequality during the 1980s.

Dixon, 2000, page 115

M.1 Introduction

The country has not changed its boundaries over the period. New Zealand switched from pounds to NZ dollars on 10 July 1967, at the ratio of £1 = $2.

Previous Coverage

Lydall (1968) contains eight tables of earnings distributions for New Zealand, based on census of population data and on income tax data from *Income and Income-Tax Statistics of New Zealand.* They relate to 1925–6, 1935, 1944–5, 1950–1, 1960–1 (Census of Population data), and 1945–6, 1949–50, 1954–5, and 1956–7 (income tax data).

New Zealand is included in two of the three OECD compilations:

1996 (Table M.1): 1984, 1986, 1988, 1990, 1992, and 1994, males and females and all workers; the figures relate to usual gross weekly earnings of full time employees, from the Household Economic Survey (the figures coincide with those of Dixon (1996)).

LMS (Table M.2): 1984, 1986, 1988, 1990, 1992, and 1994–7, all workers and men and women; the figures relate to usual gross weekly earnings of full time employees, from the Household Economic Survey.

Official Publications

No statistics on the distribution of earnings are included in the Official Yearbook.

M.2 Data Sources

The primary sources of information about the distribution of earnings in New Zealand are from household surveys. These are discussed below, together with the earlier income tax information.

Household Economic Survey

The Household Economic Survey is the successor to the Household Sample Survey (from 1973/4 to 1982/3), and the Household Expenditure and Income Survey (from 1983/4 to 1992/3). It is referred to here as HES throughout. The survey commenced on 1 July 1973 and operated on a July to June year until June 1975. It was then changed to an April to March year for the survey ended March 1976. The HES was carried out on an annual basis until 1997/8, when it became a three-yearly survey, the following ones covering 2000/1 and 2003/4.

The HES samples approximately 3,000 households annually, on a continuing basis during the survey year. It collects information on household structure, socio-economic characteristics, labour market participation. In the HES, all household members aged 15 and over are asked about their income. In the early years, no attempt was made to obtain precise income details; respondents were only asked to place themselves in one of a given range of income groups. The income questions were expanded in the early 1980s, and the survey today contains very detailed income questions—see Statistics New Zealand (2005). Information is collected on the earnings received in currently held and previously held jobs. In the studies by Dixon (1996 and 1998), she uses data on the total earnings in all current jobs, including overtime payments, allowances, and non-repeating bonuses and commission. Both full time and part time workers are included; part time workers account for about 20 per cent of the sample (Dixon, 1996, page 52). The results for weekly earnings in Table M.4 relate to full time workers only. Hourly earnings (shown in Table M.4, which includes part time workers) are calculated using information provided by respondents on their usual weekly hours of work. As Dixon notes, measurement error may be particularly important for the hourly earnings calculation. Between 1984 and 1997 the percentage of men in the HES reporting working 45 hours or more a week rose from 29 to 50 per cent, whereas the Labour Force Survey showed a much smaller increase. There are reasons, such as more flexible work arrangements, to expect reporting errors to have become more serious over time, so that any bias may have increased in importance. As Dixon (1998) emphasizes, this is a reason to regard the estimates with caution.

The HES collects income data from around 7,000 people, of whom about 3,000–4,000 are current wage or salary earners (Dixon, 1996, page 50). The sample is therefore relatively small. I have already quoted the discussion by Dixon (1998) of sampling errors. Her conclusion is that 'most of the year-to-year movements in the various measures of ... earnings inequality are not statistically significant. However, the longer-term changes occurring over periods of five years or more generally *are* large enough to exceed the relevant confidence intervals, and therefore can be treated as meaningful changes' (1998, page 75).

New Zealand Income Survey

The New Zealand Income Survey (NZIS) is a supplement attached to the Household Labour Force Survey (HLFS), which is a quarterly survey of around 15,000 households, containing some 30,000 individuals aged 15 and over. The NZIS supplement has been conducted every June quarter since June 1997. The sample excludes long

Table M.A1. Percentage changes relative to the growth of the median

	Hourly earnings		Weekly FT earnings	
	Male	Female	Male	Female
P10	3.8	2.5	0.5	1.8
P25	1.5	−3.5	1.0	−1.1
P75	−0.5	3.2	1.1	3.6
P90	5.5	4.7	6.9	5.0

term residents in institutions, members of the permanent armed forces, overseas diplomats, overseas visitors who expect to be resident for less than 12 months, and people living on offshore islands (except Waiheke Island). In June 2003, of the 92 per cent of eligible households that responded to the HLFS, over 84 per cent of eligible individuals gave a valid response to the NZIS. According to Statistics New Zealand (2005b), 'some groups of the population are more difficult to survey, for example young males tend to be under covered.'

The NZIS collects information on wages and salaries earned in a reference period (typically the week prior to the survey). Approximately 15 per cent of the wage and salary responses are imputed. Following the 1997 survey, the wage and salary section was substantially revised, and changes were made to the editing of usual earnings, for which Dixon (2004) makes an adjustment. I understand from Statistics New Zealand that there are no SNZ-published measures of earnings dispersion based on the NZIS. Dixon (2004, Table 4) reports the growth of different percentiles of earnings between 1997/8 and 2002/3. Expressed relative to the growth of the median, the percentage changes are as shown in Table M.A1.

The NZIS data are used by Dixon to examine changes in the gender wage differential between 1997 and 2003, and by Hyslop and Yahanpath (2005) to examine income growth from 1998 to 2004.

Comparison of the HES and NZIS

The two surveys are compared by Dixon (2000). She concludes that,

on balance, the IS is likely to produce a more accurate and representative picture of the characteristics and earnings of New Zealand employees than the HES. There are several reasons for rating the quality of the IS data above that of the HES data. These include the larger sample size, the higher response rate of households, and the fact that the questionnaire used to capture information on employees' current earnings and hours worked was specifically designed for this purpose. (2000, page 35)

She notes for example that the higher response rate in the IS (around 90 rather than 80 per cent in the HES) means that the IS contains a higher proportion of younger workers, who typically have a lower response rate in surveys. At the same time, the IS reports a substantially lower proportion of secondary jobs than the HES, possibly because the IS is a telephone, rather than face-to-face, survey.

Income Tax Data

Since 1921, classifications have been published of the incomes of personal taxpayers (prior to that date, the incomes of persons and companies were not distinguished separately). The tax records were used by Lydall (1968). While he restricted attention to persons whose principal source was wages or salaries, the published statistics relate to the total gross income of these persons, not just their earnings. (The same problem arises with the Census of Population data that he also uses; these data relate to total market income, and are not discussed here.) From 1958, however, data have been published classifying wage and salary earners according to the total salaries and wages taxed at source. (Since 1953, the New Zealand income tax has been assessed on an individual basis.) These have been used by Easton (1983), who constructed a control total for the total employee labour force. The total, N, is equal to the official labour force at the end of the tax year omitting self-employed workers as defined by census data. He then took the top N persons in the distribution of salaries and wages taxed at source. In this way, he sought to reduce the impact of part year and part time workers, although he concluded that only the top eight deciles appeared to be full year workers. The income tax statistics are based on a sample of tax returns: 5 per cent (10 per cent to 1967–8) with a complete enumeration of all persons with incomes above a certain level. There are no data for 1961 (information not processed).

Summary

Evidence about the distribution of earnings in New Zealand is patchy. As may be seen from Figures M.1 and M.2, the available information starts earlier than in a number of other countries, with the series of Easton from the 1950s. But there is a gap, until we can make use of the results from the household survey from 1984. But this too comes to an end in 1997.

M.3 What Happened?

There is a widespread view that earnings dispersion has increased substantially in New Zealand, particularly during the 1980s. Let us however begin with the 1950s and 1960s. Easton concluded that 'trends in the [male] earnings distribution over time [1958 to 1973] are complex. In essence the top quartile of the distribution is moving away from the middle but the top of the distribution itself is getting more equal' (Easton, 1983, page 56). It is true that the upward trend in the upper quartile (for males) shown in Figure M.1 is not sufficient to register, and that the top percentile, not shown, did not rise. At the same time, the top decile did rise from 1958 to 1973 by 5 per cent. There is some indication that the Golden Age in New Zealand benefited the top decile relative to the median. The downward movement in the lower quartile in Figure M.2 is not sufficient to register.

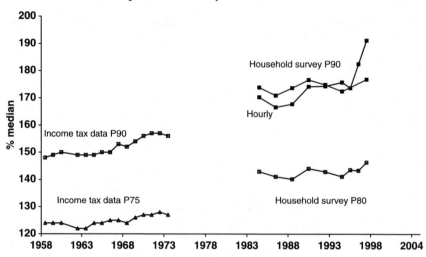

Figure M.1 NEW ZEALAND upper part of the distribution 1958–2004

Sources: Table M.2, columns C and D; Table M.3, columns B and C; Table M.4, column E.

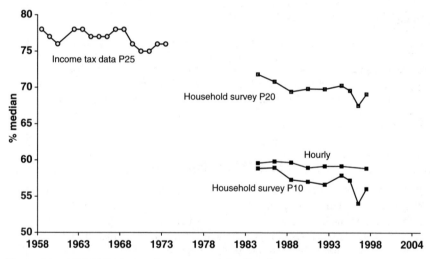

Figure M.2 NEW ZEALAND lower part of the distribution 1958–2004

Sources: Table M.2, columns A and B; Table M.3, column A; Table M.4, column B.

Jumping to the 1980s, we can see that Figures M.1 and M.2 do indeed show a widening during the period 1984 to 1997. The bottom decile for all workers fell from 59 per cent in 1984 to 56 per cent in 1997, a fall of 5 per cent, which is the criterion adopted here, and, lies on the boundary of the 95 per cent confidence interval suggested by Dixon (1998). The fall is larger for male workers—see Table M.1. The top decile rose over the same period by 12 per cent, a significant increase according to the criteria adopted here. Together these changes caused the decile ratio to rise from 2.89 in 1984 to 3.41 in 1997. But the picture is not totally transparent. As Dixon stresses, the hourly distribution shows less of a decline in the bottom decile: indeed, 'if it is agreed that hourly earnings are the most meaningful measure of unit returns to labour, it must be concluded that there was not a dramatic increase in total earnings inequality between 1984 and 1994' (Dixon, 1996, page 61). The bulk of the rise in the top decile is indeed from 1995 to 1997; before that date there has been no registrable change. So that, while there was undoubtedly an increase in the dispersion of weekly earnings for men in New Zealand, with the decile ratio widening from 2.72 in 1984 to 3.56 in 1997, the picture is less clear-cut than would be suggested by this stark statistic.

What has happened since 1997? As explained earlier, we cannot draw on published distributions. The growth in different percentiles between 1997/8 and 2002/3 was shown above. As explained by Dixon (2004), growth was more rapid at the top and the bottom, but the former predominated, and she refers to the decile ratio rising by 'a little'. The analysis of the NZIS 1998 and 2004 by Hyslop and Yahanpath (2005) leads them to conclude that 'there have been comparatively steady increases in earnings and incomes for both individuals and households, and little evidence of any dramatic localized changes in the distributions' (2005, page 11). They note that the relative contributions of employment changes and wage changes vary across the distribution, with employment changes being more important at the lower end of the distribution.

Summary

New Zealand is often presented as having experienced dramatic distributional changes. The evidence about the distribution of earnings—as opposed to household incomes—is, however, limited in its coverage of the post-war period. Estimates exist for the period 1984 to 1997, during which the bottom decile fell and the top decile rose significantly. Going back to the 1970s and earlier, there is some indication that the Golden Age in New Zealand benefited the top decile relative to the median.

Table M.1. New Zealand: OECD (1996)

	Column					
	A	B	C	D	E	F
	All		Males		Females	
	P10	P90	P10	P90	P10	P90
1984	59	170	61	166	64	154
1986	59	167	59	161	61	155
1988	57	168	57	164	61	153
1990	57	174	57	176	57	156
1992	56	174	56	175	60	162
1994	58	176	56	179	60	157

Coverage	All
Industry	All
Age	All
Sex	See headings
Occupation	All
Definition	Usual gross earnings
Intensity	FT
Period	Weekly
Limits	None
Source	OECD (1996, Table 3.1)
Original source	*Household Economic Survey*
Note	Provided by the NZ Department of Labour

Table M.2. New Zealand: OECD (LMS)

	A	B	C	D	E	F	G	H	I	J	K	L
							Column					
			All				Males				Females	
	P10	P20	P80	P90	P10	P20	P80	P90	P10	P20	P80	P90
1984	58.9	71.8	142.9	170.3	61.1	72.4	140.5	166.1	63.6	75.4	131.6	154.4
1986	59.0	70.8	141.1	166.6	59.1	71.6	136.5	160.6	61.3	75.7	133.7	155.5
1988	57.3	69.4	140.2	167.8	57.6	70.4	139.3	164.2	61.0	73.4	132.9	153.2
1990	57.0	69.8	144.0	174.2	57.0	70.1	145.5	175.6	57.5	70.3	135.0	155.7
1992	56.6	69.8	142.9	174.3	56.0	68.8	143.8	175.1	59.8	72.3	138.8	161.5
1994	57.9	70.3	141.1	175.8	56.5	69.2	141.6	179.0	59.8	72.0	134.1	156.9
1995	57.2	69.6	143.6	173.7	55.8	68.0	144.0	174.0	60.4	72.9	133.5	158.3
1996	54.0	67.5	143.3	182.5	56.6	68.3	144.4	182.5	58.2	69.5	141.5	165.0
1997	56.1	69.1	146.3	191.2	54.8	69.0	147.1	194.6	59.8	70.6	141.1	168.3

Coverage	All
Industry	All
Age	All
Sex	See headings
Occupation	All
Definition	Usual gross earnings; non-regular payments are included
Intensity	FT
Period	Weekly
Limits	None
Source	Downloaded from OECD website December 2005
Original source	*Household Economic Survey*
Note	Provided by the NZ Department of Labour

Table M.3. New Zealand: Income tax (Easton)

	Column			
	A	B	C	D
	P25	P75	P90	P99
1958	78	124	148	269
1959	77	124	149	267
1960	76	124	150	273
1962	78	122	149	273
1963	78	122	149	269
1964	77	124	149	265
1965	77	124	150	256
1966	77	125	150	249
1967	78	125	153	261
1968	78	124	152	266
1969	76	126	154	253
1970	75	127	156	249
1971	75	127	157	262
1972	76	128	157	265
1973	76	127	156	255

Coverage	All
Industry	All
Age	All
Sex	Male
Occupation	All
Definition	Gross wages and salaries taxed at source
Intensity	FT and PT
Period	Annual
Limits	None
Source	Easton (1983, Table 4.8)
Original source	Income tax data
Note	Covers employed labour force, exc. the self employed, taking top wage and salary recipients in tax records, defined in terms of tax assessed at source

Table M.4. New Zealand: Household Economic Survey (Dixon)

	A	B	C	D	E	F	G	H	I	J	K	L	M	N	O	P	Q	R	S	T	U
											Column										
			All							Hourly FT and PT											
										Male							Female				
	P05	P10	P20	P80	P90	P95	Gini	P05	P10	P20	P80	P90	P95	Gini	P05	P10	P20	P80	P90	P95	Gini
1984	47.5	59.6	73.4	144.1	173.9	204.9	24	46.8	58.9	71.9	143.2	171.2	201.0	24	51.2	63.6	77.6	135.7	166.0	195.2	22
1986	46.9	59.8	73.1	142.9	170.9	199.4		43.9	58.9	73.1	143.0	164.5	196.1		51.9	63.9	76.9	137.8	161.6	190.2	
1988	48.0	59.7	72.2	143.3	173.7	204.6		46.3	57.7	70.2	140.2	167.9	199.7		50.5	62.2	75.0	136.5	161.5	194.9	
1990	44.5	59.0	70.8	144.9	176.7	213.5	26	42.2	55.6	69.3	145.8	176.6	215.0	27	48.2	61.0	74.8	138.4	164.8	193.7	24
1992	46.0	59.2	71.4	143.3	174.9	210.5		39.6	56.9	72.1	148.4	179.9	214.8		52.8	61.6	73.1	137.4	166.0	192.8	
1994	45.1	59.2	72.2	141.8	172.5	212.3		39.4	55.8	70.5	144.2	179.1	222.8		49.3	61.9	75.9	137.1	163.3	194.5	
1997		58.9			176.8		27		56.0			182.2		28		61.9			171.6		24

(*Continued*)

Table M.4. (*Continued*)

							Column						
V	W	X	Y	Z	AA	AB	AC	AD	AE	AF	AG	AH
						FT weekly							
			All					Male			Female		
P05	P10	P20	P80	P90	P95	Gini	P10	P90	Gini	P10	P90	Gini
1984 50.5	58.9	71.9	142.8	170.3	201.1	23	61.3	166.5	23	63.8	153.7	19
1986 47.8	59.0	70.8	141.0	166.6	193.0							
1988 47.3	57.3	69.3	140.1	167.8	195.6							
1990 46.8	57.0	69.8	144.0	174.2	211.0	26	57.1	175.1	26	57.7	155.3	22
1992 47.0	56.6	69.7	142.9	174.3	206.2							
1994 47.4	57.9	70.3	141.2	175.8	212.6							
1997	56.0			191.6		28	54.9	195.4	29	60.0	168.2	24

Coverage	All
Industry	All
Age	All
Sex	See headings
Occupation	All
Definition	Gross
Intensity	See headings
Period	See headings
Limits	None
Sources	Columns A–U from Dixon (1998, Tables A3, A4, and A5); columns V–AH from Dixon (1996, Tables A2) and (1998, Table 2)
Original source	Household Economic Survey

Bibliography

Borland, J, 1999, 'Economic explanations of earnings distribution trends in the international literature and application to New Zealand', Report prepared for the New Zealand Treasury.

Dixon, S, 1996, 'The distribution of earnings in New Zealand 1984–94', *Labour Market Bulletin*, 1: 45–100.

—— 1998, 'Growth in the dispersion of earnings: 1984–97', *Labour Market Bulletin* 1&2: 71–107.

—— 2000, 'Pay inequality between men and women in New Zealand', New Zealand Department of Labour, Occasional Paper Series, 2000/1.

—— 2004, 'Understanding reductions in the gender wage differential 1997–2003', New Zealand Conference on Pay and Employment Equity for Women, Wellington.

Easton, B, 1983, *Income distribution in New Zealand*, New Zealand Institute of Economic Research, Wellington.

Hyslop, D and Maré, D., 2005, 'Understanding New Zealand's changing income distribution, 1983–1998', *Economica*, vol 72: 469–95.

—— Yahanpath, S, 2005, 'Income growth and earnings variations in New Zealand, 1998–2004', Treasury Working Paper Series 05/11, New Zealand Treasury, Wellington.

Ministry of Social Development, 2005, *The Social Report 2005*, Wellington.

Ministry of Social Policy, 2001, *The Social Report 2001*, Wellington.

Podder, N and Chatterjee S, 2002, 'Sharing the national cake in post reform New Zealand: Income inequality trends in terms of income sources', *Journal of Public Economics*, vol 86: 1–27.

Statistics New Zealand, 1999, *New Zealand Now: Incomes*, Statistics New Zealand, Wellington.

—— 2001, 'The introduction of integrated weighting to the 2000/01 household economic survey', Statistics New Zealand, Wellington.

—— 2005, 'Information about the Household Economic Survey', Statistics New Zealand website.

—— 2005a, 'Survey of Family, Income and Employment Dynamics (Year ended 30 September 2003): Reference Reports', Statistics New Zealand website.

—— 2005b, 'Information about the New Zealand Income Survey', Statistics New Zealand website.

N

Norway

Earnings inequality is remarkably low and stable in Norway [and] the increases which have been evident in the United States and the UK are not repeated here.

Salvanes, Burgess, and Lane, 1998, page 9

N.1 Introduction

The union of Norway with Sweden ended in June 1905. The geographic boundaries have remained unchanged.

Previous Coverage

Norway is included in two of the OECD compilations (no information is included in the LMS dataset):

1993 (Table N.1): all workers, 1980, 1987, and 1991, supplied by Erling Barth and Halvor Mehlum, Institute for Social Research, Oslo.

1996 (Tables N.1 and N.2): the same data as OECD (1993), with the addition of information for 1983; in addition the Annex contained data for 1989 and 1993 from the Norwegian Survey of Organizations and Employees, which are shown in Table N.2.

Official Publications

The income data published in the Official Yearbook does not include the distribution of individual earnings. Earnings distribution information has been published in *Income and Property Statistics (Inntekt- og Formuesstatistikk)*, the earliest data covering 1970, 1973, and 1979.

N.2 Data Sources

The principal source of earnings distribution data is the income tax register, with register information typically being attached to a survey, such as the Income Distribution Survey, or to the Population and Housing Census, both described below.

Income Distribution Surveys

The Income Distribution Surveys (IDS) (*Inntekt- og Formuesundersøkelsen for hus-holdninger*) are sample surveys that collect most of their data from income tax records. Household composition is established after a household interview (in the case of non-response, the missing information on household composition is replaced by information from the National Population Register). The first survey was conducted in 1958 (when information from the Population Register was used) and in 1970, 1973, and 1979 the published tables included a distribution of earnings, distinguishing full year workers. Household interviews were conducted for the first time in 1982. For the years 1979, 1982, 1986, and 1990, the IDS was coordinated with the Level of Living Survey (see below). The IDS became annual in 1984. The sample was based on the panel population of the IDS and the households covered by the Survey of Consumer Expenditure, totalling some 3,000–4,000 households, with the addition every four years of the Living Conditions Survey sample. Since 1994 the sample has consisted of the IDS panel population, the Income and Property Survey for the Self-Employed, and the revolving subject Living Condition Surveys. The resulting sample for 2000 was 12,919 households and 34,851 individuals. (Information from the website of the Luxembourg Income Study.)

The earnings are recorded gross of taxes and contributions. They include sickness benefits. It should be noted that the definition of income in the registers changes over time. As pointed out by Statistics Norway, 'there will always be changes to income registers . . . as a result of administrative regulations. Although the income terms remain unchanged, the content can vary from one year to the next' (2005, page 40). In particular, the tax reform of 1992 may have led to changes in the content.

Population and Housing Census

The first complete population census in Norway was conducted in 1769 (Utne, 2005), and since 1890 the census has been decennial (except that for 1940, postponed to 1946). Since 1970, details have been taken from the National Population Register; and since 1980 income information has been obtained from the tax register. In 1990, the census was based on a sample of approximately 28 per cent of the population.

The censuses since 1980 have published tables of the distribution of earned in-come—see Table N.5. The definition in 1980 and 1990 included the self-employed and self-employment income. The published tables contain a relatively small number of ranges: eight in the case of 2001. For these reasons, the results on Table N.5 are classified as B, but they are included in view of the paucity of published information. The results for the 2001 Census show salaried employees and self-employed separately, so that the percentiles may be compared. The lower quartile is 56.7 per cent of the median for salaried workers, but 55.8 per cent if the self-employed are included; the upper quartile and top decile are, respectively, 136.4 and 180.3 per cent of the median for salaried workers, but 137.5 and 183.0 per cent if the self-employed are included. (Self-employed account for some 7 per cent of the total in 2001.)

According to Statistics Norway, 'all income variables in Census 2001 fully correspond with the Income Distribution Survey' (2005, page 40). They are not, however,
fully comparable across censuses. In particular, the 1980 and 1990 data relate to
pensionable earnings, whereas the 2001 figures also include non-pensionable employment income (Statistics Norway, 2005, page 40).

Level of Living Survey

The first Level of Living Survey was conducted in 1973. It was a general welfare survey,
repeated in 1980, 1983, and then at four-year intervals up to 1995. Since 1996 there
has been an annual Survey of Living Conditions. The 1996 reorganization is described
by Alvheim (1997), who provides a tabular overview of the primary micro-data
sources. They have been used by, for example, Kahn (1998) in studies of wage
determination in Norway.

Summary

Norway has excellent register information, which has been widely used to study the
distribution of total income, but relatively little has been published on the distribution
of earnings. The data in Figures N.1 and N.2 are shown as being based on tax data, but
they are a combination of survey (to determine the sample) and register data. The
differences that are evident in Figures N.1 and N.2 are due, at least in part, to the
differences in the populations covered in the different samples.

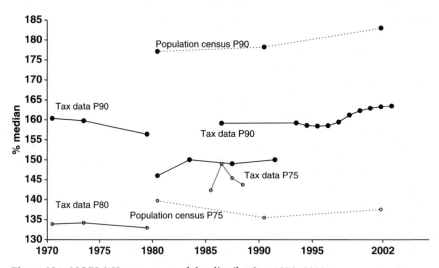

Figure N.1 NORWAY upper part of the distribution 1970–2002

Sources: Table N.1, column B; Table N.3, calculated from columns C–F, taking decile limits as average of
adjacent means, and fitting Pareto distribution to two top shares; Table N.4, columns D, E, and F; Table N.5,
column F.

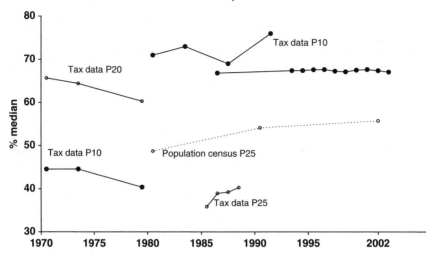

Figure N.2 NORWAY lower part of the distribution 1970–2002

Sources: Table N.1, column A; Table N.3, calculated from columns A–D, taking decile limits as average of adjacent means; Table N.4, columns A, B, and C; Table N.5, column C.

N.3 What Happened?

In his article entitled 'Against the Wind', Kahn describes the Norwegian experience as follows: 'even though Norway was faced with similar supply and demand conditions to those of other OECD nations, Norway's wage distribution changed in ways very different from other countries. In particular, workers at the bottom gained relative to the middle during the 1987–91 period, at the same time that low wage workers in other countries were losing ground' (1998, page 633). He argues that, during the 1960s and 1970s, bargaining took place largely at the national level, with lower paid workers receiving larger percentage increases. This was tempered by local wage drift, but the evidence of Holden (1989) suggests that the central wage settlements continued to have a strong impact on relative wages. However, in 1981 there was a change to a conservative government (the first for nearly 50 years). The government decided not to take part in the 1982 wage round and the Norwegian Federation of Trade Unions (LO) agreed to more decentralized negotiations. There was a return to centralized wage bargaining in 1988, leading Kahn to call the period 1988–91 a period of 'recentralization'.

How far is this reflected in the observed changes over time in the distribution of earnings? As already indicated, in the absence of a single consistent series this a difficult question to answer. The period up to 1980 shows changes at the top that are not sufficiently large to register, and a decline of some 10 per cent in the bottom decile relative to the median, which may be due to changes in the composition of the population covered. For the early 1980s, we lack the annual data necessary to track the impact of decentralization of bargaining. From 1987 to 1991, the OECD data show a 10 per cent rise in the bottom decile, consistent with recentralization having reduced dispersion. The population census data, comparing 1990 with 1980, show an 11 per cent rise in the lower quartile. The changes in the top decile were again not large enough to register. The data for the 1990s show a rise in the upper percentiles, but again this is not large enough to register.

Summary

The picture of earnings dispersion in Norway is far from clear, but there is nothing in the data assembled here to disprove the hypothesis that there have been only limited changes since 1970.

Table N.1. Norway: OECD (1993)

	Column	
	A	B
	P10	P90
1980	71	146
1983	73	150
1987	69	149
1991	76	150

Coverage	All
Industry	All
Age	Aged 19–55
Sex	All
Occupation	All
Definition	Gross
Intensity	All
Period	Hourly
Limits	Observations of less than 25 kroner per hour or more than 1000 kroner per hour (in 1991 prices) omitted
Source	OECD (1993, Table 5.2).
Original source	Level of Living Survey
Notes	(1) supplied by Erling Barth and Halvor Mehlum, Institute for Social Research, Oslo; (2) 1983 added from OECD (1996)

Table N.2. Norway: OECD (1996) Annex Data

	Column					
	A	B	C	D	E	F
	All		Male		Female	
	P10	P90	P10	P90	P10	P90
1989	75	150	75	149	78	138
1993	75	149	73	151	78	135

Coverage	Excludes firms with fewer than 2 employees
Industry	All
Age	19–55
Sex	See headings
Occupation	All
Definition	Gross
Intensity	FT and FY
Period	Annual
Limits	None
Source	OECD, 1996, Annex 3.A
Original source	*Norwegian Survey of Organisations and Employees*
Note	Supplied by Erling Barth and Halvor Mehlum, Institute for Social Research, Oslo

Table N.3. Norway: Income Distribution Survey

	Column					
	A	B	C	D	E	F
	Share of bottom 10%	Share of bottom 20%	Share of fifth 10%	Share of sixth 10%	Share of top 20%	Share of top 10%
1986	5.6	12.2	8.7	9.5	32.2	19.0
1993	5.6	12.2	8.7	9.4	32.7	19.6
1994	5.6	12.2	8.7	9.4	32.5	19.5
1995	5.7	12.3	8.7	9.4	32.5	19.5
1996	5.7	12.3	8.7	9.4	32.6	19.6
1997	5.6	12.2	8.7	9.4	32.9	19.9
1998	5.5	12.0	8.7	9.4	33.2	20.1
1999	5.6	12.2	8.6	9.3	33.2	20.1
2000	5.6	12.1	8.6	9.3	33.5	20.4
2001	5.5	12.0	8.6	9.3	33.6	20.5
2002	5.5	12.0	8.6	9.3	33.5	20.4

Coverage	All
Industry	All
Age	All
Sex	All
Occupation	All
Definition	Gross including over time, sickness payments
Intensity	Persons earning more than 60% of average industrial wage
Period	Annual
Limits	See above
Source	Statistics Norway

Table N.4. Norway: Income Distribution Survey II

	A	B	C	D	E	F	G	H	I	J	K	L	M	N	O	P	Q	R	
			All						Male						Female				
	P10	P20	P25	P75	P80	P90	P10	P20	P25	P75	P80	P90	P10	P20	P25	P75	P80	P90	Source*
1970	25.3	45.2			146.7	181.6	39.6	65.2			136.6	171.8	28.1	45.3			169.0	205.4	IS 1970, page 50
1970 FY	44.5	65.7			133.9	160.3	65.7	77.7			130.8	156.3	40.9	58.2			141.2	162.9	IS 1970, page 59
1973	24.1	44.7			145.2	175.9	37.9	64.6			134.5	161.0	25.0	42.7			161.0	195.2	IS 1973, page 78
1973 FY	44.6	64.4			134.2	159.8	65.8	78.0			130.5	154.9	42.3	59.6			139.6	165.9	IS 1973, page 78
1979	19.2	43.7			140.2	167.4	43.8	71.8			130.2	154.4	14.3	34.7			164.6	188.9	IS 1979, page 102
1979 FY	40.4	60.3			133.0	156.4	66.2	80.2			127.8	150.3	32.1	56.5			139.5	157.3	IS 1979, page 102
1985			35.8	142.3	151.2	187.3			51.2	130.4	139.3					163.5	176.2	206.9	IS 1985, page 49
1986			39.0	149.0	161.4			32.4	47.9	132.3	141.0				41.0	162.4	176.1	208.2	IS 1986, page 68
1987			39.2	145.4	157.0			32.2	50.4	131.4					40.8	159.5	171.4	201.6	IS 1987, page 68
1988			40.3	143.7	154.6			32.4	51.0	130.8			31.0		43.0	155.6	166.4	196.9	IS 1988, page 68

Coverage	All
Industry	All
Age	17 and over
Sex	See headings
Occupation	All
Definition	Gross earnings in cash and kind
Intensity	See headings
Period	Annual
Limits	None
Source	See last column
Note	*IS = Inntekts-Statistikk

Table N.5. Norway: Population and Housing Census

	A	B	C	D	E	F
				Column		
				All		
	P10	P20	P25	P75	P80	P90
1980		37.5	48.7	139.7	147.5	177.1
1990	16.9	42.7	54.2	135.5	147.3	178.2
2001		43.9	55.8	137.5	145.5	183.0

Coverage	All
Industry	All
Age	16 and over
Sex	See headings
Occupation	All
Definition	Pensionable income. Including self employment income
Intensity	All
Period	Annual
Limits	None
Source	*Population and Housing Census 1980,* volume II, page 109, and 1990, Documentation and Main Figures, page 56

Bibliography

Alvheim, A, 1997, 'A reorganisation of the collection of level of living data', *NSD Newsletter*, 96.

Colbjørnsen, T and Kalleberg, A L, 1988, 'Spillover, standardisation and stratification: Earnings determination in the United States and Norway', *European Sociological Review*, vol 4: 20–31.

Holden, S, 1989, 'Wage drift and bargaining: Evidence from Norway', *Economica*, vol 56: 419–32.

Kahn, L M, 1998, 'Against the wind: Bargaining, recentralisation and wage inequality in Norway 1987–91', *Economic Journal*, vol 108: 603–45.

Salvanes, K G, Burgess, S, and Lane, J, 1998, 'Sources of earnings dispersion in a linked employer–employee dataset: Evidence from Norway', unpublished.

—— and Førre, S E, 2003, 'Effects on employment of trade and technical change: Evidence from Norway', *Economica*, vol 70: 293–329.

Statistics Norway, 2005, *Population and Housing Census 2001: Documentation and Main Figures*, Statistics Norway, Oslo.

Strøm, B, 1995, 'Envy, Fairness and Political Influence in Local Government Wage Determination: Evidence from Norway', *Economica*, vol 62: 389–409.

Utne, H, 2005, 'The Population and Housing Census Handbook 2001', Department of Social Statistics, Statistics Norway, Document 2005/2.

O

Poland

Polish dispersion—of manual workers as well as of all employees—declined significantly from 1957 to 1960, after which there was little change.

Lydall, 1968, page 198

O.1 Introduction

Point 13 of President Woodrow Wilson's *Fourteen Points* was the restitution of Poland, and in 1919 Poland regained its independence. In 1939 Poland was invaded. After the Second World War, it was reconstituted as a country with its borders shifted substantially westward and 20 per cent smaller in area. The Soviet Union instituted a communist government, and the People's Republic was proclaimed in 1952. Formation of the independent trade union, Solidarity, eroded the dominance of the Communist Party, and won Parliamentary elections in 1989, beginning a process of transition. Poland joined the European Union on 1 May 2004.

Previous Coverage

Lydall (1968) contains seven tables of earnings distributions for Poland, based on data from the Statistical Yearbook 1959 (page 332), 1962, 1963 (page 430), and 1965 (page 469). The data relate to 1956, 1957, 1958, 1960, 1961, 1963, and 1964.

Poland was not included in OECD (1993) or (1996), but is covered by the OECD (LMS) dataset. See Table O.1 which contains data for the years 1980 to 1999: that is, years both before and after the transition from communism. The OECD (LMS) data are obtained from published tabulations of the results of enterprise surveys.

Official Publications

For many years, data on the distribution of earnings in Poland based on enterprise wage surveys has been published in the Official Yearbook (*Rocznik Statystyczny*). The results from 1992 to 2004 are summarized in Table O.2, which provides in effect a continuation of Table O.1. The results for deciles are in many cases given directly in the Yearbook; in other cases they have been interpolated.

O.2 Data Sources

In addition to the enterprise wage surveys, other sources are the Household Budget Survey, held since 1957, and the Labour Force Survey, which started in 1992.

Enterprise Wage Surveys

An annual enquiry has been made since the 1950s on the distribution of earnings of full time workers. The information requested from the employers was the number of employees in discrete earnings bands in that month. In only some years were employers required to distinguish men and women workers separately. Up to 1989 this September enquiry covered the socialized sector: state-owned and cooperative enterprises. At that date, the socialized sector accounted for two-thirds of the labour force. The bulk of agricultural workers in Poland were always in the private sector: in 1989 3.6 million were in private employment or self-employment in agriculture, compared with 0.8 million in the socialized sector of agriculture (Atkinson and Micklewright, 1992, page 257). The armed forces, police, senior government officials were not covered, nor were employees in the sector 'Political Organisations, trade unions, and other'. Those not working a full month were excluded. Until 1980, the enquiry was a full census of employers; after 1981 it was based on a sample from the list of business establishments, all employees in a sampled enterprise being included in the survey. The results for the period from 1956 to 1989 are shown in Table O.3. In the pre-1990 period, the published tabulations up to 1970 related to the distribution of 'gross' earnings; from 1970 the distributions are described as 'net'. Figures are given on both bases for 1970, which show that there is distinctly less dispersion on a net basis: the decile ratio is 2.84, compared with 3.14 on a gross basis.

In 1991 the survey was extended to cover private firms, although those with fewer than six employees are omitted. It is now carried out for the month of October (since 1998). Gross earnings are defined to include basic pay, overtime, allowances for hazardous work, managerial responsibilities, long service, profit shares, bonuses, and premia. All payments which are not monthly are converted to a monthly equivalent.

Results spanning the communist and post-1989 periods are given in Tables O.1 and O.4, the latter based on the work of Rutkowski (1996 and 2001). In considering the impact of the transition, we have to take account of the introduction of the personal income tax in Poland in 1992. In that year, earnings were increased to adjust for the effect of personal income taxation. According to Rutkowski, 'were the net earnings concept still used, the inequality—given the progressive nature of the tax system—would be lower. On the other hand, however, the error should not be significant as the vast majority of workers fall into the lowest tax bracket' (1996a, page 91). Since 1999 the difference between gross and net earnings has been further widened by the introduction of compulsory contributions by employees to social security.

Household Budget Survey (HBS)

The HBS was initiated in 1957 and has been held annually, but with significant changes in the survey design. Until 1972, the HBS was restricted to the households of employees in the socialized sector excluding agriculture (so that its coverage was more restricted than that of the earnings surveys). Indeed, up until 1962 the HBS focused solely on the households of industrial workers. From 1973 the HBS was radically changed, being conducted on a territorial basis, with a sampling frame of households rather than enterprises. Certain households continued to be omitted, such as households in which the principal income was from employment or self-employment in the private agricultural sector. In 2003, the HBS covered 32,452 households. The results from recent HBS used by Keane and Prasad (2002a) are reproduced in Table O.6.

Labour Force Survey

The Polish Labour Force Survey (LFS) is a quarterly household survey, which started in May 1992 (Duffy and Walsh, 2001, page 13). It now has a rotating sample. It includes all persons aged 15 and over, with the exception of those living in military barracks and dormitories, and those resident abroad. It contains questions on individual characteristics, and net earnings in the previous month from the main job. The LFS earnings data have been used by Newell (2001)—see Table O.5—and Sibley and Walsh (2002).

Summary

The data for Poland are summarized in Figures O.1 and O.2. There is a distinct break at 1990, shown by the right hand vertical line, in that the statistics prior to that date relate to the socialized sector, which accounted for some two-thirds of employment. This is particularly important in view of the role attributed to the developing private sector in generating a rise in earnings dispersion during the process of transition to a market economy—see, for example, Aghion and Commander (1999). At the same time, as explained by Rutkowski (1996a, page 90), the immediate effect of the change was small. The left hand vertical line marks the break in the earlier series at 1970 when the form of the statistics changed; at that date, the definition changed from gross earnings to net earnings.

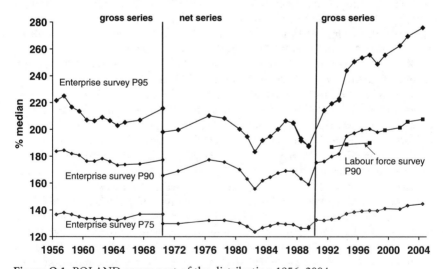

Figure O.1 POLAND upper part of the distribution 1956–2004

Sources: Table O.1, columns D and F; Table O.2, columns D, F, and G; Table O.3, columns D, E, and F; Table O.5, column B.

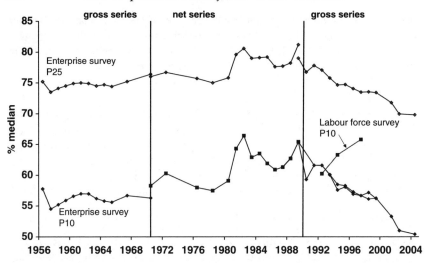

Figure O.2 POLAND lower part of the distribution 1956–2004

Sources: Table O.1, columns A and C; Table O.2, columns A and C; Table O.3, columns B and C; Table O.5, column A.

O.3 What Happened?

In the first two decades of the period, up to 1978, there appear to have been first a fall and then a rise in the upper percentiles. The top decile fell by some 6 per cent up to 1964, and the top vintile fell by 10 per cent. Piecing together the gross and net series, we can see that from 1964 to 1978 the top decile rose by 8 per cent and the vintile by 12 per cent. The lower part of the distribution was more stable.

This was followed by the labour unrest at the start of the 1980s and the Gdansk Accord of August 1980, which led to relatively equalizing wage adjustments. The bottom decile in Figure O.2 rises by 7 percentage points, and the lower quartile by 5 percentage points. Flakierski (1986) argues that 'the spectacular drop in relative dispersion of earnings between 1980 and 1982 claimed by the official statistics is probably exaggerated, because the official statistical data in this period of turmoil are particularly unreliable' (1986, page 72). But he goes on to say that 'there is no doubt that even the partial implementation of Solidarity's wage and incomes policies has reduced inequalities' (1986, page 72). The gains, whether real or a statistical illusion, were not retained. By 1986 both top and bottom deciles had returned to within 5 per cent of their 1980 values. On the other hand, the end of the 1980s saw a renewed rise in the bottom decile and reduction in the top decile. Figure O.1 shows how the top percentiles cycled, peaking in the mid-1950s, the mid-1970s, and the mid-1980s.

The cycles pre-1989 make it difficult to choose a base year for any comparison of the last years of the communist regime with the post-transition distribution of earnings. It makes a difference whether we take 1989, or, like Rutkowski, take 1987 as 'the last "normal" year preceding the incipient fall of the communist economy' (Rutkowski, 1996a, page 93). He goes on to discuss the problems of making comparisons during and after communism. He notes the differences in coverage of the enterprise wage surveys, and the impact of the introduction of personal income taxation. He discusses the role of non-cash remuneration, noting that 'the actual distributional role of fringe benefits during the communist period is not easy to determine' (1996a, page 91). There were benefits going to manual workers and there were in-kind benefits for managers. He suggests that the view that 'actual inequality was higher than the measured one … is based more on conventional wisdom than on reliable research findings' (1996a, page 91). On the other hand, he believes that in the post-communist period taking account of fringe benefits would lead to wider earnings dispersion. Overall, his conclusion is that the 'biases seem to be of the second order and do not alter the main results' (1996a, page 91).

What are the main results? In general, it seems agreed that there was a rise in earnings dispersion but that it was relatively modest. Rutkowski (1996a) shows the Gini coefficient as rising from 23.0 in 1987 to 25.7 in 1993. The top decile rose by 8 per cent relative to the median. Keane and Prasad, using a different data source (the Household Budget Survey), and examining net, rather than gross, earnings, found that the Gini coefficient increased from 21.8 in 1987 to 23.9 in 1992 (2002a, Table A1). Moreover, it has been argued that '[in Poland] the growth in inequality was strongly concentrated during the early stage of the transition' (Rutkowski, 2001, page 11). 'Poland and Slovenia are examples of countries which still experience some increases in earnings inequality but at a very modest rate. In both these countries the Decile Ratio hardly increased since the mid 1990s, suggesting that a new equilibrium was reached' (Rutkowski, 2001, page 7). He attributes this in part to the fact that Poland is a country 'where strong trade unions are successful in protecting the relative earnings position of low paid workers' (2001, page 13). Indeed, evidence from the Labour Force Survey (LFS) data for hourly wages suggests that in the mid-1990s, the widening had been reversed: according to Newell, 'household labour income became more unevenly distributed in Poland through the 1990s, but this was not caused by increasing individual wage inequality' (2001, page 8).

From Figure O.2 the reader can see that the LFS data for the 1990s look rather different from the employer surveys. The top decile rose less, and the bottom decile went in the opposite direction. These different findings may reflect differences in the source or the fact that the LFS results are for hourly earnings. The employer surveys, which are used in the Statistical Yearbook (Table O.2), indicate that the widening continued, at least up to 2004. The bottom decile has fallen by 18 per cent between 1992 and 2004, and the lower quartile by 9.5 per cent. Figure O.1 shows the 'fanning out' of the distribution, with the top decile (rising by 15.5 per cent between 1992 and 2004) outstripping the upper quartile (rising by 9 per cent), and the top vintile (rising by 26 per cent) shooting ahead of the top decile.

Summary

In contrast to the view expressed in the quotation from Lydall with which this chapter opened, the period since 1960 has not been one of stability in the distribution of earnings in Poland. There appear to have been distinct cycles during the communist period, notably associated with the Solidarity Movement and its aftermath, and the employer surveys indicate that the post-communist period saw a large fall in the bottom decile relative to the median, and a fanning out of the upper part of the distribution. But this evidence has to be interpreted in the light of changing definitions and coverage of the statistics, and of differing findings from different sources.

Table O.1. Poland: OECD (LMS)

	A	B	C	D	E	F	G	H	I	J	K	L	M	N	O	P	Q	R
				Column														
			All				Male						Female					
	P10	P20	P25	P75	P80	P90	P10	P20	P25	P75	P80	P90	P10	P20	P25	P75	P80	P90
1980	59.3					170.4												
1981	64.3					162.9												
1982	67.0					156.3												
1983	62.8					161.2												
1984	63.8					164.4												
1985	61.7					167.2												
1986	60.9					169.1												
1987	61.3					169.1												
1988	62.8					163.2												
1989	65.4	74.6	79.0	127.3	131.7	159.0												
1990	59.3	71.1	76.7	132.5	142.3	175.3												
1991	61.6	73.4	77.8	132.2	141.0	176.1	61.7	72.9	77.4	132.8	143.6	178.7	64.0	74.1	79.0	126.3	133.4	159.8
1992	61.6	72.7	77.1	133.0	143.2	179.8	60.9	72.1	76.8	135.3	146.9	183.8	64.0	74.1	78.1	127.8	135.4	162.9
1993	60.1	71.0	75.8	134.1	145.1	181.9	58.7	70.7	75.8	135.6	147.3	183.5	63.4	73.4	77.8	129.4	137.9	166.9
1994	57.6	69.3	74.6	137.2	150.4	195.0	54.9	68.1	73.5	142.7	156.5	202.3	61.4	71.7	76.4	130.7	141.0	172.0
1995	58.1	69.5	74.7	138.4	151.7	197.3	54.5	67.4	72.9	142.2	156.3	201.1	62.4	72.4	77.1	130.9	140.8	173.9

(Continued)

Table O.1. (*Continued*)

			All						Male						Female			
	A	B	C	D	E	F	G	H	I	J	K	L	M	N	O	P	Q	R
	P10	P20	P25	P75	P80	P90	P10	P20	P25	P75	P80	P90	P10	P20	P25	P75	P80	P90
1996	56.9	68.5	74.1	139.1	152.7	199.5	53.2	66.8	72.6	143.0	157.5	202.6	61.3	71.7	76.3	132.1	142.5	177.2
1997	56.7	68.2	73.5	139.7	153.1	200.5	52.9	66.0	72.0	143.0	158.0	205.0	60.6	71.3	76.0	133.4	144.2	179.8
1998	56.1	68.1	73.5	139.4	155.8	198.0	53.8	67.3	73.0	143.7	155.8	198.1	59.6	70.6	75.5	136.2	146.2	187.3
1999	56.3	68.1	73.4	141.1	155.4	199.5	53.1	65.9	71.7	142.1	154.9	201.6	58.9	70.0	74.7	137.3	146.0	183.9

Coverage	Prior to 1990 refers to socialized sector only; from 1990 excludes employees of firms with fewer than six employees
Industry	All
Age	All
Sex	See headings
Occupation	All
Definition	Gross (including monthly equivalent of periodic bonuses)
Intensity	FT
Period	Month
Limits	None
Source	Downloaded from OECD website December 2005
Original source	Enterprise survey
Note	OECD interpolations of published data

Table O.2. Poland: Data from Statistical Yearbook

	A	B	C	D	E	F	G	H		I	J	K	L	M	N	O
				All				Column					Male			
	P10	P20	P25	P75	P80	P90	P95	P98		P10	P20	P25	P75	P80	P90	P95
1992	61.6	72.6	76.9	132.6	143.3	179.8	219.2			60.9	72.1	76.8	135.7	146.9	183.8	219.7
1993	60.1	71.0	75.8	133.8	145.0	181.9	222.8			58.7	70.8	75.6	136.4	147.3	183.5	220.6
1994	57.7	69.4	74.2	137.7	150.4	195.1	243.9	315.4		54.9	68.1	73.3	142.2	156.2	202.1	247.3
1995	58.1	69.5	74.8	138.6	151.7	197.3	250.5	324.2		54.5	67.4	72.8	142.3	156.3	201.1	257.8
1996	56.9	68.6	73.9	140.2	152.7	199.5	253.4	332.7		53.2	66.8	72.3	143.9	157.5	202.6	255.4
1997	56.7	68.0	73.4	141.7	154.0	203.3	255.6	336.8		52.7	65.9	71.8	142.3	160.8	207.4	258.6
1998	56.1	68.0	73.5	139.4	155.8	198.0	248.8	328.5		53.8	67.3	73.0	143.7	155.8	198.1	244.3
1999	56.3	68.1	73.4	141.1	155.4	199.5	255.5			53.1	65.9	71.7	142.2	154.8	201.6	255.4
2001	53.3	66.0	71.8	140.7	154.2	201.4	262.5			51.8	66.0	71.7	143.7	157.1	207.6	267.3
2002	51.0	64.1	69.9	143.4	157.6	205.9	269.5			48.7	63.4	69.9	147.4	161.5	215.2	277.4
2004	50.4	63.9	69.8	144.6	158.9	207.7	275.9			48.4	63.4	69.8	146.3	161.0	216.6	293.7

(*Continued*)

Table O.2. (*Continued*)

	P	Q	R	S	T	U	V	Source*
				Column				
				Female				
	P10	P20	P25	P75	P80	P90	P95	
1992	64.0	74.0	78.2	127.6	135.4	162.9	195.2	SY 1993, Tables 9(313) and 10(314)
1993	63.4	73.3	77.6	129.2	138.0	166.9	201.1	SY 1994, Tables 9(303) and 10(304)
1994	61.4	71.8	76.0	131.6	140.9	172.2	210.7	SY 1995, Tables 8(227) and 9(228)
1995	62.4	72.5	76.9	131.1	140.7	173.9	214.5	SY 1996, Tables 6(228) and 7(229)
1996	61.3	71.7	76.4	132.5	142.5	177.2	221.8	SY 1997, Tables 7(236) and 8(237)
1997	60.6	71.3	76.0	134.1	145.2	181.7	228.8	SY 1998, Table 6(178)
1998	59.6	70.6	75.6	136.2	146.3	187.3	231.7	SY 1999, Table 7(183)
1999	58.9	70.0	74.8	137.3	146.1	183.9	237.0	SY 2001, Table 7(184)
2001	55.8	67.5	72.6	138.3	149.9	187.1	237.6	SY 2002, Table 6(181)
2002	53.9	65.9	71.1	141.6	152.5	190.4	240.0	SY 2003, Table 6(192)
2004	53.1	65.5	70.8	143.8	155.4	197.1	247.0	SY 2006, Table 6(197)

Coverage	Excluding employees of firms with fewer than six employees
Industry	All
Age	All
Sex	See headings
Occupation	All
Definition	Gross
Intensity	FT
Period	Month of September (October since 1998)
Limits	None
Sources	See final column
Original source	Enterprise survey
Notes	(1) Figures in italics interpolated; (2) Deciles same as Table O.1.
	*Statistical Yearbook (SY)

Table O.3. Poland: Census of enterprises

	A	B	C	D	E	F	G	H	I	J	K	L	M	N	O	P	Q	R	S	T	U	V
Column																						
				All								Male							Female			
	P05	P10	P25	P75	P90	P95	P99	Gini	P05	P10	P25	P75	P90	P95	Gini	P05	P10	P25	P75	P90	P95	Gini
1956	49.4	57.8	75.2	136.6	183.7	221.5	322.3	25.9														
1957	45.6	54.5	73.5	138.0	184.5	224.9	314.0	26.6														
1958	45.2	55.2	74.1	136.7	181.9	216.6	306.8	26.0														
1959	45.9	55.9	74.5	135.0	180.7	213.5	309.6	25.8														
1960	47.2	56.6	74.9	133.6	176.3	207.0	295.8	25.0														
1961	48.5	57.0	75.0	133.5	176.3	206.4	295.5	24.7														
1962	48.0	57.0	74.9	133.8	178.2	209.1		25.1														
1963	47.5	56.2	74.5	133.1	176.1	206.6		24.9														
1964	46.7	55.8	74.7	132.3	173.3	202.9		24.7														
1965	46.7	55.6	74.4	133.9	173.8	205.3		25.0														
1967	48.0	56.7	75.2	136.9	174.3	207.0		25.1														
1970	47.5	56.3	76.4	136.9	177.3	215.7		26.2														
1970 net		58.3	76.0	129.7	165.7	198.1	274.9	23.2														
1972	51.0	60.3	76.7	129.7	168.9	199.7	282.7	23.2	54.2	63.0	79.5	128.5	164.0	196.1	21.5		62.7	79.2	122.9	148.6	170.4	19.4
1976	49.9	58.0	75.7	132.2	177.3	210.2	287.1	24.1														

(Continued)

Table O.3. (*Continued*)

	A	B	C	D	E	F	G	H	I	J	K	L	M	N	O	P	Q	R	S	T	U	V
				All							Male							Female				
	P05	P10	P25	P75	P90	P95	P99	Gini	P05	P10	P25	P75	P90	P95	Gini	P05	P10	P25	P75	P90	P95	Gini
1978	49.2	57.5	75.0	132.3	175.6	208.3	286.8	24.2														
1980	51.4	59.1	75.8	130.2	170.1	200.2	269.2	22.9														
1981	57.2	64.3	79.6	127.6	163.0	194.6	292.2	21.8														
1982	58.6	66.4	80.6	123.5	155.7	183.4	276.8	20.2														
1983	55.2	62.9	79.0	126.7	161.9	191.9		22.0														
1984	55.9	63.5	79.1	128.1	164.4	194.8		22.0														
1985	54.3	61.9	79.2	129.9	167.5	200.1	279.3	22.4	54.4	62.9	78.8	128.7	166.8	208.8	23.9	58.5	65.8	80.5	122.6	147.3	164.8	17.5
1986	51.9	60.9	77.6	129.3	169.1	206.5		24.2														
1987	52.5	61.3	77.7	129.0	168.8	204.7	293.5	23.0														
1988	55.4	62.7	78.2	126.3	163.3	191.6	258.8	21.2														
1989	57.8	65.4	81.2	126.3	159.0	188.1		20.7														

Coverage   Socialized sector, excluding those working in private sector, members of armed forces, police, senior government officials, and employees in 'Political Organisations, trade unions, and other'

Industry   All

Age   All

Sex   See headings

Occupation   All

Definition   Gross up to 1970; net from 1970

Intensity   FT

Period   Month

Limits   None

Source   Atkinson and Micklewright (AM), Tables PE2, PE3 and PE4

Original source   Census of enterprises; information provided in bands.

Notes   (1) see A+M section S.6 on interpolation method; P99 obtained by Pareto interpolation of individual ranges.; (2) 1956–60 in close agreement with Lydall, 1968, Table PO-1

Table O.4. Poland: Employer survey (Rutkowski)

	A	B	C	D	E	F	G	H	I
	P5	P10	P25	P75	P90	P95	Gini	Share of bottom 20%	Share of top 20%
1987	53.0	61.3	77.7	129.4	168.8	205.0	23.0	10.7	33.9
1988	54.9	62.7	78.7	127.7	163.3	193.3	21.4	11.2	32.7
1989	57.4	65.4	80.3	125.7	159.0	187.3	20.5	11.5	32.3
1990								11.1	33.7
1991	53.6	61.6	77.9	130.9	176.1	214.2	24.2	10.6	35.1
1992	53.8	61.6	77.3	132.4	179.8	219.3	24.7	10.5	35.6
1993	52.4	60.1	75.9	133.8	181.9	221.8	25.7	10.2	36.2
1994		58.5			196.5		28.1		
1995		58.3			197.0		28.8		
1996		57.3			198.4		29.5		
1997		56.7			200.3		30.1		
1998		57.2			193.6		29.3		
1999		56.2			199.2		30.5		

Coverage	All
Industry	All
Age	All
Sex	All
Occupation	All
Definition	Gross (inc. monthly equivalent of bonuses and allowances)
Intensity	FT
Period	Monthly
Limits	None
Source	Rutkowski 1996, Tables 3 and 4, Annex, and 2001, Table 1.
Original source	September enterprise survey

Table O.5. Poland: Labour Force Survey (Newell)

	A	B	C
	P10	P90	Gini
1992	60	187	26.2
1994	63	189	25.5
1997	66	190	24.7

Coverage	All
Industry	All
Age	All
Sex	All
Occupation	All
Definition	Gross (inc. monthly equivalent of bonuses and allowances)
Intensity	FT
Period	Hourly
Limits	None
Source	Newell, 2001, Table 7.
Note	Labour Force Survey

Table O.6. Poland: Household Budget Survey (Keane and Prasad)

	A	B	C	D	E	F	G
	All			Male		Female	
	P90/P10	P75/P25	Gini	P90/P10	P75/P25	P90/P10	P75/P25
1985	2.61	1.63	21.6	2.51	1.57	2.32	1.54
1986	2.64	1.65	22.0	2.48	1.58	2.36	1.55
1987	2.61	1.63	21.8	2.48	1.57	2.34	1.54
1988	2.64	1.65	22.1	2.56	1.60	2.34	1.55
1989	2.83	1.70	23.1	2.72	1.67	2.64	1.67
1990	2.80	1.68	22.8	2.75	1.68	2.66	1.65
1991	2.80	1.70	22.9	2.77	1.70	2.59	1.62
1992	2.94	1.75	23.9	2.92	1.73	2.69	1.67
1994	3.03	1.75	25.9	3.13	1.79	2.69	1.65
1994 unadj.	3.16	1.79					
1995	3.06	1.79	26.2	3.10	1.82	2.69	1.65
1995 unadj.	3.19	1.82					
1996	3.06	1.80	26.1	3.16	1.80	2.72	1.67
1996 unadj.	3.16	1.84					

Coverage	All
Industry	All
Age	All
Sex	See headings
Occupation	All
Definition	Net
Intensity	FT
Period	Quarterly until 1992, then monthly (adjusted and unadj.)
Limits	None
Source	Keane and Prasad 2002a, Tables 2, 7 and A1.
Original source	Household Budget Survey
Note	Keane and Prasad argue that the move to a monthly, rather than quarterly, survey period led to a rise in the error variance; they adjust as shown

Bibliography

Aghion, P and Commander, S, 1999, 'On the dynamics of inequality in the transition', *Economics of Transition*, vol 7: 275–98.

Atkinson, A B and Micklewright, J, 1992, *Economic Transformation in Eastern Europe and the Distribution of Income*, Cambridge University Press, Cambridge.

Domanski, H, 1988, 'Labor market segmentation and income determination in Poland', *Sociological Quarterly*, vol 29: 47–62.

Duffy, F and Walsh, P P, 2001, 'Individual pay and outside options: Evidence from the Polish Labour Force Survey', IZA Discussion Paper 295.

Flakierski, H, 1986, *Economic Reform and Income Distribution*, M E Sharpe, Armonk.

Flemming, J S and Micklewright. J, 1999, 'Income distribution, economic systems and transition', in A B Atkinson and F Bourguignon, editors, *Handbook of Income Distribution*, Elsevier, Amsterdam.

Keane, M P and Prasad, E S, 2002, 'Inequality, transfers and growth: New evidence from the economic transition in Poland', *Review of Economics and Statistics*, vol 84: 324–41.

—— and—— 2002a, 'Changes in the structure of earnings during the Polish transition', IZA Discussion Paper 496.

Newell, A, 2001, 'The distribution of wages in transition countries', IZA Discussion Paper 267.

—— and Socha, M, 1998, 'Wage distribution in Poland: The roles of privatisation and international trade', *Economics of Transition*, vol 6: 47–65.

Rutkowski, J, 1993, 'Wage determination in historically planned economies: The case of Poland', CEPR Discussion Paper 164.

—— 1994, 'Wage determination in late socialism: The case of Poland', *Economics of Planning*, vol 27: 135–64.

—— 1996, *Changes in the Wage Structure during Economic Transition in Central and Eastern Europe*, World Bank Technical Paper 340.

—— 1996a, 'High skills pay-off: The changing wage structure during economic transition in Poland', *Economics of Transition*, vol 4: 89–112.

—— 2001, 'Earnings inequality in transition economies of Central Europe: Trends and patterns during the 1990s', World Bank SP Discussion Paper 0117.

Sibley, C W and Walsh, P P, 2002, 'Earnings inequality and transition: A regional analysis of Poland', IZA Discussion Paper 441.

Svejnar, J, 1996, 'Enterprises and workers in the transition: Econometric evidence', *American Economic Review, Papers and Proceedings*, vol 86: 123–7.

P

Portugal

Rising inequality characterized the evolution of labour returns in Portugal during the 1980s and early 1990s. The pattern of change in inequality in the labour market reinforced the main characteristic detected for the Portuguese earnings distribution at the beginning of the decade—a stretched top, where dispersion increased remarkably.

Cardoso, 1998, page 340

P.1 Introduction

The First Portuguese Republic was established in 1910, replacing the Portuguese monarchy. In 1926, a military *coup d'état* installed the 'Second Republic' that became an authoritarian right-wing dictatorship and later evolved into a type of single party corporate regime. In April 1974 there was a left-wing military coup, and in 1975 Portugal held its first free multi-party elections since 1926. Portugal became a member of the European Communities in 1986, and adopted the euro in 2002.

Previous Coverage

Lydall (1968) contains no data for Portugal.

Portugal is not covered by the downloaded OECD (LMS) data. It was covered by the earlier OECD compilations:

1993 (Table P.1): Data for all workers 1985 and 1995 from a sample of the *Quadros de Pessoal*, an annual census of the personnel records of employers with at least one employee.

1996 (Table P.2): Data for all workers, and men and women separately, 1985 to 1993 (with gaps) from a sample of the *Quadros de Pessoal*.

Official Publications

No earnings distribution data are published in the Statistical Yearbook.

P.2 Data Sources

The source used since 1982 is the *Quadros de Pessoal*, an annual census of the personnel records of employers with at least one employee. For earlier years, information on the upper part of the earnings distribution is available from the wage tax records (*Imposto Profissional*).

Quadros de Pessoal

Employers are required by law to provide information about their employees to the Quadros de Pessoal. It is carried out in November of each year, requiring information about the month of October (previously March). The census covers all firms employing paid labour, and provides information for over 2 million workers each year. Employees in public administration and domestic service are not within the remit of the survey, and in practice agriculture is not covered.

Information is collected about the establishment, the firm, and the worker, including monthly earnings. 'Salario' refers to basic wages; 'ganho' includes overtime and bonuses. Individuals for whom the survey has complete information number around 1.5 million each year (Machado and Mata, 2001, page 117). The Direcção-Geral de Estudios, Estatistica e Planeamento (DGEEP) of the Ministry of Labour and Social Solidarity publishes a report on the results, and there is a chronological series, but this does not contain results on earnings dispersion. The data were first collected in 1982. No data on the dispersion of earnings are available for 1990 or for 2001. The data are the basis for Tables P.1, P.2, and P.3.

Household Budget Survey (IOF)

The household budget survey is known as the Inquéritos aos Orçamentos Familiares. The first such survey took place between April 1967 and March 1968, but did not contain income information. The second survey took place between July 1973 and June 1974, and did contain income information. Unfortunately the micro-data no longer survive. The income information from the next survey (1980/1), and from 1989/90, 1994/5, and 2000/1 have been used by Rodrigues (1994, 2005)—see also Jimeno et al (2000).

Imposto Profissional

The Imposto Profissional was introduced in 1929 as a tax on the earnings of employees (including agriculture but not public administration) and liberal professionals (including the self-employed). From 1936 tabulations have been published of the number of taxed individuals by intervals of tax paid. Alvaredo (2007) has used the tax code to recover the implied brackets of earnings and average earnings by bracket. The wage tax data only covered a small fraction of employees (under 10 per cent until 1965), and the results in Table P.4 only relate to the top income shares. From 1989, the same information is available in the income tax tabulations (see Alvaredo, 2007).

Summary

From 1982 we have information on the distribution of earnings in Portugal from the employer survey, and the results are summarized in Figures P.1 and P.2. Before that date, we have evidence about the top earnings shares going back to 1936.

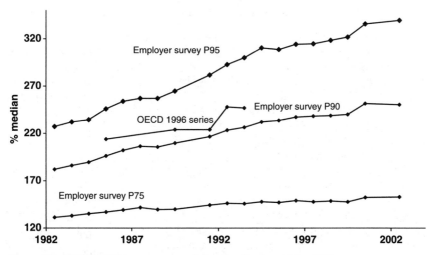

Figure P.1 PORTUGAL upper part of the distribution 1982–2002
Sources: Table P.2, column B; Table P.3, columns D, E, and F.

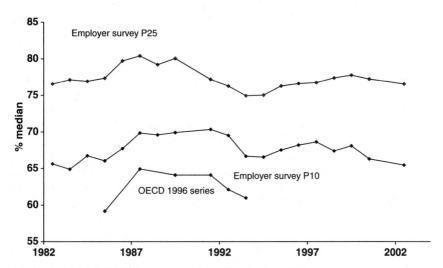

Figure P.2 PORTUGAL lower part of the distribution 1982–2002
Sources: Table P.2, column A; Table P.3, columns B and C.

P.3 What Happened?

The early data are limited to the top of the earnings distribution but show no sign of compression in the period 1936 to 1950; if anything, the share of the top 1 per cent rose in this period. Much clearer is the significant fall in the top earnings shares after 1968. The share of the top 1 per cent fell from 9.2 per cent in 1968 to 5.9 per cent in 1977, and that of the top 10 per cent from 24 per cent to 19.5 per cent. The post-1968 decade was eventful for top earners as well as politically.

The decade of the 1980s saw a great deal of change in the Portuguese economy, particularly associated with Portugal joining the European Communities in 1986. There was considerable modernization. One study of European skill levels noted that 'the greatest change [in the qualifications of young people] has taken place in Portugal where the proportion of 25–27 year olds with [only primary education] was reduced by 17 percent from 1986 to 1996' (Murray and Steedman, 1998, page 12). From Figure P.2, we can see that in the early part of the 1980s there was a definite improvement in the relative position of the bottom decile, which rose by 6.6 per cent between 1982 and 1987. This improvement was broadly maintained until the end of the decade. At the top, on the other hand, as Cardoso (1998) indicated, the distribution was widening: the top decile rose from 182 per cent of the median in 1982 to 217 per cent in 1991, causing the decile ratio to rise from 2.8 to 3.1.

In the 1990s, the decile ratio rose faster, since there was a decline between 1991 and 1994 in the bottom decile of some 5 per cent. Indeed at the end of the period the bottom decile in 2002 was virtually identical to its value 20 years earlier. Taking the period 1982 to 2002 as a whole, therefore, we could say that there has been no long run trend in the bottom decile, although such a summary would miss the rise in the 1980s and the fall in the 1990s. In contrast, in the upper part of the distribution (Figure P.1) the pattern is clear. There has been a distinct fanning-out of the distribution. Over the 20 year period, the upper quartile rose, relative to the median, by 16 per cent, the top decile rose by 38 per cent and the top vintile by 49 per cent. The decile ratio rose, from 1982 to 2002, from 2.78 to 3.82, an increase of over a third.

The different forces influencing the distribution of earnings in Portugal are considered by, among others, Gouveia and Tavares (1995), and Cardoso (1998 and 1998a). Gouveia and Tavares make the interesting observation that the standard trade/earnings argument may apply in reverse to Portugal. In the context of the EU, Portugal may be relatively well-endowed with unskilled labour. Increased trade within Europe may therefore increase the relative demand for unskilled workers. There is, however, little sign of a decline in the skill premium. Indeed the study by Hartog, Pereira, and Vieira (2001) found that the returns to education have increased, especially since Portugal joined the EU.

Summary

The top earnings shares show no sign of a compression from 1936 to 1950, but there was a very definite fall in the decade following 1968. Over the period from 1982 to 2002, the bottom decile rose and then fell, but the top percentiles rose steadily. The decile ratio rose by more than a third, and there was an evident fanning-out in the upper part of the distribution.

Table P.1. Portugal: OECD (1993)

	Column	
	A	B
	P10	P90
1985	70	180
1995	71	187
Coverage	All	
Industry	Exc. agriculture	
Age	All	
Sex	All	
Occupation	All	
Definition	Gross earnings	
Intensity	FT	
Period	Monthly	
Limits	None	
Source	OECD (1993, Table 5.2)	
Original source	A sample of *Quadros de Pessoal*, personnel records of employers with at least one employee	
Note	Provided by Professor Alberto Castro, Universidade do Porto	

Table P.2. Portugal: OECD (1996)

			Column			
A	B	C	D	E	F
All		Male		Female	
P10	P90	P10	P90	P10	P90
1985	59	214	64	213	66	184
1987	65		62		75	212
1989	64	224	58	224	75	210
1991	64	224	57	239	80	227
1992	62	248	58	243	76	229
1993	61	247	58	240	72	234

Coverage	All
Industry	Exc. agriculture and public administration
Age	All
Sex	All
Occupation	All
Definition	Gross earnings
Intensity	FT
Period	Monthly
Limits	None
Source	OECD (1996, Table 3.1)
Original source	A sample of *Quadros de Pessoal,* personnel records of employers with at least one employee

Table P.3. Portugal: Employer survey (Rodrigues)

	A	B	C	D	E	F	G	H	I	J	K	L	M	N	O	P	Q	R	S	T	U	V	W	X
		All						Male							Female							All hourly		
	P05	P10	P25	P75	P90	P95	Gini	P05	P10	P25	P75	P90	P95	Gini	P05	P10	P25	P75	P90	P95	Gini	P10	P90	Gini
1982	50.6	65.6	76.6	131.3	182.1	227.3	25.8	49.4	62.3	79.1	131.8	181.6	228.4	25.7	58.6	72.6	87.5	133.5	178.1	214.8	21.9			
1983	51.9	64.9	77.1	133.0	186.2	232.2	26.0	49.8	64.4	79.2	133.5	186.7	232.7	26.0	60.0	72.7	88.0	133.3	184.7	223.5	22.2	63	235	32.41
1984	52.9	66.7	76.9	135.1	189.6	234.5	26.1	51.6	65.7	78.7	134.7	189.5	236.1	26.2	59.0	72.6	87.2	134.4	184.4	224.9	22.3			
1985	54.2	66.0	77.4	136.9	196.3	246.0	27.1	52.6	66.7	78.9	139.2	198.3	247.7	27.3	60.5	74.4	89.3	136.3	188.5	234.9	22.9			
1986	54.4	67.7	79.7	139.1	202.2	254.0	27.4	52.8	67.5	78.6	141.5	204.8	255.5	27.9	60.5	76.2	87.9	135.5	194.1	239.6	23.1	67	243	33.40
1987	56.8	69.9	80.4	141.7	206.4	257.1	27.6	55.4	65.8	78.3	142.3	207.6	259.3	28.1	62.4	76.3	86.9	134.2	194.9	241.5	23.2			
1988	57.0	69.6	79.2	139.6	205.7	257.1	27.6	55.7	64.4	78.1	142.0	206.3	260.4	28.2	64.6	77.4	87.1	133.1	195.0	243.6	22.9			
1989	58.3	69.9	80.1	139.9	209.8	264.8	28.3	57.4	63.8	77.9	142.2	211.0	267.7	28.9	67.4	79.8	87.2	134.0	200.8	251.3	23.6	64	256	35.23
1991	61.4	70.4	77.2	144.3	216.7	281.8	30.2	58.3	63.6	77.6	145.9	217.7	285.5	30.7	71.0	83.3	88.4	136.7	213.0	267.6	25.5			
1992	62.5	69.5	76.3	146.2	223.4	292.8	31.2	56.4	62.6	77.4	147.7	222.3	295.3	31.6	73.0	79.5	87.3	138.3	219.3	280.5	26.9	63	270	37.53
1993	63.6	66.7	75.0	145.7	226.4	300.0	32.3	56.9	61.3	76.7	147.1	223.1	300.2	32.6	74.2	77.7	85.6	139.6	226.4	289.6	28.5			
1994	66.3	66.6	75.0	147.8	232.2	310.5	33.1	59.7	60.8	76.7	148.4	228.8	309.0	33.4	76.6	79.8	84.2	141.7	233.2	300.6	29.9			
1995	67.5	67.5	76.3	146.9	233.8	308.7	32.3	60.5	62.6	76.7	149.1	231.9	309.2	33.0	77.0	80.1	84.4	139.4	230.7	295.8	28.2			

(Continued)

Table P.3. (*Continued*)

	A	B	C	D	E	F	G	H	I	J	K	L	M	N	O	P	Q	R	S	T	U	V	W	X
	All							Male							Female							All hourly		
	P05	P10	P25	P75	P90	P95	Gini	P05	P10	P25	P75	P90	P95	Gini	P05	P10	P25	P75	P90	P95	Gini	P10	P90	Gini
1996	68.2	76.6		149.0	237.4	314.3	32.6	60.7	62.8	77.1	148.2	231.6	313.7	33.3	78.8	79.7	83.6	139.3	229.1	297.7	28.6			
1997	68.6	76.8		147.7	238.3	314.8	32.3	61.6	63.4	77.5	151.0	235.3	317.8	33.2	79.9	80.6	84.3	141.0	228.5	298.5	28.0			
1998	67.3	77.4		148.5	238.9	318.5	32.3	60.7	64.2	77.2	151.9	238.7	322.0	33.2	78.9	78.9	83.3	139.4	230.5	300.1	28.1			
1999	68.1	77.8		147.6	240.1	321.9	32.2	61.3	64.8	78.0	150.0	240.3	326.2	33.4	78.8	78.8	82.5	139.3	229.0	299.5	27.7			
2000	60.5	77.2		152.3	251.6	335.8	33.8	56.2	63.5	76.1	155.0	252.8	340.0	34.8	70.4	71.9	83.0	143.1	235.8	312.4	29.4			
2002	59.3	76.6		152.8	250.5	339.5	34.2	55.6	63.3	76.2	154.5	251.5	346.2	35.2	67.8	70.3	81.2	145.7	244.5	323.3	30.8			

Coverage   All except public administration
Industry   All
Age   All
Sex   See headings
Occupation   All
Definition   Gross
Intensity   FT
Period   Monthly, except columns V, W and X (hourly)
Limits   None
Source   A sample of *Quadros de Pessoal*, personnel records of employers with at least one employee, data supplied by Carlos Farinha Rodrigues, except columns V, W, and X from Cardoso (1998, Figure 1)
Note   March until 1993, October from 1994

Table P.4. Portugal: Income tax data (Alvaredo)

| | Column | | |
	A	B	C
	Share of top 10%	Share of top 5%	Share of top 1%
1936			6.15
1937			6.11
1938			6.48
1939			7.21
1940			7.46
1941			7.42
1942			6.79
1943			6.27
1944			6.14
1945			6.52
1946			6.50
1947			6.90
1948			7.78
1949			7.83
1950			8.40
1951			7.96
1952			8.31
1953			8.02
1954			6.98
1955			7.92
1956			8.08
1957			8.46
1958			8.97
1959		18.60	8.49
1960		18.41	8.45
1961		18.03	8.35
1962			8.24
1964		13.99	6.78
1965	21.88	17.01	8.40
1966	21.79	16.85	8.36
1967	21.53	16.31	8.20
1968	23.96	18.08	9.21
1969	23.74	17.90	8.89
1970	22.51	16.76	7.97
1971	19.83	15.17	7.58
1972	20.22	15.52	7.98
1973	18.98	14.27	6.91
1974	19.59	13.80	6.73
1975	17.75	12.70	6.30
1976	17.45	12.70	6.84

(Continued)

Table P.4. (*Continued*)

| | Column | | |
| | A | B | C |
	Share of top 10%	Share of top 5%	Share of top 1%
1977	19.48	13.88	5.91
1989	25.71	16.05	5.18
1990	27.16	17.18	5.62
1991	28.41	18.01	5.91
1992	30.50	18.90	6.17
1993	28.79	18.38	6.16
1994	29.27	18.69	6.41
1995	30.43	19.48	6.82
1996	28.40	18.25	6.43
1997	29.28	18.95	6.78
1998	30.58	19.93	7.18
1999	30.97	20.42	7.61
2000	28.49	18.68	6.82

Coverage	Mainland Portugal
Industry	All
Age	All
Sex	All
Occupation	All
Definition	Gross wages and salaries taxed at source
Intensity	All
Period	Annual
Limits	None
Source	Alvaredo (2007)
Original source	Wage tax (IP) tabulations
Notes	(1) Includes self-employed liberal professionals; (2) Earnings brackets reconstructed from tax code

Bibliography

Alvaredo, F, 2007, 'Top incomes and earnings in Portugal 1936–2004', forthcoming.

Cantó, O, Cardoso, A R, and Jimeno, J F, 2002, 'Earnings inequality in Portugal and Spain: Contrasts and similarities', in D Cohen, T Piketty, and G Saint-Paul, editors, *The Economics of Rising Inequalities*, Oxford University Press, Oxford.

Cardoso, A R, 1998, 'Earnings inequality in Portugal: High and rising?', *Review of Income and Wealth*, series 44: 325–43.

—— 1998a, 'Workers or employers: Who is shaping wage inequality?', *Oxford Bulletin of Economics and Statistics*, vol 59: 523–47.

—— 1999, 'Firms' wage policies and the rise in labor market inequality: The case of Portugal', *Industrial and Labor Relations Review*, vol 53: 87–102.

Gouveia, M and Tavares, J, 1995, 'The distribution of household income and expenditure in Portugal: 1980 and 1990', *Review of Income and Wealth*, series 41: 1–17.

Hartog, J, Pereira, P T, and Vieira, J A C, 1999, 'Inter-industry wage dispersion in Portugal: High but falling', IZA Discussion Paper 53.

—— —— and —— 2001, 'Changing returns to education in Portugal during the 1980s and early 1990s: OLS and quantile regression estimators', *Applied Economics*, vol 33: 1021–37.

Jimeno, J F, Cantó, O, Rute, A, Izquierdo, M, and Rodrigues, C A Farinha, 2000, 'Integration and inequality: Lessons from the accessions of Portugal and Spain to the EU', FEDEA.

Machado, J A F and Mata, J, 2001, 'Earning functions in Portugal 1982–1994: Evidence from quantile regressions', *Empirical Economics*, vol 26: 115–34.

Murray, A and Steedman, H, 1998, 'Growing skills in Europe: The changing skills profiles of France, Germany, the Netherlands, Portugal, Sweden and the UK', CEP Discussion Paper 399, London School of Economics.

Rodrigues, C A Farinha, 1994, 'Repartição do rendmento e disigualdade: Portugal nos anos 80', *Estudios de Economia*, vol 14: 399–427.

—— 2005, *Distribuição do Rendimento, Desigualdade e Pobreza: Portugal nos anos 90*, PhD thesis, Universidade Técnica de Lisboa.

—— and Albuquerque, J L, 2000, 'Pobreza e exclusão social: Percursos e perspectivas da investigação em Portugal', in *Actas do Seminário Pobreza e Exclusão Social: Percursos e Perspectivas da Investigação em Portugal*, CESIS, Lisbon.

Vieira, J, 1999, 'The evolution of wage structures in Portugal 1982–1992', PhD thesis, Tinbergen Institute, Amsterdam.

Q

Sweden

Wage inequality declined precipitously during the 1960s and 1970s. There was a sharp reduction in overall wage dispersion ... The trend of decline in wage inequality was broken in the 1980s. Wage differentials have widened along several dimensions from the mid-1980s to the early 1990s.

Edin and Holmlund, 1995, page 307

Q.1 Introduction

The union of Sweden and Norway was dissolved in 1905. Since then Sweden has had the same geographical boundaries. Sweden joined the European Union in 1995.

Previous Coverage

Sweden is included in all three OECD compilations:

1993 (Table Q.1): all workers, and male and female separately, 1974, 1981, 1984, 1986, 1988, and 1991, supplied by Per-Anders Edin from surveys.

1996 (Table Q.2): all workers, and male and female separately, 1980 to 1993, from Income Distribution Survey.

LMS (Table Q.3): all workers, and male and female separately, 1980 to 1998, from Income Distribution Survey.

Official Publications

The Statistical Yearbook (*Statistisk Årsbok för Sverige*) has published tables with the distribution of earned income, or income from employment and business income, but these cover only certain periods. Earnings data based on the Income Distribution Survey are published in *Statistiska Meddelanden* (see Table Q.5). Earnings distribution data from employer surveys have been published in recent years in the Statistical Yearbook of Salaries and Wages (*Lönstatistisk Årsbok*) and are available from the Statistics Sweden website (see Table Q.4).

Q.2 Data Sources

Lydall (1968) gives an extensive account of distributional changes in Sweden since 1920, but this is based largely on census of population tabulations that relate to total income, not earnings. According to the criteria adopted here, these data are not acceptable. Here I draw on data tabulated according to earnings (not including self-employment income), drawing on the Income Distribution Survey, the Pensionable Income Register, and the earnings surveys of employers.

Income Register Data

A central element in Swedish income data is the information available in the Income Registers (Inkomst- och Förmögenhets-statistiken), available annually from 1968.

The data from the registers are used in the Income Distribution Survey (Inkomst-fördelningsundersökningen or HINK) that is the basis for the earnings distributions in Tables Q.2 and Q.3, and for the Luxembourg Income Study (LIS) data used by Gottschalk and Joyce (1998), reproduced in Table Q.7. The Income Distribution Survey (IDS) is an annual survey of a national sample of adults that has been conducted every year since 1975. In 2000, the interviewed sample contained some 33,000 individuals. The data combine a household survey and the income data available from the income registers. The central idea is that the survey allows, for the sampled individuals, additional information to be attached to the income tax based data derived from the complete enumeration of the income statistics. The non-response rate to the survey in 2000 was 25.5 per cent, but the retrieval of information from the registers was almost complete. The survey non-response does not appear to have affected the total income from employment: according to the checks reported on the LIS website, the total was only 0.5 per cent different. The earnings data in the IDS are the basis for the distributions published in *Statistiska Meddelanden* and reproduced in Table Q.5.

The data from the Income Registers start in 1968. For this reason, Gustavsson (2004) makes use of the earlier data from the Pensionable Income Register (PIR). He has kindly made calculations based on these data available and they are reproduced in Table Q.6, allowing coverage of the 1960s. As he notes, the data are affected by top coding, and the percentage of earnings that are top-coded increases over time (so that the top decile is not available after 1965). The data exclude those earning less than a specified amount (about 10 per cent of the sample) and those in receipt of a pension. The sample selected was also unrepresentative in that it includes only those alive in 1990. For these reasons, Gustavsson suggests that the proportion of low earners is understated, and he shows that this is indeed the case when compared with the Income Registers (Gustavsson, 2004, Figure 1). On the other hand, the data relate to annual earnings and are not restricted to full year workers. Moreover, the PIR data do not include sickness benefits.

Employer Surveys

The earnings distribution data published in recent years in the Statistical Yearbook of Salaries and Wages (*Lönstatistisk Årsbok*) are based on surveys of employers in the public (census) and private sectors (sample). Surveys of employers requesting data on individual employees have been carried out for many years. For example, since 1955 surveys have been conducted of the earnings of salaried employees in the mining,

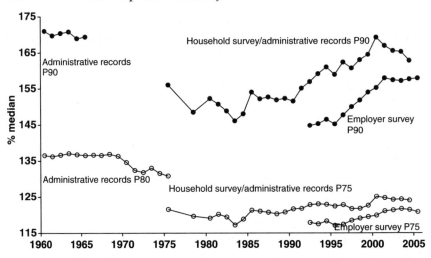

Figure Q.1 SWEDEN upper part of the distribution 1960–2005

Sources: Table Q.4, columns C and D; Table Q.5, columns C and D; Table Q.6, columns C and D.

manufacturing, building and construction industries (published in *Löner 19xx, Del 1 Industritjänstemän, handelsanställda m fl*). Other surveys covered employees in hotels and restaurants, pharmacies, commercial and savings banks, and insurance. Only in recent years have these been brought together, as in Table Q.4.

Summary

The earnings distribution data for Sweden are summarized in Figures Q.1 and Q.2. These begin with the administrative data from the Pensionable Income Register; they continue with the Income Distribution Survey data, combining register and survey data, and for the most recent years there are data from the combined employer surveys.

Q.3 What Happened?

The quotation at the beginning of this chapter summarizes concisely the history of wage dispersion since 1960, but certain aspects may be elaborated. The information about earnings in Figures Q.1 and Q.2 commences in 1960. During the decade of the 1960s, the earnings distribution appears to have been broadly stable. The downward movement in the bottom decile was less than 5 per cent and the two quintiles were little changed. According to Edin and Holmlund (1995), the solidarity wage policy pursued by the Swedish trade union movement gradually came into effect in the 1950s, following the first centralized wage rounds. The impact was described by one of the architects of the policy as follows: 'the history of wages policy is the story of the efforts on the part of a pragmatic trade union movement to transform a sophisticated

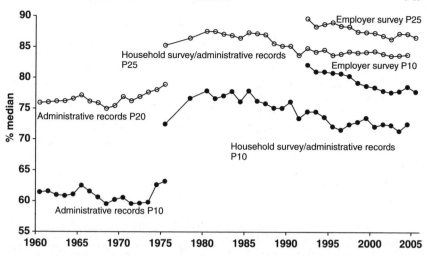

Figure Q.2 SWEDEN lower part of the distribution 1960–2005

Sources: Table Q.4, columns A and B; Table Q.5, columns A and B; Table Q.6, columns A and B.

ideology of equality into a reality for the labour market' (Meidner, 1974, page 30). To the extent that a policy of 'equal pay for equal work' reduced differences in pay that reflected differences in profitability, pay compression may have been expected. On the other hand, there was sizeable 'wage drift' (the difference between actual wage increases and the industry agreements) that may have offset the compression (see Hibbs and Locking, 1996).

'Around the middle of the 1960s, wage solidarity took a more radically egalitarian form' (Hibbs, 1990, page 182). Using data for blue-collar and white-collar workers, he finds that 'the biggest earnings compressions came between the mid-1960s and the mid-1970s' (1990, page 183). A starting date of 1968 is taken by Edin and Holmlund (1995), who describe the subsequent changes as 'dramatic'. Combining the PIR and IDS series in Figures Q.1 and Q.2, we can see that between 1968 and 1983 the bottom decile rose by 14 per cent, and the upper quintile/quartile fell by 8.5 per cent. Both changes clearly register on the conventions adopted here, and the change for the bottom decile is significant.[21]

The compression was reversed after 1983, when the wage bargaining moved much more to an industry level. Between 1983 and 1996, the bottom decile fell by 8 per cent. Again linking the PIR and IDS series, we can see that this fall still left the bottom decile at a higher percentage of the median than in 1968. The changes in the quintiles were less than 5 per cent, but the top decile rose by 16 per cent between 1983 and 2000. Gustavsson (2006) has used data from the income registers to investigate changes in

[21] Although it should be noted that the PIR data show a *decline* in the bottom decile after 1975.

the wage structure during the 1990s. He concludes that dispersion increased in both the lower and the upper halves of the distribution. The IDS data in Figure Q.2 however show the bottom decile falling between 1990 and 2004 by 4.8 per cent. When we allow for the fact that 1990 was a local peak, we have some grounds for concluding that the increased dispersion is more evident at the top. This is supported by the employer survey data in Figures Q.1 and Q.2. From 1992 to 2005, the bottom decile fell by 5.2 per cent, or just enough to register as a fall on the criteria adopted here. The top decile, over the same period, rose by 9 per cent.

Finally, we may note that the rise in the top decile either paused (employer survey data) or was reversed (IDS data) since 2000. The latter data show the Gini coefficient for earnings as falling from 22.6 per cent in 2000 to 21.1 per cent in 2004.

Summary

The experience of Sweden over the period since 1960 can be summarized as stability, followed by compression, and then reversal, with a significant rise in the top decile. As in other countries, the bottom decile has retained part of the gains from compression.

Table Q.1. Sweden: OECD (1993)

	Column					
	A	B	C	D	E	F
	All		Male		Female	
	P10	P90	P10	P90	P10	P90
1974	74	152	76	157	75	140
1981	77	154	78	168	81	137
1984	77	148	76	150	76	134
1986	74	148	76	149	75	137
1988	76	152	76	156	79	138
1991	74	154	73	157	77	140

Coverage	All
Industry	All
Age	Adult
Sex	See headings
Occupation	All
Definition	Gross
Period	Hourly
Limits	None
Source	OECD (1993, Table 5.2).
Original source	Level of Living Survey (LNU) for 1974 and 1981, and Household and Nonmarket Activities Survey (HUS) for 1984, 1986, and 1988

Table Q.2. Sweden: OECD (1996)

	Column					
	A	B	C	D	E	F
	All		Male		Female	
	P10	P90	P10	P90	P10	P90
1980	77	157	76	161	80	132
1981	76	155	75	156	76	135
1982	76	153	76	157	78	134
1983	77	150	77	155	79	136
1984	75	152	76	155	78	135
1985	77	159	74	158	78	136
1986	76	157	75	160	75	135
1987	75	157	75	158	75	139
1988	75	156	75	157	77	139
1989	74	157	74	160	78	138
1990	76	152	75	156	82	140
1991	74	155	74	160	78	142
1992	75	157	74	162	77	140
1993	75	159	74	162	77	140

Coverage	All
Industry	All
Age	23 and over
Sex	See headings
Occupation	All
Definition	Gross
Intensity	FT and FY
Period	Annual
Limits	None
Source	OECD (1996, Table 3.1)
Original source	*Income Distribution Survey*

Table Q.3. Sweden: OECD (LMS)

		All					Male						Female				
A	B	C	D	E	F	G	H	I	J	K	L	M	N	O	P	Q	R
	P20	P25	P75	P80	P90	P10	P20	P25	P75	P80	P90	P10	P20	P25	P75	P80	P90
P10																	
1975	71.8	81.5			132.3	160.7	74.4	81.6			133.7	162.2	73.5	83.5			121.7	139.2
1978	75.9	83.1			129.5	153.0	76.3	83.3			130.1	155.5	80.6	86.4			122.5	139.6
1980	77.1	84.9			129.1	156.9	76.5	83.1			133.0	161.0	80.2	86.2			116.5	131.8
1981	75.9	84.6			129.5	155.2	75.0	82.3			130.1	156.0	76.6	85.8			117.0	134.6
1982	76.3	84.0			128.5	153.3	75.7	82.2			130.6	157.1	77.6	85.4			117.6	133.7
1983	77.0	84.3			126.1	150.5	76.7	82.6			129.1	154.9	79.1	87.8			120.4	135.6
1984	75.4	83.5			128.8	152.4	76.1	82.3			129.9	154.9	77.3	86.3			120.0	134.8
1985	77.1	84.2			130.6	158.6	74.3	81.5			131.8	158.1	78.1	87.3			117.6	135.7
1986	75.5	83.6			130.5	156.7	74.6	81.7			132.3	160.5	75.3	85.5			118.9	134.7
1987	75.0	83.6			130.6	157.3	75.2	82.5			132.4	158.4	75.1	84.9			121.4	139.1
1988	74.4	82.1			130.6	156.3	74.7	81.8			131.9	157.0	77.0	85.3			122.7	138.8
1989	74.3	81.7			131.0	157.1	73.9	81.2			131.8	159.7	77.6	86.3			123.1	138.3
1990	75.8	82.1			130.0	152.3	75.4	81.7			130.2	156.3	81.7	86.8			124.1	140.3

(Continued)

Table Q.3. (*Continued*)

										Column								
			All					Male						Female			
	A	B	C	D	E	F	G	H	I	J	K	L	M	N	O	P	Q	R
	P10	P20	P25	P75	P80	P90	P10	P20	P25	P75	P80	P90	P10	P20	P25	P75	P80	P90
1991	73.4	80.6			129.1	155.1	73.3	81.5			131.1	159.9	77.7	86.1			128.0	141.9
1992	74.5	81.8			130.7	157.1	73.9	81.2			131.8	162.2	76.7	86.1			124.4	139.9
1993	74.5	81.1			131.4	159.1	73.5	80.7			133.6	162.3	76.9	85.6			123.8	139.6
1994	73.6	81.6			130.9	160.9	72.8	81.7			133.6	168.7	77.3	85.6			123.2	139.5
1995	72.1	80.4			129.9	158.9	71.6	81.2			131.4	163.0	77.1	85.1			124.7	142.4
1996	71.5	80.4			131.4	162.5	71.2	80.8			134.5	168.1	74.7	82.8			123.5	142.7
1997	72.6	81.1			129.4	160.6	72.8	81.3			132.9	168.3	76.1	84.3			124.8	141.4
1998	72.9	80.9	84.1	121.7	129.7	162.0	72.7	81.8	85.0	124.5	134.4	170.6	77.0	84.5	87.2	120.0	125.6	143.9

Coverage	All
Industry	All
Age	All
Sex	See headings
Occupation	All
Definition	Gross
Intensity	FT and FY
Period	Annual
Limits	None
Source	Downloaded from OECD website December 2005
Original source	*Income Distribution Survey*
Note	New basis, consistent with 1991 change in tax base, and spliced onto old series prior to 1989

Table Q.4. Sweden: Data from Statistical Yearbook of Salaries and Wages

								Column							
	A	B	C	D	E	F	G	H	I	J	K	L	M	N	O
			All					Male					Female		
	P10	P25	P75	P90	P90/P10	P10	P25	P75	P90	P90/P10	P10	P25	P75	P90	P90/P10
1992	82.1	89.6	117.9	144.8	1.77	79.2	87.5	122.2	156.3	1.98	84.3	91.3	115.0	133.1	1.58
1993	81.0	88.3	117.5	145.3	1.80	78.2	87.8	122.5	157.8	2.01	83.9	90.8	113.9	132.3	1.58
1994	81.0	88.7	118.3	146.5	1.81	78.3	86.8	121.7	158.6	2.03	83.7	90.4	114.8	133.3	1.60
1995	80.8	89.0	117.1	145.2	1.80	78.7	88.4	121.3	158.1	2.01	82.1	90.0	113.6	131.4	1.59
1996	80.7	88.4	117.4	147.7	1.83	78.8	87.9	121.2	160.6	2.04	83.6	90.4	115.1	133.6	1.60
1997	80.3	88.3	118.5	150.0	1.87	78.6	87.9	122.5	161.9	2.06	83.0	90.2	114.4	133.3	1.61
1998	79.2	87.5	119.1	151.8	1.91	77.8	87.2	122.8	166.1	2.12	82.8	89.8	115.3	135.7	1.64
1999	78.7	87.4	119.5	154.0	1.95	76.9	86.6	123.7	166.7	2.16	81.7	89.6	116.5	137.2	1.69
2000	78.5	87.3	119.9	155.2	1.98	77.3	86.6	123.2	167.5	2.17	81.2	88.8	116.5	138.8	1.71
2001	77.9	86.8	121.1	157.9	2.03	76.7	86.1	124.3	170.3	2.22	81.4	89.3	118.1	141.2	1.74
2002	77.7	86.3	121.3	157.4	2.03	76.2	85.7	123.8	168.6	2.21	80.5	88.6	117.3	141.6	1.75
2003	77.8	87.2	121.7	157.1	2.02	76.0	85.7	124.0	165.9	2.18	80.2	88.5	117.7	141.7	1.76
2004	78.6	87.1	121.4	157.6	2.01	76.4	85.8	124.0	168.0	2.20	80.4	88.4	117.6	141.2	1.76
2005	77.8	86.6	120.8	157.9	2.03	75.7	85.7	124.3	168.7	2.23	80.4	88.7	117.6	142.2	1.77

Coverage   All
Industry   All
Age   All
Sex   See headings
Occupation   All
Definition   Gross wages and salaries
Intensity   All
Period   Monthly average
Limits   None
Source   Statistics Sweden website, downloaded 3 March 2007 and information supplied by Statistics Sweden; see also *Lönestatistisk årsbok* 2000, Tabell 1, 2001 Tabell 1a, 2002, Tabell 1a, and 2003 Tabell 1a

Table Q.5. Sweden: Income Distribution Survey

	Column											
	A	B	C	D	E	F	G	H	I	J	K	L
	All				Male				Female			
	P10	P25	P75	P90	P10	P25	P75	P90	P10	P25	P75	P90
1975	72.5	85.3	121.5	156.0	75.6	86.1	123.4	159.4	73.6	86.9	115.6	136.2
1978	76.7	86.4	119.7	148.5	77.7	87.5	121.0	152.8	80.7	88.8	115.3	136.5
1980	77.9	87.5	119.1	152.3	77.8	87.2	121.3	158.1	80.3	88.6	111.8	128.8
1981	76.6	87.5	120.2	150.7	76.2	86.3	120.6	153.2	76.7	89.1	112.5	131.7
1982	77.1	87.1	119.4	148.9	76.9	86.8	120.4	154.3	77.7	88.8	111.8	130.8
1983	77.8	86.9	117.2	146.1	78.0	87.2	118.2	152.1	79.2	90.6	114.4	132.7
1984	76.1	86.4	118.8	148.0	77.4	86.3	120.7	152.1	77.5	89.8	114.1	131.8
1985	77.9	87.3	121.3	154.1	75.6	85.5	121.1	155.3	78.2	89.8	112.4	132.7
1986	76.2	87.2	121.0	152.2	75.9	86.2	121.7	157.7	75.4	88.4	113.2	131.8
1987	75.8	87.0	120.7	152.7	76.5	86.3	121.9	155.6	75.1	88.4	115.0	136.2
1988	75.1	85.6	120.3	151.9	76.0	86.1	122.0	154.3	77.1	88.8	116.1	135.8
1989	75.1	85.2	120.8	152.3	75.2	85.2	121.4	156.8	77.7	89.2	116.1	135.4
1990	76.1	85.2	121.7	151.6	75.8	84.8	121.1	155.4	81.8	89.2	117.7	139.2
1991	73.5	83.7	121.8	155.1	73.3	84.5	122.7	159.8	77.7	88.7	120.9	142.0
1992	74.5	84.8	122.8	156.9	73.8	83.9	123.6	162.1	76.6	88.6	118.2	139.9
1993	74.5	84.2	123.0	159.1	73.5	83.7	124.8	162.3	77.0	88.2	118.5	139.9
1994	73.6	84.6	122.9	161.0	72.8	84.6	124.7	168.7	77.4	88.1	117.8	139.6
1995	72.1	83.7	122.4	158.9	71.6	84.8	122.7	163.0	77.1	88.2	119.3	142.5
1996	71.6	83.9	122.8	162.3	71.7	84.0	125.8	168.2	74.4	85.8	118.6	143.4

1997	72.5	84.3	121.7	160.7	72.7	84.5	123.8	168.5	75.9	87.1	119.4	141.8
1998	72.9	84.1	121.8	163.0	72.3	84.8	124.7	171.0	76.8	87.1	119.7	143.9
1999	73.5	84.2	122.6	164.5	73.0	84.6	125.0	170.5	77.5	87.4	119.4	146.5
2000	72.1	84.3	125.1	169.2	71.3	83.8	127.3	174.2	74.3	86.0	119.9	147.1
2001	72.5	83.9	124.7	166.9	71.4	83.5	126.3	172.4	75.9	86.6	120.9	151.5
2002	72.4	83.6	124.2	165.5	72.0	84.0	126.5	170.2	76.2	85.6	120.9	149.9
2003	71.4	83.6	124.3	165.3	69.9	83.4	125.8	171.6	74.3	86.1	121.9	151.6
2004	72.5	83.8	124.0	162.8	71.8	83.6	126.6	170.1	75.4	85.9	120.3	147.2

Coverage	All
Industry	All
Age	Age 20–64
Sex	See headings
Occupation	All
Definition	Gross wages and salaries, including sickness allowance
Intensity	FT FY
Period	Annual
Limits	None
Source	*Statistiska Meddelanden* HE21SM0601, Tabeller 27, 28, and 29
Original source	Income Distribution Survey

Table Q.6. Sweden: Pensionable Income Register (Gustavsson)

| | Column | | | |
| | A | B | C | D |
	P10	P20	P80	P90
1960	61.4	75.9	136.5	171.0
1961	61.6	76.0	136.2	169.8
1962	61.0	76.2	136.6	170.4
1963	60.9	76.2	137.1	170.8
1964	61.1	76.6	136.8	169.0
1965	62.6	77.2	136.5	169.4
1966	61.6	76.2	136.6	
1967	60.6	75.9	136.6	
1968	59.5	75.0	136.9	
1969	60.2	75.5	136.3	
1970	60.6	76.9	134.6	
1971	59.6	76.2	132.4	
1972	59.6	76.9	131.8	
1973	59.8	77.7	133.0	
1974	62.7	78.1	131.5	
1975	63.2	78.9	130.8	
1976	60.8	78.7	128.1	
1977	61.0	78.1	128.3	
1978	60.2	78.6	128.5	
1979	59.6	78.3	129.3	
1980	58.2	77.7	129.4	
1981	58.2	77.6	129.7	
1982	57.4	78.0	129.7	
1983	58.1	77.9	130.1	
1984	57.7	77.9	129.7	
1985	59.0	78.1	130.8	
1986	58.8	77.9	131.1	
1987	57.8	77.3	131.3	
1988	58.3	77.2	131.2	
1989	58.3	76.9		
1990	58.4	76.3		

Coverage	All
Industry	All
Age	26 to 53
Sex	Male
Occupation	All
Definition	Earnings from all jobs including self-employment
Intensity	All with earnings above basic amount
Period	Annual
Limits	None
Source	Percentiles supplied by Magnus Gustavsson
Original source	Pensionable Income Register
Note	Earnings top-coded

Table Q.7. Sweden: Income Distribution Survey (Gottschalk and Joyce)

| | Column | |
	A	B
	P10	P90
1981	73	154
1987	72	159
1992	71	164

Coverage	Heads of household
Industry	All
Age	25 to 54
Sex	Male
Occupation	All
Definition	Gross wages and salaries
Intensity	FT Year round workers
Period	Annual
Limits	None
Source	Gottschalk and Joyce, 1998, Table 1.
Original source	Luxembourg Income Study (Income Distribution Survey)

Bibliography

Björklund, A, 1986, 'Assessing the decline in wage dispersion in Sweden', in *The Economics of Institutions and Markets*, IUI Yearbook 1986–87, IUI, Stockholm.

—— 2000, 'Going different ways: Labour market policy in Denmark and Sweden', in G Esping-Andersen and M Regini, editors, *Why Deregulate Labour Markets?*, Oxford University Press, Oxford.

Edin, P-A and Holmlund, B, 1995, 'The Swedish wage structure: The rise and fall of solidarity wage policy', in R B Freeman and L F Katz, editors, *Differences and Changes in Wage Structures*, University of Chicago Press, Chicago.

—— and Zetterberg, J, 1992, 'Interindustry wage differentials: evidence from Sweden and a comparison with the United States', *American Economic Review*, vol 82: 1341–9.

Gottschalk, P and Joyce, M, 1998, 'Cross-national differences in the rise in earnings inequality: Market and institutional factors', *Review of Economics and Statistics*, vol 80: 489–502.

Gustavsson, M, 2004, 'Trends in the transitory variance of earnings: Evidence from Sweden 1960–1990 and a comparison with the United States', Working Paper 2004:11, Department of Economics, Uppsala Universitet.

—— 2006, 'The evolution of the Swedish wage structure: New evidence for 1992–2001', *Applied Economics Letters*, vol 13: 279–86.

—— 2007, 'The 1990s rise in Swedish earnings inequality: Persistent or transitory?' *Applied Economics*, vol 39: 25–30.

Hibbs, D A, 1990, 'Wage dispersion and trade union action in Sweden', in I Persson, editor, *Generating Equality in the Welfare State*, Norwegian University Press, Oslo.

—— and Locking, H, 1996, 'Wage compression, wage drift and wage inflation in Sweden', *Labour Economics*, vol 3: 109–41.

—— and —— 2000, 'Wage dispersion and productive efficiency: Evidence for Sweden', *Journal of Labor Economics*, vol 18: 755–82.

Meidner, R, 1974, *Co-ordination and Solidarity: An Approach to Wages Policy*, Prisma, Stockholm.

Zanchi, L, 1992, 'The inter-industry wage structure: Empirical evidence for Germany and a comparison with the U.S. and Sweden', EUI Working Paper ECO 92/76.

R

Switzerland

Studying the Swiss labour market is interesting because it is rather non-European as far as labour-market institutions are concerned . . . unions are weak, membership and coverage are low, and employment protection measures are not far-reaching. Nevertheless, the Swiss labour market resembles a typical continental European country in terms of low and rather stable wage inequality.

Winter-Ebmer and Zweilmüller, 1999, page 89

R.1 Introduction

The neutrality of Switzerland was guaranteed at the Congress of Vienna in 1815, and the boundaries have remained unchanged since then. It is a federal state.

Previous Coverage

No data are given by Lydall (1968) for Switzerland.

Earnings data were not included in the OECD (1993) compilation, but are included in:

1996 (Table R.1): all workers, and men and women separately, for 1991 to 1995, based on the *Enquête Suisse de la Population Active*, ESPA.

LMS (Table R.2): all workers, and men and women separately, for 1991 to 1998, based on the *Enquête Suisse de la Population Active*, ESPA.

Official Publications

The Swiss Federal Statistical Office has begun including in the Official Yearbook (*Annuaire Statistique*) the distributions of earnings based on the employer Structure of Earnings Survey, which is an alternative source to the ESPA.

R.2 Data Sources

As in a number of other countries, there are both surveys sampling households and surveys of enterprises. In the case of Switzerland, a significant feature of these sources is that the household-based survey (ESPA/SAKE) covers the resident population, some of whom may work outside Switzerland, whereas the enterprise survey considers those employed in Switzerland, regardless of their domicile, which therefore includes those entering Switzerland daily to work. The number of cross-border workers in 2005 was some 180,000, or around 5 per cent of total employment.

Swiss Labour Force Survey

The Swiss Labour Force Survey, *Schweizerische Arbeitskräfteerhebung* (SAKE), *Enquête Suisse de la Population Active* (ESPA), is a nationwide survey, launched in 1991, and conducted annually by 20-minute telephone interviews in the second quarter of the year by the Swiss Federal Statistical Office. A summary of the survey and key findings is provided in English by the Swiss Federal Statistical Office (2005). The questions covered professional activity, including earnings, and a variety of related topics. It is a five-year rotating panel, in which each person is interviewed for five consecutive years.

The survey covers all persons who officially reside in Switzerland for the entire year ('the permanent resident population'). In the 2004 survey, for example, 39,000 households were randomly selected from the telephone directory, and one person aged 15 and over was then randomly selected from the household. (Up to 2001, the sample was approximately 16,000.) Following a decision in 2003, the sample was supplemented with a sample of 15,000 foreigners selected from the Central Aliens Register. The survey results are grossed up to be representative of the Swiss permanent resident population, taking account of the two sample sources. On average, each respondent to the 2004 survey represented some 100 members of the population aged 15 and over. Participation in the ESPA/SAKE is not compulsory. In 2003, the response rate to the initial interview was 70 per cent, and to the panel element 85 per cent, giving an overall response rate of 77 per cent (*Annuaire Statistique 2005*, page 182).

The Swiss Federal Statistical Office notes that the earnings information supplied in telephone interviews is less precise than that obtained in other sources, such as the Structure of Earnings Survey (*Annuaire Statistique 2005*, page 182). Moreover, a significant proportion of those interviewed do not respond to the questions on earnings: 14 per cent in 1998 (Bolzani and Abul Naga, 2002, page 117n). The issue of item non-response has been investigated by Henneberger and Sousa-Poza (1998) and Sousa-Poza and Henneberger (2000). Their findings suggest that non-response did not cause serious selectivity problems in the estimation of wage equations, but it does not follow that the degree of earnings dispersion is unaffected.

The ESPA/SAKE data are used by, among others, Bonjour and Gerfin (2001), Bolzani and Abul Naga (2002), and Bonjour and Pacelli (1998), the latter a comparative study also using the INPS data for Italy.

Structure of Earnings Survey

The *Enquête Suisse sur la structure des salaires (ESS)*, or *Schweizerische Lohnstruktur-rhebung (LSE)*, has been carried since 1994 at two-yearly intervals in the month of October, the most recent being 2004. It is a sample survey of some 42,000 undertakings (*Annuaire Statistique 2005*, page 182), with some 1.1 million employees. Where the sampled enterprise has 3–19 employees (the survey excludes enterprises with only 1 or 2 employees), information is requested for all employees. Where the enterprise has 20 or more employees, a sample is drawn (1 in 2 for those employing fewer than

50, 1 in 6 for larger enterprises). The response rate has risen from 58 per cent in 1996 to 71 per cent in 2000. In 2002, the response rate was 85 per cent (*Annuaire Statistique 2005*, page 181). In 1996, the results were based on returns for some 560,000 employees (Bolzani and Abul Naga, 2002, page 122n).

The survey excludes home workers, apprentices, 'stagiaires', temporary workers, workers paid solely on commission, and persons whose professional activities are largely abroad. The survey does not cover agriculture. It covers federal government employees and public enterprises (such as the postal service and the railways), and since 1998 has covered employees of the cantonal governments.

Income Tax Data

The income tax tabulations show employees separately, but these are classified by total taxable income, not by earned income. The first two federal income taxes were, however, levied only on earned income, and could be used to study the distribution of total earned income. These taxes were in force for incomes earned from 1911 to 1914 (the Impôt de Guerre) and 1917 to 1928 (Nouvel Impôt de Guerre Extraordinaire)—see Dell, Piketty, and Saez (2007).

Summary

The earnings distribution data available for Switzerland on Figures R.1 and R.2 date from 1991, which limits what can be said, but the Labour Force Survey and the Structure of Earnings Survey now provide valuable sources of evidence. The two results from the two sources seem reasonably coherent. The bottom decile is higher

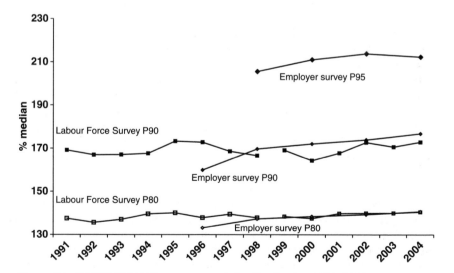

Figure R.1 SWITZERLAND upper part of the distribution 1991–2004

Sources: Table R.2, columns C and D; Table R.3, columns C and D; Table R.4, columns C, D, and E.

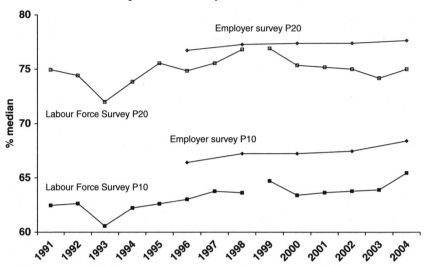

Figure R.2 SWITZERLAND lower part of the distribution 1991–2004

Sources: Table R.2, columns A and B; Table R.3, columns A and B; Table R.4, columns A and B.

for the structure of earnings survey, which may reflect differences in coverage of lower-earners in the two types of inquiry. It should also be noted that earnings are net of social security contributions in the structure of earnings survey.

R.3 What Happened?

The quotation from Winter-Ebmer and Zweilmüller with which this chapter opens identifies a number of specific features of the Swiss labour market, such as limited union membership and employment protection. It is also the case that Switzerland enjoyed until the 1990s a very low rate of unemployment, typically under 1 per cent. Since then, however, unemployment has risen to 4 per cent: 'since the beginning of the 1990s, Switzerland has undergone an economic recession of exceptional length. During this period of time [up to 1998] the unemployment rate has increased significantly, much more than in other European countries' (Flückiger, 1998, page 369).

The evolution of earnings dispersion in Switzerland during the recession of the 1990s has been examined using data from the *Enquête Suisse sur la Population Active* (ESPA) for 1992 and 1997 by Küng Gugler and Blank (2000), and by Bolzani and Abul Naga (2002). These authors reach rather different conclusions. The subtitle of the former summarizes their conclusion that there was no significant increase in wage inequality: 'despite a long recession and technological progress, wage inequality has increased very little in Switzerland during the period 1992–1997' (2000, page 316). In contrast, Bolzani and Abul Naga find (see Table R.5) that, while the decile ratio is unchanged, the Lorenz curve for salaried workers (and that for the self-employed) shifts significantly towards the line of equality. The Gini coefficient falls from 27 per cent to 22 per cent, which is a large fall, and the share of the top 10 per cent is reduced from 24.9 per cent to 19.8 per cent. There are a number of reasons for the different findings, including the fact that Küng Gugler and Blank consider hourly earnings and Bolzani and Abul Naga consider annual earnings.

What has happened since 1997? Here we may note the conclusion of the Swiss Federal Statistical Office that 'In general, the inequality of earnings has increased between 1996 and 2002. This growth in inequality is principally due to the fact that the increase of earnings has been most marked for the very high salaries' (*L'enquête Suisse sur la structure des salaires 2002*, my translation). The evidence in Figure R.1 bears out this conclusion to the extent that the top decile in the employer survey (ESS) rose by 11 per cent between 1998 and 2004. There was a fanning out, in that the next decile rose by only 6 per cent. At the same time, the Labour Force Survey results do not suggest a rise in the top decile of any magnitude. At the bottom, shown in Figure R.2, there are also conflicting tendencies, but none of the changes (the rise in the bottom decile and the fall of the second decile) exceed 5 per cent. The picture is therefore a mixed one.

Summary

The evidence for the distribution of earnings in Switzerland is of too short a duration to allow strong conclusions to be drawn about the long-run evolution, and the differences between the two sources complicate the interpretation of shorter run movements.

Table R.1. Switzerland: OECD (1996)

	Column					
	A	B	C	D	E	F
	All		Male		Female	
	P10	P90	P10	P90	P10	P90
1991	62	169	69	168	58	157
1992	63	167	68	166	63	157
1993	62	167	66	165	63	156
1994	63	168	67	164	64	156
1995	63	171	66	168	63	159

Coverage	All
Industry	All
Age	All
Sex	See headings
Occupation	All
Definition	Gross
Intensity	FT, FY equivalent workers
Period	Annual
Limits	None
Source	OECD (1996, Table 3.1)
Original source	*Enquete Suisse de la Population Active*, ESPA
Note	Decile calculations supplied by the Federal Statistics Office

Table R.2. Switzerland: OECD (LMS)

	Column											
	A	B	C	D	E	F	G	H	I	J	K	L
	All				Male				Female			
	P10	P20	P80	P90	P10	P20	P80	P90	P10	P20	P80	P90
1991	62.5	75.0	137.6	169.2	69.4	79.6	139.6	168.1	59.1	73.4	133.5	157.1
1992	62.6	74.4	135.7	167.0	67.6	78.1	137.8	165.7	63.2	75.3	134.9	155.3
1993	60.6	72.0	137.1	167.1	65.0	74.3	138.2	165.0	61.5	73.8	134.2	154.4
1994	62.2	73.8	139.6	167.7	66.1	76.4	136.4	164.0	62.5	75.0	134.6	156.0
1995	62.6	75.6	140.1	173.3	65.5	76.4	139.9	167.8	62.7	74.3	134.1	158.4
1996	63.0	74.8	137.9	172.8	67.0	77.0	141.6	172.7	64.7	74.4	134.8	156.3
1997	63.8	75.6	139.5	168.6	65.9	76.9	137.8	169.0	64.4	75.0	138.4	161.9
1998	63.6	76.8	137.9	166.7	68.2	76.9	139.9	164.2	63.8	75.5	131.0	154.0

Coverage	All
Industry	All
Age	All
Sex	See headings
Occupation	All
Definition	Gross
Intensity	FT, FY equivalent workers
Period	Annual
Limits	None
Source	Downloaded from OECD website December 2005
Original source	*Enquete Suisse de la Population Active*, ESPA
Note	Decile calculations supplied by the Federal Statistics Office

Table R.3. Switzerland: Labour Force Survey

	Column											
	A	B	C	D	E	F	G	H	I	J	K	L
	All				Male				Female			
	P10	P20	P80	P90	P10	P20	P80	P90	P10	P20	P80	P90
1999	64.7	76.9	138.5	169.1	69.5	78.1	138.9	167.9	62.9	72.7	133.3	157.3
2000	63.4	75.4	137.5	164.3	67.5	76.9	135.2	163.2	58.4	71.6	135.0	157.8
2001	63.6	75.2	139.9	167.8	67.8	76.3	137.4	164.1	60.9	72.8	137.5	160.5
2002	63.8	75.0	140.0	172.8	66.4	76.7	139.5	167.3	64.0	73.9	136.4	162.9
2003	63.9	74.2	140.0	170.7	66.7	76.7	141.2	171.9	63.9	74.8	135.6	159.7
2004	65.5	75.0	140.6	173.0	67.8	76.7	141.0	172.8	65.7	75.8	138.3	161.9

Coverage	All
Industry	All
Age	All
Sex	See headings
Occupation	All
Definition	Gross
Intensity	FT
Period	Monthly standardized
Limits	None
Source	Supplied by central statistical office
Original source	*Enquête Suisse de la Population Active*, ESPA/SAKE

Table R.4. Switzerland: Structure of Earnings Survey

	Column													
	All					Male				Female				Sources*
	A	B	C	D	E	F	G	H	I	J	K	L	M	
	P10	P20	P80	P90	P95	P10	P20	P80	P90	P10	P20	P80	P90	
1996	66.4	76.7	133.2	159.9		71.2	80.2	132.2	160.3	72.3	78.8	132.0	150.7	OY 2001, page 201
1998	67.2	77.3	137.4	169.7	205.6	71.1	79.8	138.3	171.5	70.4	78.3	134.2	158.8	OY 2003, page 210
2000	67.2	77.4	138.4	172.1	211.1	71.0	79.6	139.3	174.2	70.5	78.5	135.2	160.7	ESS 2002 page 66
2002	67.5	77.4	139.4	174.0	213.9	71.1	79.6	140.5	176.0	71.1	78.6	136.3	163.0	ESS 2004 page 23
2004	68.4	77.6	140.7	176.8	212.4	71.0	79.3	141.9	178.6	72.0	79.2	136.7	164.4	

Coverage   All

Industry   Excludes agriculture and cantonal employees prior to 1998

Age   All

Sex   See headings

Occupation   All

Definition   Salary net of compulsory social security contributions, including that part above the minimum, includes supplements, overtime, and 1/12 of annual bonuses

Intensity   FT

Period   Monthly (October)

Limits   None

Source   Quantiles, except P95, supplied by Swiss Central Statistical Office

Original source   Employer survey, *Enquête Suisse sur la structure des salaires*

Note   P95 interpolated logarithmically from tabulations (for sources see final column).

*OY = Statistical Yearbook; ESS = Report of Survey

Table R.5. Switzerland: Labour Force Survey (Bolzani and Abul Naga)

	A	B	C	D	E	F	G	H	I	J	K	L	M
								Column					
	Gini	P90/P10	P75/P25	Bottom	2	3	4	5	6	7	8	9	Top
								Shares of decile groups					
1992	27	2.63	1.59	4.3	5.9	6.9	7.4	8.2	8.9	−9.7	11.0	12.8	24.9
1997	22	2.63	1.63	4.6	6.3	7.2	8.0	8.7	9.5	10.4	11.8	13.7	19.8

Coverage	Excludes apprentices, family workers, and military
Industry	All
Age	All
Sex	All
Occupation	All
Definition	Gross
Intensity	FT
Period	Annual
Limits	None
Source	Bolzani and Abul Naga, 2002, Tables 1 and 2.
Original source	*Enquête Suisse de la Population Active*, ESPA

Bibliography

Abul Naga, R H and Bolzani, E, 2002, 'Dynamique des salaires et de l'emploi en période de récession: le cas Suisse', discussion paper, University of Lausanne.

Bolzani, E, 2001, 'Distribution des salaires et dynamique de l'emploi en Suisse: 1992–1997', Doctoral thesis, University of Lausanne.

—— and Abul Naga, R H, 2002, 'La distribution des salaires en Suisse: Quelques observations sur la récession des années 90', *Revue Suisse d'économie et de Statistique, Schweizerische Zeitschrift für Volkswirtschaft und Statistik*, vol 138: 115–36.

Bonjour, D and Gerfin, M, 2001, 'The unequal distribution of unequal pay: An empirical analysis of the gender wage gap in Switzerland', *Empirical Economics*, vol 26: 407–27.

—— and Pacelli, L, 1998, 'Wage formation and the gender wage gap: Do institutions matter? Italy and Switzerland Compared', UCL Discussion Paper 98-12, University College London.

Dell, F, Piketty, T, and Saez, E, 2007, 'Income and wealth concentration in Switzerland over the 20th Century', in A B Atkinson and T Piketty, editors, *Top Incomes over the Twentieth Century*, Oxford University Press, Oxford.

Flückiger, Y, 1998, 'The labour market in Switzerland: The end of a special case?', *International Journal of Manpower*, vol 19: 369–95.

Henneberger, F and Sousa-Poza, A, 1998, 'Estimating wage functions and wage discrimination using data from the 1995 Swiss labour force survey: A double selectivity approach', *International Journal of Manpower*, vol 19: 486–506.

Küng Gugler, A and Blank, S, 2000, 'Inégalité des salaires en Suisse: pas d'augmentation sensible durant les années 90', *Revue Suisse d'Economie et de Statistique*, vol 136: 307–17.

Sousa-Poza, A and Henneberger, F, 2000, 'Wage data collected by telephone interviews: An empirical analysis of the item nonresponse problem and its implications for the estimation of wage functions', *Revue Suisse d'économie et de Statistique, Schweizerische Zeitschrift für Volkswirtschaft und Statistik*, vol 136: 79–98.

Swiss Federal Statistical Office, 2005, *Swiss Labour Force Survey 2004 in Brief*, Neuchâtel.

Winter-Ebmer, R and Zweilmüller, J, 1999, 'Firm-size wage differentials in Switzerland: Evidence from job-changers', *American Economic Review*, vol 89: 89–93.

S

United Kingdom

> Possibly the most striking phenomenon in the British labour market over the last couple of decades has been the massive rise in wage inequality. Wage differentials have risen to a degree that pay inequality is now higher than at any time over the last century.
>
> Dickens, 2000, page 27

S.1 Introduction

The United Kingdom of Great Britain and Northern Ireland has retained the same geographical structure since 1921, when what is now the Republic of Ireland became independent. Some data relate to Great Britain (i.e. excluding Northern Ireland). Decimal currency was introduced in 1971. In 1973 the United Kingdom joined the European Communities.

Previous Coverage

Lydall (1968) included ten tables for the United Kingdom, based on income tax data (1954/5, 1958/9, 1960/1, and 1961/2), employer surveys (1906, 1938, and 1960), and household surveys (1953–4 and 1964).

The United Kingdom is included in all three OECD compilations:

1993 (Table S.1): 1973 to 1991, men and women separately, various years, from *New Earnings Survey (NES)*.

1996 (Table S.2): 1979–1995, from NES.

LMS (Table S.3): 1970–2000, from NES.

Official Publications

Summary results from the NES are published in the *Annual Abstract of Statistics*; fuller results were published in annual reports, consisting of several parts; this was replaced by publication on the website of the Office for National Statistics (ONS). The NES has now been replaced by the *Annual Survey of Hours and Earnings (ASHE)*, the results of which are published on the ONS website.

S.2 Data Sources

New Earnings Survey (NES)

The major source of earnings data in the UK in recent decades, and that underlying the OECD estimates, has been the NES. The survey, introduced experimentally in 1968, was established on an annual basis in 1970, and ran until 2003 when it was replaced by the *Annual Survey of Hours and Earnings* (see below). Many of the NES results relate to Great Britain; there was a separate but similar survey for Northern Ireland, and in recent years results were published for the United Kingdom as a whole. Information from the NES is given in Table S.4.

The unit of analysis is the individual employee, but information is collected from *employers*. The NES is a 1 per cent sample of employees, from 1975 this sample was formed by persons with National Insurance numbers ending in 14. The survey is obtained largely from the income tax (Pay As You Earn) records, supplemented by data supplied by large employers. Questionnaires are issued for all identified employees, requesting employers to provide detailed information for the employee, covering the hours worked and earnings in the pay period including a specified date in April. The records from different employers are not linked to give total individual earnings from all employments.

The coverage of the NES is incomplete as a result of non-identification of the employer or non-response by the employer. In 1990, 77.3 per cent of the questionnaires issued were returned and useable for tabulations. In a sizeable proportion of cases, non-response was associated with the employee having recently left the employer. See Atkinson and Micklewright (1992, pages 270–2) for further discussion. A sizeable fraction of those earning less than the lower earnings limit for National Insurance are not covered by returns, causing the low paid to be under-represented. According to Wilkinson, 'the main limitation of the *NES* is the undersampling of employees earning below the weekly PAYE threshold' (1998, page 231). This affects particularly part time workers: Orchard and Sefton (1996) estimate that the NES covers around 70 per cent of part time men and 80 per cent of part time women. Employees out of scope include those in private domestic service, non-salaried directors, clergymen holding pastoral appointments, persons working for their spouses, and the armed forces.

Annual Survey of Hours and Earnings (ASHE)

The Annual Survey of Hours and Earnings, which replaced the NES from 2004, is similar in design, in that the unit of analysis is the individual *employee*, with information being collected from *employers*. ASHE collects information for a 1 per cent sample. Again a similar survey is carried out for Northern Ireland, and results are published for the United Kingdom as a whole. Information from ASHE is given in Table S.5.

The principal differences from the NES are (see Bird, 2004 and Dobbs, 2005):

1 ASHE results are weighted to the number of jobs given by the Labour Force Survey.

2 ASHE imputes for item non-response.

3 From 2004 onwards, the coverage is improved by the use of supplemental information on businesses not registered for VAT and employees who changed or started new jobs between sample selection and the survey reference period. As a result the series from 2004 onwards is not fully comparable (the tables show the effect for 2004 of excluding this supplementary information).

Family Expenditure Survey

In addition to the employer surveys described above, household surveys provide corroborative evidence and, most importantly, allow one to go back before 1968. The *Family Expenditure Survey (FES)*, now replaced by the *Expenditure and Food Survey*,[22] was a household budget survey, which began as a continuous survey in 1957, collecting information on the income and expenditure of a representative sample of UK households. The income information is detailed (in 1985 the Income questionnaire contained 91 questions) and was collected on an individual basis. The FES contained relatively small samples (some 4,000 employees in 1963—see Thatcher, 1968, page 137). The response rate has varied but has been about 70 per cent. Results from the FES are presented in Table S.8. FES data on earnings 1978 to 1995 are analysed by Gosling, Machin, and Meghir (2000).

General Household Survey

The *General Household Survey (GHS)* is a continuous multi-purpose survey carried out by the Office for National Statistics. It was launched in 1971 and in the early years (until 1979) contained only broad questions on income. From 1979 to 1992, questions were asked more similar to those in the FES, but this resulted in a sizeable proportion of missing values (see Thomas, 1999). In 1992 the questions were again revised to adopt a mid-way position, where individuals are asked about their usual gross and take-home earnings. Income questions have been asked annually from 1979 to 1996, in 1998, and then 2000–3. Results from the GHS are shown in Table S.6. GHS data on earnings 1974 to 1988 are analysed by Schmitt (1995); data on earnings 1978 to 1991 are analysed by Gosling, Machin, and Meghir (2000).

Labour Force Survey

The *Labour Force Survey (LFS)* was carried out every two years from 1979 to 1983; from 1984 to 1991 it was an annual survey. In spring 1992, it became a continuous survey, conducted by ONS, in which households are interviewed for five quarters.

---

[22] It has also been replaced by the *Family Resources Survey (FRS)*, which is a continuous survey launched in 1992, commissioned by the Department for Work and Pensions. It has a larger sample size than the FES or the GHS, interviewing some 24,000 (Great Britain), 29,000 (UK) households annually.

Each wave consists of some 12,000 households, so that 60,000 households are covered in any quarter. Since 1992 it has contained income data. Wage data were collected in the final wave until 1996, since when data have been sought at both the first and fifth interviews. For use of the LFS data, see Gregg and Wadsworth (2000).

British Household Panel Survey

The *British Household Panel Survey* (*BHPS*) is a longitudinal study carried out by NOP for the Centre for Study of Micro-Social Change at the University of Essex. It covers some 4,000 households. For use of the BHPS data on earnings, see, for example, Booth and Frank (1996), Stewart and Swaffield (1999), Dickens (2000a), and Ramos (2003).

Schedule E Income Tax Data

Prior to the introduction of the New Earnings Survey, researchers made considerable use of the data on annual incomes collected by the Inland Revenue (IR).[23] Information about the distributions of annual *principal source Schedule E income* began to be published in the IR *Annual Reports* from 1954/5. The series does not appear to have been published for years after 1979/80, but this provides an overlap with the NES series. The IR principal source series covers individuals for whom pay-as-you-earn cards had been issued, and hence treats husbands and wives as separate units. It relates to annual earnings from the person's principal employment; where the person changes job, it is the sum of earnings from successive principal employments in the tax year. It excludes those below the tax deduction limit (£190 a year in 1958/9), but there is no restriction to full time or full year workers: part time or part year workers earning more than this amount are included. The data relate to the United Kingdom. There is no reason to expect the distribution generated by the Schedule E data to be the same as that from the NES. NES data relate to the current pay period; the Schedule E data to annual earnings. The coverage differs in terms of both people and earnings.

In Table S.7 are assembled the percentile distributions from the IR Schedule E data for the full run of years available. The sources are described in Table S.A1. The series covers the period 1954 to 1971, and 1975 to 1979. In view of the interval in publication, it is possible that the results for the second sub-period are not fully comparable with those for the earlier sub-period. The percentiles are calculated from independent control totals, based on total civilian employment, described in the final column of Table S.A1. It should be noted that this differs from the treatment of Lydall (1968), who took the total recorded in the IR Schedule E statistics. I have not followed him in this respect on the grounds that the IR total includes a number of part year incomes. The form in which the data are published means that interpolation has to be made over quite wide intervals. For example, in 1979 the typical interval around the top decile was £1,000 a year, when the median was around £4,000. As explained in

---

[23] Routh (1965) used the data for 1958/9. Lydall (1968, page 351) employed the same source for 1954/5, 1958/9, 1960/1, and 1961/2. The Royal Commission on the Distribution of Income and Wealth (1976) in its Report on *Higher Incomes from Employment* made use of similar data covering 1959/60 and the period 1964/5 to 1973/4. Data for 1954/5, 1959/60, and 1964/5 were used by Thatcher (1968).

Table S.A1. Sources of data on Schedule E Principal Employment

Year	Source of earnings data	Source for control total of total employees
1954/5	First given in AR 1956/7, page 81, derived from SPI; slightly revised in AR 1957/8, page 68 (source used)	Mitchell (1988, pages 115–16) adjusted to be on same basis as 1971 figures (multiplied by 0.952)
1955/6	AR 1958/9, page 71	As above
1956/7 and 1957/8	AR 1959/60, page 73	As above
1958/9 to 1968/9	IRS 1970, Table 21	1958/9 as above; from 1959/60 from Mitchell (1988, pages 117–18) adjusted to be on same basis as 1971 figures (multiplied by 0.952).
1969/70 to 1971/2	IRS 1974, Table 6	As above, except 1971/2 from Mitchell (1988, pages 119–20).
1972/3	Not available	
1973/4	Available information only covers top part of the distribution	
1974/5	Not available	As above
1975/6 and 1976/7	SPI 1975/6 and 1976/7, Tables 66 and 133	As above
1977/8	SPI 1977/8, Table 73	As above
1978/9	SPI 1978/9, Table 76	As above
1979/80	SPI 1979/80, Table 66	*Department of Employment Gazette*, December 1981, page S7

AR denotes Annual Report of the Inland Revenue; IRS denotes the publication *Inland Revenue Statistics*; SPI denotes Survey of Personal Incomes (in some cases published as a separate publication; in others included in AR).

Atkinson (2005), it is not possible to place the same bounds on percentiles as for shares of total earnings; and the matter is complicated by the fact that they are expressed as a percentage of the median. Given that we know the interval mean, I have used this information to fit a split histogram.

Earlier Sources

The history of earnings surveys in the United Kingdom has been concisely described by Thatcher as follows:

The earliest surveys of the distribution of weekly earnings were known as 'Wage Censuses'. These were confined to manual workers, and were made by obtaining details from large numbers of employers about the earnings of each of the manual workers on their payrolls. This method was first used by the Board of Trade in 1886. Owing to the expense involved, full-scale surveys of this type have been very infrequent and only three others have been held, in 1906, 1938 and 1960. Their coverage was extensive but not complete: in particular they did not include agriculture, coal mining, distributive trades or miscellaneous services, though in 1960 distributions for coal miners and agricultural workers were available separately. (1968, page 135)

In addition to these official wage surveys, information on earnings was obtained in household surveys, although these were not on a national scale. The survey by Rowntree of York was used by Bowley (1902) to obtain an estimated distribution of earnings; Bowley's own survey of Reading provides another example (Bowley, 1913). As far as I know, the only national household surveys conducted outside government are the Oxford surveys of income and savings (Hill, 1959) and the poverty survey of Townsend (1979).

Comparison of Sources

The *Family Expenditure Survey (FES)* data on earnings and hours have been compared with those from the *New Earnings Survey (NES)* by Atkinson, Micklewright, and Stern (1988) and by Wilson (1995). The former considered data for the period 1971 to 1977, and concluded that the recorded degree of earnings dispersion was sufficiently similar to be reassuring to the users of both surveys. Wilson examined the FES for 1991 to 1993, and found that for the first two years, but not for 1993, there is 'remarkable similarity in the relative dispersion of weekly earnings from the two surveys' (1995, page 26). For 1993, relative dispersion is greater in the FES.

Machin (1998) makes use of data on earnings for the period 1975 to 1996 drawn from three sources: the FES, the NES, and the *General Household Survey*. He does not highlight any major differences between the changes recorded in the three sources.

Laux and Marshall (1994) compare the *Labour Force Survey (LFS)* earnings data with those from the NES (they also provide a good summary of other sources of earnings data). They find that the LFS estimates of earnings are lower, and that the differences are greater at the bottom of the distribution than at the top. They attribute differences to under-reporting in the LFS and to under-representation of the low paid in the NES. The differences are not however large. The two sources are further compared by Orchard and Sefton (1996), Wilkinson (1998), and Williams (2003). The conclusion of Wilkinson is that 'for full time employees the NES should be considered the primary source of earnings data. The LFS is preferred for analysis of part time employees and for estimates of the number of employees earning below a low threshold' (1998, page 223).

Summary

The employer surveys (ASHE, and earlier NES) provide the main source of earnings data in the UK since 1968, as summarized in Figures S.1 and S.2. Before 1968, the evidence is patchier. The figures shown in Figures S.1 and S.2 are from the income tax data, which are not comparable with those from the NES (the income tax data are

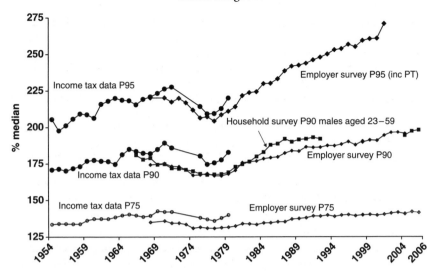

Figure S.1 UNITED KINGDOM upper part of the distribution 1954–2006

Sources: Table S.4, columns D, E, and G; Table S.7, columns C, D, and E; Table S.8, column V.

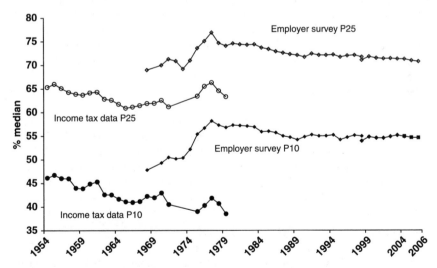

Figure S.2 UNITED KINGDOM lower part of the distribution 1954–2006

Sources: Table S.4, columns B and C; Table S.7, columns A and B.

similar to those of Lydall, 1968). One series based on household survey data (FES) is shown in Figure S.1.

S.3 What Happened?

The quotation at the beginning of this chapter highlights the most striking feature of the UK earnings distribution: the substantial rise in dispersion since the late 1970s. The increased dispersion has however to be seen in historical context. The widening followed a period when differentials had been compressed, as is brought out in the account of the period 1966 to 1992 given by Gosling, Machin, and Meghir, 1994:

(1) a period (1966–72) when there was no change in the wage structure; there was wage growth throughout the distribution;

(2) a short period (1972–5) when relative differentials were falling and all wages growing;

(3) the two-year period when the social contract was at its toughest when all wages were falling but wages were hit hardest at the top;

(4) a long sustained period from 1978 to 1992 when growth rates diverged across the distribution ... the 10th percentile wage did not change ... while the median grew by 35 per cent and the 90th percentile by over 50 per cent. (Gosling, Machin, and Meghir, 1994, pages 1 and 2)

We can however start further back. The income tax data in Figures S.1 and S.2 show that the decile ratio was widening from the mid-1950s to the mid-1960s. The bottom decile fell by over a tenth, and the lower quartile by 7 per cent. This may be due in part to the expansion of part time work and increased labour force participation by women,[24] but it seems likely that in the UK, as in a number of other countries, the Golden Age of the 1950s and early 1960s was a period of widening dispersion—except for the very top, where earnings shares were falling (Atkinson and Voitchovsky, 2003). The Prime Minister, Harold Macmillan, famously said in 1957 that 'most of our people have never had it so good', but he did not claim that the rise in real earnings had been equal for all.

In contrast, the 1970s saw, as described by Gosling, Machin, and Meghir (1994), a narrowing of wage differentials. Between 1968 and 1977 the bottom decile rose by over a fifth and the top decile fell by about 5 per cent (the NES and FES evidence agree on this). This has to be borne in mind when considering the subsequent rise in dispersion. Moreover, the effect is different at the top and bottom. It is clear from Figure S.2 that the subsequent fall in the bottom decile did not erase the gains of the 1970s. The 1998 value for the bottom decile relative to the median was 15 per cent higher than that in 1968. Whereas the rises in the top vintile, decile, and quartile

---

[24] It may be noted that the estimates of Hill (1959, Table 1) from the Oxford national survey of incomes and savings show upper and lower deciles for men working full time and full year that are close (68.3% and 159.4%, respectively) to those from the FES for 1963. These sources are not of course fully comparable.

shown in Figure S.1 have taken top earnings well above the relative level of 1968. In neither case therefore can it be said that the recent changes have simply reversed those of the 1970s.

Figures S.1 and S.2 show that the period since 1977 can in fact be divided into two sub-periods. During the 1980s there was a distinct fall in the bottom decile of some 7 percentage points between 1977 and the end of the 1980s, but since the end of the 1980s, the bottom decile for all workers, and for men, has remained broadly stable. There has not been a continuing decline in earnings at the bottom. In contrast, the top decile has continued to rise. In 1977 the top decile was below 170 per cent of the median according to the NES series; it rose to 185 per cent in the next decade, but has neared 200 per cent in the early years of the present millennium.

The widening of the earnings dispersion in the UK has indeed taken a particular form. As shown by Figure 8 in Part I, the deciles below the median all showed a reduction, relative to the median, in the 1980s, but there has then followed a 15-year period of stability for the lower half of the UK earnings distribution. The bottom decile is, taking account of the join in the series, 1.5 per cent higher in 2006 than in 1991. But the values of P20, P30, P40, and P60 are less than 1 per cent different in 2005 from their values in 1991. The widening has taken the form of a fanning out at the top. The top decile is 6.5 per cent higher in 2005 than in 1991. The fanning out at the top is illustrated in Figure S.1 by the sharper rise in the top vintile (P95), compared with the top decile, and the less sharp rise in the top quartile.

Summary

The story of the distribution of earnings in the UK over the 50 years ending in 2005 may be summarized as follows:

- There is evidence of widening dispersion from the mid 1950s to the mid-1960s.
- Narrowing of the deciles from the late-1960s to 1977, with a large rise in the bottom decile.
- A fall in the bottom decile from 1977 to the end of the 1980s, after which it has stabilized, along with the rest of the bottom half of the distribution.
- The top decile has continued to rise, with a fanning out of the upper half of the earnings distribution.

Table S.1. United Kingdom: OECD (1993)

	Column			
	A	B	C	D
	Male		Female	
	P10	P90	P10	P90
1973	68	170	68	175
1975	70	166	68	172
1979	69	167	71	165
1980	68	172	70	168
1981	67	178	68	178
1985	63	184	67	177
1986	63	186	66	182
1987	62	189	65	180
1988	61	193	64	187
1989	61	195	64	193
1990	61	196	63	190
1991	59	199	62	193

Coverage	Described as relating to UK
Industry	All
Age	Prior to 1983 men aged 21+ and women aged 18+; from 1983 those paid at adult rates
Sex	See headings
Occupation	All
Definition	Gross
Intensity	FT earnings not affected by absence
Period	Current week or month
Limits	None
Source	OECD (1993, Table 5.2)
Original source	*New Earnings Survey*

Table S.2. United Kingdom: OECD (1996)

	Column					
	A	B	C	D	E	F
	All		Male		Female	
	P10	P90	P10	P90	P10	P90
1979	59.2	165.0	64.5	158.0	69.9	158.0
1980	59.9	167.0	64.5	162.0	68.5	160.0
1981	59.5	173.0	64.1	168.0	68.0	172.0
1982	58.8	174.0	62.9	169.0	67.1	168.0
1983	58.8	175.0	62.5	170.0	66.7	167.0
1984	58.1	177.0	61.7	171.0	66.2	166.0
1985	57.8	177.0	61.0	171.0	65.8	164.0
1986	57.5	178.0	60.2	173.0	64.9	170.0
1987	56.5	181.0	59.5	176.0	64.1	172.0
1988	56.2	182.0	58.8	178.0	63.3	178.0
1989	55.9	183.0	58.5	180.0	62.9	180.0
1990	55.9	184.0	58.1	181.0	62.5	179.0
1991	56.5	185.0	57.8	183.0	61.7	181.0
1992	55.9	185.0	57.5	184.0	61.0	183.0
1993	55.9	186.0	57.5	186.0	60.6	182.0
1994	56.2	186.0	57.5	186.0	60.6	182.0
1995	55.2	187.0	56.2	186.0	59.5	182.0

Coverage	Described as relating to UK
Industry	All
Age	Paid at adult rates
Sex	See headings
Occupation	All
Definition	Gross
Intensity	FT earnings not affected by absence
Period	Weekly or monthly earnings
Limits	None
Source	OECD (1996, Table 3.1)
Original source	*New Earnings Survey*

Table S.3. United Kingdom: OECD (LMS)

										Column												
				All							Male						Female					
A	B	C	D	E	F	G	H	I	J	K	L	M	N	O	P	Q	R	S	T	U	V
P10	P20	P25	P30	P40	P60	P70	P75	P80	P90	P10	P20	P25	P75	P80	P90	P10	P20	P25	P75	P80	P90
1970	47.8	60.9	69.6	73.9	87.0	113.0	126.1	134.8	143.5	173.9	61.5	73.1	76.9	130.8	138.5	165.4	64.3	71.4	78.6	128.6	142.9	171.4
1971	52.0	64.0	72.0	76.0	88.0	112.0	128.0	136.0	144.0	176.0	62.1	72.4	79.3	127.6	134.5	162.1	62.5	75.0	81.3	131.3	137.5	168.8
1972	50.0	64.3	71.4	78.6	89.3	114.3	128.6	135.7	146.4	175.0	62.5	75.0	78.1	128.1	137.5	165.6	61.1	72.2	77.8	127.8	138.9	172.2
1973	50.0	65.6	71.9	78.1	87.5	112.5	128.1	134.4	143.8	171.9	59.5	73.0	78.4	127.0	135.1	162.2	65.0	75.0	80.0	130.0	140.0	170.0
1974	54.1	64.9	73.0	78.4	89.2	110.8	124.3	132.4	140.5	170.3	61.9	76.2	81.0	128.6	135.7	161.9	66.7	75.0	79.2	129.2	137.5	162.5
1975	56.3	68.8	75.0	79.2	89.6	112.5	125.0	133.3	141.7	168.8	63.0	75.9	79.6	127.8	135.2	161.1	66.7	75.8	81.8	127.3	136.4	166.7
1976	56.1	70.2	75.4	80.7	91.2	110.5	124.6	131.6	140.4	168.4	62.5	75.0	79.7	126.6	134.4	162.5	63.4	75.6	80.5	129.3	136.6	168.3
1977	58.7	69.8	76.2	81.0	90.5	109.5	122.2	130.2	139.7	166.7	64.3	75.7	80.0	127.1	134.3	160.0	67.4	76.1	80.4	126.1	134.8	163.0
1978	57.7	69.0	74.6	78.9	88.7	109.9	122.5	129.6	139.4	166.2	62.5	73.8	78.8	125.0	133.8	158.8	66.7	76.5	80.4	125.5	133.3	162.7
1979	57.5	68.8	73.8	78.8	88.8	111.3	123.8	131.3	140.0	167.5	61.5	73.6	78.0	126.4	134.1	159.3	66.7	77.2	80.7	126.3	135.1	159.6
1980	56.7	69.1	74.2	79.4	89.7	111.3	123.7	132.0	141.2	170.1	61.8	73.6	78.2	127.3	135.5	162.7	66.2	76.1	80.3	126.8	135.2	162.0
1981	57.8	69.7	74.3	79.8	89.9	111.9	125.7	133.9	144.0	177.1	61.5	73.8	78.7	131.1	140.2	171.3	65.4	75.3	80.2	130.9	140.7	174.1
1982	57.1	68.9	74.8	79.8	89.9	111.8	126.1	134.5	144.5	177.3	60.7	72.6	77.0	130.4	140.0	171.1	65.2	75.3	78.7	129.2	139.3	169.7
1983	57.4	69.0	74.4	79.8	89.9	112.4	125.6	134.1	145.0	177.5	60.3	72.6	77.4	130.8	141.1	171.2	64.3	74.5	78.6	129.6	140.8	168.4
1984	56.1	68.3	73.4	79.1	89.2	112.9	126.6	135.3	146.0	179.1	59.5	71.5	76.6	132.3	141.8	173.4	64.8	74.3	78.1	130.5	141.0	167.6
1985	56.4	68.5	73.8	78.5	89.3	112.8	126.2	134.9	145.6	179.2	58.8	71.2	75.9	131.8	142.4	173.5	63.7	74.3	77.9	131.0	141.6	166.4
1986	55.3	67.7	72.7	78.3	88.8	112.4	126.7	135.4	146.6	180.1	58.2	70.3	75.8	133.0	143.4	176.9	64.5	74.4	78.5	133.9	143.8	172.7

Year																						
1987	55.2	67.4	72.7	77.9	88.4	112.8	127.3	136.0	147.1	182.6	57.4	69.7	75.4	133.8	144.1	178.5	63.4	72.5	77.1	133.6	144.3	172.5
1988	54.3	66.5	72.3	77.7	88.3	113.3	128.7	137.2	148.4	184.0	57.1	69.8	75.0	134.9	146.7	180.7	62.9	72.0	76.9	137.1	149.0	179.0
1989	54.6	66.8	72.2	77.1	88.3	113.7	129.3	138.5	148.8	185.4	56.5	69.0	74.1	134.5	145.7	181.5	62.4	72.6	77.1	138.9	151.0	183.4
1990	54.2	66.7	72.0	77.3	88.4	113.8	129.3	138.2	149.3	185.8	56.3	68.9	74.0	135.8	147.2	182.3	61.7	72.0	76.6	137.7	150.9	180.0
1991	55.1	67.5	72.4	77.8	88.9	114.0	130.5	139.5	150.2	186.4	56.2	68.6	73.7	136.1	147.4	183.9	61.1	72.0	76.7	139.4	152.3	182.4
1992	55.2	67.0	72.4	77.4	88.5	113.8	130.3	139.5	150.6	186.6	56.2	68.2	73.6	136.6	149.0	184.9	60.3	71.3	76.1	140.2	153.6	185.2
1993	55.2	67.4	72.2	77.4	88.5	113.7	130.7	140.0	151.5	187.8	56.1	68.1	73.8	137.5	150.2	187.4	59.5	70.5	75.5	139.5	152.7	182.3
1994	55.2	67.0	72.0	77.4	87.8	113.6	129.7	138.7	150.5	187.1	56.3	68.3	73.5	137.2	149.8	186.7	59.6	70.6	75.9	139.5	152.2	182.5
1995	54.2	66.7	71.9	77.1	87.8	113.5	130.2	139.2	151.4	187.5	55.3	67.5	73.1	138.4	149.7	186.9	59.1	70.2	75.3	141.3	154.0	182.6
1996	54.7	66.8	72.1	77.5	88.3	113.8	130.9	140.3	152.3	190.3	55.6	67.7	72.8	138.7	150.8	190.0	58.3	69.6	74.9	140.1	153.0	181.0
1997	55.1	67.0	72.1	77.2	88.1	114.4	130.4	139.4	151.9	188.1	55.8	67.6	73.1	138.4	150.0	188.7	58.7	69.9	74.9	140.2	152.9	181.9
1998	55.2	66.7	71.9	77.2	88.3	114.2	130.6	139.8	151.9	189.8	55.7	67.7	72.7	138.2	150.1	189.7	59.1	70.3	75.1	140.1	153.2	182.5
1999	55.4	67.0	72.0	77.4	88.4	114.0	131.0	140.8	152.7	191.1	55.5	67.4	72.8	138.5	150.7	191.1	59.2	70.2	74.8	140.4	153.2	184.0
2000	55.9	67.4	72.3	77.5	88.5	114.1	130.5	140.1	152.2	189.6	55.5	67.4	72.7	138.3	150.0	188.5	59.9	70.5	75.7	140.8	152.7	182.9

Coverage	Described as relating to UK
Industry	All
Age	All
Sex	See headings
Occupation	All
Definition	Gross, including overtime and supplementary payments
Intensity	FT earnings not affected by absence
Period	Current week or month
Limits	None
Source	Downloaded from OECD website December 2005
Original source	New Earnings Survey

Table S.4. United Kingdom: New Earnings Survey (NES)

	A	B	C	D	E	F	G	H	I	J	K	L	M	N	O
				All				Column All (inc. PT)		Sample with hourly earnings			Male aged 21 and over		
	P05	P10	P25	P75	P90	P95	P95	P99	P995	P10	P90	P10	P25	P75	P90
1968	39.1	47.8	69.0	135.0	174.4	207.6	220.2	338.9	418.9			65.7	80.0	126.7	161.4
1970	40.8	49.3	70.0	135.9	175.3	208.1	220.2	340.4	416.3			65.4	79.7	126.7	160.6
1971	41.1	50.5	71.3	134.4	173.3	206.4	217.4	331.3	400.4			66.1	80.3	126.5	160.7
1972	41.4	50.2	70.9	134.4	173.1	206.9	220.0	333.2				65.5	79.7	126.4	160.9
1973	41.0	50.4	69.2	133.5	171.0	203.3	216.9	321.1				65.6	79.9	125.3	158.5
1974	44.1	52.2	71.0	130.9	167.2	197.2	211.9	316.5	375.9			66.8	80.7	124.6	157.0
1975	47.0	55.4	73.6	131.6	167.5	196.5	206.5	295.2	344.7			67.0	81.0	125.3	157.6
1976	47.9	56.7	75.1	131.0	168.4	197.2	207.3	297.7	345.0			67.6	81.3	125.6	159.5
1977	49.3	58.2	76.9	130.8	166.9	195.1	204.4	291.6	340.0			68.1	81.4	125.6	157.7
1978	49.1	57.3	74.7	131.3	166.8	196.2	208.7	299.1	351.7			66.8	80.6	125.1	157.9
1979	48.9	56.8	74.1	131.6	168.1	196.2	211.1	305.7	360.6			66.0	80.3	125.1	156.9
1980	49.2	57.3	74.6	132.4	170.6	203.1	214.1	316.1	364.0			65.9	80.1	126.5	161.6
1981	49.4	57.2	74.4	134.0	175.8	208.6	221.7	327.7	383.1			65.6	79.8	129.5	167.7
1982	49.5	57.1	74.3	133.9	176.4	211.2	223.8	333.2	389.3			64.5	79.0	129.8	168.1
1983	48.8	56.9	74.4	133.4	176.9	211.5	224.4	334.6	393.5			64.1	78.8	129.8	169.7
1984	48.4	55.9	73.7	134.5	178.5	214.3	229.9	345.5	406.6						

Year											
1985	48.3	56.0	73.4	134.6	179.2	215.3	230.1	346.9	414.9		
1986	48.4	55.7	72.9	135.3	179.7	217.3	233.2	357.3	427.0		
1987	47.5	55.0	72.6	135.3	182.3	221.4	238.6	376.9	453.3		
1988	47.3	54.7	72.3	137.1	183.9	225.9	241.8	384.7	468.7		
1989	46.2	54.2	72.1	137.5	183.6	226.5	242.4	395.2	484.8		
1990	47.3	54.8	71.7	138.0	186.5	228.0	243.8	395.5	481.8		
1991		55.2	72.4	139.2	186.1		246.1	400.5	488.7	58.0	199.5
1992		55.0	72.1	139.1	186.3		248.0	401.6	486.4	57.9	201.6
1993		55.0	72.1	139.8	187.5		250.1	410.1	504.4	57.3	201.7
1994		55.2	72.2	138.9	187.3		253.1	417.7	522.2	58.0	202.3
1995		54.2	71.7	139.8	188.3		253.8	413.2	518.7	56.4	205.0
1996		54.7	72.0	140.1	190.1		256.8	424.6	527.1	56.4	205.3
1997		55.1	72.1	139.4	187.9		255.2	427.7	531.7	56.5	203.8
1998		54.9	71.7	140.0	190.4		259.4	435.7	550.4	56.6	205.6
1999		55.5	72.2	140.6	191.7		260.6	447.4	560.0	56.9	207.3
2000		55.4	72.0	140.0	191.9		260.9	452.2	569.3	57.1	207.5
2001		55.3	72.0	141.2	195.6		271.0	476.5	595.0	56.8	211.4
2002		55.7	72.2	141.3	197.3					57.3	212.8
2003		56.1	72.1	141.8	196.1					57.5	211.7

Sources

1969 to 1990 from Atkinson and Micklewright, 1992, Tables BE1 and BE3, 1991 onwards from NES 2001, 2002, and 2003, Table A30

Atkinson and Voitchovsky (2003)

NES 2001, 2002 and, 2003, Table A31.2

(*Continued*)

Table S.4. (*Continued*)

	Column															
	P	Q	R	S	T	U	V	W	X	Y	Z	AA	AB	AC	AD	AE
	Males paid on adult rates				Female aged 18 and over				Females paid on adult rates				Male weekly earnings Gini	Male hourly earnings Gini	Female weekly earnings Gini	Female hourly earnings Gini
	P10	P25	P75	P90	P10	P25	P75	P90	P10	P25	P75	P90				
1968					67.0	80.0	129.7	171.2								
1970					66.4	79.8	129.3	170.4								
1971					66.6	80.2	127.3	165.8								
1972					65.6	79.6	128.6	167.1								
1973					67.4	80.7	127.6	164.7								
1974					67.7	81.0	126.4	159.1								
1975					67.4	81.5	125.2	164.5					23.6	22.3	28.1	21.5
1976					66.1	80.2	125.9	165.9					23.9	22.9	29.4	22.5
1977					68.6	82.1	124.7	162.1					23.3	22.1	28.8	20.6
1978					69.1	82.2	125.3	161.4					23.9	22.7	29.0	20.5
1979					69.4	82.1	124.7	158.6					24.5	22.8	29.5	20.3
1980					68.4	81.3	126.1	161.3					24.5	23.3	30.0	21.0
1981					68.0	80.6	129.8	172.6					25.1	24.6	31.3	23.1
1982					66.9	79.7	129.4	169.0					25.4	24.8	31.5	22.7
1983	62.7	78.2	130.2	170.4	66.4	79.7	129.9	168.3	66.5	79.9	129.9	167.4	26.0	25.3	32.3	23.0
1984	61.6	77.2	130.6	171.5					66.2	79.2	130.2	166.3	27.4	26.1	33.7	23.6
1985	60.8	76.9	131.0	171.5					65.8	78.7	130.9	164.5	27.5	26.1	33.5	23.6
1986	60.2	76.6	131.6	173.3					65.1	78.6	132.7	170.0	27.9	26.6	34.0	23.7
1987	59.4	75.7	132.5	176.2					64.2	78.1	133.5	171.7	28.9	27.7	34.8	24.0
1988	59.0	75.5	134.0	178.3					63.4	77.2	136.6	177.5	29.5	28.4	35.5	25.0

1989	58.5	75.1	134.0	179.9	63.1	77.1	138.0	180.5	29.8	28.8	36.2	26.0
1990	58.3	74.9	134.6	181.1	62.5	76.7	137.9	178.6	29.9	28.9	36.6	26.0
1991	57.9	74.6	135.7	183.0					30.3	29.4	37.0	26.8
1992	57.5	74.1	135.8	183.9					30.6	29.6	37.7	27.0
1993	57.3	74.1	137.0	186.3	60.6	75.8	139.8	181.9	31.1	30.1	37.7	27.7
1994	57.5	73.7	136.6	185.9	60.7	76.0	139.6	182.1	31.6	30.8	38.0	27.8
1995	56.1	73.2	137.2	186.7	59.2	75.4	140.4	181.9	32.2	31.7	38.6	28.9
1996	56.4	73.2	137.6	188.8	59.1	75.3	139.9	181.2	32.5	31.8	38.8	28.8
1997	56.8	73.3	137.2	187.8	59.3	75.3	140.0	181.3				
1998	56.1	73.0	137.7	189.5	59.5	75.4	140.4	183.1				
1999	56.3	73.3	138.3	190.8	59.6	75.1	140.3	183.1				
2000	56.5	73.1	138.0	191.2	59.8	75.4	140.7	184.1				
2001	56.2	72.7	139.2	196.0	59.3	74.7	142.6	186.6				
2002	56.5	72.7	139.5	199.3	59.6	74.5	142.2	187.8				
2003	56.4	72.7	140.0	197.9	59.7	74.6	141.8	187.3				
Sources	NES 2001, 2002, and 2003, Table A28				NES 2001, 2002 and 2003, Table A28				Machin (1998, Table 1a)		Machin (1998, Table 1b)	

Coverage	GB
Industry	All
Age	See headings
Sex	See headings
Occupation	All
Definition	Gross wages and salaries primary job
Intensity	FT (apart from col G–I) earnings not affected by absence
Period	Current week or month, unless otherwise indicated
Limits	None
Sources	Indicated below columns
Original source	New Earnings Survey

Table S.5. United Kingdom: Annual Survey of Hours and Earnings (ASHE)

	Column																	
	A	B	C	D	E	F	G	H	I	J	K	L	M	N	O	P	Q	R
						All							Male					Female	
	P10	P20	P25	P30	P40	P60	P70	P75	P80	P90	P10	P25	P75	P90	P10	P25	P75	P90
1998	53.9	65.7	71.1	76.6	87.6	114.0	129.9	139.8	151.3	189.8	54.6	72.2	138.1	189.4	57.8	73.8	141.2	182.1
1999	54.8	66.6	71.8	77.3	88.3	114.2	130.6	140.2	152.0	191.2	55.1	72.5	138.4	190.6	58.3	74.0	141.6	183.6
2000	54.5	66.3	71.5	76.9	87.8	114.1	130.3	139.8	151.6	190.9	55.3	72.4	138.2	191.1	58.5	74.4	141.8	184.3
2001	54.5	66.1	71.3	76.6	87.7	114.4	130.9	140.4	153.2	194.5	55.2	72.1	138.5	195.6	58.3	73.6	143.0	186.3
2002	54.8	66.2	71.4	76.6	87.9	114.3	131.2	141.2	153.1	196.4	55.6	72.1	139.5	199.4	58.1	73.1	143.3	188.6
2003	55.1	66.3	71.3	76.5	87.6	114.5	131.4	141.7	153.7	196.6	55.5	72.0	140.1	199.4	58.7	73.4	142.9	188.3
2004	54.8	66.0	71.3	76.7	87.5	114.0	131.1	140.7	153.4	195.7	55.0	72.0	139.9	198.0	58.4	73.5	142.9	188.1
2004new	54.9	65.9	71.1	76.3	87.2	114.3	131.2	140.9	153.1	194.4	54.3	71.6	139.3	196.0	58.7	73.6	143.1	188.9
2005	54.6	65.8	70.9	76.0	87.3	114.4	132.0	142.2	155.0	197.3	54.3	71.2	141.3	199.0	58.6	73.3	143.9	190.8
2006	54.6	65.6	70.7	76.3	87.3	114.4	131.7	141.6	154.3	198.2	54.3	71.2	141.5	202.2	58.6	73.2	143.6	188.4

Coverage	UK
Industry	All
Age	All
Sex	See headings
Occupation	All
Definition	Gross all wages and salaries
Intensity	FT earnings not affected by absence
Period	Current week or month
Limits	None
Source	ONS website, downloaded December 2005
Original source	ASHE
Note	Results from 2004new make use of supplementary information collected from 2004

Table S.6. United Kingdom: General Household Survey (GHS)

| | Column | | | |
| | A | B | C | D |
	Male aged 16–64 FT employed when interviewed P10	Male aged 16–64 FT employed when interviewed P90	Male All Gini	Female All Gini
1974	60.41	160.96		
1975	60.29	160.00	24.9	34.9
1976	60.65	160.00	24.2	35.0
1977	62.06	156.99	24.0	34.9
1978	62.13	159.20	23.7	34.7
1979	61.69	159.20	23.1	34.2
1980	61.57	163.89	24.4	35.0
1981	59.45	165.37	25.0	36.5
1982	61.57	172.12	27.7	37.1
1983	60.41	170.92	25.6	36.4
1984	57.64	174.54	28.1	37.5
1985	57.01	177.89	28.3	39.0
1986	56.84	176.47	29.4	39.0
1987	53.74	180.94	30.1	40.0
1988	55.77	180.58	29.8	39.2
1989			30.2	39.4
1990			30.1	39.5
1991			31.3	40.1
1992			31.6	40.2
1993			31.4	41.4
1994			32.4	40.3
1995			32.5	40.4
	Schmitt (1992, Table 1)	Schmitt (1992, Table 1)	Machin (1998, Table 1a)	Machin (1998, Table 1a)

Coverage	GB
Industry	All
Age	See headings
Sex	See headings
Occupation	All
Definition	Gross
Intensity	See headings
Period	Annual earnings divided by weeks worked for 1974–8; usual weekly earnings from 1979
Limits	None
Sources	Indicated below columns
Original source	GHS
Note	There was a major change in the income questions in 1979

Table S.7. United Kingdom: Income tax data (Schedule E)

| | | | | Column | | |
	A	B	C	D	E	F
	P10	P25	P75	P90	P95	P99
1954	46.1	65.3	133.5	170.9	205.5	374.6
1955	46.7	66.0	134.0	171.5	197.7	361.5
1956	46.0	65.1	133.9	170.2	201.2	349.9
1957	46.0	64.3	133.8	171.8	205.8	362.8
1958	44.0	63.9	133.8	173.2	209.3	376.9
1959	43.9	63.7	136.2	176.9	208.8	383.3
1960	44.9	64.2	137.3	177.5	206.3	382.9
1961	45.3	64.3	137.3	176.9	215.9	377.5
1962	42.6	62.8	137.3	176.6	218.0	366.5
1963	42.6	62.6	138.4	174.7	220.0	378.8
1964	41.7	61.7	139.7	181.3	218.7	393.0
1965	41.1	60.9	140.4	185.0	218.3	387.9
1966	41.0	61.1	139.6	183.5	215.5	378.6
1967	41.1	61.4	138.7	182.3	219.3	375.5
1968	42.2	61.9	139.4	182.0	220.9	373.8
1969	41.9	61.9	142.6	184.9	223.3	367.6
1970	42.9	62.6	142.1	189.2	226.3	382.5
1971	40.5	61.2	142.1	185.9	227.6	377.8
1975	39.0	63.4	138.1	180.4	214.3	335.1
1976	40.3	65.5	137.0	174.6	209.3	322.5
1977	41.8	66.3	135.9	175.7	209.5	325.2
1978	40.7	64.6	137.9	177.7	212.9	326.6
1979	38.5	63.3	139.9	182.8	220.0	342.8

Coverage	UK
Industry	All
Age	All
Sex	All
Occupation	All
Definition	Gross wages and salaries primary job
Intensity	All
Period	Annual
Limits	None
Source	Own calculations from Schedule E data—see text

Table S.8. United Kingdom: Family Expenditure Survey (FES)

	A	B	C	D	E	F	G	H	I	J	K	L	M	N	O	P	Q	R	S	T
	Male				Female				Column Male						Female					
	Normal earnings				Normal earnings				Actual weekly earnings				Actual hourly		Actual weekly earnings				Actual hourly	
	P10	P25	P75	P90	P10	P25	P75	P90	P10	P25	P75	P90	P10	P90	P10	P25	P75	P90	P10	P90
1963	68.9	81.4	124.0	161.1	66.5	82.0	129.9	179.0												
1964	68.9	81.1	129.4	159.7	62.2	79.1	130.1	172.0												
1965	68.1	81.3	124.9	157.1	64.9	80.3	127.0	172.5												
1966	67.0	80.9	125.4	159.5	67.6	81.5	128.2	170.8												
1971									65.5	79.2	127.0	165.2	66.7	173.5	65.4	79.2	130.8	170.4	63.9	178.7
1972									65.1	79.2	128.4	167.3	66.4	172.9	62.6	78.0	128.6	170.3	64.1	182.3
1973									64.5	80.0	126.1	161.3	67.9	172.2	62.9	79.2	129.2	168.8	62.6	174.2
1974									66.4	80.5	127.1	162.9	68.5	170.8	67.6	80.9	130.3	165.1	67.7	166.4
1975									66.1	80.6	126.0	162.0	68.5	166.7	64.5	78.9	127.7	171.7	64.2	178.3
1976									67.2	81.6	124.6	161.9	68.8	165.5	65.2	79.7	126.1	165.4	64.5	171.8
1977									67.0	81.2	125.0	160.5	68.9	168.1	67.3	82.3	125.0	161.3	66.8	170.4

Source: Thatcher (1968, Table 12)

Source: Atkinson, Micklewright, and Stern (1982, Tables 7, 9 and 11) (Sample 3)

(Continued)

Table S.8. (*Continued*)

	U	V	W	X	Y	Z	AA	AB	AC	AD	AE	AF	AG	AH	AI	AJ	AK	AL	AM	AN	AO	AP
	Male aged 23–59 Usual weekly earnings divided by usual hours		Male									Column	Female									
			Hourly earnings									Weekly	Hourly earnings									Weekly
	P10	P90	P10	P20	P30	P40	P60	P70	P80	P90	Gini	Gini	P10	P20	P30	P40	P60	P70	P80	P90	Gini	Gini
1966	68.0	181.0																				
1967	68.5	178.0																				
1968	68.7	179.0																				
1969	68.7	174.5																				
1970	67.7	174.8																				
1971	67.3	172.0																				
1972	67.5	171.7																				
1973	67.9	171.0																				
1974	69.0	170.0																				
1975	69.2	168.2	59.3	73.4	82.4	91.4	109.0	120.2	137.3	169.5	23.9	24.4	61.2	72.0	82.0	91.4	110.5	122.4	140.7	177.8	25.6	35.6
1976	69.4	167.5	60.4	74.1	83.2	91.7	109.2	120.9	136.6	167.7	23.5	24.0	60.5	72.3	82.4	91.5	108.3	119.7	135.5	172.5	26.1	36.0
1977	68.5	167.8	61.7	73.6	83.3	91.6	109.4	120.5	137.2	170.3	23.6	23.8	63.0	75.8	85.2	93.2	108.8	119.4	136.5	170.7	24.4	35.3
1978	67.3	168.0	60.7	72.8	82.8	91.3	110.0	122.1	139.9	170.7	24.4	24.4	62.6	74.5	85.5	91.6	109.2	120.6	138.2	178.3	25.8	35.3
1979	66.7	169.2	55.6	69.4	80.3	90.1	110.6	122.4	138.5	165.7	24.0	24.6	64.0	75.5	83.5	91.2	110.1	123.7	141.3	175.2	25.2	35.5
1980	65.8	173.0	56.1	70.5	80.9	90.4	111.4	124.6	141.1	173.7	25.6	26.2	61.9	76.4	83.6	91.7	110.2	123.3	143.4	185.8	25.3	35.9
1981	65.3	174.7	54.2	69.3	80.0	89.3	111.8	124.6	144.4	177.9	26.4	26.6	62.6	75.3	82.5	91.0	111.7	127.9	148.5	189.7	27.9	37.7
1982	64.3	176.5	53.9	69.0	79.5	89.5	110.8	124.2	143.9	173.4	25.8	26.0	63.1	75.2	81.9	90.8	110.8	125.9	150.9	197.0	27.0	38.1

Gosling, Machin, and Meghir (1994, Figure 1.2)

Year		
1983	64.5	180.0
1984	63.7	183.0
1985	61.9	187.9
1986	59.3	188.7
1987	58.0	192.0
1988	57.4	190.0
1989	57.1	191.5
1990	56.2	192.0
1991	55.4	193.0
1992	54.8	192.0

Machin (1998, Tables 1a and 2a)

Year										
1983	52.7	68.0	79.4	89.6	111.7	126.3	145.7	179.6	27.6	27.9
1984	53.5	68.7	79.7	89.1	111.5	126.1	146.6	183.6	27.3	27.6
1985	52.1	67.2	79.1	89.3	111.9	127.6	149.4	184.6	28.5	29.2
1986	52.7	66.5	77.8	88.8	112.6	127.6	150.8	190.2	28.7	29.8
1987	49.6	64.9	77.0	88.5	113.0	128.5	151.6	191.4	30.5	31.9
1988	50.1	65.1	76.8	87.8	112.9	129.5	151.5	191.3	29.9	31.1
1989	49.3	64.6	77.0	88.5	111.9	128.4	150.8	186.8	29.1	30.2
1990	49.1	65.7	77.6	88.4	113.9	131.3	156.0	194.7	31.2	32.4
1991	49.7	63.1	75.6	86.7	113.3	130.4	154.0	191.7	30.1	32.1
1992	48.9	61.1	74.5	87.2	114.9	131.6	152.1	190.3	30.9	33.0
1993	47.2	61.6	74.4	86.1	113.7	131.1	155.0	194.8	31.9	33.8
1994	47.5	62.7	75.1	86.9	113.5	131.1	154.8	192.8	32.0	33.8
1995	49.3	63.3	75.7	87.6	113.1	129.0	151.2	189.8	35.8	32.6
1996	48.7	62.6	74.9	87.3	114.3	133.0	155.4	193.1	33.5	32.9

Machin (1998, Tables 1b and 2b)

Year										
1983	61.8	74.1	81.8	90.3	113.6	130.0	151.0	200.8	28.1	38.8
1984	63.2	74.1	81.6	89.2	112.3	128.5	152.1	195.7	27.7	38.1
1985	62.1	72.6	80.0	89.3	113.2	129.4	153.1	198.5	28.3	38.7
1986	61.9	74.0	81.3	89.6	113.2	130.0	155.6	205.7	29.8	38.6
1987	60.9	71.4	79.5	87.9	111.8	129.5	156.5	202.2	31.1	39.7
1988	60.1	70.4	78.1	89.1	113.9	131.8	159.4	206.2	31.0	39.4
1989	56.6	69.1	77.2	87.7	112.1	130.0	157.9	206.2	29.5	39.3
1990	58.2	69.5	77.5	87.8	112.6	132.8	160.3	210.7	32.0	40.1
1991	58.0	69.6	77.5	87.2	113.2	130.2	158.4	200.4	30.0	39.6
1992	55.6	67.1	75.7	86.8	112.8	130.0	157.4	207.7	30.6	40.9
1993	56.1	67.7	76.9	87.3	112.7	132.3	159.7	204.5	30.6	40.3
1994	56.9	67.6	76.6	88.0	112.7	132.2	159.5	204.2	30.7	40.3
1995	57.0	66.1	75.8	87.0	112.6	131.6	157.6	203.1	30.0	40.7
1996	56.7	66.5	76.7	87.5	114.4	133.8	158.2	200.8	31.2	40.0

Coverage	UK
Industry	Exc. HM Forces
Age	21 and over
Sex	See headings
Occupation	All
Definition	Gross
Intensity	FT
Period	See headings
Limits	None
Sources	Indicated below columns
Original source	FES

Bibliography

Adams, M, 1988, *The distribution of earnings 1973 to 1986*, Research Paper No 64, London: Department of Employment.

—— and Owen, J, 1989, 'The New Earnings Survey Panel Dataset', New Earnings Survey Panel Project Working Paper 1, EMRU, Department of Employment, London.

—— Maybury, R, and Smith, W, 1988, 'Trends in the distribution of earnings, 1973 to 1986', *Department of Employment Gazette*, February: 75–82.

Allen, R G D, 1957, 'Changes in the Distribution of Higher Incomes', *Economica*, vol 24: 138–53.

Atkinson, A B, 2005, 'Top incomes in the UK over the 20th century', *Journal of the Royal Statistical Society*, vol 168, Part 2: 325–43.

—— and Micklewright, J, 1992, *Economic Transformation in Eastern Europe and the Distribution of Income*, Cambridge University Press, Cambridge.

—— —— and Stern, N H, 1988, 'A comparison of the Family Expenditure Survey and the New Earnings Survey 1971–1977' in A B Atkinson and H Sutherland, editors, *Tax-Benefit Models*, STICERD Occasional Paper 10, London School of Economics.

—— and Voitchovsky, S, 2003, 'The distribution of top earnings in the UK since the Second World War', discussion paper.

Bird, D, 2004, 'Methodology for the 2004 Annual Survey of Hours and Earnings', *Labour Market Trends*, November: 457—64.

Booth, A L, and Frank, J, 1996, 'Seniority, earnings and unions', *Economica*, vol 63: 673–86.

Bowley, A L, 1902, 'Wages in York in 1899', *Journal of the Royal Statistical Society*, vol 65: 359–61.

—— 1913, 'Working-class households in Reading', *Journal of the Royal Statistical Society*, vol 76: 672–701.

Daffin, C, 'An analysis of historical ASHE data 1998–2003', *Labour Market Trends*, December: 493–504.

Dickens, R, 2000, 'The evolution of individual male earnings in Great Britain: 1975–95', *Economic Journal*, vol 110: 27–49.

—— 2000a, 'Caught in a trap: Wage mobility in Great Britain: 1975–94', *Economica*, vol 67: 477–98.

Dobbs, C, 2005, 'Patterns of pay: Results of the Annual Survey of Hours and Earnings 1998 to 2004', *Labour Market Trends*, September: 387–96.

Forth, J and Millward, N, 2000, 'The determinants of pay levels and fringe benefit provision in Britain', NIESR Discussion Paper 171.

Gosling, A, Machin, S, and Meghir, C, 1994, 'What has happened to the wages of men since the mid-1960s?', *Fiscal Studies*, vol 15: 63–87.

—— —— and —— 1996, 'What has happened to the wages of men since 1966?', in J Hills, editor, *New Inequalities*, Cambridge University Press, Cambridge.

Gosling, A, Machin, S, and Meghir, C, 2000, 'The changing distribution of male wages in the U.K.', *Review of Economic Studies*, vol 67: 635–66.

Gottschalk, P and Joyce, M, 1998, 'Cross-national differences in the rise in earnings inequality: Market and institutional factors', *Review of Economics and Statistics*, vol 80: 489–502.

Gregg, P and Machin, S, 1994, 'Is the UK rise in inequality different?' in R Barrell, editor, *The UK Labour Market*, Cambridge University Press, Cambridge.

—— and Wadsworth, J, 2000, 'Mind the gap, please: The changing nature of entry jobs in Britain', *Economica*, vol 67: 499–524.

Gregory, M, 1990, 'A perspective on pay', in M Gregory and A Thomson, editors, 1990, *A Portrait of Pay*, Oxford University Press, Oxford.

—— and Elias, P, 1994, 'Earnings transitions of the low paid in Britain, 1976–91: A longitudinal study', *International Journal of Manpower*, vol 15: 170–88.

—— Zissimos, B, and Greenhalgh, C, 2001, 'Jobs for the skilled: How technology, trade and domestic demand changed the structure of UK employment, 1979–1990', *Oxford Economic Papers*, vol 53: 20–41.

Harmon, C and Walker, I, 1995, 'Estimates of the economic return to schooling for the United Kingdom', *American Economic Review*, vol 85: 1278–86.

—— and —— 1999, 'The marginal and the average returns to schooling', *European Economic Review*, vol 43: 879–87.

—— and —— 2000, 'The returns to quantity and quality of education: Evidence for men in England and Wales', *Economica*, vol 67: 19–35.

Hill, T P, 1959, 'An analysis of the distribution of wages and salaries in Great Britain', *Econometrica*, vol 27: 355–81.

Laux, R and Marshall, N, 1994, 'Income and earnings data from the LFS: Data quality and initial findings from winter 1992/3 to winter 1993/4', *Employment Gazette*, December: 461–71.

Leslie, D and Pu, Y, 1996, *What Caused Rising Earnings Inequality in Britain? Evidence from Time Series 1970–1993*, Peter Lang, Frankfort.

Machin, S, 1996, 'Wage inequality in the UK', *Oxford Review of Economic Policy*, vol 12, Number 1: 47–64.

—— 1998, 'Recent shifts in wage inequality and the wage returns to education in Britain', *National Institute Economic Review*, No 166: 87–96.

McKnight, A, 2000, 'Trends in earnings inequality and earnings mobility, 1977–1997: The impact of mobility on long-term inequality', DTI Employment Relations Research Series, No 8.

Meghir, C and Whitehouse, E, 1992, 'The Evolution of Wages in the UK: Evidence from Microdata', IFS Working Paper W92/16.

Mitchell, B R, 1988, *British Historical Statistics*, Cambridge University Press, Cambridge.

Orchard, T and Sefton, R, 1996. 'Earnings data from the Labour Force Survey and the New Earnings Survey', *Labour Market Trends*, April: 161–74.

Ramos, X, 2003, 'The covariance structure of earnings in Great Britain, 1991–1999', *Economica*, vol 70: 353–74.

Routh, G, 1965, *Occupation and Pay in Great Britain 1906–60*, Cambridge University Press, Cambridge.

—— 1980, *Occupation and Pay in Great Britain 1906–79*, second edition, Macmillan, London.

Royal Commission on the Distribution of Income and Wealth, 1976, *Higher Incomes from Employment*, Report No. 3, Cmnd 6383, HMSO, London.

Schmitt, J, 1995, 'The changing structure of male earnings in Britain, 1974–1988', in R Freeman and L Katz, editors, *Differences and Changes in Wage Structures*, University of Chicago Press, Chicago.

Stewart, M B and Swaffield, J, 1999, 'Low pay dynamics and transition probabilities', *Economica*, vol 66: 23–42.

Thatcher, A R, 1968, 'The distribution of earnings of employees in Great Britain', *Journal of the Royal Statistical Society*, series A, vol 131: 133–80.

—— 1971, 'Year-to-year variations in the earnings of individuals', *Journal of the Royal Statistical Society*, series A, vol 134: 374–82.

—— 1976, 'The New Earnings Survey and the distribution of earnings', in A B Atkinson, editor, *The Personal Distribution of Incomes*, Allen and Unwin, London.

Thomas, R, 1999, 'Income—Commentary', Qb, University of Surrey website.

Townsend, P B, 1979, *Poverty in the United Kingdom*, Allen Lane, London.

Wilkinson, D, 1998, 'Towards reconciliation of the *NES* and LFS earnings data', *Labour Market Trends*, vol 106: 223–31.

Williams, R D, 2003, 'Earnings growth 1997 to 2002: A guide to measurements', *Labour Market Trends*, vol 111: 77–88.

Wilson, M, 1995, 'Earnings distributions from the Family Expenditure Survey and the New Earnings Survey compared', DAE Working Paper MU 9505, Cambridge.

T

United States

Researchers using several data sources—including household survey data from the Current Population Survey, other household surveys, and establishment surveys—have documented that wage inequality and skill differentials in earnings and employment increased sharply in the United States from the mid-1970s through the 1980s and into the 1990s.

Freeman, 1995, pages 17 and 18

T.1 Introduction

The United States of America has had the same geographic boundaries over the period covered.

Previous Coverage

Lydall (1968) contains no fewer than 23 tables for the United States, based largely on the Censuses of Population 1940, 1950, and 1960. His estimates for the full-period labour force in all industries are shown in Table T.8.

The US is included in all OECD compilations:

1993 (Table T.1): all workers, and men and women separately, various years 1975–92, from the March Supplement to the *Current Population Survey* (estimates of Karoly, 1993).

1996 (Table T.2): men and women separately, 1979–95, and all workers, 1993–5, from the March Supplement to the *Current Population Survey*.

LMS (Table T.3): all workers, and men and women separately, 1973–2000, from the March Supplement to the *Current Population Survey*.

Official Publications

No earnings distribution data are published regularly in the *Statistical Abstract of the United States*,

T.2 Data Sources

'Public understanding of trends in the income distribution depends mainly on measures of income and inequality developed by the Bureau of the Census. The

Bureau [uses] data collected in the March Current Population Survey' (Karoly and Burtless, 1995, page 381). Historically, the collection of national data began with the Census of Population, and it is with this that I begin. I go on to consider the Current Population Survey (both the March Supplement and the Outgoing Rotation Groups), the Social Security Administration earnings records, the Survey of Income and Program Participation (SIPP), and the income tax returns.

Population Census

The first census of the US population, carried out in 1790, asked six questions, but these did not include earnings. Questions about income were first asked in the census of 1940, relating to incomes in the year 1939. The census today continues to ask questions about income for a sample of about one in six (who receive the so-called 'long form'). The census is sent by mail, and the national response rate in 2000 was 67 per cent.

The census of population provides a series of decennial observations on the distribution of earnings, and the US Census Bureau has made the data and the results widely available. Public-use samples are available free from the Integrated Public Use Microdata Series (IPUMS) database at the Minnesota Population Center, University of Minnesota. The data have been used by Goldin and Margo (1992) in their study of the 'great compression' of wage differentials from 1939: see Tables T.9 and T.14. The published reports have been scanned and are available up to and including 1970 on the US Census Bureau website. The tabulated data were used by Lydall (1968), and these are reproduced in Table T.8, where I have added further results obtained by interpolating from the published tables.

Current Population Survey

The Current Population Survey is a national survey of some 50,000 households carried out monthly, designed to represent the civilian non-institutional population. It is conducted by the Bureau of the Census for the Bureau of Labor Statistics. The CPS is the primary source of statistics on the labour force composition of the US population. The CPS uses a complex multistage stratified sample design. It is a rolling panel, in which households participate for four consecutive months, are dropped for eight months, and then re-enter for four months. The Outgoing Rotation Group (ORG) files consist of those in the fourth or eighth month of the CPS. In any given month, these people make up a quarter of the CPS sample.

The CPS has a long history. It had its origins in the need to measure unemployment that became particularly acute during the 1930s Depression. During the latter half of the 1930s the Work Projects Administration (WPA) developed sampling techniques to measure unemployment that led to the institution in March 1940 of the monthly sample survey of the unemployed by the WPA. Responsibility was transferred to the US Census Bureau in 1942, and it became the Current Population Survey (see Hansen and Hurwitz, 1944). There is therefore a long run of data. At the same time, there have been major changes in the survey. From the mid-1950s, the CPS sample has undergone substantial revision when the results have become available from the most recent decennial census of population. The US Census Bureau (2002) has published a list of nearly 50 'important modifications' to the CPS starting in the mid-1940s and going up to 2002. These include the extension of coverage in 1960 to Alaska and Hawaii, which added about half a million to the working age population. Of major importance was the switch in 1992/3 to computer-assisted interviewing and a revised questionnaire. According to the US Census Bureau (2002, pages 2–5), the redesign significantly increased the employment/population ratio for women, and significantly reduced that for men, with consequences for the proportion reported to be working part time. Lerman cites C T Nelson, from the US Census Bureau, as believing that 'the computer-assisted method stimulated more responses to earnings questions—especially from respondents with high-earning individuals in their households—and more reports of very high earnings' (1997, page 20).

Annual CPS Supplement

In addition to the regular monthly survey, the CPS is used as the basis for Supplemental inquiries, notably, in the case of earnings and income, the Annual Social and Economic Supplement (ASEC). This is also known as the Annual Demographic Supplement or March CPS Supplement. The basis for the ASEC sample is the March CPS sample, data being collected in this month because it is 'thought that since March is the month before the deadline for filing federal income tax returns, respondents were likely to have recently prepared tax returns or be in the midst of preparing such returns and could report their income more accurately than at any other time of the year' (US Census Bureau, 2002, pages 11–14).[25] To this sample are added a number of Hispanic households, non-Hispanic non-White households, and non-Hispanic White households with children. The ASEC Supplemental survey contains additional detailed questions on the amounts of money income received from a variety of sources during the preceding calendar year. These include money wages and salary. In the current form of the survey, these annual earnings can be converted to weekly earnings using the response to the question concerning weeks worked last year. Although prior to 1975, the variable 'weeks worked last year' was reported only in seven categories, which limits any adjustment to a weekly basis (see Buchinsky, 1994). The same applies to hourly earnings which are calculated from weeks worked and from a further question on 'usual weekly hours of work'. The Supplement dates in effect back to April 1946 (providing data for 1945). Until 1956 it took place in April. The Supplement has undergone two major redesigns: in March 1968 and March 1980.

Micro-data from the March CPS Supplement are available in a public-use file, starting with March 1964, providing data for 1963 (Katz and Autor, 1999, page 1470), and this forms the basis for most academic research. The Supplement to the CPS has been widely used in econometric studies of the structure of wages: see, among others,

---

[25] The increase in sample from 2002 has meant that some interviews now take place in February or April; most of the data collection however takes place in March (US Census Bureau, 2002, pages 11–14).

Katz and Murphy (1992), Murphy and Welch (1992), Juhn, Murphy, and Pierce (1993), and Buchinsky (1994), In order to protect the confidentiality of respondents, the public-use version is top-coded.[26] Moreover, the top code has not been indexed, but adjusted at irregular intervals. Until March 1989, for example, a single top code was applied to total earnings from all jobs; it had been raised from $50,000 to $75,000 in the survey year 1982, then to $99,999 in the year 1985. Beginning in 1989, separate top codes of the same amount were applied to 'main' and 'other' jobs, revised to $150,000 for the main job and $25,000 for the second job in March 1996. (Source: Lemieux, 2006, page 494.) Furthermore, in 1995 the US Census Bureau changed its top-coding procedures for public-use data, for the first time assigning cell means (rather than the threshold value). The results of Burkhauser et al (2004) indicate that the maximum percentage affected is 1.3 per cent of wage and salary earners. Burkhauser, Feng, and Jenkins (2007) examine the implications for wage and salary income of full time full year workers, and their results suggest that for the top decile of all workers top coding has only a minor effect (although it will have a larger impact on sub-groups such as male full year full time workers). Top coding still causes summary measures of dispersion such as the Gini coefficient to be understated, and affects trends in these measures. For this reason, Karoly and Burtless (1995), for example, took care to apply a consistent top-coding procedure to all years of the data used in their study.

The ASEC Supplement forms the basis for the estimates of the earnings distribution in Tables T.1 (from 1975), T.2 (from 1979), T.3 (from 1973), T.6 (from 1958 but only Gini coefficient), T.7 (from 1963), T.11 (from 1967), and T.12 (in part). The results in terms of percentiles in these tables relate back only to 1963, reflecting the availability of micro-data. Tabulations were, however, published in the Current Population Reports (P-60) for nearly all years since 1945. These were used by Burtless (see 1990) to document the changes in the distribution of annual wage and salary earnings over the period 1947 to 1986. The Gini coefficients for male and female workers published in Burtless (1990) are given in Table T.10, where I have used the same P-60 sources to interpolate the percentiles. Since the lower ranges are quite broad, the estimates in Table T.10 do not include the bottom decile, but they do include the lower quartile. Miller (1958 and 1968) used unpublished tabulations to calculate the earnings shares in Table T.15.

The response rate to the monthly CPS is high: around 92–3 per cent in recent years. However, only around 80–2 per cent of the eligible households have completed the March Supplement. The issue of non-reporting in the census of population and in the Current Population Survey has been examined by Lillard, Smith, and Welch, who summarized the situation as follows:

if experience with recent decennial censuses and their annual Current Population Survey (CPS) counterparts is a useful guide, 15–20 percent of those who have wage

---

[26] This top coding is in addition to that applied in recording the raw responses. For example in 1999 a respondent was only allowed to report $999,999 of wage and salary income—see Burkhauser et al (2004, page 296).

and salary earnings...will not have reported the relevant amounts. The Census Bureau has expanded its efforts, with limited success, to offset this increasing tendency for Americans not to respond to inquiries about income. Before the 1960 Census and the 1962 CPS, such nonreporters were simply excluded from census tabulations. Since then, and in all public-use tapes provided to the research community, nonreporters amounts have been assigned by a procedure known as the 'hot deck'. (1986, page 490)

As they show, non-response was low in the case of the 1940 census (only 2.5 per cent), but has increased steadily over time. This is an example where the quality of earlier data is higher than that of more recent data. To compound the difficulties, the public-use micro-datasets for the first years released (1968 to 1975) did not identify the observations for which wages had been assigned. Where the observations are flagged, then it is possible for users of micro-data to discard these observations, but this affects the measured degree of dispersion unless non-reporters are a random drawing from the population. In fact, Lillard, Smith, and Welch conclude that the propensity to report earnings falls with income. (The non-response rate reaches a third for dentists and doctors.) They conclude that 'CPS and census data appear to understate significantly actual income levels in many occupations' (1986, page 505). This qualification needs to be borne in mind, as does the more general warning that users of tabulated results (as in this book) are not in general told how non-responding households (or employers) are treated. It is only because of the intensive study of the CPS data in the US that we have some idea what lies beneath the surface.

Outgoing Rotation Groups (ORG)

A number of researchers have chosen to work, not with the March CPS Supplement, but with the Outgoing Rotation Groups (ORG) in the CPS, described above. In any month, they represent a quarter of the total CPS sample, giving for the year as a whole a sample of between 160,000 and 180,000 observations in the period 1979 to 1995. ORG respondents are asked a set of questions about hours worked, weekly earnings, and, where paid by the hour, hourly wages, in the week prior to the survey. In *The State of Working America*, Mishel et al (1993–2005) argue that the CPS ORG files provide a better basis for investigating changes in earnings dispersion. Mishel and Bernstein (1997) emphasize, in addition to the larger sample size, the fact that about two-thirds of respondents report an hourly wage, so that this variable does not need to be constructed, and that questions about the preceding week are less subject to recall bias. Lemieux, after a detailed comparison of the two sources (see below), concludes that 'the May/ORG CPS provides a more accurate measure of both the level and the growth in residual wage inequality than the March CPS' (2006, page 486). The CPS ORG data are used in Table T.4 for the years from 1979.

Social Security Administration (SSA) Earnings Records

The social security data come directly from the information reported by employers to the SSA on the W-2 form. The advantage offered over household surveys is stressed by Utendorf, 'it is believed that individuals towards the upper end of the earnings distribution have a higher tendency to incorrectly report their earnings in surveys. [Social security data] do not have this problem since individuals generally do not have a choice regarding what is reported on their W-2 forms' (1998, page 14). In addition, the sample sizes are much larger. In the analysis of the earnings distribution by Utendorf (1998), the smallest annual sample consists of 982,510 observations.

The data contain multiple measures of total earnings, as described by Utendorf (1999, pages 16 and 17). The Old Age, Survivors and Disability Insurance (OASDI) taxable earnings shows earnings up to the annual maximum; total wages and salaries include earnings above the maximum and are indicated regardless of whether or not the person is covered by social security. The total wages and salaries is in general the higher figure, and this is used by Utendorf. There can however be cases where the total is lower (for example where the person is contributing to a tax-deferred saving plan, or where a correction has been made to social security earnings but not carried over to the total variable). In these cases, Utendorf uses the maximum. From 1994, Medicare (H1) taxable earnings are also reported, and these include deferred compensation. Using the highest value of the previous two variables, of H1 taxable earnings, and of total wages and salaries plus deferred compensation has a noticeable effect on the results. In 1994, the top decile rises from 294.2 to 295.3, and the estimated top decile share rises from 36.1 to 36.9 per cent. There have been changes in the data over time. In 1978 there was a change from quarterly to annual reporting. As a result, Utendorf starts his study in 1981, noting that 'there were difficulties in the years immediately following the change ... with late posting, duplicate reports, and other processing problems' (1998, page 14).

The SSA publishes tabulations of net compensation by intervals in its *Wage Statistics*. These are highly detailed. The 2004 distribution has nearly 60 ranges, the top being $50 million and upwards (containing 96 workers). The SSA has made earnings micro-data available for outside researchers (for example, Brittain, 1972, used SSA tabulations), and the data have been studied by internal researchers. The latter have enjoyed privileged access, in that the data are not, for example, top-coded, but the raw data still need considerable work. As is noted wryly by Utendorf, 'researchers within SSA, in effect, have access to these data as an afterthought and thus necessarily spend a great deal of time making them useful for research purposes'(1999, page 16).

Survey of Income and Program Participation (SIPP)

The SIPP is a continuous series of national panels, the duration of each panel lasting from two-and-a-half to four years. All household members aged 15 and over are interviewed, and information is collected about income, labour force activity, and participation in social security programmes. The SIPP grew out of the Income Survey Development Program, conducted between 1977 and 1981. It was launched in 1983 and redesigned in 1996. The cost in 2002 was $31 million. The target sample is 37,000 households. This means that it is a little smaller than the Current Population Survey (CPS), but a lot larger than the Panel Study of Income Dynamics. The data were used by Lerman (1997) to study the evolution of dispersion over the period 1984 to 1995, and his results are summarized in Table T.12

Income Tax Returns

The income tax returns have been used by Piketty and Saez (2003 and 2007) in their study of top incomes. For this purpose they use published tabulations classifying tax returns by the size of total wages and salaries, and micro-data from 1966 onwards. The data have the great advantage of providing evidence about the pre-war period: they start in 1927. On the other hand, they are limited to the upper part of the distribution. The results are summarized in Table T.13, which shows the top decile, top vintile, and top percentile, expressed as percentages of the mean (not the median, which is not available). Moreover, the estimates differ from those discussed elsewhere in that they relate to tax units, rather than individuals. Although prior to 1948 there was an incentive for two-wage earning couples to file separately, after that date very few married women filed separately. For this reason, the tax data do not yield distributions of individual earnings.

Comparison of Different Sources

The tables in this chapter draw on five sources: the Census of Population, the Current Population Survey, the social security data, the Survey of Income and Program Participation, and the income tax records. As just explained, the tax data relate to tax units and are not directly comparable. The social security data on earnings (Table T.5) cover the entire population with wage and salary earnings in a particular year. It is not therefore surprising that the lower quantiles are much lower than in those CPS estimates where attention is restricted to full time workers (Table T.3) or where earnings are divided by hours worked (Table T.4).

A comparison may also be made with the Survey of Income and Program Participation (SIPP). According to the US Census Bureau, compared with SIPP, 'the CPS has gaps in the area of income measurement. A yearlong reference period means that CPS respondents are more likely than SIPP respondents to forget or misreport certain asset income or irregular income sources' ('Introduction to SIPP' on US Census Bureau website, 13 January 2006). This objection to the CPS data is, however, less applicable to earnings, although, as noted by Lerman (1997), a smaller proportion of cases in SIPP require imputation of earnings. His comparison of his results (Table T.15) with the CPS shows the decile ratio as being lower. He concludes that his results 'cast doubt on the prevailing view that [earnings dispersion] continued rising through the 1980s and into the mid-1990s' (1997, page 24), drawing attention in particular to the break in comparability in CPS data in 1993.

Katz and Autor (1999) compare the changes in earnings dispersion in the March CPS (on which they focus) with those in the Census of Population and in the CPS Outgoing Rotation Groups (ORG), covering the period 1959 to 1996. The conclusions for different periods are discussed in Section T.3, but for the 1980s they find that 'overall inequality expands dramatically across all data sources' (1999, page 1484). They also compare findings for the weekly earnings of full time workers and for hourly earnings, concluding that these are 'largely comparable' (1999, page 1485). A more critical evaluation of the accuracy of hourly wages in the March CPS and CPS ORG data from 1973 to 2003 is provided by Lemieux (2006). He exploits the fact that hourly paid workers are asked directly in the CPS ORG about their hourly wage, whereas for other workers the hourly wage has to be calculated in both sources. He shows that, for those who are hourly paid, the variance of the logarithm of the hourly wage rate is less in the CPS ORG, whereas there is no difference for other workers, and argues that the CPS ORG data are less 'noisy'. The distance is increasing over time, leading him to conclude that 'both the level of and growth in residual wage inequality are overstated in the March CPS' (Lemieux, 2006, page 462).

Summary

The Millennial publication of *Historical Statistics of the United States* (Carter et al, 2006) contains a table of 'summary measures of wage inequality, 1939–1989' (which is reproduced in Table T.14), based on the Censuses of Population (for earlier years) and on the Current Population Survey. The same two sources underlie our summary in Figures T.1 and T.2, although I have taken the figures up to 2005. It seems puzzling that a reference work published in 2006 should be content with a series ending in 1989, and considerable interest attaches to the period since then, as discussed below. Moreover, where there is a choice, I have, for reasons explained above, used CPS results based on the Outgoing Rotation Group.

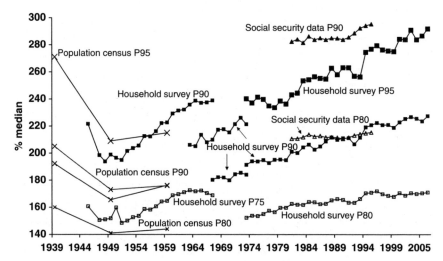

Figure T.1 UNITED STATES upper part of the distribution 1939–2005

Sources: Table T.4, columns C, D, and E; Table T.5, columns C and D; Table T.7, column D; Table T.8, columns D and E; Table T.9, column B; Table T.10, columns B and C; Table T.11, column C.

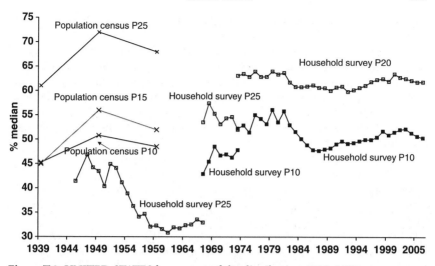

Figure T.2 UNITED STATES lower part of the distribution 1939–2005

Sources: Table T.4, columns A and B; Table T.7, column B; Table T.8, columns A and B; Table T.9, column A; Table T.10, column A; Table T.11, column B.

T.3 What Happened?

In considering the evolution of the earnings distribution in the US, I consider four main periods: the 'Great Compression' of the 1940s identified by Goldin and Margo (1992), the Golden Age of the 1950s, the 1960s and 1970s, and the period since 1980 on which recent attention had focused.

'Great Compression' is the term used by Goldin and Margo to describe the narrowing in the US wage structure in the 1940s: 'when the United States emerged from war and depression, it had not only a considerably lower rate of unemployment, it also had a wage structure more egalitarian than at any time since' (1992, page 2). Goldin and Margo make use of an impressive variety of sources, with a key role being played by the earnings deciles for male full year workers obtained from the census of population, shown by the crosses in Figures T.1 and T.2. The population census data are also used by Juhn, who refers to the 1940s as 'a decade in which there was a large reduction in wage inequality' (1994, page 6). And, long before these authors, Lydall (1968) had used the census data to conclude that 'it is clear that there was a substantial fall in dispersion of employee earnings in the United States from 1939 to 1949' (page 177). His estimates for full year workers (for P15, P25, P90, and P95) are shown in Figures T.1 and T.2, although it should be noted that the 1939 figures include part time workers.

How large was the compression? Between 1939 and 1949, the top decile, using the figures of Goldin and Margo shown in Figure T.1, fell by 16 per cent. In other words, according to the criteria used here, the fall was 'significant' but not 'large'.

The fall exhibited by the estimates of Lydall is similar, although we should note that the fall in P95 was in excess of 20 per cent. The bottom decile, again using the figures of Goldin and Margo shown in Figure T.2, rose from 45 to 51 per cent of the median, an increase of about one eighth, again 'significant' but not 'large'. The expression 'Great Compression' provides a neat counterpoint to the 'Great Depression'. It may be an overstatement, but the phenomenon described was clearly a significant one.

It is generally agreed that the 1940s compression has been unwound. As put by Katz and Autor, we have returned to the degree of differentiation observed in 1939: 'the entire compression of the wage structure in the 1940s is undone by 1990' (1999, page 1500). When, however, did the unwinding take place? According to Goldin and Margo, 'the movement toward equality in the 1940s was reversed in the post-1970 period' (1992, page 3). Here it is instructive to make use of the tabulations of the March CPS that date back to the 1940s (see Table T.10). These have the disadvantage of relating to all workers, full time and part time, and part year as well as full year. The lower quartile, shown in Figure T.2, is therefore a lot below the figures for full year workers. Nonetheless, the lower quartile and the upper quartile and top decile (in Figure T.1) exhibit a very clear pattern. Using the annual data provided by the Current Population Survey tabulations, we can see that there was a sharp turnaround in 1951. The U initiated by the Great Compression was not a flat-bottomed U but a V. The top decile began to rise immediately in 1952 and the rise continued unchecked until 1964. The rise from 195 per cent of the median in 1951 to 239 per cent in 1964 qualifies as 'large'. The lower quartile fell steadily throughout the 1950s. Again the change can be described as large. The 'Golden Age' was therefore in the US a period of widening earnings dispersion on a large scale. Since this conclusion is at odds with what is commonly believed, and with some contemporary accounts, I devoted some time in the Lecture to the corroborative evidence.

Was the experience of the 1960s the same? Katz and Autor (1999), using the population censuses for 1959 and 1969, and the March CPS from 1963, note the divergent movements according to different sources and definitions. The Census 'indicates modest expansion in overall weekly earnings inequality in the 1960s for men and women separately and combined, the bulk of which is accounted for by [the increase in the top decile]' (1999, page 1484). From Figure T.1, we can see that the early years of the 1960s involved a continuation of the widening at the top that had characterized the 1950s. A more natural break point would be 1963, when the March CPS micro-data become available, although Katz and Autor caution against using the early years of these micro-data, since the results may be affected by the inclusion of workers with extremely low reported earnings. This may be responsible for the differences indicated by the series shown for the 1960s in Figures T.1 and T.2. It does not seem unreasonable, however, to conclude that the significant rise in the US top decile had come to an end by the early 1960s, and that the significant fall in the bottom decile had ended by 1960. In this sense, the experience of the period from the mid-1960s to the late 1970s is rather different, representing a hiatus between the widening of the 1950s and that of the 1980s.

What happened next is well known. There was a large fall in the bottom decile: between 1980 and 1987 the bottom decile in the CPS ORG data shown in Figure T.2 fell from 53.6 per cent of the median to 47.7 per cent. There was a rise over the same period in the top decile, which went from 194.9 per cent of the median in 1980 to 208.7 per cent in 1987. It is these changes that have attracted so much attention. A not-unrepresentative statement being that of Buchinsky: 'the 1980's witnessed rapid and massive changes in the structure of wages in the United States. In particular one observes sharp changes in wage inequality' (1994, page 405). At the same time, there is some disagreement as to whether the process continued steadily. On the basis of the CPS ORG data, Mishel and Bernstein (1997) argued that the increase in earnings dispersion had tapered off in the late 1980s. Lerman (1997), on the basis of Survey of Income and Program Participation data, was led to doubt whether the rise in earnings dispersion continued into the mid-1990s. Using the Social Security administrative (SSA) data, Utendorf (1999) found that earnings dispersion widened in the early 1980s, decreased somewhat from 1988 to 1991, and increased from 1991 to 1995 (the SSA data are shown in Figure T.1).

In order to make sense of these different views, we need to consider separately the top and bottom of the distribution. From Figure T.2, we can see that the bottom decile of hourly earnings for all workers trended upwards from 1987 to 2002. Even allowing for the fall from 2002 to 2005, the overall change from 1987 to 2005 is a rise of 5.5 per cent. The lowest quintile also rose, but not enough to register according to the criteria adopted here. If therefore the decile ratio has continued to widen, it is on account of what has taken place in the upper part of the distribution. From Figure T.1, we can see that there was indeed a pause in the late 1980s but that the upward trend then continued. Between 1987 and 2005 the top decile rose by 9 per cent. Linking the series for men (Census of Population, Current Population Survey tabulations, and Current Population Survey results given by the Census Bureau and EPI), we find that the top decile fell from 210 per cent of the median in 1939 to 160 per cent in 1951 and then rose, with a pause from 1965 to 1979 (and in the late 1980s), to 233 per cent in 2005. At the same time, we have to bear in mind the fact that we are looking at money wages and salaries, and that in recent years total compensation may have changed rather differently on account of the growth of employer financed health insurance and pension contributions.

Figure T.1 shows how the upper part of the earnings distribution in the US has 'fanned out' since 1980: the upper quintile rose by 7.1 per cent between 1980 and 2005, the top decile rose by 16.7 per cent, and P95 rose by 23.4 per cent. The income tax data of Piketty and Saez (Table T.13) reinforce this picture. They show the top decile (relative to the mean) as rising by 15 per cent between 1980 and 2002, P99 as rising by 25.5 per cent, and the top percentile as rising by 50.5 per cent.

Summary

The data for the distribution of earnings in the US over the past two-thirds of a century are best described as a 'patchwork'. The results, as we have seen, vary to some degree according to sources and definitions. Nonetheless, the following broad conclusions emerge:

- The 1940s were a period of wage compression (even if 'great' is too strong an adjective).
- The 1950s saw a large reversal of this compression, continuing at the top into the early 1960s.
- The mid-1960s and 1970s were a period of hiatus.
- The bottom decile fell in the 1980s, but then recovered some of the lost ground in the 1990s.
- The top decile rose in the 1980s, paused, and then continued its upward path, so that by 2005 it was above the equivalent of its 1939 value.
- There has been a distinct 'fanning out' of the upper part of the US earnings distribution.

Table T.1. United States: OECD (1993)

			Column			
	A	B	C	D	E	F
	All		Male		Female	
	P10	P90	P10	P90	P10	P90
1975	43	214	41	193	47	197
1979	46	219	41	193	49	196
1980	45	216	41	195	50	196
1981	45	221	41	198	50	201
1985	43	227	38	210	47	209
1986	41	224	37	208	45	212
1987	41	226	37	209	44	210
1988	40	223	38	210	44	211
1989	40	222	38	214	44	215
1990	42	223	39	218	44	214
1991	41	222	39	217	45	216
1992	42	225	39	217	45	218

Coverage	All
Industry	All
Age	All
Sex	See headings
Occupation	All
Definition	Gross hourly earnings, calculated as annual earnings divided by (annual weeks worked × usual weekly hours)
Intensity	FT
Period	See above
Limits	None
Source	OECD (1993, Table 5.2).
Original source	Annual Demographic Supplement to the March Current Population Survey, as published by Karoly (1993, Table 2B.2)—see Table T.7
Note	Extended to 1992 using OECD 1996, page 103.

Table T.2. United States: OECD (1996)

	Column					
	A	B	C	D	E	F
	All		Male		Female	
	P10	P90	P10	P90	P10	P90
1979			54	173	56	173
1980			54	176	60	176
1981			52	174	62	185
1982			51	180	56	177
1983			50	178	56	179
1984			51	186	55	180
1985			49	184	54	180
1986			48	187	53	185
1987			49	191	53	187
1988			49	199	50	177
1989			49	197	53	192
1990			50	196	99	192
1991			50	195	53	194
1992			49	200	53	196
1993	49	203	49	200	53	196
1994	48	207	47	201	51	203
1995	48	210	47	204	51	203

Coverage	All
Industry	All
Age	Aged 25 and over
Sex	See headings
Occupation	All
Definition	Gross weekly earnings
Intensity	FT
Period	Month
Limits	None
Source	OECD (1996, Table 3.1)
Original source	Annual Demographic Supplement to the March Current Population Survey

Table T.3. United States: OECD (LMS)

	A	B	C	D	E	F	G	H	I	J	K	L	M	N	O	P	Q	R
				All					Male	Column						Female		
	P10	P20	P25	P75	P80	P90	P10	P20	P25	P75	P80	P90	P10	P20	P25	P75	P80	P90
1973	52.2	64.8	70.4	142.1	152.2	190.6	54.8	67.6	73.9	133.5	146.3	186.2	58.1	70.9	75.2	133.3	141.9	170.9
1974	53.5	65.3	70.6	141.2	152.9	195.9	53.7	67.3	73.2	133.2	143.4	181.0	63.2	72.8	76.8	132.8	141.6	178.4
1975	52.4	63.8	69.7	140.5	153.0	196.2	52.0	66.5	71.9	132.6	145.7	179.2	60.9	70.3	75.4	133.3	144.2	176.8
1976	52.8	63.5	69.5	141.1	151.8	194.4	52.1	66.2	71.4	136.8	149.6	183.3	61.6	71.9	76.0	134.9	147.3	177.4
1977	51.2	62.9	69.0	140.4	156.3	190.6	51.2	64.6	70.1	138.2	148.0	183.1	61.1	71.3	75.2	136.3	147.8	179.0
1978	51.1	63.0	68.7	144.5	157.7	195.2	50.9	63.7	71.1	136.6	144.7	180.2	63.3	71.7	75.9	138.6	147.6	178.9
1979	51.4	64.1	70.2	142.4	156.3	194.7	51.2	65.2	70.9	135.1	145.2	182.3	60.4	69.5	74.3	132.6	144.4	175.9
1980	51.3	64.0	70.0	143.4	155.8	196.6	50.8	65.0	70.3	135.0	145.8	181.7	58.5	70.2	75.6	135.1	144.9	177.1
1981	52.1	63.8	69.7	143.8	153.8	196.6	50.3	63.8	69.5	136.2	148.6	184.2	57.3	70.2	75.1	135.1	146.7	179.6
1982	51.0	63.5	69.0	142.6	156.5	196.1	49.2	62.1	68.0	138.4	150.5	185.2	56.4	69.1	74.5	137.4	147.7	180.2
1983	50.5	63.5	68.7	146.4	158.5	201.9	48.2	60.8	67.0	139.7	150.5	189.7	56.9	69.0	74.5	137.6	150.6	186.7
1984	50.0	63.1	68.5	147.0	161.3	205.4	48.1	60.0	66.4	140.0	151.1	191.4	56.1	68.0	74.0	139.8	152.8	187.7
1985	49.7	62.6	67.7	148.0	161.4	205.1	47.9	59.2	66.4	139.6	153.3	196.7	54.8	67.5	73.1	141.0	155.1	190.8
1986	49.2	61.5	66.9	147.5	160.1	203.0	47.1	59.0	66.1	140.5	154.9	201.1	53.9	67.3	72.1	142.4	155.6	190.6
1987	49.0	61.0	66.5	146.6	159.4	207.3	47.1	59.6	66.7	143.1	156.4	204.4	53.2	66.8	71.6	144.2	155.5	190.6
1988	49.0	60.6	66.4	146.2	161.4	212.1	46.7	59.6	66.3	144.3	156.8	207.1	53.1	65.7	71.0	143.8	154.6	194.4
1989	49.3	60.2	66.5	146.1	162.6	212.6	46.6	59.7	66.2	145.4	156.7	205.3	53.6	66.1	71.1	144.9	158.6	200.9
1990	49.3	60.7	66.7	147.9	162.6	213.7	46.9	60.6	66.7	145.6	160.4	206.5	54.7	65.7	71.1	145.3	159.8	201.4
1991	49.2	60.9	67.1	148.1	161.5	213.0	46.8	60.3	66.2	145.0	162.7	209.4	54.5	65.2	70.9	145.2	157.2	198.1

(*Continued*)

Table T.3. (*Continued*)

			Column															
	A	B	C	D	E	F	G	H	I	J	K	L	M	N	O	P	Q	R
			All						Male						Female			
	P10	P20	P25	P75	P80	P90	P10	P20	P25	P75	P80	P90	P10	P20	P25	P75	P80	P90
1992	48.7	60.7	66.8	148.7	161.4	213.1	46.2	59.6	65.4	144.6	164.0	210.8	53.5	64.5	70.2	145.2	158.9	202.3
1993	48.4	60.5	66.4	148.6	162.8	212.3	45.9	59.4	65.5	147.8	165.5	211.6	52.8	63.6	69.3	144.5	159.5	205.9
1994	47.5	60.0	65.9	151.3	168.0	214.6	45.4	58.5	64.5	151.8	168.3	213.5	51.2	62.8	68.7	145.3	161.8	211.1
1995	47.2	60.0	65.8	151.3	169.8	217.2	45.3	58.6	64.8	152.4	167.9	213.0	51.3	63.0	68.8	146.0	163.2	213.1
1996	47.4	60.3	66.0	151.4	171.3	219.4	45.3	58.5	65.1	152.8	167.6	212.7	50.9	62.6	68.5	146.7	162.6	212.6
1997	47.7	60.3	66.0	153.4	172.1	220.2	45.6	58.4	65.3	153.2	167.0	214.7	51.2	62.8	68.7	147.4	162.6	212.5
1998	48.0	60.4	66.0	153.7	170.7	218.8	46.3	58.9	66.0	152.7	165.7	219.6	51.1	63.2	68.6	147.2	160.4	209.5
1999	48.2	60.5	66.8	154.9	170.4	220.4	46.7	59.5	66.1	151.1	166.5	220.4	51.7	63.9	69.1	148.7	164.5	209.9
2000	48.4	60.3	66.9	154.8	169.2	224.6	46.5	59.4	65.6	150.0	167.0	221.4	52.2	64.0	69.2	148.2	166.2	211.9

Coverage All
Industry All
Age All aged 16 and over
Sex See headings
Occupation All
Definition Gross usual weekly earnings
Intensity FT
Period Month
Limits None
Source Downloaded from OECD website December 2005
Original source OECD interpolations from unpublished Bureau of Labor Statistics (BLS) tabulations by earnings class

Table T.4. United States: Economic Policy Institute (EPI)

							Column							
		All					Male					Female		
A	B	C	D	E	F	G	H	I	J	K	L	M	N	O
P10	P20	P80	P90	P95	P10	P20	P80	P90	P95	P10	P20	P80	P90	P95
1973	52.27	63.10	152.33	191.42	240.20	50.86	65.28	143.56	182.85	220.38	56.73	70.53	146.20	180.77	213.62
1974	52.91	63.48	153.81	194.04	237.13	50.94	64.84	140.60	178.36	217.72	63.52	70.79	146.84	180.42	213.76
1975	51.48	62.87	153.57	193.88	241.42	49.50	62.96	144.33	178.68	216.38	61.06	69.84	149.82	181.93	216.39
1976	55.06	63.96	155.07	194.93	239.76	50.88	63.62	146.18	184.95	217.26	63.94	74.20	151.21	184.11	221.36
1977	54.27	62.87	157.54	192.78	234.85	49.52	62.06	145.42	180.53	218.63	66.56	73.22	149.64	183.82	219.15
1978	53.19	62.89	156.44	195.18	233.58	49.66	62.48	145.94	179.70	213.08	64.64	73.05	150.41	184.60	216.45
1979	56.12	64.00	159.71	195.34	238.57	49.09	62.41	147.95	180.12	216.00	67.91	73.61	147.30	183.33	216.70
1980	53.57	63.36	159.68	194.86	236.36	48.48	62.15	144.99	175.67	213.24	63.61	70.91	148.41	182.20	217.84
1981	55.84	63.68	162.61	201.10	243.11	48.07	61.84	148.63	181.96	222.27	66.35	71.83	150.84	188.57	220.16
1982	52.99	61.72	161.97	200.14	244.37	46.45	60.10	152.00	185.83	228.19	63.72	69.74	154.76	190.95	228.06
1983	51.61	60.84	161.76	204.30	253.47	45.46	58.75	152.52	191.55	238.58	61.01	67.37	154.70	191.86	225.49
1984	50.12	60.78	163.94	206.35	254.23	45.45	58.46	154.02	196.37	242.63	58.75	66.03	156.27	193.41	230.70
1985	48.86	60.92	163.71	202.60	256.43	44.79	57.41	155.01	196.28	251.98	57.26	65.64	161.06	199.15	237.22
1986	47.85	61.16	162.38	204.98	255.25	43.85	56.83	155.39	193.46	238.52	55.49	64.85	159.05	197.60	236.04
1987	47.70	60.66	162.65	208.69	254.75	44.16	57.63	154.09	198.78	247.51	53.39	63.73	158.02	196.07	235.84
1988	48.00	60.59	165.17	211.72	262.77	45.62	58.66	157.66	201.13	252.76	52.35	64.21	157.17	199.74	241.85
1989	48.22	60.05	166.13	209.85	257.94	47.20	59.11	159.50	199.80	248.06	52.51	64.70	161.23	202.39	244.08
1990	49.05	60.73	165.48	211.10	263.07	47.23	59.28	162.59	206.78	252.73	52.94	64.29	160.56	202.97	246.70

(*Continued*)

Table T.4. (Continued)

	Column	All					Male					Female			
	A	B	C	D	E	F	G	H	I	J	K	L	M	N	O
	P10	P20	P80	P90	P95	P10	P20	P80	P90	P95	P10	P20	P80	P90	P95
1991	49.67	60.92	163.52	211.21	263.12	46.49	58.57	162.20	206.82	255.98	53.83	63.96	161.04	206.35	248.76
1992	49.16	59.84	163.41	206.62	256.82	46.20	58.30	163.01	208.63	259.99	54.42	63.44	162.26	209.39	252.36
1993	49.32	60.19	166.17	211.51	256.31	46.26	59.17	164.40	212.88	267.17	54.13	63.83	165.42	209.75	255.98
1994	49.68	60.65	170.38	219.11	274.45	46.79	60.10	168.06	216.39	272.38	54.19	63.79	167.73	215.69	265.28
1995	49.98	61.10	170.79	220.71	276.79	47.23	59.66	164.18	214.05	267.69	54.30	64.76	167.29	214.98	267.17
1996	49.96	61.87	171.88	222.37	279.36	47.94	59.70	166.60	213.18	270.00	53.91	64.64	167.27	216.53	267.86
1997	50.47	62.30	169.71	220.78	276.22	48.57	60.35	165.57	216.84	274.92	53.48	63.73	165.20	213.88	261.54
1998	51.76	62.49	168.53	220.89	275.39	48.30	61.09	165.43	217.70	270.46	55.25	64.99	167.57	215.06	265.48
1999	50.93	61.95	167.78	218.75	274.97	49.18	60.63	165.67	217.19	271.31	56.01	66.27	168.75	219.19	271.52
2000	51.54	63.46	170.44	222.79	284.16	49.25	60.38	166.14	221.34	277.13	55.16	65.66	166.37	218.64	268.55
2001	52.07	62.77	168.63	225.25	283.73	49.14	61.05	166.26	220.99	280.84	54.63	65.70	165.56	217.47	270.73
2002	52.22	62.50	170.45	226.67	290.87	48.88	60.70	167.84	225.13	285.21	54.64	65.41	166.28	214.80	271.10
2003	51.35	62.12	169.86	225.44	283.69	49.63	61.32	169.59	226.42	289.13	54.76	65.20	165.86	218.54	274.25
2004	50.66	61.80	170.42	223.51	286.53	49.82	61.28	170.69	233.50	298.90	54.38	64.42	168.10	221.80	274.85
2005	50.35	61.84	170.98	227.32	291.78	49.81	61.64	170.78	230.71	296.74	53.68	63.78	169.91	225.23	279.65

Coverage   All
Industry   All
Age   18–64
Sex   See headings
Occupation   All
Definition   Gross wages and salaries primary job
Intensity   All
Period   Hourly
Limits   None
Source   The State of Working America 2006–07, Table 3.4.
Original source Current Population Survey, Outgoing Rotation Group from 1979; May CPS for 1973–78
Note   Wage percentiles smoothed to allow for 'clumps' in the distribution

Table T.5. United States: Social Security Administration (SSA) data

	A	B	C	D	E	F	G	H	I	J	K	L	M
							Shares						Dispersion
	P10	P20	P80	P90	P99	P999	S10	S20	ST20	ST10	ST01	ST001	Gini
1981	10.2	26.3	210.7	282.3			0.35	1.73	49.59	30.79			48.4
1982	9.7	25.6	210.8	284.0	642.6	1724.9	0.31	1.59	51.39	33.14	8.2	2.0	50.3
1983	9.3	25.1	211.8	281.4	620.3	1718.3	0.30	1.56	51.22	32.96	8.3	2.2	50.2
1984	9.2	25.0	213.8	286.3	633.6	1821.4	0.30	1.53	51.68	33.42	8.7	2.5	50.7
1985	9.7	25.8	212.3	283.7	632.6	1807.4	0.31	1.60	51.37	33.20	8.5	2.3	50.3
1986	9.2	24.8	212.8	285.0	645.6	1941.2	0.30	1.53	51.81	33.69	8.9	2.5	50.8
1987	9.3	25.0	211.7	283.8	667.6	2378.9	0.29	1.49	52.82	35.09	10.7	3.8	51.8
1988	9.4	25.3	211.8	284.9	686.0	2514.7	0.29	1.51	53.05	35.42	10.9	3.8	52.0
1989	9.5	25.6	211.6	284.9	686.0	2357.0	0.30	1.55	52.71	34.97	10.3	3.3	51.6
1990	9.9	26.5	210.6	283.7	679.7	2422.5	0.31	1.60	52.54	34.84	10.3	3.3	51.3
1991	9.9	26.7	211.6	285.6	684.0	2327.8	0.31	1.61	52.59	34.85	10.1	3.2	51.3
1992	9.5	26.2	213.1	288.6	705.2	2601.4	0.29	1.53	53.30	35.67	11.0	3.8	52.1
1993	9.3	25.9	214.1	292.3	727.8	2500.9	0.27	1.48	53.52	35.84	10.8	3.6	52.3
1994	9.0	25.3	214.8	294.2	725.1	2422.8	0.27	1.45	53.75	36.08	11.1	3.9	52.6
1995	9.0	25.3	215.4	295.3	746.2	2480.5	0.26	1.42	54.37	36.89	10.7	3.3	53.2

Coverage   All
Industry   All
Age   All aged 13 to 86
Sex   All
Occupation   All
Definition   Gross wages and salaries
Intensity   All
Period   Annual
Limits   None
Source   Utendorf 1999 Tables 1 and 2, and Utendorf 2001/2, Tables 1 and 2
Original source SSA data
Note   P99 and P999 calculated using median from Utendorf 1999

Table T.6. United States: Current Population Survey (Henle and Ryscavage)

	Column			
	A	B	C	D
	Male		Female	
Gini coefficient	All	FY and FT	All	FY and FT
1958	32.7	25.4	38.9	
1959	32.4	26.2	38.5	
1960	33.7	27.5	38.4	
1961	34.3	27.4	39.9	
1962	33.6	27.0	39.3	
1963	33.6	27.0	39.6	
1964	33.6	27.5	39.1	
1965	33.4	27.6	39.6	
1966	34.2	28.1	39.2	
1967	33.5	27.4	39.5	26.4
1968	33.7	27.3	39.0	25.6
1969	34.4	27.2	39.5	24.6
1970	35.0	27.8	40.2	25.5
1971	35.7	28.1	40.0	25.1
1972	36.5	28.1	40.3	25.2
1973	36.0	28.7	40.4	25.4
1974	35.9	28.6	39.5	25.2
1974 rev.	36.1	28.1	39.5	23.7
1975	36.7	28.2	40.0	24.5
1976	37.1	28.4	40.1	24.5
1977	37.4	28.7	39.9	24.5

Coverage	All wage and salary workers (in March) with wage and salary income the previous year
Industry	All
Age	All
Sex	See headings
Occupation	All
Definition	Gross hourly earnings, calculated as annual earnings divided by (annual weeks worked × usual weekly hours)
Intensity	See headings
Period	Month
Limits	None
Source	Henle and Ryscavage (1980, Tables 1 and 5), revised version of Henle (1972, Table 1)
Original source	Annual Demographic Supplement to the March Current Population Survey
Notes	(1) There is a break in the FY FT series after 1966, as a result of a change in the method of calculating the Gini coefficient; (2) A revision to the processing methods was made in 1974

Table T.7. United States: Current Population Survey (Karoly)

	Column																							
	A	B	C	D	E	F	G	H	I	J	K	L	M	N	O	P	Q	R	S	T	U	V	W	X
	All Weekly				Male				Female				All Hourly				Male				Female			
	P10	P25	P75	P90	P10	P25	P75	P90	P10	P25	P75	P90	P10	P25	P75	P90	P10	P25	P75	P90	P10	P25	P75	P90
1963	22.3	54.7	150.0	206.1	28.4	64.9	135.1	184.8	19.9	51.1	149.8	204.5												
1964	21.7	54.5	150.3	205.2	28.4	64.0	136.8	177.7	20.5	51.0	150.4	209.3												
1965	21.8	54.5	152.5	213.5	29.1	62.9	133.3	180.0	20.0	49.3	150.0	206.1												
1966	22.1	53.0	151.6	208.0	29.1	64.7	137.5	184.4	22.0	51.3	154.3	210.5												
1967	21.6	53.5	152.0	210.0	28.6	63.6	138.5	184.6	21.5	50.9	157.2	214.9												
1968	23.1	57.4	153.8	217.3	28.6	64.3	138.6	185.7	21.8	53.3	147.8	207.1												
1969	23.8	55.3	156.0	217.7	29.0	63.5	137.0	186.5	23.2	52.8	147.2	201.1												
1970	23.4	53.2	154.1	215.4	27.8	62.5	137.5	187.5	22.5	51.8	149.2	203.6												
1971	23.6	54.4	158.9	221.4	27.4	61.0	140.6	190.2	22.1	53.1	150.2	206.6												
1972	23.5	54.7	156.9	226.2	27.5	59.5	138.0	190.8	23.5	53.0	151.6	205.9												
1973	22.3	52.0	157.1	221.4	26.5	59.8	139.5	189.5	23.8	52.5	152.5	211.3												
1974	23.8	53.5	161.8	226.2	26.3	60.0	142.0	195.0	23.3	51.9	152.0	204.8												
1975	25.5	53.8	159.2	225.5	27.5	60.0	140.1	186.7	26.1	55.6	152.1	212.9	42.4	63.7	151.3	212.4	40.4	63.8	142.5	191.1	46.9	70.0	144.3	196.0
1976	25.4	55.6	163.4	229.2	27.1	59.4	142.6	191.3	25.6	53.2	151.2	204.7	43.2	63.5	152.9	211.8	39.8	63.1	142.5	190.3	47.9	71.5	144.1	197.1
1977	25.9	55.8	162.9	225.6	29.1	59.5	148.3	198.3	26.0	56.9	154.1	211.5	43.8	64.1	154.8	216.2	40.2	62.4	143.9	191.4	47.4	71.0	143.1	199.1
1978	26.8	54.7	161.1	231.6	28.6	59.2	146.2	194.7	27.2	56.2	147.6	205.5	44.3	64.2	154.3	215.9	41.7	63.3	146.0	194.7	48.4	71.1	141.1	195.5
1979	27.4	57.5	166.7	235.3	28.0	58.8	146.3	195.8	27.0	56.9	146.5	205.0	45.5	65.7	155.7	217.8	40.5	63.0	147.1	191.1	49.3	71.8	142.0	195.2
1979 new	27.3	57.5	166.7	235.3	28.2	58.7	146.7	197.4	27.1	57.0	146.5	205.6	45.7	66.0	155.6	219.0	40.6	62.8	147.8	192.1	49.3	71.7	142.3	195.5

(Continued)

Table T.7. (Continued)

	Column																							
	A	B	C	D	E	F	G	H	I	J	K	L	M	N	O	P	Q	R	S	T	U	V	W	X
	All Weekly				Male				Female				All Hourly				Male				Female			
	P10	P25	P75	P90	P10	P25	P75	P90	P10	P25	P75	P90	P10	P25	P75	P90	P10	P25	P75	P90	P10	P25	P75	P90
1980	27.0	56.1	165.4	233.9	28.3	58.8	150.3	196.1	27.9	57.3	150.8	213.2	44.9	64.9	155.5	215.9	40.3	61.7	145.6	194.5	50.2	71.1	139.8	194.8
1981	26.0	56.5	166.7	237.1	27.4	57.8	151.7	201.2	27.1	55.6	152.0	211.1	44.9	64.1	159.3	221.0	40.4	62.5	149.7	196.9	49.9	70.9	145.6	200.0
1982	24.8	54.8	164.4	234.9	26.3	57.8	151.9	210.4	25.9	53.5	154.4	213.7	44.4	64.1	157.6	226.2	39.6	60.3	149.9	204.5	48.0	69.2	146.0	202.0
1983	25.3	54.7	167.1	242.6	25.4	55.6	150.0	207.6	25.8	55.5	157.0	220.0	43.2	63.2	156.1	221.7	39.4	60.6	151.4	205.1	47.3	68.3	146.3	202.0
1984	25.0	53.5	166.5	242.0	26.1	54.0	154.9	213.7	25.0	55.5	160.0	228.1	41.9	62.6	159.2	222.6	37.5	58.9	150.2	205.5	45.6	66.7	147.5	205.3
1985	24.6	53.2	167.1	236.5	25.7	53.6	151.5	209.6	26.4	54.4	163.3	226.8	42.7	63.1	160.0	226.7	37.4	59.1	152.3	209.4	46.8	66.1	149.6	207.8
1986	25.1	52.5	167.3	243.4	26.3	55.0	157.5	220.0	25.6	52.9	160.3	230.0	41.1	62.3	157.7	223.6	37.1	59.1	153.7	206.9	45.3	65.4	153.8	211.5
1987	25.0	53.1	164.2	243.8	26.3	54.8	153.8	214.3	25.0	54.0	161.8	226.5	41.2	62.1	159.4	225.6	36.4	60.0	150.0	208.1	44.3	64.9	148.1	209.0
1987 new	25.1	53.1	164.2	243.8	26.0	55.2	156.0	216.3	25.5	54.2	161.8	226.6	41.3	62.1	159.4	225.8	36.7	60.0	151.6	209.1	44.1	64.9	148.8	209.8
1988	24.8	52.9	164.7	235.3	25.5	54.5	154.5	213.6	25.7	53.8	161.5	230.8	40.3	60.7	157.0	223.4	37.5	60.0	152.0	209.9	44.1	65.4	152.2	210.9
1989	25.4	53.2	164.5	235.3	26.9	56.4	156.9	224.1	26.0	53.6	157.1	228.6	40.0	61.7	157.5	222.2	38.1	61.2	155.2	214.2	43.9	65.9	151.6	215.0
1990													41.8			223.0	39.1			218.0	43.7			214.0
1991													41.3			222.0	38.8			217.0	45.0			216.0
1992													41.7			225.0	39.1			217.0	44.8			218.0

Coverage   All
Industry   All
Age   16 and over
Sex   See headings
Occupation   All
Definition   Gross
Intensity   All who worked at least 1 week in year
Period   See headings
Limits   None
Source   Karoly (1993, Table 2B.2)
Original source   Annual Demographic Supplement to the March Current Population Survey
Notes   (1) Extended to 1992 using OECD 1996, page 103; (2) Estimates up to 1979 (first figure) based on 1970 population weights; later estimates based on 1980 population weights; (3) Figures from 1987 (second figure) using new processing system

Table T.8. United States: Census of Population (Lydall)

	Column																		
	A	B	C	D	E	F	G	H	I	J	K	L	M	N	O	P	Q	R	S
			All						Men						Women				
	P15	P25	P80	P90	P95	P98	P15	P25	P80	P90	P95	P98	P15	P25	P80	P90	P95	P98	P99
1939	45	61	160	205	271	403	48	65	155	199	267	270	45	67	156	191	231	294	367
1949	56	72	141	173	209	278	61	74	135	168	206	278	55	71	134	157	177	215	252
1959	52	68	144	176	215	288	59	74	137	168	206	278	52	70	139	161	182	216	248

Coverage	All
Industry	All
Age	All aged 14+
Sex	See headings
Occupation	All
Definition	Gross wages and salaries
Intensity	In 1939, those who worked FT throughout the year; in 1949 and 1959, those who worked 50+ weeks whether FT or PT
Period	Annual
Limits	None
Source	Lydall (1968, Tables US-4, US-5 and US-6)
Original sources	Census of Population 1940, vol iii, Table 72; Census of Population 1950, Report P-E No 1B, Table 23; Census of Population 1960, Final Report PC(2)-7A, Table 28

Table T.9. United States: Census of Population (Goldin and Margo)

	A	Column B	C
	39+ weeks P10	P90	FT adults P90/P10
1939	45.2	192.3	4.26
1949	50.8	165.5	2.89
1959	48.5	176.3	
1960			3.16
1970			3.25
1980			3.74
1985			4.31

Coverage	All wage and salary workers (in March) with wage and salary income the previous year
Industry	All
Age	See heading
Sex	Men
Occupation	All
Definition	Gross
Intensity	See heading
Period	Weekly
Limits	Earning more than half the minimum wage on a FT basis
Source	Goldin and Margo (1992, Table 1)
Original source	Census of Population, public-use microdata samples

Table T.10. United States: Current Population Reports

	A	B	C	D	E	F	G	H	I	J	K	
		All			Male					Female		
	P25	P75	P90	P25	P75	P90	Gini	P25	P75	P90	Gini	Source*
1939	47.4	174.4	259.9	48.1	163.2	237.6		44.1	166.7	241.6		CPR P-60 No 6, Table 18
1945	41.5	160.7	221.6	45.9	143.0	188.2			164.2	210.6		CPR P-60 No 2, Table 14
1947	46.9	150.6	198.5	56.0	149.3	178.8	32.7	38.9	160.1	205.9	40.3	CPR P-60 No 5, Table 21
1948	44.2	151.0	193.9	55.1	152.2	177.3	32.8	37.5	166.7	211.7	40.3	CPR P-60 No 6, Tables 18 and 20
1949	43.5	151.8	198.9	53.5	138.0	177.8	33.3		170.5	219.4	41.0	CPR P-60 No 7, Table 25
1950	40.4	159.8	196.6	54.6	150.4	176.6	33.5	32.5	176.4	225.8	43.2	CPR P-60 No 9, Table 23
1951	44.9	148.5	195.0	61.0	132.1	170.8	30.7		168.4	221.5	41.5	CPR P-60 No 11, Table 12
1952	44.1	150.1	201.6	58.9	134.4	171.9	31.5		171.2	225.7	42.4	CPR P-60 No 14, Table 11
1953	41.2	152.6	203.7	58.4	136.3	175.3	32.5	35.0	175.4	231.0	42.1	CPR P-60 No 16, Table 10
1954	38.9	153.6	205.6	53.4	137.9	177.4	33.6		183.6	242.1	43.1	CPR P-60 No 19, Table 10
1955	36.3	158.8	212.6		137.6	176.3	34.1		190.7	258.2	44.6	CPR P-60 No 23, Table 10
1956	34.1	158.3	212.3	52.5	138.2	176.8	34.3		196.7	265.2	45.3	CPR P-60 No 27, Table 27
1957	34.7	160.7	216.2	50.8	139.3	178.3	35.0		194.5	261.1	45.2	CPR P-60 No 30, Table 27
1958	32.1	164.3	222.1	45.4	142.2	183.4	36.5		202.8	278.5	46.7	CPR P-60 No 33, Table 39
1959	32.3	164.7	222.7	48.8	141.0	183.9	36.1		202.5	277.0	46.6	CPR P-60 No 35, Table 36
1960	31.6	168.8	229.2	46.9	143.3	188.5	37.0		200.2	274.5	46.5	CPR P-60 No 37, Table 36
1961	30.8	169.6	231.4	45.9	144.3	190.8	37.6		202.9	284.2	47.3	CPR P-60 No 39, Table 40

(Continued)

Table T.10. (*Continued*)

	A	B	C	D	E	F	G	H	I	J	K	
		All			Male				Female			
	P25	P75	P90	P25	P75	P90	Gini	P25	P75	P90	Gini	Source*
1962	31.9	171.1	232.2	45.3	142.1	188.3	37.2		199.4	279.1	46.7	CPR P-60 No 41, Table 28
1963	31.7	172.6	235.9	45.1	142.1	188.9	37.3		195.0	277.5	46.8	CPR P-60 No 43, Table 32
1964	32.4	171.8	238.8	45.4	143.8	194.5	37.6	28.9	191.2	268.8	46.5	CPR P-60 No 47, Table 32
1965	32.5	172.4	237.2	44.3	144.5	192.6	37.8	29.1	187.1	263.3	46.7	CPR P-60 No 51, Table 32
1966	33.6	170.4	237.6	47.9	140.9	189.9	36.8	30.4	185.1	258.0	45.8	CPR P-60 No 53, Table 32
1967	33.0	168.9	239.0	49.8	143.1	192.1	36.9	30.4	184.8	259.4	45.8	CPR P-60 No 60, Table 16

Coverage   All
Industry   All
Age   All
Sex   See headings
Occupation   All
Definition   Gross
Intensity   All
Period   Year
Limits   None
Source   See final column, the Gini coefficients in columns G and K are from Burtless, 1990, Table A-1
Original source April/March Supplement to the Current Population Survey
Notes   (1) The 1939 figure is given in the Current Population Report for comparison but is based on the 1940 Census report; (2) In 1945 it is particularly important that the figures relate only to the civilian population; (3) Where certain entries are blank for a year that means that the top or bottom range is too large to allow interpolation; (4) Linear interpolation of cumulative frequency, Pareto interpolation for P90

* CPR denotes Current Population Report

Table T.11. United States: Census Bureau Historical Tables

				Column					
	A	B	C	D	E	F	G	H	I
	All	Male				Female			
	Gini	P10	P90	Dec ratio	Gini	P10	P90	Dec ratio	Gini
1967	34.0	42.9	180.3	4.20	31.4	37.5	174.9	4.67	29.8
1968	33.3	45.5	182.3	4.01	30.8	43.5	173.5	3.99	27.9
1969	32.6	48.5	182.0	3.75	30.5	50.5	166.7	3.30	26.4
1970	32.6	46.7	179.9	3.85	30.5	51.3	174.9	3.41	27.2
1971	32.8	46.9	184.5	3.93	30.9	51.5	174.7	3.39	26.8
1972	33.6	46.3	185.6	4.01	31.6	51.5	171.6	3.33	27.1
1973	33.0	47.8	184.2	3.85	30.9	51.5	174.2	3.38	26.1
1974	32.6	46.5	178.6	3.84	30.9	56.2	169.1	3.01	25.0
1975	32.7	49.0	187.7	3.83	30.8	54.3	170.7	3.14	26.0
1976	32.8	45.2	188.7	4.17	31.1	55.2	171.8	3.11	25.9
1977	33.2	44.1	181.5	4.12	31.5	53.5	174.9	3.27	26.0
1978	33.3	45.2	187.3	4.14	31.6	55.6	177.8	3.20	25.9
1979	33.5	45.9	183.9	4.01	31.7	54.9	174.7	3.18	26.4
1980	33.1	43.9	192.1	4.38	31.5	54.6	178.7	3.27	26.5
1981	33.4	43.7	187.3	4.29	32.1	54.1	174.6	3.23	26.6
1982	34.0	43.9	194.7	4.44	33.0	53.5	178.6	3.34	27.8
1983	34.0	41.8	195.4	4.67	33.2	50.8	181.2	3.57	28.0
1984	34.2	40.8	195.5	4.79	33.2	49.8	179.6	3.61	28.5
1985	34.8	41.7	200.0	4.80	34.3	50.0	187.0	3.74	28.9
1986	35.5	40.0	200.0	5.00	34.9	48.1	187.5	3.90	29.9

(Continued)

Table T.11. (*Continued*)

	A	B	C	D	E	F	G	H	I
	All	Male				Female			
	Gini	P10	P90	Dec ratio	Gini	P10	P90	Dec ratio	Gini
1987	35.3	41.7	200.4	4.81	34.7	47.6	190.5	4.00	30.0
1988	35.5	42.4	202.1	4.77	35.0	46.3	191.7	4.14	30.6
1989	36.2	42.6	207.2	4.87	36.1	48.1	194.2	4.04	31.0
1990	35.9	41.3	208.3	5.04	36.1	46.5	189.3	4.07	30.8
1991	35.5	41.3	206.6	5.00	35.4	49.5	195.0	3.94	31.1
1992	36.0	40.0	204.8	5.12	36.3	47.6	190.5	4.00	31.2
1993	38.9	40.0	216.8	5.42	39.7	46.5	195.3	4.20	33.6
1994	39.5	40.0	226.8	5.67	40.3	45.5	204.5	4.50	34.3
1995	38.8	42.0	223.1	5.31	39.8	44.8	200.0	4.46	33.2
1996	39.3	40.7	220.3	5.42	40.1	46.3	201.9	4.36	34.3
1997	39.4	42.0	225.2	5.36	40.3	44.8	200.0	4.46	34.1
1998	39.3	41.2	218.5	5.31	40.1	48.1	208.2	4.33	34.5
1999	39.9	41.7	222.1	5.33	40.8	46.1	207.4	4.50	34.4
2000	40.6	40.5	229.6	5.67	42.0	44.4	207.6	4.67	34.1
2000	40.5	40.5	229.6	5.67	41.8	44.4	207.6	4.67	34.5
2001	40.9	41.0	236.5	5.77	41.9	44.8	207.2	4.62	36.2

Coverage   All
Industry   All
Age   All
Sex   See headings
Occupation   All
Definition   Gross
Intensity   FT FY
Period   Year
Limits   None
Source   US Census Bureau website, downloaded 12 January 2007; see also US Census Bureau (2000)
Original source   Annual Demographic Supplement to the March Current Population Survey
Notes   (1) Break in 1993 as a result of change in data collection methodology; (2) From 2000 (second figure) implementation of 28,000 household sample expansion

Table T.12. United States:
Survey of Income and
Program Participation (SIPP)

	Column A
	P90/P10
1984	4.10
1986	4.22
1987	4.30
1988	4.35
1989	4.20
1990	4.17
1991	4.21
1992	4.25
1993	4.20
1994	4.20
1995	4.18

Coverage	All
Industry	All
Age	All aged 13 to 86
Sex	All
Occupation	All
Definition	Gross wage rate for all hours worked
Intensity	All
Period	Hourly
Limits	None
Source	Lerman, 1999, Chart 1
Original source	SIPP
Note	Read from graph

Table T.13. United States: Income tax data (tax units)

		Column					Column	
	A	B	C		A	B	C
		Tax units					Tax units	
Year	P90	P95	P99	Year	P90	P95	P99
1927	166.0	213.9	439.1	1968	256.9	310.0	490.2
1928	173.7	232.8	475.5	1969	257.8	311.2	483.9
1929	174.1	228.1	464.5	1970	252.8	306.0	478.4
1930	174.8	224.2	482.7	1971	252.3	305.8	482.1
1931	186.4	237.1	476.0	1972	258.4	311.3	493.2
1932	191.9	247.7	460.7	1973	255.7	310.6	494.6
1933	191.2	244.5	457.0	1974	241.5	295.6	480.6
1934	182.2	247.8	461.4	1975	237.7	288.8	458.6
1935	190.3	253.1	469.5	1976	241.3	293.1	471.1
1936	183.1	241.0	476.2	1977	239.1	290.9	468.5
1937	193.9	248.6	466.3	1978	233.4	284.4	466.0
1938	197.9	252.0	461.0	1979	227.5	276.8	455.5
1939	206.4	261.4	464.5	1980	229.1	279.6	466.2
1940	214.6	260.4	463.3	1981	231.1	284.0	469.9
1941	206.6	247.8	430.8	1982	230.4	283.8	474.2
1942	192.6	234.3	393.3	1983	234.4	290.7	492.0
1943	195.1	231.4	362.4	1984	237.1	294.7	505.7
1944	193.0	228.7	339.6	1985	247.2	309.5	529.2
1945	185.2	219.8	343.0	1986	263.2	330.5	567.1
1946	182.4	221.3	404.6	1987	264.8	333.3	595.3
1947	184.7	218.6	401.3	1988	263.6	335.7	617.5
1948	182.7	228.6	392.1	1989	258.3	330.7	598.5
1949	184.9	231.3	396.1	1990	253.7	324.1	593.2
1950	189.2	234.1	400.6	1991	250.1	322.6	589.4
1951	192.4	232.1	396.0	1992	247.7	318.5	598.4
1952	190.5	231.8	396.1	1993	243.9	315.3	592.5
1954	191.7	234.4	408.1	1994	243.3	314.0	588.8
1956	207.3	257.8	453.7	1995	250.3	324.2	616.3
1958	202.2	256.3	439.0	1996	250.4	329.6	639.3
1960	214.3	272.7	448.0	1997	255.6	334.7	671.2
1961	222.5	280.2	456.6	1998	257.1	340.2	678.9
1962	234.8	289.3	466.0	1999	264.2	349.8	709.5
1964	243.6	293.0	462.8	2000	267.7	356.6	736.2
1966	252.5	303.4	479.0	2001	269.5	358.1	720.3
1967	255.4	309.3	492.5	2002	263.6	351.0	700.8

Coverage	All
Industry	All
Age	All
Sex	All
Occupation	All
Definition	Gross
Intensity	All
Period	Year
Limits	None
Source	Piketty and Saez, 2007, Tables 5B.1 and 5B.3
Original source	Income tax returns
Note	Percentiles expressed relative to the mean

Table T.14. United States Historical Statistics

			Column		
	A	B	C	D	E
	Male P90/P10 Census	Male P90/P10 CPS	Male Std dev of log	Male Var of log	Female Var of log
1939	4.25				
1949	3.26				
1959	3.49	2.86	0.450		
1963		2.91	0.453	1.471	2.125
1964		3.01	0.456	1.494	2.143
1965		2.97	0.459	1.408	2.021
1966		3.00	0.453	1.342	1.921
1967		2.90	0.446	1.354	1.867
1968		2.88	0.446	1.343	1.847
1969		3.00	0.448	1.357	1.858
1970		3.06	0.455	1.428	1.890
1971		3.15	0.467	1.408	1.838
1972		3.23	0.483	1.397	1.821
1973		3.28	0.477	1.402	1.770
1974		3.23	0.481	1.401	1.754
1975		3.23	0.479	1.380	1.729
1976		3.41	0.490	1.411	1.717
1977		3.40	0.495	1.426	1.700
1978		3.43	0.499	1.395	1.685
1979		3.47	0.504	1.430	1.852
1980		3.59	0.509	1.471	1.814
1981		3.66	0.520	1.536	1.755
1982		3.94	0.530	1.471	1.814
1983		3.90	0.540	1.724	1.917
1984		4.17	0.550	1.624	1.910
1985		4.25	0.560	1.579	1.867
1986		4.29	0.563	1.606	1.872
1987		4.18	0.562	1.641	1.902
1988		4.28	0.567		
1989		4.44	0.578		

Coverage	All
Industry	All
Age	18–65 (64 col. A) or 16+ (cols. D and E)
Sex	See headings
Occupation	All
Definition	Gross
Intensity	Working more than 39 weeks (col. A in 1939) and earning more than 50% minimum wage; working 35 hours or more a week (cols. B and C); with positive earnings (cols. D and E)
Period	Weekly (cols. A and B); hourly (col. C); annual (cols. D and E)
Limits	None
Source	Carter et al, 2006, Table Ba426-4430
Original source	Census of population and Current Population Survey

Table T.15. United States: Income of the American People (Miller)

						Column					
A	B	C	D	E	F	G	H	I	J	K	L
		All				Male				Female	
S20	S40	ST40	ST20	S20	S40	ST40	ST20	S20	S40	ST40	ST20
1939 3.4	11.8	73.2	49.3	3.5	12.5	72.0	48.7	3.0	12.2	71.0	46.5
1945 2.9	13.0	69.6	43.9	3.8	16.2	65.3	39.9	4.5	14.8	66.7	39.7
1947 2.9	13.2	69.0	44.3	4.5	16.4	65.7	39.3	2.8	11.5	70.5	43.8
1948 2.9	13.1	68.3	42.8	3.9	16.6	64.4	39.7	3.0	11.5	70.1	41.5
1949 2.6	12.7	68.6	42.4	3.6	15.9	64.9	40.1	2.2	10.2	71.5	42.9
1950 2.3	12.0	69.7	44.0	3.5	16.0	65.3	41.0	2.0	9.5	72.9	43.4
1951 3.0	13.6	67.5	41.6	4.9	18.0	62.7	38.3	3.3	11.1	70.6	42.9
1953 2.6	12.3	69.6	44.3	3.6	16.1	65.1	41.1	3.0	10.5	72.0	43.8
1954 2.5	11.7	70.3	45.0	3.4	15.4	65.9	41.6	2.9	10.1	72.9	44.9
1955 2.2	10.9	71.2	45.0	3.2	15.1	65.9	40.9	2.9	9.4	74.5	46.7
1956 2.1	10.5	72.2	46.3	3.0	14.9	66.5	42.1	2.8	9.1	75.0	46.5
1957 2.1	10.4	72.4	46.5	2.8	14.3	67.3	42.8	2.7	9.1	74.6	46.4
1958 1.8	9.5	73.7	47.9	2.4	13.0	68.8	44.8	2.6	8.1	75.9	47.7
1959 1.9	10.0	72.7	45.9	2.7	14.1	67.0	41.5	2.5	8.2	75.6	47.6
1960 1.8	9.6	73.4	46.8	2.5	13.4	67.7	42.5	2.4	8.3	75.5	47.3

Coverage	All
Industry	All
Age	All
Sex	See headings
Occupation	All
Definition	Gross
Intensity	All
Period	Annual
Limits	None
Source	Miller (1968, page 77)
Original source	Census of population and April/March Supplement to Current Population Survey
Note	S20 denotes the share of the bottom 20 per cent, and ST20 denotes the share of the top 20 per cent

Table T.16. United States: Social Security Administration data (Brittain)

| | Column | |
| | A | B |
	Gini	ST05
1951	46.9	21.2
1952	46.3	20.5
1953	46.1	20.0
1954	46.4	20.5
1955	46.7	19.5
1956	47.1	20.7
1957	47.0	20.4
1958	47.4	20.6
1959	47.6	20.7
1960	47.9	20.8
1961	47.7	20.5
1962	47.8	20.5
1963	48.0	20.6
1964	47.9	20.2
1965	48.0	20.3
1966	49.2	21.5
1967	48.9	21.7
1968	48.9	21.3
1969	46.5	21.1

Coverage	All wage and salary workers contributing to Old Age, Survivors, Disability and Health Insurance
Industry	All
Age	All
Sex	All
Occupation	All covered
Definition	Taxable earnings
Intensity	All
Period	Annual
Limits	None
Source	Brittain (1972, page 107)
Original source	Social Security Administration (SSA)
Notes	Interpolated by Brittain from tabulations supplied by SSA; STO5 denotes the share of the top 5 per cent

Bibliography

Alvey, W and Cobleigh, C, 1980, 'Exploration of differences between linked social security and CPS earnings data for 1972', in *Studies from Interagency Data Linkages*, Report No 11, US Department of Health, Education and Welfare, Washington, DC.

Beach C M, Chaykowski, R P, and Slotsve, G A, 1997, 'Inequality and polarization of male earnings in the United States, 1968–1990', *North American Journal of Economics and Finance*, vol 8: 135–51.

Blackburn, M, 1990, 'What can explain the increase in earnings inequality among males?', *Industrial Relations*, vol 29: 441–56.

—— and Bloom, D, 1987, 'Earnings and income inequality in the United States', *Population and Development Review*, vol 13: 575–609.

—— —— and Freeman, R B, 1990/1, 'An era of falling earnings and rising inequality?' *Brookings Review*, vol 9: 38–43.

—— —— and —— 1991, 'Changes in earnings differentials in the 1980's: Concordance, convergence, causes and consequences', Discussion Paper 554, Department of Economics, Columbia University.

Brittain, J A, 1972, *The Payroll Tax for Social Security*, The Brookings Institution, Washington, DC.

Buchinsky, M, 1994, 'Changes in the U.S. wage structure 1963 to 1987: An application of quantile regression', *Econometrica*, vol 62: 405–58.

Burkhauser, R V, Butler, J S, Feng, S, and Houtenville, A J, 2004, 'Long term trends in earnings inequality: What the CPS can tell us', *Economics Letters*, vol 82: 295–9.

—— Feng, S, and Jenkins, S P, 2007, 'Using the P90/P10 index to measure US inequality trends with Current Population Survey data: A view from inside the Census Bureau vaults', ISER Working Paper 2007–14, University of Essex, Colchester.

Burtless, G, 1990, 'Earnings inequality over the business and demographic cycles', in G Burtless, editor, *A Future of Lousy Jobs?*, Brookings Institution, Washington, DC.

—— editor, 1990a, *A Future of Lousy Jobs?*, Brookings Institution, Washington, DC.

Carter, S B, Gartner, S S, Haines, M R, Olmstead, A L, Sutch, R, and Wright, G, 2006, editors, *Historical Statistics of the United States: Earliest Times to the Present, Millennial Edition*, Cambridge University Press, Cambridge.

Dooley, M and Gottschalk, P, 1982, 'Does a younger male labor force mean greater earnings inequality?' *Monthly Labor Review*, vol 105, issue 11: 42–5.

—— and—— 1984, 'Earnings inequality among males in the United States: Trends and effects of labor force growth', *Journal of Political Economy*, vol : 59–89.

—— and—— 1985, 'The increasing proportion of men with low earnings in the United States', *Demography*, vol 22: 25–34.

Freeman, R B, 1995, 'Are your wages set in Beijing?', *Journal of Economic Perspectives*, vol 9: 15–32.

Gittleman, M and Joyce, M, 1995, 'Earnings mobility in the United States, 1967–91', *Monthly Labor Review*, vol 118: 3–13.

—— and —— 1996, 'Earnings mobility and long-run inequality: An analysis using matched CPS data', *Industrial Relations*, vol 35: 180–96.

Goldin, C and Margo, R, 1992, 'The Great Compression: The wage structure in the United States at mid-century', *Quarterly Journal of Economics*, vol 107: 1–34.

Gottschalk, P and Moffitt, R, 1992, 'Earnings and wage distributions in the NLS, CPS and PSID', Part 1, Final Report to the US Department of Labor, Brown University.

—— and —— 1994, 'The growth of earnings instability in the U.S. labor market', *Brookings Papers on Economic Activity*, No 2: 217–72.

—— and —— 1995, 'Trends in the covariance structure of earnings in the US: 1969–1987', Brown University.

Grubb, W and Wilson, R, 1989, 'Sources of increasing inequality in wages and salaries, 1960–1990', *Monthly Labor Review*, vol 112: 3–13.

Hansen, M H and Hurwitz, W N, 1944, 'A new sample of the population', US Census Bureau, Washington, DC.

Henle, P, 1972, 'Exploring the distribution of earned income', *Monthly Labor Review*, vol 95, December: 16–27.

—— and Ryscavage, P, 1980, 'The distribution of earned income among men and women, 1958–1977', *Monthly Labor Review*, vol 103, issue 4: 3–10.

Hyslop, D R, 2001, 'Rising U.S. earnings inequality and family labor supply: The covariance structure of intrafamily earnings', *American Economic Review*, vol 91: 755–77.

Jones, A F and Weinberg, D H, 2000, *The Changing Shape of the Nation's Income Distribution*, Current Population Report P60–204, US Census Bureau, Washington DC.

Juhn, C, 1994, 'Wage inequality and industrial change: Evidence from five decades', NBER Working Paper 4684.

—— Murphy, K M, and Pierce, B, 1993, 'Wage inequality and the rise in returns to skill', *Journal of Political Economy*, vol 101: 410–42.

Karoly, L A, 1992, 'Changes in the distribution of individual earnings in the United States, 1967–1986', *Review of Economics and Statistics*, vol 74: 107–15.

—— 1994, 'The trend in inequality among families, individuals, and workers in the United States: A twenty-five year perspective' in S Danziger and P Gottschalk editors, *Uneven Tides*, Russell Sage Foundation, New York.

—— and Burtless, G, 1995, 'Demographic change, rising earnings inequality and the distribution of personal well-being, 1959–1989', *Demography*, vol 32: 379–405.

—— and Klerman, J A, 1994, 'Using Regional Data to Reexamine the Contribution of Demographic and Regional Changes to Increasing U.S. Wage Inequality', in J H Bergstrand et al, editors, *The Changing Distribution of Income in an Open U.S. Economy*, Elsevier, Amsterdam.

Katz, L F and Autor, D H, 1999, 'Changes in the wage structure and earnings inequality', in O Ashenfelter and D Card, editors, *Handbook of Labor Economics*, vol 3.

—— and Murphy, K M, 1992, 'Changes in relative wages, 1963–1987: Supply and demand factors', *Quarterly Journal of Economics*, vol 107: 35–78.

Keat, P, 1960, 'Long-run changes in occupational wage structure, 1900–1956', *Journal of Political Economy*, vol 73: 584–600.

Lemieux, T, 2006, 'Increasing residual wage inequality: Composition effects, noisy data, or rising demand for skill?', *American Economic Review*, vol 96: 461–98.

Lerman, R, 1997, 'Reassessing trends in U.S. earnings inequality', *Monthly Labor Review*, vol 120, No 12: 17–25.

Levy, F, 1989, 'Recent trends in U.S. earnings and family incomes', in O J Blanchard and S Fischer, editors, *NBER Macroeconomics Annual*, vol 4, MIT Press, Cambridge.

Lillard, L, Smith, J P, and Welch, F, 1986, 'What do we really know about wages? The importance of nonreporting and census imputation', *Journal of Political Economy*, vol 94: 489–506.

Miller, H P, 1958, *Income of the American People*, John Wiley, New York.

—— 1968, *Income Distribution in the United States*, Bureau of the Census, Washington, DC.

Mishel, L R and Bernstein, J, 1993, *The State of Working America: 1992–93*, Sharpe, Armonk, New York.

—— —— and Allegretto, S, 2005, *The State of Working America: 2004/2005*, ILR Press, New York.

—— —— and Schmitt, J, 1997, *The State of Working America: 1996–97*, Sharpe, Armonk, New York.

—— —— and —— 1999, *The State of Working America: 1998–99*, ILS Press, Ithaca.

—— —— and —— 2001, *The State of Working America: 2000–2001*, ILR Press, New York.

—— —— and —— 2003, *The State of Working America: 2002/2003*, ILS Press, Ithaca.

Moffitt, R A and Gottschalk, P, 2002, 'Trends in the transitory variance of earnings in the United States', *Economic Journal*, vol 112: C68–C73.

Murphy, K M and Welch, F, 1992, 'The structure of wages', *Quarterly Journal of Economics*, vol 107: 285–326.

Ober, H, 1948, 'Occupational wage differentials, 1907–1947', *Monthly Labor Review*, August: 127–34.

Pierce, B and Welch, F, 1994, 'Dimensions of inequality in labor income', in J H Bergstrand et al, editors, *The Changing Distribution of Income in an Open U.S. Economy*, Elsevier, Amsterdam.

Piketty, T and Saez, E, 2003, 'Income inequality in the United States', *Quarterly Journal of Economics*, vol 118: 1–39.

—— and —— 2007, 'Income and wage inequality in the United States, 1913–2002', in A B Atkinson and T Piketty, editors, *Top Incomes over the Twentieth Century*, Oxford University Press, Oxford.

Pischke, J-S, 1995, 'Measurement error and earnings dynamics: Some estimates from the PSID validation study', *Journal of Business and Economic Statistics*, vol 13: 305–14.

Plotnick, R D, 1982, 'Trends in male earnings inequality', *Southern Economic Journal*, vol 48: 724–32.

Polivka, A E, 1996, 'Data watch: The redesigned Current Population Survey', *Journal of Economic Perspectives*, vol 10, No 3: 169–80.

—— 2000, 'Using earnings data from the monthly Current Population Survey', Bureau of Labor Statistics, Washington, DC.

Schwartz, S, 1986, 'Earnings capacity and the trend in inequality among black men', *Journal of Human Resources,* vol 21 : 44–63.

US Census Bureau, 2002, 'Current Population Survey: Design and methodology', Technical Paper 63RV, US Census Bureau, Washington.

Utendorf, K R, 1998, 'Recent changes in earnings distributions in the United States', *Social Security Bulletin*, vol 61, No 2: 12–28.

—— 1999, 'Recent changes in earnings distributions in the United States: Age and cohort effects', *Social Security Bulletin*, vol 62, No 2: 14–28.

—— 2001/2002, 'The upper part of the earnings distribution in the United States: How has it changed?' *Social Security Bulletin*, vol 64, No 3: 1–11.

Weinberg, D H, 2006, 'Income data quality issues in the CPS', *Monthly Labor Review,* June: 38–45.

General Bibliography

As explained in the Introduction, the literature on individual countries is contained in the Bibliographies to Chapters A–T in Part III. This General Bibliography contains all the references cited in Parts I and II, as well as a number of other items that may be of interest to the reader, including those that deal with subjects not covered in this volume, and earlier literature that retains, in my judgement, much of value.

Books, Articles, and Essays

The Bibliography includes a number of books and survey articles on the distribution of individual earnings, and collections of essays. These are listed below.

Books and Survey Articles

Acemoglu (2002), Aghion, Caroli, and Garcia-Peñalosa (1999), Bjerke (1961 and 1970), Bowles, Gintis, and Osborne (2001), Burtless (1995), Gottschalk and Smeeding (1997), Katz and Autor (1999), Levy and Murnane (1992), Lydall (1968), Mincer (1970), Morris and Western (1999), Phelps Brown (1977), Reder (1962, 1968, and 1969), Sahota (1978), Sattinger (1993), and Willis (1986).

Collections of Essays

Arrow, Bowles, and Durlauf (2000), Auerbach and Beleous (1998), Bergstrand et al (1994), Bhagwati and Kosters (1994), Burtless (1990), Cohen, Piketty, and Saint-Paul (2002), Freeman and Katz (1995), Kosters (1991), and Peoples (1998).

Topics not Treated in the Lecture

In the Lecture, I identified several important topics not treated adequately in the text but for which a selection of references are included in the Bibliography. These are listed below in alphabetical order.

Collective Bargaining

Asher and DeFina (1997), Bell and Pitt (1998), Betcherman (1991), Blanchflower (1984), Booth (1995), Booth and Frank (1996), Boyer (1988), Boyer and Hatton (1994), Bratsberg and Ragan (1997), Card (1996), Carruth and Oswald (1989), Christofides and Oswald (1992), Dillon and Gang (1987), Duncan and Stafford (1980), Eichengreen (1987), Freeman (1980, 1982, 1984, and 1993), Freeman and Medoff (1984), Geroski and Stewart (1986), Gosling and Machin (1995), Green (1988), Hatton, Boyer, and Bailey (1994), Hibbs (1990), Jakubson (1991), Kahn

(1998), Kahn and Curme (1987), Lemieux (1993 and 1997), Lewis (1986), Mellow (1981), Metcalf (1982), Metcalf, Hansen, and Charlwood (2000), Moene and Wallerstein (1997), Muller (1989), Oswald (1985), Pencavel (1991), Pencavel and Hartsog (1984), Pettengill (1979 and 1980), Riddell (1995), Shah (1984), and Stewart (1983, 1990, 1991, and 1995).

Gender Differentials

Bernhardt, Morris, and Handcock (1995), Blackburn, Jarman, and Brooks, (2000), Blau and Beller (1988), Blau and Kahn (1992, 1994, 1995, 1997, and 2000), Butcher and Case (1994), Fortin and Lemieux (1995 and 2000), Groschen (1991a), Harkness (1996), Harkness, Machin, and Waldfogel (1996), Main and Reilly (1992), Miller, Mulvey, and Martin (1997), O'Neill and Polachek (1993), and Rosenfeld and Kalleberg (1990).

Minimum Wages

Bazen (1991 and 2000), Brown (1999), Brown, Gilroy, and Kohen (1982), Card and Krueger (1995), Dickens, Machin, and Manning (1994), Freeman (1996), Horrigan and Mincy (1993), Lee (1999), Machin and Manning (1994), Manning (2003, Chapter 12), Metcalf (2007), and Stewart (2004).

Product Market Power, Regulation, and Privatization

Abowd and Lemieux (1993), Card (1996), Hendricks (1994), Hirsch (1988), Nickell, Vainiomaki, and Wadhwani (1994), Peoples (1989/90 and 1998), Rose (1987), and Weiss (1966).

Bibliography

Abel-Smith B and Townsend, P, 1965, *The Poor and the Poorest*, Bell, London.

Abowd, J M and Bognanno, M, 1995, 'International differences in executive and managerial compensation', in R Freeman and L Katz, editors, *Differences and Changes in Wage Structures*, University of Chicago Press, Chicago.

—— and Card, D, 1989, 'On the covariance structure of earnings and hours changes', *Econometrica*, vol 57: 411–45.

—— and Kaplan, D S, 1999, 'Executive compensation', *Journal of Economic Perspectives*, vol 13, No 4: 145–68.

—— and Kramarz, F, 1999, 'The analysis of labor markets using matched employer–employee data', in O Ashenfelter and D Card, editors, *Handbook of Labor Economics*, vol 3B, North-Holland, Amsterdam.

—— —— and Margolis, D, 1999, 'High wage workers and high wage firms', *Econometrica*, vol 67: 251–333.

—— and Lemieux, T, 1993, 'The effects of product market competition on collective bargaining agreements: The case of foreign competition in Canada', *Quarterly Journal of Economics*, vol 108: 983–1014.

Abraham, K G and Farber, H S, 1987, 'Job duration, seniority and earnings', *American Economic Review*, vol 77: 278–97.

Acemoglu, D, 1996, 'A microfoundation for increasing returns in human capital accumulation', *Quarterly Journal of Economics*, vol 111: 779–804.

—— 1998, 'Why do new technologies complement skills? Directed technical change and wage inequality', *Quarterly Journal of Economics*, vol 113: 1055–89.

—— 1999, 'Changes in unemployment and wage inequality: An alternative theory and some evidence', *American Economic Review*, vol 89: 1259–78, republished in D Cohen, T Piketty, and G Saint-Paul, editors, *The Economics of Rising Inequalities*, Oxford University Press, Oxford.

—— 2001, 'Good jobs vs. bad jobs: Theory and some evidence', *Journal of Labor Economics*, vol 19: 1–21.

—— 2002, 'Technical change, inequality and the labor market', *Journal of Economic Literature*, vol 40: 7–72.

—— 2003, 'Technology and Inequality', *NBER Reporter*, Winter 2002/3.

—— and Pischke, J S, 1999, 'The structure of wages and investment in general training', *Journal of Political Economy*, vol 107: 539–72.

—— and Shimer, R, 2000, 'Wage and technology dispersion', *Review of Economic Studies*, vol 67: 585–607.

Adler, M, 1985, 'Stardom and talent', *American Economic Review*, vol 75: 208–12.

Agell, J and Lundborg, P, 1995, 'Theories of pay and unemployment: Survey evidence from Swedish manufacturing firms', *Scandinavian Journal of Economics*, vol 97: 295–307.

Aghion, P, 2002, 'Schumpeterian growth theory and the dynamics of income inequality', *Econometrica*, vol 70: 855–82.

—— Caroli, E, and Garcia-Peñalosa, C, 1999, 'Inequality and economic growth: The perspective of the new growth theories', *Journal of Economic Literature*, vol 37: 1615–60.

—— Howitt, P, and Violante, G L, 2002, 'General purpose technology and wage inequality', *Journal of Economic Growth*, vol 7: 315–45.

Akerlof, G, 1980, 'A theory of social custom, of which unemployment may be one consequence', *Quarterly Journal of Economics*, vol 95: 749–75.

—— and Yellen, J, 1990, 'The fair wage/effort hypothesis and unemployment', *Quarterly Journal of Economics*, vol 105: 255–83.

Albaek, K, Arai, M, Asplund, R, Barth, E, and Strøyer Madsen, E, 1998, 'Measuring wage effects of plant size', *Labour Economics*, vol 5: 425–8.

Albrecht, J and Vroman, S, 2002, 'A matching model with endogenous skill requirements', *International Economic Review*, vol 43: 283–305.

Allen, S, 2001, 'Technology and wage structure', *Journal of Labor Economics*, vol 19: 440–83.

Altonji, J and Shakotko, R A, 1987, 'Do wages rise with job seniority?', *Review of Economic Studies*, vol 54: 437–59.

Anderton, R and Brenton, P, 1998, 'The dollar, trade, technology and inequality in the USA', *National Institute Economic Review*, No 166: 78–86.

—— 1998a, 'Trade with the NICs and wage inequality: Evidence from the UK and Germany', in P Brenton and J Pelkmans, editors, *Global Trade and European Workers*, Macmillan, London.

—— and —— 1998b, 'Did outsourcing to low-wage countries hurt less-skilled workers in the UK?', in P Brenton and J Pelkmans, editors, *Global Trade and European Workers*, Macmillan, London.

—— and —— 1999, 'Outsourcing and low-skilled workers in the UK', *Bulletin of Economic Research*, vol 51: 267–85.

Arai, M, 1994, 'Compensating wage differentials versus efficiency wages: An empirical study of job autonomy and wages', *Industrial Relations*, vol 33: 249–61.

—— 1994a, 'An empirical analysis of wage dispersion and efficiency wages', *Scandinavian Journal of Economics*, vol 96: 31–50.

—— 2003, 'Wages, profits, and capital intensity: Evidence from matched worker–firm data', *Journal of Labor Economics*, vol 21: 593–618.

Arkes, J, 1998, 'Trends in long-run versus cross-section earnings inequality in the 1970s and 1980s', *Review of Income and Wealth*, series 44: 199–213.

Arrow, K J, 1960, 'Price-quantity adjustments in multiple markets with rising demands', in K J Arrow, S Karlin, and P Suppes, editors, *Mathematical Methods in the Social Sciences, 1959*, Stanford University Press, Stanford.

—— Bowles, S, and Durlauf, S, editors, 2000, *Meritocracy and Economic Inequality*, Princeton University Press, New Jersey.

—— and Capron, W M, 1959, 'Dynamic shortages and price rises: The engineer-scientist case', *Quarterly Journal of Economics*, vol 73: 235–52.

Arthur, W B, 1983, 'Age and earnings in the labour market: Implications of the 1980s labour bulge', in P Streeten, editor, *Human Resources, Employment and Development*, Macmillan, London.

Ashenfelter, O, Harmon, C, and Oosterbeek, H, 1999, 'A review of estimates of the schooling/earnings relationship, with tests of publication bias', *Labour Economics*, vol 6: 453–70.

—— and Zimmerman, D J, 1997, 'Estimates of the returns to schooling from sibling data: Fathers, sons, and brothers', *Review of Economics and Statistics*, vol 79: 1–9.

Asher, M A and DeFina, R, 1997, 'The impact of changing union density on earnings inequality: Evidence from the private and public sectors', *Journal of Labor Research*, vol 18: 425–38.

Askenazy, P, 2005, 'Trade, services and wage inequality', *Oxford Economic Papers*, vol 57: 674–92.

Atkinson, A B, 1999, *Is Rising Inequality Inevitable? A Critique of the Transatlantic Consensus*, WIDER Annual Lecture 3, UNU/WIDER, Helsinki.

—— 1999a, 'The distribution of income in industrialized countries', in *Income Inequality: Issues and Policy Options*, Kansas City, Federal Reserve Bank of Kansas City.

—— 2000, 'The changing distribution of income: Evidence and explanations', *German Economic Review*, vol 1: 3–18.

—— 2005, 'Top incomes in the UK over the twentieth century', *Journal of the Royal Statistical Society*, series A, vol 168: 325–43.

Atkinson, A B, 2007, 'The long run earnings distribution in five countries: "remarkable stability", U, V or W?', *Review of Income and Wealth*, series 53: 1–24.

—— 2007a, 'The distribution of earnings in OECD countries', *International Labour Review*, vol 146:

—— and Brandolini, A, 2006, 'The panel-of-countries approach to explaining income inequality: An interdisciplinary research agenda', in S L Morgan, D B Grusky, and G S Fields, editors, *Mobility and Inequality*, Stanford University Press, Stanford.

—— and Micklewright, J, 1992, *Economic Transformation in Eastern Europe and the Distribution of Income*, Cambridge University Press, Cambridge.

—— and Voitchovsky, S, 2003, 'The distribution of top earnings in the UK since the Second World War', discussion paper.

Audas, R, Barmby, N, and Treble, J, 2004, 'Luck, effort, and reward in an organizational hierarchy', *Journal of Labor Economics*, vol 22: 379–95.

Auerbach, J and Beleous, R, editors, 1998, *The Inequality Paradox*, National Planning Association, Washington, DC.

Autor, D H, Katz, L F, and Krueger, A B, 1998, 'Computing inequality: Have computers changed the labor market?', *Quarterly Journal of Economics*, vol 113: 1169–213.

—— Levy, F, and Murnane, R J, 2002, 'Upstairs, downstairs: Computers and skills on two floors of a large bank', *Industrial and Labor Relations Review*, vol 55: 432–47.

—— —— and —— 2003, 'The skill content of recent technological change: An empirical exploration', *Quarterly Journal of Economics*, vol 118: 1279–333.

Baker, G P, Gibbons, R, and Murphy, K J, 1994, 'Subjective performance measures in optimal incentive contracts', *Quarterly Journal of Economics*, vol 109: 1125–56.

—— Gibbs, M, and Holmstrom, B, 1993, 'Hierarchies and compensation: A case study', *European Economic Review*, vol 37: 366–78.

—— —— and —— 1994, 'The internal economics of the firm: Evidence from personnel data', *Quarterly Journal of Economics*, vol 109: 881–919.

—— —— and —— 1994a, 'The wage policy of a firm', *Quarterly Journal of Economics*, vol 109: 921–55.

—— and Holmstrom, B, 1995, 'Internal labor markets: Too many theories, too few facts', *American Economic Review, Papers and Proceedings*, vol 85: 255–9.

—— Jensen, M C and, Murphy, K J, 1988, 'Compensation and incentives: Practice vs. theory', *Journal of Finance*, vol 43: 593–616.

Baker, M, 1997, 'Growth-rate heterogeneity and the covariance structure of life-cycle earnings', *Journal of Labor Economics*, vol 15: 338–475.

Baldwin, R E and Cain, G G, 1997, 'Shifts in relative wages: The role of trade, technology and factor endowments', NBER Working Paper 5934.

Baron, J N and Bielby, W T, 1980, 'Bringing the firms back in: Stratification, segmentation, and the organization of work', *American Sociological Review*, vol 45: 737–65.

Bartel, A P and Lichtenberg, F, 1987, 'The comparative advantage of educated workers in implementing new technology', *Review of Economics and Statistics*, vol 64: 1–11.

—— and Sicherman, N, 1999, 'Technological change and wages: An inter-industry analysis', *Journal of Political Economy*, vol 107: 285–325.

Barth, E and Zweimüller, J, 1995, 'Relative wages under decentralised and corporatist bargaining systems', *Scandinavian Journal of Economics*, vol 97: 369–84.

Bartlett, S, 1978, 'Education, experience and wage inequality: 1939–1969', *Journal of Human Resources*, vol 13: 349–65.

Bazen, S, 1991, 'The impact of the minimum wage on earnings and employment in France', *OECD Economic Studies*, vol 16: 199–221.

—— 2000, 'The impact of the regulation of low wages on inequality and labour-market adjustment: A comparative analysis', *Oxford Review of Economic Policy*, vol 16, No 1: 57–69.

Beach, C M, Finnie, R, and Gray, D, 2003, 'Earnings variability and earnings instability of women and men in Canada: How do the 1990s compare to the 1980s?', *Canadian Public Policy*, vol 29: S41–S63.

Beamish, A, Levy, F, and Murnane, R J, 1999, 'Computerization and skills: Examples from a car dealership', MIT Department of Urban Studies.

Beaudry, P and Green, D, 1998, 'What is driving U.S., and Canadian wages: Endogenous technical change or endogenous choice of technique?', NBER Working Paper 6853.

—— and —— 2000, 'Cohort patterns in Canadian earnings: Assessing the role of skill premia in inequality trends', *Canadian Journal of Economics*, vol 33: 907–36.

—— and —— 2003, 'Wages and employment in the United States and Germany: What explains the differences?', *American Economic Review*, vol 93: 573–602.

Becker, G S, 1964, *Human Capital*, Columbia University Press, New York.

—— 1967, *Human Capital and the Personal Distribution of Income*, W S Woytinsky Lecture, University of Michigan Press, Ann Arbor.

—— and Chiswick, B R, 1966, 'Education and the distribution of earnings', *American Economic Review, Papers and Proceedings*, vol 56: 358–69.

Beckmann, M J, 1978, *Rank in Organizations*, Springer Verlag, Berlin.

Behrman, J, Taubman, P, and Wales, T, 1977, 'Controlling for and measuring the effects of genetics and family environment in equations for schooling and labor market success', in P Taubman, editor, *Kinometrics*, North-Holland, Amsterdam, 35–96.

Bell, B D and Pitt, M K 1998, 'Trade union decline and the distribution of wages in the UK: Evidence from kernel density estimation', *Oxford Bulletin of Economics and Statistics*, vol 60: 509–28.

—— Hunter, L, and Danson, M, 1990, 'The distribution of earnings', in M B Gregory and A W J Thompson, editors, *A Portrait of Pay, 1970–1982*, Clarendon Press, Oxford.

Ben-Porath, Y, 1967, 'The production of human capital and the life-cycle of earnings', *Journal of Political Economy*, vol 75: 353–65.

Beramendi, P and Anderson, C J, 2005, 'Economic inequality, redistribution and political inequality', paper presented at APSA meeting.

Berger, M, 1984, 'Cohort size and the earnings growth of young workers', *Industrial and Labor Relations Review*, vol 37: 582–91.

—— 1985, 'The effect of cohort size on earnings growth: A re-examination of the evidence', *Journal of Political Economy*, vol 93: 561–73.

Bergstrand, J H et al, editors, 1994, *The Changing Distribution of Income in an Open U.S. Economy*, Elsevier, Amsterdam.

Berman, E, Bound, J, and Griliches, Z, 1994, 'Changes in the demand for skilled labor within U.S. manufacturing: Evidence from the Annual Survey of Manufactures', *Quarterly Journal of Economics*, vol 109: 367–97.

—— —— and Machin, S, 1998, 'Implications of skill-biased technological change: International evidence', *Quarterly Journal of Economics*, vol 113: 1245–80.

—— and Machin, S, 2000, 'Skill-biased technology transfer around the world', *Oxford Review of Economic Policy*, vol 16, No 3: 12–22.

Bernard, A B and Jensen, J B, 1997, 'Exporters, skill upgrading and the wage gap', *Journal of International Economics*, vol 42: 3–31.

Bernhardt, A, Morris, M, and Handcock, M, 1995, 'Women's gains or men's losses? A closer look at the shrinking gender gap in earnings', *American Journal of Sociology*, vol 101: 302–28.

Bernstein, J and Mishel, L, 1997, 'Has wage inequality stopped growing?', *Monthly Labor Review*, December, 3–16.

Bertola, G and Felli, L, 1993, 'Job matching and the distribution of producer surplus', *Richerche Economiche*, vol 47: 65–92.

—— and Ichino, A, 1995, 'Wage inequality and unemployment: United States vs. Europe', in B S Bernanke and J J Rotemberg, editors, *NBER Macroeconomics Annual 1995*, MIT Press, Cambridge.

—— and Rogerson, R, 1997, 'Institutions and labor reallocation', *European Economic Review*, vol 41: 1147–71.

Betcherman, G, 1991, 'Does technological change affect union wage bargaining power?', *British Journal of Industrial Relations*, vol 29: 447–62.

Bewley, T F, 1998, 'Why not cut pay?', *European Economic Review*, vol 42: 459–90.

—— 1999, *Why Wages Don't Fall During a Recession*, Harvard University Press, Cambridge.

Bhagwati, J and Dehejia, V, 1994, 'Free trade and wages of the unskilled: Is Marx striking again?', in J Bhagwati and M Kosters, editors, *Trade and Wages*, American Enterprise Institute, Washington, DC.

—— and Kosters, M, editors, 1994, *Trade and Wages: Leveling Wages Down?*, American Enterprise Institute, Washington, DC.

Binswanger, H, 1974, 'The measurement of technical change biases with many factors of production', *American Economic Review*, vol 64: 964–76.

Bishop, J, 1991, 'Achievements, test scores, and relative wages', in M H Kosters, editor, *Workers and Their Wages: Changing Patterns in the United States*, American Enterprise Institute, Washington, DC.

Bjerke, K, 1961, 'Some income and wage distribution theories', *Weltwirtschaftliches Archiv*, vol 86: 46–66.

—— 1970, 'Income and wage distributions, Part I: A survey of the literature', *Review of Income and Wealth*, series 16: 235–52.

Björklund, A, 2000, 'Going different ways: Labour market policy in Denmark and Sweden', in G Esping-Andersen and M Regini, editors, *Why Deregulate Labour Markets?*, Oxford University Press, Oxford.

Blackburn, M and Bloom, D, 1987, 'Earnings and income inequality in the United States', *Population and Development Review*, vol 13: 575–609.

—— —— and Freeman, R B, 1990, 'The declining position of the less-skilled American males', in G Burtless, editor, *A Future of Lousy Jobs?*, Brookings Institution, Washington, DC.

—— and Neumark, D, 1993, 'Omitted ability bias and the increase in the return to schooling', *Journal of Labor Economics*, vol 11: 521–43.

Blackburn, R, Jarman, J, and Brooks, B, 2000, 'The puzzle of gender segregation and inequality: A cross-national analysis', *European Sociological Review*, vol 16: 119–36.

Blanchard, O, 1997, *Macroeconomics*, Prentice-Hall, London.

Blanchflower, D G, 1984, 'Union wage effects: A cross-section analysis using establishment data', *British Journal of Industrial Relations*, vol 22: 311–32.

—— and Oswald, A J, 1988, 'Internal and external influences upon pay determination', *British Journal of Industrial Relations*, vol 26: 363–70.

—— and —— 1994, *The Wage Curve*, MIT Press, Cambridge.

—— —— and Garrett, M D, 1990, 'Insider power in wage determination', *Economica*, vol 57: 143–70.

—— —— and Sanfey, P, 1996, 'Wages, profits, and rent-sharing', *Quarterly Journal of Economics*, vol 111: 227–52.

Blau, F D and Beller, A H, 1988, 'Trends in earnings differentials by gender', *Industrial and Labor Relations Review*, vol 41: 513–29.

—— and Kahn, L M, 1992, 'The gender earnings gap: Learning from international comparisons', *American Economic Review, Papers and Proceedings*, vol 82: 533–8.

—— and —— 1994, 'Rising wage inequality and the U.S. gender gap', *American Economic Review*, vol 84: 23–8.

—— and —— 1995, 'The gender earnings gap: Some international evidence', in R B Freeman and L F Katz, editors, *Differences and Changes in Wage Structures*, University of Chicago Press, Chicago.

—— and —— 1996, 'International differences in male wage inequality: Institutions versus market forces', *Journal of Political Economy*, vol 104: 791–36.

—— and —— 1997, 'Swimming upstream: Trends in the gender wage differential in the 1980s', *Journal of Labor Economics*, vol 15: 1–42.

—— and —— 2000, 'Gender differences in pay', *Journal of Economic Perspectives*, vol 14, No 4: 75–99.

Blinder, A S, 1976, 'On dogmatism in human capital theory', *Journal of Human Resources*, vol 11: 8–22.

Bluestone, B, 1994, 'Old theories in new bottles: Toward an explanation of growing world-wide income inequality', in J H Bergstrand et al, editors, *The Changing Distribution of Income in an Open U.S. Economy*, Elsevier, Amsterdam.

—— and Harrison, B, 1988, *The Great U-Turn: Corporate Restructuring and the Polarizing of America*, Basic Books, New York.

Bluestone, B and Harrison, B, 1988a, 'The growth of low-wage employment 1963–1986', *American Economic Review, Papers and Proceedings*, vol 78:

Bonhomme, S and Robin, J-M, 2004, 'Modeling individual earnings trajectories using copulas with an application to the study of earnings inequality: France, 1990–2002', discussion paper, CREST, Paris.

Booth, A L, 1995, *The Economics of the Trade Union*, Cambridge University Press, Cambridge.

—— 1993, 'Private sector training and graduate earnings', *Review of Economics and Statistics*, vol 76: 164–70.

Borjas, G, 1999, 'The economic analysis of immigration', in O Ashenfelter and D Card, editors, *Handbook of Labor Economics*, vol 3A, North-Holland, Amsterdam.

—— Freeman, R B, and Katz, L F, 1997, 'How much do immigration and trade affect labor market outcomes?' *Brookings Papers on Economic Activity*, vol 1: 1–90.

—— and Ramey, V, 1994, 'Time-series evidence on the sources of trends in wage inequality', *American Economic Review, Papers and Proceedings*, vol 84: 10–16.

—— and —— 1994a, 'The relationship between wage inequality and international trade', in J H Bergstrand et al, editors, *The Changing Distribution of Income in an Open U.S. Economy*, Elsevier, Amsterdam.

—— and —— 1995, 'Foreign competition, market power and wage inequality', *Quarterly Journal of Economics*, vol 110: 1075–110.

Borland, J, 1997, 'Earnings and inequality in Australia', RSSS Annual Report, Australian National University, Canberra.

—— and Wilkins, R, 1996, 'Earning inequality in Australia', *Economic Record*, vol 72: 7–23.

Bosch, G, 2004, 'Towards a new standard employment relationship in Western Europe', *British Journal of Industrial Relations*, vol 42: 617–36.

Boudarbat, B, Lemieux, T, and Riddell, W C, 2003, 'Recent trends in wage inequality and the wage structure in Canada', discussion paper, University of British Columbia.

Bound, J, Brown, C, Duncan, G, and Rodgers, W, 1990, 'Measurement error in cross-sectional and longitudinal labor market surveys: Results from two validation studies', in J Hartog et al, editors, *Panel Data and Labor Market Studies*, North-Holland, Amsterdam.

—— Griliches, Z, and Hall, B H, 1986, 'Wages, schooling and IQ of brothers and sisters: Do family factors differ?', *International Economic Review*, vol 27: 77–105.

—— and Johnson, G, 1991, 'Wages in the United States during the 1980s and beyond', in M Kosters, editor, *Workers and their Wages*, American Enterprise Institute, Washington, DC.

—— and —— 1992, 'Changes in the structure of wages in the 1980s: An evaluation of alternative explanations', *American Economic Review*, vol 82: 371–92.

—— and Krueger, A B, 1991, 'The extent of measurement error in longitudinal earnings data: Do two wrongs make a right?', *Journal of Labor Economics*, vol 9: 1–24.

Bover, O, Bentolila, S, and Arellano, M, 2002, 'The distribution of earnings in Spain during the 1980s: The effects of skill, unemployment, and union power', in D Cohen, T Piketty, and G Saint-Paul, editors, *The Economics of Rising Inequalities*, Oxford University Press, Oxford.

Bowles, S and Gintis, H, 1976, *Schooling in Capitalist America*, Basic Books, New York.

—— —— and Osborne, M, 2001, 'The determinants of individual earnings: Skills, preferences and schooling', *Journal of Economic Literature*, vol 39: 1137–76.

—— —— and —— 2001a, 'Incentive-enhancing preferences: Personality, behavior and earnings', *American Economic Review, Papers and Proceedings*, vol 91: 155–8.

—— and Nelson, V L, 1974, ' "The inheritance of IQ" and the intergenerational reproduction of economic inequality', *Review of Economics and Statistics*, vol 56: 39–51.

Boyer, G R, 1988, 'What did unions do in nineteenth-century Britain?', *Journal of Economic History*, vol 48: 319–32.

—— and Hatton, T J, 1994, 'Did Joseph Arch raise agricultural wages? Rural trade unions and the labour market in late-nineteenth-century England', *Economic History Review*, vol 47: 310–34.

Brandolini, A, Cipollone, P, and Sestito, P, 2002, 'Earnings dispersion, low pay and household poverty in Italy, 1977–98', in D Cohen, T Piketty, and G Saint-Paul, editors, *The Economics of Rising Inequalities*, Oxford University Press, Oxford.

Brandt, M, Burniaux, J M, and Duval, R, 2005, 'Assessing the OECD Jobs Strategy: Past developments and reforms', Economics Department Working Paper 429, OECD, Paris.

Bratsberg, B and Ragan, J F, 1997, 'Have unions implied growing wage dispersion among young workers?', *Journal of Labor Research*, vol 18: 593–612.

Brauer, D A and Hickok, S, 1995, 'Explaining the growing inequality in wages across skill levels', *Economic Policy Review*, vol 1: 61–75.

Brenton, P and Pinna, A M, 2002, 'Trends in disaggregated import and export prices in Europe: Implications for the trade and wages debate', *Scottish Journal of Political Economy*, vol 49: 1–21.

Bresnahan, T F, 1999, 'Computerisation and wage dispersion', *Economic Journal*, vol 109: F390–F415.

—— Brynjolfson, E, and Hitt, L M, 2002, 'Information technology, workplace organization and the demand for skilled labor: Firm-level evidence', *Quarterly Journal of Economics*, vol 107: 339–76.

Brittain, J A, 1972, *The Payroll Tax for Social Security*, The Brookings Institution, Washington, DC.

Brown, C, 1980, 'Equalizing differences in the labor market', *Quarterly Journal of Economics*, vol 94: 113–34.

—— 1999, 'Minimum wages, employment and the distribution of income', in O Ashenfelter and D Card, editors, *Handbook of Labor Economics*, vol 3B, North-Holland, Amsterdam.

—— Gilroy, C, and Kohen, A, 1982, 'The effect of the minimum wage on employ-ment and unemployment', *Journal of Economic Literature*, vol 20: 487–528.

Brown, C, and Medoff, J L, 1989, 'The employer size wage effect', *Journal of Political Economy*, vol 97: 1027–59.

—— and —— 2003, 'Firm age and wages', *Journal of Labor Economics*, vol 21: 677–97.

Brown, J N, 1989, 'Why do wages rise with seniority?', *American Economic Review*, vol 79: 971–91.

Brown, W A, 1976, 'Incomes policies and pay differentials', *Oxford Bulletin of Economics and Statistics*, vol 38: 27–49.

—— 1979, 'Engineering wages and the Social Contract 1975–77', *Oxford Bulletin of Economics and Statistics*, vol 41: 51–61.

Bry, G, 1960, *Wages in Germany, 1871–1945*, Princeton University Press, Princeton.

Buch, H and Rühmann, P, 1998, 'Atypical work as a form of low-wage employment in the German labour market', in S Bazen, M Gregory, and W Salverda, editors, *Low-Wage Employment in Europe*, Edward Elgar, Cheltenham.

Buchinsky, M, 1994, 'Changes in the U.S. wage structure 1963 to 1987: An application of quantile regression', *Econometrica*, vol 62: 405–58.

—— and Hunt, J, 1999, 'Wage mobility in the United States', *Review of Economics and Statistics*, vol 81: 351–68.

Buckberg, E and Thomas, A, 1996, 'Wage dispersion in the 1980s: Resurrecting the role of trade through the effects of durable employment changes', *IMF Staff Papers*, vol 43: 336–54.

Bulow, J and Summers, L H, 1986, 'A theory of dual labor markets with applications to industrial policy, discrimination and Keynesian unemployment', *Journal of Labor Economics*, vol 4: 376–414.

Burdett, K and Mortensen, D T, 1998, 'Wage differentials, employer size, and unemployment', *International Economic Review*, vol 39: 257–73.

Burfisher, M E, Robinson, S, and Thierfelder, K E, 1994, 'Wage changes in a US–Mexico free trade area: Migration versus Stolper–Samuelson effects', in J Francois and C R Shiells, editors, *Modelling Trade Policy*, Cambridge University Press, Cambridge.

Burkhauser, R V, Feng, S, and Jenkins, S P, 2007, 'Using the P90/P10 index to measure US inequality trends with Current Population Survey data: A view from inside the Census Bureau vaults', ISER Working Paper 2007–14, University of Essex, Colchester.

Burtless, G, editor, 1990, *A Future of Lousy Jobs?*, Brookings Institution, Washington, DC.

—— 1990a, 'Earnings inequality over the business and demographic cycles', in G Burtless, editor, *A Future of Lousy Jobs?*, Brookings Institution, Washington, DC.

—— 1995, 'International trade and the rise in earnings inequality', *Journal of Economic Literature*, vol 33: 800–16.

—— 1998, 'Technological change and international trade: How well do they explain the rise in U.S. income inequality?', in J Auerbach and R Beleous, editors, *The Inequality Paradox*, National Planning Association, Washington, DC.

—— 1999, 'Effects of growing wage disparities and changing family composition on the U.S. income distribution', *European Economic Review*, vol 43: 853–65.

—— 2007, 'Income progress across the American income distribution, 2000–2005', Testimony for the Committee on Finance, US Senate, 10 May 2007.

Butcher, K and Case, A, 1994, 'The effect of sibling sex composition on women's education and earnings', *Quarterly Journal of Economics*, vol 109: 531–63.

Calvo, G A and Wellisz, S, 1979, 'Hierarchy, ability and income distribution', *Journal of Political Economy*, vol 87: 991–1010.

Cameron, D R, 1984, 'Social democracy, corporatism, labour quiescence and the representation of economic interest', in J H Goldthorpe, editor, *Order and Conflict in Contemporary Capitalism*, Oxford University Press, Oxford.

Cantó, O, Cardoso, A R, and Jimeno, J F, 2002, 'Earnings inequality in Portugal and Spain: Contrasts and similarities', in D Cohen, T Piketty, and G Saint-Paul, editors, *The Economics of Rising Inequalities*, Oxford University Press, Oxford.

Cao, M and Shi, S, 2000, 'Coordination, matching, and wages', *Canadian Journal of Economics*, vol 33: 1009–33.

Cappelli, P, 1996, 'Technology and skill requirements: Implications for establishment wage structures', *New England Economic Review*, May–June: 139–54.

Card, D, 1995, 'Earnings, schooling and ability revisited', *Research in Labor Economics*, vol 14: 23–48.

—— 1996, 'The effect of unions on the structure of wages: A longitudinal analysis', *Econometrica*, vol 64: 957–79.

—— 1996a, 'Deregulation and labor earnings in the airline industry', NBER Working Paper 5687.

—— and DiNardo, J E, 2002, 'Skill-biased technological change and rising wage inequality: Some problems and puzzles', *Journal of Labor Economics*, vol 20: 733–83.

—— and Krueger, A, 1995, *Myth and Measurement: The New Economics of the Minimum Wage*, Princeton University Press, Princeton.

—— Kramarz, F, and Lemieux, T, 1999, 'Changes in the structure of wages and employment: A comparison of the United States, Canada and France', *Canadian Journal of Economics*, vol 32: 705–46.

—— and Lemieux, T, 2001, 'Can falling supply explain the rising return to college for younger men? A cohort-based analysis', *Quarterly Journal of Economics*, vol 116: 1449–92.

Caroli, E, 2001, 'New technologies, organizational change and the skill bias: What do we know?', in P Petit and L Soete, editors, *Technology and the Future Employment of Europe*, Edward Elgar, London.

—— and van Reenen, J, 2001, 'Skill-biased organizational change? Evidence from a panel of British and French establishments', *Quarterly Journal of Economics*, vol 116: 1449–92.

Carruth, A A and Oswald, A J, 1989, *Pay Determination and Industrial Prosperity*, Clarendon Press, Oxford.

Cawley, J, Heckman, J J, and Vytlacil, E, 1999, 'Meritocracy in America: Wages within and across occupations', *Industrial Relations*, vol 38: 250–96.

—— —— and —— 2001, 'Three observations on wages and measured cognitive ability', *Labour Economics*, vol 8: 419–42.

Centre d'Etudes des Revenus et des Coûts (CERC), 1976, *Dispersion et disparité de salaires en France au cours des vingt dernières années*, Document 25/26, Paris.

—— 1990, *Formation, mobilité et disparités de salaires depuis quarante ans*, Notes et Graphiques, No 10, Paris.

Chamberlain, G, 1993, 'Quantile regressions, censoring and the structure of wages', in C Sims, editor, *Advances in Econometrics*, vol 1, Cambridge University Press, Cambridge.

Chater, R E J, 1981, 'The differentials dilemma', in R E H Chater, A Dean, and R F Elliott, editors, *Incomes Policy*, Clarendon Press, Oxford.

Chennells, L and van Reenen, J, 1997, 'Technical change and earnings in British establishments', *Economica*, vol 64: 587–604.

—— and —— 1998, 'Establishment level earnings, technology and the growth of inequality: Evidence from Britain', *Economics of Innovation and New Technologies*, vol 5: 139–64.

—— and —— 2000, 'The effects of technical change on skills, wages, and employment: A survey of the micro-economic evidence', in J Mairesse and N Greenan, editors, *Information and Communication Technologies: Productivity, Employment and Earnings*, MIT Press, Cambridge.

Chiswick, B R, 1968, 'Schooling and intra-regional income inequality', *American Economic Review*, vol 58: 495–500.

—— 1974, *Income Inequality: Regional Analysis within a Human Capital Framework*, Columbia University Press, New York.

—— and Mincer, J, 1972, 'Time-series changes in personal income inequality in the United States from 1939, with projections to 1985', *Journal of Political Economy*, vol 80: S34–S66.

Chowdhury, G and Nickell, S J, 1985, 'Individual earnings data in the US: Another look at unionization, schooling, sickness, and unemployment using panel data', *Journal of Labor Economics*, vol 3: 38–69.

Christofides, L N and Oswald, A J, 1992, 'Real wage determination and rent-sharing in collective bargaining agreements', *Quarterly Journal of Economics*, vol 107: 985–1002.

Cohen, D, Piketty, T, and Saint-Paul, G, editors, 2002, *The Economics of Rising Inequalities*, Oxford University Press, Oxford.

Cohn, E and Kahn, S P, 1995, 'The wage effects of overschooling revisited', *Labour Economics*, vol 2: 67–76.

Colbjørnsen, T and Kalleberg, A L, 1988, 'Spillover, standardisation and stratification: Earnings determination in the United States and Norway', *European Sociological Review*, vol 4: 20–31.

Coles, S, 2001, *An Introduction to Statistical Modeling of Extreme Values*, Springer Verlag, London.

Connor, W D, 1979, *Socialism, Politics and Equality: Hierarchy and Change in Eastern Europe and the USSR*, Columbia University Press, New York.

Corcoran, M, Gordon, R, Laren, D, and Solon, G, 1992, 'The association between men's economic status and their family and community origins', *Journal of Human Resources*, vol 27: 575–601.

—— Jencks, C, and Olneck, M, 1976, 'The effects of family background on earnings', *American Economic Review*, vol 66: 430–35.

Cornia, G A, 2003, 'The impact of liberalization and globalization on income inequality in developing and transitional economies', CES/Ifo Working Paper 843.

Cotton, J, 1988, 'On the decomposition of wage differentials', *Review of Economics and Statistics*, vol 70: 236–43.

Cowell, F A and Mehta, F, 1982, 'The estimation and interpolation of inequality measures', *Review of Economic Studies*, vol 49: 273–90.

Creedy, J and Hart, P E, 1979, 'Age and the distribution of earnings', *Economic Journal*, vol 89: 280–93.

Cullen, D E, 1956, 'The inter-industry wage structure, 1899–1950', *American Economic Review*, vol 46: 353–69.

Dalmazzo, A and Scaramozzino, P, 2000, 'It takes two to tango: Process integration and wages', University of Siena.

Davis, D R, 1998, 'Does European unemployment prop up American wages? National labor markets and global trade', *American Economic Review*, vol 88: 478–94.

—— 1998a, 'Technology, unemployment and relative wages in a global economy', *European Economic Review*, vol 42: 1613–33.

Davis, S J, 1992, 'Cross-country patterns of change in relative wages', in O J Blanchard and S Fischer, editors, *NBER Macroeconomic Annual*, MIT Press, Cambridge.

—— and Haltiwanger, J, 1991, 'Wage dispersion within and between manufacturing plants', *Brookings Papers on Economic Activity: Microeconomics*, 115–80.

—— and —— 1996, 'Employer Size and the wage structure in U.S. manufacturing', *Annales d'Economie et Statistique*, No 41/42: 323–67.

—— and Topel, R H, 1993, 'International trade and American wages in the 1980s: Giant sucking sound or small hiccup? Comment', *Brookings Papers on Economic Activity*, issue 2: 214–21.

Dean, A J H, 1978, 'Incomes policies and differentials', *National Institute Economic Review*, August: 40–8.

Dearden, L, 1999, 'The effects of families and ability on men's education and earnings in Britain', *Labour Economics*, vol 6: 551–67.

Deardorff, A and Hakura, D, 1994, 'Trade and wages: What are the questions?', in J Bhagwati and M Kosters, editors, *Trade and Wages*, American Enterprise Institute, Washington, DC.

Desjonqueres, T, Machin, S, and van Reenen, J, 1999, 'Another nail in the coffin? Or can the trade based explanation of changing skill structures be resurrected?', *Scandinavian Journal of Economics*, vol 101: 533–54.

Dewatripont, M, Sapir, A, and Sekkat, K, 1999, *Trade and Jobs in Europe*, Oxford University Press, Oxford.

Diamond, P A, 1982, 'Wage determination and efficiency in search equilibrium', *Review of Economic Studies*, vol 49: 217–27.

Dickens, R, Machin, S, and Manning, A, 1994, 'Estimating the effect of minimum wages on employment from the distribution of wages: A critical review', Centre for Economic Performance Discussion Paper No 203, London School of Economics.

Dickens, W T and Katz, L F, 1987, 'Inter-industry wage differences and industry characteristics', in K Lang and J S Leonard, editors, *Unemployment and the Structure of Labour Markets*, Blackwell, Oxford.

—— and Lang, K, 1987, 'Where have all the good jobs gone? Deindustrialization and labour market segmentation', in K Lang and J S Leonard, editors, *Unemployment and the Structure of Labour Markets*, Blackwell, Oxford.

Dillon, P and Gang, I, 1987, 'Earnings effects of labor organizations in 1890', *Industrial and Labor Relations Review*, vol 40: 501–15.

DiNardo, J, Fortin, N, and Lemieux, T, 1996, 'Labour market institutions and the distribution of wages, 1977–1992', *Econometrica*, vol 64: 1001–44.

—— and Lemieux, T, 1997, 'Diverging male wage inequality in the United States and Canada, 1981–1988: Do institutions explain the difference?', *Industrial and Labor Relations Review*, vol 50: 629–51.

—— and Pischke, J-S, 1997, 'The returns to computer use revisited: Have pencils changed the wage structure too?', *Quarterly Journal of Economics*, vol 112: 291–303.

DiPrete, T A, de Graaf, P M, Luijkx, R, Tahlin, M, and Blossfeld, H-P, 1997, 'Collect-ivist versus individualist mobility regimes? Structural change and job mobility in four countries', *American Journal of Sociology*, vol 103: 318–58.

Dixon, S, 1998, 'Growth in the dispersion of earnings: 1984–97', *Labour Market Bulletin* 1&2: 71–107.

Doeringer, P B and Piore, M, 1971, *Internal Labor Market and Manpower Analysis*, D C Heath, Lexington.

Doms, M, Dunn, T, and Troske, K, 1997, 'Workers, wages and technology', *Quarterly Journal of Economics*, vol 112: 253–90.

Donald, S G, Green, D A, and Paarsch, H J, 2000, 'Differences in wage distributions between Canada and the United States: An application of a flexible estimator of distribution functions in the presence of covariates', *Review of Economic Studies*, vol 67: 609–33.

Dugé de Bernonville, L, 1912–13, 'Distribution des salaires et de revenus en divers pays', *Bulletin de la Statistique Générale de la France*, vol 2: 400–36.

Duguet, E and Greenan, N, 1997, 'Skill biased technical change: An econometric study at the firm level', *Revue Economique*, vol 48: 1061–89.

Duncan, G J and Hill, D, 1985, 'An investigation of the extent and consequences of measurement error in labor-economic survey data', *Journal of Labor Economics*, vol 3: 508–32.

—— and Hoffman, S D, 1981, 'The incidence and wage effects of overeducation', *Economics of Education Review*, vol 1: 75–86.

—— and Mathiowetz, N, 1985, *A Validation Study of Economic Survey Data*, University of Michigan Survey Research Center, Ann Arbor.

—— and Stafford, F P, 1980, 'Do union members receive compensating wage differ-entials?', *American Economic Review*, vol 70: 355–71.

Dunlop, J and Rothbaum, M, 1955, 'International comparisons of wage structures', *International Labour Review*, vol 71: 347–63.

Dunne, T, Foster, L, Haltiwanger, J, and Troske, K R, 2004, 'Wage and productivity dispersion in United States manufacturing: The role of computer investment', *Journal of Labor Economics*, vol 22: 397–429.

—— and Schmitz, J A, 1995, 'Wages, employment structure and employer size-wage premia: Their relationship to advanced-technology usage at U.S. manufacturing establishments', *Economica*, vol 62: 89–107.

Dustmann, C and Meghir, C, 1998, 'Wages, experience and seniority', IFS Discussion Paper.

Edin, P-A and Holmlund, B, 1995, 'The Swedish wage structure: The rise and fall of solidarity wage policy', in R B Freeman and L F Katz, editors, *Differences and Changes in Wage Structures*, University of Chicago Press, Chicago.

—— and Topel, R H, 1997, 'Wage policy and restructuring: The Swedish labor market since 1960', in R B Freeman, B Swedenborg, and R H Topel, editors, *The Welfare State in Transition*, University of Chicago Press, Chicago.

—— and Zetterberg, J, 1992, 'Interindustry wage differentials: Evidence from Sweden and a comparison with the United States', *American Economic Review*, vol 82: 1341–9.

Eichengreen, B J, 1987, 'The impact of late nineteenth century unions on labor earnings and hours: Iowa in 1894', *Industrial and Labor Relations Review*, vol 40: 501–15.

Eicher, T S, 1996, 'Interaction between endogenous human capital and technological change', *Review of Economic Studies*, vol 63: 127–44.

Embrechts, P, Klüppelberg, C, and Mikosch, T, 1997, *Modelling Extremal Events*, Springer Verlag, Berlin.

Entorf, H, Gollac, M, and Kramarz, F, 1999, 'New technologies, wages and worker selection', *Journal of Labor Economics*, vol 17: 464–91.

—— and Kramarz, F, 1997, 'Does unmeasured ability explain the higher wage of new technology workers?', *European Economic Review*, vol 41: 1489–510.

—— and ——, 1998, 'The impact of new technologies on wages and skills: Lessons from matching data on employees and their firms', *Economics of Innovation and New Technologies*, vol 5: 169–97.

Erickson, C L and Ichino, A C, 1995, 'Wage differentials in Italy: Market forces, institutions and inflation', in R B Freeman and L F Katz, editors, *Differences and Changes in Wage Structures*, University of Chicago Press, Chicago.

Eriksson, T and Jäntti, M, 1997, 'The distribution of earnings in Finland 1971–1990', *European Economic Review*, vol 41: 1736–79.

European Commission, 2005, *Employment in Europe 2005*, European Commission, Brussels.

Evans, D S and Leighton, L S, 1989, 'Why do smaller firms pay less?', *Journal of Human Resources*, vol 24: 299–318.

Farber, H and Gibbons, R, 1997, 'Learning and wage dynamics', *Quarterly Journal of Economics*, vol 112: 907–40.

Feenstra, R C and Hanson, G H, 1996, 'Globalization, outsourcing and wage inequality', *American Economic Review*, vol 86: 240–5.

Feenstra, R C and Hanson, G H, 1996a, 'Foreign investment, outsourcing and relative wages', in R C Feenstra, G M Grossman, and D A Irwin, editors, *The Political Economy of Trade Policy*, MIT Press, Cambridge.

—— and —— 1999, 'Productivity measurement and the impact of trade and technology on wages: Estimates for the US, 1972–1990', *Quarterly Journal of Economics*, vol 114: 1007–47.

Fehr, E and Schmidt, K M, 1999, 'A theory of fairness, competition, and cooperation', *Quarterly Journal of Economics*, vol 114: 817–68.

Felli, L and Harris, C, 1996, 'Learning, wage dynamics, and firm-specific human capital', *Journal of Political Economy*, vol 104: 838–68.

Fernandez, R, 2001, 'Skill-biased technological change and wage inequality: Evidence from a plant retooling', *American Journal of Sociology*, vol 107: 273–320.

Flabbi, L and Ichino, A, 2001, 'Productivity, seniority and wages: New evidence from personnel data', *Labour Economics*, vol 8: 359–87.

Flakierski, H, 1979, 'Economic reform and income distribution in Hungary', *Cambridge Journal of Economics*, vol 3: 15–32.

—— 1986, *Economic Reform and Income Distribution*, M E Sharpe, Armonk.

Flemming, J S and Micklewright, J, 2000, 'Income distribution, economic systems and transition', in A B Atkinson and F Bourguignon, editors, *Handbook of Income Distribution*, North-Holland, Amsterdam.

Flinn, C, 1986, 'Wages and job mobility of young workers', *Journal of Political Economy*, vol 94: S88–S110.

Flinn, C J, 2002, 'Labour market structure and welfare: A comparison of Italy and the U.S.', *Review of Economic Studies*, vol 69: 611–45.

Fogarty, M P, 1959, 'The white-collar pay structure in Britain', *Economic Journal*, vol 69: 55–70.

Forslund, A, 1994, 'Wage setting at the firm level: Insider versus outsider forces', *Oxford Economic Papers*, vol 46: 245–61.

Fortin, N and Lemieux, T, 1995, 'Rank regressions, wage distributions, and the gender gap', *Journal of Human Resources*, vol 33: 610–43.

—— and —— 1997, 'Institutional changes and rising wage inequality: Is there a linkage?', *Journal of Economic Perspectives*, vol 11, No 2: 75–96.

—— and —— 2000, 'Are women's wage gains men's losses? A distributional test', *American Economic Review, Papers and Proceedings*, vol 90: 456–60.

Fourastié, J, 1979, *Les Trentes Glorieuses, ou la révolution invisible de 1946 à 1975*, Fayard, Paris.

Frank, R H, 1984, 'Are workers paid their marginal products?', *American Economic Review*, vol 74: 549–71.

—— and Cook, P J, 1995, *The Winner Take-All Society*, Free Press, New York.

Freeman, R B, 1976, *The Overeducated American*, Academic Press, New York.

—— 1979, 'The effect of demographic factors on the age–earnings profile in the United States', *Journal of Human Resources*, vol 14: 289–318.

—— 1980, 'Unionism and the dispersion of wages', *Industrial and Labor Relations Review*, vol 34: 3–23.

—— 1982, 'Union wage practices and wage dispersion within establishments', *Industrial and Labor Relations Review*, vol 36: 3–21.

—— 1984, 'Longitudinal analyses of the effects of trade unions', *Journal of Labor Economics*, vol 2: 1–26.

—— 1993, 'How much has de-unionization contributed to the rise in male earnings inequality?', in S Danziger and P Gottschalk, editors, *Uneven Tides*, Russell Sage, New York.

—— 1995, 'Are your wages set in Beijing?', *Journal of Economic Perspectives*, vol 9, No 3: 15–32.

—— 1996, 'The minimum wage as a redistributive tool', *Economic Journal*, vol 108: 639–49.

—— 1996a, 'Labor market institutions and earnings inequality', *New England Economic Review*, May/June: 157–68.

—— and Katz, L F, 1994, 'Rising wage inequality: The United States versus other advanced countries', in R B Freeman, editor, *Working Under Different Rules*, Russell Sage Foundation, New York.

—— and —— 1995, editors, *Differences and Changes in Wage Structures*, University of Chicago Press, Chicago.

—— and Medoff, J L, 1984, *What Do Unions Do?*, Basic Books, New York.

—— and Needles, K, 1993, 'Skill differentials in Canada in an era of rising labor market inequality', in D Card and R Freeman, editors, *Small Differences that Matter*, University of Chicago Press, Chicago.

Friedman, M, 1953, 'Choice, chance, and the personal distribution of income', *Journal of Political Economy*, vol 61: 277–90.

—— and Kuznets, S, 1945, *Income from Independent Professional Practice*, National Bureau of Economic Research, New York.

Friez, A and Julhès, M, 1998, *Séries Longues sur les Salaires*, Emploi-Revenus, No 36 (Paris: INSEE).

Galor, O and Moav, O, 2000, 'Ability biased technological transition, wage inequality within and across groups, and economic growth', *Quarterly Journal of Economics*, vol 115: 469–98.

—— and Tsiddon, D, 1997, 'Technological progress, mobility, and economic growth', *American Economic Review*, vol 87: 363–82.

Garen, J E, 1985, 'Worker heterogeneity, job screening and firm size', *Journal of Political Economy*, vol 93: 715–39.

Gaston, N and Nelson, D, 2000, 'Immigration and labour-market outcomes in the United States: A political-economy puzzle', *Oxford Review of Economic Policy*, vol 16, No 3: 104–14.

Geroski, P A and Stewart, M B, 1986, 'Specification-induced uncertainty in the estimation of trade union wage differentials from industry-level data', *Economica*. vol 53: 29–39.

Gibbons, R and Katz, L, 1992, 'Does unmeasured ability explain inter-industry wage differentials?', *Review of Economic Studies*, vol 59: 515–35.

Gibbs, M, 1994, 'Testing tournaments? An appraisal of the theory and the evidence', *Labor Law Journal*, vol 45: 493–500.

Giles, C, Gosling, A, Laisney, F, and Geib, T, 1998, *The Distribution of Income and Wages in the UK and West Germany 1982–1992*, IFS Research Report, London.

Gintis, H, 1971, 'Education, technology, and the characteristics of worker productivity', *American Economic Review, Papers and Proceedings*, vol 61: 266–79.

Goldin, C and Katz, L F, 1995, 'The decline of non-competing groups: Changes in the premium to education, 1890 to 1940', NBER Working Paper 5202.

—— and —— 1996, 'Technology, skill, and the wage structure: Insights from the past', *American Economic Review, Papers and Proceedings*, vol 86: 252–7.

—— and —— 1998, 'The origins of technology-skill complementarity', *Quarterly Journal of Economics*, vol 113: 693–732.

—— and —— 1999, 'The returns to skill in the United States across the twentieth century', NBER Working Paper 7126.

—— and —— 2000, 'Education and income in the early twentieth century: Evidence from the Prairies', *Journal of Economic History*, vol 60: 782–818.

—— and —— 2001, 'The legacy of U.S. educational leadership: Notes on distribution and economic growth in the 20th Century', *American Economic Review, Papers and Proceedings*, vol 91: 18–23.

—— and Margo, R, 1992, 'The Great Compression: The wage structure in the United States at mid-century', *Quarterly Journal of Economics*, vol 107: 1–34.

Goldthorpe, J H, 1984, 'The end of convergence: Corporatist and dualist tendencies in modern Western societies', in J H Goldthorpe, editor, *Order and Conflict in Contemporary Capitalism*, Oxford University Press, Oxford.

Görg, H, Hijzen, A, and Hine, R C, 2001, 'International fragmentation and relative wages in the UK', Research Paper 2001/33, GEP, Nottingham.

Gosling, A, Johnson, P, McCrae, J, and Paull, J, 1997, *The Dynamics of Low Pay and Unemployment in Early 1990s Britain*, Institute for Fiscal Studies, London.

—— and Machin, S, 1995, 'Trade unions and the dispersion of earnings in UK establishments, 1980–90', *Oxford Bulletin of Economics and Statistics*, vol 57: 167–84.

—— —— and Meghir, C, 1994, 'What has happened to wages?', IFS Commentary No 43.

—— —— and —— 1994a, 'What has happened to the wages of men since the mid-1960s?', *Fiscal Studies*, vol 15: 63–87.

—— —— and —— 1996, 'What has happened to the wages of men since 1966?' in J Hills, editor, *New Inequalities*, Cambridge University Press, Cambridge.

—— —— and —— 2000, 'The changing distribution of male wages in the U.K.', *Review of Economic Studies*, vol 67: 635–66.

Gottschalk, P, 1997, 'Inequality in income, growth and mobility: the basic facts', *Journal of Economic Perspectives*, vol 11, No 2: 21–40.

—— and Danziger, S, 2005, 'Inequality of wage rates, earnings and family income in the United States, 1975–2002', *Review of Income and Wealth*, series 51: 231–54.

—— and Joyce, M, 1992, 'Is earnings inequality also rising in other industrialized countries?', Boston College Working Paper No 223.

—— and —— 1998, 'Cross-national differences in the rise in earnings inequality: Market and institutional factors', *Review of Economics and Statistics*, vol 80: 489–502.

—— and Smeeding, T M, 1997, 'Cross-national comparisons of earnings and income inequality', *Journal of Economic Literature*, vol 35: 633–87.

Gould, E D, 2002, 'Rising wage inequality, comparative advantage, and the growing importance of general skills in the United States', *Journal of Labor Economics*, vol 20: 105–47.

—— Moav, O, and Weinberg, B A, 2001, 'Precautionary demand for education, inequality, and technological progress', *Journal of Economic Growth*, vol 6: 285–315.

Goux, D and Maurin, E, 1999, 'Persistence of inter-industry wage differentials: A reexamination on matched worker–firm panel data', *Journal of Labor Economics*, vol 17: 492–533.

—— and —— 2000, 'The decline in demand for unskilled labour: An empirical method and its application to France', *Review of Economics and Statistics*, vol 82: 596–607.

Green, F, 1988, 'The trade union wage gap in Britain: Some new estimates', *Economics Letters*, vol 27: 183–7.

Green, G, Coder, J, and Ryscavage, P, 1992, 'International comparisons of earnings inequality for men in the 1980s', *Review of Income and Wealth*, series 38: 1–16.

Greenaway, D, Reed, G V, and Winchester, N, 2002, 'Trade and rising wage inequality in the UK: Results from a CGE analysis', GEP Research Paper 2002/29, University of Nottingham.

Greenwood, J, Hercowitz, Z, and Krusell, P, 1997, 'Long-run implications of investment-specific technological change', *American Economic Review*, vol 87: 342–62.

—— and Yorukoglu, M, 1997, '1974', *Carnegie–Rochester Conference Series on Public Policy*, vol 46: 49–95.

Griliches, Z, 1969, 'Capital-skill complementarity', *Review of Economics and Statistics*, vol 51: 465–8.

—— and Mason, W M, 1972, 'Education, income and ability', *Journal of Political Economy*, vol 80: S74–S103.

Grill, P and Quiquerez, G, 1998, 'Sentiment d'equité et effort', GREQAM Document de Travail No 98C08, Universités d'Aix-Marseille II and III.

Grogger, J and Eide, E, 1995, 'Changes in college skills and the rise in the college wage premium', *Journal of Human Resources*, vol 30: 280–310.

Groot, W, 1996, 'The incidence of, and returns to, overeducation in the UK', *Applied Economics*, vol 28: 1345–50.

Groshen, E, 1991, 'Sources of wage dispersion: How much do employers matter?', *Quarterly Journal of Economics*, vol 106: 869–84.

—— 1991a, 'The structure of the female/male wage differential: Is it who you are, what you do, or where you work?', *Journal of Human Resources*, vol 26: 457–72.

Groshen, E L, 1991, 'Rising inequality in a salary survey: Another piece of the puzzle' Federal Reserve Bank of Cleveland Working Paper 9121.

Groshen, E L, 1996, 'American employer salary surveys and labor economics research', *Annales d'Economie et de Statistique*, vol 41/2: 412–42.

Grubb, D, 1985, 'Earnings inequality in OECD countries', preliminary version, London School of Economics.

—— 1985a, 'Ability and power over production in the distribution of earnings', *Review of Economics and Statistics*, vol 67: 188–94.

Grund, C, 2002, 'The wage policy of firms—comparative evidence for the U.S. and Germany from personnel data', IZA Discussion Paper 685.

Guiso, L, Jappelli, T, and Pistaferri, L, 1998, 'What determines earnings and employment risk?', Working Paper No 8, Centre for Studies in Economics and Finance, University of Salerno.

Gustavsson, M, 2004, 'Trends in the transitory variance of earnings: Evidence from Sweden 1960–1990 and a comparison with the United States', Working Paper 2004:11, Department of Economics, Uppsala Universitet.

Haider, S J, 2001, 'Earnings instability and earnings inequality of males in the United States: 1967–1991', *Journal of Labor Economics*, vol 19: 799–836.

Haisken-DeNew, J P and Schmidt, C M, 1997, 'Inter-industry and inter-region wage differentials', *Review of Economics and Statistics*, vol 79: 516–21.

Hall, B J and Liebman, J B, 1998, 'Are CEOs paid like bureaucrats?', *Quarterly Journal of Economics*, vol 113: 653–91.

Haller, M, 1987, 'Positional and sectoral differences in income: Germany, France and the USA', *International Journal of Sociology*, vol 17: 172–90.

Hamlen, W A, Jr, 1991, 'Superstardom in popular music: Empirical evidence', *Review of Economics and Statistics*, vol 73: 729–33.

Handcock, M S, Morris, M, and Bernhardt, A, 2000, 'Comparing earnings inequality using two major surveys', *Monthly Labor Review*, March, 48: 61.

Handel, M and Levine, D I, 2004, 'Editor's introduction: The effect of new work practices on workers', *Industrial Relations*, vol 43: 1–43.

Harkness, S, 1996, 'The gender earnings gap: Evidence from the UK', *Fiscal Studies*, vol 17: 1–36.

—— Machin, S, and Waldfogel, J, 1996, 'Women's pay and family incomes in Britain 1979–1991', in J Hills, editor, *New Inequalities*, Cambridge University Press, Cambridge.

Harrigan, J, 2000, 'International trade and American wages in general equilibrium, 1967–1995', in R C Feenstra, editor, *The Impact of International Trade on Wages*, University of Chicago Press, Chicago.

Hartog, J, 1986, 'Allocation and the earnings function', *Empirical Economics*, vol 1: 97–110.

—— and Oosterbeek, H, 1988, 'Education, allocation and earnings in the Netherlands: Overschooling', *Economics of Education Review*, vol 7: 185–94.

—— Opstal, R van, and Teulings, C, 1997, 'Inter-industry wage differentials and tenure effects in the Netherlands and the US', *De Economist*, vol 145: 91–9.

Haskel, J, 1999, 'Small firms, contracting-out, computers and wage inequality: Evidence from UK manufacturing', *Economica*, vol 66: 1–21.

—— and Heden, Y, 1999, 'Computers and the demand for skilled labour: Industry and establishment panel evidence for the UK', *Economic Journal*, vol 109: 68–79.

—— and Slaughter, M E, 1998, 'Does the sector bias of skill-biased technical change explain changing wage inequality?', *European Economic Review*, vol 46: 1757–83.

—— and —— 2001, 'Trade, technology and UK wage inequality', *Economic Journal*, vol 111: 163–87.

Hatton, T J, Boyer, G R, and Bailey, R E, 1994, 'The union wage effect in late nineteenth century Britain', *Economica*, vol 61: 435–56.

Hause, J, 1980, 'The fine structure of earnings and the on-the-job training hypothesis', *Econometrica*, vol 48: 1013–29.

Haveman, R H and Buron, L, 1994, 'The growth in male earnings inequality, 1973–1988: The role of earnings capacity and utilization', in J H Bergstrand et al, editors, *The Changing Distribution of Income in an Open U.S. Economy*, Elsevier, Amsterdam.

Heckman, J J and Honore, B, 1990, 'The empirical content of the Roy model', *Econometrica*, vol 58: 1121–49.

—— and Krueger, A B, 2004, *Inequality in America: What Role for Human Capital Policies?*, MIT Press, Cambridge.

—— Layne-Farrar, A, and Todd, P, 1996, 'Human capital pricing equations with an application to estimating the effect of schooling quality on earnings', *Review of Economics and Statistics*, vol 78: 563–610.

—— Lochner, L, and Taber, C, 1998, 'Explaining rising wage inequality: Explorations with a dynamic general equilibrium model of labor earnings with heterogeneous agents', *Review of Economic Dynamics*, vol 1: 1–58.

—— and Polachek, S, 1974, 'Empirical evidence on the functional form of the earnings–schooling relationship', *Journal of the American Statistical Association*, vol 69: 350–4.

—— and Robb, R, 1985, 'Using longitudinal data to estimate age, period and cohort effects in earnings equations', in W M Mason and S E Feinberg, editors, *Cohort Analysis in Social Research*, Springer-Verlag, New York.

Hedström, P, 1991, 'Organizational differentiation and earnings dispersion', *American Journal of Sociology*, vol 97: 96–113.

Hendricks, W, 1994, 'Deregulation and labor earnings', *Journal of Labor Research*, vol 15: 207–34.

Henle, P, 1972, 'Exploring the distribution of earned income', *Monthly Labor Review*, vol 95, December: 16–27.

—— and Ryscavage, P, 1980, 'The distribution of earned income among men and women, 1958–1977', *Monthly Labor Review*, vol 103, issue 4: 3–10.

Hibbs, D A, 1990, 'Wage dispersion and trade union action in Sweden', in I Persson, editor, *Generating Equality in the Welfare State*, Norwegian University Press, Oslo.

—— and Locking, H, 2000, 'Wage dispersion and productive efficiency: Evidence for Sweden', *Journal of Labor Economics*, vol 18: 755–82.

Hildreth, A and Oswald, A, 1997, 'Rent-sharing and wages: Evidence from company and establishment panels', *Journal of Labor Economics*, vol 15: 318–37.

Hill, T P, 1959, 'An analysis of the distribution of wages and salaries in Great Britain', *Econometrica*, vol 27: 355–81.

Hirsch, B T, 1988, 'Trucking regulation, unionization, and labor earnings: 1973–85', *Journal of Human Resources*, vol 23: 296–317.

Hodson, R, 1984, *Workers' Earnings and Corporate Economic Structure*, Academic Press, New York.

Holmlund, B and Zetterberg, J, 1991, 'Insider effects in wage determination', *European Economic Review*, vol 35: 1009–34.

Holzer, H, Katz, L, and Krueger, A, 1991, 'Job queues and wages', *Quarterly Journal of Economics*, vol 106: 739–68.

Horrigan, M W and Mincy R B, 1993, 'The minimum wage and earnings and income inequality', in S Danziger and P Gottschalk, editors, *Uneven Tides*, Russell Sage, New York.

Hosios, A, 1990, 'On the efficiency of matching and related models of search and unemployment', *Review of Economic Studies*, vol 57: 279–98.

Houthakker, H, 1972, 'The size distribution of labour incomes derived from the distribution of aptitudes', in W Sellekaerts, editor, *Selected Readings in Econometrics and Economic Theory: Essays in Honour of Jan Tinbergen*, Macmillan, London.

Howell, D R, Houston, E, and Milberg, W, 1999, 'Demand shifts and earnings inequality: Wage and hours growth by occupation in the U.S., 1970–97', CEPA Working Paper 6, New School for Social Research.

—— and Wieler, S S, 1998, 'Skill-biased demand shifts and the wage collapse in the United States', *Eastern Economic Journal*, vol 24: 343–66.

—— and Wolff, E N, 1991, 'Trends in the growth and distribution of skills in the U.S. workplace, 1960–1985', *Industrial and Labor Relations Review*, vol 41: 486–502.

Ichniowski, C and Shaw, K, 2003, 'Beyond incentive pay: Insiders' estimates of the value of complementary human resource management practices', *Journal of Economic Perspectives*, vol 17: 155–80.

Idson, T L and Feaster, D J, 1990, 'A selectivity model of employer size–wage differentials', *Journal of Labor Economics*, vol 8: 99–122.

Ishikawa, T, 1981, 'Dual labour market hypothesis and long-run income distribution', *Journal of Development Economics*, vol 9: 1–30.

Iversen, T and Wren, A, 1998, 'Equality, employment and budgetary restraint', *World Politics*, vol 46: 527–55.

Jacobs, B, 2004, 'The lost race between schooling and technology', *De Economist*, vol 152: 47–78.

Jakubson, G, 1991, 'Estimation and testing of the union wage effect using panel data', *Review of Economic Studies*, vol 58: 971–91.

Jensen, M C and Murphy K J, 1990, 'CEO incentives: It's not how much you pay, but how', *Harvard Business Review*, May–June: 138–53.

Johnson, G E, 1997, 'Changes in earnings inequality: The role of demand shifts', *Journal of Economic Perspectives*, vol 11, No 2: 41–54.

—— and Stafford, F P, 1993, 'International competition and real wages', *American Economic Review*, vol 83: 127–31.

Jones A F and Weinberg, D H, 2000, 'The changing shape of the nation's income distribution, 1947–1998', Current Population Report P60–204, US Census Bureau, Washington, DC.

Jorgenson, D W and Pachon, A, 1983, 'Lifetime income and human capital', in P Streeten and H Maier, editors, *Human Resources, Employment, and Development*, vol 2, Macmillan, London.

Juhn, C, 1994, 'Wage inequality and industrial change: Evidence from five decades', NBER Working Paper 4684.

—— and Murphy, K M, 1997, 'Wage inequality and family labor supply', *Journal of Labor Economics*, vol 15: 72–97.

—— —— and Pierce, B, 1993, 'Wage inequality and the rise in returns to skill', *Journal of Political Economy*, vol 101: 410–42.

Kahn, J A and Lim, J-S, 1998, 'Skilled labor-augmenting technical progress in U.S. manufacturing', *Quarterly Journal of Economics*, vol 113: 1281–308.

Kahn, L M, 1998, 'Collective bargaining and the interindustry wage structure: International evidence', *Economica*, vol 65: 507–34.

—— and Curme, M, 1987, 'Unions and nonunion wage dispersion', *Review of Economics and Statistics*, vol 69: 600–7.

Kalachek, E and Raines, F, 1976, 'The structure of wage differences among mature male workers', *Journal of Human Resources*, vol 11: 484–506.

Kalleberg, A L, 1988, 'Comparative perspectives on work structures and inequality', *Annual Review of Sociology*, vol 14: 203–25.

—— and Sørensen, A B, 1979, 'The sociology of labor markets', *Annual Review of Sociology*, vol 5: 351–79.

—— Wallace, M, and Althauser, R P, 1981, 'Economic segmentation, worker power and income inequality', *American Journal of Sociology*, vol 87: 651–83.

Karoly, L A, and Burtless, G, 1995, 'Demographic change, rising earnings inequality and the distribution of personal well-being, 1959–1989', *Demography*, vol 32: 379–405.

Katz, L F, 1986, 'Efficiency wage theories: A partial evaluation', in S Fischer, editor, *NBER Macroeconomics Manual 1986*, MIT Press, Cambridge.

—— and Autor, D H, 1999, 'Changes in the wage structure and earnings inequality', in O Ashenfelter and D Card, editors, *Handbook of Labor Economics*, vol 3A, North-Holland, Amsterdam.

—— Loveman, G, and Blanchflower, D, 1995, 'An international comparison of changes in the structure of wages: France, the United Kingdom and the United States', in R Freeman and L Katz, editors, *Differences and Changes in Wage Structures*, University of Chicago Press, Chicago.

—— and Murphy, K M, 1992, 'Changes in relative wages, 1963–1987: Supply and demand factors', *Quarterly Journal of Economics*, vol 107: 35–78.

—— and Revenga, A L, 1989, 'Changes in the structure of wages: The United States vs. Japan', *Journal of the Japanese and International Economies*, vol 3: 522–53.

—— and Summers, L H, 1989, 'Industry rents: Evidence and implications', *Brookings Papers on Economic Activity: Microeconomics*, 207–75.

Keating, M, 2003, 'The labour market and inequality', *Australian Economic Review*, vol 36: 374–96.

Kenworthy, L, 2004, *Egalitarian Capitalism*, Russell Sage Foundation, New York.

Kiley, M T, 1999, 'The supply of skilled labour and skill-biased technological progress', *Economic Journal*, vol 109: 708–24.

Kosters, M, editor, 1991, *Workers and their Wages: Changing Patterns in the United States*, American Enterprise Institute, Washington, DC.

—— 1998, *Wage Levels and Inequality*, American Enterprise Institute, Washington, DC.

Kremer, M and Maskin, E, 1996, 'Wage inequality and segregation by skill', NBER Working Paper 5718.

Krueger, A B, 1993, 'How computers changed the wage structure: Evidence from micro data', *Quarterly Journal of Economics*, vol 108: 33–60.

—— and Summers, L H, 1987, 'Reflections on the inter-industry wage structure', in K Lang and J S Leonard, editors, *Unemployment and the Structure of Labour Markets*, Blackwell, Oxford.

—— and —— 1988, 'Efficiency wages and the inter-industry wage structure', *Econometrica*, vol 56: 259–94.

Krugman, P, 1994, 'Past and prospective causes of high unemployment', in *Reducing Unemployment: Current Issues and Policy Options*, Kansas City, Federal Reserve Bank of Kansas City.

—— 1995, 'Growing world trade: Causes and consequences', *Brookings Papers*, 1: 327–62.

—— and Lawrence, R Z, 1993, 'Trade, jobs and wages', *Scientific American*, 270(4): 44–9.

Krusell, P, Ohanian, L E, Rios-Rull, J-V, and Violante, L, 2000, 'Capital-skill complementarity and inequality: A macroeconomic analysis', *Econometrica*, vol 68: 1029–53.

Kuznets, S, 1955, 'Economic growth and income inequality', *American Economic Review*, vol 45: 1–28.

Lawler, E E and O'Gara, P W, 1967, 'The effect of inequity produced by underpayment on work output, work quality, and attitude toward work', *Journal of Applied Psychology*, vol 51: 407–10.

Lawrence, R Z and Slaughter, M J, 1993, 'International trade and American wages in the 1980s: Giant sucking sound or small hiccup?', *Brookings Papers on Economic Activity*, issue 2: 161–210.

Lazear, E P, 1976, 'Age, experience and wage growth', *American Economic Review*, vol 66: 548–58.

—— 1989, 'Pay equality and industrial politics', *Journal of Political Economy*, vol 97: 561–80.

—— 1999, 'Personnel economics: Past lessons and future directions', *Journal of Labor Economics*, vol 17: 199–236.

—— 2000, 'Performance pay and productivity', *American Economic Review*, vol 90: 1346–61.

—— and Rosen, S, 1981, 'Rank-order tournaments as optimum labor contracts', *Journal of Political Economy*, vol 89: 841–64.

Leamer, E E, 1996, 'Wage inequality from international competition and technological change: Theory and country experience', *American Economic Review, Papers and Proceedings*, vol 86: 309–14.

Lee, D S, 1999, 'Wage inequality in the U.S. during the 1980s: Rising dispersion or falling minimum wage?', *Quarterly Journal of Economics*, vol 114: 977–1023.

Lemieux, T, 1993, 'Unions and wage inequality in Canada and the United States', in D Card and R Freeman, editors, *Small Differences that Matter*, University of Chicago Press, Chicago.

—— 1998, 'Estimating the effects of unions on wage inequality in a panel data model with comparative advantage and non-random selection', *Journal of Labor Economics*, vol 16: 261–91.

—— 2006, 'Increasing residual wage inequality: Composition effects, noisy data, or rising demand for skill?', *American Economic Review*, vol 96: 461–98.

Lester, R A, 1952, 'A range theory of wage differentials', *Industrial and Labor Relations Review*, vol 5: 483–500.

Leuven, E, Oosterbeek, H, and van Ophem, H, 2004, 'Explaining international differences in male skill wage differentials by differences in demand and supply of skill', *Economic Journal*, vol 114: 466–86.

Levine, D I, 1991, 'Fairness, markets, and ability to pay: Evidence from compensation executives', *American Economic Review*, vol 81: 1241–59.

—— 1991a, 'Cohesiveness, productivity, and wage dispersion', *Journal of Economic Behavior and Organization*, vol 15: 237–55.

Levy, F and Murnane, R J, 1992, 'U.S. earnings levels and earnings inequality: A review of recent trends and proposed explanations', *Journal of Economic Literature*, vol 30: 1333–81.

—— and —— 1996, 'With what skills are computers a complement?', *American Economic Review*, vol 86: 258–62.

Lewis, H G, 1986, *Union Relative Wage Effects: A Survey*, University of Chicago Press, Chicago.

Lillard, L A, 1977, 'Inequality: Earnings vs. human wealth', *American Economic Review*, vol 67: 42–53.

—— Smith, J P, and Welch, F, 'What do we really know about wages? The importance of nonreporting and census imputation', *Journal of Political Economy*, vol 94: 489–506.

—— and Weiss, Y, 1979, 'Components of variation in panel earnings data: American scientists 1960–70', *Econometrica*, vol 47: 437–54.

—— and Willis, R J, 1978, 'Dynamic aspects of earnings mobility', *Econometrica*, vol 46: 985–1012.

Lindbeck, A and Snower, D J, 1990, 'Interindustry wage structure and the power of incumbent workers', in R Brunetta and C Dell' Aringa, editors, *Labour Relations and Economic Performance*, Macmillan, London.

Lindbeck, A and Snower, D J, 1996, 'Reorganization of firms and labor market inequality', *American Economic Review, Papers and Proceedings*, vol 86: 315–21.

—— and —— 2000, 'Multitask learning and the reorganization of work: From tayloristic to holistic organization', *Journal of Labor Economics*, vol 18: 353–76.

Lloyd-Ellis, H, 1999, 'Endogenous technological change and wage inequality', *American Economic Review*, vol 89: 47–77.

Loury, G C, 1981, 'Intergenerational transfers and the distribution of earnings', *Econometrica*, vol 49: 843–67.

Loveman, G W and Tilly, C, 1988, 'Good jobs or bad jobs: What does the evidence say?', *New England Economic Review*, Jan–Feb: 46–65.

Lucas, R E B, 1977, 'Is there a human capital approach to income inequality?', *Journal of Human Resources*, vol 12: 387–95.

Lucifora, C, 2000, 'Wage inequalities and low pay: The role of labour market institutions', in M Gregory, W Salverda, and S Bazen, editors, *Labour Market Inequalities*, Edward Elgar: Cheltenham.

Lücke, M, 1999, 'Trade with low-income countries and the relative wages and employment opportunities of the unskilled: An exploratory analysis for West Germany and the UK', in P Brenton and J Pelkmans, editors, *Global Trade and European Workers*, Macmillan, London.

Lydall, H F, 1959, 'The distribution of employment incomes', *Econometrica*, vol 27: 110–15.

—— 1968, *The Structure of Earnings*, Clarendon Press, Oxford.

MacDonald, G M, 1988, 'The economics of rising stars', *American Economic Review*, vol 78: 155–66.

MacLeod, W B and Malcomson, J M, 1998, 'Motivation and markets', *American Economic Review*, vol 88: 388–411.

Machin, S, 1996, 'Wage inequality in the UK', *Oxford Review of Economic Policy*, vol 12, No 1: 47–64.

—— 1996a, 'Changes in the relative demands for skills', in A Booth and D J Snower, editors, *Acquiring Skills*, Cambridge University Press, Cambridge.

—— 1997, 'The decline in labour market institutions and the rise of wage inequality in Britain', *European Economic Review*, vol 41: 647–57.

—— 1999, 'Wage inequality in the 1970s, 1980s and 1990s', in P Gregg and J Wadsworth, editors, *The State of Working Britain*, Manchester University Press, Manchester.

—— 2001, 'The changing nature of labour demand in the new economy and skill biased technology change', *Oxford Bulletin of Economics and Statistics*, vol 63: 753–76.

—— 2003, 'Wage inequality since 1975', in R Dickens, P Gregg, and J Wadsworth, editors, *The Labour Market under New Labour*, Macmillan, London.

—— and Manning, A, 1994, 'Minimum wages, wage dispersion, and employment: Evidence from the UK wages councils', *Industrial and Labor Relations Review*, vol 47: 319–29.

—— and van Reenen, J, 1998, 'Technology and changes in skill structure: Evidence from seven OECD countries', *Quarterly Journal of Economics*, vol 113: 1215–44.

Macunovich, D J, 1998, 'Relative cohort size and inequality in the United States', *American Economic Review*, vol 88: 259–64.

Maddison, A, 2005, 'Measuring and interpreting world economic performance 1500–2001', *Review of Income and Wealth*, series 51: 1–35.

Mahler, V, Jesuit, D, and Roscoe, D, 1999, 'Exploring the impact of trade and investment on income inequality', *Comparative Political Studies*, vol 32: 363–95.

Main, B G M and Reilly, B, 1992, 'Women and the union wage gap', *Economic Journal*, vol 102: 49–66.

—— O'Reilly, C A and Wade, J, 1993, 'Top executive pay: Tournament or teamwork?', *Journal of Labor Economics*, vol 11: 606–28.

Manacorda, M, 2004, 'Can the Scala Mobile explain the fall and rise of earnings inequality in Italy? A Semiparametric Analysis, 1977–1993', *Journal of Labor Economics*, vol 22: 585–613.

Manasse, P and Turrini, A, 1999, 'Trade, wages and superstars', *Journal of International Economics*, vol 54: 97–117.

Mandelbrot, B, 1962, 'Paretian distributions and income maximization', *Quarterly Journal of Economics*, vol 76: 57–85.

Manning, A, 1994, 'Labour markets with company wage policies', Discussion Paper 214, Centre for Economic Performance, LSE, London.

—— 2003, *Monopsony in Motion*, Princeton University Press, Princeton.

March, L, 1898, 'Quelques exemples de distribution des salaires', *Journal de la Société Statistique de Paris*, vol 39: 193–206.

Margolis, D, 1996, 'Cohort effects and returns to seniority in France', *Annales d'Economie et de Statistique*, vol 41/2: 443–64.

Marshall, A, 1920, *Principles of economics: An introductory volume*, 8th edition, Macmillan, London.

Mayer, T, 1960, 'The distribution of ability and earnings', *Review of Economics and Statistics*, vol 42: 189–95.

Mellow, W, 1981, 'Unionism and wage rates: A longitudinal analysis', *Review of Economics and Statistics*, vol 63: 43–52.

—— 1982, 'Employer size and wages', *Review of Economics and Statistics*, vol 64: 495–501.

—— and Sider, H, 1983, 'Accuracy of response in labor market surveys: Evidence and implications', *Journal of Labor Economics*, vol 1: 331–44.

Mendez, R, 2002, 'Creative destruction and the rise of inequality', *Journal of Economic Growth*, vol 7: 259–81.

Metcalf, D H, 1982, 'Unions and the distribution of earnings', *British Journal of Industrial Relations*, vol 20: 163–9.

—— 2007, 'Why has the British national minimum wage had little or no impact on employment?', CEP Discussion Paper 781, London School of Economics.

—— Hansen, K, and Charlwood, A, 2000, 'Unions and the Sword of Justice: Unions and Pay Systems, Pay Inequality, Discrimination and Low Pay', CEP Discussion Paper 452.

Meyers, F, 1950, 'Notes on changes in the distribution of manufacturing wage earners by straight-time hourly earnings, 1941–48', *Review of Economics and Statistics*, vol 32: 352–5.

Miller, H P, 1958, *Income of the American People*, John Wiley, New York.

—— 1968, *Income Distribution in the United States*, Bureau of the Census, Washington, DC.

Miller, P, Mulvey, C, and Martin, N, 1997, 'Family characteristics and the returns to schooling: Evidence on gender differences from a sample of Australian twins', *Economica*, vol 64: 119–36.

Mincer, J, 1958, 'Investment in human capital and personal income distribution', *Journal of Political Economy*, vol 66: 281–301.

—— 1970, 'The distribution of labor incomes: A survey with special reference to the human capital approach', *Journal of Economic Literature*, vol 8: 1–26.

—— 1974, *Schooling, Experience and Earnings*, Columbia University Press, New York.

—— 1991, 'Human capital, technology and the wage structure: What do time series show?', NBER Working Paper 3581.

Mittag, H-J, 2007, 'Earnings disparities across European countries and regions', *Statistics in Focus*, 7/2007.

Moene K O and Wallerstein, M, 1997, 'Pay inequality', *Journal of Labor Economics*, vol 15: 403–30.

Montgomery, J D, 1991, 'Equilibrium wage dispersion and interindustry wage differentials', *Quarterly Journal of Economics*, vol 106: 163–79.

Morris, M and Western, B, 1999, 'Inequality in earnings at the close of the twentieth century', *Annual Review of Sociology*, vol 25: 623–57.

Mortensen, D and Pissarides, C, 1994, 'Job creation and job destruction in the theory of unemployment', *Review of Economic Studies*, vol 61: 397–415.

Muller, E N, 1989, 'Distribution of income in advanced capitalist states: Political parties, labor unions, and the international economy', *European Journal of Political Research*, vol 17: 367–400.

Murnane, R, Willet, J, and Levy, F, 1995, 'The growing importance of cognitive skills in wage determination', *Review of Economics and Statistics*, vol 77: 251–66.

Murphy, K J, Plant, M, and Welch, F, 1988, 'Cohort size and earnings in the United States', in R Lee, editor, *Economics of Changing Age Distributions in Developed Countries*, Clarendon Press, Oxford.

—— Riddell, W C, and Romer, P M, 1998?, 'Wages, skill and technology in the United States and Canada', in E Helpman, editor, *General Purpose Technologies*, MIT Press, Cambridge.

Murphy, K M and Topel, R H, 1987, 'Unemployment, risk and earnings: Testing for equalizing wage differences in the labour market', in K Lang and J S Leonard, editors, *Unemployment and the Structure of Labour Markets*, Blackwell, Oxford.

—— and Welch, F, 1989, 'Wage premiums for college graduates: Recent growth and possible explanations', *Educational Researcher*, vol 18: 17–26.

—— and —— 1990, 'Empirical age–earnings profiles', *Journal of Labor Economics*, vol 8: 202–29.

—— and —— 1992, 'The structure of wages', *Quarterly Journal of Economics*, vol 107: 285–326.

—— and —— 1993, 'Occupational change and the demand for skill, 1940–1990', *American Economic Review, Papers and Proceedings*, vol 83: 122–6.

—— and ——1993a, 'Industrial change and the rising importance of skill', in S Danziger and P Gottschalk, editors, *Uneven Tides*, Russell Sage, New York.

Neugart, M and Tuinstra, J, 2004, 'Endogenous fluctuations in the demand for education', *Journal of Evolutionary Economics*, vol 13: 29–51.

Nevile, J W and Saunders, P, 1998, 'Globalization and the return to education in Australia', *Economic Record*, vol 74: 279–85.

Nickell, S J and Bell, B, 1996, 'Changes in the distribution of wages and unemployment in OECD Countries', *American Economic Review, Papers and Proceedings*, vol 86: 302–9.

—— Vainiomaki, J, and Wadhwani, S, 1994, 'Wages and product market power', *Economica*, vol 61: 457–73.

OECD, 1993, *Employment Outlook*, OECD, Paris.

—— 1994, *The Jobs Study*, OECD, Paris.

—— 1996, *Employment Outlook*, OECD, Paris.

—— 1997, *Employment Outlook*, OECD, Paris.

Oi, W and Idson, T, 1999, 'Firm size and wages', in O Ashenfelter and D Card, editors, *Handbook of Labor Economics*, vol 3B, North-Holland, Amsterdam.

O'Neill, J and Polachek, S, 1993, 'Why the gender gap in wages narrowed in the 1980s', *Journal of Labor Economics*, vol 11: 205–28.

Ortín-Ángel, P and Salas-Fumás, V, 2002, 'Compensation and span of control in hierarchical organizations', *Journal of Labor Economics*, vol 20: 848–76.

Osberg, L, 1977, 'Stochastic process models and the distribution of earnings', *Review of Income and Wealth*, series 23: 205–15.

Oster, G, 1979, 'A factor analytic test of the theory of the dual economy', *Review of Economics and Statistics*, vol 61: 33–9.

Osterman, P, 1975, 'An empirical study of labour market segmentation', *Industrial and Labor Relations Review*, vol 28: 508–23.

Oswald, A J, 1985, 'The economic theory of the trade union', *Scandinavian Journal of Economics*, vol 87: 160–93.

—— and Turnbull, P, 1985, 'Pay and employment determination in Britain: What are labour contracts really like?', *Oxford Review of Economic Policy*, 80–97.

Pencavel, J, 1991, *Labour Markets under Trade Unionism*, Basil Blackwell, Oxford.

—— and Hartsog, C E, 1984, 'A reconsideration of the effects of unionism on relative wages and employment in the United States, 1920–1980', *Journal of Labor Economics*, vol 2: 193–232.

Peoples, J H, 1989/90, 'Wage outcomes following the divestiture of AT&T', *Information Economics and Policy Journal*, vol 4: 105–26.

—— editor, 1998, *Regulatory Reform and Labor Markets*, Kluwer, Boston.

Petersen, T, 1989, 'The earnings function in sociological studies of earnings inequality: Functional form and hours worked', *Research in Social Stratification and Mobility*, vol 8: 221–50.

Pettengill, J S, 1979, 'Labour unions and the wage structure: A general equilibrium analysis', *Review of Economic Studies*, vol 46: 675–93.

Pettengill, J S, 1980, *Labor Unions and the Inequality of Earned Incomes*, North-Holland, Amsterdam.

Petzina, D, 1977, *Die deutsche Wirtschaft in der Zwischenkriegszeit*, Franz Steiner Verlag, Wiesbaden.

Pfeffer, J and Davis-Blake, A, 1992, 'Salary dispersion, location in the salary distribution, and turnover among college administrators', *Industrial and Labor Relations Review*, vol 45: 753–63.

Phelps Brown, E H, 1977, *The Inequality of Pay*, Oxford University Press, Oxford.

—— 1979, 'The inequalities of earnings— an unexplained uniformity', Seventh Joan Woodward Memorial Lecture, Imperial College, London.

Pierce, B, 2001, 'Compensation inequality', *Quarterly Journal of Economics*, vol 116: 1493–525.

Piketty, T, 2001, *Les hauts revenus en France au 20ème siècle*, Grasset, Paris.

—— 2003, 'Income inequality in France, 1901–1998', *Journal of Political Economy*, vol 111: 1004–42.

—— and Saez, E, 2003, 'Income inequality in the United States', *Quarterly Journal of Economics*, vol 118: 1–39.

—— and —— 2007, 'Income and wage inequality in the United States, 1913–2002', in A B Atkinson and T Piketty, editors, *Top Incomes over the Twentieth Century*, Oxford University Press, Oxford.

Pontusson, J, Rueda, D, and Way, C R, 2002, 'Comparative political economy of wage distribution: The role of partisanship and labour market institutions', *British Journal of Political Science*, vol 32: 281–308.

Postlewaite, A, 1997, 'The social basis of interdependent preferences', CARESS Working Paper 97-14, University of Pennsylvania.

Prasad, E S, 2004, 'The unbearable stability of the German wage structure: Evidence and interpretation', *IMF Staff Papers*, vol 51: 354–85.

Pudney, S, 1994, 'Earnings inequality in Hungary: A comparative analysis of household and enterprise survey data', *Economics of Planning*, vol 27: 251–76.

Ransom, M R, 1993, 'Seniority and monopsony in the academic labor market', *American Economic Review*, vol 83: 221–33.

Rao, M J M and Datta, R C, 1985, 'Human capital and hierarchy', *Economics of Education Review*, vol 4: 67–76.

Reder, M W, 1962, 'WAGES: Structure', *International Encyclopedia of the Social Sciences*, vol 16, Macmillan, New York.

—— 1968, 'The size distribution of earnings', in J Marchal and B Ducros, editors, *The Distribution of National Income*, Macmillan, London.

—— 1969, 'A partial survey of the theory of income size distribution', in L Soltow, editor, *Six Papers on the Size Distribution of Income and Wealth*, Columbia University Press, New York.

Revanga, A, 1992, 'Exporting jobs? The impact of import competition on employment and wages in U.S. manufacturing', *Quarterly Journal of Economics*, vol 107: 255–84.

Richardson, J D, 1995, 'Income inequality and trade: How to think, what to conclude', *Journal of Economic Perspectives*, vol 9, No 3: 33–55.

Riddell, W C, 1995, 'Unionization in Canada and the United States: A tale of two countries', in D Card and R Freeman, editors, *Small Differences that Matter*, University of Chicago Press, Chicago.

Ritzen, J M M, 1977, *Education, Economic Growth and Income Distribution*, North-Holland, Amsterdam.

Roberts, D R, 1956, 'A general theory of executive compensation based on statistically tested propositions', *Quarterly Journal of Economics*, vol 70: 270–94.

Rose, N L, 1987, 'Labor rent and regulation: Evidence from the trucking industry', *Journal of Political Economy*, vol 95: 1146–78.

Rosen, S, 1978, 'Substitution and division of labour', *Economica*, vol 45: 235–50.

—— 1981, 'The economics of superstars', *American Economic Review*, vol 71: 845–58.

—— 1982, 'Authority, control, and the distribution of earnings', *Bell Journal of Economics*, vol 13: 311–23.

—— 1986, 'The theory of equalizing differences', in O Ashenfelter and R Layard, editors, *Handbook of Labor Economics*, vol 1, North-Holland, Amsterdam.

—— 1986a, 'Prizes and incentives in elimination tournaments', *American Economic Review*, vol 76: 701–15.

Rosenbaum, J E, 1980, 'Hierarchical and individual effects on earnings', *Industrial Relations*, vol 19: 1–14.

Rosenfeld, R A and Kalleberg, A L, 1990, 'A cross-national comparison of the gender gap in income', *American Journal of Sociology*, vol 96: 69–106.

Rotemberg, J J, 2002, 'Perceptions of equity and the distribution of income', *Journal of Labor Economics*, vol 20: 249–88.

Routh, G, 1965, *Occupation and Pay in Great Britain 1906–60*, Cambridge University Press, Cambridge.

—— 1980, *Occupation and Pay in Great Britain 1906–79*, Macmillan, London.

—— 1980a, 'The morals of pay', in Routh, G, Wedderburn, D, and Wootton, B, *The Roots of Pay Inequalities*, Low Pay Unit Discussion Series No 1.

Rowthorn, R E, 1992, 'Corporatism and labour market performance', in J Pekkarinen, M Pohjola, and R E Rowthorn, editors, *Social Corporatism: A Superior Economic System?*, Clarendon Press, Oxford.

Roy, A D, 1950, 'The distribution of earnings and individual output', *Economic Journal*, vol 60: 489–505.

—— 1951, 'Some thoughts on the distribution of earnings', *Oxford Economic Papers*, vol 3: 235–46.

Rubery, J, 1978, 'Structured labour markets, worker organization and low pay', *Cambridge Journal of Economics*, vol 2: 17–36.

Rueda, D and Pontusson, J, 2000, 'Wage inequality and varieties of capitalism', *World Politics*, vol 52: 350–83.

Rumberger, R W, 1987, 'The impact of surplus schooling on productivity and earning', *Journal of Human Resources*, vol 22: 1–50.

Rutkowski, J, 2001, 'Earnings inequality in transition economies of Central Europe: Trends and patterns during the 1990s', World Bank SP Discussion Paper 0117.

Sachs, J D and Shatz, H J, 1994, 'Trade and jobs in U.S. manufacturing', *Brookings Papers on Economic Activity*, 1–84.

Sahota, G S, 1978, 'Theories of personal income distribution', *Journal of Economic Literature*, vol 16: 1–55.

Salverda, W, 1998, 'Incidence and evolution of low-wage employment in the Netherlands and the United States, 1979–1989', in S Bazen, M Gregory, and W Salverda, editors, *Low-Wage Employment in Europe*, Edward Elgar, Cheltenham.

Sattinger, M, 1975, 'Comparative advantage and the distribution of earnings and abilities', *Econometrica*, vol 43: 455–68.

—— 1979, 'Differential rents and the distribution of earnings', *Oxford Economic Papers*, vol 31: 60–71.

—— 1980, *Capital and the Distribution of Labor Earnings*, North-Holland, Amsterdam.

—— 1993, 'Assignment models of distribution of earnings', *Journal of Economic Literature*, vol 31: 831–80.

Saunders, C T and Marsden, D, 1981, *Pay Inequalities in the European Communities*, Butterworth, London.

Schelling, T, 1978, *Micromotives and Macrobehavior*, Norton, New York.

Schlicht, E, 1998, *On Custom in the Economy*, Clarendon Press, Oxford.

Scitovsky, T, 1966, 'An international comparison of the trend of professional earnings', *American Economic Review*, vol 56: 25–42.

Seiver, D A, 1979, 'A note on the measurement of income inequality with interval data', *Review of Income and Wealth*, series 25: 229–33.

Shah, A, 1984, 'Job attributes and the size of the union/non-union differential', *Economica*, vol 51: 437–46.

Shi, S, 2002, 'Product market and the size–wage differential', *International Economic Review*, vol 43: 21–54.

—— 2002a, 'A directed search model of inequality with heterogeneous skills and skill-biased technology', *Review of Economic Studies*, vol 69: 467–91.

—— and Wen, Q, 1999, 'Labour market search and the dynamic effects of taxes and subsidies', *Journal of Monetary Economics*, vol 43: 457–95.

Sicherman, N, 1991, 'Overeducation in the labor market', *Journal of Labor Economics*, vol 9: 101–22.

—— and Galor, O, 1990, 'A theory of career mobility', *Journal of Political Economy*, vol 98: 169–92.

Siegel, D S, 1999, *Skill-Biased Technological Change*, W E Upjohn Institute, Kalamazoo.

Simon, H A, 1957, 'The compensation of executives', *Sociometry*, vol 20: 32–5.

Slaughter, M, 1998, 'International trade and labour market outcomes: Results, questions and policy options', *Economic Journal*, vol 108: 1452–62.

—— 1999, 'Globalization and wages: A tale of two perspectives', *The World Economy*, vol 22: 609–30.

Slichter, S H, 1950, 'Notes on the structure of wages', *Review of Economics and Statistics*, vol 32: 80–91.

Sloane, PJ and Theodossiou, I, 1996, 'Earnings mobility, family income and low pay', *Economic Journal*, vol 106: 657–66.

Slottje, D J, 1989, *The Structure of Earnings and the Measurement of Income Inequality in the U.S.*, North-Holland, Amsterdam.

Snower, D, 1999, 'Causes of changing earnings inequality', in *Income Inequality: Issues and Policy Options*, Kansas City, Federal Reserve Bank of Kansas City.

Solow, R M, 1990, *The Labour Market as a Social Institution*, Basil Blackwell, Oxford.

Somermeyer, W H, 1977, 'A general market model of labour income distribution', Report 7708/E, Erasmus University, Rotterdam.

Soskice, D, 1990, 'Wage determination: The changing role of institutions in advanced industrialized countries', *Oxford Review of Economic Policy*, vol 6: 36–61.

Spence, M, 1973, 'Job market signaling', *Quarterly Journal of Economics*, vol 87: 355–74.

Stark, T, 1977, *The Distribution of Income in Eight Countries*, Background Paper No 4, Royal Commission on the Distribution of Income and Wealth, HMSO, London.

Statistischen Reichsamt, 1929, *Der Steuerabzug vom Arbeitslohn im Jahre 1926*, Statistik des Deutschen Reichs, Band 359, Reimar Hobbing, Berlin.

Stewart, F and Berry, A, 1999, 'Globalization, liberalization, and inequality: Expectations and experience', in A Hurrell and N Woods, editors, *Inequality, Globalization, and World Politics*, Oxford University Press, Oxford.

Stewart, M B, 1983, 'Relative earnings and individual union membership in the United Kingdom', *Economica*, vol 50: 111–25.

—— 1990, 'Union wage differentials, product market influences and the division of rents', *Economic Journal*, vol 100: 1122–37.

—— 1991, 'Union wage differentials in the face of changes in the economic and legal environment', *Economica*, vol 58: 155–72.

—— 1995, 'Union wage differentials in an era of declining unionization', *Oxford Bulletin of Economics and Statistics*, vol 57: 143–66.

—— 2004, 'The impact of the introduction of the UK minimum wage on the employment probabilities of low wage workers', *Journal of the European Economic Association*, vol 2: 67–97.

Strøm, B, 1995, 'Envy, fairness and political influence in local government wage determination: Evidence from Norway', *Economica*, vol 62: 389–409.

Sweezy, M Y, 1939, 'Distribution of wealth and income under the Nazis', *Review of Economics and Statistics*, vol 21: 178–84.

Taber, C R, 2001, 'The rising college premium in the 1980s: Return to college or return to unobserved abilities?', *Review of Economic Studies*, vol 68: 665–91.

Teichova, A, 1988, *The Czechoslovak Economy 1918–1980*, Routledge, London.

Teulings, C N, 1995, 'The wage distribution in a model of assignment of skills to jobs', *Journal of Political Economy*, vol 103: 280–315.

Teulings, C N, and Hartog, J, 1998, *Corporatism or Competition? Labour Contracts, Institutions and Wage Structures in International Comparison*, Cambridge University Press, Cambridge.

Thaler, R, 1989, 'Interindustry wage differentials', *Journal of Economic Perspectives*, vol 3: 181–93.

Thatcher, A R, 1968, 'The distribution of earnings of employees in Great Britain', *Journal of the Royal Statistical Society*, Series A, vol 131: 133–80.

Theodossiou, T, 1995, 'Wage determination for career and non-career workers in the UK: Is there labour market segmentation?', *Economica*, vol 62: 195–211.

Thurow, L C, 1975, *Generating Inequality*, Basic Books, New York.

Tinbergen, J, 1956, 'On the theory of income distribution', *Weltwirtschaftliches Archiv*, vol 77: 155–75.

—— 1974, 'Substitution of graduate by other labor', *Kyklos*, vol 27: 217–26.

—— 1975, *Income Distribution: Analysis and Policies*, North-Holland, Amsterdam.

—— 1975a, *Income Differences: Recent Research*, North-Holland, Amsterdam.

Tombazos, C G, 1999, 'The role of imports in expanding the demand gap between skilled and unskilled labour in the US', *Applied Economics*, vol 31: 509–16.

—— 2003, 'A production theory approach to the imports and wage inequality nexus', *Economic Inquiry*, vol 41: 42–61.

Topel, R H, 1991, 'Specific capital, mobility and wages: Wages rise with job seniority', *Journal of Political Economy*, vol 99: 145–76.

—— 1993, 'Regional labor markets and the determinants of wage inequality', *American Economic Review, Papers and Proceedings*, vol 83: 110–15.

—— 1997, 'Factor proportions and relative wages: The supply-side determinants of wage inequality', *Journal of Economic Perspectives*, vol 11, No 2: 55–74.

—— and Ward, M P, 1992, 'Job mobility and the careers of young men', *Quarterly Journal of Economics*, vol 107: 439–79.

Trivanovitch, V, 1937, *Economic Development of Germany under National Socialism*, National Industrial Conference Board, New York.

Troske, K, 1999, 'Evidence on the employer size–wage premium from worker–establishment matched data', *Review of Economics and Statistics*, vol 81: 15–26.

Tsakloglou, P and Cholezas, I, 2006, 'Earnings inequality in Europe: Structure and patterns of inter-temporal changes', discussion paper, Athens University of Economics and Business.

Tsang, M C and Levin, H M, 1985, 'The economics of overeducation', *Economics of Education Review*, vol 4: 93–104.

Turner, H A and Jackson, D A S, 1969, 'On the stability of wage differences and productivity-based wage policies: An international analysis', *British Journal of Industrial Relations*, vol 7: 1–18.

Tyers, R, Duncan, R, and Martin, W, 1999, 'Trade, technology and labor markets: General equilibrium perspectives', *Journal of Economic Integration*, vol 14: 226–64.

—— and Yang, Y, 1998, 'Trade with Asia and skill upgrading effects on labour markets in the older industrial countries', *Weltwirtschaftliches Archiv*, vol 133: 383–417.

Tyers, R, and Yang, Y, 2000, 'Capital–skill complementarity and wage outcomes following technical change in a global model', *Oxford Review of Economic Policy*, vol 16, No 3: 23–41.

US Census Bureau, 2006, *Income, Earnings, and Poverty Data From the 2005 American Community Survey*, Document ACS-02, US Census Bureau, Washington, DC.

Utendorf, K R, 1998, 'Recent changes in earnings distributions in the United States', *Social Security Bulletin*, vol 61, No 2: 12–28.

Van Reenen, J, 1996, 'The creation and capture of economic rents: Wages and innovation in a panel of UK companies', *Quarterly Journal of Economics*, vol 111: 195–26.

Vartiainen, J, 1998, *The Labour Market in Finland: Institutions and Outcomes*, Prime Minister's Office, Publications Series 1998/2, Helsinki.

Večernik, J, 1991, 'Earnings distribution in Czechoslovakia: Intertemporal changes and international comparison', *European Sociological Review*, vol 7: 237–52.

—— 1995, 'Changing earnings distribution in the Czech Republic: Survey evidence from 1988–1994', *Economics of Transition*, vol 3: 355–71.

—— 2001, 'Earnings disparities in the Czech Republic: Evidence of the past decade and cross-national comparison', William Davidson Institute Working Paper No 373, May 2001.

Villiers, A, 1949, *The Set of the Sails*, Hodder and Stoughton, London.

Violante, G L, 2002, 'Technological acceleration, skill transferability and the rise in residual inequality', *Quarterly Journal of Economics*, vol 117: 297–338.

Wälde, K, 2000, 'Egalitarian and elitist education systems as the basis for international differences in wage inequality', *European Journal of Political Economy*, vol 16: 445–68.

Waldman, M, 1984, 'Worker allocation, hierarchies and the wage distribution', *Review of Economic Studies*, vol 51: 95–109.

Wallerstein, M, 1999, 'Wage-setting institutions and pay inequality in advanced industrial societies', *American Journal of Political Science*, vol 43: 649–80.

Wasmer, E, 1999, 'Competition for jobs in a growing economy and the emergence of dualism', *Economic Journal*, vol 109: 349–71.

Weick, K E, 1966, 'The concept of equity in the perception of pay', *Administrative Science Quarterly*, vol 11: 414–39.

Weiss, L, 1966, 'Concentration and labor earnings', *American Economic Review*, vol 56: 96–117.

Welch, F, 1969, 'Linear synthesis of skill distribution', *Journal of Human Resources*, vol 4: 312–27.

—— 1979, 'Effects of cohort size on earnings: The baby boom babies' financial bust', *Journal of Political Economy*, vol 87: S65–S97.

Wilkinson, F, 1981, *The Dynamics of Labour Market Segmentation*, Academic Press, London.

Willis, R J, 1986, 'Wage determinants: A survey and reinterpretation of human capital earnings functions', in O Ashenfelter and R Layard, editors, *Handbook of Labor Economics*, vol 1, North-Holland, Amsterdam.

Wolff, E N, 2002, 'Productivity, computerization and skill change', NBER Working Paper 8743.

Wong, L Y, 2003, 'Can the Mortensen-Pissarides model with productivity changes explain U.S. wage inequality?', *Journal of Labor Economics*, vol 21: 70–105.

Wood, A, 1978, *A Theory of Pay*, Cambridge University Press, Cambridge.

—— 1991, 'The factor content of North–South trade in manufactures reconsidered', *Weltwirtschaftliches Archiv*, vol 127: 719–43.

—— 1991a, 'How much does trade with the South affect workers in the North?', *World Bank Research Observer*, vol 6: 19–36.

—— 1994, *North–South Trade, Employment, and Inequality*, Clarendon Press, Oxford.

—— 1995, 'How trade hurt unskilled workers', *Journal of Economic Perspectives*, vol 9: 57–80.

—— 1997, 'Openness and wage inequality in developing countries: The Latin American challenge to East Asian conventional wisdom', *World Bank Economic Review*, vol 11: 33–57.

—— 1998, 'Globalisation and the rise in labour market inequalities', *Economic Journal*, vol 108: 1463–82.

—— 2002, 'Globalisation and wage inequalities: A synthesis of three theories', *Weltwirtschaftliches Archiv*, vol 138: 54–82.

Wootton, B, 1955, *The Social Foundations of Wage Policy*, Allen and Unwin, London.

Zweimüller, J and Barth, E, 1994, 'Bargaining structure, wage determination, and wage dispersion in six OECD countries', *Kyklos*, vol 47: 81–93.

Index